Foundations of Empirical Software Engineering

Barry Boehm · Hans Dieter Rombach
Marvin V. Zelkowitz (Eds.)

Foundations of Empirical Software Engineering

The Legacy of Victor R. Basili

With 103 Figures and 21 Tables

Springer

Editors

Barry Boehm
University of Southern California
Center for Software Engineering
941 W 37th Place
CA 90089-0781, Los Angeles, USA
boehm@sunset.usc.edu

Hans Dieter Rombach
Fraunhofer IESE
Sauerwiesen 6
67661 Kaiserslautern, Germany
rombach@iese.fraunhofer.de

Marvin V. Zelkowitz
University of Maryland and Fraunhofer CESE
4321 Hartwick Road, Suite 500
College Park, MD 20742-3290, USA
mvz@cs.umd.edu

ACM Computing Classification (1998): D.2.8, D.2.9, D.2.1

ISBN-13 978-3-642-06389-3 e-ISBN-13 978-3-540-27662-3

Springer is a part of Springer Science+Business Media

springeronline.com

Printed in Germany

Cover design: KünkelLopka, Heidelberg

Printed on acid-free paper 45/3142/YL - 5 4 3 2 1 0

Preface

Although software engineering can trace its beginnings to a NATO conference in 1968, it cannot be said to have become an empirical science until the 1970s with the advent of the work of Prof. Victor Robert Basili of the University of Maryland. In addition to the need to engineer software was the need to *understand* software. Much like other sciences, such as physics, chemistry, and biology, software engineering needed a discipline of observation, theory formation, experimentation, and feedback. By applying the scientific method to the software engineering domain, Basili developed concepts like the Goal-Question-Metric method, the Quality-Improvement-Paradigm, and the Experience Factory to help bring a sense of order to the ad hoc developments so prevalent in the software engineering field.

On the occasion of Basili's 65th birthday, we present this book containing reprints of 20 papers that defined much of his work. We divided the 20 papers into 6 sections, each describing a different facet of his work, and asked several individuals to write an introduction to each section.

Instead of describing the scope of this book in this preface, we decided to let one of his papers, the keynote paper he gave at the International Conference on Software Engineering in 1996 in Berlin, Germany to lead off this book. He, better than we, can best describe his views on what is experimental software engineering.

This book was developed for a symposium honoring Basili, which was held during the International Conference on Software Engineering in St. Louis, MO, USA in May 2005. Whether you attended this symposium or are reading this later, we are confident that you will find these papers to be an important compendium of experimental software engineering literature.

Barry Boehm
H. Dieter Rombach
Marvin V. Zelkowitz
January 2005

Table of Contents

---

* Permission to reprint granted by respective copyright holders.

The Role of Experimentation in Software Engineering: Past, Current, and Future

Victor R. Basili

Institute for Advanced Computer Studies and Department of Computer Science, University of Maryland

Abstract. Software engineering needs to follow the model of other physical sciences and develop an experimental paradigm for the field. This paper proposes the approach towards developing an experimental component of such a paradigm. The approach is based upon a quality improvement paradigm that addresses the role of experimentation and process improvement in the context of industrial development. The paper outlines a classification scheme for characterizing such experiments.

1. Introduction

Progress in any discipline depends on our ability to understand the basic units necessary to solve a problem. It involves the building of models[1] of the application domain, e.g., domain specific primitives in the form of specifications and application domain algorithms, and models of the problem solving processes, e.g., what techniques are available for using the models to help address the problems. In order to understand the effects of problem solving on the environment, we need to be able to model various product characteristics, such as reliability, portability, efficiency, as well as model various project characteristics such as cost and schedule. However, the most important thing to understand is the relationship between various process characteristics and product characteristics, e.g., what algorithms produce efficient solutions relevant to certain variables, what development processes produce what product characteristics and under what conditions.

Our problem solving ability evolves over time. The evolution is based upon the encapsulation of experience into models and the validation and verification of those models based upon experimentation, empirical evidence, and reflection. This

[1] We use the term model in a general sense to mean a simplified representation of a system or phenomenon; it may or may not be mathematical or even formal.

encapsulation of knowledge allows us to deal with higher levels of abstraction that characterize the problem and the solution space. What works and doesn't work will evolve over time based upon feedback and learning from applying the ideas and analyzing the results.

This is the approach that has been used in many fields, e.g., physics, medicine, manufacturing. Physics aims at understanding the behavior of the physical universe and divides its researchers into theorists and experimentalists. Physics has progressed because of the interplay between these two groups.

Theorists build models to explain the universe - models that predict results of events that can be measured. These models may be based upon theory or data from prior experiments. Experimentalists observe and measure. Some experiments are carried out to test or disprove a theory, some are designed to explore a new domain. But at whatever point the cycle is entered, there is a modeling, experimenting, learning and remodeling pattern.

Science to the early Greeks was observation followed by logical thought. It took Galileo, and his dropping of balls off the tower at Pisa, to demonstrate the value of experimentation. Modern physicists have learned to manipulate the physical universe, e.g. particle physicists. However, physicists cannot change the nature of the universe [8].

Another example is medicine. Here we distinguish between the researcher and the practitioner. Human intelligence was long thought to be centered in the heart. The circulation of the blood throughout the body was a relatively recent discovery. The medical researcher aims at understanding the workings of the human body in order to predict the effects of various procedures and drugs and provide knowledge about human health and well-being. The medical practitioner aims at applying that knowledge by manipulating the body for the purpose of curing it. There is a clear relationship between the two and knowledge is often built by feedback from the practitioner to the researcher.

Medicine began as an art form. Practitioners applied various herbs and curing processes based upon knowledge handed down, often in secret, from generation to generation. Medicine as a field did not really progress, until various forms of learning, based upon experimentation and model building, took place. Learning from the application of medications and procedures formed a base for evolving our knowledge of the relationship between these solutions and their effects. Experimentation takes on many forms, from controlled experiments to case studies. Depending on the area of interest, data may be hard to acquire. However, our knowledge of the human body has evolved over time. But both grew based upon our understanding of the relationship between the procedures (processes) and its effects on the body (product). The medical practitioner can and does manipulate the body, but the essence of the body, which is physical, does not change. Again, the understanding was based upon model building, experimentation, and teaming.

A third and newer example is manufacturing. The goal of manufacturing is to produce a product that meets a set of specifications. The same product is generated, over and over, based upon a set of processes. These processes are based upon models of the problem domain and solution space and the relationship between the two. Here the relationship between process and product characteristics is generally well understood. But since the product is often a man-made artifact, we can improve on the artifact itself, change its essence. Process improvement is performed by experimenting with variations in the process, building models of what occurs, and measuring its effect on the revised product. Models are built with good predictive capabilities based upon a deep understanding of the relationship between process and product.

2. The nature of the software engineering discipline

Like physics, medicine, manufacturing, and many other disciplines, software engineering requires the same high level approach for evolving the knowledge of the discipline; the cycle of model building, experimentation and teaming. We cannot rely solely on observation followed by logical thought. Software engineering is a laboratory science. It involves an experimental component to test or disprove theories, to explore new domains. We must experiment with techniques to see how and when they really work, to understand their limits, and to understand how to improve them. We must learn from application and improve our understanding.

The researcher's role is to understand the nature of processes and products, and the relationship between them. The practitioner's role is to build "improved" systems, using the knowledge available. Even more than in the other disciplines, these roles are symbiotic. The researcher needs 'laboratories'; they only exist where practitioners build software systems. The practitioner needs to understand how to build better systems; the researcher can provide the models to make this happen.

Unlike physics and medicine, but like manufacturing, we can change the essence of the product. Our goal is to build improved products. However, unlike manufacturing, software is development not production. We do not re-produce the same object, each product is different from the last. Thus, the mechanisms for model building are different; we do not have lots of data points to provide us with reasonably accurate models for statistical quality control.

Most of the technologies of the discipline are human based. It does not matter how high we raise the level of discourse or the virtual machine, the development of solutions is still based upon individual creativity, and so differences in human ability will always create variations in the studies. This complicates the experimental aspect of the discipline. Unlike physics, the same experiment can provide different results depending on the people involved. This is a problem found in the behavioral sciences.

Besides the human factor, there are a large number of variables that affect the outcome of an experiment. All software is not the same; process is a variable, goals are variable, context is variable. That is, one set of processes might be more effective for achieving certain goals in a particular context than another set of processes. We have often made the simplifying assumption that all software is the same, i.e., the same models will work independent of the goals, context size, application, etc. But this is no more true than it is for hardware. Building a satellite and a toaster are not the same thing, anymore than developing the micro code for a toaster and the flight dynamic software for the satellite are the same thing.

A result of several of the above observations is that there is a lack of useful models that allow us to reason about the software process, the software product and the relationship between them. Possibly because we have been unable to build reliable, mathematically tractable models, like in physics and manufacturing, we have tended not to build any. And those that we have, are not always sensitive to context. Like medicine, there are times when we need to use heuristics and models based upon simple relationships among variables, even if the relationships cannot be mathematically defined.

3. The available research paradigms

There are various experimental and analytic paradigms used in other disciplines. The analytic paradigms involve proposing a set of axioms, developing a theory, deriving results and, if possible, verifying the results with empirical observations. This is a deductive model which does not require an experimental design in the statistical sense, but provides an analytic framework for developing models and understanding their boundaries based upon manipulation of the model itself. For example the treatment of programs as mathematical objects and the analysis of the mathematical object or its relationship to the program satisfies the paradigm. Another way of verifying the results is by an existence proof, i.e., the building of a software solution to demonstrate that the theory holds. A software development to demonstrate a theory is different from building a system ad hoc. The latter might be an excellent art form but does not follow a research paradigm.

The experimental paradigms involve an experimental design, observation, data collection and validation on the process or product being studied. We will discuss three experimental models; although they are similar, they tend to emphasize different things.

First we define some terms for discussing experimentation. A hypothesis is a tentative assumption made in order to draw out and test its logical or empirical consequence. We define study broadly, as an act or operation for the purpose of discovering something unknown or of testing a hypothesis. We will include various forms of experimental, empirical and qualitative studies under this heading. We will use the term experiment to mean a study undertaken in which the researcher has control over some of the conditions in which the study takes place and control over (some aspects of) the independent variables being studied. We will use the term controlled experiment to mean an experiment in which the subjects are randomly assigned to experimental conditions, the researcher manipulates an independent variable, and the subjects in different experimental conditions are treated similarly with regard to all variables except the independent variable.

The experimental paradigm of physics is epitomized by the scientific method: observe the world, propose a model or a theory of behavior, measure and analyze, validate hypotheses of the model or theory (or invalidate them), and repeat the procedure evolving our knowledge base.

In the area of software engineering this inductive paradigm might best be used when trying to understand the software process, product, people, or environment. It attempts to extract from the world some form of model which tries to explain the underlying phenomena, and evaluate whether the model is truly representative of the phenomenon being observed. It is an approach to model building. An example might be an attempt to understand the way software is being developed by an organization to see if their process model can be abstracted or a tool can be built to automate the process. The model or tool is then applied in an experiment to verify the hypotheses. Two variations of this inductive approach can be used to emphasize the evolutionary and revolutionary modes of discovery.

The experimental paradigm in manufacturing is exemplified by an evolutionary approach: observe existing solutions, propose better solutions, build/develop, measure and analyze, and repeat the process until no more improvements appear possible.

This evolutionary improvement oriented view assumes one already has models of the software process, product, people and environment and modifies the model or aspects of the model in order to improve the thing being studied. An example might be the study of improvements to methods being used in the development of software or the demonstration that some tool performs better than its predecessor relative to certain characteristics. Note that a crucial part of this method is the need for careful analysis and measurement.

It is also possible for experimentation to be revolutionary, rather than evolutionary, in which case we would begin by proposing a new model, developing statistical/qualitative methods, applying the model to case studies, measuring and analyzing, validating the model and repeating the procedure.

This revolutionary improvement oriented view begins by proposing a new model, not necessarily based upon an existing model, and attempts to study the effects of the process or product suggested by the new model. The idea for the new model is often based upon problems observed in the old model or approach. An example might be the proposal of a new method or tool used to perform software development in a new way. Again, measurement and analysis are crucial to the success of this method.

These approaches serve as a basis for distinguishing research activities from development activities. If one of these paradigms is not being used in some form, the study is most likely not a research project For example, building a system or tool alone is development and not research. Research involves gaining understanding about how and why a certain type of tool might be useful and by validating that a tool has certain properties or certain effects by carefully designing an experiment to measure the properties or to compare it with alternatives. An experimental method can be used to understand the effects of a particular tool usage in some environment and to validate hypotheses about how software development can best be accomplished.

4. Software engineering model building

A fair amount of research has been conducted in software engineering model building, i.e., people are building technologies, methods, tools, life cycle models, specification languages, etc. Some of the earliest modeling research centered on the software product, specifically mathematical models of the program function. There has also been some model building of product characteristics, such as reliability models. There has been modeling in the process domain; a variety of notations exist for expressing the process at different levels for different purposes. However, there has not been much experimenting on the part of the model builders: implementation yes, experimentation no. This may in part be because they are the theorists of the discipline and leave it to the experimenters to test their theories. It may in part be because they view their "models" as not needing to be tested - they see them as self-evident.

For example, in defining a notation for abstracting a program, the theorist may find it sufficient to capture the abstraction perfectly, and not wonder whether it can be applied by a practitioner, under what conditions its application is cost effective, what kind of training is needed for its successful use, etc. Similar things might be said about the process modeler.

It may also be that the theorists view their research domain as the whole unit, rather than one component of the discipline. What is sometimes missing is the big picture, i.e., what is the collection of components and how do they fit together? What are the various program abstraction methods and when is each appropriate? For what applications are they not effective? Under what conditions are they most effective? What is the relationship between processes and product? What is the effect of a particular technique on product reliability, given an environment of expert programmers in a new domain, with tight schedule constraints, etc.

One definition of science is the classification of components. We have not sufficiently enumerated or emphasized the roles of different component models, e.g., processes, products, resources, defects, etc., the logical and physical integration of these models, the evaluation and analysis of the models via experimentation, the refinement and tailoring of the models to an application environment, and the access and use of these models in an appropriate fashion, on various types of software projects from an engineering point of view. The majority of software engineering research has been bottom-up, done in isolation. It is the packaging of technology rather than the solving of a problem or the understanding of a primitive of the discipline.

5. What will our future look like?

We need research that helps establish a scientific and engineering basis for the software engineering field. To this end, researchers need to build, analyze and evaluate models of the software processes and products as well as various aspects of the environment in which the software is being built, e.g. the people, the organization, etc. It is especially important to study the interactions of these models. The goal is to develop the conceptual scientific foundations of software engineering upon which future researchers can build. This is often a process of discovering and validating small but important concepts that can be applied in many different ways and that can be used to build more complex and advanced ideas rather than merely providing a tool or methodology without experimental validation of its underlying assumptions or careful analysis and verification of its properties.

This research should provide the software engineering practitioner with the ability to control and manipulate project solutions based upon the environment and goals set for the project, as well as knowledge based upon empirical and experimental evidence of what works and does not work and when. The practitioner can then rely on a mix of scientific and engineering knowledge and human ingenuity.

But where are the laboratories for software engineering? They can and should be anywhere software is being developed. Software engineering researchers need industry-based laboratories that allow them to observe, build and analyze models. On the other hand, practitioners need to build quality systems productively and profitably, e.g., estimate cost track progress, evaluate quality. The models of process and product generated by researchers should be tailored based upon the data collected within the organization and should be able to continually evolve based upon the organization's evolving experiences. Thus the research and business perspectives of software engineering have a symbiotic relationship. From both perspectives we need a top down experimental, evolutionary framework in which research and development can be logically and physically integrated to produce and take advantage of models of the discipline that have been evaluated and tailored to the application environment. However, since each such laboratory will only provide local, rather than global, models, we need many experimental laboratories at multiple levels. These will help us generate the basic models and metrics of the business and the science.

This allows us to view our usable knowledge as growing over time and provides some insight into the relationship between software development as an art and as an engineering discipline. As we progress with our deeper understanding of the models and relationships, we can work on harder and harder problems. At the top is always the need to create new ideas, to go where models do not exist. But we can reach these new heights based upon our ability to build on packages of knowledge, not just packages of technologies.

6. Can this be done?

There have been pockets of experimentation in software engineering but there is certainly not a sufficient amount of it [5, 9, 11]. One explicit example, with which the author is intimately familiar, is the work done in the Software Engineering Laboratory at NASA/GSFC [6]. Here the overriding experimental paradigm has been the Quality Improvement Paradigm [1, 4], which combines the evolutionary and revolutionary experimental aspects of the scientific method, tailored to the study of software. The steps of the QIP are:

Characterize the project and environment, i.e., observe and model the existing environment.

Set goals for successful project performance and improvement and organizational learning.

Choose the appropriate **processes** and supporting methods and tools for this project and for study.

Execute the processes, construct the products, collect and validate the prescribed data based upon the goals, and analyze it to provide real-time feedback for corrective action.

Analyze the data to evaluate the current practices, determine problems, record findings, and make recommendations for future project improvements.

Package the experience in the form of updated and refined models and other forms of structured knowledge gained from this and prior projects and save it in an experience base for future projects.

To help create the laboratory environment to benefit both the research and the development aspects of software engineering, the Experience Factory concept was created. The Experience Factory represents a form of laboratory environment for software development where models can be built and provide direct benefit to the projects under study. It represents an organizational structure that supports the QIP by providing support for learning through the accumulation of experience, the building of experience models in an experience base, and the use of this new knowledge and understanding in the current and future project developments [2].

7. The maturing of the experimental discipline

In order to identify patterns in experimental activities in software engineering from the past to the present, I relied on my experience, discussions with the Experimental Software Engineering Group here at the University of Maryland, and some observations in the literature of experimental papers, i.e., papers that reported on studies that were carried out.

This identified some elements and characteristics of the experimental work in software engineering, specifically (1) identification of the components and purposes of the studies, (2) the types and characteristics of the experiments run, and (3) some ideas on how to judge if the field is maturing. These have been formulated as three questions. First, what are the components and goals of the software engineering studies? Second, what kinds of experiments have been performed? Third, how is software engineering experimentation maturing?

7.1. What are the components and goals of the software engineering studies?

Our model for components method is the Goal/Question/Metric (GQM) Goal Template [4]. The GQM method was defined as a mechanism for defining and interpreting a set of operation goals, using measurement. It represents a systematic approach for tailoring and integrating goals with models of the software processes, products and quality perspectives of interest, based upon the specific needs of a project and organization. However, here, we will only use the parameters of a goal to characterize the types of studies performed. There are four parameters: the object of study, the purpose, the focus, and the point of view. A sample goal might be: analyze **perspective based reading** (object of interest), in order to **evaluate** (purpose) it with respect to **defect detection** (focus) from the point of view of **quality assurance** (point of view). Studies may have more than one goal but the goals are usually related, i.e. there are several focuses of the same object being analyzed or a related set of objects are being studied. In experimental papers, the point of view is usually the researcher trying to gain some knowledge.

object of study: a process, product, or any form of model

purpose: to characterize (what is it?), evaluate (is it good?), predict (can I estimate something in the future?), control (can I manipulate events?), improve (can I improve event?)

focus: the aspect of the object of study that is of interest, e.g., reliability of the product, defect detection/prevention capability of the process, accuracy of the cost model

point of view: the person who benefits from the information, e.g., the researcher in understanding something better

In going through the literature, there appeared to be two patterns of empirical studies, those I will call *human factor* studies, and those that appear to be more broad-based software engineering. The first class includes studies aimed at understanding the human cognitive process, e.g., how individual programmers perceive or solve problems. The second set of studies appear to be aimed more at understanding how to aid the practitioner, i.e., building models of the software process, product, and their relationship. We will call these *project-based* studies. The reason for making the distinction is that they appear to have different patterns. Many of the human factor studies were done by or with cognitive psychologists who were comfortable with the experimental paradigm. The object of study tended to be small, the purpose was evaluation with respect to some performance measure. The point of view was mostly the researcher, attempting to understand something about programming.

Although the project-based studies are also often from the point of view of the researcher, it is clear that the perspectives are often practitioner based, i.e. the point of view represented by the researcher is that of the organization, the manager, the developer, etc. The object of study is often the software process or product in some form. If we are looking at breadth, there have been an enormous variety of objects studied. The object set which once included only small, specific items, like particular programming language features, has evolved to include entire development processes, like Cleanroom development

Although the vast majority of such studies are also aimed at evaluation, and a few at prediction; more recently, as the recognition of the complexity of the software domain has grown, there are more studies that simply try to characterize and understand something, like effort distribution, rather than evaluate whether or not it is good.

7.2. What kinds of experiment have been performed?

There are several attributes of an experiment. Consider the following set:

(1) Does the study present results which are descriptive, correlational, cause-effect?

Descriptive: there may be patterns in the data but the relationship among the variables has not been examined

Correlational: the variation in the dependent variable(s) is related to the variation of the independent variable(s)

Cause-effect: the treatment variable(s) is the only possible cause of variation in the dependent variable(s)

Most of the human factor studies were cause-effect. This appears to be a sign of maturity of the experimentalists in that area as well as the size and nature of the problem they were attacking. The project-based studies were dominated by correlational studies early on but have evolved to more descriptive (and qualitative) style studies over time. I believe this reflects early beliefs that the problem was simpler than it was and some simple combination of metrics could easily explain cost, quality, etc.

(2) Is the study performed on novices or experts or both?

novice: students or individuals not experienced in the study domain

experts: practitioners of the task or people with experience in the study domain

There seems to be no pattern here, except possibly that there are more studies with experts in the project based study set. This is especially true with the qualitative studies of organizations and projects, but also with some of the controlled experiments.

(3) Is the study performed in vivo or in vitro?

In vivo: in the field under normal conditions

In vitro: in the laboratory under controlled conditions

Again, for project-based studies, there appear to be more studies under normal conditions (in vivo).

(4) Is it an experiment or an observational study? Although the term experiment is often used to be synonymous with controlled experiment, as defined earlier, I have taken a broader definition here. In this view, we distinguish between *experiments,* where at least one treatment or controlled variable exists, and *observational studies* where there are no treatment or controlled variables.

Experiments can be characterized by the number of teams replicating each project and the number of different projects analyzed. As such, it consists of four different experimental classes, as shown in Table 1: blocked subject-project, replicated project, multi-project variation, and a single project. Blocked subject-project and replicated project experiments represent controlled experiments, as defined earlier. Multi-project variation and single project experiments represent what have been called quasi-experiments or pre-experimental designs [7].

In the literature, typically, controlled experiments are in vitro. There is a mix of both novice and expert treatments, most often the former. Sometimes, the novice subjects are used to "debug" the experimental design, which is then run with professional subjects. Also, controlled experiments can generate stronger statistical confidence in the conclusions. A common approach in the blocked subject-project study is the use of fractional factorial designs. Unfortunately, since controlled experiments are expensive and difficult to control if the project is too large, the projects studied tend to be small.

Quasi-experiments can deal with large projects and be easily done in vivo with experts. These experiments tend to involve a qualitative analysis component, including at least some form of interviewing.

		# Projects	
		One	*More than one*
# of Teams per Project	***One***	Single Project	Multi-Project Variation
	More than one	Replicated Project	Blocked Subject-Project

Table 1: Experiments

Observational studies can be characterized by the number of sites included and whether or not a set of study variables are determined a priori, as shown in Table 2. Whether or not a set of study variables are predetermined by the researcher separates the pure qualitative study (no a priori variables isolated by the observer), from the mix of qualitative and quantitative analysis, where the observer has identified, a priori, a set of variables for observation.

In purely qualitative analysis, deductions are made using non-mathematical formal logic, e.g., verbal propositions [10]. I was only able to find one study that fit in this category and since it involved multiple sites would be classified as a Field Qualitative Study. On the other hand, there are a large number of case studies in the literature and some field studies. Almost all are in vivo with experts and descriptive.

7.3. How is software engineering experimentation maturing?

One sign of maturity in a field is the level of sophistication of the goals of an experiment and its relevance to understanding interesting (e.g., practical) things about the field. For example, a primitive question might be to determine experimentally if various software processes and products could be measured and their characteristics differentiated on the basis of measurement. This is a primitive question but needed to be answered as a first step in the evolution of experimentation. Over time, the questions have become more sophisticated, e.g., Can a change in an existing process produce a measurable effect on the product or environment? Can the measurable characteristics of a process be used to predict the measurable characteristics of the product or environment, within a particular context? Can we control for product effects, based upon goals, given a particular set of context variables?

Another sign of maturity is to see a pattern of knowledge building from a series of experiments. This reflects the discipline's ability to build on prior work (knowledge, models, experiments). There are various ways of viewing this. We can ask if the study was an isolated event, if it led to other studies that made use of the information obtained from this particular study. We can ask if studies have been replicated under similar or differing conditions. We can ask if this building of knowledge exists in one research group or environment, or has spread to others, i.e., researchers are building on each other's work.

In both these cases we have begun to see progress. Researchers appear to be asking more sophisticated questions, trying to tackle questions about relationships between processes and product characteristics, using more studies in the field than in the controlled laboratory, and combining various experimental classes to build knowledge.

There are several examples of the evolution of knowledge over time, based upon experimentation and learning, within a particular organization or research group. The SEL at NASA/GSFC offers several examples [6]. One particular example is the evolution of the SEL knowledge of the effectiveness of reading related techniques and methods [3]. In fact, inspections, in general, are well studied experimentally.

		Variable Scope	
		defined a priori	*not defined a priori*
# of Sites	***One***	**Case Study**	**Case Qualitative Study**
	More than one	**Field Study**	**Field Qualitative Study**

Table 2: Observational Studies

There is also growing evidence of the results of one research group being used by others. At least one group of researchers have organized explicitly for the purpose of sharing knowledge and experiments. The group is called ISERN, the International Software Engineering Research Network. Its goal is to share experiences on software engineering experimentation, by experimenting, learning, remodeling and farther experimenting to build a body of knowledge, based upon empirical evidence. They have begun replicating experiments, e.g., various forms of replication of the defect-based reading have been performed, and replications of the perspective-based reading experiment are being performed. Experiments are being run to better understanding the parameters of inspection. ISERN has membership in the U.S., Europe, Asia, and Australia representing both industry and academia.

Another sign of progress for experimental software engineering is the new journal by Kluwer, the International Journal of Empirical Software Engineering, whose aim is to provide a forum for researchers and practitioners involved in the empirical study of software engineering. It aims at publishing artifacts and laboratory manuals that support the replication of experiments. It plans to encourage and publish replicated studies, successful and unsuccessful, highlighting what can be learned from them for improving future studies.

Acknowledgements: I would like to thank the members of the Experimental Software Engineering Group at the University of Maryland for their contributions to the ideas in this paper, especially, Filippo Lanubile, Carolyn Seaman, Jyrki Kontio, Walcelio Melo, Yong-Mi Kim, and Giovanni Cantone.

8. References

[1] Victor R. Basili, Quantitative Evaluation of Software Methodology, Keynote Address, First Pan Pacific Computer Conference, Melbourne, Australia, September 1985.

[2] Victor R. Basili, Software Development: A Paradigm for the Future, COMPSAC '89, Orlando, Florida, pp. 471-485, September 1989.

[3] Victor R. Basili and Scott Green, Software Process Evolution at the SEL, IEEE Software, pp. 58-66, July 1994.

[4] Victor R. Basili and H. Dieter Rombach, The TAME Project: Towards Improvement-Oriented Software Environments, IEEE Transactions on Software Engineering, vol. 14, no. 6, June 1988.

[5] V. R. Basili, R. W. Selby, D. H. Hutchens, "Experimentation in Software Engineering," IEEE Transactions on Software Engineering, vol. SE-12, no. 7, pp. 733-743, July 1986.

[6] Victor Basili, Marvin Zelkowitz, Frank McGarry, Jerry Page, Sharon Waligora, Rose Pajerski, SEL's Software Development Process Improvement Program, IEEE Software Magazine, pp. 83-87, November 1995.

[7] Campbell, Donald T. and Julian C. Stanley, Experimental and Quasi-experimental Designs for Research, Houghton Mifflin, Boston, MA.

[8] Lederman, Leon, "The God Particle", Houghton Mifflin, Boston, MA, 1993

[9] Norman Fenton, Shari Lawrence Pfleeger, and Robert L. Glass, Science and Substance: A Challenge to Software Engineers, IEEE Software, pp. 86 – 94, July 1994.

[10] A. S. Lee, "A scientific methodology for MIS Case Studies", MIS Quarterly, pp.33-50 March 1989.

[11] W. L. Tichy, P. Lukowicz, L. Prechelt, and E. A. Heinz, Experimental Evaluation in Computer Science: A Quantitative Study, Journal of Systems and Software, vol. 28, pp. 1

Section1: Programming Languages and Formal Methods

Marvin V. Zelkowitz

Computer Science Department, University of Maryland and
Fraunhofer Center for Experimental Software Engineering

Professor Victor Basili is best known for his work in the areas of software engineering experimentation and measurement, highlighted by the twenty-five year history of the NASA Goddard Space Flight Center Software Engineering Laboratory (SEL) from 1976 until 2002. However, his early work was along more traditional programming language issues in the semantics of programming languages and concepts on the design of compilers. His dissertation research at the University of Texas at Austin, under the direction of Professor Terry Pratt, was on programming language semantics using a graphical model called hierarchical graphs or H-graphs. In this section of the book, we highlight three papers from his work in this area from the 1970s through the early 1980s.

Soon after Prof. Basili arrived at the University of Maryland in 1970, he became interested in programming language design issues and the problems in designing a simple to use language. At that time, the major educational languages were still FORTRAN, with its artificial and obtuse syntax, and BASIC, in its original form too simple for complex program development. About the same time that Niklaus Wirth was developing Pascal, Basili became interested in a language design using a simple BNF grammar that would be easy to learn and simple for a compiler to parse. The result of this was SIMPL-T, the language used for several years as the programming language for freshman computer science majors at the University.

The goal for the SIMPL family of languages was to have a series of extendable compilers using a common base syntax. SIMPL-T was the teaching language, which limited data types to strings and integers. An extension to SIMPL was SIMPL-R, which added real arithmetic for more complex programs. An extension by Dick Hamlet and myself led to SIMPL-XI, a language for systems programming for the PDP-11 minicomputer.

The SIMPL-T compiler was written in SIMPL-T. The first paper in this section, "A transportable extendable compiler," describes the structure of these SIMPL compilers and describes the process of bootstrapping the compiler onto a system where there is no SIMPL-T compiler initially available upon which to compile the original source files. Using a SNOBOL4 translator to convert the SIMPL-T compiler into FORTRAN and then compiling the FORTRAN, they constructed a first version of the compiler. Then this compiler, written in SIMPL, could now compile the original source. By improving on the code generation process in the SIMPL-T source files, once one had a running compiler, improved code could be generated. Although the process is well understood today, one must remember that in the early 1970s, compiler design was only developing into a mature technology. (Recall that the major paper by Jay Earley defining a simple parsing method for SLR and LALR languages first appeared in 1971!)

The second paper, "Iterative enhancement: A practical technique for software development," describes an aspect of the SIMPL-T project that has had a larger impact than the SIMPL family of languages. Data was collected on the development of the SIMPL-T compiler, previously mentioned. An iterative process evolved where design decisions were implemented, and for successive releases of the compiler if a modification required too much effort, the module was redesigned. Rather than simply adding code to add functionality, significant effort was devoted to redesign and redevelopment in order to keep the structure simple and understandable.

The importance of this paper was twofold: For one, it was an early example of the need to collect data during program development. The large store of data was the background for some of the ideas later developed during the SEL days, described later in this book. Secondly, the concept of iterative enhancement was rediscovered years later with the advent of "agile development." Agile's emphasis on refactoring, redesign, and short development cycle are just a 2001 restatement of the iterative enhancement principles Basili espoused 26 years earlier.

By the 1980s, Pascal had replaced SIMPL-T as the freshman programming language at the University. A project by Basili, Harlan Mills, Dick Hamlet and John Gannon took Pascal and reduced it to a minimal set of operators, called CF-Pascal (Character-File Pascal). In essence it made CF-Pascal into a Turing machine using files as the infinite tape and characters as the only data type. This reduced programming to its simplest level with only very few operators and data types to manipulate. For several years this was the programming course for Freshmen.

The final paper in this section, "Understanding and documenting programs," was a description of the programming process used in CF-Pascal to allow for verification of programs in a mechanical manner – a goal we are still seeking. The examples in the paper use FORTRAN as the language for wider readership, but the underlying research was done using Pascal.

Using the concepts of a program as a flowchart, and using the ideas of the prime program decomposition of these flowcharts, a method is described for decomposing programs into its prime components and then verifying the correctness of each prime subcomponent until the entire program is proven correct. Building upon the earlier verification work of Hoare and Dijkstra, a method is described which is applicable to this restricted form of FORTRAN (and Pascal).

A Transportable Extendable Compiler

Victor R. Basili* and Albert J. Turner

Computer Science Department, University of Maryland,
College Park, Maryland U.S.A.

Abstract. This report describes the development of a transportable extendable self-compiler for the language SIMPL-T. SIMPL-T is designed as the base language for a family of languages. The structure of the SIMPL-T compiler and its transportable bootstrap are described. In addition, the procedures for generating a compiler for a new machine and for bootstrapping the new compiler on to the new machine are demonstrated.

Key Words: Transportable, Extendable, Compiler, Bootstrapping, SIMPL-T, SIMPL family

Introduction

The differences in computer architecture and in operating systems make the development of a transportable compiler for a programming language a formidable task. This paper describes the development of a reasonably transportable and extendable compiler for the language SIMPL-T.1

Most compilers that are designed to be transportable are self-compiling; that is, they are written in the language that they compile. The NELIAC compilers2 were among the first self-compiling compilers, and more recent efforts include the XPL3, 4 and BCPL5 compilers. The effort required to transport these compilers includes the rewriting of the code generation portion of the compiler to generate object code for the new machine and the design and programming of run-time support routines. An existing implementation can then be used for the debugging

---

* This research was supported in part by the Office of Naval Research under Grant N00014-67-A-0239-0021 (NR-044-431) to the Computer Science Center of the University of Maryland, and in part by the Computer Science Center of the University of Maryland.

Received 16 January 1974
Revised 21 October 1974

and generation of a compiler for the new machine. As an alternate procedure, the BCPL design allows the bootstrap process to be performed without using an existing implementation by writing (and debugging) two code generators, one in BCPL and another in an existing language already implemented on the target machine.

The SIMPL-T compiler is also self-compiling and the effort required to transport it to a new machine consists of the design and programming of a new code generator and a run-time environment for SIMPL-T programs executing on the new machine.

This paper discusses three features of the transportable, extendable SIMPL-T compiler.

Firstly, there is a transportable bootstrap which permits the SIMPL-T compiler to be transported to most machines without using an existing implementation of the language. Moreover, this bootstrap requires no extra effort such as writing a temporary code generator for the bootstrap that will not be used in the final implementation on the new machine. This transportable bootstrap distinguishes the SIMPL-T bootstrap procedure from that required for most other self-compiling compilers.

Secondly, the highly modular design of the compiler, along with the features of the SIMPL-T language itself, minimizes the effort required to write and interface the new code generator and run-time environment. A reasonably competent systems programmer should be able to bootstrap SIMPL-T to a new machine in one to three months. The actual time required depends mostly on the quality of the object code to be produced by the compiler.

Finally, the compiler has been designed to permit extensions so that other compilers may be built out of it.

The SIMPL-T Language

SIMPL-T is a member of the SIMPL family of structured programming languages.[6] The SIMPL family is a set of languages each of which contains common features, such as a common set of data types and control structures. The fundamental idea behind the family is to start with a base language and a base compiler and then to build each new language in the family as an extension to the base compiler. Thus, each new language and its compiler are bootstrapped from some other language and compiler in the family.

SIMPL-T was designed to be the transportable extendable, base language for the family. The transportable extendable base compiler for SIMPL-T was written in SIMPL-T to permit the entire family of languages to be implemented on various machines in a relatively straightforward manner, as suggested by Waite.[7] (The extensibility scheme is thus similar to that used for Babel and SOAP.[8])

Other members of the SIMPL family include a typeless compiler-writing language, SIMPL-X,[9] a standard mathematically-oriented language, SIMPL-JR[10], a systems implementation language for the PDP-11, SIMPL-XI[11] and the graph algorithmic language GRAAL.[12] The original design and implementation of the SIMPL family of languages and compilers were done at the University of Maryland for the UNIVAC 1100 series computers.

SIMPL-T and other members of the SIMPL family have been used in research projects and in classes at a variety of levels in the Computer Science Department at the University of Maryland. SIMPL-T is being used as an implementation language by the Defense Systems Division, Software Engineering Transference Group at Sperry Univac. SIMPL-R is being used in the development of a transportable system for solving large spare matrix problems.[10]

The salient features of SIMPL-T are:

1. Every program consists of a sequence of procedures that can access a set of global variables, parameters or local variables.
2. The statements in the language are the assignment, if-then-else, while, case, call, exit and return statements. There are compound statements in the language, but there is no block structure.
3. There is easy communication between separately compiled programs by means of external references and entry points.
4. There is an integer data type and an extensive set of integer operations including arithmetic, relational, logical, shift, bit and part word operations.
5. There are string and character data types. Strings are of variable length with a declared maximum. The range of characters is the full set of ASCII characters. The set of string operators includes concatenation, the substring operator, an operator to find an occurrence of a substring of a string and the relational operators.
6. Strong typing is imposed and there are intrinsic functions that convert between data types.
7. There is a one-dimensional array data structure.
8. Procedures and functions may be recursive but may not have local procedures or functions. Only scalars and structures may be passed as parameters. Scalars are passed by value or reference and structures are passed by reference.
9. There is a facility for interfacing with other languages.
10. There is a simple set of read and write stream I/O commands.
11. The syntax and semantics of the language are relatively simple, consistent and uncluttered.

It seems prudent to emphasize here that SIMPL-T programs are not necessarily transportable. The language contains some highly machine-dependent operations, such as bit manipulation operators. The merits and disadvantages of having such operations in the language will not be discussed here. However, it is not difficult to write SIMPL-T programs that are transportable, and this is what was done in writing the SIMPL-T compiler.

A simple stack is adequate for the run-time environment in an implementation of SIMPL-T. This together with the simple I/O facilities in the language and the lack of reels makes the design and implementation of support routines easier than for languages such as FORTRAN and ALGOL.

The availability of external procedures in SIMPL-T means that operating systems interfaces that may be desired for a compiler can easily be managed by writing the interface as an external procedure. Such external interfaces are needed only for uses involving individual operating system idiosyncrasies, however, as SIMPL-T is sufficiently powerful to allow the compiler to be written entirely within itself. (Examples of such uses are the obtaining of date and time, the interchanging of files, etc.)

The SIMPL-T Compiler

Although SIMPL-T programs can be compiled in one pass, the compiler was written as a three-pass compiler with separate scan, parse and code generation phases. The separate code generator is needed for the portability scheme, and separate scan and parse phases promote modularity and provide more flexibility for implementing later extensions.

The scanner and parser are designed and programmed to be machine independent so that the compiler can be transported to a new machine by writing only the code generation pass for that machine. The parser generates a file containing a machine-independent intermediate form of a SIMPL-T program that can readily be converted into machine code for most computers. (This approach is similar to that used for the BGPL compiler.)

Extendibility in the scanner and parser is provided by using a modular approach that avoids the use of obscure programming 'tricks'. In order to enhance the clarity and ease of extendibility, occasional inefficiency and repetition of code has been allowed. The parser uses a syntax-directed approach that is based on an optimized SLR(1)[13] algorithm and uses an operator precedence[14] scheme for parsing expressions.

An additional optimization pass is planned that will perform machine-independent optimization on the intermediate output from the parser. (Such an optimizer was written for an earlier version of the compiler but has not been updated for the latest version.) The design of the compiler permits the use of a variety of machine-independent optimization techniques, such as those suggested by Hecht and Ullman,[15] and Kildall.[16] In order to provide more efficient usage of storage on a variety of machines the scan and parse phases of the compiler are written in macro code. A macro preprocessor[17] is used to generate different versions of these phases for different word sizes on the target machines. The differences mostly involve the symbol table, whose entries consist of several 16-bit fields. For machines having a word size of less than 32 bits, these fields are allocated one per word; for larger words, one field is right-justified in each half word.

All implementation-dependent decisions in the compiler are delayed until the code generation phase. These include the assignment of addresses, decisions on immediate constants, generation of object output for initialized variables and the handling of entry points and external references. These actions could be performed more efficiently during the scan phase, but delaying them until code generation facilitates a new implementation of the compiler.

The intermediate form generated by the parser is a quadruple[18]

OP, A, B, R

consisting of an operation field, an A-operand, a B-operand and a result field. The quads represent high-level operations that make no assumptions about the architecture of the machine for which the compiler is to generate code. Some redundancy is introduced into the quads so that writing a straightforward code generator is made easier.

The quads are generally of two types: operation quads and structure quads. The operation quads correspond to the primitive operators of the SIMPL-T language, and the structure quads represent the program structure. As examples, the operation X + Y would be represented by the quad

+, X, Y, t

where t is an integrator for the result; a statement beginning

IF X > Y THEN

would generate the quads

>, X, Y, t

IF, t, ,

The choice of quads over a polish string representation was made primarily to enhance the writing of a machine-independent optimization pass. Quads also allow more flexibility in the design of a code generator since, for example, no stack is required. Quads were chosen over two-address codes (triples)18 for the same reasons, although the same arguments apply to a lesser degree. We believed that there would be less bookkeeping effort required for quads than for triples. Our experience thus far has shown the choice of quads to be satisfactory in every way.

The high level of the quads allows a great deal of flexibility as to the efficiency of the object code generated. For example, the original 1108 code generator, designed and implemented in three weeks, was fairly straightforward and generated mediocre to poor object code. However, an extensive revision of the code generator, requiring a six-week effort, yielded a compiler that provides good object code comparing favorably with the code that is produced by other compilers on the 1108. Thus, the time and effort expended on a new implementation of SIMPL-T depends a great deal on the quality of the object code to be produced for the new machine.

Table I gives a comparison of the core requirements for the ALGOL, FORTRAN and SIMPL-T compilers on the UNIVAC 1108. The FORTRAN figures are for the smaller of the two standard FORTRAN compilers supported by UNIVAC, and the ALGOL compiler used is the NUALGOL compiler from Norwegian University. Both the ALGOL and FORTRAN compilers are coded in assembly language.

Comprehensive comparisons have not been made between object programs produced by the different compilers. However, the results of one comparison between the object programs generated by the FORTRAN and SIMPL-R compilers is given in Table II. (The SIMPL-R compiler is an extension of the SIMPL-T compiler and the two compilers generate identical code for SIMPL-T programs.) For this comparison, a sparse matrix problem was coded in both FORTRAN and SIMPL-R and executed on several sets of data.[10] Both programs consisted of about 750 source cards (360 SIMPL-R statements), and the execution timings are for a typical set of test data.

Table I. Size comparisons for UNIVAC 1108 compilers. K =1,000 words

Compiler	Overlay segments	Space required Instructions	Data	Total	Non-overlayed size Instructions	Data	Total
ALGOL	3	13K	9K	22K	30K	17K	47K
FORTRAN	6	16K	19K	35K	53K	39K	92K
SIMPL-T	4	15K	14K	29K	30K	20K	50K

Table II. Comparison between a sample program coded in FORTRAN and SIMPL-R. The timings are CPU times, and the program sizes include library routines

Language	Compile time	Object program size Instructions	Data	Execution time
FORTRAN	6·9 sec	6,873	21,862	7·7 sec
SIMPL-R	7·0 sec	5,339	20,875	6·6 sec

The performance figures in Tables I and II illustrate some success in achieving the SIMPL-T design criterion of generating efficient object code. The favorable comparisons are in spite of the fact that the FORTRAN compiler has a good optimizer, while the SIMPL-T and SIMPL-R compilers have only local optimization.

The figures also show reasonable results in compile time for the SIMPL compilers when compared with FORTRAN. This is in spite of the facts that the SIMPL compilers are designed for portability rather than for fast compilation and are coded in a high-level language rather than in assembly language.

Bootstrapping SIMPL-T

Plans for transporting a compiler from computer M to a new computer N must include a procedure for bootstrapping on to the target machine N unless the compiler is written in a language that already exists on the target machine. Since the SIMPL-T compiler is written in SIMPL-T, a bootstrap is required in order to transport the compiler.

Two procedures for bootstrapping SIMPL-T on to a new machine are illustrated in Figures 1 and 2. The notation

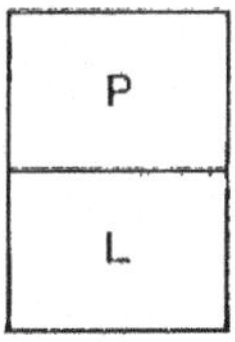

denotes program P coded in language L and

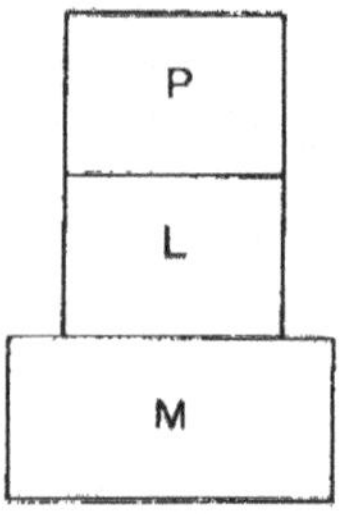

denotes program P, in language L, executing on machine M (so that L would be machine language for M). ζ(L, M) denotes a language L compiler for machine M, and ML(M) denotes machine language for machine M. Thus the objective of a bootstrap of SIMPL-T to a new machine N is to obtain

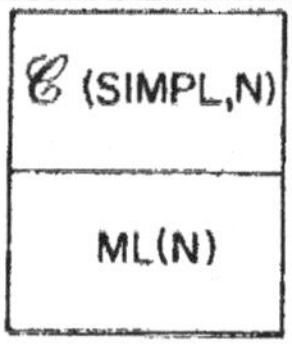

Finally, T(L1, L2) denotes a translator from language L1 to language L2, and

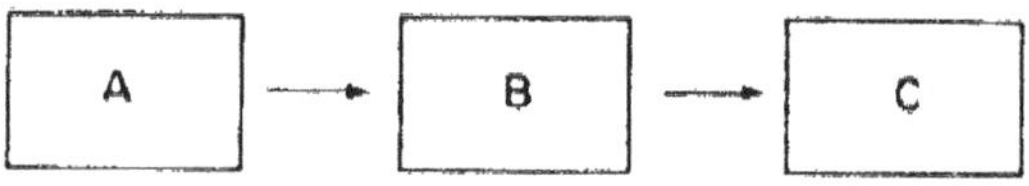

indicates that A is input to processor B and the output is C. It is worth noting that the code generation module of

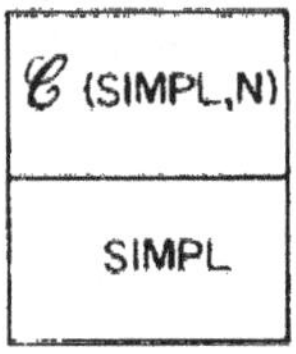

represents the major effort required to transport the SIMPL-T compiler to a new machine N.

One method of bootstrapping that could be used for SIMPL-T is to compile the new compiler for machine N using the existing SIMPL-T compiler on machine M and then transport the object code to the new machine. This procedure, illustrated in Figure 1, has the advantage that no intermediate language is involved, and it is possibly the best procedure to use if a system that supports an existing SIMPL-T compiler is conveniently available. As an alternative to using an existing SIMPL-T compiler for the bootstrap, and as a means of bootstrapping SIMPL-T on to our 1108 initially, it was decided to write a transportable bootstrap compiler. This required that the bootstrap compiler be written in a transportable language and that the compiler produce transportable output.

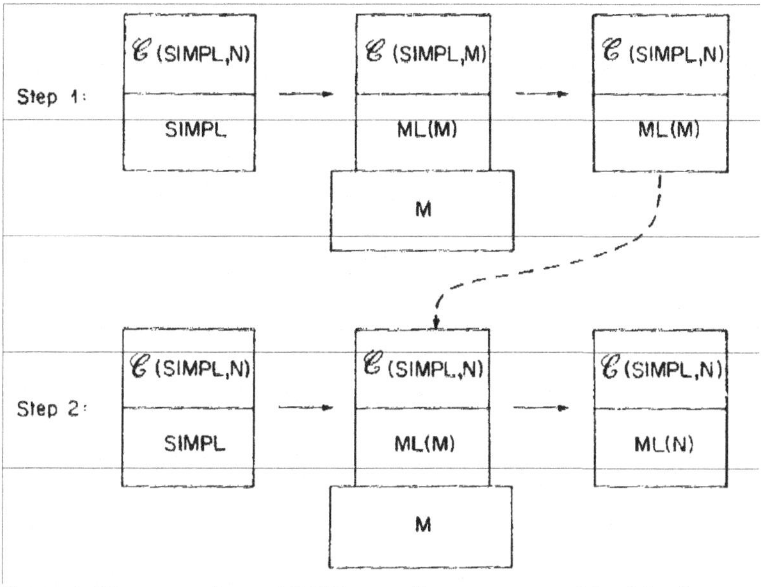

Figure 1. Bootstrapping a SIMPL compiler on to a machine N using an existing implementation on machine M

Of the languages available only FORTRAN and SNOBOL satisfied the main requirements of portability and availability. SNOBOL was preferred because of its recursion and string handling facilities, but the lack of compiler versions of SNOBOL is a disadvantage for several reasons.19 SNOBOL interpreters are usually large and slow and are not designed for easily debugging large modular programs.

On the other hand, FORTRAN provides convenient facilities for working with separately compiled modules, but it is undesirable for writing portable string manipulation programs. It was thus desired to find a solution that would provide the ease of programming a translator in SNOBOL and the ease of working with programs written in FORTRAN.

The solution obtained was to write a translator in SNOBOL4 that translates a SIMPL-T program into ANSI FORTRAN IV. This would yield a bootstrap procedure that would enable SIMPL-T programs to be run on a machine that has no SIMPL-T compiler, provided the machine has SNOBOL4 and FORTRAN IV available. The SNOJBOL bootstrap translator would be used to convert a SIMPL-T program into a FORTRAN program, and the FORTRAN program could then be compiled and executed. This procedure is illustrated in Figure 2.

To facilitate the use of the bootstrap, string handling and I/O packages (written in FORTRAN) are included. Thus the only effort required to transport the bootstrap (in addition to the effort required for the compiler) is to write a few machine-dependent subroutines, such as bit manipulation and system interface subroutines. This practically negligible effort yields the desired bootstrap package for a new machine.

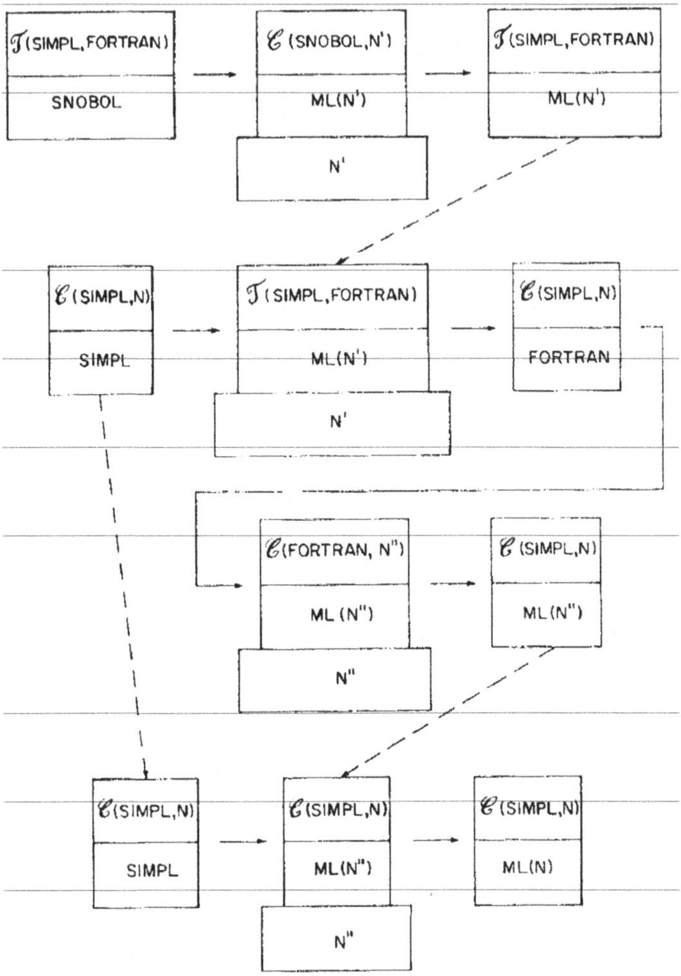

Figure 2. Bootstrapping a SIMPL compiler on to machine N using the SNOBOL translator. Machines N' and N" would normally (but need not) be the same as machine N. Note that if N" = N, the last step is still needed to produce a more efficient compiler. Note also that Steps 1 and 2 would be combined if a SNOBOL interpreter (instead of a compiler) were used

It should be noted that the SNOBOL translator produces transportable FORTRAN code through such devices as allocating strings one character per word. Essentially all of the features of SIMPL-T are supported by the translator, including recursion; call by value and reference, and externals.

Some variation on the bootstrap procedure using the SNOBOL translator may be desirable if SNOBOL, FORTRAN or both are not available on the target machine. Either the translation of a SIMPL-T program into FORTRAN, or the compilation and execution of the resulting FORTRAN program (or both) could be done on another machine. (This might be the case, for example, in bootstrapping to a small machine for which SNOBOL is not available.) Thus, the bootstrap process is rather flexible due to the portability of the SNOBOL translator and of the FORTRAN programs that it produces.

Results and Comments

The bootstrap procedure described here was used initially to bootstrap the type less language SIMPL-X on to the UNIVAC 1108 at the University of Maryland Computer Science Center. This bootstrap was facilitated by the fact that the variables of SIMPL-X translated directly into FORTRAN integer variables.

A code generator for the PDP-11 has also been written in order to implement the systems programming language SIMPL-XI mentioned earlier. This code generator was interfaced with the existing scanner and parser with no problems. SIMPL-XI, which also required some extensions to the compiler, is being run as a cross-compiler on the 1108 for the PDP-11.

The SIMPL-T compiler was bootstrapped from SIMPL-X and has been extended to yield a compiler for SIMPL-R, a language that has reels. The SIMPL-R implementation10 was a six-week effort by a programmer who was not familiar with either the SIMPL-T compiler or the 1108 computer and operating system.

Currently, efforts are under way to bootstrap SIMPL-T on to the IBM 360/370 machines. The SNOBOL-FORTRAN bootstrap for SIMPL-T was recently completed and has been used to run the scan and parse passes of the compiler on a 360.

While the bootstrap procedure has been successful in general, there have been some problems. No compiler version of SNOBOL was available for the 1108, and the available interpreter versions proved to be inadequate and required local modification. SPITBOL on the 360 has been a vast improvement and would have more than adequately solved this problem had a working version been available for the 1108.

The other problems were primarily due to the inadequacies and restrictions of FORTRAN. Again, if SPITBOL were generally available, most of these problems could have been eliminated by translating SIMPL-T into SNOBOL (SPITBOL). This would have made available such features as recursion and string data, thereby facilitating the translation.

Although these problems were foreseen, they were underestimated. The large amount of time and memory required for the SNOBOL programs and the size of the FORTRAN programs generated (about 90K words for the scanner and parser on the 1108) made the development of the bootstrap an expensive and time-consuming process. Furthermore, these requirements make the bootstrap procedure impractical (if not impossible) for small machines.

Yet these were the only languages available for which there was reasonable expectation of producing portable programs. This is a rather sad commentary on the availability of reasonable general-purpose languages and compilers, and indicates a need for widespread implementation of languages and compilers such as SIMPL-T and its compiler.

On the basis of our experience, we believe that this approach to bootstrapping a language on to a variety of machines would be quite satisfactory if a suitable language were already available on the target machines. Even with the drawbacks mentioned, we know of no alternative that would provide an easier means of performing a stand-alone bootstrap.

Acknowledgements

The bootstrap for SIMPL-X was written by Mike Kamrad, and the bootstrap for SIMPL-T was written by Bruce Carmichael. The system routines for the UNIVAC 1108 compilers were written by Hans Breitenlohner. C. Wrandle Barth at Goddard Space Flight Center and Robert Knight at Princeton University are bootstrapping SIMPL-T to a 360.

References

[1] V. R. Basili and A. J. Turner, SIMPL-T: A Structured Programming Language, CN-14, University of Maryland Computer Science Center, 1974.
[2] M. Halstead, Machine-independent Computer Programming, Spartan Books; Rochelle Park, New Jersey, 1962.
[3] W. M. McKeeman, J. J. Horning and D. B. Wortman, A Compiler Generator, Prentice-Hall, Englewood Cliffs, New Jersey, 1970.
[4] G. Leach and H. Golde, 'Bootstrapping XPL to an XDS sigma 5 computer', Software— Practice and Experience, 3, No. 3, 235-244 (1973).
[5] M. Richards, 'BCPL: a tool for compiler writing and system programming', AFIPS Proceedings, 34, 557-566 (SJCC 1969).
[6] V. R. Basili, The SIMPL Family of Programming Languages and Compilers, TR-305, University of Maryland Computer Science Center, 1974.
[7] W. M. Waite, 'Guest editorial', Software— Practice and Experience, 3, No. 3, 195-196 (1973).
[8] R. S. Scowen, 'Babel and SOAP, applications of extensible compilers', Software— Practice and Experience, 3, No. 1, 15-27 (1973).
[9] V. R. Basili, SIMPLEX, A Language for Writing Structured Programs, TR-223, University of Maryland Computer Science Center, 1973.
[10] J. McHugh and V. R. Basili, SIMPL-R and Its Application to Large Sparse Matrix Problems, TR-310, University of Maryland Computer Science Center, 1974.

[11] R. G. Hamlet and M. V. Zelkowitz, 'SIMPL systems programming on a minicomputer', Micros and Minis Applications and Design, Proc. of 9th Annual IEEE COMPCON, 203-206, 1974.

[12] W. C. Rheinboldt, V. R. Basili and C. K; Mesztenyi, 'On a programming language for graph algorithms', BIT, 12, No. 2, 220-241 (1972).

[13] F. L. De Remer, 'Simple LR(k) grammars', Comm. ACM, 14, No, 7, 453-460 (1971).

[14] R. W. Floyd, 'Syntactic analysis and operator precedence', JnlACM, 10, No. 3, 316-333 (1963).

[15] M. S. Hecht and J. D. Ullman, 'Analysis of a simple algorithm for global flow problems', ACM Symposium on Principles of Programming Languages, 1973

[16] G. A. Kildall, 'A unified approach to global problem optimization', ACM Symposium on Principles of Programming Languages, 1973.

[17] J. A. Verson and R, E. Noonan, A High-level Macro Processor, TR-297, University of Maryland Computer Science Center, 1974.

[18] D. Gries, Compiler Construction for Digital Computers, Wiley, New York, 1971.

[19] R. Dunn, 'SNOBOL4 as a language for bootstrapping a compiler', SIGPLAN Notices, 8, No. 5, 28-32 (1973).

Iterative Enhancement: A Practical Technique for Software Development

Victor R. Basili and Albert J. Turner

Abstract. This paper recommends the "iterative enhancement" technique as a practical means of using a top-down, stepwise refinement approach to software development. This technique begins with a simple initial implementation of a properly chosen (skeletal) subproject which is followed by the gradual enhancement of successive implementations in order to build the full implementation. The development and quantitative analysis of a production compiler for the language SIMPL-T is used to demonstrate that the application of iterative enhancement to software development is practical and efficient, encourages the generation of an easily modifiable product, and facilitates reliability.

Key Words: Iterative enhancement, SIMPL, software analysis, software development, software evaluation measures, top-down design.

1. Introduction

Several techniques have been suggested as aids for producing reliable software that can be easily updated to meet changing needs [1]-[4]. These include the use of a top-down modular design, a careful design before coding, modular, well-structured components, and a minimal number of implementers. Although it is generally agreed that the basic guideline is the use of a top-down modular approach using "stepwise refinement" [5], this technique is often not easy to apply in practice when the project is of reasonable size. Building a system using a well-modularized, top-down approach requires that the problem and its solution be well understood. Even if the implementers have previously undertaken a similar project, it is still difficult to achieve a good design for a new system on the first try.

Manuscript received August 5, 1975. This work was supported in part by the Office of Naval Research under Grant N00014-67-A-0239-0021 (NR-044-431) to the Computer Science Center of the University of Maryland, and in part by the Computer Science Center of the University of Maryland.
V. R. Basili is with the Department of Computer Science, University of Maryland, College Park, Md. 20742.
A. J. Turner is with the Department of Mathematical Sciences, Clemson University, Clemson, S. C.

Furthermore, design flaws often do not show up until the implementation is well underway so that correcting the problems can require major effort.

One practical approach to this problem is to start with a simple initial implementation of a subset of the problem and iteratively enhance existing versions until the full system is implemented. At each step of the process, not only extensions but also design modifications can be made. In fact, each step can make use of stepwise refinement in a more effective way as the system becomes better understood through the iterative process. As these iterations converge to the full solution, fewer and fewer modifications need be made. "Iterative enhancement" represents a practical means of applying stepwise refinement.

This paper discusses the heuristic iterative enhancement algorithm and its application to the implementation of a fully instrumented production compiler for the programming language SIMPL-T [6]. The SIMPL-T project represents a successful practical experience in using the approach in conjunction with several of the standard informal techniques to develop a highly reliable and easily modifiable product in a relatively short amount of time.

The next section of this paper contains a discussion of the basic iterative enhancement method, independent of a specific application. The following section discusses the application of the method as used in the development of the compiler for SIMPL-T, and includes some initial results from a quantitative analysis of the SIMPL-T project.

2. Overview of the method

The first step in the application of the iterative enhancement technique to a software development project consists of a simple initial implementation of a skeletal sub problem of the project. This skeletal implementation acts as an initial guess in the process of developing a final implementation which meets the complete set of project specifications. A project control list is created that contains all the tasks that need to be performed in order to achieve the desired final implementation. At any given point in the process, the project control list acts as a measure of the "distance" between the current and final implementations.

In the remaining steps of the technique the current implementation is iteratively enhanced until the final implementation is achieved. Each iterative step consists of selecting and removing the next task from the list, designing the implementation for the selected task (the design phase), coding and debugging the implementation of the task (the implementation phase), performing an analysis of the existing partial implementation developed at this step of the iteration (the analysis phase), and updating the project control list as a result of this analysis. The process is iterated until the project control list is empty, i.e., until a final implementation is developed that meets the project specifications.

Although the details of the algorithm vary with the particular problem class and implementation environment, a set of guidelines can be given to further specify the various steps in the process. The development of the first step, the skeletal initial implementation, may be achieved by defining the implementation of a skeletal, subset of the problem. A skeletal subset is one that contains a good sampling of the key aspects of the problem, that is simple enough to understand and implement easily, and whose implementation would make a usable and useful product available to the user. This subset should be devoid of special case analysis and should impose whatever restrictions might be necessary to facilitate its implementation without seriously affecting its usability. The implementation itself should be simple and straightforward in overall design and straightforward and modular at lower levels of design and coding so that it can be modified easily in the iterations leading to the final implementation.

The project control list guides the iterative process by keeping track of all the work that needs to be done in order to achieve the final implementation. The tasks on the list include the redesign or receding of components in which flaws have been discovered, the design and implementation of features and facilities that are missing from the current implementation, and the solution of unsolved problems. The sequence of lists corresponding to the sequence of partial implementations is a valuable component of the historical documentation of the project.

Each entry in the project control list is a task to be performed in one step of the iterative process. It is important that each task be conceptually simple enough to be completely understood in order to minimize the chance of error in the design and implementation phases of the process.

A major component of the iterative process is the analysis phase that is performed on each successive implementation. The project control list is constantly being revised as a result of this analysis. This is how redesign and receding work their way into the control list. Specific topics for analysis include such items as the structure, modularity, modifiability, usability, reliability and efficiency of the current implementation as well as an assessment of the achievement of the goals of the project. One approach to a careful analysis is the use of an appropriate set of guidelines as follows.

1) Any difficulty in design, coding, or debugging a modification should signal the need for redesign or receding of existing components.
2) Modifications should fit easily into isolated and easy-to-find modules. If not, then some redesign is needed.
3) Modifications to tables should be especially easy to make. If any table modification is not quickly and easily done, then a redesign is indicated.
4) Modifications should become easier to make as the iterations progress. If not, then there is a basic problem such as a design flow or a proliferation of "patches."
5) "Patches" should normally be allowed to exist for only one or two iterations. Patches should be allowed, however, in order to avoid redesigning during an implementation phase.
6) The existing implementation should be analyzed frequently to determine how well it measures up to the project goals.
7) Program analysis facilities should be used whenever available to aid in the analysis of the partial implementations.
8) User reaction should always be solicited and analyzed for indications of deficiencies in the existing implementation.

Certain aspects of the iteration process are dependent on the local environment in which the work is being performed, rather than on the specific project. Although the techniques used in the design and implementation phases of each iteration step should basically be top-down step-wise refinement techniques, the specifics can vary depending on such factors as installation standards and the number of people involved. Much has been written elsewhere about such techniques, and they will not be discussed further here. The procedures used in the analysis phase for each partial implementation are dependent upon such local factors as the program analysis facilities available, the programming languages used, and the availability of user feedback. Thus, to some extent the efficient use of the iterative enhancement technique must be tailored to the implementation environment.

In summary, iterative enhancement is a heuristic algorithm that begins with the implementation of a sub-problem and proceeds with the iterative modification of existing implementations based on a set of informal guidelines in order to achieve the desired full implementation. Variants of this technique have undoubtedly been used in many applications. However, iterative enhancement is different from the iterative techniques often discussed in the literature, in which the entire problem is initially implemented and the existing implementations are iteratively refined or reorganized [2] to achieve a good final design and implementation.

3. Application of the method to compiler development

Compiler development falls into a class of problems that can be called *input directed*. Such problems have well-defined inputs that determine the processing to be performed. The application of the iterative enhancement method to compiler development will be discussed in this section. In order to be more specific, it is assumed that the syntax of the language L to be compiled is defined by a context free grammar G.

Since a compiler is input directed, the skeletal compiler to be initially implemented can be specified by choosing a skeletal language, L_o, for L. The language L_o may be slightly modified sublanguage of L with a grammar G_o that is essentially a sub grammar of G.

In choosing L_o, a small number of features of L are chosen, as a basis. For example, this basis might include one data type, three or four statement types, one parameter mechanism, a few operators, and other features needed to give L_o the overall general flavor of L. The language derived from this basis can then be modified for ease of implementation and improved usability to obtain L_o.

The remainder of this section describes the use of iterative enhancement in an actual compiler implementation.

3.1 A Case Study: the SIMPL-T Project

The iterative enhancement method was used at the University of Maryland in the implementation of a compiler for the procedure-oriented algorithmic language SIMPL-T [6] on a Univac 1108. The SIMPL-T project is discussed in this section, beginning with a brief illustration of the scope of the project.

Overview: SIMPL-T is designed to be the base language for a family of programming languages [7]. Some of its features are as follows.

1) A program consists of a set of separately compiled modules.
2) Each module consists of a set of global variables and a set of procedures and functions.
3) The statement types are assignment, if-then-else, while, case, call, exit, and return.
4) The data types are integer, character, and character string.
5) There are extensive sets of operators and intrinsics for data manipulation.
6) There is a one-dimensional array of any data type.
7) Procedures and functions may optionally be recursive.
8) Scalar arguments may be passed by reference or by value; arrays are passed by reference.
9) Procedures and functions may not have internal procedures or functions; neither procedures nor functions may be passed as parameters.
10) There is no block structure (but there are compound statements).
11) Procedures, functions, and data may be shared by separately compiled modules.

Characterizing the overall design of the language, its syntax and semantics are relatively conservative, consistent and uncluttered. There are a minimal number of language constructs, and they are all rather basic. A stack is adequate for the run-time environment. These design features contributed to a reasonably well-defined language design which permitted the development of a reasonably well-understood compiler design.

The following are characteristics and facilities of the SIMPL-T compiler:

1) It is programmed in SIMPL-T and is designed to be transportable by rewriting the code generation modules [8].
2) It generates very good object code on the 1108. (In the only extensive test [9], the code produced was better than that generated by the Univac optimizing Fortran compiler.)
3) Good diagnostics are provided at both compile and runtimes.
4) An attribute and cross-reference listing is available.
5) There are traces available for line numbers, calls and returns, and variable values.
6) Subscript and case range checking are available.
7) There are facilities for obtaining statistics both at compile time and after a program execution.
8) Execution timing for procedures, functions, and separately compiled modules is available.

In summary, the compiler is a production compiler that generates efficient object code, provides good diagnostics, and has a variety of testing, debugging, and program analysis facilities. The compiler itself consists of about 6400 SIMPL-T statements, and the library consists of about 3500 (assembly language) instructions. (The statement count does not include declarations, comments, or spacing. The compiler consists of 17 000 lines of code.)

The *Initial Implementation*: The skeletal language implemented initially in the SIMPL-T project was essentially the language SIMPL-X [10]. Some of the restrictions (with respect to SIMPL-T) imposed for the initial implementation were:

1) There was only one data type (integer).
2) Only call by value was allowed for scalar parameters.
3) All procedures and functions were recursive.
4) Only the first 12 characters of an identifier name were used.
5) Case numbers were restricted to the range 0-99.
6) Both operands of a logical operator (•AND•,•OR•) were always evaluated.

Since the compiler was to be self-compiling, some character handling facility was needed. This was provided by an extension that allowed character data to be packed in an integer variable just as in Fortran.

Restrictions were also made on compiler facilities for the initial implementation. Only a source listing and reasonable diagnostics were provided, leaving the debugging and analysis facilities for later enhancements.

The design of the initial skeletal implementation was a rather straightforward attempt to provide a basis for future enhancements. This allowed the initial implementation to be completed rather quickly so that the enhancement process could get underway. It is instructive to note that while most of the higher level design of the compiler proved to be valid throughout the implementation, most of the lower level design and code was redone during the enhancement process. This illustrates the difficulty in doing a good complete project design initially, especially in light of the fact that the initial implementation was an honest attempt to achieve a good basis upon which to build later extensions.

The importance of using a simple approach in the initial implementation was illustrated by the experience with the initial SIMPL-X code generation module. Although it was not intended to generate really good code, far too much effort was expended in an attempt to generate moderately good code. As a result, most of the initial debugging effort was spent on the code generator (which was later almost completely rewritten anyhow). A simple straightforward approach would have allowed the project to get underway much faster and with much less effort.

A final comment on the skeletal implementation is that it is clear in retrospect that had the compiler not been self-compiling it would have been better to use an even more restricted subset of SIMPL-T. This was not considered at the time because programming the compiler in the initial subset would have been more difficult.

The design and implementation phases of each iteration were performed using a basic top-down approach. Every attempt was made to ensure a high level of clarity and logical construction.

It is worth noting that the SIMPL-T language itself was also being iteratively enhanced in parallel with the compiler development. As experience was gained by using the language to program the compiler, new features were added and old features were modified on the basis of this experience. Thus user experience played a major role not only in the implementation of the software project (i.e., the compiler) but also in the specification of the project (i.e., the language design).

The Analysis Phase: The analysis performed at the end of each iterative step was basically centered around the guidelines given above in the overview of the method. Some of the specific techniques used are briefly discussed below.

Since the intermediate compilers were mostly self-compiling, a large amount of user experience was available from the project itself. This user experience together with the valuable test case provided by the compiler for itself represent two of the advantages of self-compilers.

A second source of user experience in the SIMPL-T project was derived from student use in the classroom. Since classroom projects are not generally ongoing, there was normally no inconvenience to students in releasing the intermediate versions of the compiler as they were completed. These two sources of user experience are examples of how the details of applying iterative enhancement can be tailored to the resources available in the implementation environment.

Testing the intermediate compilers was done by the usual method of using test data. Again the self-compiling feature of the compiler was valuable since the compiler was often its own best test program. The bug farm and bug contest techniques [11] were also used and some of the results are given below.

Timing analyses of the compiler were first done using the University of Maryland Program Instrumentation Package (PIP). PIP provides timing information based on a partition of core and is thus more suitable for assembly language programs than for programs written in higher level languages. However the information obtained from PIP was of some value in locating bottlenecks, especially in the library routines.

When the timing and statistics facilities for object programs were added to the compiler, new tools for analysis of the compiler itself became available. The timing facility has been used to improve the execution speed through the elimination of bottlenecks, and the statistics facilities have been used to obtain information such as the frequency of hashing collisions. Future plans call for further use of the timing information to help improve compiler performance. The statistical facilities were also used to obtain the quantitative analysis discussed at the end of this section.

Project Summary: The SIMPL-T project was completed during a 16 calendar month period. Since other activities took place in parallel with the implementation effort, it is difficult to accurately estimate the total effort, but a fairly accurate effort for the language and compiler design, implementation, and maintenance (excluding the bootstrap and library implementations) is 10 man-months. Counting only the code in the final compiler, this time requirement represents an average output of almost 30 statements (75 lines) of debugged code per man-day. It is felt that the use of iterative enhancement was a major contributing factor in this achievement.

Experience has thus far indicated that the compiler is reasonably easy to modify. Two fairly large modifications have been made by people not previously participating in the compiler implementation. One of these efforts involved the addition of a macro facility and in the other, single and double precision reels were added [9]. Both efforts were accomplished relatively easily even though there was little documentation other than the compiler source listing.

Finally, the reliability of the compiler has been quite satisfactory. During the two and one-half month duration of the bug contest a total of 18 bugs were found, many of which were quite minor. (All bugs regardless of severity were counted.) Of course, several additional bugs had been found before the contest and some have been found since, but overall their number has been small. As could be predicted, most of the bugs occurred in the least well understood components: error recovery and code generation.

Project Analysis: In an attempt to justify that the heuristic iterative enhancement algorithm gives quantitative results, an extensive analysis of four of the intermediate compilers plus the final compiler was performed. As of this writing (June 1975) the analysis is only in the early stages, but some of the preliminary statistics computed are given in Table I. The interpretation of some of these statistics has not been completed, but they have been included as a matter of interest.

The compilers referenced in Table I are

1) One of the early SIMPL-X compilers (SIMPL-X 2.0).
2) The SIMPL-X compiler after a major revision to correct some structural defects (SIMPL-X 3.1).
3) The first SIMPL-T compiler, written in SIMPL-X (SIMPL-X 4.0).
4) Compiler (3), rewritten in SIMPL-T (SIMPL-T 1.0).
5) The current SIMPL-T compiler at the time of the analysis (SIMPL-T 1.6).

The statistics were computed by using the existing statistical facilities of the SIMPL-T compiler, and by adding some new facilities.

An explanation of the statistics given is as follows.

1) Statements are counted as defined by the syntax. A compound statement such as a WHILE statement counts as one statement plus one for each statement in its statement list.
2) A separately compiled module is a collection of globals, procedures, and functions that is compiled independently of other separately compiled modules and combined with the other modules for execution.
3) A token is a syntactic entity such as a keyword, identifier, or operator.
4) Globals were only counted if they were ever modified. That is, named constants and constant tables were not counted.
5) A data binding occurs when a procedure or function *P* modifies a global *X* and procedure or function *Q* accesses (uses the value of) *X*. This causes a binding *(P,X,Q)*. It is also possible to have the (different) binding *(Q,X,P)*; however *(P,X,P)* is not counted. The counting procedure was modified so that if P and *Q* execute only in separate passes and the execution of *P* precedes that of *Q*, then *(P,X,Q)* is counted but *(Q,X,P)* is not counted.

The reasons for choosing these statistics were based on intuition and a desire to investigate quantitatively the data and control structure characteristics of the sequence of compilers.

It is interesting to note that the statistics indicate a trend towards improvement in the compiler with respect to many generally accepted theories of good programming principles, even though the redesign and receding efforts that caused this trend were done only on the basis of the informal guidelines of the iterative enhancement algorithm. As the project progressed, the trend was toward more procedures and functions with fewer statements, more independently compiled segments, less nesting of statements, and a decrease in the use of global variables. These improvements occurred even though the changes were being made primarily to correct difficulties that were encountered in incorporating modifications during the iterative enhancement process.

The meaning of many of the trends indicated in Table I is clear. For example, due to the difficulties encountered in working with larger units of code, the number of procedures and functions and the number of separately compiled modules increased much more than did the number of statements. Similarly, the decrease in nesting level corresponds to the increase in the number of procedures and functions.

One of the harder to explain sequences of statistics is the average number of tokens per statement. The probable cause for the large jump between compilers 1) and 2) is the relaxation of several Fortran-like restrictions imposed for the initial bootstrap. The more interesting jump between compilers 3), written in SIMPL-X, and 4), written in SIMPL-T, seems to suggest that writing in a more powerful language (SIMPL-T) may also affect the writing style used by a programmer. That is, with more powerful operators more operators are used per statement.

The statistics for globals, locals, and parameters indicate a clear trend away from the use of globals and toward increased usage of locals and parameters. The large drop in the number of globals accessible to the average procedure or function between compilers 3) and 4) and compilers 4) and 5) corresponds to the increase in the number of separately compiled modules for 4) and 5). Splitting one separately compiled module into several modules decreases the number of accessible globals because the globals are also divided among the modules and are usually not made accessible between modules.

The notion of data binding is more complex than the notions considered above and the data binding statistics require more effort to interpret. Note, for example, that if the number of procedures and functions doubles, then the data binding count would most likely more than double due to the interactions between the new and old procedures and functions. Similarly, splitting a separately compiled module into several modules would tend to decrease the number of possible bindings due to the decrease in the number of accessible globals.

In light of these considerations, the data binding counts in Table I seem reasonable except for the decrease in actual bindings from compiler 4) to compiler 5). A more detailed investigation of this decrease revealed that it was primarily due to the elimination of the improper usage of a set of global variables in the code generation component of the compiler. The sharing of these variables by two logically independent sets of procedure had caused several problems in modifying the code generator, and the data accessing was restructured in an attempt to eliminate these problems.

Finally, the percentage of possible data bindings that actually occurred can be interpreted as an indication of how much variables that are declared globally are really used as globals. (If every procedure and function both modified and accessed all its accessible globals, then the percentage would be 100.) As with the other measures, ideal values (in an absolute sense) are not clear, but the trend toward higher values that is shown in Table I is the desired result.

4. Conclusion

Two major goals for the development of a software product are that it be reasonably modifiable and reliable.

This paper recommends the iterative enhancement technique as a methodology for software development that for many projects facilitates the achievement of these goals and provides a practical means of using a top-down step-wise refinement approach.

The technique involves the development of a software product through a sequence of successive design and implementation steps, beginning with an initial "guess" design and implementation of a skeletal sub problem. Each step of the iterative process consists of either a simple, well-understood extension, or a design or implementation modification motivated by a better understanding of the problem obtained through the development process.

It is difficult to make a nonsubjective qualitative judgment about the success of a software technique. However the preliminary statistics from an analysis of the SIMPL-T project do indicate some desirable quantitative results. These statistics suggest that the informal guidelines of the heuristic iterative enhancement algorithm encourage the development of a software product that satisfies a number of generally accepted evaluation criteria.

The measure of accomplishment for the SIMPL-T project was based upon relative improvement with respect to a set of measures. A question remains as to what are absolute measures that indicate acceptable algorithm termination criteria. More work on several different projects and studies of the implications of these measures are needed to help determine some quantitative characteristics of good software.

A need also exists for developing a formal basis for software evaluation measures. An analytical basis for evaluation would not only increase the understanding of the meaning of the measures but should also shed some light on appropriate absolute values that indicate the achievement of good characteristics.

TABLE I

MEASURES MADE ON FIVE DIFFERENT COMPILERS IN THE SIMPL-T PROJECT

	(1)	(2)	(3)	(4)	(5)
Number of Statements	3404	4217	5181	5847	6350
Number of Procedures and Functions	89	189	213	240	289
Number of Separately Compiled Modules	4	4	7	15	37
Average Number of Statements per Proc/Func	38.2	22.3	24.3	24.4	22.0
Average Nesting Level	3.4	2.9	2.9	2.9	2.8
Average Number of Tokens per Statement	5.7	6.3	6.6	7.2	7.3
Number of Data Variables:					
Globals	155	132	151	180	193
Locals	112	381	496	550	621
Parameters	35	184	215	257	388
Average Number of Data Variables per Proc/Func:					
Globals	1.7	0.7	0.7	0.8	0.7
Locals	1.3	2.0	2.3	2.3	2.1
Parameters	0.4	1.0	1.0	1.1	1.3
Percentage of:					
Globals	51.3	18.9	17.5	18.2	16.1
Locals	37.1	54.7	57.5	55.7	51.7
Parameters	11.6	26.4	24.9	26.0	32.3
Average Number of Globals Accessible by a Proc/Func	52.0	52.2	57.4	33.9	22.3
Number of Actual Data Bindings	2610	6662	8759	12006	10442
Number of Possible Data Bindings	243780	814950	1337692	497339	342727
Percentage of Possible Bindings that Occurred	1.1	0.8	0.7	2.4	3.0

The implementation and analysis of the SIMPL-T system have demonstrated that not only is the iterative enhancement technique an effective means of applying a modular, top-down approach to software implementation, but it is also a practical and efficient approach as witnessed by the time and effort figures for the project. The development of a final product which is easily modified is a by-product of the iterative way in which the product is developed. This can be partially substantiated by the ease with which present extensions and modifications can be made to the system. A reliable product is facilitated since understanding of the overall system and its components is aided by the iterative process in which the design and code are examined and reevaluated as enhancements are made.

References

[1] H,D. Mills, "On the development of large, reliable programs," *Rec. 1973 IEEE Symp. Comp. Software Reliability*, Apr. 1973, pp. 155-159

[2] ——, "Techniques for the specification and design of complex programs," in *Proc. 3rd Texas Conf. Computing Systems*, Univ. Texas, Austin, Nov. 1974, pp. 8.1.1-8.1.4.

[3] O. J. Dahl, E. W. Dijkstra, and C. A. R. Hoare, *Structured Programming*. London: Academic, 1972.
[4] D. L. Parnas, "On the criteria to be used in decomposing systems into modules," *Commun. Ass. Comput. Mach.*, vol. 15, pp. 1053-1062, Dec. 1972.
[5] N. Wirth, "Program development by stepwise refinement, *Commun. Ass. Comput. Mach.*, vol. 14. pp. 221-227, Apr. 1971.
[6] V. R. Basili and A. J. Turner, "SIMPL-T: a structured programming language," Univ. of Maryland, Comp. Sci. Ctr., CN-14, Jan. 1974.
[7] V. R. Basili, "The SIMPL family of programming languages and compilers," Univ. of Maryland, Comp. Sci. Ctr., TR-305, June 1974.
[8] V. R. Basili and A. J. Turner, "A transportable extendable compiler," *in Software—Practice and Experience*, vol. 5, 1975, pp. 269-278.
[9] J. McHugh and V. R. Basili, "SIMPL-R and its application to large, sparse matrix problems," Univ. of Maryland, Comp. Sci. Ctr., TR-310, July 1974.
[10] V. R. Basili, "SIMPL-X, a language for writing structured programs," Univ. Maryland, Comp. Sci. Ctr., TR-223, Jan. 1973.
[11] M. Rain, "Two unusual methods for debugging system software," in *Software—Practice and Experience*, vol. 3, pp. 61-63, 1973.

Understanding and Documenting Programs

Victor R. Basili and Harlan D. Mills

Abstract. This paper reports on an experiment in trying to understand an unfamiliar program of some complexity and to record the authors' understanding of it. The goal was to simulate a practicing programmer in a program maintenance environment using the techniques of program design adapted to program understanding and documentation; that is, given a program, a specification and correctness proof were developed for the program. The approach points out the value of correctness proof ideas in guiding the discovery process. Toward this end, a variety of techniques were used: direct cognition for smaller parts, discovering and verifying loop invariants for larger program parts, and functions determined by additional analysis for larger program parts. An indeterminate bounded variable was introduced into the program documentation to summarize the effect of several program variables and simplify the proof of correctness.

Key Words: Program analysis, program correctness, program documentation, proof techniques, software maintenance.

I. Introduction

Understanding Programs

We report here on an experiment in trying to understand an unfamiliar program of some complexity and to record our understanding of it. We are as much concerned with recording our understanding as with understanding. Every day programmers are figuring out what existing programs do more or less accurately. But most of this effort is lost, and repeated over and over, because of the difficulty of capturing

---

Manuscript received June 10, 1980; revised September 3, 1981 and November 6, 1981. This work was supported in part by the U.S. Air Force Office of Scientific Research under Grant AFOSR-77-3181B.
V. R. Basili is with the Department of Computer Science, University of Maryland, College Park, MD 20742.
H. D. Mills is with the Department of Computer Science, University of Maryland, College Park, MD 20742 and the Federal Systems Division, IBM Corporation, Bethesda, MD 20034.

this understanding on paper. We want to demonstrate that the very techniques of good program design can be adapted to problems of recording hard-won understandings about existing programs.

In program design we advocate the joint development of design and correctness proof, as shown in [2], [4], [6], rather than *a posteriori* proof development. Nevertheless, we believe that the idea of program correctness provides a comprehensive *a posteriori* strategy for developing and recording an understanding of an existing program. In fact, we advocate another kind of joint development, this time, of specification and correctness proof. In this way, we have a consistent approach dealing always with three objects, namely, 1) a specification, 2) a program, and 3) a correctness proof. In writing a program, we are given 1) and develop 2) and 3) jointly; in reading a program, we are given 2) and develop 1) and 3) jointly. In either case, we end up with the same harmonious arrangement of 1) and 2) connected by 3) which contain our understanding of the program.

In the experiment at hand, our final understanding exceeded our most optimistic initial expectations, even though we have seen these ideas succeed before. One new insight from this experiment was how little we really had to know about the program to develop a complete understanding and proof of what it does (in contrast to how it does it). Without the correctness proof ideas to guide us, we simply would not have discovered how little we had to know. In fact, we know a great deal more than we have recorded here about how the program works, which we chalk up to the usual dead ends of a difficult discovery process. But the point is, without the focus of a correctness proof, we would still be trying to understand and record a much larger set of logical facts about the program than is necessary to understand precisely what it does.

In retrospect, we used a variety of discovery techniques. For simpler parts of the program, we used direct cognition. In small complex looping parts, we discovered and verified loop invariants. In the large, we organized the effect of major program parts as functions to be determined by additional analysis. We also discovered a new way to express the effect of a complex program part by introducing a bounded indeterminate variable which radically simplified the proof of correctness of the program part.

The Program

We were interested in a short but complex program. Our goal was to simulate a practicing programmer in a program maintenance environment. The program was chosen by Prof. J. Vandergraft of the University of Maryland as a difficult program to understand. It was a Fortran program called ZEROIN which claimed to find a zero of a function given by a Fortran subroutine. We were given the program and told its general function. The problem then was to understand it, verify its correctness, and possibly modify it, to make it more efficient or extend its applicability. We were not given any more about the program than the program itself. The program given to us is shown in Fig. 1, the original Fortran ZEROIN.

```
***** ZEROIN.PROGRAM *****

      REAL FUNCTION ZEROIN (AX, BX, F, TOL, IP)
      REAL AX, BX, F, TOL
C
C
      REAL A, B, C, D, E, EPS, FA, FB, FC, TOL1, XM, P, Q, R, S
C
C  COMPUTE EPS, THE RELATIVE MACHINE PRECISION
C
      EPS = 1.0
   10 EPS = EPS/2.0
      TOL1 = 1.0 + EPS
      IF (TOL1 .GT. 1.0) GO TO 10
C
C  INITIALIZATION
C
        IF (IP .EQ. 1) WRITE (6, 11)
 11     FORMAT(' THE INTERVALS DETERMINED BY ZEROIN ARE')
      A = AX
      B = BX
      FA = F(A)
      FB = F(B)
C
C  BEGIN STEP
C
   20 C = A
      FC = FA
      D = B - A
      E = D
 30    IF (IP .EQ. 1) WRITE(6,31) B,C
 31    FORMAT (2E15.8)
      IF (ABS(FC) .GE. ABS(FB) ) GO TO 40
      A = B
      B = C
      C = A
      FA = FB
      FB = FC
      FC = FA
C
C  CONVERGENCE TEST
C
   40 TOL1 = 2.0*EPS*ABS(B) + 0.5*TOL
      XM =  .5*(C - B)
      IF (ABS(XM) .LE. TOL1) GO TO 90
      IF (FB .EQ. 0.0) GO TO 90
C
C  IS BISECTION NECESSARY
C
      IF (ABS(E) .LT. TOL1) GO TO 70
      IF (ABS(FA) .LE. ABS(FB)) GO TO 70
C
C  IS QUADRATIC INTERPOLATION POSSIBLE
C
      IF (A .NE. C) GO TO 50
C
C  LINEAR INTERPOLATION
C
      S = FB/FA
      P = 2.0*XM*S
      Q = 1.0 - S
      GO TO 60
C
C  INVERSE QUADRATIC INTERPOLATION
C
   50 Q = FA/FC
      R = FB/FC
      S = FB/FA
      P = S*(2.0*XM*Q*(Q - R) - (B - A) * (R - 1.0))
      Q = (Q - 1.0)*(R - 1.0)*(S - 1.0)
C
C  ADJUST SIGNS
C
   60 IF (P .GT. 0.0) Q = -Q
      P = ABS(P)
C
C  IS INTERPOLATION ACCEPTABLE
C
      IF ((2.0*P) .GE. (3.0*XM*Q - ABS(TOL1*Q))) GO TO 70
      IF (P .GE. ABS(0.5*E*Q)) GO TO 70
      E = D
      D = P/Q
      GO TO 80
C
C  BISECTION
C
   70 D = XM
      E = D
C
C  COMPLETE STEP
C
   80 A = B
      FA = FB
      IF (ABS(D) .GT. TOL1) B = B + D
      IF (ABS(D) .LE. TOL1) B = B + SIGN(TOL1, XM)
      FB = F(B)
      IF ((FB*(FC/ABS (FC))) .GT. 0.0) GO TO 20
      GO TO 30
C
C  DONE
C
   90 ZEROIN = B
      RETURN
      END

***** ZEROIN.INFO *****

      ZEROIN IS A FUNCTION SUBPROGRAM WHICH FINDS
      A ZERO OF THE FUNCTION F(X) IN THE INTERVAL AX, BX .
      THE CALLING STATEMENT SHOULD HAVE THE FORM

          X* = ZEROIN(AX, BX, F, TOL, IP)
    WHERE THE PARAMETERS ARE DEFINED AS FOLLOWS.

     INPUT

     AX    LEFT ENDPOINT OF INITIAL INTERVAL
     BX    RIGHT ENDPOINT OF INITIAL INTERVAL
     F     FUNCTION SUBPROGRAM WHICH EVALUATES F(X) FOR ANY X IN
           THE INTERVAL AX, BX
     TOL   DESIRED LENGTH OF THE INTERVAL OF UNCERTAINTY OF THE
           FINAL RESULT ( .GE. 0.0)
    IP     AN INTEGER PRINT FLAG.  WHEN SET TO 0, NO PRINTING
           WILL BE DONE BY ZEROIN.  IF SET TO 1, THEN
           ALL OF THE INTERVALS COMPUTED BY ZEROIN WILL
           BE PRINTED OUT.


     OUTPUT

      ZEROIN ABCISSA APPROXIMATING A ZERO OF F IN THE INTERVAL AX, BX


         IT IS ASSUMED THAT F(AX) AND F(BX) HAVE OPPOSITE SIGNS
      WITHOUT A CHECK.  ZEROIN RETURNS A ZERO X IN THE GIVEN INTERVAL
      AX, BX TO WITHIN A TOLERANCE 4*MACHEPS*ABS(X) + TOL, WHERE MACHEPS
      IS THE RELATIVE MACHINE PRECISION.
         THIS FUNCTION SUBPROGRAM IS A SLIGHTLY MODIFIED TRANSLATION OF
      THE ALGOL 60 PROCEDURE ZERO GIVEN IN RICHARD BRENT, ALGORITHMS FOR
      MINIMIZATION WITHOUT DERIVATIVES, PRENTICE - HALL, INC. (1973).
    THIS VERSION IS COPIED FROM "COMPUTER METHODS FOR MATHEMATICAL
    COMPUTATIONS" BY FORSYTHE, MALCOLM, AND MOLER.  THE ONLY CHANGE
    IS THE INCLUSION OF THE PRINT FLAG IP.
```

Fig. 1. Original Fortran ZEROIN.

Prof. Vandergraft played the role of a user of the program and posed four questions regarding the program.

1) I have a lot of equations, some of which might be linear. Should I test for linearity and then solve the equation directly, or just call ZEROIN? That is, how much work does ZEROIN do to find a root of a linear function?
2) What will happen if I call ZEROIN with F(AX) and F(BX) both positive? How should the code be changed to test for this condition?
3) It is claimed that the inverse quadratic interpolation saves only 0.5 function evaluations on the average. To get a shorter program, I would like to remove the inverse quadratic interpolation part of the code. Can this be done easily? How?
4) Will ZEROIN find a triple root?

II. Techniques for Understanding Programs

Flowcharts

Any flow chartable program can be analyzed in a way we describe next for better understandability and documentation. For a fuller discussion, see [6]. We consider flowcharts as directed graphs with nodes and lines. The lines denote flow of control and the nodes denote tests and operations on data. Without loss of generality, we consider flowcharts with just three types of nodes, namely,

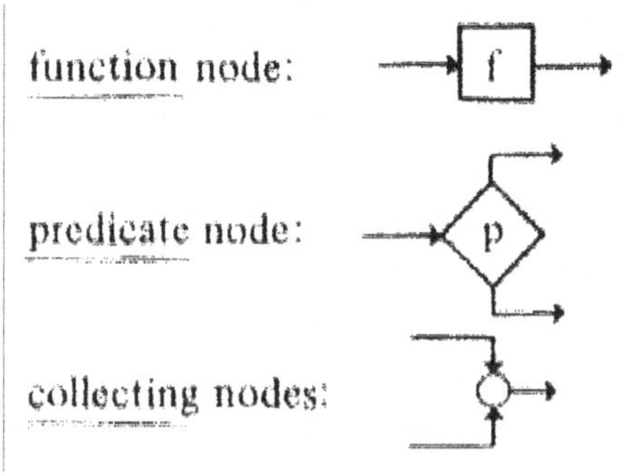

where f is any function mapping the data known to the program to new data, e.g., a simple Fortran assignment statement, and p is any predicate on the data known to the program, e.g., a simple Fortran test. An entry line of a flowchart program is a line adjacent to only one node, its head; an exit line is adjacent to only one node, its tail.

Functions and Data Assignments

Any function mapping the data known to a program to new data can be defined in a convenient way by generalized forms of data assignment statements. For example, an assignment, denoted

$$x := e \quad (\text{e.g., } x := x + y)$$

where x is a variable known to the program and e is an expression in variables known to the program, means that the value of e is assigned to x. Such an assignment also means that no variable except x is to be altered. The concurrent assignment, denoted

$$x1, x2, \cdots, xn := e1, e2, \cdots, en$$

means that expressions el, e2, •••, en are evaluated independently, and their values assigned simultaneously to xl, x2, • • •, xn, respectively. As before, the absence of a variable on the left side means that it is unchanged by the assignment. The conditional assignment, denoted

$$(p1 \rightarrow A1 | p2 \rightarrow A2 | \cdots | pn \rightarrow An)$$

where p1, p2, • • •, pn are predicates and A1, A2, • • •, An are assignments (simple, concurrent, or conditional) means that particular assignment Ai associated with the first pi, if any, which evaluates true; otherwise, if no pi evaluates true, then the conditional assignment is undefined.

An expression in an assignment may contain a function value, e.g.,

x := max (x, abs(y))

where max and abs are functions. But the function defined by the assignment statement is different, of course, from max or abs.

We note that many programming languages permit the possibility of so-called side effects, which alter data not mentioned in assignment statements or in tests. Side effects are specifically prohibited in our definition of assignments and tests.

Proper Programs

We define a proper program to be a program whose flowchart has exactly one entry line, one exit line, and, further, for every node a path from the entry through that node to the exit. For example,

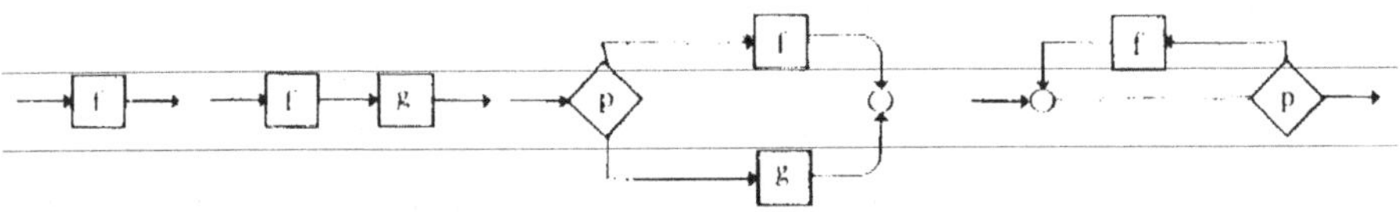

are proper programs, but

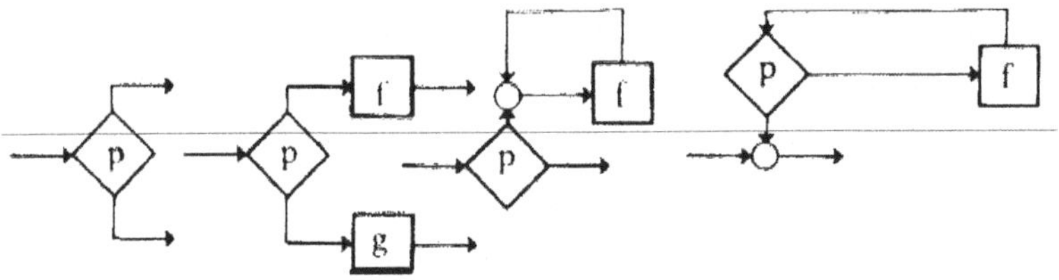

are not proper programs.

Program Functions

We define a program function of a proper program P, denoted [P], to be the function computed by all possible executions of P which start at its entry and terminate at its exit. That is, a program function [P] is a set of ordered pairs, the first member being a state of the data on entry to P and the second being the resulting state on exit. Note that the state of data includes input and output files, which may be read from or written to intermittently during execution. Also note that if a program does not terminate by reaching its exit line from some initial data at its entry, say by looping indefinitely or by aborting, no such pair will be determined and no mention of this abnormal execution will be found in its program function.

Proper programs are convenient units of documentation. Their program functions abstract their entire effect on the data known to the program. Within a program, any subprogram that is proper can be also abstracted by its program function, that is, the effect of the subprogram can be described by a single function node whose function is the program function of the subprogram.
We say two programs are function equivalent if their program functions are identical. For example, the programs

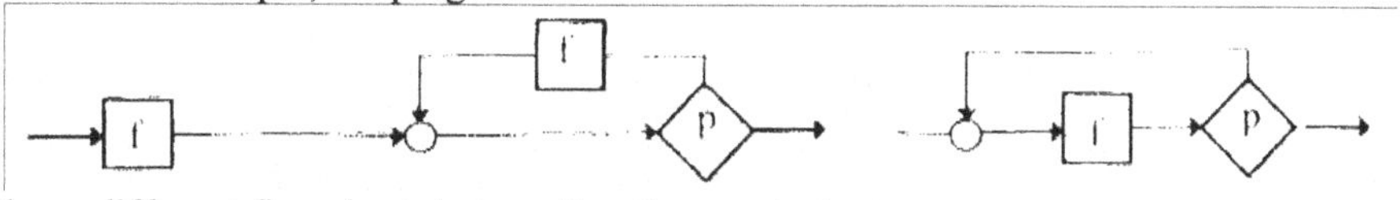

have different flowcharts but are function equivalent.

Prime Programs

We define a *prime program* to be a proper program that contains no subprogram that is proper, except for itself and function nodes. For example,

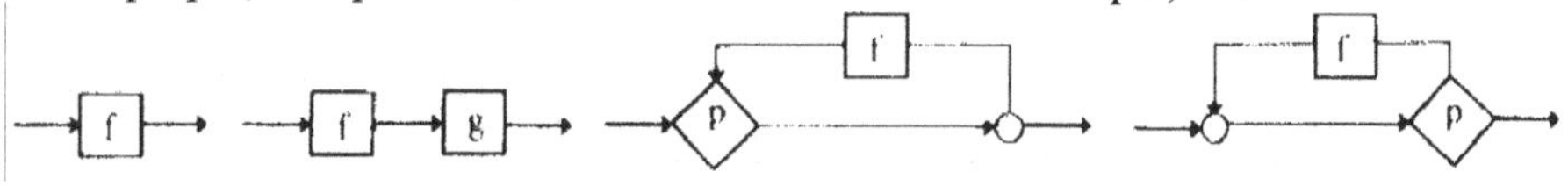

are primes, while

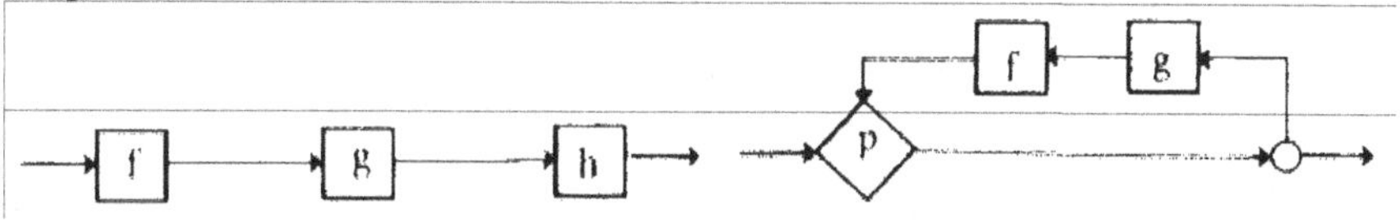

are not prime (*composite programs*), the first (of the composites) having subprograms

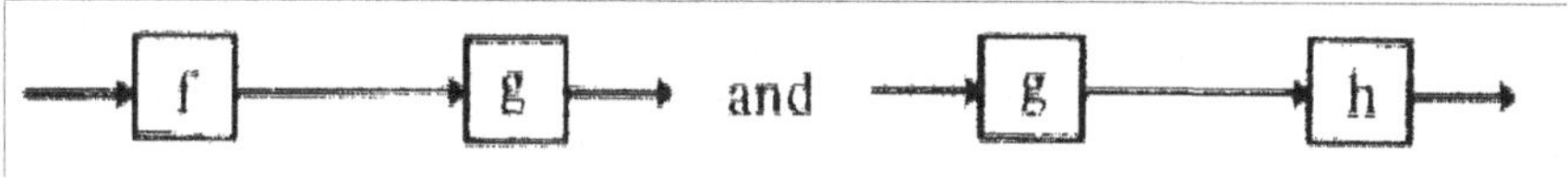

Any composite program can be decomposed into a hierarchy of primes, a prime at one level serving as a function node at the next higher level. For example, the composite programs above can be decomposed as shown next:

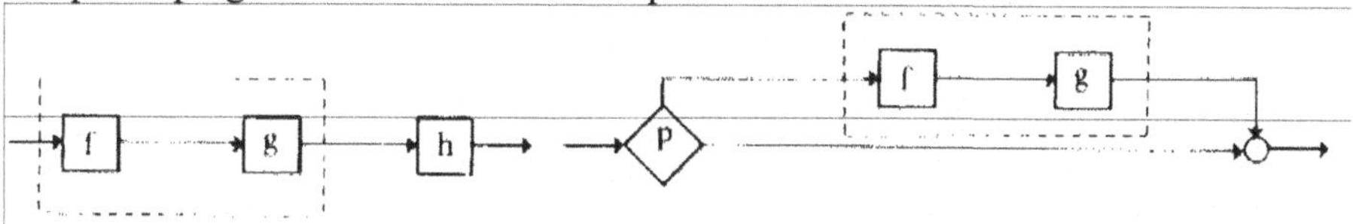

In each case, a prime is identified to serve as a function node in another prime at the next level. Note also that the first composite can also be decomposed as

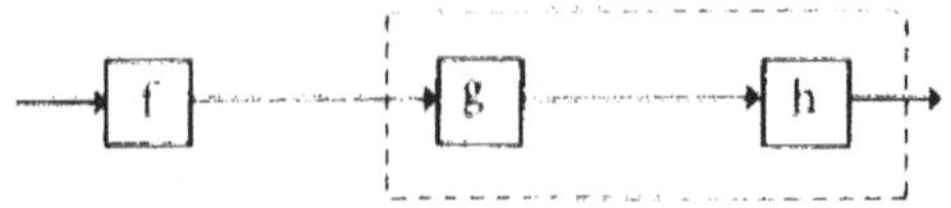

so that the prime decomposition of proper programs is not necessarily unique.

Prime Programs in Text Form

There is a striking resemblance between prime programs and prime numbers, with function nodes playing the role of unity, and subprograms the role of divisibility. Just as for numbers, we can enumerate the control graphs of prime programs and give a text description of small primes in PDL (Process Design Language) [6] as follows:

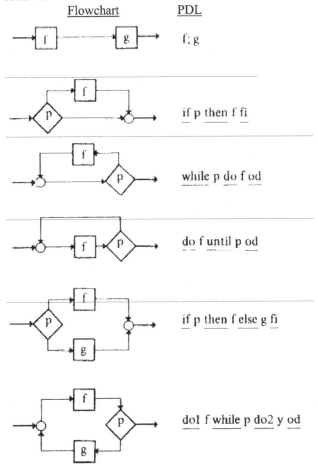

Flowchart	PDL
	f; g
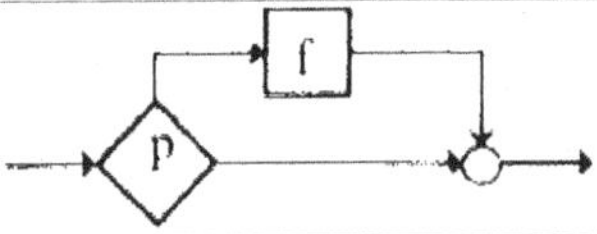	if p then f fi
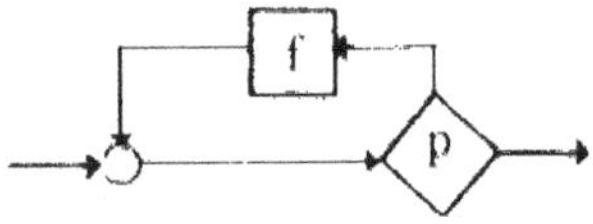	while p do f od
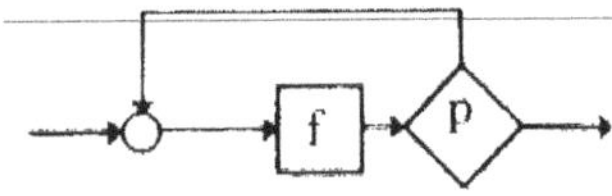	do f until p od
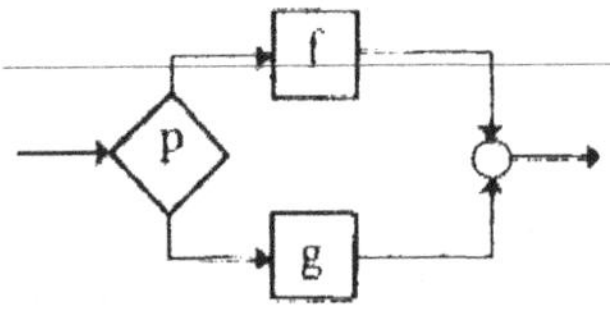	if p then f else g fi
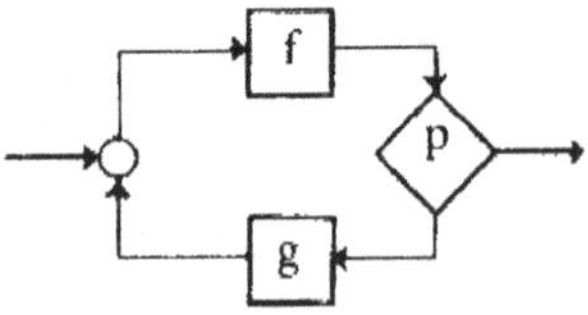	do1 f while p do2 y od

Larger primes will go unnamed here, although the case statement of Pascal is a sample of a useful larger prime. All the primes above, except the last (dowhiledo), are common to many programming languages. Prime programs in text form can be displayed with standard indentation to make the subprogram structure and control logic easily read, which we will illustrate for ZEROIN.

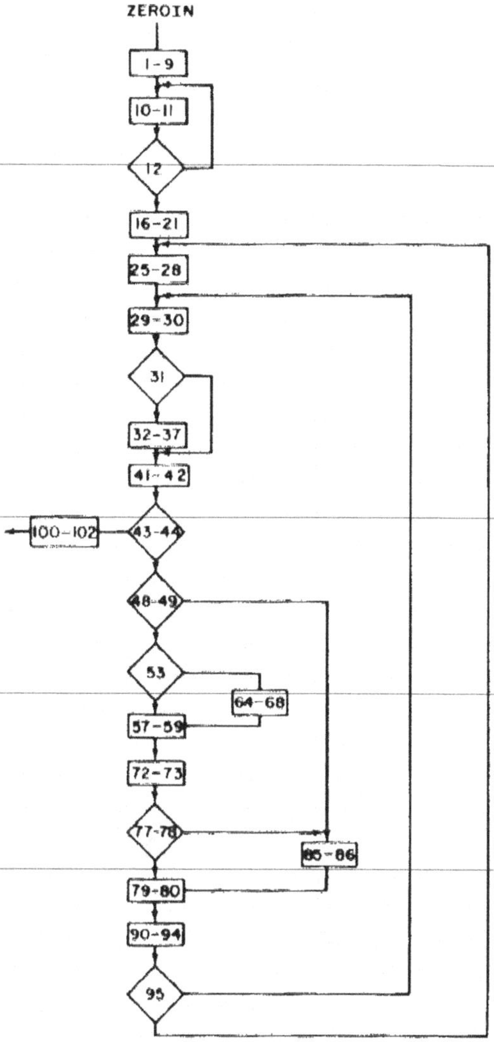

Fig.2. Flowchart of Fortran ZEROIN

III. Understanding ZEROIN

Our overall approach in understanding ZEROIN is carried out in the following steps.

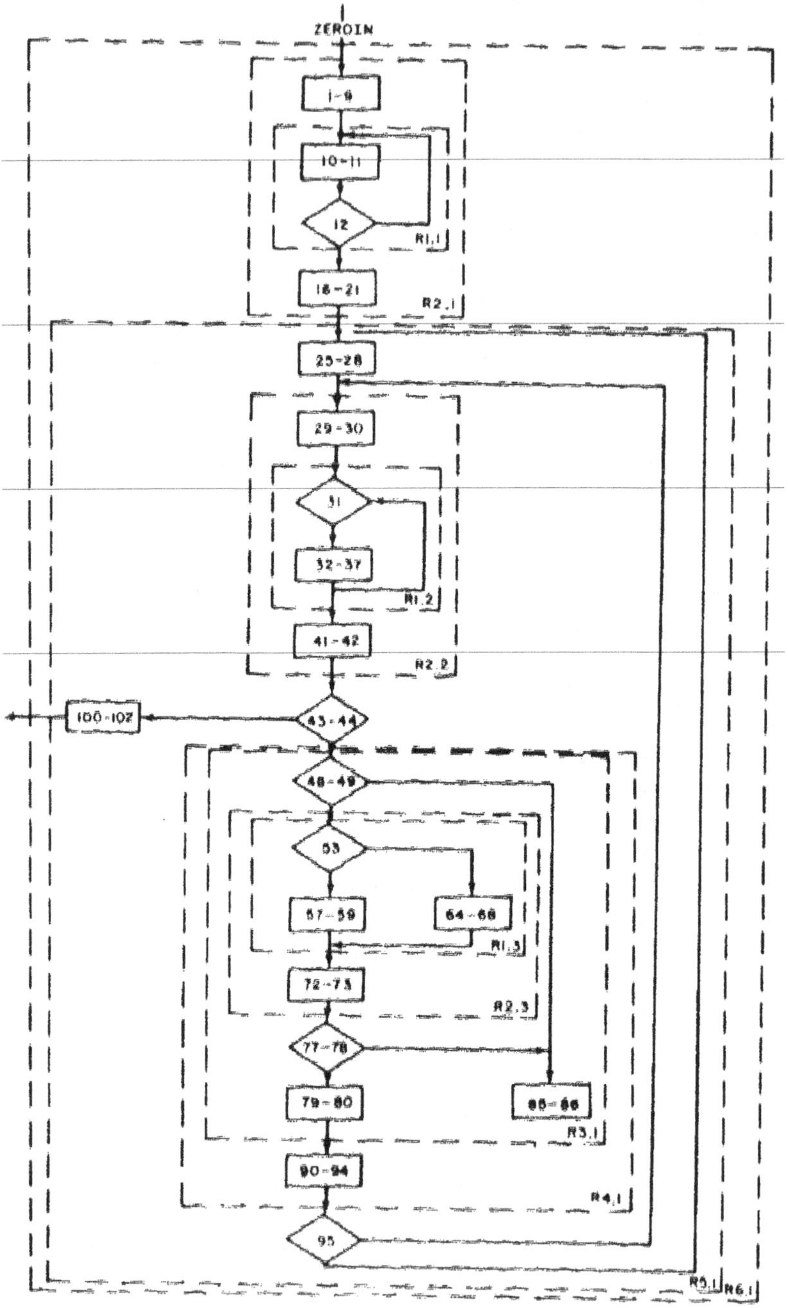

Fig. 3. Prime decomposition of Fortran ZEROIN

1) Perform a prime program decomposition which involves a restructuring of the program into a set of simple constituents which are represented by the single predicate prime programs discussed in the last section.
2) Develop a data reference table and analyze the data references from the point of view of where variables have been set and referenced. This provides insights into the inputs and outputs of the various prime program segments.
3) Perform a function decomposition of the program associating functions with each of the prime program segments. In this way, step by step, the whole program function can be determined by whatever correctness techniques are available. In what follows, the authors have used axiomatic correctness techniques, creating loop invariants along the way, and functional correctness techniques.

The Prime Program Decomposition of ZEROIN

Our first step in understanding ZEROIN was to develop a prime program decomposition of its flowchart. After a little experimentation, the flowchart for ZEROIN was diagrammed as shown in Fig. 2. The numbers in the nodes of the flowchart represent contiguous segments of the Fortran program of Fig. 1, so all lowest level sequence primes are already identified and abstracted.

The flowchart program of Fig. 2 was then reduced, a step at a time, by identifying primes therein and replacing each such prime by a newly numbered function node, e.g., R.2.3 names prime 3 in reduction 2 of the process. This prime decomposition of the Fortran ZEROIN is shown in Fig. 3, leading to a hierarchy of six levels. Of all primes shown in Fig. 3, we note only two that contain more than one predicate, namely R.3.1 and R.5.1, and each of these is easily transformed into a composite made up of primes with no more than one predicate. These transformations are shown in Fig. 4. We continue the reduction of these new composite programs to their prime decompositions in Fig. 5. In each of these two cases, a small segment of programs is duplicated to provide a new composite that clearly executes identically to the prime. Such a modification, which permits a decomposition into one predicate primes, is always possible provided an extra counter is used. In this case, it was fortunate that no such counter was required. It was also fortunate that the duplicated segments were small; otherwise, a program call in two places to the duplicated segment might be a better strategy.

A Structured Design of ZEROIN

Since a prime program decomposition of a program equivalent to ZEROIN has been found with no primes of more than one predicate, we can reconstruct this program in text form in the following way. The final reduced program of ZEROIN is given in Reduction 6 of Fig. 3, namely, that R.6.1 is a sequence, repeated here,

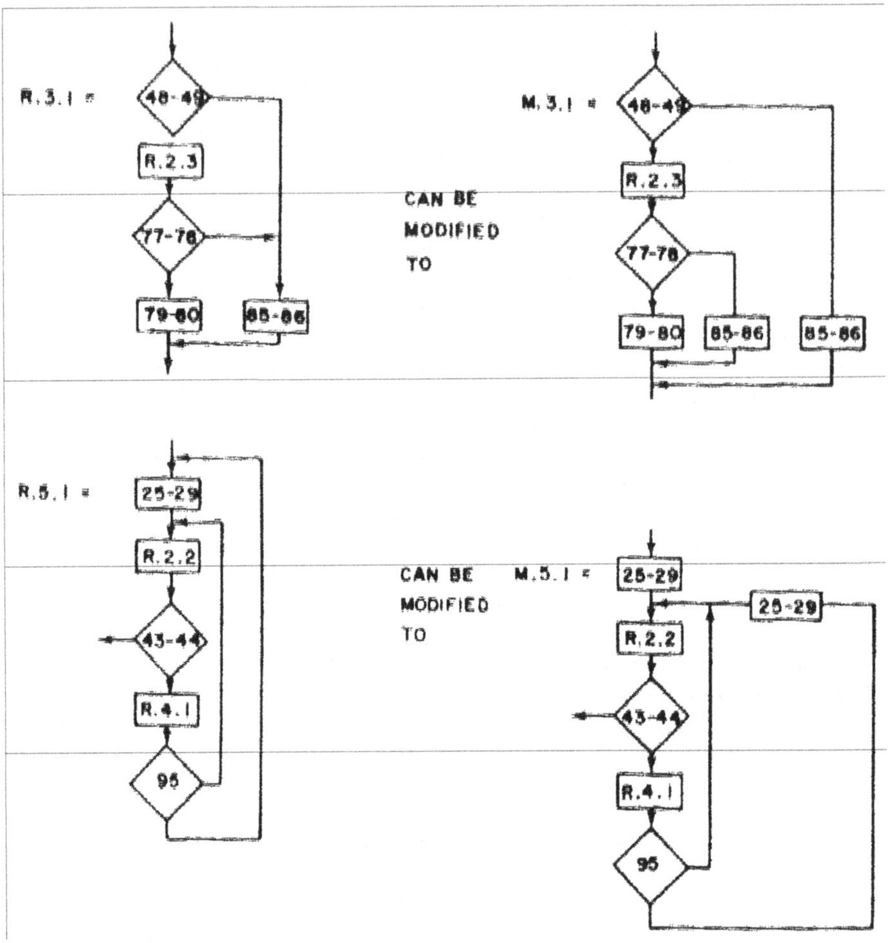

Fig. 4. Transformation to single predicate primes.

R.6.1 =

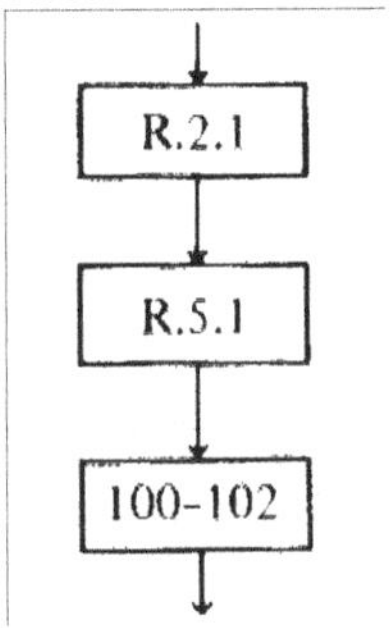

Now R.2.1 can be looked up, in turn, as

R.2.1 =

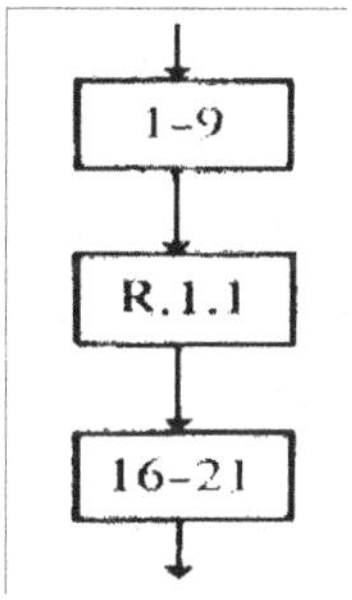

etc., until all intermediate reductions have been eliminated. Recall that R.5.1 and R.3.1 was further reduced in Fig. 5. When these intermediate reductions have all been eliminated, we obtain a structured program [2], [6], in PDL for ZEROIN shown in Fig. 6. Note there are three columns of statement numberings. The first column holds the PDL statement number; the second holds the Fortran line numbering of Fig. 1; the third holds the Fortran statement numbering of Fig. 1. The Fortran comments have been kept intact in the newly structured program and appear within square brackets [,]. From here on, statement numbers refer to the PDL statements of Fig. 6.

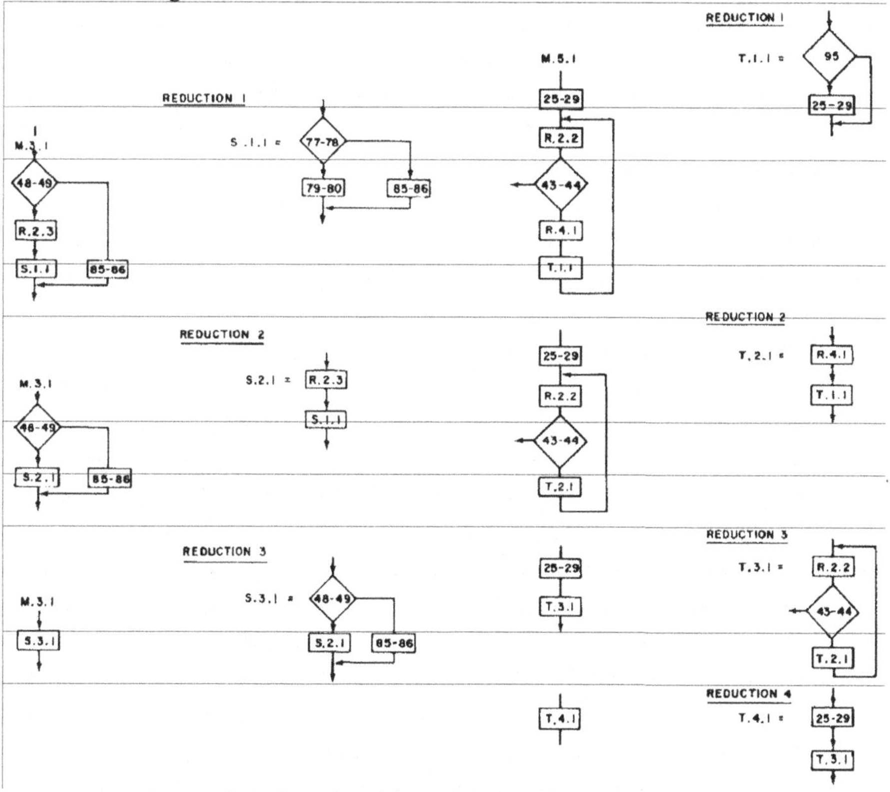

Fig. 5. Prime decomposition of the transformed ZEROIN.

The duplication of code introduced in Fig. 4 can be seen in PDL 72, 73, and PDL 96-99. It should be noted, however, that in PDL 87-91 the second IF STATEMENT in Fortran 93 can be eliminated by use of the if-then-else. This permits an execution time improvement to the code. A second improvement can be seen in PDL 62-66. The use of the absolute value function can be eliminated by using the else part of an if-then-else to change the sign of a negative p.

By construction, the PDL program of Fig. 6 is function equivalent to the Fortran program of Fig. 1. But the structured PDL program will be simpler to study and understand.

Data References in ZEROIN

Our next step in understanding ZEROIN was to develop a data reference table for all data identifiers. While straightforward and mechanical, there is still much learning value in carrying out this step, in becoming familiar with the program in the new structured form. The results are given in Fig. 7. This familiarization led to the following observations about the data references in ZEROIN (in no particular order of significance, but as part of a chronological, intuitive, discovery process).

1) ax, bx, f, ip, tol are never set, as might be expected, since they are all input parameters (but this check would discover initialized data if they existed, and the presence of side effects by the program on its parameters if passed by reference).
2) Zeroin is never used, but is returned as the purported zero found for f (since Zeroin is set to b just before the return of the program, it appears that b may be a candidate for this zero during execution).
3) eps is set by the dountil loop 6-11 at the start of program execution, and then used as a constant at statement 36 from then on.
4) tol 1 is used for two different unrelated purposes, namely, as a temporary in the dountil loop 6-11 which sets eps, then reset at statement 36 as part of a convergence consideration in 36-88.
5) Function f is called only three times, at 16, 17 to initailize fa, fb, and at 92 to reset fb to f(b) (more evidence that b is the candidate zero to be returned).
6) Identifiers a, c are set to and from b, and the triple a, b, c seems to be a candidate for bracketing the zero that b (and zeroin) purports to approach.
7) Identifiers fa, fb, fc are evidently stand-ins for f(a), f(b), f(c), and serve to keep calls on function f to a minimum.
8) Identifiers p, q, r, s are initialized and used only in the section of the program that the comments indicate is concerned with interpolation.
9) Focusing on b, aside from initialization at statement 15 and as part of a general exchange among a, b, c at statement 28-29, b is updated only in the ifthenelse 83-90, incremented by either d or tol 1.
10) d is set to xm or p/q (as a result of a more complex bisection and interpolation process); xm is set only at statement 37 to the half interval of (b, c) and appears to give a bisection value for b.

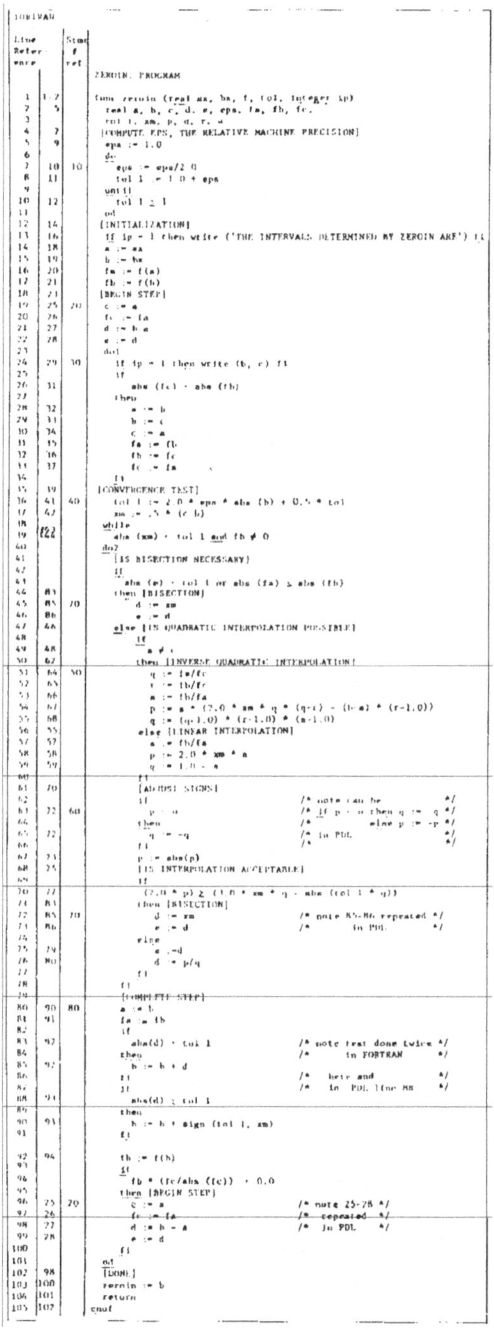

```
FORTRAN
Line   Stmt
Refer- #
ence   ref

                 ZEROIN  PROGRAM

  1   1-7        func zeroin (real ax, bx, f, tol, integer ip)
  2    5           real a, b, c, d, e, eps, fa, fb, fc,
  3                tol 1, xm, p, q, r, s
  4    7          [COMPUTE EPS, THE RELATIVE MACHINE PRECISION]
  5    9           eps := 1.0
  6                do
  7   10   10        eps := eps/2.0
  8   11             tol 1 := 1.0 + eps
  9                until
 10   12             tol 1 ≤ 1
 11                od
 12   14          [INITIALIZATION]
 13   16           if ip = 1 then write ('THE INTERVALS DETERMINED BY ZEROIN ARE') fi
 14   18           a := ax
 15   19           b := bx
 16   20           fa := f(a)
 17   21           fb := f(b)
 18   23          [BEGIN STEP]
 19   25   20      c := a
 20   26           fc := fa
 21   27           d := b-a
 22   28           e := d
 23                do1
 24   29   30        if ip = 1 then write (b, c) fi
 25                  if
 26   31                abs (fc) < abs (fb)
 27                  then
 28   32                a := b
 29   33                b := c
 30   34                c := a
 31   35                fa := fb
 32   36                fb := fc
 33   37                fc := fa
 34                  fi
 35   39          [CONVERGENCE TEST]
 36   41   40        tol 1 := 2.0 * eps * abs (b) + 0.5 * tol
 37   42             xm := .5 * (c-b)
 38                while
 39   ?22            abs (xm) > tol 1 and fb ≠ 0
 40                do2
 41                  [IS BISECTION NECESSARY]
 42                  if
 43                    abs (e) < tol 1 or abs (fa) ≤ abs (fb)
 44   83             then [BISECTION]
 45   85   70           d := xm
 46   86                e := d
 47   46             else [IS QUADRATIC INTERPOLATION POSSIBLE]
 48                     if
 49   48                  a ≠ c
 50   62                then [INVERSE QUADRATIC INTERPOLATION]
 51   64   50              q := fa/fc
 52   65                   r := fb/fc
 53   66                   s := fb/fa
 54   67                   p := s * (2.0 * xm * q * (q-r) - (b-a) * (r-1.0))
 55   68                   q := (q-1.0) * (r-1.0) * (s-1.0)
 56   55                else [LINEAR INTERPOLATION]
 57   57                   s := fb/fa
 58   58                   p := 2.0 * xm * s
 59   59                   q := 1.0 - s
 60                     fi
 61   70                [ADJUST SIGNS]
 62                     if                              /* note can be           */
 63   72   60             p > 0                         /* if p > 0 then q := -q */
 64                     then                            /*         else p := -p  */
 65   72                  q := -q                     /* in PDL               */
 66                     fi                              /*                       */
 67   73                p := abs(p)
 68   75                [IS INTERPOLATION ACCEPTABLE]
 69                     if
 70   77                  (2.0 * p) ≥ (3.0 * xm * q - abs (tol 1 * q))
 71   83                then [BISECTION]
 72   85   70              d := xm                     /* note 85-86 repeated */
 73   86                   e := d                      /*       in PDL        */
 74                     else
 75   79                   e := d
 76   80                   d := p/q
 77                     fi
 78                  fi
 79                  [COMPLETE STEP]
 80   90   80        a := b
 81   91             fa := fb
 82                  if
 83   92               abs(d) > tol 1                  /* note test done twice */
 84                  then                              /*      in FORTRAN      */
 85   92               b := b + d
 86                  fi                                /*   here and           */
 87                  if                                /*   in PDL line 88     */
 88   93               abs(d) ≤ tol 1
 89                  then
 90   93               b := b + sign (tol 1, xm)
 91                  fi

 92   94             fb := f(b)
 93                  if
 94                    fb * (fc/abs (fc)) > 0.0
 95                  then [BEGIN STEP]
 96   25   20          c := a                         /* note 25-28 */
 97   26               fc := fa                       /* repeated   */
 98   27               d := b - a                     /* in PDL     */
 99   28               e := d
100                  fi
101              od
102   98         [DONE]
103  100         zeroin := b
104  101         return
105  102       cnuf
```

Fig. 6. Transformed PDL ZEROIN.

A Function Decomposition of ZEROIN

The prime program decomposition and the familiarity developed by the data reference tabulation and observations suggest the identification of various intermediate prime or composite programs in playing important roles in summing up a functional structure for ZEROIN. Each such intermediate prime or composite program computes values of a function. The inputs (function arguments) of this function are defined by the initial value of all identifiers that are inputs (function arguments) for statements that make up the intermediate program. The outputs (function values) of this function are defined by the final values of all identifiers that are outputs (function values) for statements that make up the intermediate program. Of course, further analysis may disclose that such a function is independent of some inputs, if, in fact, such an identifier is always initialized in the intermediate program before its use.

On the basis of this prime decomposition and data analysis, we reformulated ZEROIN of Fig. 6 as zeroin 1, a sequence of four intermediate programs, as shown in Fig. 8, with function statements using the form f. n-m where n, m are the boundary statements of the intermediate programs of ZEROIN from Fig.

6. Identifier *outfile in the output lists refers to the fact that data are being transferred to an outfile by an intermediate program. The phrase (x,z,v) projection of some function x, y, z, u, v, w: = p,q,r,s,t,u means the new function x,z,v := p,r,t.

In the following program descriptions, all arithmetic operations are assumed to represent machine arithmetic. However, we will occasionally apply normal arithmetic axioms in order to simplify expressions. We next look at the intermediate programs.

f.5-11: The intermediate program that computes the values of f.5-11 is a sequence, namely, an initialized dountil, i.e.,

```
5  eps := 1.0
6  do
7      eps := eps/2.0
8      tol 1 := 1.0 +eps
9  until
10     tol 1 ≤ 1
11 od
```

After some thinking, we determine that at PDL 6, an invariant of the form

$$I6 = (\exists\, k \geq 0\ (eps = 2^{-k}))\ \Lambda\ 1 + eps > 1$$

must hold, since entry to PDL 6 must come from PDL 5 or PDL 10 (and in the latter case tol 1 > 1, having just been set to 1.0 + eps, so 1.0 +eps >1). Furthermore, at PDL 9 the invariant

	Assigned	Used
a	14,28,80	16,19,21,30,49,54,96,98
ax		14
b	15,29,85,90	17,21,24,28,36,37,54,80,85,90,92,98,103
bx		15
c	19,30,96	29,37,49
d	21,45,72,76,98	22,46,73,75,83,85,88,99
e	22,46,73,75,99	43
eps	5,7	7,8,36
f		16,17,92
fa	16,31,81	20,33,43,51,53,57,97
fb	17,32,92	26,31,39,43,52,53,57,81,94
fc	20,33,97	26,32,51,52,94
ip		13,24
p	54,58,67	63,67,70,76
q	51,55,59,65	54,55,65,70,76
r	52	54,55
s	53,57	54,55,58,59
tol		36
tol 1	8,36	10,39,43,70,83,88
xm	37	39,45,54,58,70,72,90
zeroin	101	

Fig. 7. Data references of PDL ZEROIN

```
1  func zeroin 1 (real ax, bx, f, tol, integer ip)
2      real a, b, c, d, e, eps, fa, fb, fc, p, q, r, s, tol 1, xm
3      integer ip
4      [compute eps, the relative machine precision]
5         eps, tol 1 := f. 5-11
6      [initialize data]
7         a, b, c, d, e, fa, fb, fc, *outfile := f. 13-22 (ip, ax, bx, f)
8      [estimate b as a zero of f]
9         a, b, c, d, e, fa, fb, fc, p, q, r, s, tol 1, xm, *outfile :=
          f. 23-101 (a, b, c, d, e, f, fa, fb, fc, ip, p, q, r, s, tol 1, xm)
10     [set zeroin for return, zeroinl := b]
11        zeroinl := f. 103-103(b)
12 cnuf
```

Fig. 8. Top level function / data partition of PDL ZEROIN.

$$I9 = (\exists\, k \geq 1\ (eps = 2^{-k}))\ \Lambda\ tol\ 1 = 1 + eps$$

must hold, by observing the effect of PDL 7, 8 on the invariant I6 at PDL 6. Therefore, at exit (if ever) from the segment PDL 5-11, we must have the condition I9 Λ PDL 10, namely,

$$(\exists\, k \geq 1\ (eps = 2^{-k}))\ \Lambda\ 1 + 2\ eps > 1\ \Lambda\ tol\ 1 = 1 + eps \leq 1.$$

Thus we have the following.

Lemma 5-11: The program function of f.5-11 is the constant function:

$$\{(\emptyset, (eps, tol\ 1)) \mid (\exists\, k \geq 1\ (eps = 2^{-k}))\ \Lambda\ 1 + 2\ eps > 1\ \Lambda\ tol\ 1 = 1 + eps \leq 1\}.$$

Since tol 1 is reassigned (in PDL 36) before it is used again, f.5-11 can be thought of as computing only eps.

f.13-22: The intermediate program that computes the value of f.13-22 can be written directly as a multiple assignment. It is convenient to retain the single output statement PDL 13, and write

f.13-22 = f.13-13;f.14-22

yielding the following.

Lemma 13-22: The (a,b,c,d,e,*outfile) projection of f.13-22 is function equivalent to the sequence

f.13-13;f.14-22

where f.13-13 = <u>if</u> ip=l then write ('THE INTERVALS DETERMINED BY ZEROIN ARE') and

f.14-22 = a,b,c,d,e,fa,fb,fc
:= ax,bx,ax,bx-ax,bx-ax, f(a),f(b),f(a).

f.23-101: The intermediate program that computes the value of f.23-101 is a bit more complicated than the previous program segments and will be broken down into several sub-segments. We begin by noticing that several of the input and output parameters may be eliminated from the list. Specifically, as noted earlier, p, q, r, and s are local variables to f.23-101 since they are always recalculated before they are used in f.23-101 and they are not used outside of f.23-101. The same is true for xm and tol 1. fa, fb, and fc can be eliminated since they are only used to hold the values of f(a), f(b) and f(c).

After considerable analysis and a number of false starts leading into a great deal of detail, we discovered an amazing simplification, first as a conjecture, then as a more precise hypothesis, and finally as a verified result. This simplification concerned the main body of the iteration of zeroin, namely, PDL 41-92, and obviated the need to know or check what kind of interpolation strategy was used, step by step. This discovery was that the new estimate of b always lay strictly within the interval bracketed by the previous b and c. That is, PDL 41-92, among other effects, has the (b) projection

b:=b + α (c-b),   for some α, 0 < α < 1

so that the new b was a fraction α of the distance from the previous b to c. With a little more thought, it became clear that the precise values of d, e could be ignored, their effects being captured in the proper (but precisely unknown) value of α. Furthermore, this new indeterminate (but bounded) variable α could be used to summarize the effect of d, e in the larger program part PDL 23-101, because d, e are never referred to subsequently. Thus, we may rewrite f.23-101 at this level as

a, b, c *outfile := f.23-101 (a, b, c, f, ip)

and we define it as an initialized while loop.

Lemma 23-101: The (a, b, c, *outfile) projection of f.23-101 is function equivalent to

```
(ip = 1 → write (b, c) | true → I);                    [Lemma 24]
(abs(f(c)) < abs(f(b)) → a,b,c := b.c.b | true → I);   [Lemma 25-34]
while
f(b) ≠ 0 Λ (abs(c-b)/2) > 2 eps abs(b) + tol/2
do
a,b, c :=b,b + α(c-b),c    where 0 < α < l;            [Lemma 41-92]
(f(b) * f(c) > 0 → a, b, c := a, b, a | true → I);     [Lemma 93-100]
(ip = 1 → write (b, c) | true → I);                            [Lemma 24]
(abs(f(c)) < abs(f(b)) → a,b,c := b,c,b | true → I)    [Lemma 25-34]
od
```

where I is the identity mapping.

The structure of f.23-101 corresponds directly to the structure of PDL 23-101 except for a duplication of segment PDL 23-34 in order to convert the dowhiledo into a whiledo. The proof of the correctness of the assignments of f.23-101 is given in separate lemmas as noted in the comments attached to the functions in Lemma 23-101. The while test is obtained by direct substitution of values for tol 1 and xm defined in PDL 36-37 into the test in PDL 39 using eps as defined in Lemma 5-11.

Lemma 24: PDL 24 is equivalent to

(ip = 1 → write (b, c) | true → 1).

Proof: By direct inspection.

Lemma 25-34: The (a, b, c) projection of the program function of PDL 25-34 is function equivalent to

(abs(f(c)) < abs(f(b)) → a,b,c := b,c,b | true → I).

Proof: By direct inspection of PDL 25-34.

Lemma 41-92: The (a, b, c) projection of the program function of PDL 41-92 is function equivalent to

a, b, c :=b,b + α (c-b), c where $0 < \alpha < 1$.

The proof will be done by examining the set of relationships that must hold among the variables in PDL 41-92 and analyzing the values of p and q only. That is, it is not necessary to have any knowledge of which interpolation was performed to be able to show that the new b can be defined by

b:=b + α (c-b), $0 < \alpha < 1$.

We will ignore the test on PDL 48 since it will be immaterial to the lemma whether linear or quadratic interpolation is performed. We will examine only the key tests and assignments and do the proof in two basic cases—interpolation and bisection— to show that the (d) projection of the program function of PDL 41-78 is

d = (c-b)(α) where $0 < \alpha < 1$.

Case 1 — Interpolation: If interpolation is done, an examination of Fig. 6 shows that the following set of relations holds at PDL 78:

• **I1 ≡ tol 1 = 2 * eps * abs (b) + .5 * tol**	**(PDL 36)**
• **I2 ≡ xm = (c - b)/2**	**(PDL 37)**
• **I3 ≡ abs (xm) > tol 1**	**(PDL 39)**
• **I4 ≡ p ≥ 0**	**(PDL 67)**
• **I5 ≡ 2 * p < 3 * xm * q - abs(tol 1 * q)**	**(PDL 70)**
• **I6 ≡ d = p / q**	**(PDL 76)**
• **I7 ≡ abs(d) > tol 1**	**(PDL 83)**

Now let us examine the set of cases on p and q.

$p > 0 \wedge q < 0$: We have d = p/q < 0 (by hypotheses), p/q > 3/2xm + tol 1/2 (by I5), and tol 1>0 (by I1). Since abs(xm) > tol 1 (by I3) and 3/2 xm + tol 1/2 < 0 (since p/q < 0) we have xm < 0 implying 0 > d > p/q > 3/2 xm > 3/4 (c-b) > (c-b). Thus 0 > d > (c-b) yielding d = α (c-b) where $0 < \alpha < 1$.

$p > 0 \wedge q > 0$: We have d = p/q > 0 (by hypotheses), p/q < 3/2 xm - tol 1/2 < 3/2 xm = 3/4 (c-b) < (c-b) (by I5, I1, I2) implying 0 < d < (c-b). Thus d = α (c-b) where $0 < \alpha < 1$.

$P > 0 \wedge q = 0$; q = 0 implies 0 > 2 * p (by I5) and we know p > 0 (by hypotheses), implying a contradiction.

$p = 0 \wedge$ q= *anything*: abs(p/q) > tol 1 (by I6, I7) and tol 1 ≥ 0 (by I1) implies p cannot be 0.

$p < 0 \wedge$ q = *anything*: p ≥ 0 (by 14) implies a contradiction.

Case 2 — Bisection: If bisection is done, an examination of Fig. 6 shows that the following set of relations holds at PDL 78:

B1 ≡ xm = (c − b)/2 (PDL 37)
B2 ≡ abs(xm) > tol 1 (PDL 39)
B3 ≡ d = xm (PDL 45 or PDL 72).

Here d = xm (by B3) implies $\alpha = 1/2$ (by Bl) and thus d = (c-b)(α) where $0 < \alpha < 1$.

PDL 82-91 implies if $|d| \leq$ tol 1 (i.e., if d is too small) then increment b by tol 1 with the sign adjusted appropriately, i.e., set

$$\alpha = \begin{cases} d & \text{abs}(d) > \text{tol } 1 \\ \text{sign (tol 1, sm)} & \text{otherwise} \end{cases}$$

But tol 1 < abs(xm) (by I3 and B2) = abs((c-b)/2) and the sign (tol 1) is set to the sign (xm) implying

tol 1= α (c-b) where $0 < \alpha < 1$.

Thus, in PDL 82-91 b is incremented by d or tol 1, both of which are of the form α (c- b) where $0 < \alpha < 1$. Thus we have

b := b + α (c-b), $0 < \alpha < 1$

and since in PDL 80-81 we have a, fa := b, fb we get the statement of the lemma. Once again, the reader is reminded that the proof of Lemma 41-92 was done by examining cases on p and q only. No knowledge of the actual interpolations was necessary. Only tests and key assignments were examined. Also, the program function was abstracted to only the key variables a, b, c and α represented the effect of all other significant variables.

Lemma 93-100: The (a,b,c) projection of PDL 93-100 is function equivalent to

(f(b) * f(c) > 0 → a, b, c := a, b, a | <u>true</u> → I).

Proof: By direct inspection, PDL 93-100 is an ifthen statement with if test equivalent to the condition shown above and assignments that include the assignments above.

The last function in zeroin 1 (from Fig. 8) is the single statement PDL 103, which can be easily seen as Lemma 103.

Lemma 103: f.103 is function equivalent to zeroin := b.

Now that each of the pieces of zeroin 1 have been defined, the program function of ZEROIN will be given. First, let us rewrite zeroin 1, all in one place, using the appropriate functions (Fig. 9).

The program ZEROIN has the required effect of finding and returning a root if there is one between the endpoints provided to it. The conditions under which this works are when either of the endpoints are roots or there is one root or an odd number of roots between the two endpoints (i.e., the functional values of the endpoints are of opposite signs). However, if the two endpoints provided to the program are identical, their value will be returned as the root. If there are no roots or a multiple of two roots between the two endpoints, the program will return a value as a root. This value may be one of the actual roots or it may be some point lying between the two points which is arrived at by continually halving the interval and eventually choosing one of the endpoints of a halved interval when the interval gets small enough.

The behavior of the program is more formally defined in the following theorem.

Theorem 1-105:

<u>func</u> zeroin has program function [zeroin] =
  (ax = bx → root := bx |
  f(bx) = 0 → root :=bx |
  f(ax) = 0 → root := ax |
  f(ax) * f(bx) < 0 → root := approx (f, ax, bx, tol) |
  <u>true</u> → (∀ k = 1,2, • • •, $f(b_k)$ * $f(c_k)$ > 0 → root
      := unpredictable |
    ∃ k > 0($f(b_k)$ * $f(c_k)$ ≤ 0 ∧ ∀ j = 1, 2, • • • k - 1,
    $f(b_j)$ * $f(c_j)$ > 0) → root
    := approx (f, b_k, c_k, tol)

where approx (f, ax, bx, tol) is some value, x, in the interval (ax, bx) within 4 * eps * |x| + tol of some zero, x of the function f and the sequence (b_1, c_1), (b_2, c_2), • • • is defined so that each succeeding interval is a subinterval of the preceding interval; (b_1, c_1,) = (ax, bx), (b_{k+i}, c_{k+1}) defines the half interval of (b_k, c_k) such that the endpoint kept is the one that minimizes the absolute value of f.

Proof: The proof will be carried out in cases, corresponding to the conditions in the rule given in the theorem. The first three cases follow directly by inspection of zeroin1, as special cases for input values, which bypass the while loop. That is, if ax = bx, then the values of a, b, c and root can be traced in zeroin1 as follows:

	a	b	c	root
Zeroin1.8	bx	bx	bx	bx
0.11	bx	bx	bx	bx
[condition 13 fails since c-b = 0]				
0.21	bx	bx	bx	bx

Cases 2 and 3 proceed in a similar fashion.

Case 4, f(ax) * f(bx) <0, will be handled by an analysis of the whiledo loop and its results will apply to the last sub case of the last case as well. The first sub case of the last case arises when no zero of f is even bracketed and zeroin1 runs a predictable course, as will be shown.

Case 4: It will be shown that the entry condition f (ax) * f(bx) < 0 leads to the following condition at the while test of zeroin1:

  I = (a = c ≠ b ∨ a < b < c ∨ c < b < a)
    ∧ f(b) * f(c) ≤ 0 ∧ abs(f(b) ≤ abs(f(c)).

The proof is by induction. First, I holds on entry to the whiledo loop because by direct calculation

  after zeroin1.8 a = c ∧ f (b) * f (c) < 0 ∧ c ≠ b

after zeroin1.11 $a = c \wedge f(b) * f(c) < 0 \wedge abs(f(b)) \leq abs(f(c)) \wedge c \neq b$.
Next, suppose the invariant I holds at any iteration of the whiledo at the while test, and the while test evaluates true, it can be shown that I is preserved by the three-part sequence of the do part. In fact, the first part, in seeking a better estimate of a zero of f, may destroy this invariant, and the last two parts restore the invariant. It will be shown in Lemma 15-18 that

after zeroin1.15 $(a < b < c \vee c < b < a) \wedge f(a) * f(c) < 0$
after zeroin1.16 $(a = c \neq b \vee a < b < c \vee c < b < a)$
$\wedge f(b) * f(c) \leq 0$
after zeroin1.18 $(a = c \neq b \vee a < b < c \vee c < b < a)$
$\wedge f(b) * f(c) \leq 0 \wedge abs(f(b))$
$\leq abs(f(c))$

which is I. Thus, I is indeed an invariant at the while test.

Consider the question of termination of the whiledo. In Lemma 15-18T it will be shown using c_0 and b_0 as entry values to the do part, that for some α, $0 < \alpha < 1$, after zeroin1.18 $abs(c\text{-}b) < abs(c_0 - b_0)max(\alpha, 1\text{-}\alpha)$. Therefore, the whiledo must finally terminate because the condition

$$f(b) \neq 0 \wedge abs((c\text{-}b)/2) > 2 * eps * abs(b) + tol/2$$

must finally fail, because by the finiteness of machine precision abs(c-b) will go to zero if not terminated sooner.

When the whiledo terminates, the invariant I must still hold. In particular $f(b) * f(c) \leq 0$, which combined with the negation of the while test gives

$$IT = f(b) * f(c) \leq 0 \wedge (f(b)) = 0 \vee abs((c\text{-}b)/2) \leq 2 * eps * abs(b) + tol/2.$$

IT states that
1) a zero of f is bracketed by the interval (b, c);
2) either the zero is at b or the zero is at most $| c\text{-}b |$ from b, i.e., the zero is within $4 * eps * | b | + tol$ of b.

This is the definition of approx (f, b, c, tol).
Now, beginning with the interval (ax, bx), every estimate of b created at zeroin1.15 remains within the interval (b,c) current at the time.[1] Since c and b are initialized as ax and bx at zeroin1.8, the final estimate of b is given by approx (f, ax, bx, tol). The assignment zeroin := b at zeroin1.21 provides the value required by case 4.

Case 5 — Part 1: We first show that in this case the condition a = c will hold at zeroin1.15 if $f(b) * f(c) > 0$. By the hypothesis of case 5, part 1, f((b+c)/2) is of the same sign as f(b) and f(c). Therefore, the first case of zeroin1.16 will hold and the assignment c := a will be executed implying a = c when we arrive at zeroin1.15 from within the loop. Also, if we reach zeroin1.15 from outside the loop (zeroinl.8-11) we also get a = c.

[1] This is because $f(b) * f(c) \leq 0$ is part of I.

```
1  func zeroinl (real ax, bx, f, tol, integer ip)
2    real a, b, c, d, e, eps, fa, fb, fc, α
3    file *outfile
4    [compute eps, the relative machine precision]
5      eps := {x | (∃ k ≥ 1 (x = 2^-k)) ∧ 1 + 2 x > 1 ∧ 1 + eps ≤ 1} ;
6    [initialize data]
7      (ip = 1 → *outfile := 'THE INTERVALS DETERMINED BY ZEROIN
                               ARE' | true → I) ;
8      a,b,c,d,e := ax,bx,ax,bx-ax,bx-ax
9    [estimate b as a zero of f]
10     (ip = 1 → *outfile (b, c) | true → I) ;
11     (abs(f(c)) < abs(f(b)) a, b, c := b, c, b | true → I)
12     while
13       f(b) ≠ 0 ∧ abs((c-b)/2) > 2 eps abs(b) + tol/2
14     do
15       a, b, c := b, b + α (c-b), c   where  0 < α < 1;*
16       (f(b) * f(c) > 0 → a, b, c := a, b, a | true → I) ;
17       (ip = 1 → *outfile(b, c) | true → I) ;
18       (abs(f(c)) < abs(f(b)) → a, b, c := b, c, b | true → I)
19     od;
20     [set zeroinl for return, zeroinl := b]
21     zeroinl := b
22   return
23 cnuf

*  α is an indeterminate based on the current values of a, b, c, d, e, f,
   fa, fb, fc, tol and eps
```

Fig. 9. Function abstraction of PDL ZEROIN.

We now apply Lemma 15L, which states that under the above condition the (a, b, c) projection of zeroin1.15 is

$$
\begin{aligned}
&(f(b) * f(c) > 0 \rightarrow a, b, c \\
&\qquad := b, \begin{Bmatrix} b + (c-b)/2, & \text{if } abs(c-b)/2 > tol\ 1 \\ b + tol\ 1, & \text{otherwise} \end{Bmatrix}, c \\
&\underline{true} \rightarrow a, b, c := b, b + \alpha(c-b), c)
\end{aligned}
$$

which is a refinement of zeroin1.15.

Note that zeroin 1.18 may exchange b,c depending on abs(f(b)) and abs(f(c)). Thus, the (b,c) projection of the function computed by zeroin 1.15-18 in this case is

$$
b, c := \begin{Bmatrix} b + (c-b)/2 \\ b + tol\ 1 \end{Bmatrix}, b \text{ or } b, c := b, \begin{Bmatrix} b + (c-b)/2 \\ b + tol\ 1 \end{Bmatrix},
$$

i.e., the new interval (b, c) is the half interval of the initial (b_0, c_0) which includes b_0 (for increments greater than tol 1), and the new b is chosen to minimize the value abs(f(b)). The result of iterating this dopart is unpredictable unless more is known about the values of f. For example, if the values of f in (ax, bx) are of one sign and monotone increasing or decreasing, then the iteration will go to the endpoint ax or bx for which abs(f) is minimum. In general, the iteration will tend toward a minimum for abs(f), but due to the bisecting behavior, no guarantees are possible.

Case 5 — Part 2: This covers the happy accident of some intermediate pair b,c bracketing an odd number of zeros of f by happening into values b_k, c_k, such that $f(b_k) * f(c_k) \leq 0$. The tendency to move towards a minimum for abs(f(b)) may increase the chances for such a happening, but provides no guarantee. Once such a pair b_k, c_k is found, case 4 applies and some zero will be approximated.

This completes the proof of the theorem except for the proofs of the three lemmas used in the proofs which are given in the Appendix.

IV. Conclusion

Answering the Questions

We can now answer the questions originally posed by Prof. Vandergraft.

Question 1: If the equation is linear and the size of the interval (a,b) is greater than or equal to tol 1, and there is no round off problem, the program will do a linear interpolation and find the root on one pass through the loop. If the size of the interval (a,b) is smaller than tol 1, the program will perform a bisection (based upon the test at PDL43). If abs(fa) = abs(fb) at PDL 43, then bisection will also be performed. However, in this case bisection is an exact solution. The case that the size of the interval is smaller than tol 1 is unlikely, but possible.

Question 2: The theorem states that if f(a) and f(b) are both of the same sign, we will get an answer that is some point between a and b even though there is no root in the interval (a,b) (case 5a of the Theorem). If there are an even number of roots in the interval (a, b) then it is possible the program will happen upon one of the roots and return that root as an answer (case 5b of the Theorem). To check for this condition, we should put a test right at entry to the program between PDL 3 and PDL 4 of the form

```
if
    f(ax)*f(bx)>0
then
    write ('F(AX) and F(BX) ARE BOTH OF THE SAME SIGN,
    RETURN BX')
    B := BX
else
    PDL 4-102
fi
```

Unfortunately, this does not indicate an error to the calling program. One approach in handling an error indication would be to add an extra parameter to the parameter list which would be set to indicate an error. Another approach would be to return a special value for the root, e.g., the largest negative number on the machine, as an error signal.

Question 3: It would be easy to remove the inverse quadratic interpolation part of the code. We can do this simply by removing several PDL statements, i.e., PDL 47-55. However, this would not leave us with the best solution since much of the code surrounding the inverse quadratic interpolation could be better written. For example,

1) there would be no need to keep a, b, and c;
2) the test in PDL 70 could be removed if we checked in the loop that f(a) * f(b) was always greater than zero, since bisection and linear interpolation would never take us out of the interval.

Cleaning up the algorithm would probably require a substantial transformation.

Question 4: Zeroin will find a triple root, assuming it is the only root in the interval. It will not inform the user that it is a triple root, but will return it as a root because once it has a root surrounded by two points such that f(a) and f(b) are of opposite signs, it will find that root (case 4 of the theorem).

It is also worth noting that ax and bx do not have to be the left and right endpoints of the interval; they could be interchanged. Also, any value of IP other than 1 will be equivalent to zero.

Program History

Since most programs seen by practicing programmers do not have a history in the literature, we did not research the history of ZEROIN until we had completed our experiment. The plexity of the program is partially due to the fact that it was modified over a period of time by different authors, each modification making it more efficient, effective or robust. The code is based on the secant method [7]. The idea of combining it with bisection had been suggested by several people. The first careful analysis seems to have been by Dekker [3]. Brent [1] added to Dekker's algorithm the inverse quadratic interpolation option, and changed some of the convergence tests. The Brent book contains an Algol 60 program. The Fortran program of Fig. 1 is found in [5] and is a direct translation of Brent's algorithm, with the addition of a few lines that compute the machine-rounding error. We understand that ZEROIN is a significant and actively used program for calculating the roots of a function in a specific interval to a given tolerance.

Understanding and Documenting

As it turns out, we were able to answer the questions posed and discover the program function of ZEROIN. The techniques used included function specification, the discovery of loop invariants, case analysis, and the use of a bounded indeterminate auxiliary variable. The discovery process used by the authors was not as direct as it appears in the paper. There were several side trips which included proving the correctness of the inverse quadratic interpolation (an interesting result but not relevant to the final abstraction or the questions posed).

There are some implications that the algorithm of the program was robust in that it was over designed to be correct and that the tests may be more limiting than necessary. This made the program easier to prove correct, however.

In documenting this program, we learned all the details first and, in that sense, worked bottom up. The method provided a systematic way to accumulate the detailed knowledge and package it in small pieces which consisted of theorems and lemmas. Learning of the details first was necessary for the higher level understanding. This bottom-up process is typical in maintaining programs; the form of recording that understanding is not.

Unfortunately, we kept no record of time because the work was done over a rather long period of time in bits and pieces. The authors would guess that it would take several weeks for a maintenance programmer versed in these concepts to develop and document an understanding of this program, as was done here. The implication is that maintenance without good documentation is a highly expensive proposition and clearly an extremely creative process. Unfortunately, in many environments only novice programmers are put on the maintenance task. Probably it would be better for programmers to work in senior/junior pairs, devoting part-time to the problem.

The role of good maintenance should be to keep the requirements, specifications, design and code documents up to date during development so they will be available and can be updated during maintenance. This study supplies some evidence that the payoff in not having to recreate the specification and design structure during maintenance is considerable. Although this approach of formalizing the understanding and documentation process of maintenance may appear to be overdone, it is unfortunately a necessity for many environments. To maintain a program in an embedded system, it is necessary to understand it to modify it. If there is no documentation on the requirements of the current system (which has been modified over time), there is no choice but to take the approach that was taken by the authors. There do exist systems which no one really knows what they do. The only way to be able to understand them and document them so that they can be changed or updated is by going through processes similar to processes performed by the authors.

To reiterate, the process consists of reducing the program to be understood to small prime programs and then creating in a step-by-step process the functions produced by those primes, combining them at higher and higher levels until a full specification is achieved. It is the price we pay for maintenance when only the code exists as the final documentation of a system.

We believe this experience shows that the areas of program specification and program correctness have advanced enough to make them useful in understanding and documenting existing programs, and extremely important application today. In our case, we are convinced that without the focus of searching for a correctness proof relating the specification to the program, we would have learned a great deal, but would have been unable to record very much of what we learned for others.

Hamming pointed out that mathematicians and scientists stand on each other's shoulders but programmers stand on each other's toes. We believe that will continue to be true until programmers deal with programs as mathematical objects, as unlikely as they may seem to be in real life, as we have tried to do here.

Acknowledgment

The authors are grateful to D. Dunlop for his insightful review of this report and to C. Bacigaluppi for patiently typing numerous drafts.

References

[1] R. P. Brent, *Algorithms for Minimization Without Derivatives*. Englewood Cliffs, NJ: Prentice-Hall, 1973.

[2] O. J. Dahl, E. W. Dijkstra, and C. A. R. Hoare, *Structured Programming*. New York: Academic, 1972.

[3] T. J. Dekker, "Finding a zero by means of successive linear interpolation," in *Constructive Aspects of the Fundamental Theorem of Algebra*, B. Dejou and P. Henrici, Eds. Interscience, 1969.

[4] E. W. Dijkstra, *A Discipline of Programming*. Englewood Cliffs, NJ: Prentice-Hall, 1976.

[5] G. Forsythe, M. Malcolm, and M. Moler, *Computer Methods for Mathematical Computations*. Englewood Cliffs, NJ: Prentice-Hall, 1977.

[6] R. C. Linger, H. D. Mills, and B. I. Witt, *Structured Programming Theory and Practice*. Reading, MA: Addison-Wesley, 1979.

[7] J. Ortega and W. C. Rheinboldt, *Iterative Solution of Nonlinear Equations in Several Variables*. New York: Academic, 1970.

APPENDIX

Lemma 15-18: The invariant I defined as

$$I \equiv (a = c \neq b \vee a < b < c \vee c < b < a) \wedge f(b) * f(c) \leqslant 0 \wedge abs(f(b)) \leqslant abs(f(c))$$

is preserved by the execution of the loop body ZEROIN1.15-18.

Proof: We use the following abbreviations:

$$P \equiv abs(f(b)) \neq 0 \wedge abs((c-b)/2) > 2 * eps * abs(b) + tol/2$$
$$I_0 \equiv ((c < b) \vee (c > b)) \wedge f(b) * f(c) < 0$$
$$I_1 \equiv (a < b < c \vee c < b < a) \wedge f(a) * f(c) < 0$$
$$I_2 \equiv (a = c \neq b \vee a < b < c \vee c < b < a) \wedge f(b) * f(c) \leqslant 0.$$

Note that P is the loop predicate. The validity of the lemma is an immediate consequence of the following conditions:

C1: $I \wedge P \Rightarrow I_0$
C2: I_0 {ZEROIN1.15} I_1
C3: I_1 {ZEROIN1.16} I_2
C4: I_2 {ZEROIN1.18} I.

Condition C1 is straightforward. C2 can be seen by considering $c < b$ and $c > b$ as different input cases. Condition C3 follows from

$I_1 \wedge f(b) * f(c) > 0$ {c := a} I_2 (note that setting $c = a$ changes the sign of f(c))
$I_1 \wedge f(b) * f(c) \leqslant 0 \Rightarrow I_2$.

Similarly, C4 can be inferred from

$I_2 \wedge abs(f(c)) < abs(f(b))$ {a, b, c := b, c, b} I
$I_2 \wedge abs(f(c)) \geqslant abs(f(b)) \Rightarrow I$.

Lemma 15-18T: Given b_0, c_0 on entry to zeroin1.15-18 then for some α, $0<\alpha<1$

after zeroin1.15 $abs(c-b) = (1-\alpha)\, abs(c_0-b_0)$
after zeroin1.16 $abs(c-b) \leqslant abs(c_0-b_0) \max(\alpha, 1-\alpha)$
after zeroin1.18 $abs(c-b) \leqslant abs(c_0-b_0) \max(\alpha, 1-\alpha)$.

Proof: After zeroin1.15

$$abs(c-b) = abs(c_0-b_0-\alpha(c_0-b_0)) = abs(c_0-b_0)(1-\alpha) \qquad 0<\alpha<1$$

$$abs(b-a) = abs(b_0+\alpha(c_0-b_0) - b_0) = abs\, \alpha(c_0-b_0) \qquad 0<\alpha<1.$$

After zeroin1.16

$$abs(c-b) \leqslant \max(abs(c_0-b_0)(1-\alpha), abs(c_0-b_0)\alpha) \leqslant abs(c_0-b_0) \max(\alpha, 1-\alpha).$$

After zeroin1.18

$abs(c-b) \leqslant abs(c_0-b_0) \max(\alpha,1-\alpha)$ since b and c are unchanged or exchanged.

It should be noted that in the above discussion, zeroin1.17 was ignored because its effect on the calculation of the root and termination of the loop is irrelevant.
We have one last lemma to prove.

Lemma 15L: Given a = c and f(a) * f(b) > 0 then zeroin1.15 calculates the new b using the bisection method, i.e.,

$$b := b + \begin{Bmatrix} (b-c)/2 & \text{if abs(c-b)} > \text{tol 1} \\ \text{tol 1} & \text{otherwise} \end{Bmatrix}$$

Proof: **From PDL 43, either abs(f(b)) < abs(f(a)) or bisection is done (PDL 45) with d = xm = (c-b)/2. Then PDL 82-91 implies**

$$b := \begin{Bmatrix} b + d = b + (c-b)/2 & \text{if abs(c-b)/2} > \text{tol 1} \\ b + \text{tol 1} & \text{otherwise} \end{Bmatrix}.$$

Since by hypothesis a = c, PDL 49 implies inverse quadratic interpolation is not done and linear interpolation (PDL 56) is attempted. Thus

s = fb/fa and 0 < s < 1 since fb * fa > 0 and abs(fb) < abs(fa)
p = (c-b) * s, using xm + (c- b)/2
q = 1-s, implying q > 0 in PDL 59.

The proof will be done by cases on the relationship between b and c.
c > b: c > b implies p > 0 in PDL 58. Since p > 0 before PDL 62, PDL 65 sets q to -q, so q < 0. Then the test at PDL 70 is true since

2 * p=a* s is positive,
3.0 * xm * q = 3/2* (c-b) * q is negative, and
abs(tol 1 * q) is positive

implying PDL 70 evaluates to true and bisection is performed in PDL 72-73.
c < b: c < b implies p < 0 in PDL 58. Since p < 0 before PDL 62, PDL 65 leaves q alone and PDL 67 sets p > 0 implying p = (b-c) * x. Then the test at PDL 70 is true since

2 * p = 2 * (b-c) * s is positive,
3.0 * xm * q = 3/2* (c- b) * q is negative, and
abs(tol 1 * q) is positive

implying PDL 70 evaluates to true and bisection is performed in PDL 72-73.

Section 2: Measurement and GQM

David Weiss

Avaya Labs

Thomas Kuhn in his Structure of Scientific Revolutions notes that when a new field of science or technology arises no one knows what questions to ask or what experiments to perform. We don't know what to measure or how to measure it. Eventually, through many trials and perhaps some inspired guesswork, new theories and a new way of looking at the world emerge, an experimental discipline is founded, and the field starts to make progress towards explaining previously puzzling phenomena. Kuhn labels such an emergence a paradigm shift.

For software engineering to become a discipline we must know what experiments to perform to measure software development, what the critical variables in software development are, and how to use the results of our measurements to improve our development processes, making them repeatable and predictable. Although we have not yet achieved a paradigm shift, the papers in this section illustrate the progress that we have made in figuring out what to measure and how to measure it.

Early attempts to measure software were complicated by lack of theories about what was being measured, by the variability in the skills of the software developers, and by the sensitivity of the data. On one occasion in the mid-1970s I was visited by some researchers from a large aerospace company who knew I had an interest in software measurement. They proudly showed me distributions of errors made during software development, but it was nearly impossible to discern any pattern in the distributions. When I asked what questions they were trying to answer with the data I was met with blank looks. They had a random set of data from which one could deduce almost nothing. There were no hypotheses or theories being tested. The experimenters didn't know what questions to ask. Some time earlier I had seen a paper on cost estimation from a large software development company. The paper described a model that had more than 90 variables! There was no hope of using such a model in practice and the implication was that one could never hope to control enough variables to make cost estimation reliable.

At about the same time, Walston and Felix [5] published their classic study of software development at IBM, giving the reader a taste of some meaningful data about productivity. Here were data collected over a number of projects that one might use to form a baseline and that might be the basis for constructing estimates of time and effort. Unfortunately, this was the last data to come from IBM for some time, and the rumor in the community was that the authors had been censured for publishing real data about IBM projects.

The preceding are just a few examples of the many different studies and data sets that appeared throughout the 1970s and into the 1980s. Theories and data bounded about software development, coming from a variety of quarters, such as Halstead's Software Science, Barry Boehm's studies of hundreds of aerospace projects at TRW, John Musa's detailed models of software reliability, Belady and Lehman's studies of large-scale software releases, Wolverton's work on cost models, McCabe's theory of complexity, Albrecht's function points model, Putnam's work relating time, effort, and quality, and others. It was difficult to sort out what was comparable and what was not, what was repeatable and what was not, and, when you found something that seemed meaningful and useful, how to apply it to your environment. Indeed, the state of the field was such that Paul Moranda, one of the pioneers of the field, in a short letter in Computer, 1978, lamented our inability to measure quality in a meaningful way, expressed regret at having had a hand in starting the field, and suggested that we give up [4].

To make sense and progress we needed some standard measurement methods, a tested of publicly available results from real software development projects, and long-term measurement projects.

In 1976 Vic Basili played a key role in founding NASA's Software Engineering Laboratory (SEL), which would help make such sense and progress. In conjunction with Frank McGarry at NASA and Gerry Page at Computer Sciences Corporation (CSC), and with participation from Marv Zelkowitz at the University of Maryland, from project managers at Goddard Space Flight Center (GSFC), and from software developers at CSC and GSFC, as well as a few graduate students (I among them), he formed the kind of tested we needed to make sense out of software measurement and its potential role in creating a discipline of software engineering.

The two papers in this section exemplify some of the significant steps along the way. "A Methodology for Collecting Valid Software Engineering Data" provided one of the first descriptions of the GQM measurement approach and also defined a key ingredient in measurement philosophy: the need to validate the data that one collected. The paper carefully describes the GQM approach and provides details on how to collect and validate data, down to describing the forms we used at the SEL for collecting change data. Also, it contains the results of validating the data that were collected from several SEL projects. Having started out to be a physicist I was early indoctrinated in the need for estimating the error in one's measurements. I looked in vain for error estimates in measurement studies.

After validating several thousand change report forms from SEL projects, including interviewing many SEL programmers, I convinced myself, Vic, and others in the SEL that validation was crucial to good measurement. It put us in a position to say with some confidence how good our measurement was. On several occasions at conference presentations by others working in the measurement field, Vic would get up and ask the presenter how the data had been validated. If the answer was that no validation had been done, the rejoinder, in gentle tones, was "In that case, I find it hard to put trust in your results." This paper also has some sentimental value for me: much of it was taken from my PhD thesis.

Having refined and codified the GQM approach and gained considerable experience in measuring product and process, Vic and Dieter Rombach, embarked on an ambitious task: how to make measurement an integral part of process improvement. "The TAME Project: Tailoring A Measurement Environment" codifies their approach. The SEL had shown the value of baseline measurements, especially in a field where it was very difficult to conduct comparative experiments that controlled all confounding factors. Using the data from the SEL, one could look back at the historical data and observe trends, since one understood how to compare the data.

After about 12 years of progress at the SEL in learning how to decide what data to collect, how to collect it, and how to analyze it, Vic and Dieter realized that they had a way of using measurement data to guide and quantify process improvement. One had but to establish the goals of the development process, collect data to measure progress against those goals, uses the data analysis to understand what had resulted in improvement and what had not, and use that understanding to guide further improvement attempts. A straightforward plan but not simple to achieve. Engineers in other fields would recognize this as a kind of statistical process control. Its success depends on understanding the measurement process, and on working in an organization that is willing to invest in process improvement and that is willing to establish a data collection program to support process improvement.

One may think of the Hewlett Packard software measurement program as an early industrial prototype of TAME [1]. The TAME paper explains the objective of TAME, lists the principles on which a TAME project must be built, including GQM, references the templates for measurement and data collection developed at the SEL, defines a process model for software process improvement, and sketches an architecture for creating an appropriate measurement and process improvement environment. It is an ambitious program, which, if well-implemented over the industry, would take us another step towards the paradigm shift that software development needs to become an engineering discipline. It could help to answer questions such as "What's the production capacity of your software development environment?" whose analogues engineers in other fields can answer routinely.

The papers here represent milestones in creating a software measurement field by means of the following achievements:

- Introducing goal-directed techniques.
- Establishing the basis for comparative analysis to discriminate among different measurement proposals.
- Measuring both process and product, especially measuring changes to software over time.
- Creating a systematic methodology for measurement that incorporates data validation.
- Creating and using baselines to observe trends over time.
- Using measurement to quantify and guide process improvement.

They stand as signposts for those of us who wish to see software development become software engineering.

[1] Grady, R., Caswell, E.; Software metrics: establishing a company-wide program, Upper Saddle River, Prentice-Hall, 1987
[2] Halstead, M.; Elements of Software Science, New York, Elsevier North-Holland, 1977
[3] Kuhn, T.; The Structure of Scientific Revolutions, University of Chicago Press, 1962
[4] Moranda, P.; Software Quality Technology: (Sad) Status Of: (Unapproached) Limits To; (Manifold) Alternatives To, Computer, vol. 11 no.11, pp. 72-79, Nov 1978
[5] C.E.Walston, C.P.Felix, "A Method of Programming Measurement and Estimation," IBM Systems Journal, 16,1, 1977, pp.54- 73.

A Methodology for Collecting Valid Software Engineering Data

Victor R. Basili, Member, IEEE, and David M. Weiss

Abstract. An effective data collection method for evaluating software development methodologies and for studying the software development process is described. The method uses goal-directed data collection to evaluate methodologies with respect to the claims made for them. Such claims are used as a basis for defining the goals of the data collection, establishing a list of questions of interest to be answered by data analysis, defining a set of data categorization schemes, and designing a data collection form.

The data to be collected are based on the changes made to the software during development, and are obtained when the changes are made. To ensure accuracy of the data, validation is performed concurrently with software development and data collection. Validation is based on interviews with those people supplying the data. Results from using the methodology show that data validation is a necessary part of change data collection. Without it, as much as 50 percent of the data may be erroneous.

Feasibility of the data collection methodology was demonstrated by applying it to five different projects in two different environments. The application showed that the methodology was both feasible and useful.

Key Words: Data collection, data collection methodology, error analysis, error classification, software engineering experimentation.

I. Introduction

According to the mythology of computer science, the first computer program ever written contained an error. Error detection and error correction are now considered to be the major cost factors in software development [1] - [3]. Much current and recent research is devoted to finding ways of preventing software errors. This research includes areas such as requirements definition [4], automatic and semiautomatic program generation [5], [6], functional specification [7], abstract speci-

Manuscript received December 13, 1982; revised January 11, 1984. This work was supported in part by the National Aeronautics and Space Administration under Grant NSF-5123 to the University of Maryland.

V. R. Basili is with the Department of Computer Science, University of Maryland, College Park, MD 20742.

D. M. Weiss is with the Naval Research Laboratory, Washington, DC 20375.

fication [8] -[11], procedural specification [12], code specification [13]-[15], verification [16]-[18], coding techniques [19]-[24], error detection [25], testing [26], [27], and language design [16], [28] -[31].

One result of this research is that techniques claimed to be effective for preventing errors are in abundance. Unfortunately, there have been few attempts at experimental verification of such claims. The purpose of this paper is to show how to obtain valid data that may be used both to learn more about the software development process and to evaluate software development methodologies in production environments. Previous [15], [32] - [34] and companion [35] papers present data and evaluation results, obtained from two different software development environments. (Not all of the techniques previously mentioned were included in these studies.) The methodology described in this paper was developed as part of studies conducted by the Naval Research Laboratory (NRL) and by NASA's Software Engineering Laboratory (SEL) [36]. The remainder of this section discusses motivation for data collection and the attributes of a useful data collection effort. Section II is a step-by-step description of the data collection methodology. Section III describes the application of the methodology to the SEL environment. Section IV summarizes the lessons learned concerning data collection and its associated problems, limitations, and applications.

Software Engineering Experimentation

The course of action in most sciences when faced with a question of opinion is to obtain experimental verification. Software engineering disputes are infrequently settled that way. Data from experiments exist, but rarely apply to the question to be settled. There are a number of reasons for this state of affairs. Probably the two most important are the number of potential confounding factors involved in software studies and the expense of attempting to do controlled studies in an industrial environment involving medium or large scale systems.

Rather than attempting controlled studies, we have devised a method for conducting accurate causal analyses in production environments. Causal analyses are efforts to discover the causes of errors and the reasons that changes are made to software. Such analyses are designed to provide some insight into the software development and maintenance processes, help confirm or reject claims made for different methodologies, and lead to better techniques for prevention, detection, and correction of errors. Relatively few examples of this kind of study exist in the literature; some examples are [4], [15], [32], [37], [38].

Attributes of Useful Data Collection

To provide useful data, a data collection methodology must display certain attributes. Since much of the data of interest are collected during the test phase, complete analysis of the data must await project completion. For accuracy reasons, it is important that data collection and validation proceed concurrently with development.

Developers can provide data as they make changes during development. In a reasonably well-controlled software development environment, documentation and code are placed under some form of configuration control before being released to their users. Changes may then be defined as alterations to baselined design, code, or documentation.

A key factor in the data gathering process is validation of the data as they become available. Such validity checks result in corrections to the data that cannot be made at later times owing to the nature of human memory [39]. Timeliness of both data collection and data validation is quite important to the accuracy of the analysis.

Careful validation means that the data to be collected must be carefully specified, so that those supplying data, those validating data, and those performing the analyses will have a consistent view of the data collected. This is especially important for the purposes of repetition of the studies in both the same and different environments.

Careful specification of the data requires the data collectors to have a clear idea of the goals of the study. Specifying goals is itself an important issue, since, without goals, one runs the risk of collecting unrelated, meaningless data.

To obtain insight into the software development process, the data collectors need to know the kinds of errors committed and the kinds of changes made. To identify troublesome issues, the effort needed to make each change is necessary. For greatest usefulness, one would like to study projects from software production environments involving teams of programmers.

We may summarize the preceding as the following six criteria.

1. The data must contain information permitting identification of the types of errors and changes made.
2. The data must include the cost of making changes.
3. Data to be collected must be defined as a result of clear specification of the goals of the study.
4. Data should include studies of projects from production environments, involving teams of programmers.
5. Data analysis should be historical; data must be collected and validated concurrently with development.
6. Data classification schemes to be used must be carefully specified for the sake of repeatability of the study in the same and different environments.

II. Schema for the Investigative Methodology

Our data collection methodology is goal oriented. It starts with a set of goals to be satisfied, uses these to generate a set of questions to be answered, and then proceeds step-by-step through the design and implementation of a data collection and validation mechanism. Analysis of the data yields answers to the questions of interest, and may also yield a new set of questions. The procedure relies heavily on an interactive data validation process; those supplying the data are interviewed for validation purposes concurrently with the software development process. The methodology has been used in two different environments to study five software projects developed by groups with different backgrounds, using very different software development methodologies. In both environments it yielded answers to most questions of interest and some insight into the development methodologies used. Table I is a summary of characteristics of completed projects that have been studied. Definitions of the characteristics are the same as in [40]. All examples used in this paper are taken from studies of the SEL environment.

Table I Summary of Project Information

	SEL 1	SEL 2	SEL 3	NRL 1
Effort (work-months)	79.0	39.6	98.7	48.0
Number of developers	5	4	7	9
Lines of Code (K)	50.9	75.4	85.4	21.8
Developed lines of code	46.5	31.1	76.6	21.8
Number of components	502	490	639	235

The projects studied vary widely with respect to factors such as application, size, development team, methodology, hardware, and support software. Nonetheless, the same basic data collection methodology was applicable everywhere. The schema used has six basic steps, listed in the following, with considerable feedback and iteration occurring at several different places.

1. *Establish the Goals of the Data Collection*: We divide goals into two categories: those that may be used to evaluate a particular software development methodology relative to the claims made for it, and those that are common to all methodologies to be studied.

   As an example, a goal of a particular methodology, such as information hiding [41], might be to develop software that is easy to change. The corresponding data collection goal is to evaluate the success of the developers in meeting this goal, i.e., evaluate the ease with which the software can be changed. Goals in this category may be of more interest to those who are involved in developing or testing a particular methodology, and must be defined cooperatively with them.

   A goal that is of interest regardless of the methodology being used is to help understand the environment and focus attention on techniques that are useful there. Another such goal is to characterize changes in ways that permit comparisons across projects and environments. Such goals may interest software engineers, programmers, managers, and others more than goals that are specific to the success or failure of a particular methodology.

   Consequences of Omitting Goals: Without goals, one is likely to obtain data in which either incomplete patterns or no patterns are discernible. As an example, one goal of an early study [15] was to characterize errors. During data analysis, it became desirable to discover the fraction of errors that were the result of changes made to the software for some reason other than to correct an error. Unfortunately, none of the goals of the study was related to this type of change, and there were no such data available.

2. *Develop a List of Questions of Interest*: Once the goals of the study have been established, they may be used to develop a list of questions to be answered by the study. Questions of interest define data parameters and categorizations that permit quantitative analysis of the data. In general, each goal will result in the generation of several different questions of interest. As an example, if the goal is to characterize changes, some corresponding questions of interest are: "What is the distribution of changes according to the reason for the change?", "What is the distribution of changes across system components?", "What is the distribution of effort to design changes?"

   As a second example, if the goal is to evaluate the ease with which software can be changed, we may identify questions of interest such as: "Is it clear where a change has to be made in the software?", "Are changes confined to single modules?", "What was the average effort involved in making a change?" Questions of interest form a bridge between subjectively determined goals of the study and the quantitative measures to be used in the study. They permit the investigators to determine the quantities that need to be measured and the aspects of the goals that can be measured. As an example, to discover how a design document is being used, one might collect data that show how the document was being used when the need for a change to it was discovered. This may be the only aspect of the document's use that is measurable.

   In addition to forcing sharper definition of goals, questions of interest have the desirable property of forcing the investigators to consider the data analyses to be performed before any data are collected.

   Goals for which questions of interest cannot be formulated and goals that cannot be satisfied because adequate measures cannot be defined may be discarded. Once formulated, questions can be evaluated to determine if they completely cover their associated goals and if they define quantitative measures. *Consequences of Omitting Questions of Interest*: Without questions of interest, data distributions that are needed for evaluation purposes, such as the distribution of effort involved in making changes, may have to be constructed in an ad hoc way, and be incomplete or inaccurate. As a result, there may be no quantitative basis for satisfying the goals of the study. In effect, goals are not well defined if questions of interest are not or cannot be formulated.

3. *Establish Data Categories:* Once the questions of interest have been established, categorization schemes for the changes and errors to be examined may be constructed. Each question generally induces a categorization scheme. If one question is, "What was the distribution of changes according to the reason for the change?", one will want to classify changes according to the reason they are made. A simple categorization scheme of this sort is error corrections versus no error corrections (hereafter called modifications).

   Each of these categories may be further subcategorized according to reason. As an example, modifications could be subdivided into modifications resulting from requirements changes, modifications resulting from a change in the development support environment (e.g., compiler change), planned enhancements, optimizations, and others.

Such a categorization permits characterization of the changes with respect to the stability of the development environment, with respect to different kinds of development activities, etc. When matched with another categorization such as the difficulty of making changes, this scheme also reveals which changes are the most difficult to make.

Each categorization scheme should be complete and consistent, i.e., every change should fit exactly one of the subcategories of the scheme. To ensure completeness, we usually add the category "Other" as a subcategory. Where some changes are not suited to the scheme, the subcategory "Not Applicable" may be used. As an example, if the scheme includes subcategories for different levels of effort in isolating error causes, then errors for which the cause need not be isolated (e.g., clerical errors noticed when reading code) belong in the "Not Applicable" subcategory.

Consequences of Not Defining Data Categories Before Collecting Data: Omitting the data categorization schemes may result in data that cannot later be identified as fitting any particular categorization. Each change then defines its own category, and the result is an overwhelming multiplicity of data categories, with little data in each category.

4. *Design and Test Data Collection Form*: To provide a permanent copy of the data and to reinforce the programmers' memories, a data collection form is used. Form design was one of the trickiest parts of the studies conducted, primarily because forms represent a compromise among conflicting objectives. Typical conflicts are the desire to collect a complete, detailed set of data that may be used to answer a wide range of questions of interest, and the need to minimize the time and effort involved in supplying the data. Satisfying the former leads to large, detailed forms that require much time to fill out. The latter requires a short, check-off-the-boxes type of form.

Including the data suppliers in the form design process is quite beneficial. Complaints by those who must use the form are resolved early (i.e., before data collection begins), the form may be tailored to the needs of the data suppliers (e.g., for use in configuration management), and the data suppliers feel they are a useful part of the data collection process.

The forms must be constructed so that the data they contain can be used to answer the questions of interest. Several design iterations and test periods are generally needed before a satisfactory design is found.

Our principal goals in form design were to produce a form that

a) fit on one piece of paper,

b) could be used in several different programming environments, and

c) permitted the programmer some flexibility in describing the charge.

Fig. 1 shows the last version of the form used for the SEL studies reported here. (An earlier version of the form was significantly modified as a result of experience gained in the data collection and analysis processes.) The first sections of the form request textual descriptions of the change and the reason it was made. Following sections contain questions and check-off tables that reflect various categorization schemes.

As an example, a categorization of time to design changes is requested in the first question following the description of the change. The completer of the form is given the choice of four categories (one hour or less, one hour to one day, one day to three days, and more than three days) that cover all possibilities for design time.

Consequences of Not Using a Data Collection Form: Without a data collection form, it is necessary to rely on the developer's memories and on perusal of early versions of design documentation and code to identify and categorize the changes made. This approach leads to incomplete, inaccurate data.

5. *Collect and Validate Data*: Data are collected by requiring those people who are making software changes to complete a change report form for each change made, as soon as the change is completed. Validation consists of checking the forms for correctness, consistency, and completeness. As part of the validation process, in cases where such checks reveal problems, the people who filled out the forms are interviewed. Both collection and validation are concurrent with software development; the shorter the lag between completing the form and conducting the interview, the more accurate the data.

   Perhaps the most significant problem during data collection and validation is ensuring that the data are complete, i.e., that every change has been described on a form. The better controlled the development process, the easier this is to do. At each stage of the process where configuration control is imposed, change data may be collected. Where projects that we have studied use formal configuration control, we have integrated the configuration control procedures and the data collection procedures, using the same forms for both, and taking advantage of configuration control procedures for validation purposes. Since all changes must be reviewed by a configuration control board in such cases, we are guaranteed capture of all changes, i.e., that our data are complete. Furthermore, the data collection overhead is absorbed into the configuration control overhead, and is not visible as a separate source of irritation to the developers.

   Consequences of Omitting Validation: One result of concurrent development, data collection, and data validation is that the accuracy of the collection process may be quantified. Accuracy may be calculated by observing the number of mistakes made in completing data collection forms. One may then compare, for any data category, revalidation distributions with post validation distributions. We call such an analysis a validation analysis. The validation analysis of the SEL data shows that it is possible for inaccuracies on the order of 50 percent to be introduced by omitting validation. To emphasize the consequences of omitting the validation procedures, we present some of the results of the validation analysis of the SEL data in Section III.

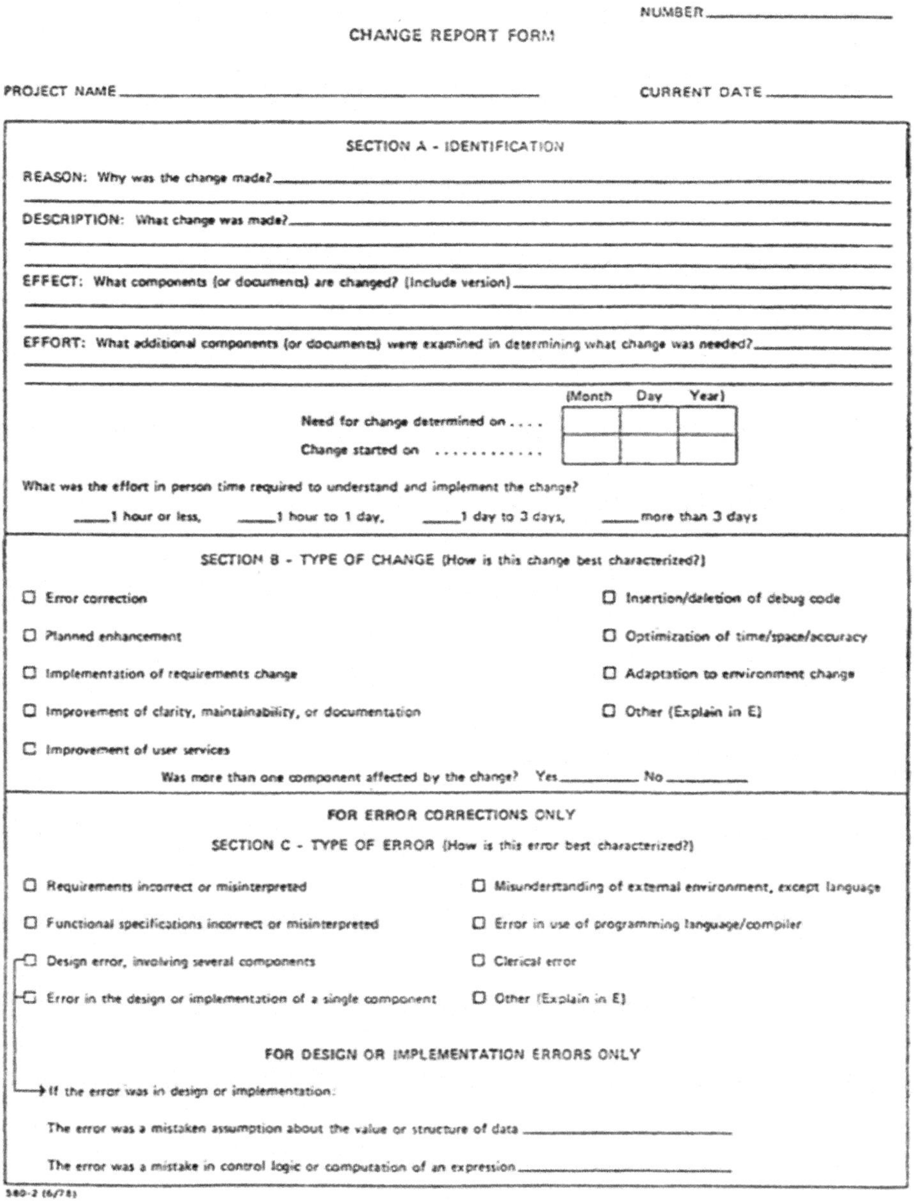

NUMBER ______

CHANGE REPORT FORM

PROJECT NAME ______ CURRENT DATE ______

SECTION A - IDENTIFICATION

REASON: Why was the change made? ______

DESCRIPTION: What change was made? ______

EFFECT: What components (or documents) are changed? (Include version) ______

EFFORT: What additional components (or documents) were examined in determining what change was needed? ______

	(Month	Day	Year)
Need for change determined on			
Change started on			

What was the effort in person time required to understand and implement the change?

____1 hour or less, ____1 hour to 1 day, ____1 day to 3 days, ____more than 3 days

SECTION B - TYPE OF CHANGE (How is this change best characterized?)

- ☐ Error correction
- ☐ Planned enhancement
- ☐ Implementation of requirements change
- ☐ Improvement of clarity, maintainability, or documentation
- ☐ Improvement of user services
- ☐ Insertion/deletion of debug code
- ☐ Optimization of time/space/accuracy
- ☐ Adaptation to environment change
- ☐ Other (Explain in E)

Was more than one component affected by the change? Yes ______ No ______

FOR ERROR CORRECTIONS ONLY

SECTION C - TYPE OF ERROR (How is this error best characterized?)

- ☐ Requirements incorrect or misinterpreted
- ☐ Functional specifications incorrect or misinterpreted
- ☐ Design error, involving several components
- ☐ Error in the design or implementation of a single component
- ☐ Misunderstanding of external environment, except language
- ☐ Error in use of programming language/compiler
- ☐ Clerical error
- ☐ Other (Explain in E)

FOR DESIGN OR IMPLEMENTATION ERRORS ONLY

→ If the error was in design or implementation:

The error was a mistaken assumption about the value or structure of data ______

The error was a mistake in control logic or computation of an expression ______

580-2 (6/78)

Fig. 1. SEL change report form. Front

FOR ERROR CORRECTIONS ONLY

SECTION D - VALIDATION AND REPAIR

What activities were used to validate the program, detect the error, and find its cause?

	Activities Used for Program Validation	Activities Successful in Detecting Error Symptoms	Activities Tried to Find Cause	Activities Successful in Finding Cause
Pre-acceptance test runs				
Acceptance testing				
Post-acceptance use				
Inspection of output				
Code reading by programmer				
Code reading by other person				
Talks with other programmers				
Special debug code				
System error messages				
Project specific error messages				
Reading documentation				
Trace				
Dump				
Cross-reference/attribute list				
Proof technique				
Other (Explain in E)				

What was the time used to isolate the cause?

___one hour or less, ___one hour to one day, ___more than one day, ___never found

If never found, was a workaround used?___Yes___No (Explain in E)

Was this error related to a previous change?

___Yes (Change Report #/Date___) ___No ___Can't tell

When did the error enter the system?

___requirements ___functional specs ___design ___coding and test ___other ___can't tell

SECTION E - ADDITIONAL INFORMATION

Please give any information that may be helpful in categorizing the error or change, and understanding its cause and its ramifications.

Name ___ Authorized: ___ Date: ___

Fig. 1. SEL change report form. Back

6. *Analyze Data*: Data are analyzed by calculating the parameters and distributions needed to answer the questions of interest. As an example, to answer the question "What was the distribution of changes according to the reason for the

change?", a distribution such as that shown in Fig. 2 might be computed from the data.

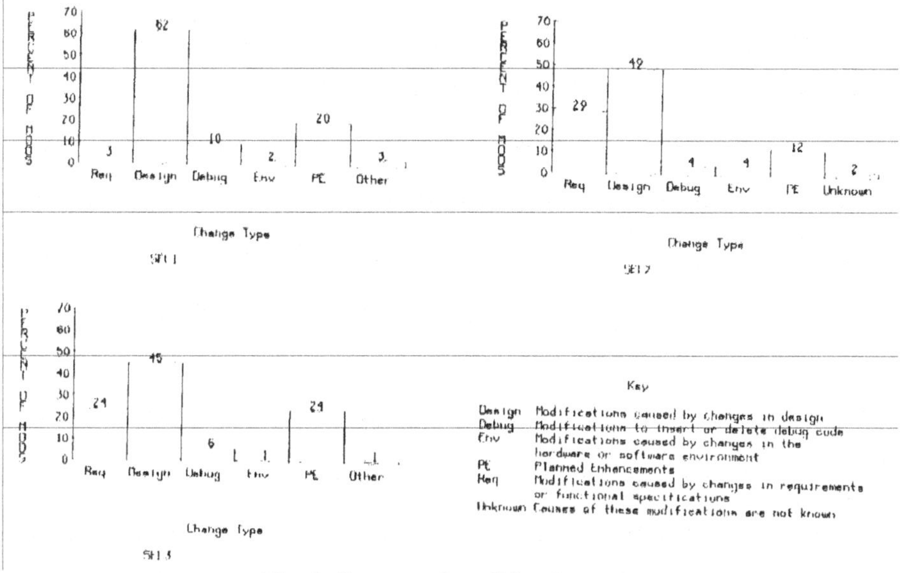

Fig. 2. Sources of modifications.

Application of the Schema

Applying the schema requires iterating among the steps several times. Defining the goals and establishing the questions of interest are tightly coupled, as are establishing the questions of interest designing and testing the form(s), and collecting and validating the data. Many of the considerations involved in implementing and integrating the steps of the schema have been omitted here so that the reader may have an overview of the process. The complete set of goals, questions of interest, and data categorizations for the SEL projects are shown in [33].

Support Procedures and Facilities

In addition to the activities directly involved in the data collection effort, here are a number of support activities and facilities required. Included as support activities are testing the forms, collection and validation procedures, training the programmers, selecting a database system to permit easy analysis of the data, encoding and entering data into the database, and developing analysis programs.

III. Details of SEL Data Collection and Validation

In the SEL environment, program libraries were used to support and control software development. There was a full-time librarian assigned to support SEL projects. All project library changes were routed through the librarian. In general, we define a change to be an alteration to baseline design, code, or documentation. For SEL purposes, only changes to code, and documentation contained in the code, were studied. The program libraries provided a convenient mechanism for identifying changes.

Each time a programmer caused a library change, he was required to complete a change report form (Fig. 1). The data presented here are drawn from studies of three different SEL projects, denoted SEL1, SEL2, and SEL3. The processing procedures were as follows.

1. Programmers were required to complete change report forms for all changes made to library routines.
2. Programs were kept in the project library during the entire test phase.
3. After a change was made a completed change report form describing the change was submitted. The form was first informally reviewed by the project leader. It was then sent to the SEL library staff to be logged and a unique identifier assigned to it.
4. The change analyst reviewed the form and noted any inconsistencies, omissions, or possible miscategorizations. Any questions the analyst had were resolved in an interview with the programmer. (Occasionally the project leader or system designer was consulted rather than the individual programmer.)
5. The change analyst revised the form as indicated by the results of the programmer interview, and returned it to the library staff for further processing. Revisions often involved cases where several changes were reported on one form. In these cases, the analyst ensured that there was only one change reported per form; this often involved filling out new forms. Forms created in this way are known as generated forms. (Changes were considered to be different if they were made for different reasons, if they were the result of different events, or if they were made at substantially different times, e.g., several weeks apart. As an example, two different requirements amendments would result in two different change reports, even if the changes were made at the same time in the same subroutine.) Occasionally, one change was reported on several different forms. The forms were then merged into one form, again to ensure one and only one change per form. Forms created in this way are known as combined forms.
6. The library staff encoded the form for entry into the (automated) SEL database. A preliminary, automated check of the form was made via a set of database support programs. This check, mostly syntactic, ensured that the proper kinds of values were encoded into the proper fields, e.g, that an alphabetic character was not entered where an integer was required.
7. The encoded data were entered into the SEL database.

8. The data were analyzed by a set of programs that computed the necessary distributions to answer the questions of interest.

Many of the reported SEL changes were error corrections. We define an error to be a discrepancy between a specification and its implementation. Although it was not always possible to identify the exact location of an error, it was always possible to identify exactly each error correction. As a result, we generally use the term error to mean error correction.

For data validation purposes, the most important parts of the data collection procedure are the review by the change analyst, and the associated programmer interview to resolve uncertainties about the data.

The SEL validation procedures afforded a good chance to discover whether valuation was really necessary; it was possible to count the number of miscategorizations of changes and associated misinformation. These counts were obtained by counting the number of times each question on the form was incorrectly answered.

An example is misclassifications of errors as clerical errors. (Clerical errors were defined as errors that occur in the mechanical translation of an item from one format to another, e.g., from one coding sheet to another, or from one medium to another, e.g., coding sheets to cards.) For one of the SEL projects, 46 errors originally classified as clerical were actually errors of other types. (One of these consisted of the programmer forgetting to include several lines of code in a subroutine. Rather than clerical, this was classified as an error in the design or implementation of a single component of the system.) Initially, this project reported 238 changes, so we may say that about 19 percent of the original reports were misclassified as clerical errors.

The SEL validation process was not good for verifying the completeness of the reported data. We cannot tell from the validation studies how many changes were never reported. This weakness can be eliminated by integrating the data collection with stronger configuration control procedures.

Validation Differences Among SEL Projects

As experience was gained in collecting, validating, and analyzing data for the SEL projects, the quality of the data improved significantly, and the validation procedures changed slightly. For SEL1 and SEL2, completed forms were examined and programmers interviewed by a change analyst within a few weeks (typically 3-6 weeks) of the time the forms were completed. For project SEL2, the task leader (lead programmer for the project) examined each form before the change analysts saw it.

Project SEL3 was not monitored as closely as SEL1 and SEL2. The task leader, who was the same as for SEL2, by then understood the data categorization schemes quite well and again examined the forms before sending them to the SEL. The forms themselves were redesigned to be simpler but still capture nearly all the same data. Finally, several of the programmers were the same as on project SEL2 and were experienced in completing the forms.

Estimating Inaccuracies in the Data

Although there is no completely objective way to quantify the inaccuracy in the validated data, we believe it to be no more than 5 percent for SKL1 and SEL2. By this we mean that no more than 5 percent of the changes and errors are misclassified in any of the data collection categories. For the major categories, such as whether a change is an error or modification, the type of change, and the type of error, the inaccuracy is probably no more than 3 percent.

For SEL3, we attempted to quantify the results of the validation procedures more carefully. After validation, forms were categorized according to our confidence in their accuracy. We used four categories.

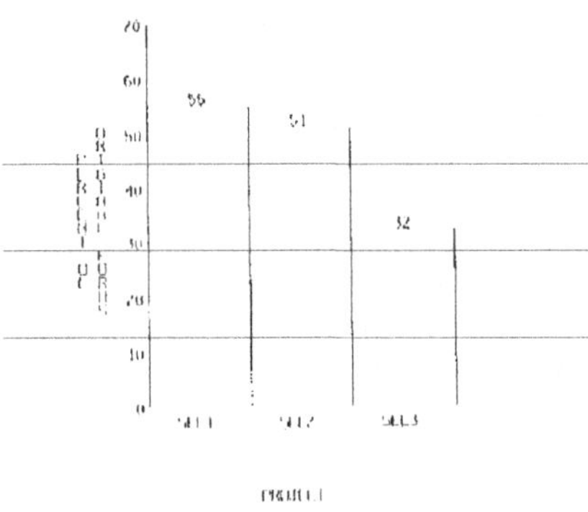

Fig. 3. Corrected forms.

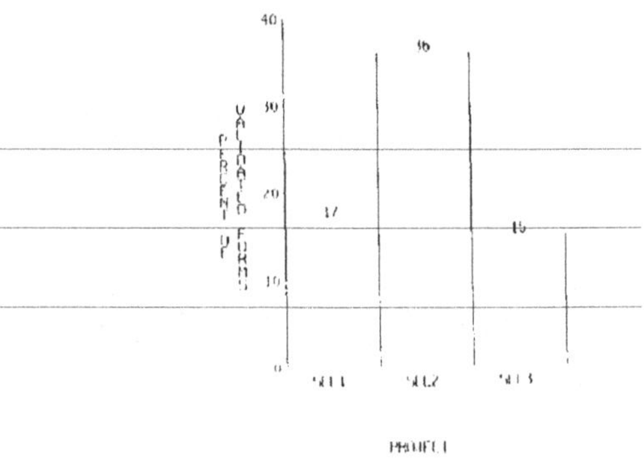

Fig. 4. Generated forms.

1. Those forms for which we had no doubt concerning the accuracy of the data. Forms in this category were estimated to have no more than a 1 percent chance of inaccuracy.
2. Those forms for which there was little doubt about the accuracy of the data. Forms in this category were estimated to have at most a 10 percent chance of an inaccuracy.
3. Those forms for which there was some uncertainty about the accuracy, with an estimated inaccuracy rate of more than 30 percent.
4. Those forms for which there was considerable uncertainty about the accuracy, with an estimated inaccuracy rate of about 50 percent.

Applying the inaccuracy rates to the number of forms in each category gave us an estimated inaccuracy of at most 3 percent in the validated forms for SEL3.

Prevalent Mistakes in Completing Forms

Clear patterns of mistakes and rnisclassifications in completing forms became evident during validation. As an example, programmers on projects SELI and SEL2 frequently included more than one change on one form. Often this was a result of the programmers sending the changes to the library as a group.

Comparative Validation Results

Fig. 3 provides an overview of the results of the validation process for the 3 SEL projects. The percentage of original forms that had to be corrected as a result of the validation process is shown. As an example, 32 percent of the originally completed change report forms for SEL3 were corrected as a result of validation. The percentages are based on the number of original forms reported (since some forms were generated, and some combined, the number of changes reported after validation is different than the number reported before validation). Fig. 4 shows the number of generated forms expressed as a percentage of total validated forms.

Fig. 3 shows that prevalidation SEL3 forms were significantly more accurate than the prevalidation SELI or SEL2 forms. Fig. 4 shows that SEL3 also had the lowest incidence of generated forms. Although not shown in the figures, combined forms represented a very small fraction of the total validated forms. Based on this analysis, the prevalidation SEL3 data are considerably better than the prevalidation data for either of the other projects. We believe the reasons for this are the improved design of the form and the familiarity of the task leader and programmers with the data collection process.

These results show that careful validation, including programmer interviews, is essential to the accuracy of any study involving change data. Furthermore, it appears that with well-designed forms and programmer training, there is improvement with time in the accuracy of the data one can obtain. We do not believe that it will ever be possible to dispense entirely with programmer interviews, however.

Erroneous Classifications

Table II shows misclassifications of errors as modifications and modifications as errors. As an example, for SEL1, 14 percent of the original forms were classified as modifications, but were actually errors. Without the validation process, considerable inaccuracy would have been introduced into the initial categorization of changes as modifications or errors.

Table III is a sampling of other kinds of classification errors that could contribute significantly to inaccuracy in the data. All involve classification of an error into the wrong subcategory. The first row shows errors that were classified by the programmer as clerical, but were later reclassified as a result of the validation process into another category. For SEL1, significant inaccuracy (19 percent) would be introduced by omitting the validation process,

Table IV is similar to Table III, but shows misclassifications involving modifications for SEL1 and SEL3 (SEL2 data were not analyzed for this purpose). The first row shows modifications that were classified by the programmer as requirements or specifications changes, but were reclassified as a result of validation.

Variation in Misclassification

Data on misclassifications of change and error type subcategories, such as shown in Table III, tend to vary considerably among both projects and subcategories. (Misclassification of clerical errors, as shown in Table III, is a good example.) This is most likely because the misclassifications represent biases in the judgments of the programmers. It became clear during the validation process that certain programmers tended toward particular misclassifications.

Table II Erroneous Modification an Error Classifications (Percent of Original Forms)

	SEL 1	SEL 2	SEL 3
Modifications classified as errors	1%	5%	< 1%
Errors classified as modifications	14%	5%	2%

Table III Typical Error Type Misclassifications (Percent of Original Forms)

Original Classification	SEL 1	SEL 2	SEL 3
Clerical Error	19%	7%	6%
(Use of) Programming Language	0%	5%	3%
Incorrect or Misinterpreted Requirements	Unavailable	0%	< 1%
Design Error	Unavailable	6%	1%

Table IV Erroneous Modification Classifications (Percent of Original Forms)

	SEL 1	SEL 3
Requirements or specification change	1%	< 1%
Design change	8%	1%
Optimization	8%	< 1%
Other	3%	< 1%

The consistency between projects SEL2 and SEL3 in Table III probably occurs because both projects had the same task leader, who screened all forms before sending them to the SEL for validation.

Conclusions Concerning Validation

The preceding sections have shown that the validation process, particularly the programmer interviews, are a necessary part of the data collection methodology. Inaccuracies on the order of 50 percent may be introduced without this form of validation. Furthermore, it appears that with appropriate form design and programmer experience in completing forms, the inaccuracy rate may be substantially reduced, although it is doubtful that it can be reduced to the level where programmer interviews may be omitted from the validation procedures.

A second significant conclusion is that the analysis performed as part of the validation process may be used to guide the data collection project; the analysis results show what data can be reliably and practically collected, and what data cannot be. Data collection goals, questions of interest, and data collection forms may have to be revised accordingly.

IV. Recommendations for Data Collectors

We believe we now have sufficient experience with change data collection to be able to apply it successfully in a wide variety of environments. Although we have been able to make comparisons between the data collected in the two environments we have studied, we would like to make comparisons with a wider variety of environments. Such comparisons will only be possible if more data become available. To encourage the establishment of more data collection projects, we feel it is important to describe a successful data collection methodology, as we have done in the preceding sections, to point out the pitfalls involved, and to suggest ways of avoiding those pitfalls.

Procedural Lessons Learned

Problems encountered in various procedural aspects of the studies were the most difficult to overcome. Perhaps the most important are the following.

1. Clearly understanding the working environment and specifying the data collection procedures were a key part of conducting the investigation. Misunderstanding by the programmer of the circumstances that require him/her to file a change report form will prejudice the entire effort. Prevention of such misunderstandings can in part be accomplished by training procedures and good forms design, but feedback to the development staff, i.e., those filling out the data collection forms, must not be omitted.
2. Similarly, misunderstanding by the change analyst of the circumstances that required a change to be made will result in misclassifications and erroneous analyses. Our SEL data collection was helped by the use of a change analyst who had previously worked in the NASA environment and understood the application and the development procedures used.
3. Timely data validation through interviews with those responsible for reporting errors and changes was vital, especially during the first few projects to use the forms. Without such validation procedures, data will be severely biased, and the developers will not get the feedback to correct the procedures they are using for reporting data.
4. Minimizing the overhead imposed on the people who were required to complete change reports was an important factor in obtaining complete and accurate data. Increased overhead brought increased reluctance to supply and discuss data. In projects where data collection has been integrated with

configuration control, the visible data collection and validation overhead is significantly decreased, and is no longer an important factor in obtaining complete data. Because configuration control procedures for the SEL environment were informal, we believe we did not capture all SEL changes.

5. In cases where an automated database is used, data consistency and accuracy checks at or immediately prior to analysis are vital. Errors in encoding data for entry into the database will otherwise bias the data.

Nonprocedural Lessons Learned

In addition to the procedural problems involved in designing and implementing a data collection study, we found several other pitfalls that could have strongly affected our results and their interpretation. They are listed in the following.

1. Perhaps the most significant of these pitfalls was the danger of interpreting the results without attempting to understand factors in the environment that might affect the data. As an example, we found a surprisingly small percentage of interface errors on all of the SEL projects. This was surprising since interfaces are an often-cited source of errors. There was also other evidence in the data that the software was quite amenable to change. In trying to understand these results, we discussed them with the principal designer of the SEL projects (all of which had the same application). It was clear from the discussion that as a result of their experience with the application, the designers had learned what changes to expect to their systems, organized the design so that the expected changes would be easy to make, and then reused the design from one project to the next. Rather than misinterpreting the data to mean that interfaces were not a significant software problem, we were led to a better understanding of the environment we were studying.
2. A second pitfall was underestimating the resources needed to validate and analyze the data. Understanding the change reports well enough to conduct meaningful, efficient programmer interviews for validation purposes initially consumed considerable amounts of the change analysts' time. Verifying that the database was internally consistent, complete, and consistent with the paper copies of reports was a continuing source of frustration and a sink for time and effort.
3. A third potential pitfall in data collection is the sensitivity of the data. Programmers and designers sometimes need to be convinced that error data will not be used against them. This did not seem to be a significant problem on the projects studied for a variety of reasons, including management support, processing of the error data by people independent of the project, identifying error reports in the analysis process by number rather than name, informing newly hired project personnel that completion of error reports was considered part of their job, and high project morale. Furthermore, project management did not need error data to evaluate performance.
4. One problem for which there is no simple solution is the Hawthorne (or observer) effect [42]. When project personnel become aware that an aspect of

their behavior is being monitored, their behavior will change. If error monitoring is a continuous, long-term activity that is part of the normal scheme of software development, not associated with evaluation of programmer performance, this effect may become insignificant. We believe this was the case with the projects studied.

5. The sensitivity of error data is enhanced in an environment where development is done on contract. Contractors may feel that such data are proprietary. Rules for data collection may have to be contractually specified.

Avoiding Data Collection Pitfalls

In the foregoing sections a number of potential pitfalls in the data collection process have been described. The following list includes suggestions that help avoid some of these pitfalls.

1. Select change analysts who are familiar with the environment, application, project, and development team.
2. Establish the goals of the data collection methodology and define the questions of interest before attempting any data collection. Establishing goals and defining questions should be an iterative process performed in concert with the developers. The developers' interests are then served as well as the data collector's.
3. For initial data collection efforts, keep the set of data collection goals small. Both the volume of data and the time consumed in gathering, validating, and analyzing it will be unexpectedly large.
4. Design the data collection form so that it may be used for configuration control, so that it is tailored to the project(s) being studied, so that the data may be used for comparison purposes, and so that those filling out the forms understand the terminology used. Conduct training sessions in filling out forms for newcomers.
5. Integrate data collection and validation procedures into the configuration control process. Data completeness and accuracy are thereby improved, data collection is unobtrusive, and collection and validation become a part of the normal development procedures. In cases where configuration control is not used or is informal, allocate considerable time to programmer interviews, and, if possible, documentation search and code reading.
6. Automate as much of the data analysis process as possible.

Limitations

It has been previously noted that the main limitation of using a goal-directed data collection approach in a production software environment is the inability to isolate the effects of single factors. For a variety of reasons, controlled experiments that may he used to test hypotheses concerning the effects of single factors do not seem practical. Neither can one expect to use the change data from goal-directed data collection to test such hypotheses.

A second major imitation is that lost data cannot be accurately recaptured. The data collected as a result of these studies represent five years of data collection. During that time there was considerable and continuing consideration given to the appropriate goals and questions of interest. Nonetheless, as data were analyzed it became clear that there was information that was never requested but that would have been useful. An example is the length of time each error remained in the system. Programmers correcting their own errors, which was the usual case, can supply these data easily at the time they correct the error. Our attempts to discover error entry and removal times after the end of development were fruitless. (Error entry times were particularly difficult to discover.) This type of example underscores the need for careful planning prior to the start of data collection.

Recommendations that May Be Provided to the Software Developer

The nature of the data collection methodology and its target environments do not generally permit isolation of the effects of particular factors on the software development process. The results cannot be used to prove that a particular factor in the development process causes particular kinds of errors, but can be used to suggest that certain approaches, when applied in the environment studied, will improve the development process. The software developer may then be provided with a set of recommended approaches for improving the software development process in his environment.

As an example, in the SEL environment neither external problems, such as requirements changes, nor global problems, such as interface design and specification, were significant. Furthermore, the development environment was quite stable. Most problems were associated with the individual programmer. The data show that in the SEL environment it would clearly pay to impose more control on the process of composing individual routines.

Conclusions Concerning Data Collection for Methodology Evaluation Purposes

The data collection schema presented has been applied in two different environments. We have been able to draw the following conclusions as a result.

1. In all cases, it has been possible to collect data concurrently with the software development process in a software production environment.
2. Data collection may be used to evaluate the application of a particular software development methodology, or simply to learn more about the software development process. In the former case, the better defined the methodology, the more precisely the goals of the data collection may be stated.
3. The better controlled the development process, the more accurate and complete the data.

4. For all projects studied, it has been necessary to validate the data, including interviews with the project developers.
5. As patterns are discerned in the data collected, new questions of interest emerge. These questions may not be answerable with the available data, and may require establishing new goals and questions of interest.

Motivations for Conducting Similar Studies

The difficulties involved in conducting large-scale controlled software engineering experiments have as yet prevented evaluations of software development methodologies in situations where they are often claimed to work best. As a result, software engineers must depend on less formal techniques that can be used in real working environments to establish long-term trends. We view goal-oriented data collection as one such technique and feel that more techniques, and many more results obtained by applying such techniques, are needed.

Acknowledgment

The authors thank the many people at NASA/GSFC and Computer Sciences Corporation who filled out forms and submitted to interviews, especially J. Grondalski and Dr. G. Page, and the librarians, especially S. DePriest.

We thank Dr. J. Gannon, Dr. R. Meltzer, F. McGarry, Dr. G. Page, Dr. D. Parnas, Dr. J. Shore, and Dr. M. Zelkowitz for their many helpful suggestions.

Deserving of special mention is F. McGarry, who had sufficient foresight and confidence to sponsor much of this work and to offer his projects for study.

References

[1] B. Boehm et al., *Information Processing/Data Automation Implications of Air Force Command and Control Requirements in the 1980's (CCIP-85)*, Space and Missile Syst. Org., Los Angeles, CA, Feb. 1972.

[2] B. Boehm, "Software and its impact: A quantitative assessment," *Datamation*, vol. 19, pp. 48-59, May 1973.

[3] R. Wolverton, "The cost of developing large scale software," *IEEE Trans. Comput.*, vol. C-23, no. 6, 1974.

[4] T. Bell, D. Bixler, and M. Dyer, "An extendable approach to computer-aided software requirements engineering," *IEEE Trans. Software Eng.*, vol. SE-3, pp. 49-60, Jan. 1977.

[5] A. Ambler, D. Good, J. Browne, et al., "GYPSY: A language for specification and implementation of verifiable programs," in *Proc. ACM Conf. Language Design for Reliable Software*, Mar. 1977, pp. 1-10.

[6] Z. Manna and R. Waldinger, "Synthesis: Dreams => programs, *IEEE Trans. Software Eng.,* vol. SE-5, pp. 294-329, July 1979.

[7] K. Heninger, "Specifying requirements for complex systems: New techniques and their application," *IEEE Trans. Software Eng.*, vol. SE-6, pp. 2-13, Jan. 1980.
[8] D. L. Parnas, "A technique for software module specification with examples," *Commun. Ass. Comput. Mach.*, vol. 15, pp. 330-336, May 1972.
[9] J. Guttag, "The specification and application to programming of abstract data types," Comput. Syst. Res. Group, Dep. Comput. Sci., Univ. Toronto, Ont., Canada, Rep. CSRG-59, 1975.
[10] —, "Abstract data types and the development of data structures," *Commun. Ass. Comput. Mach.*, vol. 20, pp. 396-404, June 1976.
[11] B. Liskov and S. Zilles, "Specification techniques for data abstraction," *IEEE Trans. Software Eng.*, vol. SE-1, pp. 7-19, Mar.1975.
[12] H. Mills, R. Linger, and B. Witt, *Structured Programming Theory and Practice*. Reading, MA: Addison-Wesley, 1979.
[13] S. Caine and E. Gordon, "PDL-A tool for software design," in *Proc. Nat. Comput. Conf.,* 1975, pp. 271-276.
[14] H. Elovitz, "An experiment in software engineering: The architecture research facility as a case study," in *Proc. 4th Int. Conf. Software Eng.*, 1579, pp. 145-152.
[15] D. Weiss, "Evaluating software development by error analysis: The data from the architecture research facility," *J. Syst. Software*, vol. 1, pp. 57-70,1979.
[16] E. W. Dijkstra, *A Discipline of Programming*. Englewood Cliffs, NJ: Prentice-Hall, 1976.
[17] R. W. Floyd, "Assigning meanings to programs," in *Proc. XIX Symp. Appl. Math.*, Amer. Math. Soc., 1967, pp. 19-32.
[18] C. A. R. Hoare, "An axiomatic basis for computer programming," *Commun. Ass. Comput. Mach.*, vol. 12, pp. 576-580, Oct. 1969.
[19] F. Baker, "Chief programmer team management of production programming," *IBM Syst. J.*, vol. 11, no. 1, pp. 56-73,1972.
[20] E. W. Dijkstra, "Notes on structured programming," in *Structured Programming*. London, England: Academic, 1972.
[21] D. E. Knuth, "Structured programming with go to statements," *Comput. Surveys*, vol. 6, pp. 261-301, Dec. 1974.
[22] H. Mills, "Chief programmer teams: Principles and procedures," IBM Fed. Syst. Div., FSC 71-5108,1971.
[23] —, "Mathematical foundations for structured programming," IBM Fed. Syst. Div., FSC 72-6012,1972
[24] N. Wirth, "Program development by stepwise refinement," *Commun. Ass. Comput. Mach.*, vol. 14, pp. 221-227, Apr. 1971.
[25] E. Satterthwaite, "Debugging tools for high-level languages," *Software—Practice and Exp.,* vol. 2, pp. 197-217, July-Sept.1972.
[26] W. Howden, "Theoretical and empirical studies of program testing," in *Proc. 3rd Int. Conf. Software Eng.*, May 1978, pp. 305-310.
[27] J. Goodenough and S. Gerhart, "Toward a theory of test data selection," in *Proc. Int. Conf. Reliable Software*, 1975, pp. 493-510.
[28] J. Gannon, "Language design to enhance programming reliability," Comput. Syst. Res. Group, Dep. Comput. Sci., Univ. Toronto, Toronto, Ont., Canada, Rep. CSRG-47, 1975.
[29] J. Gannon and Horning, "Language design for programming reliability," *IEEE Trans. Software Eng.*, vol. SE-1, June 1975.
[30] C. A. R. Hoare and N. Wirth, "An axiomatic definition of the programming language Pascal," *Acta Inform.*, vol. 2, pp. 335-355, 1973.

[31] K. Jensen and N. Wirth, *Pascal User Manual and Report*, 2nd ed. New York: Springer-Verlag, 1974.

[32] V. Basili and D. Weiss, "Evaluation of a software requirements document by analysis of change data," in *Proc. 5th Int. Conf. Software Eng.*, Mar. 1981, pp. 314-323.

[33] D. Weiss, "Evaluating software development by analysis of change data," Comput. Sci. Cen., Univ. Maryland, College Park, Rep. TR-1120, Nov. 1981.

[34] L. Chmura and E. Weiss, "Evaluation of the A-7E software requirements document by analysis of changes: Three years of data, presented at *NATO AGARD Avionics Symp.*, Sept. 1982.

[35] V. Basili and D. Weiss, "Evaluating software development by analysis of changes: Some data from the Software Engineering Laboratory," *IEEE Trans. Software Eng.*, to be published.

[36] V. Basili, M. Zelkowitz, F. McGarry, et al., "The Software Engineering Laboratory," Univ. Maryland, College Park, Rep.TR-535, May 1977.

[37] B. Boehm, "An experiment in small-scale application software engineering," TRW, Rep. TRW-SS-80-01,1980.

[38] A. Endres, "Analysis and causes of errors in systems programs", in *Proc. Int. Conf. Reliable Software*, 1975, pp. 327-336.

[39] G. Miller, 'The magical number seven, plus or minus two: Some limits on our capacity for processing information," *Psychol. Rev.*, vol. 63, pp. 81-97, Mar. 1956.

[40] J. Bailey and V. Basili, "A meta-model for software development resource expenditures," in *Proc. 5th Int. Conf. Software Eng.*, Mar. 1981, pp. 107-116.

[41] D. L. Parnas, "On the criteria to be used in decomposing systems into modules," *Commun. Ass. Comput. Mach.*, vol. 15, pp. 1053-1058, Dec. 1972.

[42] J. Brown, *The Social Psychology of Industry*. Baltimore, MD: Penguin, 1954.

The TAME Project: Towards Improvement-Oriented Software Environments

Victor R. Basili, senior member, IEEE, and H. Dieter Rombach

Abstract Experience from a dozen years of analyzing software engineering processes and products is summarized as a set of software engineering and measurement principles that argue for software engineering process models that integrate sound planning and analysis into the construction process. In the TAME (Tailoring A Measurement Environment) project at the University of Maryland we have developed such an improvement-oriented software engineering process model that uses the goal/question/metric paradigm to integrate the constructive and analytic aspects of software development. The model provides a mechanism for formalizing the characterization and planning tasks, controlling and improving projects based on quantitative analysis, learning in a deeper and more systematic way about the software process and product, and feeding the appropriate experience back into the current and future projects. The TAME system is an instantiation of the TAME software engineering process model as an ISEE (Integrated Software Engineering Environment). The first in a series of TAME system prototypes has been developed. An assessment of experience with this first limited prototype is presented including a reassessment of its initial architecture. The long-term goal of this building effort is to develop a better understanding of appropriate ISEE architectures that optimally support the improvement-oriented TAME software engineering process model.

Key Words: Characterization, execution, experience, feedback, formalizing, goal/question/metric paradigm, improvement paradigm, integrated software engineering environments, integration of construction and analysis, learning, measurement, planning, quantitative analysis, software engineering process models, tailoring, TAME project, TAME system.

Manuscript received January 15, 1988. This work was supported in part by NASA under Grant NSG-5123, the Air Force Office of Scientific Research under Grant F49620-87-0130, and the Office of Naval Research under Grant N00014-85-K-0633 to the University of Maryland. Computer time was provided in part through the facilities of the Computer Science Center of the University of Maryland.

The authors are with the Department of Computer Science and the Institute for Advanced Computer Studies, University of Maryland, College Park, MD 20742.

I. Introduction

EXPERIENCE from a dozen years of analyzing *software engineering* processes and products is summarized as a set of ten software engineering and fourteen *measurement principles*. These principles imply the need for software engineering process models that integrate sound planning and analysis into the construction process.

Software processes based upon such *improvement-oriented software engineering process models* need to be *tailorable* and *tractable*. The tailorability of a process is the characteristic that allows it to be altered or adapted to suit a set of special needs or purposes [64]. The software engineering process requires tailorability because the overall project execution model (life cycle model), methods and tools need to be altered or adapted for the specific project environment and the overall organization. The tractability of a process is the characteristic that allows it to be easily planned, taught, managed, executed, or controlled [64]. Each software engineering process requires tractability because it needs to be planned, the various planned activities of the process need to be communicated to the entire project personnel, and the process needs to be managed, executed, and controlled according to these plans. Sound tailoring and tracking require *top-down measurement* (measurement based upon operationally defined goals). The goal of a *software engineering environment* (SEE) should be to support such tailorable and tractable software engineering process models by automating as much of them as possible. In the TAME (*Tailoring a Measurement Environment*) project at the University of Maryland we have developed an improvement-oriented software engineering process model. The *TAME system* is an instantiation of this TAME software engineering process model as an ISEE (Integrated SEE).

It seems appropriate at this point to clarify some of the important terms that will be used in this paper. The term *engineering* comprises both development and maintenance. A software engineering *project* is embedded in some *project environment* (characterized by personnel, type of application, etc.) and within some *organization* (e.g., NASA, IBM). Software engineering within such a project environment or organization is conducted according to an overall software engineering *process model* (one of which will be introduced in Section II-B-3). Each individual software project in the context of such a software engineering process model is executed according to some *execution model* (e.g., waterfall model [28], [58], iterative enhancement model [24], spiral model [30]) supplemented by *techniques (methods, tools)*. Each specific instance of (a part of) an execution model together with its supplementing methods and tools is referred to as *execution process* (including the construction as well as the analysis process). In addition, the term *process* is frequently used as a generic term for various kinds of activities. We distinguish between *constructive* and *analytic* methods and tools. Whereas constructive methods and tools are concerned with building products, analytic method and tools are concerned with analyzing the constructive process and the resulting products. The body of experience accumulated within a project environment or organization is referred to as *experience base*. There exist at least three levels of formalism of such experience bases: *database* (data being individual products or processes), *information base* (information being data viewed through some superimposed structure), and *knowledge base* (knowledge implying the ability to derive new insights via deduction rules). The project personnel are categorized as either *engineers* (e.g., designers, coders, testers) or *managers.*

This paper is structured into a presentation and discussion of the improvement-oriented software engineering process model underlying the TAME project (Section II), its automated support by the TAME system (Section III), and the first TAME system prototype (Section IV). In the first part of this paper we list the empirically derived lessons learned (Section II-A) in the form of software engineering principles (Section II-A-1), measurement principles (Section II-A-2), and motivate the TAME project by stating several implications derived from those principles (Section II-A-3). The TAME project (Section II-B) is presented in terms of the improvement paradigm (Section II-B-1), the goal/question/metric paradigm as a mechanism for formalizing the improvement paradigm (Section II-B-2), and the TAME project model as an instantiation of both paradigms (Section II-B-3). In the second part of this paper we introduce the TAME system as an approach to automatically supporting the TAME software engineering process model (Section III). The TAME system is presented in terms of its requirements (Section III-A) and architecture (Section III-B). In the third part of this paper, we introduce the first TAME prototype (Section IV) with respect to its functionality and our first experiences with it.

II. Software Engineering Process

Our experience from measuring and evaluating software engineering processes and products in a variety of project environments has been summarized in the form of lessons learned (Section II-A). Based upon this experience the TAME project has produced an improvement-oriented process model (Section II-B).

A. Lessons Learned from Past Experience

We have formulated our experience as a set of software engineering principles (Section II-A-1) and measurement principles (Section II-A-2). Based upon these principles a number of implications for sound software engineering process models have been derived (Section II-A-3).

1) *Software Engineering Principles*: The first five software engineering principles address the need for developing quality *a priori* by introducing engineering discipline into the field of software engineering:

(PI) We need to clearly distinguish between the role of constructive and analytic activities. Only improved construction processes will result in higher quality software. Quality cannot be tested or inspected into software. Analytic processes (e.g., quality assurance) cannot serve as a substitute for constructive processes but will provide control of the constructive processes [27], [37], [61].

(P2) We need to formalize the planning of the construction process in order to develop quality *a priori* [3], [16], [19], [25]. Without such plans the trial and error approach can hardly be avoided.

(P3) We need to formalize the analysis and improvement of construction processes and products in order to guarantee an organized approach to software engineering [3], [25].

(P4) Engineering methods require analysis to determine whether they are being performed appropriately, if at all. This is especially important because most of these methods are heuristic rather than formal [42], [49], [66].

(P5) Software engineers and managers need real-time feedback in order to improve the construction processes and products of the ongoing project. The organization needs post-mortem feedback in order to improve the construction processes and products for future projects [66]. The remaining five software engineering principles address the need for tailoring of planning and analysis processes due to changing needs from project to project and environment to environment:

(P6) All project environments and products are different in some way [2], [66]. These differences must be made explicit and taken into account in the software execution processes and in the product quality goals [3], [16], [19], [25].

(P7) There are many execution models for software engineering. Each execution model needs to be tailored to the organization and project needs and characteristics [2], [13], [16], [66].

(P8) We need to formalize the tailoring of processes toward the quality and productivity goals of the project and the characteristics of the project environment and the organization [16]. It is not easy to apply abstractly defined methods to specific environments.

(P9) This need for tailoring does not mean starting from scratch each time. We need to reuse experience, but only after tailoring it to the project [1], [2], [6], [7], [18], [32].

(P10) Because of the constant need for tailoring, management control is crucial and must be flexible. Management needs must be supported in this software engineering process.

A more detailed discussion of these software engineering principles is contained in [17].

2) *Software Measurement Principles*: The first four measurement principles address the purpose of the measurement process, i.e., why should we measure, what should we measure, for whom should we measure:

(Ml) Measurement is an ideal mechanism for characterizing, evaluating, predicting, and providing motivation for the various aspects of software construction processes and products [3], [4], [9], [16], [21], [25], [48], [56], [57]. It is a common mechanism for relating these multiple aspects.

(M2) Measurements must be taken on both the software processes and the various software products [1], [5], [14], [29], [38], [40], [42]-[44], [47], [54]-[56],

[65], [66]. Improving a product requires understanding both the product and its construction processes.

(M3) There are a variety of uses for measurement. The purpose of measurement should be clearly stated. We can use measurement to examine cost effectiveness, reliability, correctness, maintainability, efficiency, user friendliness, etc. [8]-[10], [13], [14], [16], [20], [23], [25], [41], [53], [57], [61].

(M4) Measurement needs to be viewed from the appropriate perspective. The corporation, the manager, the developer, the customer's organization and the user each view the product and the process from different perspectives. Thus they may want to know different things about the project and to different levels of detail [3], [16], [19], [25], [66].

The remaining ten measurement principles address metrics and the overall measurement process. The first two principles address characteristics of metrics (i.e., what kinds of metrics, how many are needed), while the latter eight address characteristics of the measurement process (i.e., what should the measurement process look like, how do we support characterization, planning, construction, and learning and feedback):

(M5) Subjective as well as objective metrics are required. Many process, product and environment aspects can be characterized by objective metrics (e.g., product complexity, number of defects or effort related to processes). Other aspects cannot be characterized objectively yet (e.g., experience of personnel, type of application, understandability of processes and products); but they can at least be categorized on a quantitative (nominal) scale to a reasonable degree of accuracy [4], [5], [16], [48], [56].

(M6) Most aspects of software processes and products are too complicated to be captured by a single metric. For both definition and interpretation purposes, a set of metrics (a metric vector) that frame the purpose for measurement needs to be defined [9].

(M7) The development and maintenance environments must be prepared for measurement and analysis. Planning is required and needs to be carefully integrated into the overall software engineering process model. This planning process must take into account the experimental design appropriate for the situation [3], [14], [19], [22], [66].

(M8) We cannot just use models and metrics from other environments as defined. Because of the differences among execution models (principle P7), the models and metrics must be tailored for the environment in which they will be applied and checked for validity in that environment [2], [6]-[8], [12], [23], [31], [40], [47], [50], [51], [62].

(M9) The measurement process must be top-down rather than bottom-up in order to define a set of operational goals, specify the appropriate metrics, permit valid contextual interpretation and analysis, and provide feedback for tailorability and tractability [3], [16], [19], [25].

(M10) For each environment there exists a characteristic set of metrics that provides the needed information for definition and interpretation purposes [21].

(M11) Multiple mechanisms are needed for data collection and validation. The nature of the data to be collected (principle M5) determines the appropriate mechanisms [4], [25], [48], e.g., manually via forms or interviews, or automatically via analyzers.

(M12) In order to evaluate and compare projects and to develop models we need a historical experience base. This experience base should characterize the local environment [4], [13], [25], [34], [44], [48].

(M13) Metrics must be associated with interpretations, but these interpretations must be given in context [3], [16], [19], [25], [34], [56].

(M14) The experience base should evolve from a database into a knowledge base (supported by an expert system) to formalize the reuse of experience [11], [14].

A more detailed discussion of these measurement principles is contained in [17].

3) Implications: Clearly this set of principles is not complete. However, these principles provide empirically derived insight into the limitations of traditional process models. We will give some of the implications of these principles with respect to the components that need to be included in software process models, essential characteristics of these components, the interaction of these components, and the needed automated support. Although there is a relationship between almost all principles and the derived implications, we have referenced for each implication only those principles that are related most directly.

Based upon our set of principles it is clear that we need to *better understand* the software construction process and product (e.g., principles P1, P4, P6, M2, M5, M6, M8, M9, M10, M12). Such an understanding will allow us to *plan* what we need to do and improve over our current practices (e.g., principles P1, P2, P3, P7, P8, M3, M4, M7, M9, M14). To *make those plans operational,* we need to specify how we are going to affect the construction processes and their analysis (e.g., principles P1, P2, P3, P4, P7, P8, M7, M8, M9, M14). The *execution* of these prescribed plans involves the *construction* of products and the *analysis* of the constructive processes and resulting products (e.g., principles P1, P7).

All these implications need to be integrated in such a way that they allow for sound *learning and feedback* so that we can improve the software execution processes and products (e.g., principles P1, P3, P4, P5, P9, P10, M3, M4, M9, M12, M13, M14). This interaction requires the integration of the constructive and analytic aspects of the software engineering process model (e.g., principles P2, M7, M9).

The components and their interactions need to be formalized so they can be supported properly by an *ISEE* (e.g., principles P2, P3, P8, P9, M9). This formalization must include a *structuring of the body of experience* so that characterization, planning, learning, feedback, and improvement can take place (e.g., principles P2, P3, P8, P9, M9). An ideal mechanism for supporting all of these components and their interactions is *quantitative analysis* (e.g., principles P3, P4, M1, M2, M5, M6, M8, M9, M10, M11, M13).

B. A Process Model: The TAME Project

The TAME (Tailoring A Measurement Environment) project at the University of Maryland has produced a software engineering process model (Section II-B-3) based upon our empirically derived lessons learned. This software engineering process model is based upon the improvement (Section II-B-1) and goal/question/metric paradigms (Section II-B-2).

1) *Improvement Paradigm:* The improvement paradigm for software engineering processes reflects the implications stated in Section II-A-3. It consists of six major steps [3]:

(I1) Characterize the current project environment.

(I2) Set up goals and refine them into quantifiable questions and metrics for successful project performance and improvement over previous project performances.

(I3) Choose the appropriate software project execution model for this project and supporting methods and tools.

(I4) Execute the chosen processes and construct the products, collect the prescribed data, validate it, and provide feedback in real-time.

(I5) Analyze the data to evaluate the current practices, determine problems, record the findings, and make recommendations for improvement.

(I6) Proceed to Step I1 to start the next project, armed with the experience gained from this and previous projects.

This paradigm is aimed at providing a basis for corporate learning and improvement. Improvement is only possible if we a) understand what the current status of our environment is (step I1), b) state precise improvement goals for the particular project and quantify them for the purpose of control (step I2), c) choose the appropriate process execution models, methods, and tools in order to achieve these improvement goals (step I3), execute and monitor the project performance thoroughly (step I4), and assess it (step I5). Based upon the assessment results we can provide feedback into the ongoing project or into the planning step of future projects (steps I5 and I6).

2) *Goal/Question/Metric Paradigm*: The goal/question/metric (GQM) paradigm is intended as a mechanism for formalizing the characterization, planning, construction, analysis, learning and feedback tasks. It represents a systematic approach for setting project goals (tailored to the specific needs of an organization) and defining them in an operational and tractable way. Goals are refined into a set of quantifiable questions that specify metrics. This paradigm also supports the analysis and integration of metrics in the context of the questions and the original goal. Feedback and learning are then performed in the context of the GQM paradigm.

The process of setting goals and refining them into quantifiable questions is complex and requires experience. In order to support this process, a set of *templates* for setting goals, and a set of *guidelines* for deriving questions and metrics has been developed. These templates and guidelines reflect our experience from having applied the GQM paradigm in a variety of environments (e.g., NASA [4],

[17], [48], IBM [60], AT&T, Burroughs [56], and Motorola). We received additional feedback from Hewlett Packard where the GQM paradigm has been used without our direct assistance [39]. It needs to be stressed that we do not claim that these templates and guidelines are complete; they will most likely change over time as our experience grows. Goals are defined in terms of purpose, perspective and environment. Different sets of guidelines exist for defining product-related and process-related questions. Product-related questions are formulated for the purpose of defining the product (e.g., physical attributes, cost, changes, and defects, context), defining the quality perspective of interest (e.g., reliability, user friendliness), and providing feedback from the particular quality perspective. Process-related questions are formulated for the purpose of defining the process (quality of use, domain of use), defining the quality perspective of interest (e.g., reduction of defects, cost effectiveness of use), and providing feedback from the particular quality perspective.

• Templates/Guidelines for Goal Definition:

Purpose: To (characterize, evaluate, predict, motivate, etc.) the (process, product, model, metric, etc.) in order to (understand, assess, manage, engineer, learn, improve, etc.) it.
Example: To evaluate the system testing methodology in order to improve it.

Perspective: Examine the (cost, effectiveness, correctness, defects, changes, product metrics, reliability, etc.) from the point of view of the (developer, manager, customer, corporate perspective, etc.)
Example: Examine the effectiveness from the developer's point of view.

Environment: The environment consists of the following: process factors, people factors, problem factors, methods, tools, constraints, etc.
Example: The product is an operating system that must fit on a PC, etc.

• Guidelines for Product-Related Questions:

For each product under study there are three major sub goals that need to be addressed: 1) definition of the product, 2) definition of the quality perspectives of interest, and 3) feedback related to the quality perspectives of interest.

Definition of the product includes questions related to *physical attributes* (a quantitative characterization of the product in terms of physical attributes such as size, complexity, etc.), *cost* (a quantitative characterization of the resources expended related to this product in terms of effort, computer time, etc.), *changes and defects* (a quantitative characterization of the errors, faults, failures, adaptations, and enhancements related to this product), and *context* (a quantitative characterization of the customer community using this product and their operational profiles).

Quality perspectives of interest includes, for each quality perspective of interest (e.g., reliability, user friendliness), questions related to the *major model(s) used* (a quantitative specification of the quality perspective of interest), the *validity of the model for the particular environment* (an analysis of the appropriateness of the model for the particular project environment), the *validity of the data collected* (an analysis of the quality of data), the *model effectiveness* (a quantitative characterization of the quality of the results produced according to this model), and a *substantiation of the model* (a discussion of whether the results are reasonable from various perspectives).

Feedback includes questions related to *improving the product relative to the quality perspective of interest* (a quantitative characterization of the product quality, major problems regarding the quality perspective of interest, and suggestions for improvement during the ongoing project as well as during future projects).

• Guidelines for Process-Related Questions

For each process under study, there are three major sub goals that need to be addressed: 1) definition of the process, 2) definition of the quality perspectives of interest, and 3) feedback from using this process relative to the quality perspective of interest.

Definition of the process includes questions related to the *quality of use* (a quantitative characterization of the process and an assessment of how well it is performed), and the *domain of use* (a quantitative characterization of the object to which the process is applied and an analysis of the process performer's knowledge concerning this object).

Quality perspectives of interest follows a pattern similar to the corresponding product-oriented sub goal including, for each quality perspective of interest (e.g., reduction of defects, cost effectiveness), questions related to the *major model (s) used*, and *validity of the model for the particular environment*, the *validity of the data collected*, the *model effectiveness* and the *substantiation of the model*).

Feedback follows a pattern similar to the corresponding product-oriented sub goal.

• Guidelines for Metrics, Data Collection, and Interpretation:

The choice of metrics is determined by the quantifiable questions. The guidelines for questions acknowledge the need for generally more than one metric (principle M6), for objective and subjective metrics (principle M5), and for associating interpretations with metrics (principle M13). The actual GQM models generated from these templates and guidelines will differ from project to project and organization to organization (principle M6). This reflects their being tailored for the different needs in different projects and organizations (principle M4). Depending on the type of each metric, we choose the appropriate mechanisms for data collection and validation (principle M11). As goals, questions and metrics provide for tractability of the (top-down) definitional quantification process, they also provide for the interpretation context (bottom-up). This integration of definition with interpretation allows for the interpretation process to be tailored to the specific needs of an environment (principle M8).

3) *Improvement-Oriented Process Model*: The TAME software engineering process model is an instantiation of the improvement paradigm. The GQM paradigm provides the necessary integration of the individual components of this model. The TAME software engineering process model explicitly includes components for (Cl) the characterization of the current status of a project environment, (C2) the planning for improvement integrated into the execution of projects, (C3) the execution of the construction and analysis of projects according to the project plans, and (C4) the recording of experience into an experience base. The learning and feedback mechanism (C5) is distributed throughout the model within and across the components as information flows from one component to another. Each of these tasks must be dealt with from a constructive and analytic perspective. Fig. 1 contains a graphical representation of the improvement-oriented TAME process model. The relationships (arcs) among process model components in Fig. 1 represent information flow.

(Cl) Characterization of the current environment is required to understand the various factors that influence the current project environment. This task is important in order to define a starting point for improvement. Without knowing where we are, we will not be able to judge whether we are improving in our present project. We distinguish between the constructive and analytic aspects of the characterization task to emphasize that we not only state the environmental factors but analyze them to the degree possible based upon data and other forms of information from prior projects. This characterization task needs to be formalized.

(C2) Planning is required to understand the project goals, execution needs, and project focus for learning and feedback. This task is essential for disciplined software project execution (i.e., executing projects according to precise specifications of processes and products). It provides the basis for improvement relative to the current status determined during characterization. In the planning task, we distinguish between the constructive and analytic as well as the "what" and "how" aspects of planning. Based upon the GQM paradigm all these aspects are highly interdependent and performed as a single task. The development of quantitatively analyzable goals is an iterative process. However, we formulate the four planning aspects as four separate components to emphasize the differences between creating plans for development and making those plans analyzable, as well as between stating what it is you want to accomplish and stating how you plan to tailor the processes and metrics to do it.

(C2.1) "What" Planning deals with choosing, assigning priorities, and operationally defining, to the degree possible, the project goals from the constructive and analytic perspectives. The actual goal setting is an instantiation of the front-end of the GQM paradigm (the templates/guidelines for goal definition). The constructive perspective addresses the definition of project goals such as on-time delivery, the appropriate functionality to satisfy the user, and the analysis of the execution processes we are applying. Some of these goals might be stated as improvement goals over the current state-of-the-practice as characterized in component Cl. These goals should be prioritized and operationally defined to the extent possible without having chosen the particular construction models, methods and tools yet. The analytic perspective addresses analysis procedures for monitoring and controlling whether the goals are met. This analytic goal perspective should prescribe the necessary learning and feedback paths. It should be operationally defined to the extent allowed by the degree of precision of the constructive goal perspective.

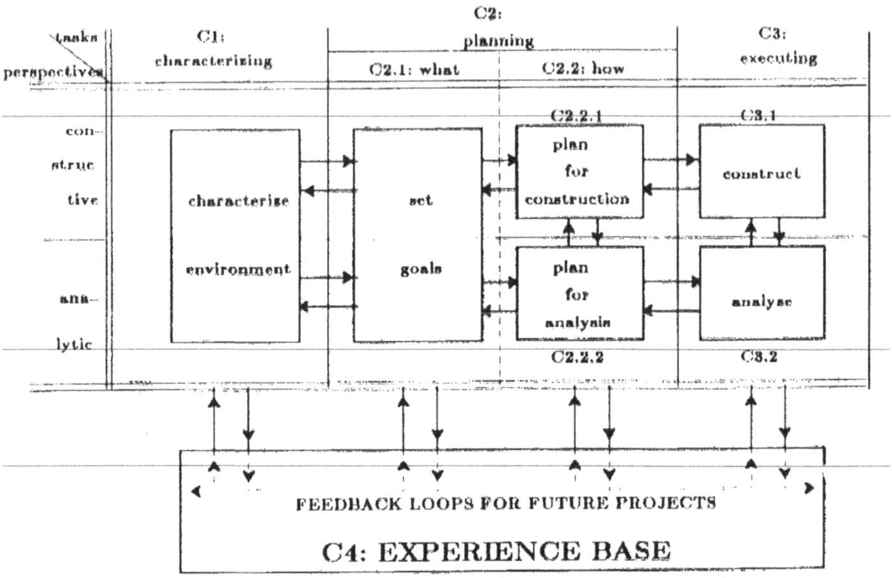

Fig. 1. The improvement-oriented TAME software process model.

(C2.2) "How" Planning is based upon the results from the "what" planning (providing for the purpose and perspective of a goal definition according to the GQM paradigm front-end) and the characterization of the environment (providing for the environment part of a goal definition according to the GQM paradigm front-end). The "how" planning involves the choice of an appropriately tailored execution model, methods and tools that permit the building of the system in such a way that we can analyze whether we are achieving our stated goals. The particular choice of construction processes, methods and tools (component C2.2.1) goes hand in hand with fine-tuning the analysis procedures derived during the analytic perspective of the "what" planning (component C2.2.2).

(C2.2.1) Planning for construction includes choosing the appropriate execution model, methods and tools to fulfill the project goals. It should be clear that effective planning for construction depends on well-defined project goals from both the constructive and analytic perspective (component C2.1).

(C2.2.2) Planning for analysis addresses the fine-tuning of the operational definition of the analytic goal perspective (derived as part of component C2.1) towards the specific choices made during planning for construction (C2.2.1). The actual planning for analysis is an instantiation of the back-end of the GQM paradigm; details need to be filled in (e.g., quantifiable questions, metrics) based upon the specific methods and tools chosen.

(C3) Execution must integrate the construction (component C3.1) with the analysis (component C3.2). Analysis (including measurement) cannot be an add-on but must be part of the execution process and drive the construction. The execution plans derived during the planning task are supposed to provide for the required integration of construction and analysis.

(C4) The Experience Base includes the entire body of experience that is actively available to the project. We can characterize this experience according to the following dimensions: a) the degree of precision/detail, and b) the degree to which it is tailored to meet the specific needs of the project (context). The precision/detail dimension involves the level of detail of the experimental design and the level and quality of data collected. On one end of the spectrum we have detailed objective quantitative data that allows us to build mathematically tractable models. On the other end of the spectrum we have interviews and qualitative information that provide guidelines and "lessons learned documents", and permit the better formulation of goals and questions. The level of precision and detail affects our level of confidence in the results of the experiment as well as the cost of the data collection process. Clearly priorities play an important role here. The context dimension involves whether the focus is to learn about the specific project, projects within a specific application domain or general truths about the software process or product (requires the incorporation of formalized experience from prior projects into the experience base). Movement across the context dimension assumes an ability to generalize experience to a broader context than the one studied, or to tailor experience to a specific project. The better this experience is packaged, the better our understanding of the environment. Maintaining a body of experience acquired during a number of projects is one of the prerequisites for learning and feedback across environments.

(C5) Learning and Feedback are integrated into the TAME process model in various ways. They are based upon the experimental model for learning consisting of a set of steps, starting with focused objectives, which are turned into specific hypotheses, followed by running experiments to validate the hypotheses in the appropriate environment. The model is iterative; as we learn from experimentation, we are better able to state our focused objectives and we change and refine our hypotheses.

This model of learning is incorporated into the GQM paradigm where the focused objectives are expressed as goals, the hypotheses are expressed as questions written to the degree of formalism required, and the experimental environment is the project, a set of projects in the same domain, or a corporation representing a general environment. Clearly the GQM paradigm is also iterative.

The feedback process helps generate the goals to influence one or more of the components in the process model, e.g., the characterization of the environment, or the analysis of the construction processes or products. The level of confidence we have in feeding back the experience to a project or a corporate environment depends upon the precision/detail level of the experience base (component C4) and the generality of the experimental environment in which it was gathered.

The learning and feedback process appears in the model as the integration of all the components and their interactions as they are driven by the improvement and

GQM paradigms. The feedback process can be channeled to the various components of the current project and to the corporate experience base for use in future projects.

Most traditional software engineering process models address only a subset of the individual components of this model; in many cases they cover just the constructive aspects of characterization (component Cl), "how" planning (component C2.2.1), and execution (component C3.1). More recently developed software engineering process models address the constructive aspect of execution (component C3.1) in more sophisticated ways (e.g., new process models [24], [30], [49], combine various process dimensions such as technical, managerial, contractual [36], or provide more flexibility as far as the use of methods and tools is concerned, for example via the automated generation of tools [45], [63]), or they add methods and tools for choosing the analytical processes, methods, and tools (component C3.2.2) as well as actually performing analysis (component C3.2) [52], [59]. However, all these process models have in common the lack of completely integrating all their individual components in a systematic way that would permit sound learning and feedback for the purpose of project control and improvement of corporate experience.

III. Automated Support through ISEES: the TAME System

The goal of an Integrated Software Engineering Environment (ISEE) is to effectively support the improvement-oriented software engineering process model described in Section II-B-3. An ISEE must support all the model components (characterization, planning, execution, and the experience base), all the local interactions between model components, the integration, and formalization of the GQM paradigm, and the necessary transitions between the context and precision/detail dimension boundaries in the experience base. Supporting the transitions along the experience base dimensions is needed in order to allow for sound learning and feedback as outlined in Section II-B-3 (component C5).

The TAME system will automate as many of the components, interactions between components and supporting mechanisms of the TAME process model as possible. The TAME system development activities will concentrate on all but the construction component (component C3.1) with the eventual goal of interfacing with constructive SEEs. In this section we present the requirements and the initial architecture for the TAME system.

A. Requirements

The requirements for the TAME system can be derived from Section II-B-3 in a natural way. These requirements can be divided into external requirements (defined by and of obvious interest to the TAME system user) and internal requirements (defined by the TAME design team and required to support the external requirements properly).

The first five (external) requirements include support for the characterization and planning components of the TAME model by automating an instantiation of the GQM paradigm, for the analysis component by automating data collection, data validation and analysis, and the learning and feedback component by automating interpretation and organizational learning. We will list for each external TAME system requirement the TAME process mode components of Section II-B-3 from which it has been derived.

External TAME requirements:

(Rl) A mechanism for defining the constructive and analytic aspects of project goals in an operational and quantifiable way (derived from components C1, C2.1, C2.2.2, C3.2).

We use the GQM paradigm and its templates for defining goals operationally and refining them into quantifiable questions and metrics. The selection of the appropriate GQM model and its tailoring needs to be supported. The user will either select an existing model or generate a new one. A new model can be generated from scratch or by reusing pieces of existing models. The degree to which the selection, generation, and reuse tasks can be supported automatically depends largely on the degree to which the GQM paradigm and its templates can be formalized. The user needs to be supported in defining his/ her specific goals according to the goal definition template. Based on each goal definition, the TAME system will search for a model in the experience base. If no appropriate model exists, the user will be guided in developing one. Based on the tractability of goals into sub goals and questions the TAME system will identify reusable pieces of existing models and compose as much of an initial model as possible. This initial model will be completed with user interaction. For example, if a user wants to develop a model for assessing a system test method used in a particular environment, the system might compose an initial model by reusing pieces from a model assessing a different test method in the same environment, and from a model for assessing the same system test method in a different environment. A complete GQM model includes rules for interpretation of metrics and guidelines for collecting the prescribed data. The TAME system will automatically generate as much of this information as possible.

(R2) The automatic and manual collection of data and the validation of manually collected data (derived from component C3.2).

The collection of all product-related data (e.g., lines of code, complexity) and certain process-related data (e.g., number of compiler runs, number of test runs) will be completely automated. Automation requires an interface with construction-oriented SEEs. The collection of many process-related data (e.g., effort, changes) and subjective data (e.g., experience of personnel, characteristics of methods used) cannot be automated. The schedule according to which measurement tools are run needs to be defined as part of the planning activity. It is possible to collect data whenever they are needed, periodically (e.g., always at a particular time of the day), or whenever changes of products occur (e.g., whenever a new product version is entered into the experience base all the related metrics are recomputed). All manually collected data need to be validated. Validating whether data are within their defined range, whether all the prescribed data are collected, and whether certain integrity rules among data are maintained will be automated. Some of the measurement tools will be developed as part of the TAME system development project, others will be imported. The need for importing measurement tools will require an effective interconnection mechanism (probably, an interconnection language) for integrating tools developed in different languages.

(R3) A mechanism for controlling measurement and analysis (derived from component C3.2).

A GQM model is used to specify and control the execution of a particular analysis and feedback session. According to each GQM model, the TAME system must trigger the execution of measurement tools for data collection, the computation of all metrics and distributions prescribed, and the application of statistical procedures. If certain metrics or distributions cannot be computed due to the lack of data or measurement tools, the TAME system must inform the user.

(R4) A mechanism for interpreting analysis results in a context and providing feedback for the improvement of the execution model, methods and tools (derived from components C3.2, C.5).

We use a GQM model to define the rules and context for interpretation of data and for feedback in order to refine and improve execution models, methods and tools. The degree to which interpretation can be supported depends on our understanding of the software process and product, and the degree to which we express this understanding as formal rules. Today, interpretation rules exist only for some of the aspects of interest and are only valid within a particular project environment or organization. However, interpretation guided by GQM models will enable an evolutionary learning process resulting in better rules for interpretation in the future. The interpretation process can be much more effective provided historical experience is available allowing for the generation of historical baselines. In this case we can at least identify whether observations made during the current project deviate from past experience or not.

(R5) A mechanism for learning in an organization (derived from components C4, C5).

The learning process is supported by iterating the sequence of defining focused goals, refining them into hypotheses, and running experiments. These experiments can range from completely controlled experiments to regular project executions. In each case we apply measurement and analysis procedures to project classes of interest. For each of those classes, a historical experience base needs to be established concerning the effectiveness of the candidate execution models, methods and tools. Feedback from ongoing projects of the same class, the corresponding execution models, methods and tools can be refined and improved with respect to context and precision/ detail so that we increase our potential to improve future projects.

The remaining seven (internal) requirements deal with user interface management, report generation, experience base, security and access control, configuration management control, SEE interface and distribution issues. All these issues are important in order to support planning, construction, learning and feedback effectively.

Internal TAME requirements:

(R6) A homogeneous user interface.

We distinguish between the physical and logical user interface. The physical user interface provides a menu or command driven interface between the user and the TAME system. Graphics and window mechanisms will be incorporated whenever useful and possible. The logical user interface reflects the user's view of measurement and analysis. Users will not be allowed to directly access data or run measurement tools. The only way of working with the TAME system is via a GQM model. TAME will enforce this top-down approach to measurement via its logical user interface. The acceptance of this kind of user interface will depend on the effectiveness and ease with which it can be used. Homogeneity is important for both the physical and logical user interface.

(R7) An effective mechanism for presenting data, information, and knowledge.

The presentation of analysis (measurement and interpretation) results via terminal or printer/plotter needs to be supported. Reports need to be generated for different purposes. Project managers will be interested in periodical reports reflecting the current status of their project. High level managers will be interested in reports indicating quality and productivity trends of the organization. The specific interest of each person needs to be defined by one or more GQM models upon which automatic report generation can be based. A laser printer and multicolor plotter would allow the appropriate documentation of tables, histograms, and other kinds of textual and graphical representations.

(R8) The effective storage and retrieval of all relevant data, information, and knowledge in an experience base.

All data, information, and knowledge required to support tailorability and tractability need to be stored in an experience base. Such an experience base needs to store GQM models, engineering products and measurement data. It needs to store data derived from the current project as well as historical data from prior projects. The effectiveness of such an experience base will be improved for the purpose of learning and feedback if, in addition to measurement data, interpretations from various analysis sessions are stored. In the future, the interpretation rules themselves will become integral part of such an experience base. The experience base should be implemented as an abstract data type, accessible through a set of functions and hiding the actual implementation. This latter requirement is especially important due to the fact that current database technology is not suited to properly support software engineering concepts [26]. The implementation of the experience base as an abstract data type allows us to use currently available database technology and substitute more appropriate technology later as it becomes available. The ideal database would be self-adapting to the changing needs of a project environment or an organization. This would require a specification language for software processes and products, and the ability to generate database schemata from specifications written in such a language [46].

(R9) Mechanisms allowing for the implementation of a variety of access control and security strategies.

TAME must control the access of users to the TAME system itself, to various system functions and to the experience base. These are typical functions of a security system. The enforced security strategies depend on the project organization. It is part of planning a project to decide who needs to have access to what functions and pieces of data, information, and knowledge. In addition to these security functions, more sophisticated data access control functions need to be performed. The data access system is expected to "recommend" to a user who is developing a GQM model the kinds of data that might be helpful in answering a particular question and support the process of choosing among similar data based on availability or other criteria.

(R10) Mechanisms allowing for the implementation of a variety of configuration management and control strategies.

In the context of the TAME system we need to manage and control three-dimensional configurations. There is first the traditional product dimension making sure that the various product and document versions are consistent. In addition, each product version needs to be consistent with its related measurement data and the GQM model that guided those measurements. TAME must ensure that a user always knows whether data in the experience base is consistent with the current product version and was collected and interpreted according to a particular model. The actual configuration management and control strategies will result from the project planning activity.

(R11) An interface to a construction-oriented SEE.

An interface between the TAME system (which automates all process model components except for the construction component C3.1 of the TAME process model) and some external SEE (which automates the construction component) is necessary for three reasons: a) to enable the TAME system to collect data (e.g., the number of activations of a compiler, the number of test runs) directly from the actual construction process, b) to enable the TAME system to feed analysis results back into the ongoing construction process, and c) to enable the construction-oriented SEE to store/retrieve products into/from the experience base of the TAME system. Models for appropriate interaction between constructive and analytic processes need to be specified. Interfacing with construction-oriented SEE's poses the problem of efficiently interconnecting systems implemented in different languages and running on different machines (probably with different operating systems).

(R12) A structure suitable for distribution. TAME will ultimately run on a distributed system consisting of at least one mainframe computer and a number of workstations. The mainframes are required to host the experience base which can be assumed to be very large. The rest of TAME might be replicated on a number of workstations.

B. Architecture

Fig. 2 describes our current view of the TAME architecture in terms of individual architectural components and their control flow interrelationships. The first prototype described in Section IV concentrates on the shaded components of Fig. 2.

We group the TAME components into five logical levels, the physical user interface, logical user interface, analysis and feedback, measurement and support level. Each of these five levels consists of one or more architectural components:

• The Physical User Interface Level consists of one component:

(Al) The User Interface Management component implements the physical user interface requirement R6. It provides a choice of menu or command driven access and supports a window-oriented screen layout.

• The Logical (GQM-Oriented) User Interface Level consists of two components:

(A2) The GQM Model Selection component implements the homogeneity requirement of the logical user interface (R6). It guarantees that no access to the analysis and feedback, measurement, or support level is possible without stating the purpose for access in terms of a specific GQM model.

(A3) The GQM Model Generation component implements requirement Rl regarding the operational and quantifiable definition of GQM models either from scratch or by modifying existing models.

• The Analysis and Feedback Level consists of two components:

(A4.1) This first portion of the Construction Interface component implements the feedback interface between the TAME system and construction-oriented SEEs (part b) of requirement R1 1).

(A5) The GQM Analysis and Feedback component implements requirement R3 regarding execution and control of an analysis and feedback session, interpretation of the analysis results, and proper feedback. All these activities are done in the context of a GQM model created by A3. The GQM Analysis and Feedback component needs to have access to the specific authorizations of the user in order to know which analysis functions this user can perform. The GQM Analysis and Feedback component also provides analysis functions, for example, telling the user whether certain metrics can be computed based upon the data currently available in the experience base. This analysis feature of the subsystem is used for setting and operationally defining goals, questions, and metrics, as well as actually performing analyses according to those previously established goals, questions, and metrics.

• The Measurement Level consists of three components:

(A4.2) This second portion of the Construction Interface component implements the measurement interface between the TAME system and SEE's (part a) of requirement R11) and the SEE's access to the experience base of the TAME system (part c) of requirement R11).

(A6) The Measurement Scheduling component implements requirement R2 regarding the definition (and execution) of automated data collection strategies. Such strategies for when to collect data via the measurement tools may range from collecting data whenever they are needed for an analysis and feedback session (on-line) to collecting them periodically during low-load times and storing them in the experience base (off-line).

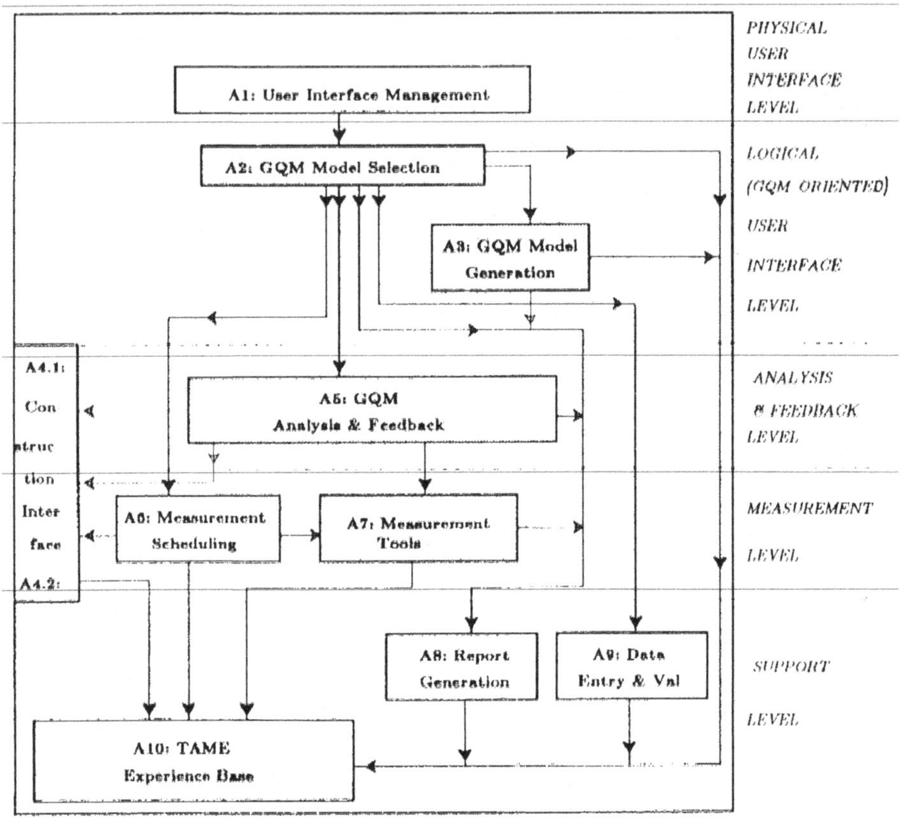

Fig. 2. The architectural design of the TAME system.

(A7) The Measurement Tools component implements requirement R2 regarding automated data collection. The component needs to be open-ended in order to allow the inclusion of new and different measurement tools as needed.

• The Support Level consists of three components:

(A8) The Report Generation component implements requirement R7 regarding the production of all kinds of reports.

(A9) The Data Entry and Validation component implements requirement R2 regarding the entering of manually collected data and their validation. Validated data are stored in the experience base component.

(A 10) The Experience Base component implements requirement R8 regarding the effective storage and retrieval of all relevant data, information and knowledge. This includes all kinds of products, analytical data (e.g., measurement data, interpretations), and analysis plans (GQM models). This component provides the infrastructure for the operation of all other components of the TAME process model and the necessary interactions among them. The experience base will also provide mechanisms supporting the learning and feedback tasks. These mechanisms include the proper packaging of experience along the context and precision/detail dimensions.

In addition, there exist two orthogonal components which for simplicity reasons are not reflected in Fig. 2:

(A11) The Data Access Control and Security component(s) implement requirement R9. There may exist a number of subcomponents distributed across the logical architectural levels. They will validate user access to the TAME system itself and to various functions at the user interface level. They will also control access to the project experience through both the measurement tools and the experience base.

(A 12) The Configuration Management and Control component implements requirement R10. This component can be viewed as part of the interface to the experience base level. Data can only be entered into or retrieved from the experience base under configuration management control.

IV. First TAME Prototype

The first in a series of prototypes is currently being developed for supporting measurement in Ada projects [15]. This first prototype will implement only a subset of the requirements stated in Section III-A because of a) yet unsolved problems that require research, b) solutions that require more formalization, and c) problems with integrating the individual architectural components into a consistent whole. Examples of unsolved problems requiring further research are the appropriate packaging of the experience along the context and precision/detail dimension and expert system support for interpretation purposes. Examples of solutions requiring more formalization are the GQM templates and the designing of a software engineering experience base. Examples of integration problems are the embedding of feedback loops into the construction process, and the appropriate utilization of data access control and configuration management control mechanisms. At this time, the prototype exists in pieces that have not been fully integrated together as well as partially implemented pieces.

In this section, we discuss for each of the architectural components of this TAME prototype as many of the following issues as are applicable: a) the particular approach chosen for the first prototype, b) experience with this approach, c) the current and planned status of implementation (automation) of the initial approach in the first TAME system prototype, and d) experiences with using the component:

(Al) The User Interface Management component is supposed to provide the physical user interface for accessing all TAME system functions, with the flexibility of choosing between menu and command driven modes and different window layouts. These issues are reasonably well understood by the SEE community. The first TAME prototype implementation will be menu-oriented and based upon the 'X' window mechanism. A primitive version is currently running. This component is currently not very high on our priority list. We expect to import a more sophisticated user interface management component at some later time or leave it completely to parties interested in productizing our prototype system.

(A2) The GQM Model Selection component is supposed to force the TAME user to parameterize each TAME session by first stating the objective of the session in the form of an already existing GQM model or requesting the creation of a new GQM model. The need for this restriction has been derived from the experience that data is frequently misused if it is accessible without a clear goal. The first prototype implementation does not enforce this requirement strictly. The current character of the first prototype as a research vehicle demands more flexibility. There is no question that this component needs to be implemented before the prototype leaves the research environment.

(A3) The GQM Model Generation component is supposed to allow the creation of specific GQM models either from scratch or by modifying existing ones. We have provided a set of templates and guidelines (Section II-B-2). We have been quite successful in the use of the templates and guidelines for defining goals, questions and metrics. There are a large number of organizations and environments in which the model has been applied to specify what data must be collected to evaluate various aspects of the process and product, e.g., NASA/GSFC, Burroughs, AT&T, IBM, Motorola. The application of the GQM paradigm at Hewlett Packard has shown that the templates can be used successfully without our guidance. Several of these experiences have been written up in the literature [4], [16], [17], [39], [48], [56], [60], [61]. We have been less successful in automating the process so that it ties into the experience base. As long as we know the goals and questions *a priori*, the appropriate data can be isolated and collected based upon the GQM paradigm. The first TAME prototype implementation is limited to support the generation of new models and the modification of existing models using an editor enforcing the templates and guidelines. We need to further formalize the templates and guidelines and provide traceability between goals and questions. Formalization of the templates and providing traceability is our most important research issue. In the long run we might consider using artificial intelligence planning techniques.

(A4.1 and A4.2) The Construction Interface component is supposed to support all interactions between a SEE (which supports the construction component of the TAME process model) and the TAME system. The model in Fig. 1 implies that interactions in both directions are required. We have gained experience in manually measuring the construction process by monitoring the execution of a variety of techniques (e.g., code reading [57], testing [20], and CLEANROOM development [61]) in various environments including the SEL [4], [48]. We have also learned how analysis results can be fed back into the ongoing construction process as well as into corporate experience [4], [48], Architectural component A4.1 is not part of this first TAME prototype. The first prototype implementation of A4.2 is limited to allowing for the integration of (or access to) external product libraries. This minimal interface is needed to have access to the objects for measurement. No interface for the on-line measurement of ongoing construction processes is provided yet.

(A5) The GQM Analysis and Feedback component is supposed to perform analysis according to a specific GQM model. We have gained a lot of experience in evaluating various kinds of experiments and case studies. We have been successful in collecting the appropriate data by tracing GQM models top-down. We have been less successful in providing formal interpretation rules allowing for the bottom-up interpretation of the collected data. One automated approach to providing interpretation and feedback is through expert systems. ARROWSMITH-P provides interpretations of software project data to managers [44]; it has been tested in the SEL/NASA environment. The first prototype TAME implementation triggers the collection of prescribed data (top-down) and presents it to the user for interpretation. The user-provided interpretations will be recorded (via a knowledge acquisition system) in order to accumulate the necessary knowledge that might lead us to identifying interpretation rules in the future.

(A6) The Measurement Scheduling component is supposed to allow the TAME user to define a strategy for actually collecting data by running the measurement tools. Choosing the most appropriate of many possible strategies (requirements Section III-A) might depend on the response times expected from the TAME system or the storage capacity of the experience base. Our experience with this issue is limited because most of our analyses were human scheduled as needed [4], [48]. This component will not be implemented as part of the first prototype. In this prototype, the TAME user will trigger the execution of measurement activities explicitly (which can, of course, be viewed as a minimal implementation supporting a human scheduling strategy).

(A7) The Measurement Tools component is supposed to allow the collection of all kinds of relevant process and product data. We have been successful in generating tools to gather data automatically and have learned from the application of these tools in different environments. Within NASA, for example, we have used a coverage tool to analyze the impact of test plans on the consistency of acceptance test coverage with operational use coverage [53]. We have used a data binding's tool to analyze the structural consistency of implemented systems to their design [41], and studied the relationship between faults and hierarchical structure as measured by the data binding's tool [60]. We have been able to characterize classes of products based upon their syntactic structure [35]. We have not, however, had much experience in automatically collecting process data. The first prototype TAME implementation consists of measurement tools based on the above three. The first tool captures all kinds of basic Ada source code information such as lines of code and structural complexity metrics [35], the second tool computes Ada data binding metrics, and the third tools captures dynamic information such as test coverage metrics [65]. One lesson learned has been that the development of measurement tools for Ada is very often much more than just a reimplementation of similar tools for other languages. This is due to the very different Ada language concepts. Furthermore, we have recognized the importance of having an intermediate representation level allowing for a language independent representation of software product and process aspects. The advantage of such an approach will be that this intermediate representation needs to be generated only once per product or process. All the measurement tools can run on this intermediate representation. This will not only make the actual measurement process less time-consuming but provide a basis for reusing the actual measurement tools to some extent across different language environments. Only the tool generating the intermediate representation needs to be rebuilt for each new implementation language or TAME host environment.

(A8) The Report Generator component is supposed to allow the TAME user to produce a variety of reports. The statistics and business communities have commonly accepted approaches for presenting data and interpretations effectively (e.g., histograms). The first TAME prototype implementation does not provide a separate experience base reporting facility. Responsibility for reporting is attached to each individual prototype component; e.g., the GQM Model Generation component provides reports regarding the models, each measurement tool reports on its own measurement data.

(A9) The Data Entry and Validation component is supposed to allow the TAME user to enter all kinds of manually collected data and validate them. Because of the changing needs for measurement, this component must allow for the definition of new (or modification of existing) data collection forms as well as related validation (integrity) rules. If possible, the experience base should be capable of adapting to new needs based upon new form definitions. We have had lots of experience in designing forms and validations rules, using them, and learning about the complicated issues of deriving validation rules [4], [48]. The first prototype implementation will allow the TAME user to input off-line collected measurement data and validate them based upon a fixed and predefined set of data collection forms [currently in use in NASA's Software Engineering Laboratory (SEL)]. This component is designed but not yet completely implemented. The practical use of the TAME prototype requires that this component provide the flexibility for defining and accepting new form layouts. One research issue is identifying the easiest way to define data collection forms in terms of a grammar that could be used to generate the corresponding screen layout and experience base structure.

(A10) The Experience Base component allows for effective storage and retrieval of all relevant experience ranging from products and process plans (e.g., analysis plans in the form of GQM models) to measurement data and interpretations. The experience base needs to mirror the project environment. Here we are relying on the experience of several faculty members of the database group at the University of Maryland. It has been recognized that current database technology is not sufficient, for several reasons, to truly mirror the needs of software engineering projects [26]. The first prototype TAME implementation is built on top of a relational database management system. A first database schema [46] modeling products as well as measurement data has been implemented. We are currently adding GQM models to the schema. The experiences with this first prototype show that the amount of experience stored and its degree of formalism (mostly data) is not yet sufficient. We need to better package that data in order to create pieces of information or knowledge. The GQM paradigm provides a specification of what data needs to be packaged. However, without more formal interpretation rules, the details of packaging cannot be formalized. In the long run, we might include expert system technology. We have also recognized the need for a number of built-in GQM models that can either be reused without modification or guide the TAME user during the process of creating new GQM models.

(A11) The Data Access Control and Security component is supposed to guarantee that only authorized users can access the TAME system and that each user can only access a predefined window of the experience base. The first prototype implements this component only as far as user access to the entire system is concerned.

(A12) The Configuration Management and Control component is supposed to guarantee consistency between the objects of measurement (products and processes), the plans for measurement (GQM models), the data collected from the objects according to these plans, and the attached interpretations. This component will not be implemented in the first prototype.

The integration of all these architectural components is incomplete. At this point in time we have integrated the first versions of the experience base, three measurement tools, a limited version of the GQM analysis and feedback component, the GQM generation component, and the user interface management component. Many of the UNIX®[1] tools (e.g., editors, print facilities) have been integrated into the first prototype TAME system to compensate for yet missing components. This subset of the first prototype is running on a network of SUN-3's under UNIX. It is implemented in Ada and C.

This first prototype enables the user to generate GQM models using a structured editor. Existing models can be selected by using a unique model name. Support for selecting models based on goal definitions or for reusing existing models for the purpose of generating new models is offered, but the refinement of goals into questions and metrics relies on human intervention. Analysis and feedback sessions can be run according to existing GQM models. Only minimal support for interpretation is provided (e.g., histograms of data). Measurement data are presented to the user according to the underlying model for his/her interpretation. Results can be documented on a line printer. The initial set of measurement tools allows only the computation of a limited number of Ada-source-code-oriented static and dynamic metrics. Similar tools might be used in the case of Fortran source code [33].

V. Summary and Conclusions

We have presented a set of software engineering and measurement principles which we have learned during a dozen years of analyzing software engineering processes and products. These principles have led us to recognize the need for

1 ® UNIX is a registered trademark of AT&T Bell Laboratories.

software engineering process models that integrate sound planning and analysis into the construction process.

In order to achieve this integration the software engineering process needs to be tailorable and tractable. We need the ability to tailor the execution process, methods and tools to specific project needs in a way that permits maximum reuse of prior experience. We need to control the process and product because of the flexibility required in performing such a focused development. We also need as much automated support as possible. Thus an integrated software engineering environment needs to support all of these issues.

In the TAME project we have developed an improvement-oriented (integrated) process model. It stresses a) the characterization of the current status of a project environment, b) the planning for improvement integrated into software projects, and c) the execution of the project according to the prescribed project plans. Each of these tasks must be dealt with from a constructive and analytic perspective.

To integrate the constructive and analytic aspects of software development, we have used the GQM paradigm. It provides a mechanism for formalizing the characterization and planning tasks, controlling and improving projects based on quantitative analysis, learning in a deeper and more systematic way about the software process and product, and feeding back the appropriate experience to current and future projects.

The effectiveness of the TAME process model depends heavily on appropriate automated support by an ISEE. The TAME system is an instantiation of the TAME process model into an ISEE; it is aimed at supporting all aspects of characterization, planning, analysis, learning, and feedback according to the TAME process model. In addition, it formalizes the feedback and learning mechanisms by supporting the synthesis of project experience, the formalization of its representation, and its tailoring towards specific project needs. It does this by supporting goal development into measurement via templates and guidelines, providing analysis of the development and maintenance processes, and creating and using experience bases (ranging from databases of historical data to knowledge bases that incorporate experience from prior projects).

We discussed a limited prototype of the TAME system, which has been developed as the first of a series of prototypes that will be built using an iterative enhancement model. The limitations of this prototype fall into two categories, limitations of the technology and the need to better formalize the model so that it can be automated.

The short range (1-3 years) goal for the TAME system is to build the analysis environment. The mid-range goal (3-5 years) is to integrate the system into one or more existing or future development or maintenance environments. The long range goal (5-8 years) is to tailor those environments for specific organizations and projects.

The TAME project is ambitious. It is assumed it will evolve over time and that we will learn a great deal from formalizing the various aspects of the TAME project as well as integrating the various paradigms. Research is needed in many areas before the idealized TAME system can be built. Major areas of study include measurement, databases, artificial intelligence, and systems. Specific activities needed to support TAME include: more formalization of the GQM paradigm, the definition of better models for various quality and productivity aspects, mechanisms for better formalizing the reuse and tailoring of project experience, the interpretation of metrics with respect to goals, interconnection languages, language independent representation of software, access control in general and security in particular, software engineering database definition, configuration management and control, and distributed system architecture. We are interested in the role of further researching the ideas and principles of the TAME project. We will build a series of revolving prototypes of the system in order to learn and test out ideas.

Acknowledgment

The authors thank all their students for many helpful suggestions. We especially acknowledge the many contributions to the TAME project and, thereby indirectly to this paper, by J. Bailey, C. Brophy, M. Daskalantonakis, A. Delis, D. Doubleday, F. Y. Farhat, R. Jeffery, E. E. Katz, A. Kouchakdjian, L. Mark, K. Reed, Y. Rong, T. Sunazuka, P. D. Stotts, B. Swain, A. J. Turner, B. Ulery, S. Wang, and L. Wu. We thank the guest editors and external reviewers for their constructive comments.

References

[1] W. Agresti, "SEL Ada experiment: Status and design experience," in *Proc. Eleventh Annu. Software Engineering Workshop,* NASA Goddard Space Flight Center, Greenbelt, MD, Dec. 1986.

[2] J. Bailey and V. R. Basili, "A meta-model for software development resource expenditures," in *Proc. Fifth Int. Conf. Software Engineering,* San Diego, CA, Mar. 1981, pp. 107-116.

[3] V. R. Basili, "Quantitative evaluation of software engineering methodology," in *Proc. First Pan Pacific Computer Conf.,* Melbourne, Australia, Sept. 1985; also available as Tech. Rep. TR-1519, Dep. Comput. Sci., Univ. Maryland, College Park, July 1985.

[4] V. R. Basili, "Can we measure software technology: Lessons learned from 8 years of trying," in *Proc. Tenth Annu. Software Engineering Workshop,* NASA Goddard Space Flight Center, Greenbelt, MD, Dec. 1985.

[5] ——, "Evaluating software characteristics: Assessment of software measures in the Software Engineering Laboratory," in *Proc. Sixth Annu. Software Engineering Workshop,* NASA Goddard Space Flight Center, Greenbelt, MD, 1981.

[6] V. R. Basili and J. Beane, "Can the Parr curve help with the manpower distribution and resource estimation problems," *J. Syst. Software,* vol. 2, no. 1, pp. 59-69, 1981.

[7] V. R. Basili and K. Freburger, "Programming measurement and estimation in the Software Engineering Laboratory." *J. Syst. Software,* vol. 2, no. 1, pp. 47-57, 1981.

[8] V. R. Basili and D. H. Hutchens, "An empirical study of a syntactic measure family," *IEEE Trans. Software Eng.,* vol. SE-9, no. 11, pp. 664-672, Nov. 1983.

[9] V. R. Basili and E. E. Katz, "Measures of interest in an Ada development," in *Proc. IEEE Comput. Soc. Workshop Software Engineering Technology Transfer,* Miami. FL, Apr. 1983, pp. 22-29.

[10] V. R. Basili, E. E. Katz, N..M. Panlilio-Yap, C. Loggia Ramsey, and S. Chang, "Characterization of an Ada software development," *Computer,* pp. 53-65, Sept. 1985.

[11] V. R. Basili and C. Loggia Ramsey, "ARROWSMITH-P: A prototype expert: system for software engineering management," in *Proc. IEEE Symp. Expert Systems in Government,* Oct. 23-25, 1985, pp. 252-264.

[12] V. R. Basili and N. M. Panlilio-Yap, "Finding relationships between effort and other variables in the SEL," in *Proc. IEEE COMPSAC,* Oct. 1985.

[13] V. R. Basili and B. Perricone, "Software errrors and complexity: An empirical investigation," *ACM, Commun.,* vol. 27, no. 1, pp. 45-52, Jan. 1984.

[14] V. R. Basili and R. Reiter, Jr., "A controlled experiment quantitatively comparing software development approaches," *IEEE Trans. Software Eng.,* vol. SE-7, no. 5, pp. 299-320, May 1981.

[15] V. R. Basili and H. D. Rombach, "TAME: Tailoring an Ada measurement environment," in *Proc. Joint Ada Conf.,* Arlington, VA, Mar. 16-19, 1987, pp. 318-325.

[16] ——, "Tailoring the software process to project goals and environments," in *Proc. Ninth Int. Conf. Software Engineering,* Monterey, CA, Mar. 30-Apr. 2, 1987, pp. 345-357.

[17] ——, "TAME: Integrating measurement into software environments," Dep. Comput. Sci., Univ. Maryland, College Park, Tech. Rep. TR-1764 (TAME-TR-1-1987), June 1987.

[18] ——, "Software reuse: A framework," in *Proc. Tenth Minnowbrook Workshop Software Reuse,* Blue Mountain Lake. NY, Aug. 1987.

[19] V. R. Basili and R. W. Selby, Jr., "Data collection and analysis in software research and management," in *Proc. Amer. Statist. Ass. and Biomeasure Soc. Joint Statistical Meetings,* Philadelphia. PA, Aug. 13-16. 1984.

[20] ——, "Comparing the effectiveness of software testing strategies," *IEEE Trans. Software Eng.*, vol. SE-13, no. 12, pp. 1278-1296, Dec. 1987.

[21] ——, "Calculation and use of an environment's characteristic software metric set," in *Proc. Eighth Int. Conf. Software Engineering,* London, England, Aug. 1985.

[22] V. R. Basili, R. W. Selby, and D. H. Hutchens, "Experimentation in software engineering," *IEEE Trans. Software Eng.,* vol. SE-12, no. 7. pp. 733-743, July 1986.

[23] V. R. Basili, R. W. Selby, and T.-Y. Phillips, "Metric analysis and data validation across Fortran projects," *IEEE Trans. Software Eng.,* vol. SE-9, no. 6, pp. 652-663, Nov. 1983.

[24] V. R. Basili and A. J. Turner, "Iterative enhancement: A practical technique for software development." *IEEE Trans. Software Eng.,* vol. SE-1, no. 4, pp. 390-396, Dec. 1975.

[25] V. R. Basili and D. M. Weiss, "A methodology for collecting valid software engineering data," *IEEE Trans. Software Eng.*, vol. SE-10, no. 3, pp. 728-738, Nov. 1984.

[26] P. A. Bernstein. "Database system support for software engineering." in *Proc. Ninth Int. Conf. Software Engineering.* Monterey. CA, Mar. 30-Apr. 2, 1987, pp. 166-178.

[27] D. Bjorner. "On the use of formal methods in software development." in *Proc. Ninth Int. Conf. Software Engineering,* Monterey, CA. Mar. 30-Apr. 2, 1987, pp. 17-29.

[28] B. W. Boehm, "Software engineering," *IEEE Trans. Comput.,* vol. C-25. no. 12, pp. 1226-1241, Dec. 1976.
[29] ——, *Software Engineering Economics.* Englewood Cliffs, NJ: Prentice-Hall, 1981.
[30] ——, "A spiral model of software development and enhancement," *ACM Software Eng. Notes,* vol. 11, no. 4, pp. 22-42, Aug. 1986.
[31] B. W. Boehm, J. R. Brown, and M. Lipow, "Quantitative evaluation of software quality." in *Proc. Second Int. Conf. Software Engineering.* 1976, pp. 592-605.
[32] C. Brophy, W. Agresti, and V. R. Basili. "Lessons learned in use of Ada oriented design methods." in *Proc. Joint Ada Conf.;* Arlington, VA, Mar. 16-19, 1987, pp. 231-236.
[33] W. J. Decker and W. A. Taylor. "Fortran static source code analyzer program (SAP)," NASA Goddard Space Flight Center, Greenbelt, MD. Tech. Rep. SEL-82-002, Aug. 1982.
[34] C. W. Doerflinger and V. R. Basili, "Monitoring software development through dynamic variables," *IEEE Trans. Software Eng.,* vol. SE-11. no. 9. pp. 978-985, Sept. 1985.
[35] D. L. Doubleday, "ASAP: An Ada static source code analyzer program," Dep. Comput. Sci., Univ. Maryland, College Park. Tech. Rep. TR-1895, Aug. 1987.
[36] M. Dowson, "ISTAR—An integrated project support environment," in *ACM Sigplan Notices (Proc. Second ACM Software Eng. Svmp. Practical Development Support Environments),* vol. 2, no. 1, Jan 1987.
[37] M. Dyer, "Cleanroom software development method," IBM Federal Systems Division, Bethesda. MD, Oct. 14, 1982.
[38] J. Gannon, E. E. Katz. and V. R. Basili, "Measures for Ada packages: An initial study," *Commun. ACM,* vol. 29, no. 7, pp 616-623, July 1986.
[39] R. B. Grady, "Measuring and managing software maintenance," *IEEE Software,* vol. 4. no. 5, pp. 35-45, Sept. 1987.
[40] M. H. Halstead, *Elements of Software Science.* New York: Elsevier North-Holland, 1977.
[41] D. H. Hutchens and V. R. Basili, "System structure analysis: Clustering with data bindings," *IEEE Trans. Software Eng.*, vol. SE-11, pp. 749-757, Aug. 1985.
[42] E. E. Katz and V. R. Basili, "Examining the modularity of Ada programs," in *Proc. Joint Ada Conf.,* Arlington, VA, Mar. 16-19, 1987, pp. 390-396.
[43] E. E. Katz, H. D. Rombach, and V. R. Basili, "Structure and maintainability of Ada programs: Can we measure the differences?" in *Proc. Ninth Minnowbrook Workshop Software Performance Evaluation.* Blue Mountain Lake, NY, Aug. 5-8, 1986.
[44] C. Loggia Ramsey and V. R. Basili. "An evaluation of expert systems for software engineering management." Dep. Comput. Sci., Univ. Maryland, College Park, Tech. Rep. TR-1708, Sept. 1986.
[45] M. Marcus, K. Sattley, S. C. Schaffner. and E. Albert. "DAPSE: A distributed Ada programming support environment," in *Proc. IEEE Second Int. Conf. Ada Applications and Environments,* 1986, pp. 115-125.
[46] L. Mark and H. D. Rombach. "A meta information base for software engineering," Dep. Comput. Sci., Univ. Maryland, College Park, Tech. Rep. TR-1765, July 1987.
[47] T. J. McCabe. "A complexity measure." *IEEE Trans. Software Eng.,* vol. SE-2, no. 4, pp. 308-320, Dec. 1976.
[48] F. E. McGarry, "Recent SEL studies." in *Proc. Tenth Annu. Software Engineering Workshop.* NASA Goddard Space Flight Center, Greenbelt, MD, Dec, 1985.
[49] L. Osterweil. "Software processes are software too." in *Proc. Ninth Int. Conf. Software Engineering.* Monterey, CA. Mar. 30-Apr. 2, 1987, pp. 2-13.

[50] F. N. Parr. "An alternative to the Rayleigh curve model for software development effort," *IEEE Trans. Software Eng.*, vol. SE-6. no. 5, pp. 291-296. May 1980.

[51] L. Putnam, "A general empirical solution to the macro software sizing and estimating problem," *IEEE Trans. Software Eng.*. vol. SE-4, no. 4, pp. 345-361, Apr. 1978.

[52] C. V. Ramamoorthy, Y. Usuda. W.-T. Tsai, and A. Prakash. "GENESIS: An integrated environment for supporting development and evolution of software," in *Proc. COMPSAC*, 1985.

[53] J. Ramsey and V. R. Basili. "Analyzing the test process using structural coverage," in *Proc. Eighth Int. Conf. Software Engineering*. London, England, Aug. 1985, pp. 306-311.

[54] H. D. Rombach, "Software design metrics for maintenance." in *Proc. Ninth Annu. Software Engineering Workshop*, NASA Goddard Space Flight Center, Greenbelt, MD, Nov. 1984.

[55] ——, "A controlled experiment on the impact of software structure on maintainability," *IEEE Trans. Software Eng.*, vol. SE-13. no. 3, pp. 344-354, Mar. 1987.

[56] H. D. Rombach and V. R. Basili. "A quantitative assessment of software maintenance: An industrial case study," in *Proc. Conf. Software Maintenance, Austin.* TX. Sept. 1987, pp. 134-144.

[57] H. D. Rombach, V. R. Basili. and R. W. Selby. Jr.. "The role of code reading in the software life cycle." in *Proc. Ninth Minnowbrook Workshop Software Performance Evaluation.* Blue Mountain Lake, NY, August 5-8, 1986.

[58] W. W. Royce, "Managing the development of large software systems: Concepts and techniques." in *Proc. WESCON.* Aug. 1970.

[59] R. W. Selby, Jr., "Incorporating metrics into a software environment." in *Proc. Joint Ada Conf.*, Arlington, VA, Mar. 16-19, 1987, pp. 326-333.

[60] R. W. Selby and V. R. Basili. "Analyzing error-prone system coupling and cohesion," Dep. Comput. Sci., Univ. Maryland, College Park. Tech. Rep., in preparation.

[61] R. W. Selby. Jr., V. R. Basili. and T. Baker. "CLEANROOM software development: An empirical evaluation," *IEEE Trans. Software Eng.*, vol. SE-13. no. 9. pp. 1027-1037, Sept. 1987.

[62] C. E. Walston and C. P. Felix. "A method of programming measurement and estimation." *IBM Syst. J.*. vol. 16, no. 1, pp. 54-73, 1977.

[63] A. I. Wasserman and P. A. Pircher. "Visible connections." *UNIX Rev.*, Oct. 1986.

[64] *Webster's New Collegiate Dictionary.* Springfield, MA: Merriam, 1981.

[65] L. Wu, V. R. Basili. and K. Reed, "A structure coverage tool for Ada software systems," in *Proc. Joint Ada Conf.*, Arlington. VA, Mar. 16-19, 1987, pp. 294-303.

[66] M. Zelkowitz, R. Yen, R. Hamlet, J. Gannon, and V. R. Basili. "Software engineering practices in the U.S. and Japan." *Computer*, pp. 57-66, June 1984.

Section 3: The Software Engineering Laboratory

Frank E. McGarry

Computer Sciences Corporation

Abstract. The Software Engineering Laboratory (SEL)—as both a concept and an operational research organization—was established in 1976 when the first formal grant was issued by NASA to the University of Maryland. The initial scope of this grant included the establishment of an operational environment for the purpose of studying production software under controlled conditions. The intent was to apply various software techniques to production projects and to analyze the impact of these techniques on the resultant software product. Not only was this concept unique, but it also became one of the linchpins of the empirical studies carried out by the staff at the University of Maryland over the subsequent 25-year period of the SEL operation. As one of the founding directors of this institution, Vic Basili established the groundwork for the concepts of empirical studies in software engineering and then directed the research arm of the SEL for its 25 year lifetime.

The SEL operated as a partnership of the three original organizations: the University of Maryland, NASA, and Computer Sciences Corporation (CSC), for approximately 25 years, during which time over 200 research papers and reports were produced. Each of those reports represented results from research conducted on NASA software development projects. Not only were there specific empirical studies reported, but the synthesis of this entire work has had a profound impact on software engineering in general and empirical studies in software in particular. As the lead researcher on the SEL activities, Basili was instrumental in essentially every one of the published results. Additionally, he was the catalyst that prompted the packaging and infusion of experience back into production use within NASA and CSC as well as in other software organizations.

Concepts

The SEL was conceived as a cooperative enterprise linking academia (University of Maryland), government (NASA), and industry (Computer Sciences Corporation). Each member of the SEL was to play a key role in the establishment and operation of the organization as well as being a significant beneficiary of all of the work and general concepts generated:

- The University was to provide the concepts, research staff, and analytical skill to lead the overall research activities.
- NASA was to define the need, allocate resources, and apply research results to improve software products within the NASA community.
- CSC was to provide the operational staff to develop and maintain software using techniques and approaches defined by the university as a concept of study.

The vision was that the SEL would apply available software techniques to selected development projects, then observe and measure the impacts on the quality or cost of the completed software, thereby establishing the framework of software engineering empirical studies. To implement this overall vision, Basili proposed several key concepts:

- Form a partnership of the three organizations to ensure that goals and benefits of each were addressed
- Develop measures to characterize environment, products, and processes
- Conduct experiments of select processes in the production environment of NASA mission software
- Continually infuse results of experiments into the process baseline of the organization

Environment

The development environment at the time the SEL was established was a software production environment. The NASA and CSC organizations were chartered to produce operational software systems to support Goddard flight missions. The support software products ranged in size from 5000 line systems to systems of well over 1 million lines with the typical being in the range of 100,000 lines. At any one time, there could be from 5 to 15 of these projects in the development stages and depending on the number of ongoing projects, the total number of development staff could range from 100 to over 300 software developers.

Activities and Significant Impacts of the SEL

Between 1976 and 2000, the SEL analyzed information from more than 100 NASA projects and reported on studies of numerous technologies, techniques, and software processes. Each of these projects is considered an experiment in software technology, and each paper or report contributed some insight into the impacts of software methods and techniques. Moreover, developers and managers who participated in the studies improved their understanding of approaches to selecting and applying variations of processes based on the nature of the problem and the specific environment.

Basili had the vision and the insight to take a more global view of all the SEL activities and results, rather than merely treating them as a series of individual studies. He advocated the capture of key principles in the form of models and theories that would lay a strong foundation for software engineering research as well as software process improvement in general. The three papers included in this section reflect some of the major contributions from the SEL.

1. The first paper, "Analyzing Medium-Scale Software Development," describes the foundation for software measurement and model building. This paper is one of the earliest to describe an approach to collecting measurement data in a production environment to generate models that improve understanding of the development process. It was published in early 1978 and represented the analysis of a collection of medium-sized projects at NASA/Goddard.

The paper describes concepts that laid the foundation for the subsequent 25 years of research carried out in the SEL: measurement, empirical studies, model building, packaging of experiences, and understanding of local environments.

Two of the projects are analyzed in detail to demonstrate the characteristics of effort distribution as compared to standard resource models such as the Rayleigh curve. The analysis demonstrates the need for software environments to tailor basic models of development to fit their own environment and more importantly demonstrates an approach for doing this. The paper describes the details of data collection forms, processes, and overall measurement analysis and it laid the framework for the SEL approach to measurement, continuous improvement and experimental software engineering.

2. The second paper, "Software Process Evolution at the SEL," presents an excellent description of the Quality Improvement Paradigm (QIP) as applied in a production environment. Three case studies examine variations of the Cleanroom methodology as applied in several projects within the SEL. Although the specific study results are significant to practitioners considering the Cleanroom technique, the major value of this set of studies is the demonstration of the QIP model. The QIP is a 6 step sequence that establishes a framework to guide an organization in defining and operating a software process improvement program. This model represents Basili's vision of how a software continuous improvement program should be structured and should operate. Basili's vision of the QIP is both described and exemplified in this paper.

   The series of studies reported demonstrates that specific tailoring of a software methodology (Cleanroom) can be carried out effectively when adhering to a structured improvement process (QIP). This continuous improvement process is used to determine appropriate and effective techniques in a particular environment. In this case, the paper concludes that Cleanroom is effective (for this environment) for 1 class of software (under 50,000 lines of code), but may not be effective for larger projects. Such insight is one value of QIP.

3. The third paper, "The Software Engineering Laboratory—An Operational Software Experience Factory," describes the structure and operation of an effective process improvement organization, and more importantly an effective learning organization. This learning organization is termed 'Experience Factory' (EF) by Basili. The concept of EF was '..introduced to institutionalize the collective learning of the organization that is at the root of continual improvement…'.

   To complement the model of process improvement (QIP) along with the foundations of structured measurement captured in the Goal-Question Metric paradigm (GQM), Basili developed this organizational model of the EF. It is an operational environment that is both developing software and capitalizing on past development activities by capturing and synthesizing lessons, insight, and general experiences. Basili derived this concept directly from the observations of the production environment operating within the guise of the SEL.

This paper describes the major roles and structure of the 2 organizations within the EF. The project organization is responsible for producing software and providing experience data to the EF organization. The EF organization is responsible for the analysis and packaging of project experiences so that it can be reused in the forms of refined models, lessons, and processes. To exemplify this organizational structure, a series of studies of Ada is described.

The significance of contributions made by the SEL is monumental, especially considering the total NASA investment of less than $6M (real-year-dollars) over 25 years. The successful forging of government, industry, and academia into an integrated partnership that meets the needs of each partner may be one of the most remarkable contributions of this endeavor. The SEL realized and exceeded the specific goals and contributions of its three organizational elements, to the benefit to all. The dedication and capabilities of the many researchers, staff, developers, and managers are primary reasons for achieving such a significant return on such a modest investment; however, the concept could not have had nearly the impact the SEL has had without the vision and dedication of Vic Basili. He nurtured the concept to maturity and dedicated time, effort, insight, and vision throughout his professional career to ensure that the software engineering community received significant value from this unique endeavor, the SEL.

Analyzing Medium-scale Software Development

Victor R. Basili and Marvin V. Zelkowitz

Department of Computer Science University of Maryland
College Park, Maryland 20742

Abstract. The collection and analysis of data from programming projects is necessary for the appropriate evaluation of software engineering methodologies. Towards this end, the Software Engineering Laboratory was organized between the University of Maryland and NASA Goddard Space Flight Center. This paper describes the structure of the Laboratory and provides some data on project evaluation from some of the early projects that have been monitored. The analysis relates to resource forecasting using a model of the project life cycle based upon the Rayleigh equation and to error rates applying ideas developed by Belady and Lehman.

1. Goals of the Laboratory

A great deal of time and money has been and will continue to be spent in developing software. Much effort has gone into the generation of various software development methodologies that are meant to improve both the process and the product [Myers, Baker, Wolverton]. Unfortunately, it has not always been clear what the underlying principles involved in the software development process are and what effect the methodologies have; it is not always clear what constitutes a better product. Thus progress in finding techniques that produce better, cheaper software depends on developing new deeper understandings of good software and the software development process. At the same time we must continue to produce software.

In order to investigate these issues, the Software Engineering Laboratory was established, in August, 1976, at NASA Goddard Space Flight Center in cooperation with the University of Maryland to promote such understandings [Basili & Zelkowitz]. The goals of the Laboratory are to analyze the software development process and the software produced in order to understand the development process, the software product, the effects of various "improvements" on the process and to develop quantitative measures that correlate well with intuitive notions of good software.

This research was sponsored in part by grant NSG-5123 from NASA Goddard Space Flight Center, Greenbelt, Maryland to the University of Maryland.

The goals of the Laboratory can be broken down into three major tasks:

1. Provide a reporting mechanism for monitoring current project progress. This goal is to provide management with up-to-date data on current project development. Better reporting procedures can pinpoint problems as they develop and help eliminate their spread and growth.
2. Collect data at as fine a level as possible that can be used to determine how the software is being developed, extend results that have been reported in the literature about very large software developments and their characteristics to medium sized projects (5 to 10 man-years), help discover what parameters can be validly isolated, expose the parameters that appear to be causing trouble, and discover appropriate milestones and techniques that show success under certain conditions.
3. By comparing data collected from several NASA projects, compare the effects of various technologies and other parameters upon system development and performance.

2. Laboratory operation

Projects for the Systems Development Section at NASA typically are produced by an outside contractor under supervision by NASA employees. Most products are in the 5 to 10 man-year range in size, and are generally large batch programs for an IBM 360 system. The programs are almost always written in FORTRAN.

To evaluate programming methodologies, a mechanism was established to collect data on each such project. The initial goal was to collect as much relevant data as possible with as little impact on the projects and software development practices as possible. It is believed that although there has been some impact and interference, it has been minimal. As we gain knowledge as to what data to collect, we hope to shorten the manual input from the project personnel, and to automate some of the tasks.

Similar to other reporting projects of this type, the principal data gathering mechanism is a set of seven reporting forms that are filled out by project personnel at various times in the development life cycle of a project [Walston & Felix]. Some of these are filled out only once or twice, while others are filled out regularly. The seven forms that are currently in use include:

1. **General Project Summary**. This form is filled out or updated at each project milestone and defines the scope of the problem, how much has been completed, estimates for the remainder of the project, and what techniques are being used. It is a top level structure of the overall organization and is filled out by the project manager.
2. **Component Summary.** This form is filled out during the design phase and describes the structure of each component (e. g. subroutine, COMMON block, etc.)
3. **Programmer Analyst Survey.** This form is filled out once by each programmer in order to provide a general background of project personnel.

4. **Resource Summary.** This form is filled out weekly by the project manager and gives manpower and other resources charged to the project during the week.
5. **Component Status Report.** This is the major accounting form that lists, for each programmer, what activities were performed on each component for the week. This is the basic form that lists what happened and when.
6. **Computer Program Run Analysis.** This form contains an entry each time the computer is used. It briefly describes what the computer is used for (e. g. compile, test, etc.) and what happened (e. g. error messages).
7. **Change Report Form.** This form is completed for each change made to the system. The reason for and a description of the change are given. If the change is made to correct an error, the method of detection, effects on other parts of the system, time to correct and type of error are noted on the form.

The data that is collected is entered into the INGRES PDP 11 data base system [Held]. This process is somewhat tedious due to the care needed to insure data validity. Almost all of the errors not detected by hand checking of the coded input are detected by the input program.

All projects that are currently being monitored can be broken down into three broad classifications:

1. **The screening experiments** are the projects that simply have the requirement to submit reporting forms. They provide a base line from which further comparisons can be made, and upon which the monitoring methodology can be tested.
2. The **semi-controlled experiments** are a set of relatively similar large scale developments. While they are different projects, they are sufficiently similar in size and scope so that comparisons can be made across these projects. In this case, specific techniques are sometimes required to be used in order to measure their effectiveness. These projects are the standard spacecraft software developed by the Systems Development Section at NASA.
3. The **controlled experiments** are a set of projects that are developed, using different methodologies. These developments are the most closely monitored and controlled of the three classifications so that the effects of methodology upon these projects can more easily be measured than in the semi-controlled experiments.

For each project, a set of factors that effect software development are extracted by the forms. Some of the factors that are of interest include:

1. **People factors** (size and expertise of development team, team organization)
2. **Problem factors** (type of problem to solve, magnitude of problem, format of specifications, constraints placed upon solution)
3. **Process factors** (specification, design and programming languages, techniques such as code reading, walkthroughs, top down design and structured programming)
4. **Product factors** (reliability, size of system, efficiency, structure of control)
5. **Resource factors** (target and development computer system, development time, budget)
6. **Tools** (Libraries, compilers, testing tools, maintenance tools)

Some of these factors can be controlled while others are inflexible. Such items as development computer system, budget, format of input specifications and type of problem to solve are mostly fixed and change very slowly year by year. On the other hand, factors like structured programming, design techniques and team organization are much more under the control of the laboratory and can be varied across different projects.

For each semi-controlled or controlled project, a set of these factors is predetermined. For example, a project may use a librarian, code reading, walkthroughs, a PDL and structured programming. The other factors that affect development will become apparent through the information obtained on the general project summary. In order to enforce these methodologies on project personnel, a training period, consisting from a two hour lecture on filling out forms up to a week's classroom training, is being utilized. Every effort is being made to use methodologies that are compatible with a project manager's basic beliefs so that no friction develops between what the manager wants to do and what he must do.

Much of the early effort in the Laboratory was expended in the organization of the operation and generation of data collection and validation procedures and forms. We have reached a point where sufficient data has been obtained to permit us to evaluate our operational procedures and to analyze data with respect to goals one and two in the introduction. In the following two sections, early evaluation of the collected data is presented. The major emphasis in these first evaluations is on reporting progress and reliability of the developing system.

3. Progress forecasting

One important aspect of project control is the accurate prediction of future costs and schedules. A model of project progress has been developed and with it estimates on project costs can be predicted.

The Rayleigh curve has been found to closely resemble the life cycle costs on large scale software projects [Norden, Putnam]. At present, we are assuming that this is true for medium scale projects as well, and are developing reporting procedures based upon this function. As data becomes available, we will be better able to test the underlying hypothesis and refine it further.

The Rayleigh curve yielding current resource expenditures (y) at time (t) is given by the equation:

$$y=2\ K\ a\ t\ \exp(-a\ t^2)$$

where the constant <u>K</u> is the total estimated project cost, and the constant <u>a</u> is equal to 1/(Td**2) where <u>Td</u> is the time when development expenditures reach a maximum. In our environment <u>K</u> and <u>a</u> are measures of hours of effort, and <u>t</u> is given in weeks.

3.1 Estimates on Initial Data

For each project in the NASA environment, the requirements phase yields estimates of the total resources and development time needed for completion. This data is obtained by the Laboratory via the General Project Summary form. From this data, a Rayleigh curve for this project can be computed.

From the General Project Summary, the following three parameters are relevant to this analysis:

1. Ka, total estimated resources needed to complete the project through acceptance testing (in hours).
2. Yd, the maximum resources needed per week to complete the project (in hours).
3. Ta, the number of weeks until acceptance testing.

Since the Rayleigh curve has only two parameters (K and a), the above system is over specified and one of the above variables can be determined from the other two. Since NASA budgets are generally fixed a year in advance, there is usually little that can be done with total resources available (K). Also, since the contractor assigns a fixed number of individuals to work on the project, the maximum resources Yd (at least for several months) is also relatively fixed. Therefore, the completion date (Ta) will vary depending upon K and Yd.

As stated above, Ka is the total estimated resources needed to develop and test the system through the acceptance testing stage. By analyzing previous NASA projects, this figure Ka is about 88% of total expenditures K. The remaining 12% goes towards last minute changes. The seemingly low figure of only 12% to cover everything other than design, coding, and testing can be explained by the following two facts local to our NASA environment:

1. the initial requirements and specifications phases are handled by different groups from the development section, and thus this data does not appear, and
2. shortly after acceptance testing, a third group undertakes the maintenance operation, and so the full maintenance costs also are not included in the estimates.

For this reason it should be clear that we have no actual data to match the Rayleigh curve in the early stage (requirements) and late stage (maintenance). However, the major central portion of the curve should be a reliable estimate of the development costs, and it is here that we hope to prove consistency between the data collected on these medium scale projects and the large scale projects in the literature. Besides, on the large scale projects, the Rayleigh curve also acts as an accurate predictor of the design, coding, and testing stages both combined and individually [Putnam]. (In the future we expect to obtain some data on the long term maintenance phase. A Maintenance Reporting Form has been developed, and the maintenance section has agreed to fill out this form and report back the data. Due to the lifetimes of these spacecraft related software systems, the data will not be available for about another year.)

Thus given the estimate of project costs Ka in hours, the total resources needed is given by:

Ka = .88 K
or
K = Ka/.88

The raw data for personnel resource estimates are not directly usable in our analyses since they include individuals of varying functions and salaries and therefore varying costs. The following normalization algorithm has been applied to the resource data in computing Ka: Each programmer hour is given a weight of 1, an hour of management time costs 1.5 while a support hour (secretary, typing, librarian, etc.) costs .5. This is a reasonable approximation to the true costs at NASA.

Then given constant a, the date of acceptance testing Ta can be computed as follows. The integral form of the Rayleigh curve is given by:

$$E = K (1 - \exp(-a t^2))$$

where E is the total expenditures until time t. From the previous discussion, we know that at acceptance testing, E is .88K. Therefore,

$$.88K = K (1 - \exp(-at^2))$$

Solving for t yields:

$$t = \mathrm{sqrt}(-\ln(.12)/a)$$

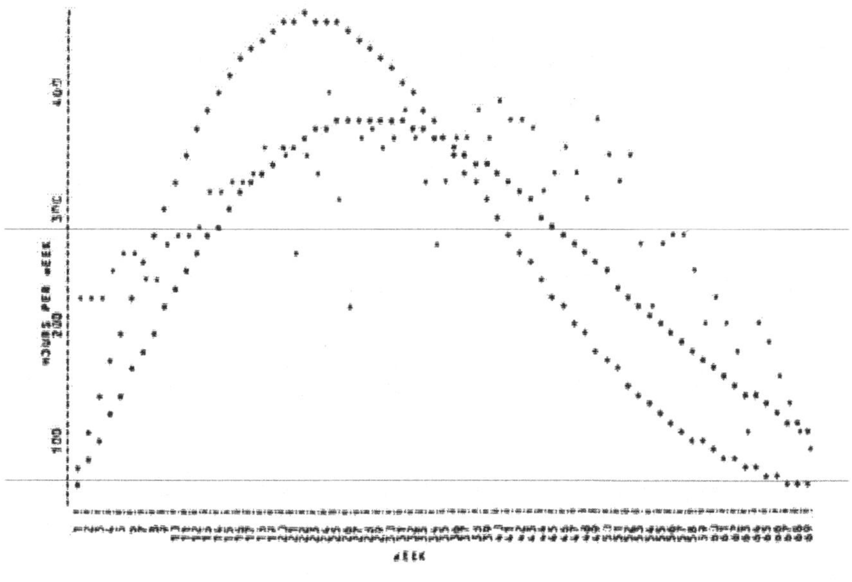

* = Estimating curve with Yd (maximum resources) fixed

\+ = Estimating curve with Ta (Completion date) fixed

. = Actual data

Figure 1. Project A – Estimated resource expenditures curves

Putnam [Putnam2] states that for development efforts only, acceptance testing (Ta) is related to the time of peak effort (Tp) by the relation:

$$Tp = \frac{Ta}{sqrt(6)}$$

or

$$Ta = Tp * sqrt(6)$$

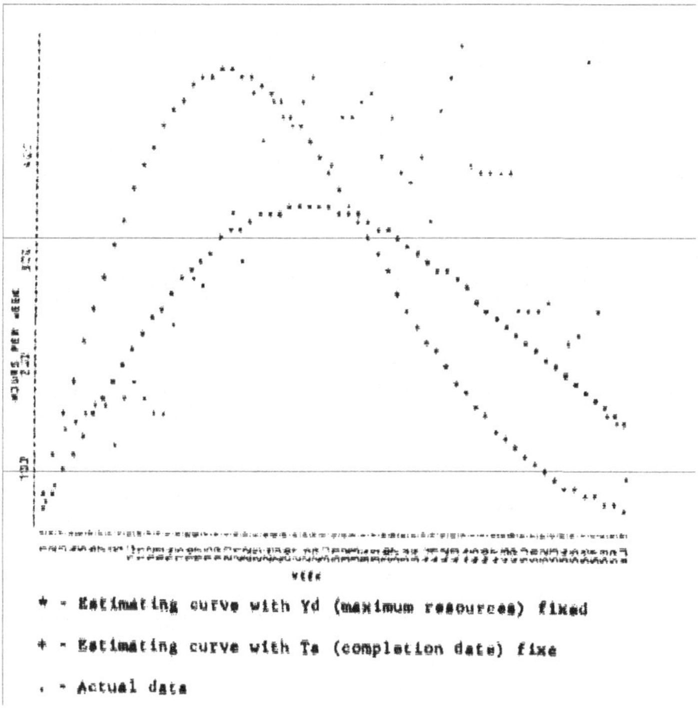

Figure 2. Project B – Estimated resource expenditures curves

From our own smaller projects, we found that this gives answers consistently higher by about 8 to 10 weeks, therefore we are using our own .88K rule to determine acceptance testing. Why our projects do not agree with the empirical evidence of large scale projects in this area is now under study.

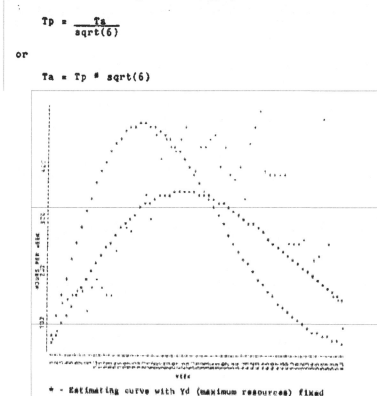

Taking the given value of K, two different Rayleigh curve estimates were plotted for each of two different projects (referred to as projects A and B) by adjusting the constant a. For one estimating curve it was assumed that the estimate for maximum resources per week Yd was accurate and that the acceptance testing date Ta could vary, while in the other case the assumed acceptance testing date Ta was fixed and the constant a could be adjusted to determine maximum weekly expenditures Yd needed to meet the target date. These plots for the two different projects are shown as figures 1 and 2.

The curve limiting maximum weekly expenditures might be considered the more valuable of the two since it more closely approximates project development during the early stages of the project. In both projects A and B, the maximum resource estimate Yd was predicted to be insufficient for completing acceptance testing by the initially estimated completion date Ta. In project A the Rayleigh curve prediction for acceptance testing was 58 weeks instead of the proposed 46 weeks. The actual date was 62 weeks - yielding only a 7% error (Figure 3). The prediction for project B showed similar results.

	Project A	Project B
Initial Estimate from General Project Summary		
Ka, Resources needed (hours)	14,213	12,997
Ta, Time to completion (weeks)	46	41
Yd, Maximum resources/week (hours)	350	320
Completion Estimates using Rayleigh Curve		
K, Resources needed (hours)	16,151	14,770
Estimated Yd with Ta fixed (hours)	440	456
Estimated Ta with Yd fixed (hours)	59	58
Actual Project Data		
K, Resourced needed (hours)	17,742	16,543
Yd, Maximum resources (hours)	371	462
Ta, Completion time (weeks)	62	54
Ta, Estimated using actual values of K and Yd (weeks)	60	43

Figure 3. Estimating Ta and Td from General Project Summary Data

As it turned out, both projects used approximately 1600 hours more than initially estimated (10% for A and 12% for B) , and maximum weekly resources did not agree exactly with initial estimates. If these corrected figures for Ka and Yd are used in the analysis, then Ta, the date for acceptance testing, is 60 weeks instead of the actual 62 weeks for project A - an error of only 3% (Figure 3).

Note however that the corrected figures for project B yield a Ta of 44 weeks instead of the actual 54. This discrepancy is due in part to the extreme variance in actual development hours allocated to the project each week, especially towards the latter period (See figure 2). If an average maximum value of 425 hours per week is substituted for the absolute maximum, the projected completion date becomes 49 weeks, yielding an error of only 5 weeks.

It is clear from the analysis of this last data, that due to the size of the project and the effect small perturbations have on the prediction of results, that there is definitely a difference in the analysis of projects of the size being studied by the Laboratory and the large scale efforts reported in the literature. To demonstrate this point even further, consider the actual data in the curve in Figure 1. The significant drop in development activities during the weeks 21, 26 and 34 can be attributed to Thanksgiving, Christmas and Washington's Birthday, all holidays for the contractor. Thus our data is quite sensitive to holidays, employee illness, and project personnel changes.

3.2 Predicting Progress

In order to test the predictability of the model, curve fitting techniques to the actual data were used. The Rayleigh curve can be rewritten as:

$$\ln \left(\frac{y}{t}\right) = \ln c - a*t^2$$

where

$$K = \frac{e^c}{2*a}$$

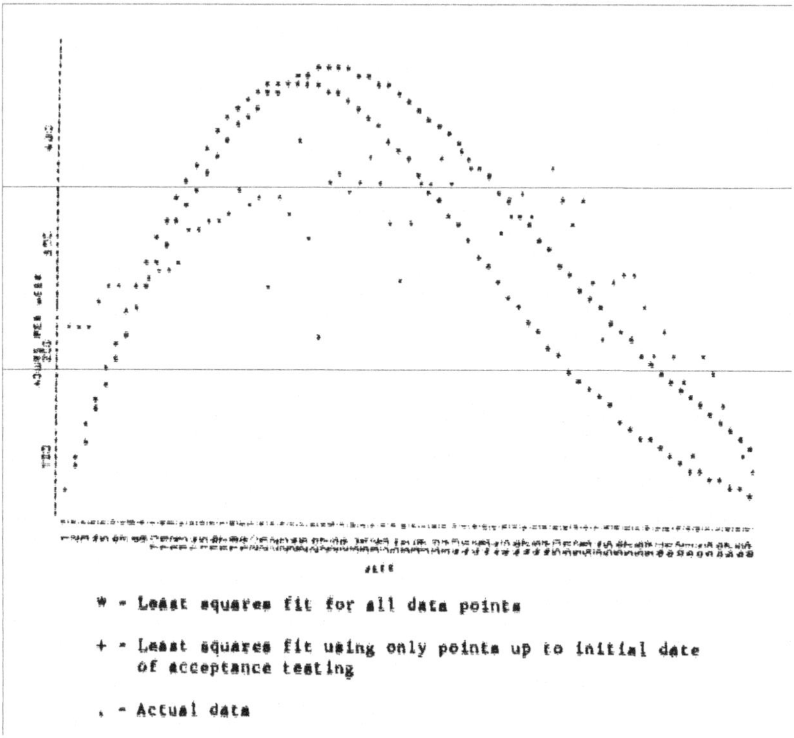

* - Least squares fit for all data points
+ - Least squares fit using only points up to initial date of acceptance testing
. - Actual data

Figure 4. Project A – Least squares fit for resource data

This equation can be used to derive the equation y=f(t) for the collected data (yi/ti, ti) using least squares techniques.

From this solution, figure 4 was plotted for project A. The * represents a best fit using all of the collected data points while the curve plotted with + represents a best fit based upon points up to the original point assumed to be acceptance testing (46 weeks for project A) to check the model's ability to predict completion.

Figure 5 summarizes the results. These are not very good, and Figure 6 is a possible explanation. On projects this small, the resource curve is mostly a step function. Thus assuming a Rayleigh curve estimate at point x results in an earlier, sharper decline while an estimate at y results in too little a decline. Starting with Norden's original assumptions that led to the Rayleigh curve as a predictor for large scale developments, current research is investigating variations to the basic curve so that it is "flatter" in its mid-range, and better approximates projects of this size.

	Project A	Project B
Least squares fit through all points		
K, in hours	20,087	17,964
Ta, in weeks	57	61
Least squares fit using points up to estimated acceptance testing date		
K, in hours	16,827	25,714
Ta, in weeks	49	61
Actual project data		
K, in hours	17,742	16,543
Ta, in weeks	62	54

Figure 5. Estimating K and Ta using least squares fit

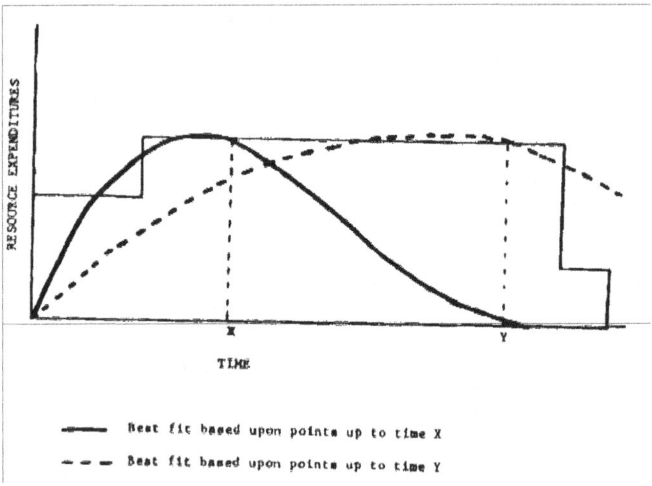

Figure 6. Rayleigh curve estimation on medium scale projects

3.3 Forecasting of Components

As part of the reporting procedure, the Component Status Report gives manpower data on each component of the system, and the Component Summary gives the necessary size and time estimates. Therefore equations can be developed for each component in the system. Thus we are able to estimate whether any piece of the system is on schedule or has slipped.

At the present time, summary data can be printed on expenditures for each component in a project. In figure 7, CM is a subsystem of the project, and the other listed components are a sample of the components of CM. The above algorithm is now being investigated to see whether all components should be checked and some indication (such as a * next to the name) made if a component seems to be slipping from its estimated schedule. In the future, more accurate predictions of K from Ka will be investigated. How well the basic Rayleigh curve fits this data is also being studied. In addition, we would like to collect data from the analysis and maintenance sections at NASA to include the requirements, specifications and maintenance phases in the lifetime of each project.

	HOURS ON EACH ACTIVITY				DATE LAST	ESTIMATED	
COMPONENT	DESIGN	CODE	TEST	TOTAL	REFERENCED	HOURS	COMPLETION
CM			79	79	9/16/77		
CMARRO		12	9	21	7/ 8/77	15	7/18/77
CMARRP		6	3	9	5/18/77	14	6/30/77
CMASP		7	1	8	2/18/77	5	5/ 1/77
CMCMP		8	10	18	2/11/77	15	6/30/77
CMDRIV		2	3	5	3/11/77	10	6/19/77
CMDTGT	1	10	11	22	4/ 1/77	5	4/15/77

Figure 7. Resource data by components (Data collection on this project began after design phase completed, so little design time shown.)

Putnam lists only two parameters affecting overall system development: total manpower needs and maximum manpower. What effects do other programming techniques have (if any) on the shape of this curve? For example, proponents of many methodologies, such as structured programming, predict a slower rise in the curve using the proposed techniques.

4. Other investigations

Besides project forecasting, several other areas are under investigation. Some of these are briefly described in the following paragraphs.

4.1 Overhead

Overhead is often an elusive item to pin down. In our projects three aspects of development have been identified: programmer effort, project management, and support items (typing, librarians, clerical, etc.). In one project programmers accounted for about 80% of total expenditures with the support activities taking about one third of the remaining resources. In addition, only about 60% of all programmer time was accountable to explicit components of the system. The remaining time includes activities like meetings, traveling, attending training sessions, and other activities not directly accountable. As others have shown, this figure must be included in computing effective workloads in hours per week.

4.2 Error Analysis

One early investigation using the collected change reports, was to test the hypothesis of Belady and Lehman [1976]. By studying several large systems, they determined that for each release of a given system, the per cent of modules altered since the previous release was constant over time ("handling rate"). Since our own data was mostly data collected during integration testing, the extension of their results was tested in our own environment. In addition, besides the handling rate, we also wanted to investigate the report rate, or the rate at which changes were reported over time on the developing system.

Figure 8(a) shows this early evaluation, which clearly does not represent a constant handling rate. The maximum rate of handling modules occurs in the middle of the testing period.

One result which was surprising, however, is the report rate of figure 8(b). This represents the number of change reports submitted each week. This figure did remain constant for almost the entire development time.

In order to test this second result further, data from a second project was plotted. It too had handling rates and report rates similar to the above project. This phenomenon will be studied in greater detail in the future.

5. Summary

The major contribution of the Laboratory to the field of software engineering is the ability to collect the kind of detailed data currently unavailable, and collect it for a class of projects (medium scale) that has not yet been well analyzed. The finer level of monitoring and data collection can yield better analysis and understanding of the details of the development process and product. The medium scale size of the projects permit us to study more projects although it is clear that good data collection techniques are more important here than in larger projects because mistakes can have a much stronger impact. The large number of projects being compared also permits various software development parameters and techniques to be analyzed and compared with quantitative assessments by correlating data across several projects.

The current status of projects in the Laboratory have permitted us to begin reporting back to management the status of projects and to begin analyzing individual aspects of projects, checking their relationships to large scale project results found in the literature. The model of resource utilization via the Rayleigh curve is an important idea that is being investigated. Error rates and their causes are also under study. Since the Laboratory only started to collect data in December of 1976, and since most projects take from 12 to 18 months to complete, the first few projects are only now being completed; however, within the next 4 to 6 months, about four more projects will be ready for analysis. This will allow for more careful comparisons with the data already collected.

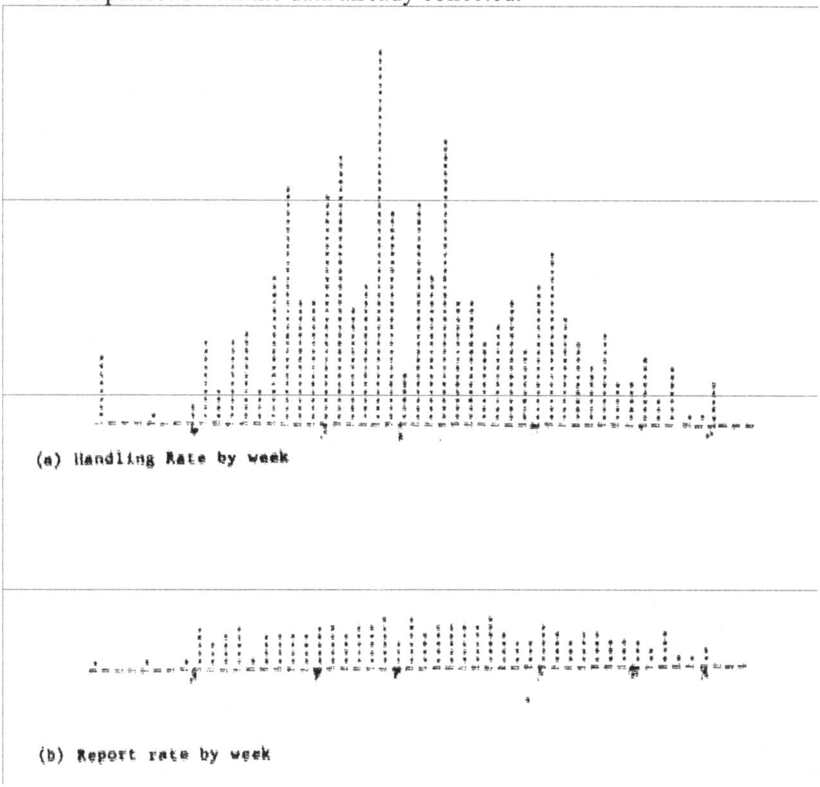

Figure 8. Handling and report rate of project A

6. Acknowledgements

We would like to acknowledge the contributions and cooperation of Mr. Frank McGarry, head of the Systems Development Section of NASA Goddard Space Flight Center. He has been instrumental in organizing the Laboratory and in interfacing with the contractor in order to see that the data is collected reliably and timely. We would also like to thank Computer Sciences Corporation for their patience during form development and their contributions to the organization and operation of the Laboratory.

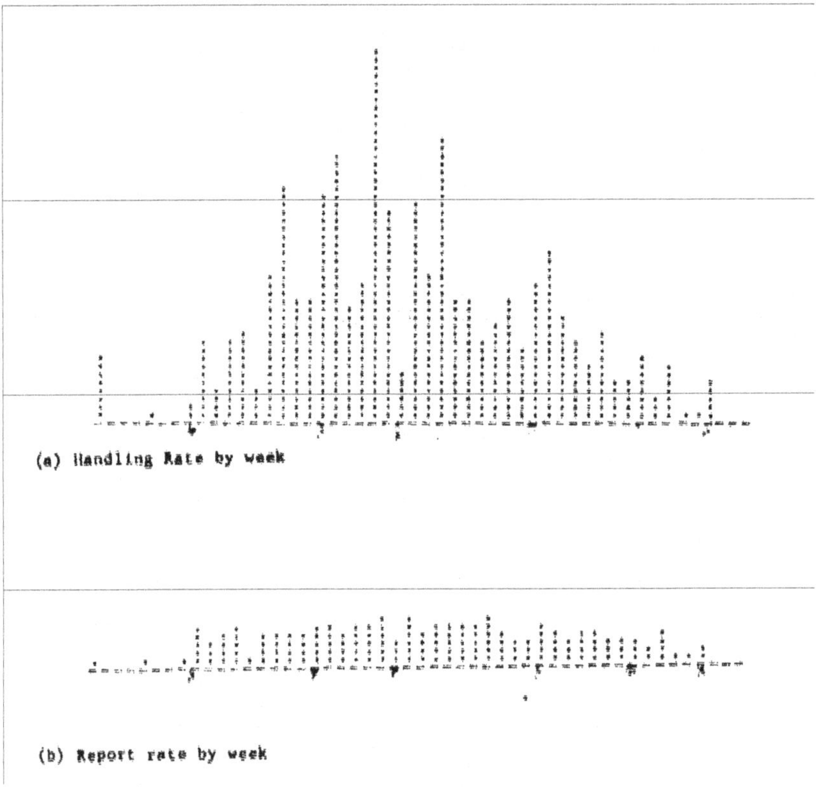

Figure 8. Handling and report rate of project A

References

[Baker] Baker F. T., Structured programming in a. production programming environment, International Conference on Reliable Software, Los Angeles, April, 1975 (SIGPLAN Notices 10, No. 6, 172-185).

[Basili & Zelkowitz] Basili V. and M. Zelkowitz, The Software Engineering Laboratory: Objectives, Proceedings of the Fifteenth Annual ACM Computer Personnel Research Conference, Washington D. C., August, 1977.

[Belady & Lehman] Belady L. A. and M. M. Lehman, A model of large program development, IBM Systems Journal 15, No. 3, 1976, 225-252.

[Held] Held G., M. Stonebraker, E. Wong, INGRES - a relational data base system, National Computer Conference, 1975, 409-416.

[Myers] Myers G., Software Reliability through composite design. Mason Charter, New York, 1975.

[Norden] Norden P., Use tools for project management, Management of Production. M. K. Starr (ed), Penguin Books, Baltimore, Md., 1970, 71-101.

[Putnam] Putnam L., A macro-estimating methodology for software development, IEEE Computer Society Compcon, Washington, D. C., September, 1976, 138-143.

[Putnam2] Putnam L., Private communication.

[Walston & Felix] Walston C. E. and C. P. Felix, A method of program measurement and estimation, IBM Systems Journal 16, No. 1, 1977, 54-73.

[Wolverton] Wolverton R. W., The cost of developing large scale software, IEEE Transactions on Computers 23, No. 6, June, 1974, 615-636.

Software Process Evolution at the SEL

Victor R. Basili and Scott Green

Abstract. The Software Engineering Laboratory has been adapting, analyzing, and evolving software processes for the last 18 years. Their approach is based on the Quality Improvement Paradigm, which is used to evaluate process effects on both product and people. The authors explain this approach as it was applied to reduce defects in code.

Since 1976, the Software Engineering Laboratory of the National Aeronautics and Space Administration's Goddard Space Flight Center has been engaged in a program of understanding, assessing, and packaging software experience. Topics of study include process, products, resource, and, defect models, as well as specific technologies and tools. The approach of the SEL – a consortium of the Software Engineering Branch of NASA Goddard's Flight Dynamics Division, the Computer Science Department of the University of Maryland, and the Software Engineering Operation of Computer Sciences Corp. - has been to gain an in-depth understanding of project and environment characteristics using process models and baselines. A process is evaluated for study, applied experimentally to a project, analyzed with respect to baselines and process model, and evaluated in terms of the experiment's goals. Then on the basis of the experiment's conclusions, results are packaged and the process is tailored for improvement, applied again, and reevaluated.

In this article, we describe our improvement approach, the Quality Improvement Paradigm, as the SEL applied it to reduce code defects by emphasizing reading techniques. The box on p.63 describes the Quality Improvement Paradigm in detail. In examining and adapting reading techniques, we go through a systematic process of evaluating the candidate and refining its implementation through lessons learned from previous experiments and studies.

As a result of this continuous, evolutionary process, we determined that we could successfully apply key elements of the Cleanroom development method in the SEL environment, especially for projects involving fewer than 50,000 lines of code (all references to lines of code refer to developed, not delivered, lines of code). We saw indications of lower error rates, higher productivity, a more complete and consistent set of code comments, and a redistribution of developer effort. Although we have not seen similar reliability and cost gains for larger efforts, we continue to investigate the Cleanroom method's effect on them.

Victor Basili is with the University of Maryland and Scott Green is with NASA Goddard Space Flight Center.

1. Evaluating candidate processes

To enhance the possibility of improvement in a particular environment, the SEL introduces and evaluates new technology within that environment. This involves experimentation with the new technology, recording findings in the context of lessons learned, and adjusting the associated processes on the basis of this experience. When the technology is notably risky - substantially different from what is familiar to the environment – or requires more detailed evaluation than would normally be expended, the SEL conducts experimentation off-line from the project environment.

Off-line experiments may take the form of either controlled experiments or case studies. Controlled experiments are warranted when the SEL needs a detailed analysis with statistical assurance in the results. One problem with controlled experiments is that the project must be small enough to replicate the experiment several times. The SEL then performs a case study to validate the results on a project of credible size that is representative of the environment. The case study adds validity and credibility through the use of typical development systems and professional staff. In analyzing both controlled experiments and case studies, the Goal/Question/Metric paradigm, described in the box on p. 63, provides an important framework for focusing the analysis.

On the basis of experimental results, the SEL, packages a set of lessons learned and makes them available in an experience base for future analysis and application of the technology.

Experiment 1; Reading versus testing. Although the SEL had historically been a test-driven organization, we decided to experiment with introducing reading techniques. We were particularly interested in how reading would compare with testing for fault detection. The goals of the first off-line, controlled experiment were to analyze and compare code reading, functional testing, and structural testing, and to evaluate them with respect to fault-detection effectiveness, cost, and classes of faults detected.

We needed to analysis from the viewpoint of quality assurance as well as a comparison of performance with respect to software type and programmer experience. Using the GQM paradigm, we generated specific questions on the basis of these goals.

We had subjects use reading by stepwise abstraction, equivalence-partitioning boundary-value testing, and statement-coverage structural testing.

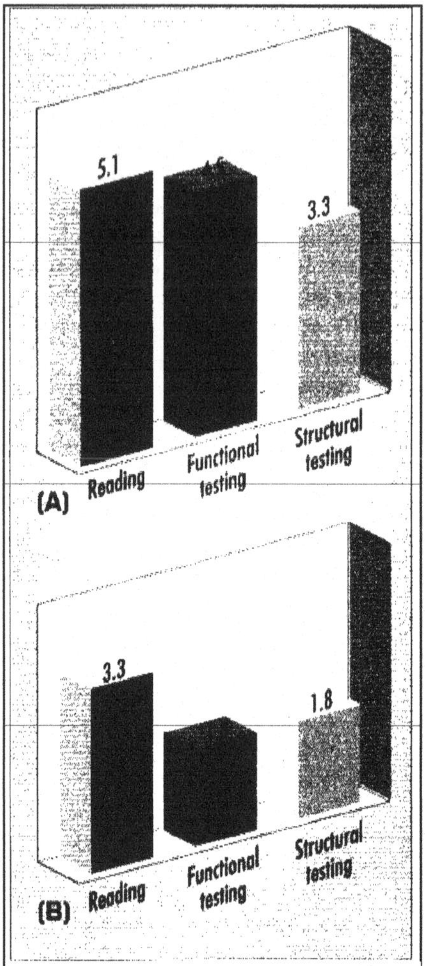

Figure 1. Results of the reading-versus-testing controlled experiment, in which reading was compared with functional and structural testing. (A) Mean number of faults detected for each technique and (B) number of faults detected per hour of use for each technique.

We conducted the experiment twice at the University of Maryland on graduate students (42 subjects) and once at NASA Goddard (32 subjects). The experiment structure was a fractional factorial design, in which every subject applied each technique on a different program. The programs included a text formatter, a plotter, an abstract data type, and a database, and they ranged from 145 to 365 lines of code. We seeded each program with faults. The reading performed was at the level of unit level.

Although the results from both experiments support the emphasis on reading techniques, we report only the results of the controlled experiment on the NASA Goddard subjects because it involved professional developers in the target environment.

Figure 1 shows the fault-detection effectiveness and rate for each approach for the NASA Goddard experiment. Reading by stepwise abstraction proved superior to the testing techniques in both the effectiveness and cost of fault detection, while obviously using fewer computer resources.

Even more interesting was that the subjects did a better job of estimating the code quality using reading than they did using testing. Readers thought they had only found about half the faults (which was nominally correct), while functional testers felt that had found essentially all the faults (which was never correct).

Furthermore, after completing the experiment, more than 90 percent of the participants thought functional testing had been the most effective technique, although the results clearly showed otherwise. This gave us some insight into the psychological effects of reading versus testing. Perhaps one reason testing appeared more satisfying was that the successful execution of multiple test cases generated a greater comfort level with the product quality, actually providing the tester with a false sense of confidence.

Reading was also more effective in uncovering most classes of faults, including interface faults. This told us that perhaps reading might scale up well on larger projects.

Experiment 2; Validation with Cleanroom. On the basis of these results, we decided to emphasize reading techniques in the SEL environment. However, we saw little improvement in overall reliability of development systems. Part of the reason may have been that SEL project personnel had developed such faith in testing that the quality of their reading was relaxed, with the assumption that testing would ultimately uncover the same faults. We conducted a small off-line experiment at the University of Maryland to test this hypothesis; the results supported our assumption. (We did this on a small scale just to verify our hypothesis before continuing with the Cleanroom experiment).

Why the Cleanroom method? The Cleanroom method emphasizes human discipline in the development process, using a mathematically based design approach and a statistical testing approach based on anticipated operational use. Development and testing teams are independent, and all development-team activities are performed without on-line testing.

Techniques associated with the method are the use of box structures and state machines, reading by stepwise abstraction, formal correctness demonstrations, and peer review. System development is performed through pipeline of small increments to enhance concentration and permit testing and development to occur in parallel.

Because the Cleanroom method removes developer testing and relies on human discipline, we felt it would overcome the psychological barrier of reliance on testing.

Applying the QIP. The first step of the Quality Improvement Paradigm is to characterize the project and its environment. The removal of developer unit testing made the Cleanroom method a high-risk technology. Again, we used off-line experimentation at the University of Maryland as a mitigating approach. The environment was a laboratory course at the university, and the project involved an electronic message system of about 1,500 LOC. The experiment structure was a simple replicated design, in which control and experiment teams are defined. We assigned 10 three-person experiment teams to use the Cleanroom method. We gave five three-person control teams the same development methodology, but allowed them to test their systems. Each team was allowed five independent test submissions of their programs. We collected data on programmer background and attitude, computer-resource activity, and actual testing results.

The second step in the Quality Improvement Paradigm is to set goals. The goal here was to analyze the effects of the Cleanroom approach and evaluate it with respect to process, product, and participants, as compared with the non-Cleanroom approach. We generated questions corresponding to this goal, focusing on the method's effect on each aspect being studied.

The next step of the Quality Improvement Paradigm involves selecting an appropriate process model. The process model selected for this experiment was the

Cleanroom approach as defined by Harlan Mills at IBM's Federal Systems Division, but modified for our environment. For example, the graduate-student assistant for the course served as each group's independent test team. Also, because we used a language unfamiliar to the subjects to prevent bias, there was a risk of errors due solely to ignorance about the language. We therefore allowed teams to cleanly compile their code before submitting it to the tester.

Because of the nature of controlled experimentation, we made few modifications during the experiment.

Cleanroom's effect on the software development process resulted in the Cleanroom developers more effectively applying the off-line reading techniques, the non-Cleanroom teams focused their efforts more on functional testing than the reading. The Cleanroom teams spent less time on-line, and were more successful in making scheduled deliveries. Further analysis revealed that the Cleanroom products had less dense complexity, a higher percentage of assignment statements, more global data, and more code comments. These products also more completely met the system requirements and had a higher percentage of successful independent test cases.

The Cleanroom developers indicated that they modified their normal software-development activities by doing a more effective job of reading, though they missed the satisfaction of actual program execution. Almost all said they would be willing to use Cleanroom on another development assignment. Through observation, it was also clear that the Cleanroom developers did not apply the formal methods associated with Cleanroom very rigorously. Furthermore, we did not have enough failure data or experience with Cleanroom testing to apply a reliability model. However, general analysis did indicate that the Cleanroom approach had potential payoff, and that additional investigation was warranted.

You can also view this experiment from the following perspective: We applied two development approaches. The only real difference between them was that the control teams had one extra piece of technology (developer testing), yet they did not perform as well as the experiment teams. One explanation might be that the control group did not use the available non-testing techniques as effectively because they knew they could rely on testing to detect faults. This supports our earlier findings associated with the reading-versus-testing experiment.

2. Evolving selected process

The positive results gathered from these two experiments gave us the justification we needed to explore the Cleanroom method in case studies, using typical development systems as data points. We conducted two case studies to examine the method, again following steps of the Quality Improvement Paradigm. A third case study was also recently begun.

First Case Study. The project we selected, Project 1, involved two subsequent systems. The system performs ground processing to determine a spacecraft's altitude, receiving and processing spacecraft telemetry data to meet the requirements of a particular mission.

The subsystems we chose are an integral part of attitude determination and are highly algorithmic. Both are interactive programs that together contain approximately 40,000 LOC, representing about 12 percent of the entire attitude ground-support system. The rest of the ground-support system was developed using the standard SEL development methodology.

The project was staffed principally by five people from the Flight Dynamics Division, which houses the SEL. All five were also working on other projects, so only part of their time was allocated to the two subsystems. Their other responsibility often took time and attention away from the case study, but this partial allocation represents typical staffing in this environment. All other projects with which the Project 1 staff were involved were non-Cleanroom efforts, so staff members would often be required to use multiple development methodologies, during the same workday.

The primary goal of the first case study was to increase software quality and reliability without increasing cost. We also wanted to compare the characteristics of the Cleanroom method with those typical of the FDD environment. A well-calibrated baseline was available for comparison that described a variety of process characteristics, including effort distribution, change rates, error rates, and productivity. The baseline represents the history of many earlier SEL studies. Figure 2 shows sample of the expected variations from the SEL baselines for a set of process characteristics.

	Sample measures	Sample baseline	Sample expectation
Process	Effort distribution Change profile	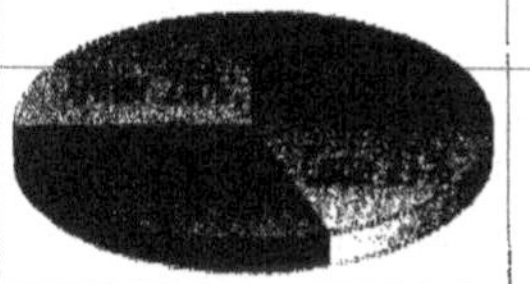	Increased design effort because of emphasis on peer-review process
Cost	Productivity Level of rework Impact of specification changes	Historically, 26 lines of code per day	No degradation from current level
Reliability	Error rate Error distribution Error source	Historically, seven errors per thousand lines of code	Decreased error rate

Figure 2. *Sample measures, baselines, and expectations for the case studies investigating the Cleanroom method.*

Choosing and tailoring processes. The process models available for examination were the standard SEL model, which represents a reuse-oriented waterfall life-cycle model; the IBM/FSD Cleanroom model, which appeared in the literature and was available through training, and the experimental University of Maryland Cleanroom model, which was used in the earlier controlled experiment [4].

We examined the lessons learned from applying the IBM and University of Maryland models. The results from the IBM model were notably positive, showing that the basic process, methods and techniques were effective for that particular environment. However, the process model had been applied by the actual developers of the methodology, in the environment for which it was developed. The University of Maryland model also had specific lessons, including the effects of not allowing developers to test their code, the effectiveness of the process on a small project, and the conclusion that formal methods appeared particularly difficult to apply and required specific skills.

Based upon these lessons and the environment within which the study was to be conducted, the initial SEL Cleanroom process model included four key elements:

On the basis of these lessons and the characteristics of our environment, we selected a Cleanroom process model with four key elements:

- separation of development and test teams
- reliance on peer review instead of unit-level testing as the primary developer verification technique
- use of informal state machines and functions to define the system design, and
- a statistical approach to testing based on operational scenarios.

We also provided training for the subjects, consistent with a University of Maryland course on the Cleanroom process model, methods, and techniques with emphasis on reading through stepwise abstraction. We also stressed code reading by multiple reviewers because stepwise abstraction was new to many subjects. Michael Dyer and Terry Baker of IBM/FSD provided additional training and motivation by describing IBM's use of Cleanroom.

To mitigate risk and address the developers' concerns, we examined back out options for the experiment. For example, because the subsystems were highly mathematical, we were afraid it would be difficult to find and correct mathematical errors without any developer testing. Because the project was part of an operational system with mission deadlines, we discussed options that ranged from allowing developer unit testing to discontinuing Cleanroom altogether. These discussions helped allay the primary apprehension of NASA Goddard management in using the new methodology. When we could not get information about process application, we followed SEL process-model activities.

We also noted other management and project-team concerns. Requirements and specifications change frequently during the development cycle in the FDD environment. This instability was of particular concern because the Cleanroom method is built on the precept of developing software right the first time. Another concern was that, given the difficulties encountered in the University of Maryland experiment about applying formal methods, how successfully could a classical Cleanroom approach be applied: Finally, there was concern about the psychological effects of separating development and testing, specifically the inability of the developers to execute their code. We targeted all these concerns for our post project analysis.

Project 1 lasted from January 1988 through September 1990. We separated the five team members into three-person development team and a two-person test team. The development team broke the total effort into six incremental builds of approximately 6,500 LOC each. An experimenter team consisting of NASA Goddard managers, SEL representatives, a technology advocate familiar with the IBM model, and the project leader monitored the overall process.

We modified the process in real time, as needed. For example, when we merged Cleanroom products into the standard FDD formal review and documentation activities, we had to modify both. We altered the design process to combine the use of state machines and traditional structured design. We also collected data for the monitoring team at various points throughout the project, although we tried to do this with as little disturbance as possible to the project team.

Analyzing and packaging results. The final steps in the QIP involve analyzing and packaging the process results. We found significant differences in effort distribution during development between the Cleanroom project and the baseline. Approximately six percent of the total project effort shifted from coding to design activities in the Cleanroom effort. Also, the baseline development teams traditionally spent approximately 85 percent of their coding effort writing code, 15 percent reading it. The Cleanroom team spent about 50 percent in each activity.

The primary goal of the first case study had been to improve reliability without increasing cost to develop. Analysis showed a reduction in change rate of nearly 50 percent and a reduction in error rate of greater than a third. Although the expectation was for a productivity equivalent to the baseline, the Cleanroom effort also improved in that area by approximately 50 percent. We also saw a decrease in rework effort, as defined by the amount of time spent correcting errors. Additional analysis of code reading revealed that three fourths of all efforts uncovered were found by only one reader. This prompted a renewed emphasis on multiple readers throughout the SEL environment.

We also examined the earlier concerns expressed by the managers and project team. The results showed increased effort in early requirements analysis and design activities and a clearer set of in-line comments. This led to a better understanding of the whole system and enabled the project team to understand and accommodate changes with greater ease than was typical for the environment.

We reviewed the application of classical Cleanroom and noted successes and difficulties. The structure of independent teams and emphasis on peer review during development was easy to apply. However, the development team did have difficulty using the associated formal methods. Also, unlike the scheme in the classical Cleanroom method, the test team followed an approach that combined statistical testing with traditional functional testing.

Finally, the psychological effects of independent testing appeared to be negligible. All team members indicated high job satisfaction as well as a willingness to apply the method in future projects.

We packaged these early results in various reports and presentations, including the SEL's 1990 Software Engineering Workshop. As a reference for future SEL Cleanroom projects, we also began efforts to produce a document describing the SEL Cleanroom process model, including details on specific activities. [6] (The completed document is now available to current Cleanroom projects).

Second Case Study. The first case study showed us that we needed better training in the use of formal methods and more guidance in applying the testing approach. We also realized that experiences from the initial project team had to be disseminated and used.

Again, we followed the Quality Improvement Paradigm. We selected two projects: one similar to the initial Cleanroom project. Project 2A and one more representative of the typical FDD contractor-support environment, Project 2B.

Project 2A involved a different subsystem of another attitude ground-support system. This subsystem focused on the processing of telemetry data, comprising 22,000 LOC. The project was staffed with four developers and two testers. Project 2B involved an entire mission attitude ground-support system, consisting of approximately 160,000 LOC. At its peak, it was staffed with 14 developers and four testers.

Setting Goals and choosing processes. The second case study had two goals. One was to verify measure from the first study by applying the Cleanroom method to Project 2A, a project of similar size and scope. The second was to verify the applicability of Cleanroom on Project 2B, a substantially larger project but one more representative of the typical environment. We also wanted to further tailor the process model to the environment by using results from the first case study and applying more formal techniques.

Packages from the SEL Experience Factory (described in the box on p. 63) were available to support project development These included an evolved training program, a more knowledgeable experimenter team to monitor the projects, and several in-process interactive sessions with the project teams. Although we had begun producing a handbook detailing the SEL Cleanroom process model, it was not ready in time to give to the teams at the start of these projects.

The project leader for the initial Cleanroom project participated as a member of the experimenter team, served as the process modeler for the handbook and acted as a consultant to the current projects.

We modified the process according to the experiences of the Cleanroom team in the first study. Project 1's team had had difficulty using state machines in system design, so we changed the emphasis to Mills' box-structure algorithm.[7] We also added a more extensive training program focusing on Cleanroom techniques, experiences from the initial Cleanroom team, and the relationship between the Cleanroom studies and the SEL's general goals. The instruction team included representatives from the SEL, members of the initial team, and Mills. Mills gave talks on various aspects of the methodology, as well as motivational remarks on the potential benefits of the Cleanroom method in the software community.

Project 2A ran from March 1990 through January 1992. Project 2B ran from February 1990 through December 1992. Again, we examined reliability, productivity, and process characteristics, comparing them to Project 1 results and the SEL baseline.

Analyzing and packaging results. As Figure 3 shows, there were significant differences between the two projects. Error and change rates for Project 2A continued to be favorable. Productivity rate, however, returned to the SEL baseline value. Error and change rates for Project 2B increased from Project 1 values, although they remained lower than SEL baseline numbers. Productivity, however, dropped below the baseline.

When we examined the effort distribution among the baseline and Projects 1, 2A and 2B, we found a continuing upward trend in the percentage of design effort, and a corresponding decrease in coding effort. Additional analysis indicated that although the overall error rates were below the baseline, the percentage of system components found to contain errors during testing was still representative of baseline projects developed in this environment. This suggests that the breadth of error distribution did not change with the Cleanroom method.

In addition to evaluating objective data for these two projects, we gathered subjective input through written and verbal feedback from project participants. In general, input from Project 2A team members, the smaller of the two projects, was very favorable, while Project 2B members, the larger contractor team, had significant reservations about the method's application. Interestingly, though, specific short-comings were remarkably similar for both teams. Four areas were generally cited in the comments. Participants were dissatisfied with the use of design abstractions and box structures, did not fully accept the rationale for having no developer compilation, had problems coordinating information between developers and testers, and cited the need for a reference to the SEL Cleanroom process model.

Again, we packaged these results into various reports and presentations, which formed the basis for additional process tailoring.

Third Case Study. We have recently begun a third case study to examine difficulties in scaling up the Cleanroom method in the typical contractor-support environment and to verify previous trends and analyze additional tailoring of the SEL process model. We expect the study to complete in September.

In keeping with this goal, we again selected a project representative of the FDD contractor-support environment, but one that was estimated at 110,000 LOC, somewhat smaller than Project 2B. The project involves development of another entire mission attitude ground-support system. Several team members have prior experience with the Cleanroom method through previous SEL studies.

Experience Factory packages available to this project include training in the Cleanroom method, an experienced experimenter team, and the SEL Cleanroom Process Model (the completed handbook). In addition to modifying the process model according to the results from the first two case studies, we are providing

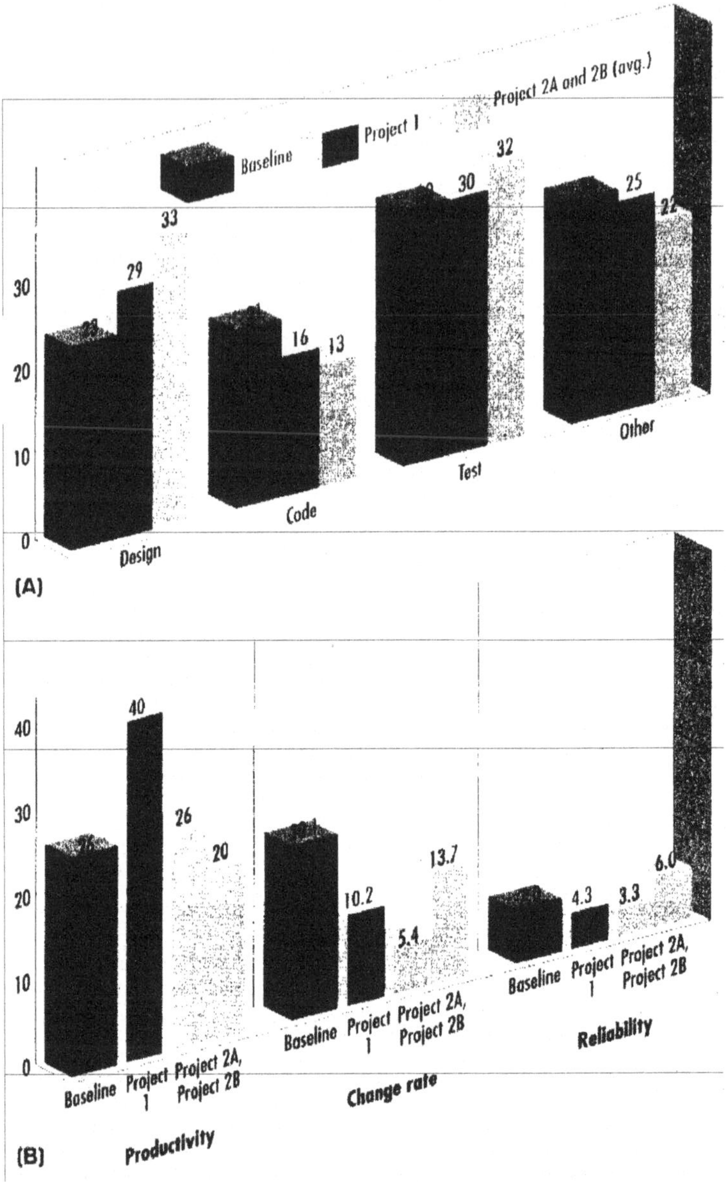

Figure 3. *Measurement comparisons for two case studies investigating Cleanroom. The first case study involved one project, Project 1. The second case study involved two projects, 2A and 2B. (A) Percentage of total development effort for various development activities, and (B) productivity in lines of code per day, change rate in changes per thousands of lines of code, and reliability in errors per thousand lines of code.*

regularly scheduled sessions in which the team members and experimenters can interact. These sessions give team members the opportunity to communicate problems they are having in applying the method, ask for clarification, and get feedback on their activities. This activity is aimed at closing a communication gap that the contractor team felt existed in Project 2B.

The concepts associated with the QIP and its use of measurement has given us an evolutionary framework for understanding, assessing, and packaging the SEL's experiences.

TABLE 1
PROJECT COMPARISONS FOR SEL TECHNOLOGY EVALUATION

Evaluation aspect	Controlled experiments		Cleanroom case studies		
	Reading vs. testing	Cleanroom	Project 1	Project 2A	Project 2B
Team size	32 participants	Three-person development teams (10 experiment teams; five control teams); common independent tester	Three-person development team; two-person test team	Four-person development team; two-person test team	Fourteen-person development team; four-person test team
Project size and application	Small (145–365 LOC) sample Fortran programs	1,500 LOC, Fortran, electronic message system for graduate laboratory course	40,000 LOC, Fortran, flight dynamics ground support system	22,000 LOC, Fortran, flight dynamics ground support system	160,000 LOC, Fortran, flight-dynamics ground support system
Results	Reading techniques appear more effective than testing techniques for fault detection	Cleanroom teams use fewer computer resources, satisfy requirements more successfully, and make higher percentage of scheduled deliveries	Project spends higher percentage of effort in design, uses fewer computer resources, and achieves better productivity and reliability than environment baseline	Project continues trend in better reliability while maintaining baseline productivity	Project reliability only slightly better than baseline while productivity falls below baseline

Table 1 shows how the evolution of our Cleanroom study progressed as we used measurements from each experiment and case study to define the next experiment or study. The SEL Cleanroom process model has evolved on the basis of results packaged through earlier evaluations. Some aspects of the target methodology continue to evolve: Experimentation with formal methods has transitioned from functional decomposition and state machines to box-structure design and again to box-structure application as a way to abstract requirements. Testing has shifted from a combined statistical/functional approach, to a purely statistical approach based on operational scenarios. Our current case study is examining the effect of allowing developer compilation.

Along the way, we have eliminated some aspects of the candidate process: we have not examined reliability models, for example, since the environment does not currently have sufficient data to seed them. We have also emphasized some aspects. For example, we are conducting studies that focus on the effect of peer reviewers and independent test teams for non-Cleanroom projects. We are also studying how to improve reading by developing reading techniques through offline experimentation.

The SEL baseline used for comparison is undergoing continual evolution. Promising techniques are filtered into the development organization as general process improvements, and corresponding measures of the modified process (effort distribution, reliability, cost) indicate the effect on the baseline.

The SEL Cleanroom process model has evolved to a point where it appears applicable to smaller projects (fewer than 50,000 LOC), but additional understanding and tailoring is still required for larger scale efforts. The model will continue to evolve as we gain more data from development projects. Measurement will provide baseline for comparison, identify areas of concern and improvement, and provide insight into the effects of process modifications. In this way, we can set quantitative expectations and evaluate the degree to which goals have been achieved.

By adhering to the Quality Improvement Paradigm, we can refine the process model from study-to-study, assessing strengths and weaknesses, experiences, and goals. However, our investigation into the Cleanroom method illustrates that the evolutionary infusion of technology is not trivial and that process improvement depends on a structured approach of understanding, assessment, and packaging.

3. Acknowledgements

This work has been supported by NASA/GSFC contract NSG-5123. We thank all the members of the SEL team who have been part of the Cleanroom experimenter teams, the Cleanroom training teams, and the various Cleanroom project teams. We especially thank Frank McGarry, Rose Pajerski, Sally Godfrey, Ara Kouchadjian, Sharon Waligora, Dr. Harlan Mills, Michael Dyer and Terry Baker for their efforts.

References

[1] Victor R. Basili, R. W. Selby, "Comparing the Effectiveness of Software Testing Strategies," IEEE Transactions on Software Engineering, Vol. SE-13, No. 12, December 1987, pp. 1278-1296.
[2] R. Linger, H. Mills, and B. Witt, Structured Programming: Theory and Practice, Addison Wesley, Reading, Mass., 1979.
[3] H. D. Mills, M. Dyer, and R. C. Linger, "Cleanroom Software Engineering," IEEE Software, September, 1987, pp. 19-24.
[4] R. W. Selby, Jr., V. R. Basili, and T. Baker, "CLEANROOM Software Development: An Empirical Evaluation," IEEE Transactions on Software Engineering, Vol. 13 no. 9, September, 1987, pp. 1027-1037.
[5] Linda Landis, Sharon Waligora, Frank McGarry, Rose Pajerski, Mike Stark, Kevin Johnson and Donna Cover, Recommended Approach to Software Development Revision 3, Software Engineering Laboratory, SEL-81-305, June 1992.
[6] Scott Green, Software Engineering Laboratory (SEL) Cleanroom Process Model, Software Engineering Laboratory, SEL-91-004, November 1991.
[7] H. D. Mills, "Stepwise Refinement and Verification in Box-Structured Systems," IEEE Software, June, 1988, pp. 23-36.

The Software Engineering Laboratory – An Operational Software Experience Factory

Victor Basili, Gianluigi Caldiera, University of Maryland
Frank McGarry, Rose Pajerski, National Aeronautics and Space Administration/Goddard Space Flight Center
Gerald Page and Sharon Waligora, Computer Science Corporation

Abstract. For 15 years the Software Engineering Laboratory (SEL) has been carrying out studies and experiments for the purpose of understanding, assessing, and improving software and software processes within a production software development environment at the National Aeronautics and Space Administration Goddard Space Flight Center (NASA/GSFC). The SEL comprises three major organizations:

- NASA/GSFC, Flight Dynamics Division
- University of Maryland. Department of Computer Science
- Computer Sciences Corporation Flight Dynamics Technology Group

These organizations have jointly carried out several hundred software studies, producing hundreds of reports, papers, and documents, all of which describe some aspect of the software engineering technology that has been analyzed in the flight dynamics environment at NASA. The studies range from small, controlled experiments (much as analyzing the effectiveness of code reading versus that of functional testing) to large, multiple-project studies (such as assessing the impacts of Ada on a production environment) The organization's driving goal is to improve the software process continually, so that sustained improvement may be observed in the resulting products. This paper discusses the SEL as a functioning example of an operational software experience factory and summarizes the characteristics of and major lessons learned from 15 years of SEL operations.

I. The Experience Factory Concept

Software engineering has produced a fair amount of research and technology transfer in the first 24 year of its existence. People have built technologies, methods, and tools that are used by many organizations in development and maintenance of software systems.

Unlike other disciplines, however, very little research has been done in the development of models for the various components of the discipline. Models have been developed primarily for the software product, providing mathematical models of its function and structure (e.g., finite state machines in object-oriented design), or, in some advanced instances, of its observable quality (e.g., reliability models). However, there has been very little modeling of several other important components of the software engineering discipline, such am processes, resources, and defects. Nor has much been done toward understanding the logical and physical integration of software engineering models, analyzing and evaluating them via experimentation and simulation, and refining and tailoring them to the characteristics and the needs of a specific application environment.

Currently, research and technology transfer in software engineering are done mostly bottom up and in isolation. To provide software engineering with a rigorous, scientific foundation and a pragmatic framework the following are needed [1]:

- A top-down, experimental, evolutionary framework in which research can be focused arid logically integrated to produce models of the discipline, which can then be evaluated and tailored to the application environment
- An experimental laboratory associated with the software artifact that is being produced and studied to develop and refine comprehensive models based upon measurement and evaluation

The three major concepts supporting this vision are

- A concept of evolution: the Quality Improvement Paradigm [2]
- A concept of measurement and control: the Gosh Question/Metric Approach [3]
- A concept of the organization: the Experience Factory [4]

The **Quality Improvement Paradigm** is a two-feedback loop process (project and organization loops) that is a variation of the scientific method It consists of the following steps:

- Characterization: Understand the environment based upon available models, data intuition etc, so that similarities to other projects can be recognized.
- Planning: Based on this characterization:
    - Set quantifiable goals for successful project and organization performance and improvement.
    - Choose the appropriate processes for improvement, and supporting methods and tools to achieve the goals in the given environment.
- Execution: Perform the processes while constructing the products and provide real-time project feedback based on the goal achievement data.
- Packaging: At the end of each specific project:
    - Analyze the data and the information gathered to evaluate the current practices, determine problems, record findings, and make recommendations for future process improvements.
    - Package the experience in the form of updated and refined models and other forms of structured knowledge gained from this and prior projects.
    - Store the packages in an experience base so they are available for future projects

The **Goal/Question/Metric Approach** is used to define measurements on the software project, process, and product in such a way that

- Resulting metrics art tailored to the organization and its goals
- Resulting in measurement data play a constructive and instructive role in the organization
- Metrics and their interpretation reflect the quality values and the different viewpoints (developers, users, operators, etc.)

Although originally tried to define and evaluate a particular project in a particular environment, the Goal/Question/Metric Approach can be used for control and improvement of a software project in the context of several projects within the

Goal/Question/Metric Approach defines a measurement model on three levels:

- Conceptual level (goal): A goal is defined for an object, for a variety of reasons with respect to various models of quality, from various points of view and relative to a particular environment.
- Operational level (question): A set of questions is used to define models of the object of study and the focuses on that object to characterize the assessment or achievement of a specific goal.
- Quantitative level (metric): A set of metrics based on the models is associated with every question in order to answer it in a quantitative way.

The concept of the Experience Factory was introduced to institutionalize the collective learning of the organization that is at the root of continual improvement and competitive advantage.

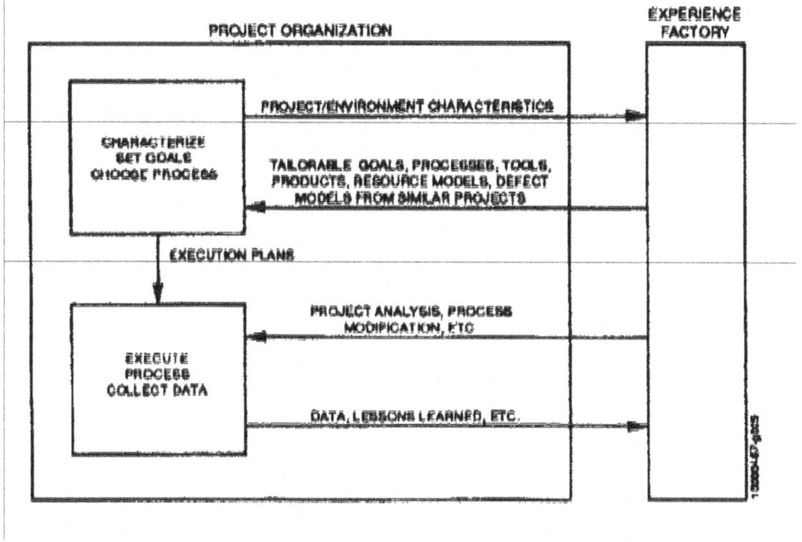

Figure 1. Project Organization Functions

Reuse of experience and collective learning cannot be left to the imagination of individual very talented, managers: they become a corporate concern, like the portfolio of a business or company assets. The experience factory is the organization that supports reuse of experience and collective learning by developing, updating, and delivering, upon request to the project organizations, clusters of competencies that the SEL refers to as experience packages. The project organizations offer to the experience factory their products, the plans used in their development, and the data gathered during development and operation (Figure 1). The experience factory transforms these objects into reusable units and supplies them to the project organizations, together with specific support that includes monitoring and consulting (Figure 2).

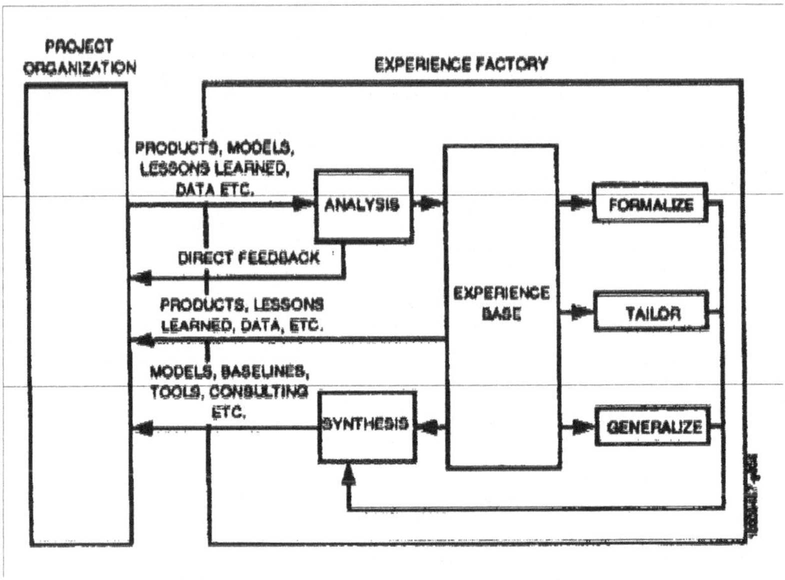

Figure 2. Experience Factory Functions

The experience factory can be a logical and/or physical organization, but it is important that its activities are separated and made independent from those of the project organization. The packaging of experience is based on tenets and techniques that are different from the problem solving activity used in project development [7].

On the one hand, from the perspective of an organization producing software, the difference is outlined in the following chart:

PROJECT ORGANIZATION (Problem Solving)	EXPERIENCE FACTORY (Experience Packaging)
Decomposition of a problem into simpler ones	Unification of different solutions and redefinition of the problem
Instantiation	Generalization, formalization
Design/implementation process	Analysis/synthesis process
Validation and verification	Experimentation

On the other hand from the perspective of software engineering research, there are the following goals:

PROJECT ORGANIZATION (Problem Solving)	EXPERIENCE FACTORY (Experience Packaging)
Develop representative languages for products processes	Develop techniques for abstraction generalization tailoring formalization analysis/synthesis
Develop techniques for design/implementation data collection/validation/ analysis validation and verification	Experiment with techniques
Build automatic support tools	Package and integrate for reuse experimental results processes/products

In a correct implementation of the experience factory paradigm, the projects and the factory will have different process models. Each project will choose its process model based on the characteristics of the software product that will be delivered whereas the factory will define (and change) its process model based upon organizational and performance tames The main product of the experience factory is the experience package There are a variety of software engineering experiences that can be packaged: resource baselines and models; change and defect baselines and models; product baselines and models; process definitions and models; method and technique models and evaluations; products; lessons learned; and quality models. The content and structure of an experience package vary based on the kind of experience clustered in the package. There is, generally, a central element that determines what the package is: a software life-cycle product or process, a mathematical relationship, an empirical or theoretical model a data base etc. This central element can be used to identify the experience package and produce a taxonomy of experience packages based on the characteristics of this central element:

- Product packages (programs, architectures, designs)
- Tool packages (constructive and analytic tools)
- Process packages (process models methods)
- Relationship packages (cost and defect models, resource models, etc)
- Management packages (guidelines decision support models)
- Data packages (defined and validated data, standardized data, etc)

The structure and functions of an efficient implementation of the experience factory concept are modeled on the characteristics and the goals of the organization it supports. Therefore different levels of abstraction best describe the architecture of an experience factory in order to introduce the specificity of each environment at the tight level without losing the representation of the global picture and the ability to compare different solutions [8].

The levels of abstraction that the SEL proposes to represent the architecture of an experience factory are as follows:

- Reference level: This first and more abstract level represents the activities in the experience factory by active objects, called architectural agents. They are specified by their ability to perform specific tasks and to interact with each other.
- Conceptual level: This level represents the interface of the architectural agents and the flows of data and control among them. They specify who communicates with whom, what is done in the experience factory, and what is done in the project organization. The boundary of the experience factory, i.e., the line that separates it front the project organization is defined at this level based on the needs and characteristics of an organization. It can evolve as these needs and characteristics evolve.
- Implementation level: This level defines the actual technical and organizational implementation of the architectural agents and their connections at the conceptual level. They are assigned process and product models synchronization and communication rules, and appropriate performers (people or computers). Other implementation details such as mapping the agents over organizational departments are included in the specifications provided at this level.

The architecture of the experience factory can be regarded as a special instance of an experience package whose design and evolution are based on the levels of abstraction just introduced and on the methodological framework of the improvement paradigm applied to the specific architecture.

The Software Engineering Laboratory (SEL) is an operating example of an experience factory. Figure 3 shows the conceptual level of the SEL experience factory, identifying the primary architectural agents and the interactions among them. The remaining sections describe the SEL implementation of the experience factory concept. They discuss its background, operations, and achievements and assess the impact it has had on the production environment it supports.

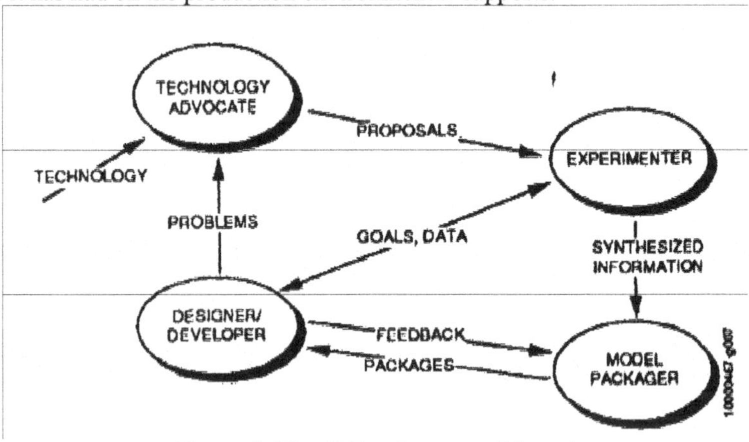

Figure 3. The SEL - Conceptual Level

2. SEL Background

The SEL was established in 1976 as a cooperative effort among the University of Maryland, the National Aeronautics and Space Administration Goddard Space Flight Center (NASA/GSFC), and Computer Sciences Corporation (CSC). Its goal was to understand and improve the software development process and its products within GSFC's Flight Dynamics Division (FDD). At that time although significant advances were being made in developing new technologies (e.g., structured development practices, automated tools, quality assurance approaches, and management tools), there was very hinted empirical evidence or guidance for applying these promising, yet immature, techniques. Additionally, it was apparent that there was very limited evidence available to qualify or to quantify the existing software process and associated products, let alone understand the impact of specific process methods Thus, the SEL staff initiated efforts to develop some means by which the software process could be understood (through measurement), qualified, and measurably improved through continually expanding understanding, experimentation, and process refinement.

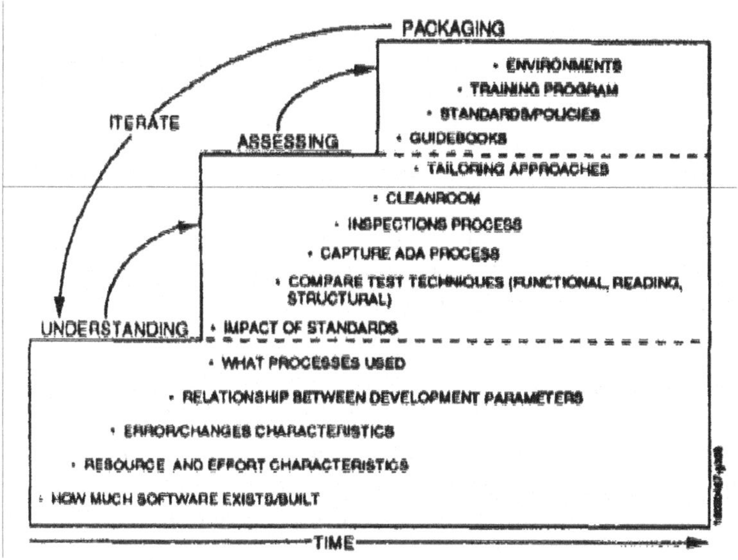

Figure 4. SEL Process Improvement Steps

This working relationship has been maintained continually since its inception with relatively little change to the overall goals of the organization. In general, these goals have matured rather than changed. They are as follows:

1. Understand: Improve insight into the software process and its products by characterizing a production environment.
2. Assess: Measure the impact that available technologies have on the software process. Determine which technologies are beneficial to the environment and,

more importantly, how the technologies must be refined to best match the process with the environment.

3. Package/infuse: After identifying process improvements, package the technology in a form that allows it to be applied in the production organization.

These goals are addressed sequentially, in an iterative fashion as shown in Figure 4.

The approach taken to attaining these goals has been to apply potentially beneficial techniques to the development of production software and to measure the process and product in enough detail to quantifiably assess the applied technology. Measures of concern, such as cost, reliability, and/or maintainability are defined as the organization determines the major near- and long-term objectives for its software development process improvement program. Once those objectives are known, the SEL staff designs the experiment; that is, it defines the particular data to be captured and the question that must be addressed in each experimental project.

All of the experiments conducted by the SEL have occurred within the production environment of the flight dynamics software development facility at NASA/GSFC. The SEL production environment consists of projects that are classified as mid-sized software systems. The average project lasts 2 to 3-1/2 years, with an average staff size of 15 software developers. The average software size is 175 thousand source lines of code (KSLOC), counting commentary, with about 25 percent reused from previous development effort. Virtually all projects in this environment are scientific ground based systems, although some embedded systems have been developed. Most software is developed in FORTRAN, although Ada is starting to be used more frequently. Other languages, such as Pascal and Assembly, are used occasionally. Since this environment is relatively consistent, it is conducive to the experimentation process. In the SEL, there exists a homogeneous class of software, a stable development environment, and a controlled consistent, management and development process.

3. SEL Operations

The following three major functional groups support the experimentation and studies within the SEL (Figure 5):

1. Software developers, who are responsible for producing the flight dynamics application software,
2. Software engineering analysts, who are the researchers responsible for carrying out the experimentation process and producing study results,
3. Data base support staff, who are responsible for collecting, chocking, and archiving all of the information collected horn the development efforts.

During the past 15 years, the SEL has collected and archived data on over 100 software development projects in the organization. The data are also used to build typical project profile, against which ongoing projects can be compared and evaluated. The SEL provides managers in this environment with tools (online and paper) for monitoring and assessing project status.

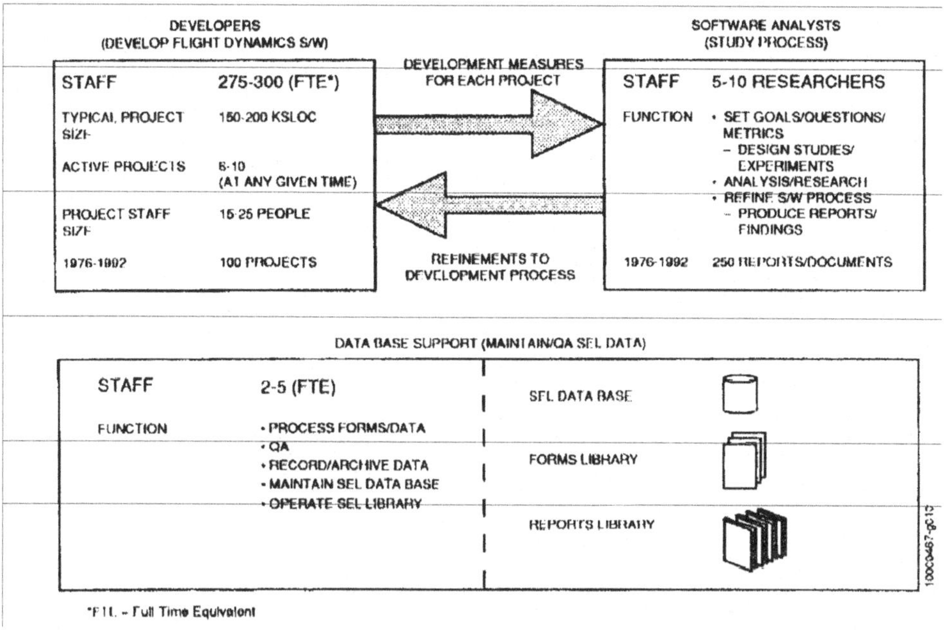

Figure 5. SEL Functional Groups

Typically, there are 6 to 10 projects simultaneously in progress in the flight dynamics environment. As was mentioned earlier, they average 175 KSLOC, ranging from small (6-8 KSLOC) to large (300-400 KSLOC), with a few exceeding 1 million-source lines of code (MSLOC). Each project is considered an experiment within the SEL, and the goal is to extract detailed information to understand the process better and to provide guidance to future projects.

To support the studies and to support the goal of continually increasing understanding of the software development process, the SEL regularly collects detailed data from its development projects. The types of data collected include cost (measured in effort), process, and product data. Process data include information about the project, such as the methodology, tools and techniques used, and information about personnel experience and training. Product data include sine (in SLOC), change and error information, and the results of post development static analysis of the delivered code.

The data may be somewhat different from one project to another since the goals for a particular experiment may be different between projects. There is a basic set of information (such as effort and error data) that is collected for every project. However, as changes are made to specific processes (e.g., Ada projects), the detailed data collected may be modified. For example, Figure 6 shows the standard error report form, used on all projects, and the modified Ada version, used for specific projects where Ada is being studied.

As the information is collected, it is quality assured and placed in a central data base. The analysis then use these data together with other information, such as subjective lessons learned, to analyze the impart of a specific software process and to measure and then feed back results to both ongoing projects and follow-on projects.

The data are used to build predictive models for future projects and to provide a rationale for refining particular software processes being used. As the data are analyzed, papers arid reports are generated that reflect results of the numerous studies. Additionally, the results of the analysis are packaged as standards, policies, training materials, and management tools.

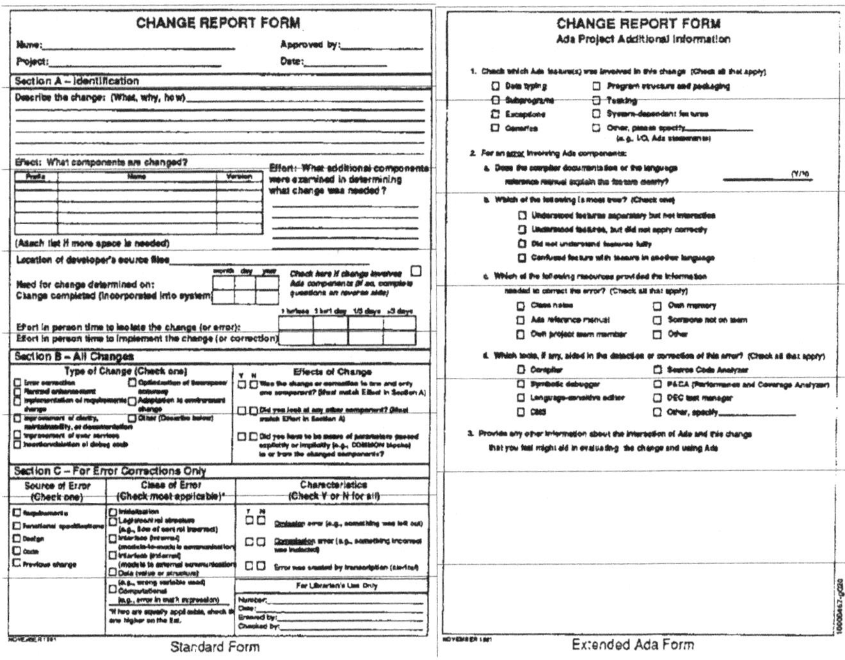

Figure 6. Error Report Forms

4. SEL Data Analysis

The overall concept of the experience factory has continually matured within the SEL as understanding of the software process has increased. The experience factory goal is to demonstrate continual improvement of the software process within an environ-merit by carrying out analysts, measurement, and feedback to projects within the environment. The steps, previously described, include understanding as assessment/refinement, and packaging. The data described in the previous section are used as one major element that supports these three activities in the SEL. In this section examples are given to demonstrate the major stages of the experience factory.

4.1 Understanding

Understanding what an organization does and how that organization operates is fundamental to any attempt to plan, manage, or improve the software process. This is especially true for software development organizations. The following two examples illustrate how understanding is supported in an operation such as the SEL.

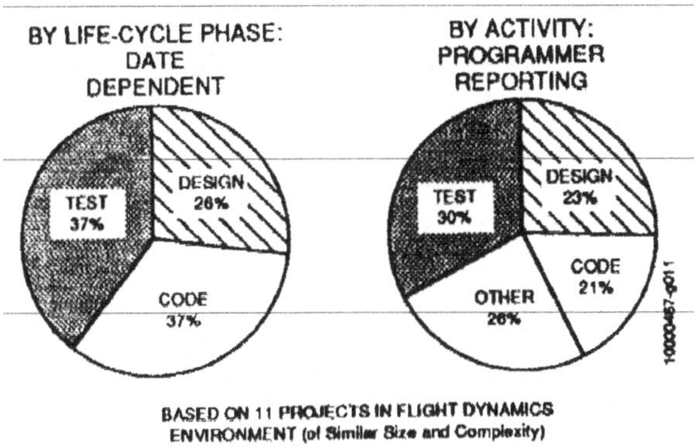

Figure 7. Effort Distribution

Effort distribution (i.e., which phases of the life cycle consume what portion of development effort) is one baseline characteristic of the SEL software development process. Figure 7 presents the effort distributions for 11 FORTRAN projects, by life-cycle phase and by activity. The phase data counts hours charged to a project during each calendar phase. The activity data count all hours attributed to a particular activity (as reported by the programmer) regardless of when in the life cycle the activity occurred. Understanding these distributions is important to assessing the similarities/differences observed on an ongoing project, planning new efforts, and evaluating new technology.

The error detection rate is another interesting model from the SEL environment. There are two types of information in this model. The first is the absolute error rate expected in each phase. By collecting the information on software errors the SEL has constructed a model of the expected error rate in each phase of the life cycle. The SEL expects about four errors per 1000 SLOC during implementation: two during system test, one during acceptance test, and one-half during operation and maintenance. Analysis of more recent projects indicates that these absolute error rates are declining as the software development process and technology improve.

The trend that can be derived from this model is that the error detection rates reduce by 50 percent in each subsequent phase (Figure 8). Thu pattern seems to be independent of the actual values of the error rates- it is still true in the recent projects where the overall error rates are declining. This model of error rates, as well as numerous other similar types of models, can be used to better predict, manage, and assess change on newly developed projects.

4.2. Assessing/Refining

In the second major stage of the experience factory, elements of the process (such as specific software development techniques) are assessed, and the evolving technologies are tailored to the particular environment. Each project in the SEL is considered to be an experiment in which some software method is studied in detail. Generally, the subject of the study is a specific modification to the standard process, a process that obviously comprises numerous software methods.

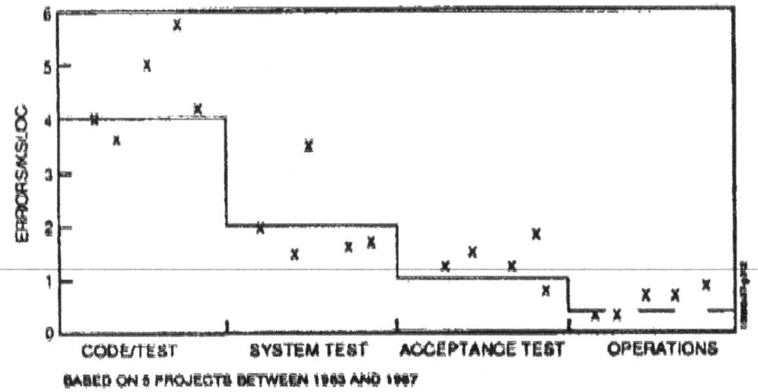

Figure 8. Derived SEL Error Model

One recent study that exemplifies the assessment stage involves the Cleanroom software methodology [9]. This methodology has been applied on three projects within the SEL, each providing additional insight into the Cleanroom process and each adding some element of "refinement" to the methodology for this one environment.

The SEL trained teams in the methodology, and then defined a modified set of Cleanroom specific data to be collected. The projects were studied in an attempt to assess the impact that Cleanroom had on the process as well as on such measures as productivity and reliability. Figure 9 depicts the characteristics of the Cleanroom changes, as well as the results of the three experiments.

The Cleanroom experiments included significant changes to the standard SEL development methodology, thereby requiring extensive training, preparation, and careful execution of the studies. Detailed experimentation plans were generated for each of the studies (as they are for all such experiments), and each included a description of the goals, the questions that had to be addressed, and the metrics that had to be collected to answer the questions.

Since this methodology consists of multiple specific methods (e.g., box structure design, statistical testing, rigorous inspections), each particular method had to be analyzed along with the full, integrated, Cleanroom methodology in general. As a result of the analysis, Cleanroom has been "assessed" as a beneficial approach for the SEL (as measured by specific goals of these studies), but specific elements of the full methodology had to be tailored to better fit the particular SEL environment. The tailoring and modifying resulted in a revised Cleanroom process model, written in the form of a process handbook [10], for future applications to SEL projects. That step is the "packaging" component of the experience factory process.

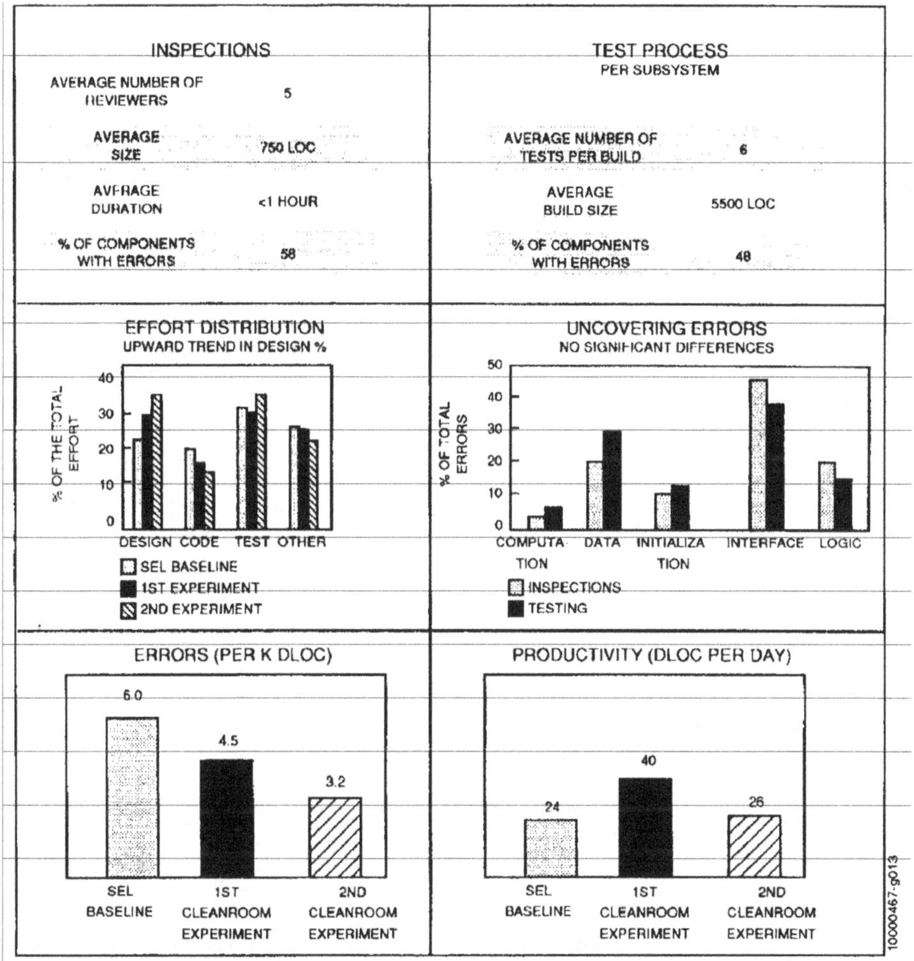

Figure 9. Cleanroom Assessment in the SEL

4.3. Packaging

The final stage of a complete experience factory is that of packaging. After beneficial methods and technologies are identified, the organization must provide feedback to ensuing projects by capturing the process in the form of standards, tools, and training. The SEL has produced a set of standards for its own use that reflect the results of the studies it has conducted. It is apparent that such standards must continually evolve to capture modified characteristics of the process (The SEE typically updates its basic standard every 5 years.) Examples of standards that have been produced as part of the packaging process include:

- *Manager's Handbook for Software Development [11]*
- *Recommended Approach* to *Software Development [121*

One additional example of an extensive packaging effort in the SEL is a management tool called the Software Management Environment (SME). The concepts of the SME, which is now an operational tool used locally in the SEL, have evolved over 8 years This tool accesses SEL project data, models, relationships, lessons teamed, and managers' rules of thumb to present project characteristics to the manager of an ongoing project. This allows the manager to gain insight into the project's consistency with or deviation from the norm for the environment (Figure 10).

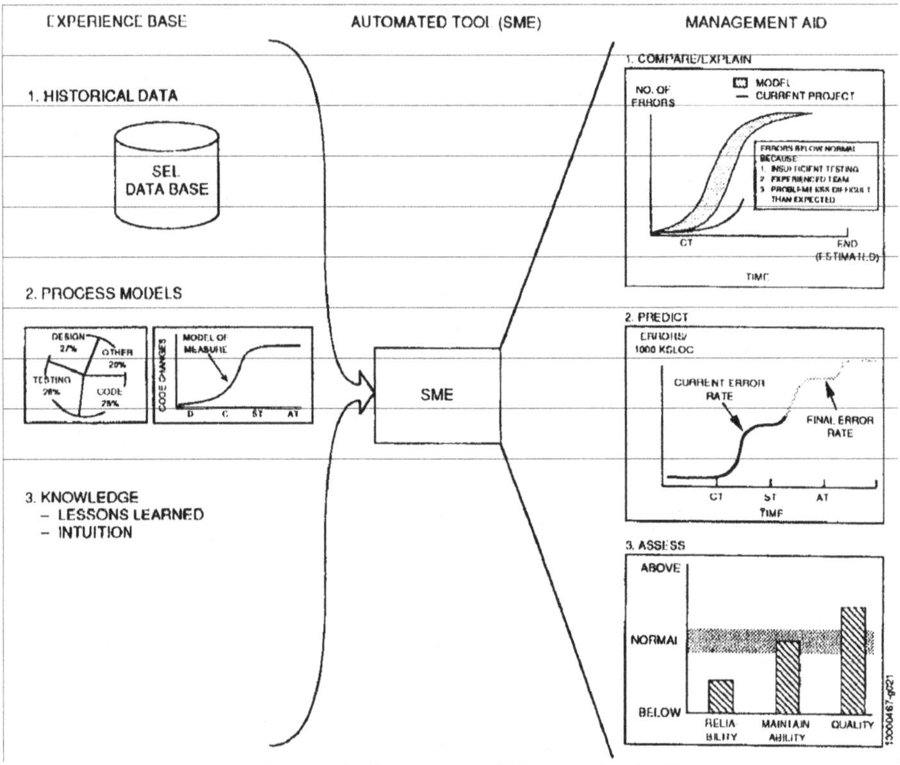

Figure 10. SME: A Tool for "Packaging"

This example of "packaging" reflects the emphasis that must be placed on making results of software projects, in the form of lessons learned, refined models, and general understanding, easily available to other follow-on development projects in a particular organization.

The tool searches the collection of 15 years of experience archived in the SEL to select appropriate, similar project data so that managers can plan, monitor, predict, and better understand their own project based on the analyzed history of similar software efforts.

As an example, all of the error characteristics of the flight dynamics projects have resulted in the error model depicted in Figure 8, where history has shown typical software error rates in the different phases of the life cycle As new projects are developed and error discrepancies arc routinely reported and added to the SEL data base, the manager can easily compare error rates on his or her project with typical error rates on completed, similar projects. Obviously, the data axe environment dependent, but the concepts of measurement, process improvement, and packaging axe applicable to all environments.

5. Ada Analysis

A more detailed example of one technology that has been studied in the SEL within the context of the experience factory is that of Ada. By 1985, the SEL had achieved a good understanding of how software was developed in the FDD; it had base lined the development process and had established rules, relationships, and models that improved the manageability of the process. It had also fine-tuned its process by adding and refining techniques within its standard methodology Realizing that Ada and object-oriented techniques offered potential for major improvement in the flight dynamics environment, the SEL decided to pursue experimentation with Ada.

The first step was to set up expectations and goals against which results would be measured. The SEL's well-established baseline and set of measures provided an excellent basis for comparison. Expectations included a change in the effort distribution of development activities (e.g., increased design and decreased testing); no greater cost per new line of code; increased reuse; decreased maintenance costs; and increased reliability (i.e., lower error rates, fewer interface errors, and fewer design errors).

The SEL started with a small controlled experiment in which two versions of the same system were developed in parallel; one was developed in FORTRAN using the standard SEL structured methodology, and the other was developed in Ada using an object oriented development (OOD) methodology. Because the Ada system would not become operational, analysts had time to investigate new ideas and learn about the new technology while extracting good calibration information for comparing FORTRAN and Ada projects, such as size ratios, average component size, error rates, and productivity. These data provided a reasonable means far planning the next set of Ada projects that even though they were small would deliver mission support software.

Over the past 6 years the SEL has completed 10 Ada/OOD projects, ranging in size from 38to 185 KSLOC. As projects completed and new ones started the methodology was continually evaluated and refined. Some characteristics of the

Ada environment emerged early and have remained rather constant; others took time to stabilize. For example, Ada projects have shown no significant change in effort distribution or in error classification when compared with the SEL FORTRAN baseline. However, reuse has increased dramatically, as shown in Figure 11.

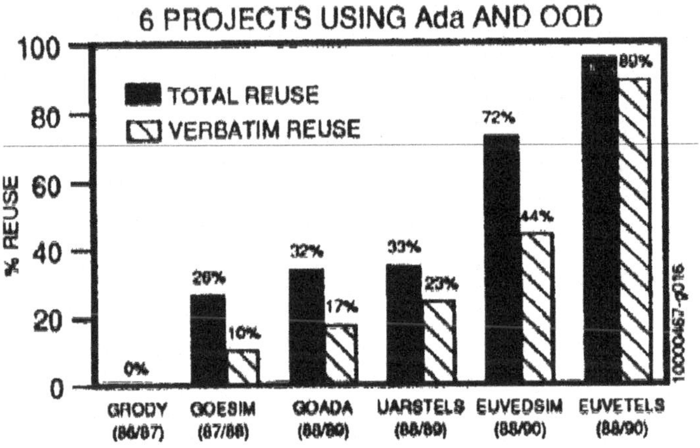

Figure 11. Reuse Trends

Over the 6-year period the use of Ada and OOD has matured. Source cods analysis of the Ada systems, grouped chronologically, revealed a maturing use of key Ada features such as genetics, strong typing, and packaging, whereas other features, such as tasking, were deemed inappropriate for the application. Generics for example, were not only used more often in the recent systems, increasing from 8 to 50 percent of the system, but they were also used in more sophisticated ways, so that parameterization increased eightfold. Moreover the use of Ada features has stabilized over the last 3 years, creating a SEL baseline for Ada development.

The cost to develop new Ada code has remained higher than the cost to develop new FORTRAN code. However, because of the high reuse, the cost to deliver an Ada system has significantly decreased and is now well below the cost to deliver an equivalent FORTRAN system (Figure 12).

Reliability of Ada systems has also improved as the environment has matured. Although the error rates for Ada systems shown in Figure 13 were significantly lower from the start than those for FORTRAN they have continued to decrease even further. Again the high level of reuse in the later systems is a major contributor to this greatly improved reliability.

During this 6-year period, the SEL went through various levels of packaging the Ada/OOD methodology. On the earliest project in 1985 when OOD was still very young in the industry the SEL found it necessary to tailor and package their own General Object-Oriented Development (GOOD) methodology [13] for use in the flight dynamics environment. This document (produced in 1986) adjusted and extended the industry standard for use in the local environment. In 1987 the SEL also developed an Ada Style Guide [14] that provided coding standards for the local environment. Commercial Ada training courses, supplemented with limited project-specific training constituted the early training in these techniques The SEL also produced lessons-learned reports on the Ada/OOD experiences, recommending refinements to the methodology.

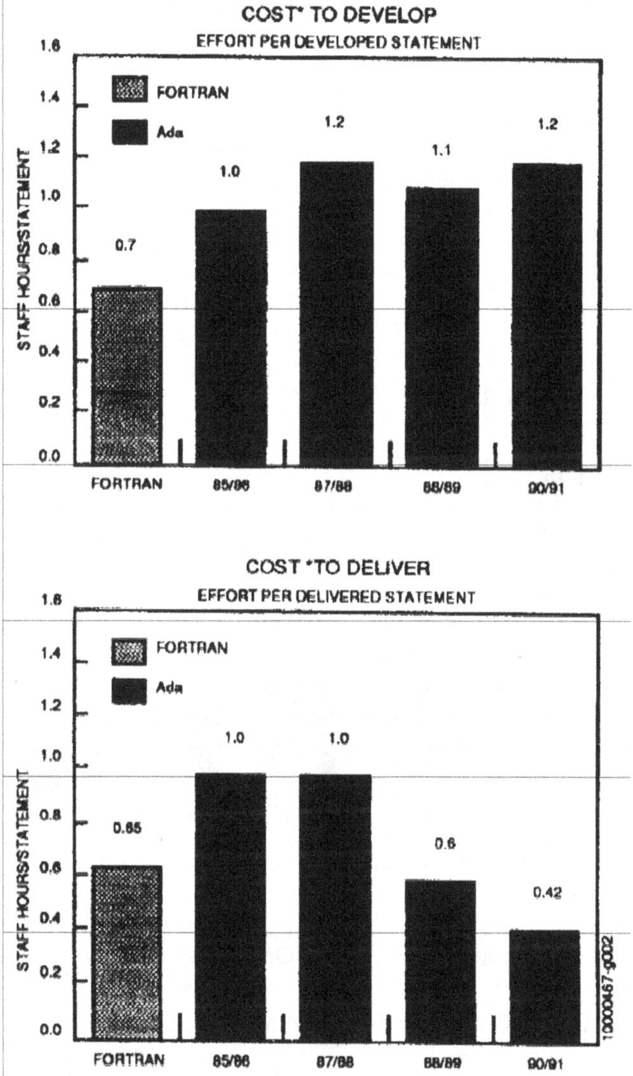

* Cost = Effort/Size
Size (developed) = New statements + 20% of reused
Size (delivered) = Total delivered statements

NOTE: Cost per statement is used here as the basis for comparison, since the SEL has found a 3-to -1 ratio when comparing Ada with FORTRAN source lines of code (carriage returns) but a 1-to-1 ratio when comparing statements.

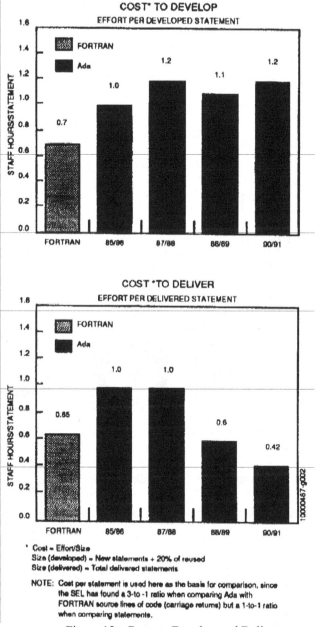

Figure 12 - Costs to Develop and Deliver

Recently, because of the stabilization and apparent benefit to the organization, Ada/OOD is being packaged as part of the baseline SEL methodology. The standard methodology handbooks [11, 12] include Ada and OOD as mainstream methods. In addition a complete and highly tailored training program is being developed that teaches Ada and OOD as an integrated part of the flight dynamics environment.

Although Ada/OOD will continue to be refined within the SEL. it has progressed through all stages of the experience factory, moving from a candidate trial methodology to a fully integrated and packaged part of the standard methodology. The SEL considers it base-lined and ready for further incremental improvement.

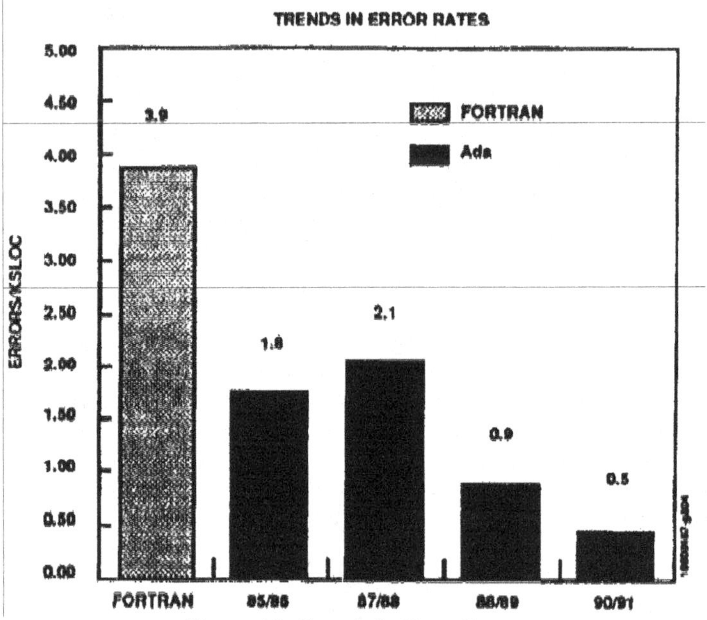

Figure 13. Trends in Error Rates

6. Implications for the Development Organization

For 15 years. NASA has been funding the efforts to carry out experiments and studies within the SEL. There have been significant cost and a certain level of overhead associated with these efforts; a logical question to ask is "Has there been significant benefit?" The historical information strongly supports a very positive answer. Not only has the expenditure of resources been a wise investment for the NASA flight dynamics environment, but members of the SEL strongly believe that inch efforts should be commonplace throughout both NASA and the software community in general. The benefits far outweigh the costs.

Since the SEL's inception in 1976, NASA has spent approximately $14 million dollars (contract support) in the three major support areas required by this type of study environment: research (defining studies and analyzing results), technology transfer (producing standards and policies), and data processing (collecting forms and maintaining data bases). Approximately 50 staff-years of NASA personnel effort have been expended on the SEL. During this same period, the flight dynamics area has spent approximately $150 million cm building operational software all of which has been putt of the study process.

During the past 15 years, the SEL has had a significant impact on the software being developed in the local environment, and there is strong reason to believe that many of die SEL studies have bad a favorable impact on a domain broader than this one environment Examples of the changes that have been observed include the following:

1. The cost per line of new code has decreased only slightly, about 10 percent, which at first glance might imply that the SEL has failed at improving productivity. Although the SEL finds that the cost to produce a new source statement is nearly as high as it was 15 years ago, there is appreciable improvement in the functionality of the software, as well as a tremendous increase in the complexity of the problems being addressed [15]. Also, there has been an appreciable increase in the reuse of software (code, design, methods, test data, etc.), which has driven the overall cost of the equivalent functionality down significantly. When the SEL merely measures the cost to produce one new source statement, the improvement is small but when it measures overall cost and productivity, the improvement is significant.
2. Reliability of the software has improved by 35 percent. As measured by the number of errors per thousand lines of code (E/KSLOC), flight dynamics software has improved from an average of 8.4 E/KSLOC in the early 1980s to approximately 5.3 E/KSLOC today. These figures cover the software phases through acceptance testing and delivery to operations. Although operations and maintenance data are not nearly as extensive as the development data, the small amount of data available indicates significant improvement in that area as well.
3. The "manageability" of software has improved dramatically. In the late 1970s and early 1980s, the environment experienced wide variations in productivity, reliability, and quality from project to project. Today, however, the SEL has excellent models of the process; it has well defined methods; and managers are better able to predict, control, and manage the cost and quality of the software being produced. This conclusion is substantiated by recent SEL data that show a continually improving set of models for planning, predicting, and estimating all development projects in the flight dynamics environment. There no longer is the extreme uncertainty in estimating such common parameters as cost, staffing, size, and reliability.
4. Other measures include the effort put forth in rework (e.g., changing and correcting) and in overall software reuse. These measures also indicate a significant improvement to the software within this one environment.

In addition to the common measures of software (e.g., cost and reliability), there are many other major benefits derived from a "measurement" program such as the SEL's. Not only has the understanding of software significantly improved within the research community, but this understanding is apparent throughout the entire development community within this environment. Not only have the researchers benefited, but the developers and managers who have been exposed to this effort are much better prepared to plan, control, assure, and, in general, develop much higher quality systems. One view of this program is that it is a major "training" exercise within a large production environment, and the 800 to 1000 developers and managers who have participated in development efforts studied by the SEL are much better trained and effective software engineers. This is due to the extensive training and general exposure all developers get from the research efforts continually in progress.

In conclusion, the SEL functions as an operational example of the experience factory concept. The conceptual model for the SEL presented to Section 1 maps to the functional groups discussed under SEL operations in Section 3. The experience base in Figure 2 is realized by the SEL data base and its archives of management models and relationships [16]. The analysis function from Figure 2 is performed by the SEL team of software engineering analysts, who analyze processes and products to understand the environment, then plan and execute experiments to **assess** and **refine** the new technologies under study. Finally, the synthesis function of the experience factory maps to the SEL's activities in packaging new processes and technology in a form tailored specifically to the flight dynamics environment. The products of this synthesis, or packaging, are the guidelines, standards, and tools the SEL produces to infuse its findings back into the project organization. These products are the experience packages of the experience factory model.

Current SEL efforts are focused on addressing two major questions. The first is "How long does it take for a new technology to move through all the stages of the experience factory?" That is, from understanding and baselining the current environment, through assessing the impacts of the technology and refining it, to packaging the process and infusing it into the project organization. Preliminary findings from the SEL's Ada and Cleanroom experiences indicate a cycle of roughly 6 to 9 years, but further data points are needed. The second question the SEL is pursuing is "How large an organization can adopt the experience factory model?" The SEL is interested in learning what the scaleup issues are when the scope of the experience factory is extended beyond a single environment. NASA is sponsoring an effort to explore the infusion of SEL-like implementations of the experience factory concept across the entire Agency.

Acknowledgement

Material for this paper represents work not only of the authors listed, but of many other SEL staff members. Special acknowledgement is given to Gerry Heller of CSC, who played a key role in editing this paper.

References

Numerous papers, reports, and studies have been generated over the SEL's 15-year existence. A complete listing of these can be found in the Annotated *Bibliography of Software Engineering Laboratory* Literature_SEl-82-1006, L. Morusiewiczand J. Valett, November 1991. The bibliography may be obtained by contacting: The SEL Library, Code 552, NASA/GSFC, Greenbelt, MD 20771

A listing of references specific to this paper follows:

[1] V. R. Basili "Towards a Mature Measurement Environment: Creating a Software Engineering Research Environment" Proceedings of the Fifteenth Annual Software Engineering Workshop, NASA/GSFC, Greenbelt, MD. SEL-90-006, November 1990.

[2] V. R. Basili, "Quantitative Evaluation of a Software Engineering Methodology," Proceedings of the First Pan Pacific Computer Conference, Melbourne Australia, September 1985.

[3] V. R. Basili and D M. Weiss, "A Methodology for Collecting Valid Software Engineering Data," IEEE Transactions on Software Engineering, November 1984, pp. 728-738.

[4] V. R. Basili, "Software Development: A Paradigm for the Future (Keynote Address), Proceedings COMPSAC '89. Orlando, Florida, September 1989 pp 471-485.

[5] V. R. Basili and H. D. Rombach, "Tailoring the Software Process to Project Goals and Environments," Proceedings of the Ninth International Conference on Software Engineering, Monterey, California, March 30— April 2. 1987, pp 345-357.

[6] V. R. Basili and H. D. Rombach, "The TAME Project; Towards Improvement-Oriented Software Environment.," IEEE Transactions on Software Engineering. Vol. 14, No 6. June 1988. pp- 758—773.

[7] V. R. Basili and G. Caldiera, "Methodological and Architectural Issues in the Experience Factory," Proceedings of the Sixteenth Annual Software Engineering Workshop. NASA GSPC, Greenbelt, Maryland. Software Engineering Laboratory Series, December 1991.

[8] V. R. Basili, G. Caldiera, and G. Cantone, "A Reference Architecture for the Component Factory," ACM Transactions on Software Engineering and Methodology, Vol. 1 No I January 1992, pp 53=80.

[9] H. D. Mills, M. Dyer, and R.C. Linger, "Cleanroom Software Engineering," IEEE Software November 1990, pp 19-24.

[10] S. Green, *Software Engineering Laboratory (SEL) Cleanroom Process Model,* SEL-91-004 November 1991.

[11] L. Landis, F. E. McGarry, S Waligora, et al,, *Manager's Handbook for Software Development (Revision1),* SEL-84-101, November 1990.

[12] F. E. McGarry, G. Page, E. Eslinger, et al, *Recommended Approach to Software Development* SEL-81-205, April 1981 Revision 3 in preparation' scheduled for publication June 1992.

[13] E. Seidewitz and M Stark, *General Object Oriented Software Development,* SEL-86-002, August 1986.

[14] E. Seidewitz et al, *Ada® Style Guide (Version 1.1),* SEL-87-002, May 1987.

[15] D. Boland et al, A *Study on Size and Reuse Trends* in *Attitude Ground Support Systems (AGSS) Developed for the Flight Dynamics Division (FDD) (1976-1988),* NASA/GSFC, CSC/ TM-89/6031, February 1989.

[16] W. Decker, R Hendrick, and J. Valett, *Software Engineering Laboratory (SEL) Relationships, Models, and Management Rules* SEL-91-001, February 1991.

Section 4: Learning Organization and Experience Factory

H. Dieter Rombach

Computer Science Department, Technical University of Kaiserslautern and Fraunhofer Institute for Experimental Software Engineering (IESE)

Sustained improvement of software development organizations requires the capture of measurement-based models, their proper storage and reuse, and their continuous improvement across projects. The foundations had been established with the GQM paradigm for goal-oriented measurement and the QIP for integrating measurement with real software development processes. The practical feasibility has been demonstrated within NASA's SEL. Lessons learned within the SEL suggested that empirically-based models needed to be augmented with context information in order to judge their suitability for reuse, and that resources outside development organizations were needed in order to create reusable models. It reflects Prof. Basili's research approach that he always alternates between doing and scientific abstraction. In the past his experiences with measurement and the pitfalls by lack of goal-orientation and integration with real projects led to the scientific GQM and QIP paradigm. This section describes how the application of the GQM and QIP paradigm in the SEL environment and the lessons learned led to the creation of a comprehensive reuse model and an the Experience Factory model providing organizational guidelines for successful QIP-based quality improvement. Once the comprehensive reuse and Experience Factory models existed, they were applied at Motorola in order to check whether these models would allow a speedy and sustained creation of a Software Learning Organization.

The first paper, "Support for comprehensive reuse," introduces a comprehensive framework of models, model-based characterization schemes, and support mechanisms aimed at better understanding, evaluating, planning, and supporting all aspects of reuse. The underlying assumptions are that practical reuse typically includes all types of software artifacts ranging from product to process and other forms of knowledge, requires modification, requires a-priori analysis of reuse candidates in order to determine when and if reuse is appropriate, and must be integrated into the specific development approach. The conclusion is that both reuse candidates as well as target reuse requirements need to be modeled. The paper proposes a reuse model, and a model-based characterization scheme. The reuse model includes the steps "identification of reuse candidates" by means of matching the models of reuse candidates against some reuse requirements model, "evaluation and selection" of the most suitable reuse candidate, and "modification" by adapting the reuse candidate to fit the reuse requirements. The characterization scheme to support this reuse model includes dimensions to characterize object (e.g., name, function, granularity, representation), interface (e.g., input/output, other dependencies), and context (e.g., application domain, solution domain, object quality). In addition, the reuse process is characterized similarly. Especially the mechanism for modification (e.g., verbatim, parameterized, template-based) has a significant impact on cost of correction. In order to illustrate the applicability, example characterizations for an Ada package, an inspection process and a cost model from the SEL environment are provided. These example schemes enable sound reasoning about the usefulness, cost and benefits of reuse.

The comprehensive reuse scheme reflects the lessons learned from storing and reusing measurement-based models within the SEL, captures them systematically and makes them available to development organizations outside the SEL. This comprehensive reuse model also provides operational support for GQM and QIP. The characterization scheme can be used to identify useful context metrics within the GQM process, and corresponds to the characteristics in step 1 of the QIP aimed at formulating reuse requirements to identify useful experience models for a new project. This paper can be considered fundamental in that it provides insights into what context information is essential for effective reuse. Without such insights continuous improvement across projects would still be an illusion. Today some of the many practical applications of the comprehensive reuse scheme include the SEL (although created earlier), the CeBASE repository for software engineering technologies (www.cebase.com), the VSEK repository for best practices in selected domains (www.software-kompetenz.de).

The second paper, "Technology Transfer at Motorola," describes the first systematic application of the GQM paradigm, QIP paradigm, and the comprehensive reuse approach outside the SEL. At Motorola, these approaches were successfully applied to introduce a software-review process. Within Motorola's corporate-wide Metrics Working Group, the QIP approach was instantiated to identify, tailor and transfer software-engineering technology into the organization. The concept of a "process package" is essential. A process package includes documents and training materials needed to bring the process to life! Examples include an overview description of the process at hand, how to use it, references to other related packages, training aids for different user groups, data and lessons learned.

The experiences from introducing a software-review process at Motorola based on GQM et al was generally positive. Specific lessons regarding the transfer approach included the importance of champions, the tailoring of data collection and analysis, and the importance of sufficient training. Other lessons relating to the review process included the importance of optimization of review guidelines based on measurements, the importance of preparedness of reviewers before entering the review meeting, the higher effectiveness of formal reviews.

This paper documents the usefulness of Vic Basili's measurement and improvement approach outside the SEL. Subsequently, many technology transfer approaches of research organizations (e.g., Fraunhofer IESE in Germany, NICTA in Australia, EASE/SEC in Japan) as well as companies (e.g., Daimler Chrysler, Robert-Bosch, Siemens, Nokia, Boeing) adopted the approach in different instantiations.

The third and final paper, "Improve Software Quality by Reusing Knowledge and Experience," defines the logical separation of project specific and organizational activities in an improvement-oriented software development organization. The resulting "Experience Factory" concept ha s since become the "architectural model" for successful software improvement programs. It distinguishes between the project-specific QIP activities of planning (characterize, set goals and choose process) and execution on the one hand, and the organizational experience factory activities of post-mortem analysis and packaging. It is clearly stated that both types of activities have to be closely intertwined, but both require different human capabilities and sources of funding. While the human capabilities of project personnel are oriented towards top-down problem solving, the capabilities of experience factory personnel are oriented towards bottom-up generalization. The funding of experience factory activities cannot come from individual project budgets, but must come from cross-project organizations which have an interest in improvement from project to project. Finally, the SEL is presented as a working Experience Factory. The Experience Factory model captures the essential activities of a Learning Organization in the software development domain. Today, the Experience Factory model is used to facilitate learning in many domains. Examples include many company-specific implementations (e.g. for subcontract management in DoD projects – source: Fraunhofer Center Maryland; failure detection at T-COM – source Fraunhofer IESE, sustained technology transfer – source: Motorola/paper 2).

The comprehensive reuse scheme and the Experience Factory model provide – together with GQM and QIP .- the integrating building blocks for Learning Organizations in the software development domain. It is important to recognize, that these models capture the essentials in a generic and abstract form. They have to be instantiated differently from environment to environment. With Vic these contributions Vic Basili has enabled the adoption of basic engineering principles such as continuous improvement via Plan-Do-Check-Act to the software domain. Thereby, Software Engineering has made significant strides towards becoming a true engineering discipline.

Support for Comprehensive Reuse

V. R. Basili and H. D. Rombach

Department of Computer Science and Institute for Advanced Computer Studies, University of Maryland

Abstract. Reuse of products, processes and other knowledge will be the key to enable the software industry to achieve the dramatic improvement in productivity and quality required to satisfy the anticipated growing demands. Although experience shows that certain kinds of reuse can be successful, general success has been elusive. A software life-cycle technology which allows comprehensive reuse of all kinds of software-related experience could provide the means to achieving the desired order-of-magnitude improvements. In this paper, we introduce a comprehensive framework of models, model-based characterization schemes, and support mechanisms for better understanding, evaluating, planning, and supporting all aspects of reuse.

1. Introduction

The existing gap between demand and our ability to produce high quality software cost-effectively calls for an improved software development technology. A reuse oriented development technology can significantly contribute to higher quality and productivity. Quality should improve by reusing all forms of proven experience including products, processes as well as quality and productivity models. Productivity should increase by using existing experience rather than creating everything from scratch.

Reusing existing experience is a key ingredient to progress in any discipline. Without reuse everything must be re-learned and re-created; progress in an economical fashion is unlikely. Reuse is less institutionalized in software engineering than in any other engineering discipline. Nevertheless, there exist successful cases of reuse, i.e. product reuse. The potential payoff from reuse can be quite high in software engineering since it is inexpensive to store and reproduce software engineering experience compared to other disciplines.

The goal of research in the area of reuse is to develop and support systematic approaches for effectively reusing existing experience to maximize quality and productivity. A number of different reuse approaches have appeared in the literature (e.g., [10, 12, 14, 17, 18, 19, 20, 27, 28, 29]).

This paper presents a comprehensive framework for reuse consisting of a reuse model, characterization schemes based upon this model, the improvement oriented TAME environment model describing the integration of reuse into the enabling software development processes, mechanisms needed to support comprehensive reuse in the context of the TAME environment model, and (partial) prototype implementations of the TAME environment model. From a number of important assumptions regarding the nature of software development and reuse we derive four essential requirements for any useful reuse model and related characterization scheme (Section 2). We illustrate that existing models and characterization schemes only partially satisfy these essential requirements (Section 3). We introduce a new reuse model which is comprehensive in the sense that it satisfies all four reuse requirements, and use it to derive a reuse characterization scheme (Section 4). Finally, we point out the mechanisms needed to support effective reuse according to this model (Section 5). Throughout the paper we use examples of reusing *generic Ada packages, design inspections*, and *cost models* to illustrate our approach.

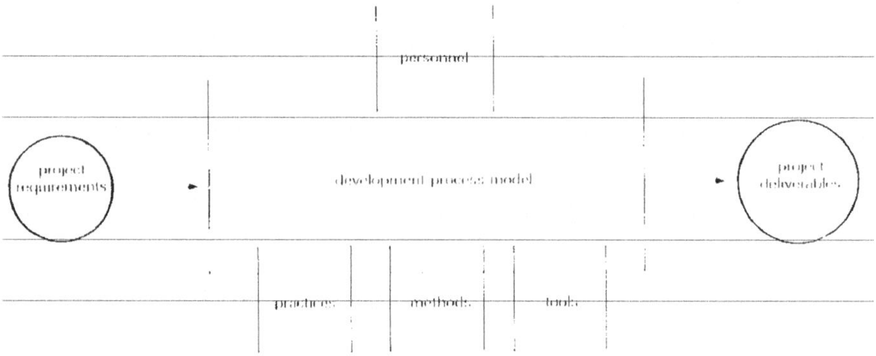

Figure 1. Software development project model

2. Scope of Comprehensive Reuse

The reuse framework presented in this paper is based on a number of assumptions regarding software development in general and reuse in particular. These assumptions are based on more than fifteen years of analyzing software processes and products [2, 5, 7, 8, 9, 23]. From these assumptions we derive four essential requirements for any useful reuse model and related characterization scheme.

2.1 Software Development Assumptions

According to a common software development project model depicted in Figure 1, the goal of software development is to produce project deliverables (i.e., project output) that satisfy project needs (i.e., project input) [30]. This goal is achieved according to some development process model which coordinates the interaction between available personnel, practices, methods and tools.

With regard to software development we make the following assumptions:

- ***Software development needs to be viewed as an 'experimental' discipline:*** An evolutionary model is needed which enables organizations to learn from each development and incrementally improve their ability to engineer quality software products. Such a model requires the ability to define project goals; select and tailor the appropriate process models, practices, methods and techniques; and capture the experiences gained from each project in reusable form. Measurement is essential.
- ***A single software development approach cannot be assumed for all software development projects:*** Different project needs and other project characteristics may suggest and justify different approaches. The potential differences may range from different development process models themselves to different practices, methods and tools supporting these development process models to different personnel.
- ***Existing software development approaches need to be tailorable to project needs and characteristics:*** In order to reuse existing development process models, practices, methods and tools across projects with different needs and characteristics, they need to be tailorable.

2.2 Software Reuse Assumptions

Reuse oriented software development assumes that, given the project-specific needs x' for an object x, we consider reusing some already existing object x_k instead of creating x from the beginning. Reuse involves identifying a set of reuse candidates x_1, ..., x_n from an experience base, evaluating their potential for satisfying x', Selecting the best-suited candidate x_k, and - if required – modifying the selected candidate x_k into x. Similar issues have been discussed in [16]. In the case of reuse oriented development, x' is not only the specification for the needed object x, but also the specification for all the mentioned reuse activities.

As we learn from each project which kinds of experience are reusable and why, we can establish better criteria for what should and what shouldn't be made available in the experience base. The term experience base suggests that anticipate storage of all kinds of software related experience, not just products. The experience base can be improved from inside as well as outside. From inside, we can record experience from ongoing projects, which satisfies current reuse criteria for future reuse, and we can re-package existing experience through various mechanisms in order to better satisfy our current reuse criteria. From outside, we can infuse experience which exists out-side the organization into the experience base. It is important to note that the remainder of this paper deals only with the reuse of experience available in an experience base and the improvement of such an experience base from inside (shaded portion of Figure 2).

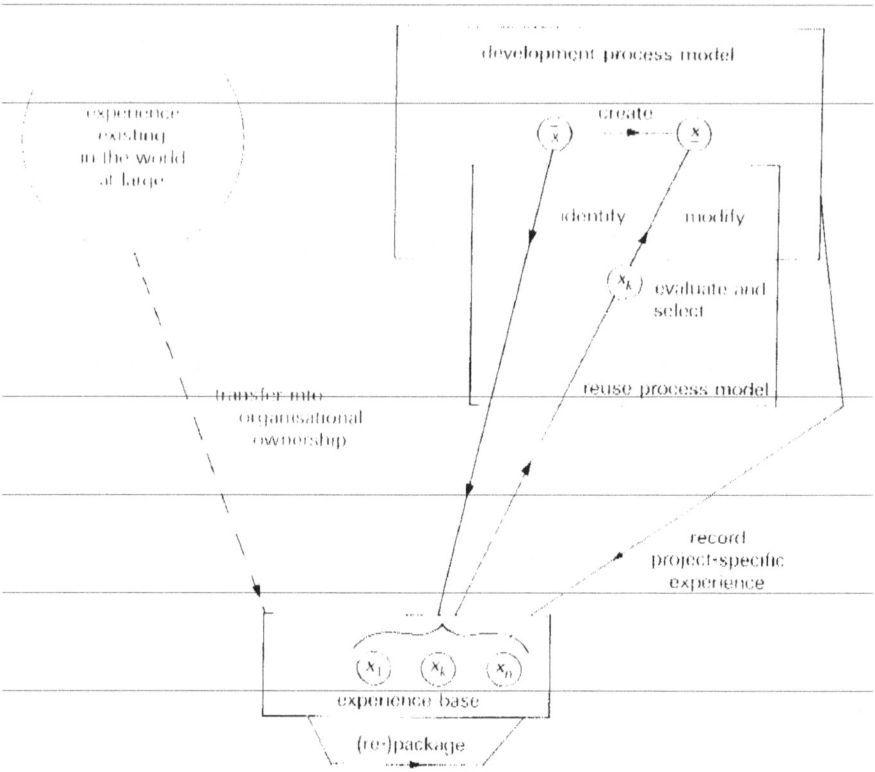

Figure 2. Reuse-oriented software development model

With regard to software reuse we make the following assumptions:

- ***All experience can be reused:*** Traditionally, the emphasis has been on reusing concrete objects of type 'source code'. This limitation reflects the traditional view that software equals code. It ignores the importance of reusing all kinds of software-related experience including products, processes, and other knowledge. The term 'product' refers to either a concrete document or artifact created during a software project, or a product model describing a class of concrete documents or artifacts with common characteristics. The term 'process' refers to either to a concrete activity or action - performed by a human being or a machine - aimed at creating some software product, or a process model describing a class of activities or actions with common characteristics. The phrase 'other knowledge' refers to anything useful for software development, including quality and productivity models or models of the application being implemented.

The reuse of 'generic Ada packages' represents an example of product reuse. Generic Ada packages represent templates for instantiating specific package objects according to a parameter mechanisms. The reuse of 'design inspections' represents an example of process reuse. Design inspections are off-line fault de-

tection and isolation methods applied during the component design phase. They can be based on different techniques for reading (e.g., ad hoc, sequential, control flow oriented, stepwise abstraction oriented). The reuse of 'cost models' represents an example of knowledge reuse. Cost models are used in the estimation, evaluation and control of project cost. They predict cost (e.g., in the form of staff-months) based on a number of characteristic project parameters (e.g., estimated product size in KLoC, product complexity, methodology level).

- ***Reuse typically requires some modification of the object being reused:*** Under the assumption that software developments may be different in some way, modification of experience from previous projects must be anticipated. The degree of modification depends on how many, and to what degree, existing object characteristics differ from the needed ones. The time of modification depends on when the reuse needs for a project or class of projects are known. Modification can take place as part of actual reuse (i.e., the 'modify' within the reuse process model of Figure 2) and/or prior to actual reuse (i.e., as part of the re-packaging activity in Figure 2).

To reuse an Ada package 'list of integers' in order to organize a 'list of reals', we need to modify it. We can either modify the existing package by hand, or we can use a generic package 'list' which can be instantiated via a parameter mechanism for any base type.

To reuse a design inspection method across projects characterized by significantly different fault profiles, the underlying reading technique may need to be tailored to the respective fault profiles. If 'interface faults' replace 'control flow faults' as the most common fault type, we can either select a different reading techniqueized by different application domains, we may have to change the number and type of characteristic project parameters used for estimating cost as well as their impact on cost. If 'commercial software' is developed instead of 'real-time software', we may have to consider re-defining 'estimated product size' to be measured in terms of 'function points' instead of 'lines of code' or re-computing the impact of the existing parameters on cost. Using a cost model effectively implies a constant updating o decision to reuse existing experience as well as how and when to reuse it needs to be based on an analysis of the payoff. Reuse payoff is not always easy to evaluate [1]. We need to understand (i) the reuse needs, (ii) how well the available reuse candidates are qualified to meet these needs, and (iii) the mechanisms available to perform the necessary modification.

Assume the existence of a set of Ada generics, which represent application-specific components of a satellite control system. The objective may be to reuse such components to build a new satellite control system of a similar type, but with higher precision. Whether the existing generics are suitable depends on a variety of characteristics: Their correctness and reliability, their performance in prior instances of reuse, their ease of integration into a new system, the potential for achieving the higher degree of precision through instantiation, the degree of change needed, and the existence of reuse the answers to these questions, they may not be reused due to lack of confidence that reuse will payoff.

Assume the existence of a design inspection method based on ad-hoc reading which has been used successfully on past satellite control software developments within a standard waterfall model. The objective may be to reuse the method in the context of the Cleanroom development method [22, 26]. In this case, the method needs to be applied in the context of a different life-cycle model, existing method can be reused depends on our ability to tailor the reading technique to the stepwise refinement oriented design technique used in Cleanroom, and the required intensity of reading due to the omission of developer testing. This results in the definition of the stepwise abstraction oriented reading technique [11].

Assume the existence of a cost model that has been validated for the development of satellite control software based on a waterfall life-cycle model, functional decomposition-oriented design techniques, and functional and structural testing. The objective may be to reuse the model in the context of Cleanroom development. Whether the cost model can be reused at all, how it needs to be calibrated, or whether a completely different model may be more appropriate depends on whether the model contains the appropriate variables needed for the prediction of cost change or whether they simply need to be re-calibrated. This question can only be answered through thorough analysis of a number of Cleanroom projects.

- ***Reuse must be integrated into the specific software development:*** Reuse is intended to make software development more effective. In order to achieve this objective, we need to tailor reuse practices, methods, and tools to the respective development process.

We have to decide when and how to identify, modify and integrate existing Ada packages. If we assume identification of Ada generics by name, and modification by the generic parameter mechanism, we require a repository consisting of Ada generics together with a description of the instantiation parameters. If we assume identification by specification, and modification of the generics code by hand, we require a suitable specification of each generic, a definition of semantic closeness[1] *of specifications so we can find suitable reuse candidates, and the appropriate source code documentation to allow for ease of modification. In the case of identification by specification we may consider identifying reuse candidates at high-level design (i.e., when the component specifications for the new product exist) or even when defining the requirements.*

We have to decide on how often, when and how design inspections should be integrated into the development process. If we assume a waterfall-based development life-cycle, we need to determine how many design inspections need to be performed and when (e.g., once for all modules at the end of module design, once for all modules of a subsystem, or once for each module). We need to state which documents are required as input to the design inspection, what results are to be produced, what actions are to be taken, and when, in case the results are insufficient; who is supposed to participate.

We have to decide when to initially estimate cost and when to update the initial estimate. If we assume a waterfall-based development life-cycle, we may estimate cost initially based on estimated product and process parameters (e.g., estimated product size). After each milestone, the estimated cost can be compared with the

[1] Definitions of semantic closeness can be derived from existing work [24].

actual cost. Possible deviations are used to correct the estimate for the remainder of the project.

2.3 Software Reuse Model Requirements

The above software reuse assumptions suggest that reuse is a complex concept. We need to build models and characterization schemes that allow us to define and understand, compare and evaluate, and plan the reuse requirements, the reuse candidates, the reuse process itself, and the potential for effective reuse. Based upon the above assumptions, such models and characterization schemes need to satisfy the following four requirements:

- **Applicable to all types of reuse objects:** We want to be able to include products, processes and all other kinds of knowledge such as quality and productivity models.
- **Capable of modeling reuse candidates and reuse needs:** We want to be able to capture the reuse candidates as well as the reuse needs in the current project. This will enable us to judge the suitability of a given reuse candidate based on the distance between the characteristics of the reuse needs and the reuse candidate, and establish criteria for useful reuse candidates based on anticipated reuse needs.
- **Capable of modeling the reuse process itself:** We want to be able to judge the ease of bridging the gap between different characteristics of reuse candidates and reuse needs, and derive additional criteria for useful reuse candidates based on characteristics of the reuse process itself.
- **Defined and rationalized so they can be easily tailored to specific project needs and characteristics:** We want to be able to adjust a given reuse model and characterization scheme to changing project needs and characteristics in a systematic way. This requires not only the ability to change the scheme, but also some kind of rationale that ties the given reuse characterization scheme back to its underlying model and assumptions. Such a rationale enables us to identify the impact of different environments and modify the scheme in a systematic way.

3. Existing Reuse Models

A number of research groups have developed (implicit) models and characterization schemes for reuse (e.g., [12, 14, 17, 27, 28]). The schemes can be distinguished as *special purpose schemes* and *meta schemes*.

The large majority of published characterization schemes have been developed for a special purpose. They consist of a fixed number of characterization dimensions. There intention is to characterize software products as they exist. Typical dimensions for characterizing source code objects in a repository are 'function', 'size', or 'type of problem'. Example schemes include the schemes published in

[14, 17], the ACM Computing Reviews Scheme, AFIPS's Taxonomy of Computer Science and Engineering, schemes for functional collections (e.g., GAMS, SHARE, SSP, SPSS, IMSL) and schemes for commercial software catalogs (e.g., ICP, IDS, IBM Software Catalog, Apple Book). It is obvious that special purpose schemes are not designed to satisfy the reuse modeling requirements of section 2.3.

A few characterization schemes can be instantiated for different purposes. They explicitly acknowledge the need for different schemes (or the expansion of existing ones) due to different or changing needs of an organization. They, therefore, allow the instantiation of any imaginable scheme. An excellent example is Ruben Prieto-Diaz's facet-based meta-characterization scheme [18, 21]. Theoretically, meta schemes are flexible enough to allow the capturing of any reuse aspect. However, based on known examples of actual uses of meta schemes, such broadness has not been utilized. Instead, most examples focus on product reuse, are limited to the reuse candidates, lustrate the capabilities of existing schemes, we give the following instance of an example meta scheme[2]:

- □ **name:** What is the product's name? (e.g., buffer.ada, queue.ada, list.pascal)
- □ **function:** What is the functional specification or purpose of the product? (e.g., integer_queue, <R: What is the product's scope? (e.g., system level, subsystem level, component level, module - package, procedure, function - level)
- □ **representation:** How is the product represented? (e.g., informal set of guidelines, schematized templates, languages such as Ada)
- □ **input/output:** What are the external input/output dependencies of the product needed to completely define/extract it as a self-contained entity? (e.g., global data referenced by a code unit, formal and actual input/output parameters of a procedure, instantiation parameters of a generic Ada package)
- □ **application domain:** what application classes was the product developed for? (e.g. ground support software for satellites, business software for banking, payroll software)

This scheme is applicable to all reuse product candidates. For example, a generic Ada package 'buffer.ada' may be characterized as having identifier 'buffer.ada', offering the function '<element>_buffer', being usable as a 'product' of type 'code document' at the 'package module level', and being represented in 'Ada'. A self contained definition of a package requires knowledge regarding the instantiation parameters, as well as its visibility of externally defined objects (e.g., explicit access through WITH clauses, implicit access according to nesting structure). In addition, effective use of the object may require some basic knowledge of the language Ada and assume thorough documentation of the object itself. It may have been developed within the application domain 'ground support software', ac-

[2] Characterization dimensions are marked with □; example categories for each dimension are listed in parentheses.

cording to a 'waterfall life-cycle' and 'functional decomposition design', and exhibiting high quality in terms of 'reliability'. In order to characterize reuse candidates of type process or knowledge, new categories need to be generated.

Such schemes have typically been used to characterize reuse candidates only. However, in order to evaluate the reuse potential of a reuse candidate in a given reuse scenario, one needs to understand the distance between its characteristics and the stated or anticipated reuse needs. In the case of the Ada package example, the required function may be different, the quality requirements with respect to reliability may be higher, or the design method used in the current project may be different from the one according to which the package has been created originally. Without understanding the distance to be bridged between reuse requirements and reuse candidates it is hard to predict the cost involved in reusing a particular object, and establish criteria for populating a reuse repository that supports cost-effective reuse.

The scheme provides no information for characterizing the reuse process. To really predict the cost of reuse we do not only have to understand the distance to be bridged between reuse candidates and reuse needs, but also the intended process to bridge it (i.e., the reuse process). For example, it can be expected that it is easier to bridge the distance with respect to function by using a parameterized instantiation mechanism rather than modifying the existing package by hand.

There is no explicit rationale for the eight dimensions of the example scheme. That makes it hard to reason about its appropriateness as well as modifies it in any systematic way. There is no guidance in tailoring the example scheme to new needs with respect to what is to changed (e.g., only some categories, dimensions, or the entire implicitly underlying model) or how it is to be changed. For example, it is not clear what needs to be changed in order to make the scheme applicable to reuse candidates of type process or knowledge.

In summary, existing schemes - special purpose as well as meta schemes - only partially satisfy the requirements laid out above. The most crucial shortcoming is the lack of rationales which makes it hard to tailor such schemes to changing needs and environment characteristics. This observation suggests the need for new, broader reuse models and characterization schemes. In the next section, we suggest a comprehensive reuse model and characterization schemes, which satisfy all four requirements.

4. A Comprehensive Reuse Model

In this section we define a comprehensive reuse model and characterization schemes, which satisfy the requirements stated in section 2.3. We start with a very general reuse model, refine it step by step until it generates reuse characterization dimensions at the level of detail needed to understand, evaluate, motivate or improve reuse. This modeling approach allows us to deal with the complexity of the modeling task itself, and document an explicit rationale for the resulting model.

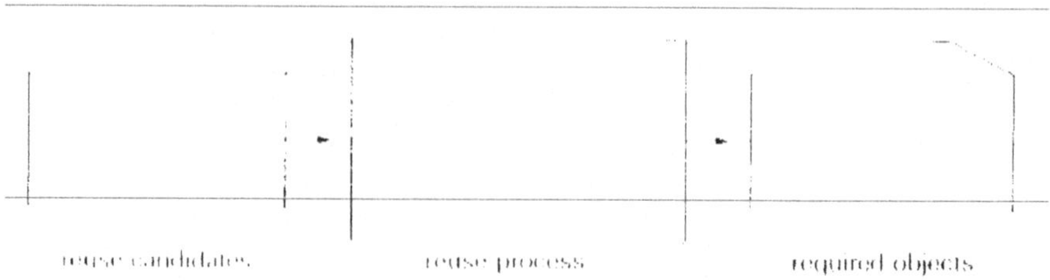

Figure 3. Abstract reuse model (refinement level 0)

4.1 Reuse Model

The comprehensive reuse model used in this section is consistent with the view of reuse represented in section 2.2. Reuse comprises the transformation of existing reuse candidates into needed objects, which satisfy established reuse needs. The transformation is referred to as reuse process. Specifications of the needed objects are an essential part of the reuse needs which guide any reuse process.

The reuse candidates represent experience from the same project, prior projects, or other sources, that have been evaluated as being of potential reuse value, and have been made available in some form of experience base. The reuse needs specify objects needed in the current project. In the case of successful reuse, these needed objects would be the potentially modified versions of reuse candidates. Both the reuse candidate and reuse needs may refer to any type of experience accumulated in the context of software projects ranging from products to processes to knowledge. The reuse process transforms reuse candidates into objects, which satisfy given reuse needs.

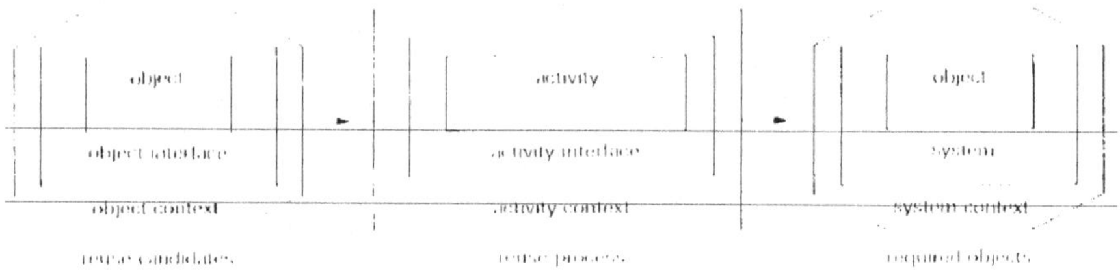

Figure 4. Reuse model (refinement level 1)

In order to better understand reuse related issues we refine each component of the reuse model further. The result of this first refinement step is depicted in Figure 4.

Each *reuse candidate* is a specific *object* considered for reuse. The object has various attributes that describe and bound it. Most objects are physically part of a system, i.e. they interact with other objects to create some greater object. If we want to reuse an object we must understand its interaction with other objects in the system in order to extract it as a unit, i.e. *object interface*. Objects were created in some environment, which leaves its characteristics on the object, even though those characteristics may not be visible. We call this the *object context*.

Given *reuse requirements* may be satisfied by a set of reuse candidates. Therefore, we may have to consider different attributes for each required object. The *system* in which the transformed object is integrated and the *system context* in which the system is developed must also be classified.

The *reuse process* is aimed at extracting a reuse candidate from a repository based on the characteristics of the known reuse needs, and making it ready for reuse in the system and context in which it will be reused. We must describe the various *reuse activities* and classify them. The reuse activities need to be integrated into the reuse-enabling software development process. The means of integration constitute the *activity interface*. Reuse requires the transfer of experience across project boundaries. The organizational support provided for this experience transfer is referred to as *activity context*.

Based upon the goals for the specific project, as well as the organization, we must assess the required qualities of the reused object as stated by the reuse needs, the quality of the reuse process, especially its integration into the enabling software evolution process, and the quality of the existing reuse candidates.

4.2 Model-Based Reuse Characterization Scheme

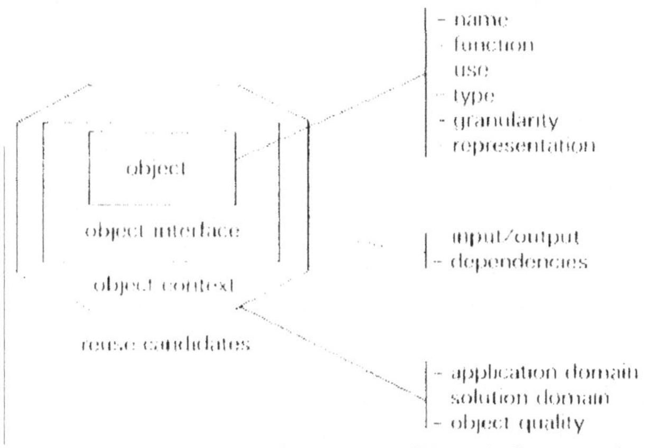

Figure 5a. Reuse model (reuse candidates/refinement level 2)

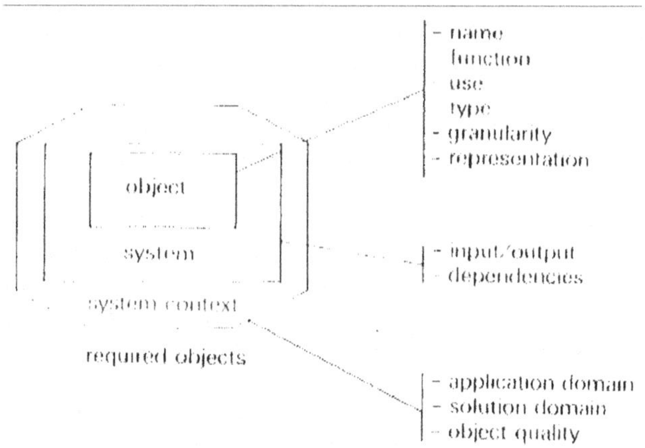

Figure 5b. Reuse model (reuse requirements/refinement level 2)

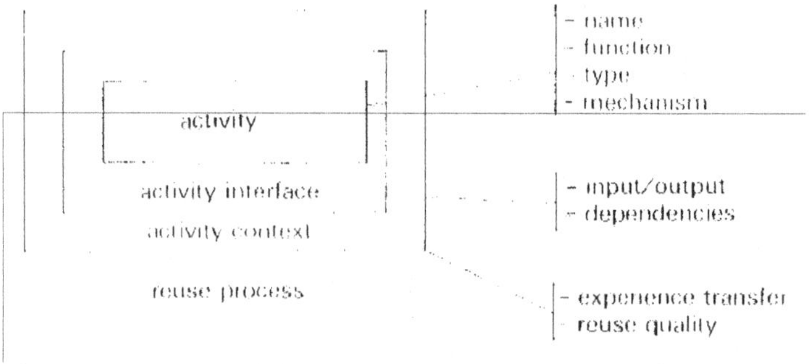

Figure 5c. Reuse model (reuse process/refinement level 2)

Each component of the First Model Refinement (Figure 4) is further refined as depicted in Figures 5(a-c). It needs to be noted that these refinements are based on our current understanding of reuse and may, therefore, change in the future.

4.2.1 Reuse Candidates: In order to characterize the object itself, we have chosen to provide the following six dimensions and supplementing categories: the object's name (e.g., buffer.ada), its function (e.g., integer_buffer), its possible use (e.g., product), its type (e.g., requirements document), its granularity (e.g., module), and its representation (e.g., Ada language). The object interface consists of such things as what are the explicit inputs/outputs needed to define and extract the object as a self-contained unit (e.g., instantiation parameters in the case of a generic Ada package), and what are additionally required assumptions and dependencies (e.g., user's knowledge of Ada). Whereas the object and object interface dimensions provide us with a snapshot of the object at hand, the object context dimension provides us with historical information such as the application classes the object was developed for (e.g., ground support software for satellites), the environment the object was developed in (e.g., waterfall life-cycle model), and its validated or anticipated quality (e.g., reliability). The resulting model refinement is depicted in Figure 5a.

Each reuse candidate is characterized in terms of

- **name**: What is the object's name? (e.g., buffer.ada, sel_inspection, sel_cost_model)
- **function:** What is the functional specification or purpose of the object? (e.g., integer_queue, <element>_buffer, sensor control system, certify appropriateness of design documents, predict project cost)
- **use**: How can the object be used? (e.g., product, process, knowledge)
- **type**: What type of object is it? (e.g., requirements document, code document, inspection method, coding method, specification tool, graphic tool, process model, cost model)
- **granularity:** What is the object's scope? (e.g., system level, subsystem level, component level, module - package, procedure, function - level, entire life cycle, design stage, coding stage)
- **representation**: How is the object represented? (e.g., data, informal set of guidelines, schematized templates, formal mathematical model, languages such as Ada, automated tools)
- **input/output**: What are the external input/output dependencies of the object needed to completely define/extract it as a self-contained entity? (e.g., global data referenced by a code unit, formal and actual input/output parameters of a procedure, instantiation parameters of a generic Ada package, specification and design documents needed to perform a design inspection, defect data produced by a design inspection, variables of a cost model)
- **dependencies:** What are additional assumptions and dependencies needed to understand the object? (e.g., assumption on user's qualification such as knowledge of Ada or qualification to read, specification document to understand a code unit, readability of design document, homogeneity of problem classes and environments underlying a cost model)
- **application domain:** What application classes was the object developed for? (e.g. ground support software for satellites, business software for banking, payroll software)
- **solution domain**: What environment classes was the object developed in? (e.g., waterfall life-cycle model, spiral life-cycle model, iterative enhancement life-cycle model, functional decomposition design method, standard set of methods)
- **object quality:** What qualities does the object exhibit? (e.g., level of reliability, correctness, user-friendliness, defect detection rate, predictability)

A subset of this scheme has been used in Section 3. In contrast to Section 3, we now have a rationale for these dimensions (see Figure 5a) and understand that they cover only part (i.e., the reuse candidate) of the comprehensive reuse model depicted in Figure 4.

4.2.2 Required Objects: In order to characterize the needed objects (or reuse needs), we have chosen the same eleven dimensions and supporting categories as for the reuse candidates. The resulting model refinement is depicted in Figure 5b:

However, an object may change its characteristics during the actual process of reuse. Therefore, its characterizations before and after reuse can be expected to be different. For example, a reuse candidate may be a compiler (type) product (use), and may have been developed according to a waterfall life-cycle approach (solution domain). The needed object is a compiler (type) process (use) integrated into a project based on iterative enhancement (solution domain).

This means that despite the similarity between the refined models of reuse candidates and needed objects, there exists a significant difference in emphasis: In the former case the emphasis is on the potentially reusable objects themselves; in the latter case, the emphasis is on the system in w which these object(s) are (or are expected to be) reused. This explains the use of different dimension names: 'system' and 'system context' instead of 'object interface' and 'object context'.

The distance between the characteristics of a reuse candidate and the needed object give an indication of the gap to be bridged in the event of reuse.

4.2.3 Reuse Process: The reuse process consists of several activities. In the remainder of this paper, we will use a model consisting of four basic activities: identification, evaluation, modification, and integration. In order to characterize each reuse activity we may be interested in its name (e.g., modify.p1), its function (e.g., modify an identified reuse candidate to entirely satisfy given reuse needs), its type (e.g., identification, evaluation, modification), and the mechanism used to perform its function (e.g., modification via parameterization). The interface of each activity may consist of such things as the explicit input/output interfaces between the activity and the enabling software evolution environment (e.g., in the case of modification: performed during the coding phase, assumes the existence of a specification), and other assumptions regarding the evolution environment that need to be satisfied (e.g., existence of certain configuration control policies). The activity context may include information about how reuse candidates are transferred to satisfy given reuse needs (experience transfer), and the quality of each reuse activity (e.g., reliability, productivity). This refinement of the reuse process is depicted in Figure 5c.

In more detail, the dimensions and example categories for each reuse activity are:

- **name**: What is the name of the activity? (e.g., identify. generics, evaluate.generics, modify.generics, integrate.generics)
- **function**: What is the function performed by the activity? (e.g., select candidate objects $\{x_i\}$ which satisfy certain characteristics of the reuse needs x'; evaluate the potential of the selected candidate objects of satisfying the given system and system context dimensions of the reuse requirements x' and pick the most suited candidate x_k; modify x_k to entirely satisfy x'; integrate object x into the current development project)
- **type:** What is the type of the activity? (e.g., identification, evaluation, modification, integration)

- **mechanism:** How is the activity performed? (in the case of identification: e.g., by name, by function, by type and function; in the case of evaluation: e.g., by subjective judgment, by evaluation of historical baseline measurement data; in the case of modification: e.g., verbatim, parameterized, template-based, unconstrained; in the case of integration: e.g., according to the system configuration plan, according to the project/process plan)
- **input/output:** What are explicit input and output interfaces between the reuse activity and the enabling software evolution environment? (in the case of identification: e.g., description of reuse needs / set of reuse candidates; in the case of modification: e.g., one selected reuse candidate, specification for the object to be reused / object to be reused)
- **dependencies:** What are other implicit assumptions and dependencies on data and information regarding the software evolution environment? (e.g., time at which reuse activity is performed - relative to the enabling development process: e.g., during design or coding stages; additional information needed to perform the reuse activity effectively: e.g., package specification to instantiate a generic package, knowledge of system configuration plan, configuration management procedures, or project plan)
- **experience transfer:** What are the support mechanisms for transferring experience across projects? (e.g., human, experience base, automated)
- **reuse quality:** What is the quality of each reuse activity? (e.g., high reliability, high predictability of modification cost, correctness, average performance)

4.3 Example Applications of the Comprehensive Reuse Model

We demonstrate the applicability of our model-based reuse scheme by characterizing the three hypothetical reuse scenarios which have been used informally throughout this paper: Ada generics, design inspections, and cost models. The resulting characterizations are summarized in tables 1-3.

5. Support Mechanisms for Comprehensive Reuse

According to the reuse oriented software development model depicted in Figure 2, effective reuse needs to take place in an environment that supports continuous improvement, i.e., recording of experience across all projects, appropriate packaging and storing of recorded experience, and reusing existing experience whenever feasible. In the TAME project at the University of Maryland, such an environment model has been proposed and (partial) prototype environments are currently being built according to this model. In the remainder of this section, we introduce the reuse oriented TAME environment model, discuss a number of mechanisms for effective reuse, and introduce several prototype environments being built according to the TAME model.

5.1 The Reuse Oriented TAME Environment Model

The important components of the reuse oriented TAME environment model are depicted in Figure 6: the project organization which performs individual development projects, the experience base which stores and actively modifies development experience from all projects, and the mechanisms for learning and reuse. The shaded areas in Figure 6 indicate how the reuse model of Figure 3 intersects with the TAME environment model.

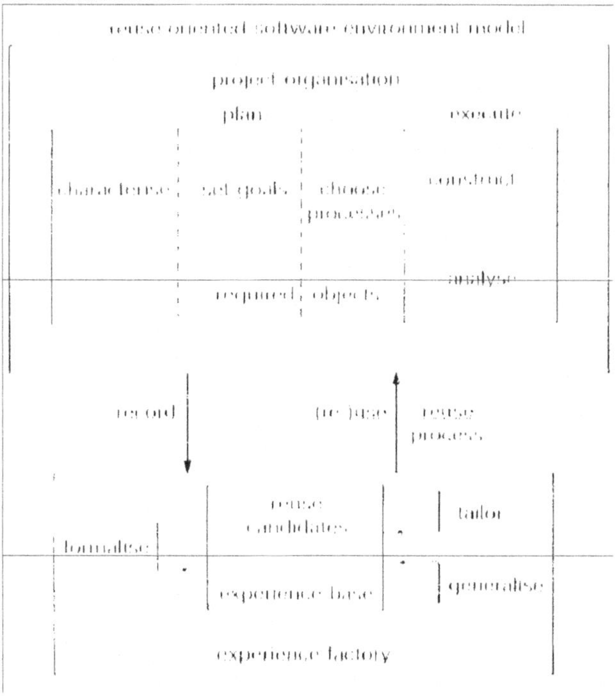

Figure 6. Reuse-oriented software environment model

Within the project organization each development project is performed according to the quality improvement paradigm [3, 9]. The quality improvement paradigm consists of the following steps:

- **Plan:** Characterize the current project environment so that the appropriate past experience can be made available to the current project. Set up the goals for the project and refine them into quantifiable questions and metrics for successful project performance and improvement over previous project performances (e.g., based upon the goal/question/metric paradigm [9, 13]). Choose the appropriate software development process model for this project with the supporting methods and tools - for both construction and analysis.
- **Execute:** Construct the products according to the chosen development process model, methods and tools. Collect the prescribed data, validate and ana-

lyze it to provide feedback in real-time for corrective action on the current project.

- **Package:** Analyze the data in a post-mortem fashion to evaluate the current practices, determine problems, record findings and make recommendations for improvement for future projects. Package the experiences in the form of updated and refined models and other forms of structured knowledge gained from this and previous projects, and save it in an experience base so it can be available to future projects.

The experience base contains reuse candidates of different types, granularity and representation. Example entries in the case of the examples described in section 4.3 include objects of type 'code document', granularity 'package' and representation 'Ada'; objects of type 'inspection method', granularity 'design stage' and representation 'schematized template'; and objects of type 'cost model', granularity 'entire life cycle' and representation 'formal mathematical model'.

During each step of a development project performed according to the quality improvement paradigm reuse needs are identified and matches made against reuse candidates available in the experience base. During the characterization step, characteristics of the current project environment can be used to identify appropriate past experience in the experience base, e.g. based on project characteristics the appropriate instantiation of a cost model can be generated. During the planning step, project goals can be used to identify existing similar goal/question/metric models or process/product/quality models in the experience base, e.g., based on project goals a goal/question/metric model can be chosen for evaluating a design inspection method. During the execution step, product specifications can be used to identify existing components from prior projects, such as Ada generics. During the feedback step, the analysis goals generated during planning are used as the basis of analysis by fitting baselines to compare against the current data. As part of the feedback step a decision is made as to which experiences are worth recording. The degree of guidance that can be provided for entering reuse candidates into the experience base depends upon the accumulated knowledge of expected reuse requests for future projects.

The experience base is part of an active organizational entity, referred to a the Experience Factory [4], that supports project developments by analyzing and synthesizing all kinds of experience, acting as a repository for such experience, and supplying that experience to various projects on demand. In the context of the reuse oriented software environment model, the Experience Factory not only stores experience in a variety of repositories, but performs the constant modification of experience to increase its reuse potential. Example modifications address the formalization of experience (e.g., building a cost model empirically based upon the data available), tailoring of experience to fit the needs of a specific project (e.g., instantiating an Ada package from a generic package), and the generalizing of experience to be applicable across project classes (e.g., developing a generic package from a specific package). It plays the role of an organizational 'server' aimed at satisfying project specific reuse requests effectively [4]. The constant collection of measurement data regarding reuse needs and the reuse processes themselves enables the judgments needed to populate the experience base effectively and select the best suited reuse candidates. The use of the quality improvement paradigm within the project organization enables the integration of measurement-based analysis and construction.

5.2 Mechanisms to Support Effective Reuse in the TAME Environment Model

Improvement in the reuse oriented TAME environment model of Figure 6 is based on the feedback of experience captured from prior projects into ongoing and future software developments. The mechanisms needed to support effective feedback are listed in Figure 7.

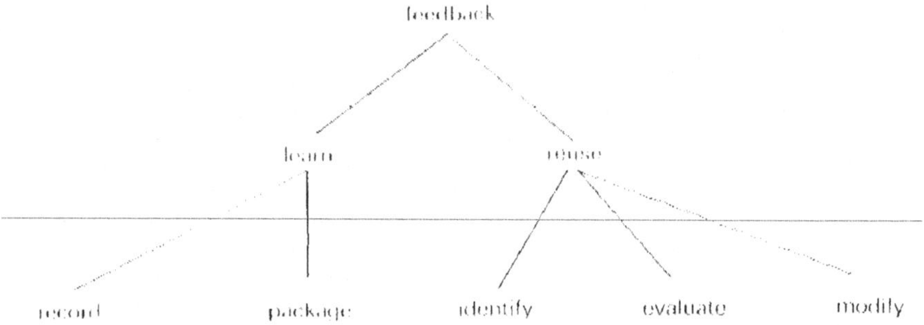

Figure 7. Mechanisms required to support effective feedback of experience

Feedback requires learning and reuse. Although learning and reuse are possible in any environment, we are interested in addressing and supporting them explicitly and systematically. Systematic learning requires support for the recording of experience in some experience base and its packaging in order to increase its reuse potential for anticipated reuse needs in future developments. Systematic reuse requires support for the identification of candidate experience, its evaluation, and modification.

Reuse and learning are possible in any environment. However, we want learning and reuse to be explicitly planned, not implicit or coincidental. In the reuse oriented software development environment, learning and reuse are explicitly modeled and become desired characteristics of software development. They are specific processes performed in conjunction with the Experience Factory.

5.3.1 Recording of Experience: The objective of recording experience is to create a repository of well-specified and organized experience. This requires a precise characterization of the reuse candidates to be recorded, the design and implementation of a comprehensive experience base, and effective mechanisms for collecting, qualifying, storing and retrieving experience. The characterization of reuse candidates is derived from characterizations of known reuse needs and reuse processes. The characterization of reuse candidates describes what information needs to be stored in addition to the objects themselves in order to make them reusable, and how it should be packaged. The experience base replaces the project database of traditional environment models by the more comprehensive concept of an experience base which is intended to capture the entire body of experience recorded during the planning and execution steps of all software projects within an organization.

Table 1 Characterisations of reuse candidates

	Reuse examples		
Dimensions	Ada generics	Design inspections	Cost models
name function use type granularity representation	buffer.ada element buffer product code document package Ada generic package	sel_inspection_waterfall certify appropriateness of design documents process inspection method design stage informal set of guidelines	sel_cost_model_fortran predict project cost knowledge cost model entire life cycle formal mathematical model
input/output	formal and actual instantiation parameters (type and number)	specification and design document required, defect data produced	estimated product size in KLOC, complexity rating, methodology level, cost in staff hours
dependencies	assumes Ada knowledge	assumes a readable design, qualified reader	assumes a relatively homogeneous class of problems and environments
application domain solution domain	ground support software for satellites waterfall (Ada) life cycle model, functional decomposition design method	ground support software for satellites waterfall Ada) life cycle model, standard set of methods	ground support software for satellites waterfall (Ada) life cycle model standard set of methods
object quality	high reliability (e.g., 0.1 defects per KLOC for a given set of acceptance tests)	average defect detection rate (e.g., 0.5 defects detected per staff hour)	average predictability (e.g., 10% prediction error)

Examples of recording experience include the storing of Ada generics, design inspection methods, and cost models. Based on our reuse model, Table 1 describes the information needed in conjunction with each of these object types in order to make them likely reuse candidates to satisfy the hypothetical reuse needs using the hypothetical reuse processes described in Tables 2 and 3, respectively. For example, in the case of Ada generics, we may require each object to be augmented with information on the number of instantiation parameters, the application and solution domain, and the expected or demonstrated reliability. If we can quantify such information (e.g., Ada generics developed within ground support software projects, Ada generics with less than 5 instantiation parameters are acceptable), we can use it to exclude inappropriate objects from being recorded in the first place.

Table 2 Characterisations of required objects

		Reuse examples	
Dimensions	Ada generics	Design inspections	Cost models
name	string buffer ada	set inspection,cleanroom	sel cost model ada
function	string buffer	certify appropriateness of design documents	predict project cost
use	product	process	knowledge
type	code document	inspection method	cost model
granularity	package	design stage	entire life cycle
representation	Ada	informal set of guidelines	formal mathematical model
input output	formal and actual instantiation parameters (type and number)	specification and design document required, defect data produced	estimated product size in KLOC, complexity rating, methodology level, cost in staff hours
dependencies	assumes Ada knowledge	assumes a readable design, qualified reader	assumes a relatively homogeneous class of problems and environments
application domain	ground support software for satellites	ground support software for satellites	ground support software for satellites
solution domain	waterfall (Ad) life cycle model, object oriented design method	Cleanroom (Fortran) development model, step wise refinement oriented design, statistical testing	waterfall (Ada) life cycle model, revised set of methods
object quality	high reliability (e.g. < 0.1 defects per KLoC for a given set of acceptance tests), high performance (e.g. max. response times for a set of tests)	high defect detection rate (e.g. > 1.0 defects detected per staff hour) wrt. interface faults	high predictability (e.g. ± 5% prediction error)

5.2.2 Packaging of Experience: The objective of packaging experience is to increase its reuse potential. This requires a precise characterization of the new reuse needs or processes, and effective mechanisms for generalizing, generalizing and formalizing experience. Packaging may take place at the time of first recording experience into the experience base or at any later time when new reuse needs reuse needs become known or our understanding of the interrelationship between reuse candidates, reuse needs and reuse processes changes.

The objective of generalizing existing experience prior to its reuse is to make a candidate reuse object useful in a larger set of potential target applications. The objective of tailoring existing experience prior to its potential reuse is to fine-tune a candidate reuse object to fit a specific task or exhibit special attributes, such as size or performance. The objective of formalizing existing experience prior to its actual reuse is to increase the reuse potential of reuse candidates by encoding them in more precise, better understood ways. These activities require a well-documented cataloged and categorized set of reuse candidates, mechanisms that support the modification process, and an understanding of the potential reuse needs. Generalization and tailoring are specifically concerned with changing the application and solution domain characteristics of reuse candidates: from project specific to domain specific to project specific and vice versa. Objectives and characteristics are different from project to project, and even more so from environment to environment. We cannot reuse past experience without modifying it to the needs of the current project. The stability of the environment in which reuse takes place, as well as the origination of the experience, determine the amount of tailoring required. Formalization activities are concerned with movement across the boundaries of the representation dimension within the experience base: from informal to schematized and then to formal.

Table 3 Characterisations of reuse processes

	Reuse examples		
Dimensions	Ada generics	Design inspections	Cost models
name	modify generics	modify inspections	modify cost models
function	modify to satisfy target specification	modify to satisfy target specification	modify to satisfy target specification
type	modification	modification	modification
mechanism	parameterised (generic mechanism)	unconstrained	template based
input output	buffer.ada, reuse specification string_buffer.ada	set_inspection_waterfall, reuse specification set_inspection_cleanroom	set_cost_model.fortran, reuse specification set_cost_model.ada
dependencies	performed during coding stage package specification required, knowledge of system configuration plan	performed during planning stage, knowledge of project plan	performed during planning stage, knowledge of historical Ada project profiles
experience transfer	automated	human and experience base	experience base
reuse quality	correctness	predictability of modification cost	efficiency

Examples of tailoring experience include the instantiation of a set of specific Ada packages from a generic package available in an object oriented experience base, the fine-tuning of a cost model to the specific characteristics of a class of projects, and the adjustment of a design inspection method to focus on the class of defects common to the application. Examples of generalizing experience include the creation of a generic Ada package from a set of specific Ada packages, the creation of a general cost model from a set of domain specific cost models, and the definition of an application and solution domain specific design inspection method based on the experience with design inspections in a number of specific projects. Examples of formalization include the writing of functional specifications for generic Ada packages, providing automated support for checking adherence to entry and exit criteria of a design inspection method, and building a cost model empirically based upon the data available in an experience base.

A misunderstanding of the importance of tailoring exists in many organizations. These organizations have specific development guidebooks which are of limited value because they 'are written for some ideal project' which 'has nothing in common with the current project and, therefore, do not apply'. All guidebooks (including standards such as DOD-STD-2167) are general and need to be tailored to each project in order to be effective.

5.2.3 Identification of Candidate Experience: The objective of identifying candidate experience is to find a set of candidates with the potential to satisfy project specific reuse needs. This requires a precise characterization of the reuse needs, some organizational scheme for the reuse candidates available in the experience base, and an effective mechanism for matching characteristics of the project specific reuse needs against the experience base.

Let's assume, for example, that we need an Ada package which implements a 'string_buffer' with high 'reliability and performance' characteristics. This need may have been established during the project planning phase based on domain analysis, or during the design or coding stages. We identify candidate objects based on some subset of the object related characteristics stated in Table 2: string_buffer.ada, string_buffer, product, code document, package, Ada [25]. The more characteristics we use for identification, the smaller the resulting set of candidate objects will be. For example, if we include the name itself, we will either find exactly one object or none. Identification may take place during any project stage. We will assume that the set of successfully identified reuse candidates contains 'buffer.ada', the object characterized in Table 1.

5.2.4 Evaluation of Experience: The objective of evaluating experience is to characterize the degree of discrepancies between a given set of reuse needs (see Table 2) and some identified reuse candidate (Table 1), and (ii) predict the cost of bridging the gap between reuse candidates and reuse needs. The first type of evaluation goal can be achieved by capturing detailed information about reuse candidates and reuse needs according to the dimensions of the presented characterization scheme. The second goal requires the inclusion of data characterizing the reuse process itself and past experience about similar reuse activities. Effective evaluation requires precise characterization of reuse needs, reuse processes and reuse candidates; knowledge about their relationships, and effective mechanisms for measurement.

The knowledge regarding the interrelationship between reuse needs, processes and candidates is the result of the proposed evolutionary learning, which takes place within the reuse oriented TAME environment model. The mechanisms used for effective measurement are based on the goal/question/metric paradigm [9,11,13]. It provides templates for guiding the selection of appropriate metrics based on a precise definition of the evaluation goal. Guidance exists at the level of identifying certain types of metrics (e.g., to quantify the object of interest, to quantify the perspective of interest, to quantify the quality aspect of interest). Using the goal/question/metric paradigm in conjunction with reuse characterizations like the ones depicted in Tables 1-3, provides very detailed guidance as to what exact metrics need to be used. For example, evaluation of the Ada generic example suggests metrics to characterize discrepancies between the reuse needs and all available reuse candidates in terms of function, use, type, granularity, and representation on a nominal scale defined by the respective categories, input/output interface on an ordinal scale 'number of instantiation params', application and solution domains on nominal scales, and qualities such as performance based on benchmark tests.

For example, we want to evaluate the reuse potential of the object 'buffer.ada' identified in the previous subsection. We need to evaluate whether and to what degree 'buffer.ada' (as well as any other identified candidate) needs to be modified and estimate the cost of such modification compared to the cost required for creating the desired object 'string_buffer' from scratch. Three characteristics of the chosen reuse candidate deviate from the expected ones: it is more general than needed (see function dimension), it has been developed according to a different design approach (see solution domain dimension), and it does not contain any information about its performance behavior (see object quality dimension). The functional discrepancy requires instantiating object 'buffer.ada' for data type 'string'. The cost of this modification is extremely low due to the fact that the generic instantiation mechanism in Ada can be used for modification (see Table 3). The remaining two discrepancies cannot be evaluated based on the information available through the characterizations in section 4.3. On the one hand, ignoring the solution domain discrepancy may result in problems during the integration phase. On the other hand, it may be hard to predict the cost of transforming 'buffer.ada' to adhere to object oriented principles. Without additional information about either the integration of non-object oriented packages or the cost of modification, we only have the choice between two risks. Predicting the cost of changes necessary to satisfy the stated object performance requirements is impossible because we have no information about the candidate's performance behavior. It is noteworthy that very often practical reuse seems to fail because of lack of appropriate information to evaluate the reuse implications a-priori, rather than because of technical infeasibility [15].

The characterization of both reuse candidates and needs and the reuse process allow us to understand some of the implications and risks associated with discrepancies between identified reuse candidates and target reuse needs. Problems arise when we have either insufficient information about the existence of a discrepancy (e.g., object performance quality in our example), or no understanding of the implications of an identified discrepancy (e.g., solution domain in our example). In order to avoid the first type of problem, one may either constrain the identification process further by including characteristics other than just the object related ones, or not have any objects without 'performance' data in the reuse repository. If we had included 'desired solution domain' and 'object performance' as additional criteria in our identification process, we may not have selected object 'buffer.ada' at all. If every object in our repository would have performance data attached to it, we at least would be able to establish the fact that there exists a discrepancy. In order to avoid the second type of problem, we need have some (semi-) automated modification mechanism, or at least historical data about the cost involved in similar past situations. It is clear that in our example any functional discrepancy within the scope of the instantiation parameters is easy to bridge due to the availability of a completely automated modification mechanism (i.e., generic instantiation in Ada). Any functional discrepancy that cannot be bridged through this mechanisms poses a larger and possibly unpredictable risk. Whether it is more costly to re-design 'buffer.ada' in order to adhere to object oriented design principles or to re-develop it from scratch is not obvious without past experience. A mechanism for modeling all kinds of experience is given in [6].

5.2.5 Modification of Experience: The objective of modifying experience is to bridge the gap between selected reuse candidates and given reuse needs. This requires a precise characterization of the reuse needs, and effective mechanisms for modification. Technically, modification mechanisms are very similar to the tailoring (and generalization) mechanism introduced for packaging experience. Tailoring here is different in that during modification the target is described by concrete, project specific reuse needs, whereas during packaging the target is typically imprecise in that it reflects anticipated reuse needs in a class of future projects. We refer to tailoring (and generalizing) as 'off-line' (during packaging) or 'on-line' (during modification) depending on whether it takes place before or as part of a concrete instance of reuse.

Examples of modifying experience - similar to the examples given earlier for tailoring – include the instantiation of a set of specific Ada packages from a generic package available in an object oriented experience base, the fine-tuning of a cost model to the specific characteristics of a class of projects, and the adjustment of a design inspection method to focus on the class of defects common to the application.

5.3 TAME Environment Prototypes

In the TAME (Tailoring A Measurement Environment) project, we investigate fundamental issues related to the reuse- (or improvement-) oriented software environment model of Figure 6 and build a series of (partial) research prototype versions [8, 9, 15].

Current research topics include the formalization of the goal/question/metric paradigm for effective software measurement and evaluation; the development of formalisms for representing software engineering experience such as quality models, lessons learned, process models, product models; the development of models for packaging experience in the experience base; and the development of effective mechanisms to support learning and reuse within the experience factory (e.g., qualification, formalization, tailoring, generalization, synthesis). In addition, various slices of an evolving TAME environment are being prototyped in order to study the definition and integration of different concepts.

Aspects of the TAME research prototypes, currently being developed at the University of Maryland, can be classified best by the different classes of experience they attempt to generate, maintain and reuse:

- Support for identifying objects by browsing through projects, goals and processes based on a facet-based characterization mechanism.
- Support for the generalization, tailoring, and integration of a variety experience types based on an object oriented experience base model.
- Support for the definition of environment specific cost and resource allocation models and their tailoring, generalization and formalization based on project experience.
- Support for the definition of test techniques in terms of entry and exit criteria that provides a method for selecting the appropriate technique for each project phase based on environment characteristics, data models, and project goals.
- Support for the definition of process models and their formalization, generalization and tailoring based on project experience.
- Support for an experience factory architecture that supports the evolution of the organization.

6. Conclusions

We have introduced a comprehensive reuse framework consisting of reuse models, model-based characterization schemes, the TAME environment model supporting the integration of reuse into software development, and ongoing research and development efforts toward a TAME environment prototype.

The presented reuse model and related model-based characterization schemes have advantages over existing models and schemes in that they

- allow us to capture the reuse of any type of experience.
- address reuse candidates and reuse needs as well as the reuse process itself.
- provide a rationale for the chosen characterizing dimensions.

We have demonstrated the advantages of such a comprehensive reuse model and related schemes by applying them to the characterization of example reuse scenarios. Especially their usefulness for defining and motivating the support mechanisms for comprehensive reuse and learning were stressed.

Finally, we introduced the TAME environment model which supports the integration of reuse into software developments. Several partial instantiations of the TAME environment model, currently being developed at the University of Maryland, have been mentioned. In order to make reuse a reality, more research is required towards understanding and conceptualizing activities and aspects related to reuse, learning and experience factory technology.

7. Acknowledgements

We thank all our colleagues and graduate students who contributed to this paper, especially all members of the TAME, CARE and LASER projects. We also thank the Guest Editors, Nazim H. Madhavji and Wilhelm Schaefer, and the anonymous referees for their excellent suggestions for improving this paper.

8. References

[1] B. H. Barnes and T. B. Bollinger, "Making Reuse Cost-Effective", IEEE Software Magazine, January 1991, pp. 13-24.

[2] V. R. Basili, "Can We Measure Software Technology: Lessons Learned from Eight Years of Trying", in Proc. Tenth Annual Software Engineering Workshop, NASA Goddard Space Flight Center, Greenbelt, MD, December 1985.

[3] V. R. Basili, "Quantitative Evaluation of Software Methodology", Dept. of Computer Science, University of Maryland, College Park, TR-1519, July 1985 [also in Proc. of the First Pan Pacific Computer Conference, Australia, September 1986].

[4] V. R. Basili, "Software Development: A Paradigm for the Future", Proc. 13th Annual International Computer Software & Applications Conference, Orlando, FL, September 20-22, 1989.

[5] V. R. Basili, "Viewing Maintenance as Reuse Oriented Software Development", IEEE Software Magazine, January 1990, pp. 19-25.

[6] V. R. Basili, G. Caldiera, and G. Cantone, "A Reference Architecture for the Component Factory", Technical Report TR-3333, Dept. of Computer Science, University of Maryland, College Park, MD 20742, March 1991.

[7] V. R. Basili and H. D. Rombach, "Tailoring the Software Process to Project Goals and Environments", Proc. Of the Ninth International Conference on Software Engineering, Monterey, CA, March 30 - April 2, 1987, pp. 345-357.

[8] V. R. Basili and H. D. Rombach, "TAME: Integrating Measurement into Software Environments", Technical Report TR-1764 (or TAME-TR-1-1987), Dept. of Computer Science, University of Maryland, College Park, MD 20742, June 1987.

[9] V. R. Basili and H. D. Rombach "The TAME Project: Towards Improvement Oriented Software Environments", IEEE Transactions on Software Engineering, vol. SE-14, no. 6, June 1988, pp. 758-773.

[10] V. R. Basili and H. D. Rombach, "Towards a Comprehensive Framework for Reuse: A Reuse-Enabling Software Evolution Environment (part I)/Model-Based Reuse Characterization Schemes (part II)", Technical Reports, Dept. of Computer Science (CS-TR-2158/CS-TR-2446) and UMIACS (UMIACS-TR-88-92/UMIACS-TR-90-47), University of Maryland, College Park, MD 20742, December 1988/April 1990.

[11] V. R. Basili and R. W. Selby, "Comparing the Effectiveness of Software Testing Strategies", IEEE Transactions on Software Engineering, vol. SE-13, no.12, December 1987, pp.1278-1296.

[12] V. R. Basili and M. Shaw, "Scope of Software Reuse", White paper, working group on 'Scope of Software Reuse', Tenth Minnowbrook Workshop on Software Reuse, Blue Mountain Lake, New York, July 1987 (in preparation).

[13] V. R. Basili and D. M. Weiss, "A Methodology for Collecting Valid Software Engineering Data", IEEE Transactions on Software Engineering, vol.SE-10, no.3, November 1984, pp.728-738.

[14] Ted Biggerstaff, "Reusability Framework, Assessment, and Directions", IEEE Software Magazine, March 1987, pp.41-49.

[15] G. Caldiera and V. R. Basili, "Reengineering Existing Software for Reusability", Technical Report (UMIACS-TR-90-30, CS-TR-2419), Dept. of Computer Science, University of Maryland, College Park, MD 20742, February 1990.

[16] S. Cardenas and M. V. Zelkowitz, "Evaluation Criteria for Functional Specifications", Proc. of the 12th IEEE International Conference on Software Engineering, Nice, France, March 26-30, 1990, pp. 26-33.

[17] P. Freeman, "Reusable Software Engineering: Concepts and Research Directions", Proc. of the Workshop on Reusability, September 1983, pp. 63-76.

[18] R. Prieto-Diaz and P. Freeman, "Classifying Software for Reusability", IEEE Software, vol.4, no.1, January 1987, pp. 6-16.

[19] IEEE Software, special issue on 'Reusing Software', vol.4, no.1, January 1987.

[2-] IEEE Software, special issue on 'Tools: Making Reuse a Reality', vol.4, no.7, July 1987.

[21] G. A. Jones and R. Prieto-Diaz, "Building and Managing Software Libraries", Proc. Compsac'88, Chicago, October 5-7, 1988, pp. 228-236.

[22] A. Kouchakdjian, V. R. Basili, and S. Green, "The Evolution of the Cleanroom Process in the Software Engineering Laboratory", IEEE Software Magazine (to appear 1990).

[23] F. E. McGarry, "Recent SEL Studies", in Proc. Tenth Annual Software Engineering Workshop, NASA Goddard Space Flight Center, Greenbelt, MD, Dec. 1985.

[24] A. Mili, W. Xiao-Yang, and Y. Qing, "Specification Methodology: An Integrated Relational Approach", Software - Practice and Experience, vol. 16, no. 11, November 1986, pp. 1003-1030.

[25] E. Ostertag, J. Hendler, R. Prieto-Diaz, and C. Braun, "Computing Similarity for Software Reuse: An AI-Based Approach", Technical Report CS-TR-3335, Dept. of Computer Science, University of Maryland, College Park, MD 20742, March 1991.

[26] R. W. Selby, Jr., V. R. Basili, and T. Baker, "CLEANROOM Software Development: An Empirical Evaluation", IEEE Transactions on Software Engineering, vol. SE-13, no. 9, September 1987, pp.1027-1037.

[27] Mary Shaw, "Purposes and Varieties of Software Reuse", Proceedings of the Tenth Minnowbrook Workshop on Software Reuse, Blue Mountain Lake, New York, July, 1987.

[28] T. A. Standish, "An Essay on Software Reuse", IEEE Transactions on Software Engineering, vol. SE-10, no. 5, September 1984, pp.494-497.

[29] W. Tracz, "Tutorial on 'Software Reuse: Emerging Technology'", IEEE Catalog Number EHO278-2, 1988.

[30] M. V. Zelkowitz (ed.), "Proceedings of the University of Maryland Workshop on 'Requirements for a Software Engineering Environment', Greenbelt, MD, May 1986", Technical Report TR-1733, Dept. of Computer Science, University of Maryland, College Park, MD 20742, December 1986 [also published by, Ablex Publ., 1988].

The paper was first received on 29th May 1990 and in revised form on 6th February 1991.

Technology Transfer at Motorola

Victor Basili, Michael Daskalantonakis and Robert Yacobellis

While developing a formal software-review process, a working group at Motorola devised a technology-transfer model that is built on process packages, each one targeted to a different user group. Their model allows for tailoring, makes training and consulting widely available, and relies on champions.

Although new processes, methods, and tools are introduced in the literature every year, few are actually adopted. Development managers in industry complain that these new ideas are either not applicable to real-world projects or that their process is not mature enough to incorporate them.

Consider a project manager who buys a tool to improve change control. The tool is virtually worthless without a well-defined, documented, and reasonable change-control process, and even if there is such a process the development team

Victor R. Basili is with the University of Maryland. Michael K. Daskalantonakis and Robert H. Yacobellis are with Motorola.

is likely to need training in both the process and the tool before they can be used on a real project. But too often the manager fails to allocate sufficient training time and doesn't anticipate the initial drop in productivity. This situation occurs time and time again.

We believe part of the problem is that the industry lacks a focused, needs-based approach to tailoring and transferring software-engineering technology. At Motorola, we have developed an approach that helps development organizations focus on the technology they really need, devise solutions, and transfer those solutions to development teams. In this article, we report our experience using this approach in the last five years and the lessons we learned.

Targeted Process Packages

Through 15 years of study at the US National Aeronautics and Space Administration's Software Engineering Laboratory and elsewhere, a set of software-engineering technology principles has evolved[1] that recommend organizations

- Develop quality-focused software-engineering technology within a business unit.
- Formalize plans to tailor, transfer, and deploy software-engineering technology.
- Evaluate software-engineering technology to improve it on the basis of feedback obtained from goal-oriented measurement.
- Experience in applying these principles, in turn, has produced recommendations for measuring software processes and products in the context of software-engineering technology:
    - Conduct goal-oriented, top-down measurement of processes and products.
    - View the measurements and their interpretation from an appropriate perspective.
    - Account for differences in project environments, processes, products, and available technology.

These principles and recommendations are embodied in two paradigms: the Quality Improvement Paradigm, a three-part process-improvement approach, and the Goal-Question-Metric paradigm,[2] a mechanism that the Quality Improvement Paradigm incorporates for establishing project and corporate goals and measuring against those goals.

Motorola's corporate-wide Metrics Working Group adopted the Quality Improvement Paradigm and instantiated it with a set of organizational procedures to identify, tailor, and transfer software-engineering technology. The Motorola version is called the Software Engineering Improvement Paradigm. It is designed to help managers focus on software-engineering technology as it applies to specific development activities, such as testing, product reviews, and management. It also provides a justification for selecting and tailoring software-engineering technology to individual projects and a mechanism for evaluating technology against a business unit's goals.

Fundamental to our approach is the *process package*, a set of documents and training material that communicates everything about the technology you are trying to transfer. A process package includes an overview of what to expect, how to use the information, references to other corporate efforts and process packages, guidelines for using the process, training aids targeted to different user groups, a set of slides for conducting training workshops, and data and lessons learned.

As Figure 1 shows, a process package evolves over time as experience is gained and feedback is incorporated. Our approach builds on the Quality Improvement Paradigm's three phases: planning, execution, and analysis and packaging. Within these three phases, we defined seven steps:

1. Characterize and evaluate the organization's current environment and technology.
2. Set organizational goals and refine them into quantifiable questions and metrics. Choose the processes that have the best chance of paying off if technology improvements are made.
3. Create documents, targeted to different audiences, that define new technology or improvements to existing technology in those high-payoff areas.
4. Pilot the technology in sample projects, analyze the data, refine the technology, and create a lessons-learned document.
5. Enhance the process package by targeting the training materials and consulting support to a particular audience.
6. Deploy the technology within a business unit, monitor its use carefully, and learn from the organization's progress.
7. Analyze data from using the process package, evaluate the practices, and improve the process package. Proceed to step 1 and, armed with the recorded, structured experience gained from this and previous cycles, start the cycle again. Package this experience to make it accessible to others involved in creating process packages.

Motorola's Three-Stage Formal Software-Review Process

Many software projects in industry use reviews to detect problems early. However, the degree to which they are an integral part of the development process and their effectiveness varies widely. At Motorola, we felt there was a need to formalize the review process and its measurement to maximize its effectiveness and efficiency.

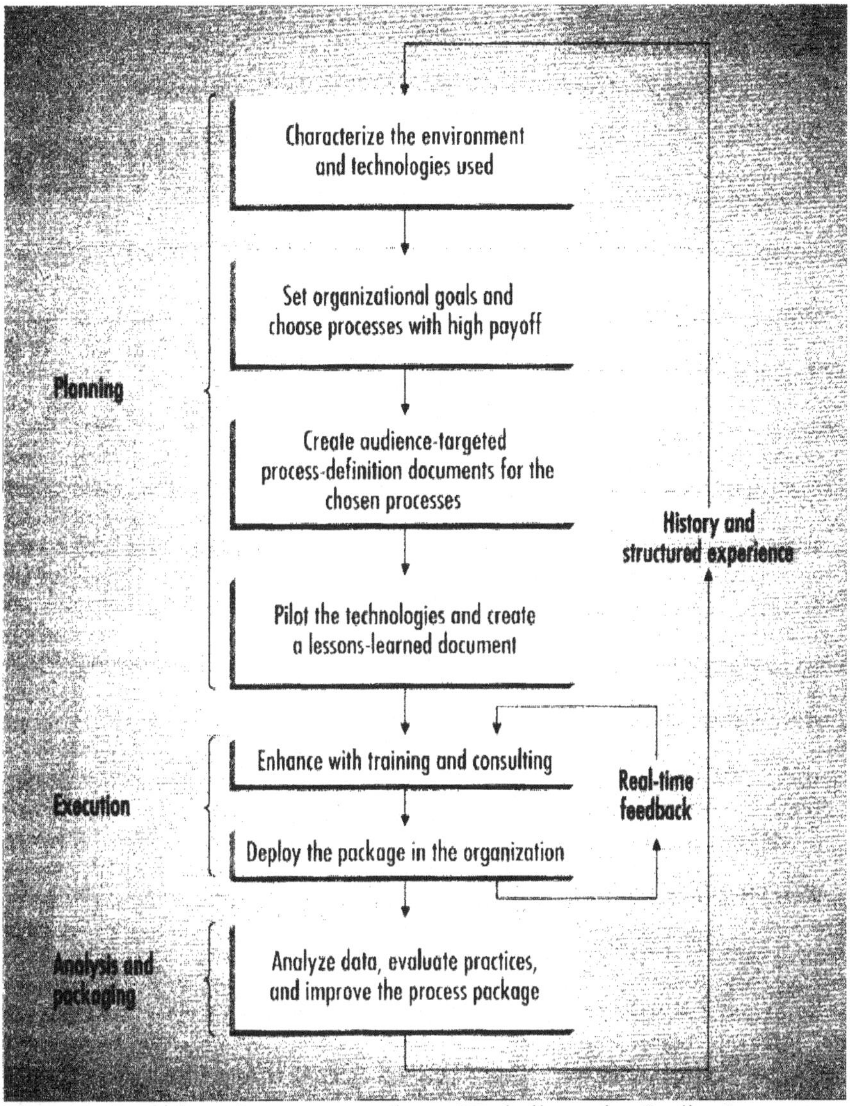

Figure 1. Evolution of a process package. We built on the Quality Improvement Paradigm's planning, execution, and analysis and packaging phases, then defined seven steps to transferring technology via process packages.

Three Stages

The review process package defines a three-stage formal process:

1. *Reviewer preparation.* Participants agree that the material is ready, select a leader and a review team, schedule a meeting, prepare material, have an op-

tional orientation meeting, study the material and inform the review leader of faults found, and decide if they should hold a meeting or if additional preparation is needed.

2. *Review meeting.* The review leader introduces the reviewers and their roles and outlines the purpose of the review. Then the presenter starts and reviewers ask questions to expose problems, the author of the reviewed material answers with clarifications only, the recorder takes notes, and the presenter starts again in a loop until the review disposition is determined. The recorder completes a report documenting the review disposition and faults found.
3. *Follow-ups.* The review meeting report is published, the developers fix errors and defects, the recorder fills out a software process-assurance form that summarizes metrics data so that it can be used to improve the process, and the review leader ensures follow-up and schedules any additional reviews.

We based this process description on existing practices within several groups in Motorola and published work. However, we tailored our process to address some major issues we identified, such as reviewer preparation.

The package also contains a set of guidelines aimed at enhancing the effectiveness and efficiency of reviews. We developed and continuously improved them by analyzing the data collected for the review metrics defined.

Review Goals

An integral part of the review process is the collection and analysis of metrics data for improving not only the review process, but also the development process and the product being reviewed.

We used the Goal-Question-Metric approach to establish quantitative goals for the review process, define the measurements that must be taken to evaluate its effectiveness, discover problems, and improve it. Although this use of GQM was tailored to our priorities, our experience is applicable to projects with different priorities.

Our primary measurement goal was

- Analyze the review process to improve its effectiveness in removing faults, from the corporation's point of view.

Our secondary goals, which used the same data, were

- Analyze the constructive and analytic process of the previous development phases to improve their ability to generate a fault-free product, from the corporation's point of view.
- Analyze the construction process of the current development phase to improve its ability to generate a fault-free product, from the corporation's point of view.
- Analyze the product before and after the review to evaluate its correctness, from the project manager's point of view.

GQM requires that you characterize the environment of the specific project to provide a framework for comparison and to expose other factors that may influence behavior. Sample factors include the number of software engineers on the project; their average expertise and familiarity with the application domain and its difficulty; development techniques, tools, and hardware; estimated project size; and target machine.

Table A: Analyzing metrics to determine project quality at end of phase								
Conditions				**Facts**				
RPC	**RPD**	**ET**	**DT**	**Score**	**Product-in**	**Product-out**	**Process-previous**	**Process-current**
C	S	LS	LS	5	good	good	effective	effective
C	S	H	LS	4	good	fixed-up	effective	not-effective
C	S	LS	H	2	Poor	fixed-up	not-effective	effective
C	S	H	H	1	Poor	fixed-up	not-effective	not-effective
N	x	x	x	0	?	?	?	?
x	U	x	x	0	?	?	?	?

x = don't care value
? = no value due to insufficient information

product-in = product received after review and changes in previous phase
product-out = product generated by current phase after review and changes
process-previous = construction and review process used in previous phase
process-current = construction process used in the current phase

Review Metrics

Using GQM to define metrics involves mapping the measurement goals to sets of questions, which in turn generates supporting questions and defines the metrics that should be collected during a review.

Some of the metrics we defined to evaluate the review process are

- *Review Process Compliance.* A subjective determination of how well the constructive process and subsequent review has complied with the review process. This subjective determination is done by the person having the SQA perspective. An RPC value is either C (compliant) or N (noncompliant).
- *Review Process Domain.* A subjective determination of how well the reviewers understood the document (based on their level of experience and the perspective they represent). This subjective determination is done by the person having the SQA perspective. An RPD value is either S (satisfactory) or U (unsatisfactory).

  We defined several metrics for evaluating faults in a product as well as the effectiveness of the fault-removal activities (an error is a fault found during a formal review of a deliverable, a defect is a fault found after the formal review of a deliverable).

- *Phase-Containment Effectiveness* is an objective determination of the reviews of the deliverables produced during a specific project phase. It is defined as the ratio of errors found in reviews to the sum of errors found in reviews and defects that escaped such reviews. The value of PCE is expressed as a percentage, where 100 percent is the best.
- *Error Trend* is an indicator of how the normalized number of errors found in a review compares with the corresponding number for past similar projects (those with similar environmental characteristics). The value of ET is either H (higher) or LS (lower, about the same).
- *Defect Trend* is an indicator of how the normalized number of defects found during a review in deliverables from previous phases compares with the corresponding number for past similar projects. The value of DT is either H (higher) or LS (lower, about the same).

Table B:
Number of defects introduced in constructive phases

Phase	Number of errors	Number of defects
Requirements specification	5	0
Requirements model	12	1
Architectural model	11	4
Pseudo code	39	33
Code	10	10

Analyzing Metrics

The review process package includes interpretation tables, defined in the context of the GQM, to help reviewers analyze these metrics. Table A shows how the RPC, RPD, ET, and DT metrics are used in measuring against the review process-measurement goals identified to determine a project´s quality. For example, in row 1 the project score is 5, indicating a high-quality project. This score holds because we have done a good review and found few old or new problems. In row 4, the project score is 1, which indicates low quality. This score holds because we have done a good review and found more than the average number of new and old problems. In row 5 and 6, a score of 0 indicates that we cannot make any conclusions because we have not done a good review.

These metrics provide managers with real-time feedback about a current project, without the need to wait for additional defect data to be collected. All the data necessary to evaluate the quality of a phase is a available at the end of that phase.

Sample Use of PCE

Phase-containment effectiveness is a key metric to quantify and track the improvement goal. You want to reach a value of 100 percent – the review is totally effective in finding all existing problems, assuming that some problems exist in the deliverable reviewed.

In this example, the data comes from reviews done according to the review process package, augmented with testing and preliminary operation data.

We conducted reviews at the end of requirements specification, requirements modeling, architectural modeling, pseudo coding, and coding. As Table B shows, we found some errors during the review and they were fixed. Reviews of subsequent deliverables and testing, however, uncovered 48 defects that had escaped detection during review, listed in Table B in the constructive phase they were traced back to.

Using this data, you can derive phase-containment effectiveness for reviews done during each phase:

- Requirements specification review = 5/(5+0) = 100.00%
- Requirements model review = 12/(12+1) = 92.31%
- Architectural model review = 11/(11+4) = 73.33%
- Pseudo code review = 39/(39+33) = 54.17%
- Code review = 10/(10+10) = 50%

These metrics indicate that pseudo code and code reviews had relatively low containment values. Perhaps the reviewers need more training or the checklists need updating. In addition, the project participants should analyze the specific errors and defects using Pareto charts to determine their process-related causes and ensure that the process gets changed.[3] This should help avoid the introduction of such faults in the future.

References

[1] D. P. Freeman and G. M. Weinberg, *Walkthroughs, Inspections and Technical Reviews*, Little Brown, New York, 1982.

[2] D. L. Parnas and D. M. Weiss, "Active Design Reviews: Principles and Practices", *Proc. 8th Int'l Conf. Software Eng.*, IEEE CS Press, Los Alamitos, Calif., 1985, pp. 215-222.

Motorola's Experience

In 1988, Motorola's Metrics Working Group[3] was formed to develop and deploy, among other items, a process package for formal software reviews. The members of the Metrics Working Group were selected to represent Motorola business units whose goal is to champion measurement-based process improvement. It was to be part of a broader Software Engineering Technology Steering Committee and funded by Corporate Software Research and Development

The Metrics Working Group is similar to a Software Engineering Process Group, as later defined by the Software Engineering Institute. It is a volunteer group whose focus is process engineering and measurement, as opposed to an organization with a budget and head count. Individual Motorola business units have their own process and metrics working groups; if an organization does not have one, it is encouraged to create one.

Selecting a Process

By applying the first two steps of the Software Engineering Improvement Paradigm, the group identified a set of improvement goals, one of which was to improve the software-review process. For several reasons, the group chose this process as the one with the highest potential payoff:

- It is an effective marriage of process and measurement.
- It covers the entire life cycle, so it provides feedback to all processes and methods and introduces the approach to every part of the organization.
- It is the most critical aspect of product evaluation, yet it was not being used widely in 1988.
- It helps find problems early.
- It provides critical defect baselines.
- It is a good first step for integrating other process packages. A review package can be instantiated for each review along the development path: requirements, design, code, and test script.

The formal software-review process, described in the box on pp. 72-73, was the first area in which we implemented the concepts embodied in the Software Engineering Improvement Paradigm and the process package.

Creating Documents

After applying step 3, the Metrics Working Group drafted seven documents that became part of the review package, each targeted to a specific audience.

- *Overview* targets everyone. It lists the process-package documents and their corresponding audiences.
- *QIP* explains the Quality Improvement Paradigm to corporate-level managers.
- *Managers* tells software managers what to expect when they use the review package.
- *SQA* describes to software quality-assurance personnel how to use the review package.
- *GQM* explains to software managers and SQA personnel how to apply GQM to the review process and defines review metrics and how to use them.
- *Definition* describes in detail to software managers, SQA personnel, and developers how to implement a formal, technical review. It includes four forms designed to document the outcome of a specific formal software review.
- *Experience* gives corporate-level managers, software managers, and SQA personnel sample results and lessons learned in using the review package on pilot projects.

Selecting Pilot Projects

Once the initial versions of these documents had been created, the group selected a small set of pilot projects within one business unit (step 4). They chose mostly small enhancement projects of (relatively) short duration so that results would be available as soon as possible. The engineers and managers tailored the reviews over time and adapted the process to their needs. Their input, in turn, was used to enhance and evolve the initial review package. Acceptance of the review package was good, so it was generalized to apply to more projects.

The business unit's representative to the Metrics Working Group carefully monitored the use of the review package in the pilot projects. The group documented these lessons in the Experience document, and the package evolved over time to address the lessons learned on the pilots.

Training and Consulting

As the review package was being implemented on pilot projects, the Metrics Working Group developed a one-day workshop that explained how to implement and measure software reviews (step 5). The first workshop was developed and taught by the authors of the review package to cover the mechanics of conducting reviews, in the context of the review package. The course covered technical and interpersonal communication issues.

Once the technical content stabilized, the course was transferred to Motorola`s training organization, Motorola University, where it is now available to all Motorola engineers. It is not required for a group project that conducts software reviews. However, several training road maps include it as a recommended course.

In the last five years, we've offered this workshop to all development groups that want to use the review package to conduct formal reviews. If the project manager so requests, this training is followed by expert consulting, to ensure effective implementation of the ideas presented in the workshop.

Deploying a Package

Over the next three years, the review package was deployed in several business units (step 6). This took about one person-year of tailoring and deployment work, primarily by the Metrics Working Group.

Package use was concentrated in smaller projects in business units where managers and developers had been trained and received follow-up consulting. Also, having an active champion to consult on how to use the package promoted wider use.

Evaluating a Package

After the package had been in use about three years the group conducted a survey of about 100 engineers and managers across the company to determine how often the review package was being used, how it had been tailored, and what improvements were necessary (step 7).

The survey indicated that the review package was successful: 90 percent of projects within the business units affected conducted formal software reviews, and 67 percent of respondents said they used the review package.

However, 74 percent of respondents said they had had to tailor the process package. The items they changed most were the forms provided to document the review process. We did (and still do) encourage such tailoring, but wanted to identify what changes were done by what types of projects, so we could provide criteria for tailoring.

The items that did seem to work well were data-collection and error-tracking forms, reviewer sign-off, and the guidelines for whether or not to hold a review meeting.

The items that did not seem to work well are the assignment of roles to reviewers, the metrics charts used for data analysis and feedback, and the guidelines for implementing the roles assigned to reviewers. We are addressing these shortcomings through additional training and by creating local procedures.

The survey revealed that the primary inhibitors to use are the lack of appropriate resources, the lack of guidelines for how to apply the package to very small projects, and the need to streamline processes.

TABLE 1
PERCENTAGE OF FAULTS IN FORMAL REVIEW

	Release			
Deliverable	1	2	3	4
System functional specification	85	80	72	80
Software functional specification	78	67	80	70
Detailed design	49	78	64	81
Code	32	25	37	44+*

*= *Release 4 is not yet complete*

Lessons Learned

The lessons we learned hint at what we can expect as we deploy other process packages and what we must do to ensure that the tailoring and transferring of software-engineering technology is done effectively. However, some of the details are specific to reviews (such as the need to evaluate the reviewers' preparedness before a review meeting).

- *Don't underestimate the importance of champions.* Involving business units that will use the process package as you develop it not only ensures its acceptance, but facilitates the transfer process. The Metrics Working Group participants who helped tailor the review package became its champions within their business units. Business units that did not have representatives in the working group did not reap the benefits of this technology as readily.

- *Don't skimp on training.* We quickly realized that the one hour of training we initially offered to pilot projects was insufficient As a result, we developed a one-day workshop and made it the first step in deploying the review package. We also conducted train-the-trainer sessions, to speed deployment in parts of Motorola that received many requests for training. We also found it was critical to follow up with expert consulting, which we discovered helped smooth the initiation of the formal review process.
- *Be prepared to be specific.* Once the developers understood the review process, they asked for more concrete guidelines. They wanted to know what role (leader, recorder, presenter, designer, and so on) each review participant should take, specific criteria for determining when they should not proceed to conduct a review meeting (due to lack of preparation, for example), and what to do with the results. To develop these role guidelines, we referred to the objective of each review type. For example, reading the requirements document from a tester's perspective assumes the reader is trying to understand if there is sufficient information to develop tests for each requirement. To develop other quantitative decision guidelines and criteria, we relied on data collected from reviews.
- *Preparation is key.* We found that the most important factor in predicting a review's effectiveness is how prepared the reviewers are when a review meeting starts. Review leaders asked for indicators to determine reviewer readiness, so we incorporated a form that asked reviewers to indicate the time they spent preparing for a review, and we tracked the number of errors found before and during a review meeting. We also found that review leaders were initially hesitant to issue a no-go decision to hold a meeting, even if the reviewers were ill-prepared or many errors were found. The consultants helped mitigate this tendency.
- *Data collection and analysis must be tailored.* The reviewers requested classification schemes to help them record defects and analyze the data for use in process improvement. We did develop classification schemes but found that they must evolve over time and are highly dependent on the type of project and product. The classification schemes provided valuable feedback to help us standardize and improve metrics collection, analysis, and reporting.
- *Formal reviews do improve quality.* When the review package was deployed, some small projects were not conducting any reviews at all, relying on testing to find faults. Formal reviews helped find and fix faults early, as the data from four successive enhancements of an internal project indicates. The data in Table 1 shows the percentage of faults found in each phase, in the early stages of deploying the review package. Note that unit and integration test found most of the faults escaping from these reviews. Reviews during the detailed design and code review phases show the biggest improvement.

Motorola's culture is such that business unit managers decide what process and technology will be used within their unit. Although senior management sets the quality-improvement goal, and the Metrics Working Group recommends formal reviews, the use of the process package is not mandatory. Data like that in Table 1 is far more effective than any mandate.

It is not easy to tailor and transfer software-engineering technology. To change the culture of the business unit so that it will accept new technology, you must employ champions and package information appropriately.

Using the Software Engineering Improvement Paradigm will help identify the process packages that should be developed first. Then, when you enjoy success on some pilot projects and publicize that success, new projects will sign up.

Many projects and locations across the company now use versions of the review package, and we have since created a testing package.

We believe our evolutionary, feedback approach has three main strengths:

- It provides quantitative guidelines that encourage the achievement of quality and productivity goals.
- It supports the development of a corporate memory because it integrates quantitative measurement.
- It provides a way to improve and tailor technology and process through data analysis.

The work done on the reviews and testing packages has evolved into an initial Best Practices and Technology Transfer Program within Motorola, which uses internal and external benchmarks and metrics to identify and promote effective, high-payoff practices to produce quality software. Motorola has also used benchmarking to establish aggressive improvement goals and metrics in software process, quality, cycle time, development technology, and customer satisfaction.

Building on the work done on the review package, Motorola business units have started to adopt, tailor, and evolve Michael Pagan's inspections-based improvement process,[4] resulting in further improvements in software quality and productivity. Motorola has begun to use education and skills training for senior and middle management as a way to enlist improvement champions across the entire corporation.

These mechanisms, coupled with the vision provided by a senior executive program, whose mission is to accelerate the pace of software improvement, are leveraging our technology-transfer initiative to bring about change much more rapidly.

Acknowledgements

We thank the many Motorola employees who participated in the Metrics Working Group over time, especially Mike Burke, Ann Miller, Ken Biss, and David Yen. Their work was a significant factor in ensuring the successful tailoring and deployment of the review package.

References

[1] V.R. Basili, "Software Development: A Paradigm for the Future," *Proc. Compsac,*, IEEE CS Press, Los Alamitos, Calif, 1989, pp. 471-485.
[2] V.R. Basili and D.H. Rombach, "The TAME Project: Towards Improvement-Oriented Software Environments," *IEEE Trans. Software Eng.,* Nov. 1984, pp. 728-738.
[3] M.K. Daskalantonakis, "A Practical View of Software Measurement and Implementation Experiences within Motorola," *IEEE Trans. Software Eng.,* Nov. 1992, pp. 998-1010.
[4] M.E. Fagan, "Design and Code Inspections to Reduce Errors in Program Development," *IBM Systems J.,* No. 3,1976, pp. 182-211.

Address questions about this article to Basili at Computer Science Dept, University of Maryland, College Park, Md. 20742; basili@cs.umd.edu or to Daskalantonakis at Motorola, 1501W Shure Dr., IL27/Rm 1315, Arlington Heights, IL 60004; dask@cig.mot.com.

Improve Software Quality by Reusing Knowledge and Experience

Victor R. Basili and Gianluigi Caldiera

THE APPROACHES FOR IMPROVING QUALITY IN MANUFACTURING PROCESSES DON'T WORK ESPECIALLY WELL FOR SOFTWARE DEVELOPMENT. The authors provide a quality improvement paradigm for the software industry that builds on manufacturing models but focuses on reused learning and experience by establishing "experience factories." Their iterative process enables an organization to acquire core competencies to support its strategic capabilities.

The quality movement that has had such a dramatic impact on all industrial sectors has finally reached the systems and software industry. Although some of the concepts of quality management originally developed for other products can be applied to software, as a product that is developed and not produced, it requires a special approach. In this paper, we introduce a quality paradigm specifically tailored to the systems and software industry. We discuss the reuse of knowledge, products, and experience as a feasible solution to the problem of developing higher-quality systems at a lower cost. In other words, how can an organization build models or package them so that it can reuse them in other projects?

Companies often achieve quality improvement by defining and developing an appropriate set of strategic capabilities and supporting core competencies. We propose a quality improvement paradigm (QIP) for developing core competencies. This process must be supported by a goal-oriented approach to measurement and control, and an organizational infrastructure that we call an experience factory. In this paper, we introduce the major concepts of our proposed approach, discuss their relationship with other approaches in the industry, and present an example of an organization that successfully applied those concepts.

Why Is Software Development Different?

Software is present in almost every activity and institution of our society. Our dependence on software becomes evident when software problems — system shutdowns, new product delays, and assorted glitches — become newspaper headlines.

Victor R Basili is a professor and Gianluigi Caldiera is a research associate at the Institute for Advanced Computer Studies, Department of Computer Science, University of Maryland.

> Problems often arise when companies try to transfer the quality lessons learned in the manufacturing process to the software development process.

The business community is aware of these problems but does not truly understand their causes. Such misunderstanding extends to the software business community itself, especially when it deals with the philosophies of quality improvement.

Problems often arise when companies try to transfer the quality lessons learned in the manufacturing process to the software development process. Quite often, manufacturers develop quality models by collecting great amounts of data from work locations where the same function is repeated over and over. In such a context, statistical quality control can be accomplished based on numerous repetitions of the manufacturing process. Because software is developed once, this type of control is impossible. Software development models, therefore, cannot be built the same way as manufacturing models, with their dependence on lessons learned from massive repetitions of the same process. Software models provide something less definitive — the ability to learn from other software development projects. To accomplish this learning, we have to distinguish what is different about these projects.

A company can manage the quality of a software system in two ways. First, it can improve the effectiveness of the software development process by reducing the amount of rework and by reusing software artifacts across segments of a project or different projects. Second, it can develop and implement plans for controlled, sustained, and continuous improvement based on facts and data.

A major problem with software engineering is that data regarding a system's quality can be observed and measured only when the system is implemented. Unfortunately, at that stage, correcting a design defect requires the expensive redesign of sometimes large, complex components. To prevent expensive defects from occurring in the final product, quality management must focus on the early stages of the engineering process. At those early stages, however, the process is less defined and controllable with quantitative data. Therefore, software engineering projects do not regularly collect data and build models based on them.

There are many successful software projects from a quality point of view. Quality management's goal is to repeat this success in other projects by transferring the knowledge and experience at the roots of that success to the rest of the organization. A software organization that manages quality should have a corporate infrastructure that links together and transcends the single projects by capitalizing on successes and learning from failures.

Organizations need to have a strategic approach to software quality management as a part of a corporate strategy for software, aimed at pursuing and improving quality on an organizational level. There is no solution that can be mechanically transferred and applied to every organization (the famous "silver bullet"). Every organization can use our proposed approach, however, after appropriate customization, to improve software quality in a controllable way.

The Problem of Software Quality

How does a company improve quality in a *development* environment instead of a *production* environment? The key is to build or package models so that they are reusable by other projects in the organization — that is, to reuse knowledge and experience.

In many disciplines, quality issues are well understood. Because of the relative newness of the software business, definitions or trade-offs aren't clear. Software users often can't articulate what qualities they really want. Do they care about reliability, user-friendliness, or ease of modification? Software doesn't really break in the normal sense, but it has to evolve. Today's system won't satisfy the user three years from now because there are constantly changing expectations.

Because software is a new field, and good, sound models are hard to build, companies have not built models to reason about what things are, how they work, and what they should look like. Quality isn't defined so that both the developer and the user can understand it and communicate it.

Of the approaches to software quality available, there are various paradigms, mostly from manufacturing. Some organizations apply an improvement process to their software processes based on the Shewart-Deming cycle[1]. This four-stage approach provides a way to manage change throughout the production process by analyzing the change's impact on the data derived from the process:

1. Plan — define quality improvement goals and targets and determine methods for reaching those goals; prepare an implementation plan.
2. Do — execute the implementation plan and collect data.
3. Check — verify the improved performance using the data collected from the process and take corrective actions when needed.
4. Act — standardize the improvements and install them into the process.

Some organizations use the total quality management (TQM) approach, which is derived from the Shewart-Deming method and applied to all the company's business processes[2]. Another approach is benchmarking, in which organizations model their improvement on an external scale that represents the best practices in quality. The goals of the improvement program are, in this case, not internally generated but suggested by the best practices.

The software industry has used these approaches — and variations on them — with mixed outcome. The major problem is that these approaches do not deal specifically with the nature of a software product. Or if they do, they assume a consistent picture of a good software product or process. This is not adequate because, to be really effective, a software quality program should deal with the nature of the software business itself. There is no such thing as an explicit, consistent picture of a good software product.

Our approach reflects an attempt to learn from the successes of the different paradigms and to avoid problems when they are applied to software environments.

We rely on the lean enterprise concept by concentrating production and resources on value-added activities that represent an organization's critical business processes[3].

Table 1 Traditional and Expanded Focus of Software Development

Traditional Focus	Expanded Focus
Delivering specific products and services	Developing capabilities
Decomposing a complex problem into simpler ones	Unifying different solutions into more general ones
Designing and implementing	Analyzing and synthesizing
Detailing	Abstracting from detail
Validating and verifying	Experimenting

Toward a Mature Software Organization

Successful management strategies of the past ten years all call for long-term investments and top management sponsorship[4]. They advocate establishing a permanent structure to develop and support the reuse of strategic capabilities. This strategy is new for the software industry, which is predominantly driven by its business units and therefore has little ability to capitalize on experiences and capabilities.

Companies that develop software have sought to apply recent management strategies in the following ways:

1. The company must understand the software process and product.
2. The company must define its business needs and its concept of process and product quality.
3. The company must evaluate every aspect of the business process, including previous successes and failures.
4. The company must collect and use information for project control.
5. Each project should provide information that allows the company to have a formal quality improvement program in place, i.e., it should be able to control its processes, tailor them to individual project needs, and learn from its own experiences.
6. Competencies must be built in critical areas of the business by packaging and reusing clusters of experience relevant to the company's business.

Software companies need to expand their focus on a new set of problems and the techniques for solving them. Unfortunately, a software project is traditionally based on a case-by-case, problem-solving approach; the development of strategic capabilities is based instead on experience reuse and organizational sharing. (Table 1 outlines the traditional focus of software development and problem solving, along with the expanded focus.)

A Strategy for Improvement

At the center of an improvement strategy is the need for reusable experience. Next we present the framework of our strategy through a process we call the quality improvement paradigm. We discuss an approach to quality improvement based on the development of strategic capabilities, on a control tool (the goal-oriented approach to measurement that addresses the support of the improvement process with quantitative information), and on an organizational tool (an infrastructure aimed at capitalization and reuse of software experience and products).[5]

Are there any practical models a company can use to develop a strategy with the new focus? Later we illustrate with an example of a practical model, which we chose because it is a unique blend of an organizational strategy aimed at continuous improvement, a data-based approach to decision making, and an experimental paradigm, along with many years of continuous operation and data collection.

The Quality Improvement Paradigm

A common problem of software development companies is that they don't think software is their business. They think they are building "telephone systems" or "switching systems" when they are really building telephony software and switching software. They have little understanding of strategic capabilities and core competencies.

In the software business, companies determine strategic capabilities by knowing whether they can reuse architectures and designs, what functionality their product has, and how to estimate the cost of adding new features or changing existing ones. Strategic capabilities are always supported by core competencies — technologies tailored to the specific needs of the organization in performing business processes.

The goal of the process we present here is the acquisition of core competencies that support strategic capabilities. The organization must own, control, and properly maintain competencies as state of the art and know how to tailor them to the characteristics of specific projects and business units.

The quality improvement process occurs in six steps (see Figure 1). By *characterizing*, a company builds models of the current environment. Next it *sets goals* for what it wants to achieve for the next product and learn about the business. To satisfy the goals relative to the current environment, it *chooses processes, methods, techniques, and tools*, tailors them to fit the problem, and *executes* them. During execution, it analyzes the intermediate results and asks if it is satisfying the goals and using appropriate processes. This feedback loop is project learning. Finally, the company *analyzes* what happened and learns from it. Then it stores and propagates the knowledge, i.e., *packaging.*

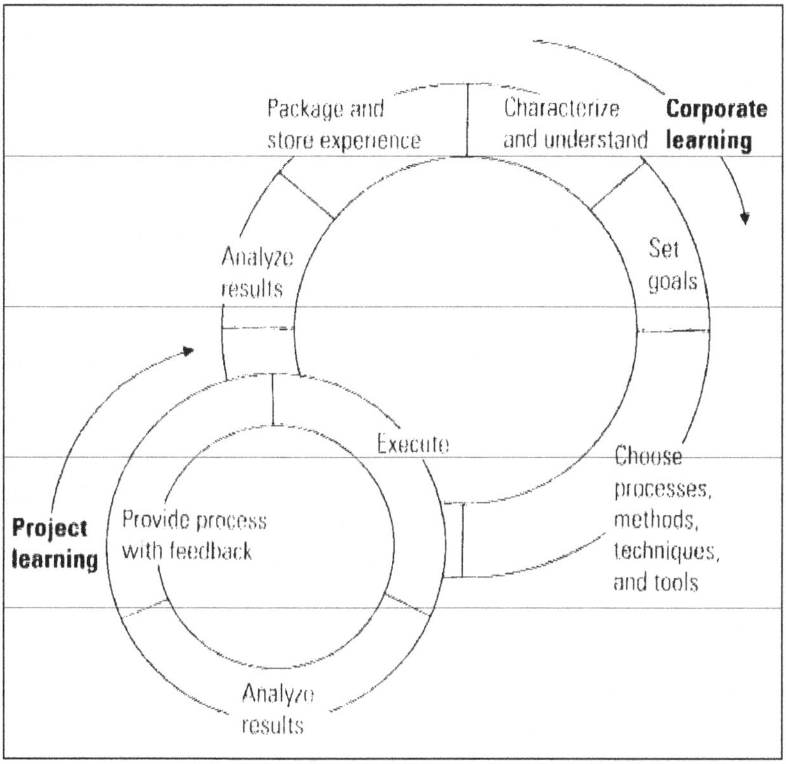

Figure 1. The Quality Improvement Paradigm

Each cycle results in better models in terms of characterization of the software business, a better articulation of goals, and a better understanding of the relationship between processes and their effects. Each time through the loop is a corporate learning event.

The quality improvement paradigm implements two major cycles:

- The control cycle is the feedback to the project during the execution phase. It provides analytic information about project performance at intermediate stages of development by comparing project data with the nominal range for similar projects. This information is used to prevent and solve problems, monitor and support the project, and realign the process with the goals.
- The capitalization cycle is the feedback to the organization. Its purpose is to understand what happened, by capturing experience and devising ways to transfer that experience across application domains and to accumulate reus-

able experience in the form of software artifacts that are applicable to other projects and are improved based on the analysis.

An organizations use of the quality improvement paradigm is an iterative process that repeatedly characterizes the environment, sets appropriate goals, and chooses the process for achieving those goals. It then proceeds with the execution and analytical phases. At each iteration, it redefines and improves characteristics and goals (see Figure 2).

Goal-Oriented Measurement

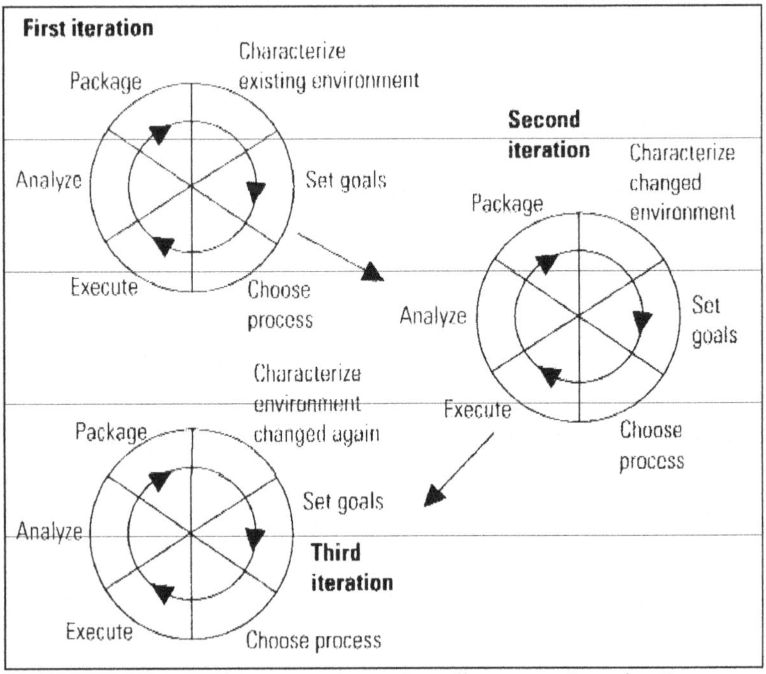

Figure 2. The Quality Improvement Paradigm as an Iterative Process

The goal/question/metric (GQM) approach provides a method to identify and control key business processes in a measurable way.[6] A company can use it to define metrics during the software project, process, and product so the resulting metrics are tailored to the organization and its goals and reflect the quality values of different viewpoints (developers, users, operators, and so on).

A GQM model is a hierarchy starting with a goal (specifying purpose of measurement, object to measure, issue to measure, and viewpoint from which to take the measurement). Suppose a company wants to improve the timeliness of change-request processing during the maintenance phase of a system's life cycle. The resulting goal will specify a purpose (improve), a process (change-request processing), a viewpoint (project manager), and a quality issue (timeliness). It then refines the goal into several questions that usually break the issue down into its major components. In the example we discuss later, the goal of the Software Engineering Laboratory can be refined to a series of questions about, for instance, turnaround time and resources used. It then refines each question into metrics. The questions in the example can be answered by metrics comparing specific turnaround times with an average. (The goal/question/metric model for our example is shown in Table 2.)

Goal	Purpose	Improve
	Issue	the timeliness of
	Object (process)	change-request processing
	Viewpoint	from the project manager's viewpoint
Question		Is the performance of the process improving?
Metrics		Current average turnaround time Baseline average turnaround time
		Subjective rating of manager's satisfaction
Question		Is the distribution of resources changing?
Metrics		Percent effort spent on: • Problem analysis • Solution identification • Solution implementation • Solution testing

Table 2. Goal/Question/Metric Model

A company can also use the GQM approach for long-range corporate goal setting and evaluation. It can enhance the evaluation of a project by analyzing it in the context of several other projects. It can expand the level of feedback and understanding by defining the appropriate synthesis procedure for transforming specific, valuable information into more general packages of experience. In implementing the quality improvement paradigm, the company can formally learn more about the definition and application of the GQM approach, just as it would about any other experiences.

The Experience Factory: A Capability-Based Organization

In a capability-based organization, reuse of experience and collective learning become a corporate concern like the business portfolio or company assets. The experience factory is the organization that supports reuse of experience and collective learning by developing, updating, and providing, on request, dusters of competencies to be used by the project organizations.[7] We call these clusters of competencies "experience packages." The project organizations supply the experience factory with the products, plans, processes, and models used in their development and the data gathered during development and operation; the experience factory transforms them into reusable units and supplies them to the project organizations, together with specific monitoring and consulting support.

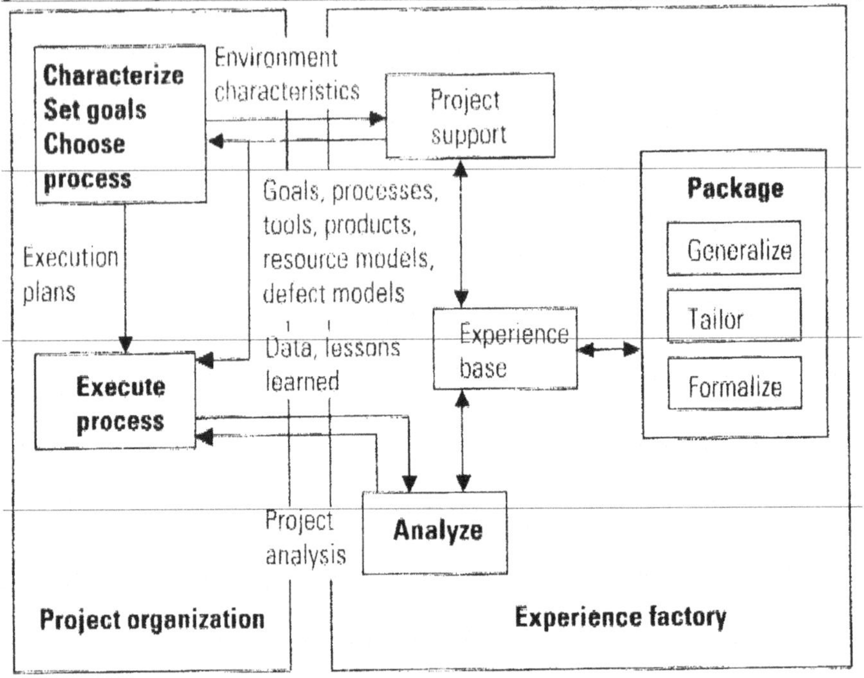

Figure 3. Synergies between Project Organization and Experience Factory

The experience factory's activities must be clearly identified and independent from those of the project organization. At the same time, the synergy and interaction between the experience factory and project organizations must be constant and effective. The project organization's goal is to produce and maintain software. The experience factory provides direct feedback to each project, together with goals and models tailored from similar projects. (Figure 3 shows the experience factory organization and highlights activities and information flows among the component sub organizations.)

The project organization provides the experience factory with project and environment characteristics, development data, resource usage information, quality records, and process information. This provides feedback on the actual performance of the models that the experience factory processes and the project utilizes. The experience factory produces and provides baselines, tools, lessons learned, and data, parameterized in some form to adapt to a project's specific characteristics. Support personnel sustain and facilitate the interaction between developers and analysts by saving and maintaining the information, making it efficiently retrievable, and controlling and monitoring its access.

The main products of the experience factory are core competencies packaged as aggregates of technologies. (For some examples of core competencies and the corresponding aggregation of technologies, see Table 3.) A company can implement core competencies in various formats or experience packages. Their content and structure vary based on the kind of experience clustered within. There is generally a central element that determines what the package is, such as a software life-cycle product or process, an empirical or theoretical model, a database, and so on.

Core Competencies	**Aggregate Technologies**
• Use of an integrated software engineering environment tailored to one or more specific application domains	• Tool integration • Domain analysis and architectures • Data sharing and communication in heterogeneous environments
• Availability of reusable components (modules, algorithms, architectures) and tools portable across different platforms	• Reuse libraries, mechanisms, and methods • Domain analysis and architectures • Object-oriented techniques
• Availability and use of a software management environment based on "local" data for estimate, control, and prediction of projects	• Measurement and data collection and analysis • Data and process modeling • Defect counting, categorization, and analysis

Table 3. Core Competencies and Corresponding Technologies

The synergy of the project organization and the experience factory is based on the quality improvement paradigm we introduced previously. Each component performs activities in all six steps, but, for each step, one component has a leadership role. (Figure 4 shows an outline of the whole organization and its mapping on the QIP.)

In the first three phases (characterize, set goals, and choose process), the operation focuses on planning. The project organization has a leading role and is supported by the experience factory analysts. The outcome of these three phases is, on the project organization side, a project plan associated with a management control framework, and on the experience factory side, a support plan also associated with a management control framework. The project plan describes the projects goals, phases, and activities, with their products, mutual dependencies, milestones, and resources. For the experience factory side, the plan describes the support that it will provide for each phase and activity and expected improvements.

In the fourth phase (execute), the operation focuses on delivering the product or service assigned to the project organization. The project organization again has a leading role, supported by the experience factory. The outcome of this phase is the product or service, which is associated with a set of potentially reusable products, processes, and experiences.

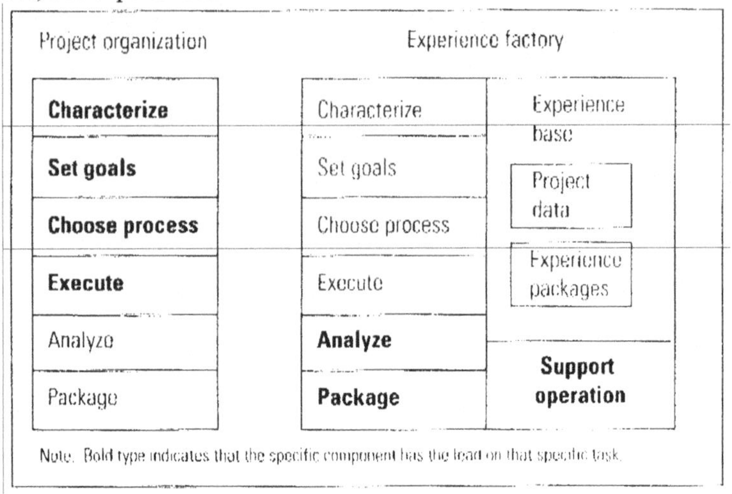

Figure 4. A Map of the Quality Improvement Paradigm for the Whole Organization

In the fifth and the sixth phases (analyze and package), the operation concentrates on capturing project experience and making it available to future similar projects. The experience factory has a leading role and is supported by the project organization that is the source of that experience. The outcomes of these phases are lessons learned with recommendations for future improvements, and new or updated experience packages incorporating the experience gained during the project execution.

Structuring a software development organization as an experience factory offers the ability to learn from every project, constantly increase the organization's maturity, and incorporate new technologies into the life cycle. In the long term, it supports the overall evolution of the organization from project-based, where all activities are aimed at the successful execution of current project tasks, to capability-based, which capitalizes on task execution.

An organization benefits from its structure as an experience factory by:

- Establishing a software improvement process substantiated and controlled by quantitative data.
- Producing a repository of software data and models that are empirically based on everyday practice.
- Developing an internal support organization that limits overhead and provides substantial cost and quality performance benefits.
- Providing a mechanism for identifying, assessing, and incorporating into the process new technologies that have proven valuable in similar contexts.
- Incorporating and supporting reuse in the software development process.

Developers' Focus	Analysts' Focus	Support Infrastructure's Focus
Software development	Experience packaging	Support developers and analysts
Single application	Application domain	Organization
Decompose a problem into simpler ones	Generalize and formalize solutions and products	Categorize and organize
Tailor and apply the process	Analyze and synthesize the process	Store and retrieve the process information
Validation and verification	Experimentation	Efficient retrieval

Table 4. Focus of the Software Engineering Lab´s Three Components

Improvement in Practice: A NASA Engineering Laboratory

Next we offer a practical example of an experience factory organization — the Software Engineering Laboratory (SEL) at NASA Goddard Space Flight Center — and show how its operation uses the quality improvement paradigm.[8]

The SEL was established in 1976 as a cooperative effort among the Department of Computer Science of the University of Maryland, the National Aeronautic and Space Administration Goddard Space Flight Center (NASA/GSFC), and Computer Sciences Corporation (CSC). The lab's goal was to understand and improve key software development processes and products in a specific organization, the Flight Dynamics Division.

The goals, structure, and operation of the SEL have evolved from an initial stage — a laboratory dedicated to experimentation and measurement—to a full-scale organization aimed at reusing experience and developing strategic capabilities. The SEL`s structure is based on three components:

- Developers, who provide products, plans used in development, and data gathered during development and operation (the project organization).
- Analysts, who transform the objects that the developers provide into reusable units and supply them to the developers; they support the projects on use of the analyzed, synthesized information, tailoring it for a current software effort (the experience factory proper).
- Support infrastructure, which provides services to the developers by supporting data collection and retrieval, and to the analysts by managing the library of stored information and its catalogs (the experience base support).

(For an outline of the differences in focus among the three sub organizations, see Table 4.)

In the late 1980s, the software engineering community was considering the use of the Ada programming language environment and technology, which the U.S. Department of Defense had developed.[9] NASA thought of using Ada technology for some major projects such as the space station. Its application was also being considered in areas outside the Department of Defense. If more and more systems used Ada as a development environment, more organizations would be involved with it, and Ada would have to be transformed from simple technology to core competence for the software development organizations within NASA.

Associated with Ada was the issue of object-oriented technologies. Some basic characteristic elements of the object-oriented approach are:

- A system is seen as a set of objects with a defined behavior and characteristics.
- Objects interact with each other by exchanging messages.
- Objects are organized into classes based on common characteristics and behaviors.
- All information about the state or the implementation of an object is held in the object itself and cannot be deliberately or accidentally used by other objects.

From the beginning, the SEL thought that the two technologies (Ada and object technology) should be packaged together into a core competence supporting the strategic capability of delivering systems with better quality and lower delivery cost. After it recognized that this capability had a strategic value for the organization, the SEL selected Ada and the object-oriented design technology for supporting it, measured its benefits, and provided data in support of its decision to use the technology.

The SEL followed these steps, according to the QIP:

1. Characterize. In 1985, the SEL developed a baseline of how the Flight Dynamics Division developed software. It defined the development processes and built models to improve the process's manageability. It integrated the standard development methodology, based on the traditional design-and-build approach, with concepts aimed at continuously evolving systems by successive enhancements.
2. Set goals. Realizing that object-oriented techniques implemented in the design and programming environments offered potential for major improvements in productivity, quality, and reusability of software products and processes, the SEL decided to develop a core competence around object-oriented design and Ada. First, it set up expectations and goals against which it measured results. The SEL's well-established baseline and measures provided an excellent basis for comparison. Its expectations included —
    - An increase in effort on early phases of development activities (design) and a decrease on late phases (testing).
    - Increased reuse of software modules.
    - Decreased maintenance costs due to the better quality, reusable components.
    - Increased reliability as a result of lower global error rates, fewer high-impact interface errors, and fewer design errors.

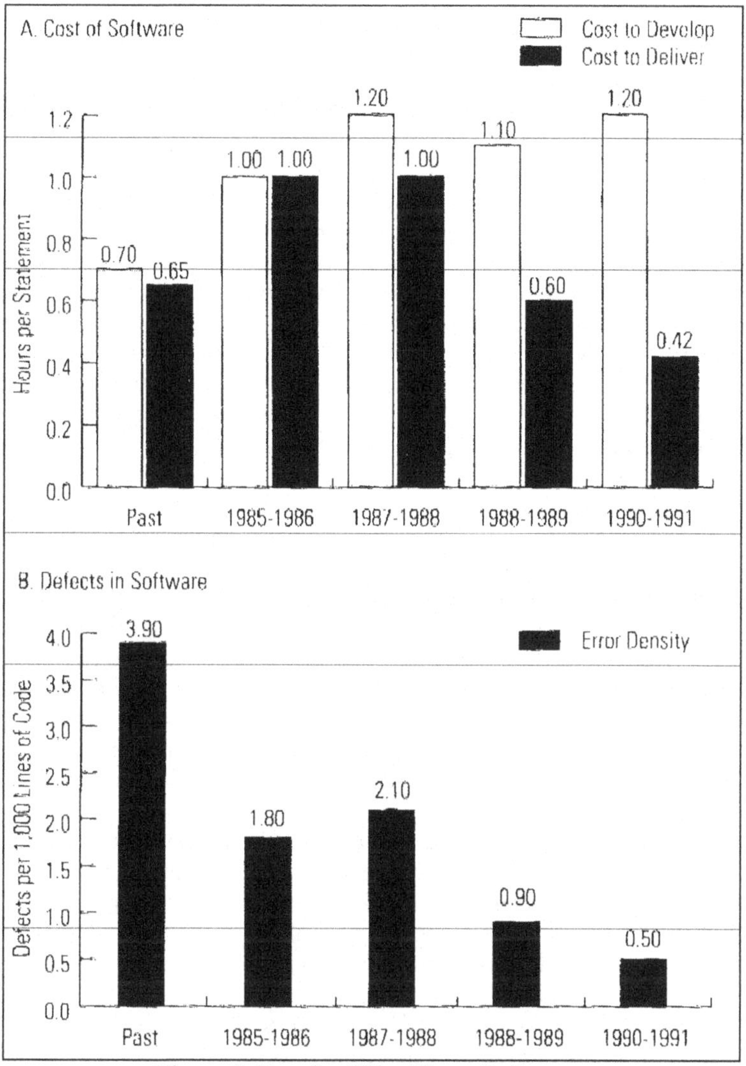

Figure 5. Trends of Significant Indicators

3. Choose process. The SEL decided to approach the development of the desired core competence by experimenting with Ada and object-oriented design in a "real" project. It developed two versions of the same system. System A used FORTRAN and followed the standard methodology based on functional decomposition. System B used Ada and followed an object-oriented methodology called HOOD. The SEL compared the data derived from the development of system B with those from system A. It devoted particular attention to quality and productivity data.
4. Execute. The SEL implemented systems A and B and collected the desired metrics.

5. Analyze. The data showed an increase in the cost to develop due to the organization's inexperience with the new technology and to the technology's intrinsic characteristics. The data also showed an increase in cost to deliver due to the same causes. The overall quality of system B showed an improvement over system A in terms of a substantially lower error density.
6. Package. The laboratory tailored and packaged an internal version of the methodology that adjusted and extended HOOD for use in a specific environment and on a specific application domain. Commercial training courses, supplemented with limited project-specific training, constituted the early training in the techniques. The laboratory also produced experience reports on the lessons learned using the new technology and recommendations for refinements to the methodology and standards.

Results of the Process. The data collected from the first execution of the process were encouraging, especially on the quality issue, but inconclusive. The SEL decided on new executions to be continued in the future. Along with the development methodology, it developed a programming language style guide that provided coding standards for the local Ada environment.

The SEL has completed at least ten projects using an object-oriented technology derived from the one used for system B but constantly modified and improved. The size of single projects, measured in thousands of lines of source code, ranges from small to large. Some characteristics of an object-oriented development, using Ada, emerged early and have remained rather constant. No significant change has been observed, for instance, in the effort distribution or in the error classification. Other characteristics emerged later and took time to stabilize. Reuse has increased dramatically after the first projects, going from a traditionally constant figure of 30 percent reuse across different projects, to a current 96 percent (89 percent reuse). (See Figure 5.)

Over the years, use of the object-oriented approach and expertise with Ada have matured. Source code analysis of the systems developed with the new technology has revealed a maturing use of Ada's key features that has no equivalent in the programming environments NASA traditionally uses. The SEL used such features not only more often in more recent systems, but also in more sophisticated ways, as revealed by specific metrics for this purpose. Moreover, the use of object-oriented design and Ada features has stabilized during the past three years, creating an SEL baseline for object-oriented developments.

The cost to develop code in the new environment has remained higher than the cost to develop code in the old one. However, because of the high reuse rates obtained through the object-oriented paradigm, the cost to deliver a system in the new environment has significantly decreased and is now well below the old cost.

The reliability of the systems developed in the new environment has improved during the maturing of the technology. The error rates were significantly lower than the traditional ones and have continued to decrease. Again, the high level of reuse in the later systems is a major contributor to this greatly improved reliability. Because of the technology's stabilization and apparent benefit, the object-oriented development methodology has been packaged and incorporated into the current technology baseline and is a core competence of the organization. Although the

SEL will continue to refine the technology of object-oriented design, HOOD has now progressed through all stages, moving from a trial methodology to a fully integrated, packaged part of the standard methodology, ready for further incremental improvement.

The SEL example also illustrates the relationship between a competence (object-oriented technology) and a target capability (deliver high quality at low cost) and shows how innovative technologies can systematically enter the production cycle of mature organizations. Although the topic of technology transfer is not specifically within our scope here, it is clear that the model we derive from the SEL example outlines a solution to some major technology-transfer issues. The purpose of an experience factory organization, however, goes beyond technology transfer to encompass capability transfer and reuse.

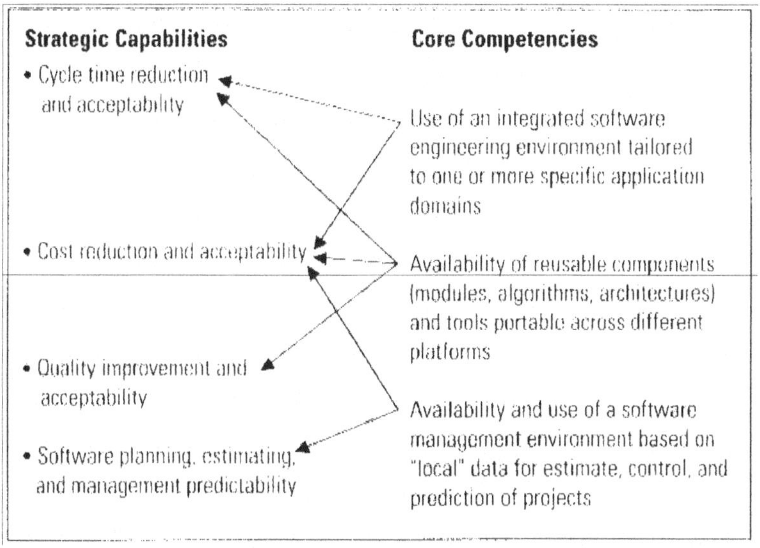

Figure 6. Relationships between Strategic Capabilities and Core Competencies

Conclusion

For software, the remainder of the 1990s will be the era of quality and cycle time. There is a growing need to develop or adapt quality improvement approaches to the software business. Our approach to software quality improvement is based on the exploitation and reuse of an organization's critical capabilities across different projects based on business needs.

The relationship between core competencies and strategic capabilities is established by the kind of products and services the organization wants to deliver and is specified by the strategic planning process. (Figure 6 gives a possible map for an organization whose main business is systems and software development for user applications.) The SEL example shows that these ideas are feasible and have been successfully applied in a production environment to create a continuously improving organization. Such an organization can manipulate its processes to achieve various product characteristics. It needs to have a process and organizational structure to:

- Understand its processes and products.
- Measure and model its business processes.
- Define process and product quality explicitly and tailor the definitions to the environment.
- Understand the relationship between process and product quality.
- Control project performance with respect to quality.
- Evaluate project success and failure with respect to quality.
- Learn from experience by repeating successes and avoiding failures.

By using the quality improvement paradigm/experience factory approach, an organization has a good chance to achieve all these capabilities and improve quality faster because it focuses on its strategic capabilities and value-added activities. The experience factory organization is the lean enterprise model for the system and software business.

References

We acknowledge the contributions of all those who participated in the experiences and discussions that originated the concepts presented here. Particular acknowledgment goes to the personnel of the Software Engineering Laboratory at NASA Goddard Space Flight Center and Frank McGarry, Jerry Page (CSC), Tony Jordano (SAIC), Bob Yacobellis (Motorola), Paolo Sigillo (Italsiel), and Mike Deutsch (Hughes Information Technology Corporation).

[1] W. Edwards Deming, *Out of the Crisis* (Cambridge, Massachusetts: MIT Press, Center for Advanced Engineering Study, 1986).

[2] A.V. Feigenbaum, *Total Quality Control* (New York: McGraw Hill, 1991).

[3] J.P. Womack, D.T. Jones, and D. Roos, *The Machine That Changed the World* (New York: Rawson Associates, 1989).

[4] G. Stalk, P. Evans, and L.E. Shulman, "Competing on Capabilities: The New Rules of Corporate Strategy," *Harvard Business Review*, March-April 1992, pp. 57-69.

[5] V.R. Basili, "Quantitative Evaluation of a Software Engineering Methodology" (Melbourne, Australia: Proceedings of the First Pan-Pacific Computer Conference, September 1985); and
V.R. Basili, "Software Development: A Paradigm for the Future" (Orlando, Florida: Proceedings of COMPSAC '89, September 1989), pp. 471-485.

[6] V.R. Basili and D.M. Weiss, "A Methodology for Collecting Valid Software Engineering Data," *IEEE Transactions on Software Engineering*, November 1984, pp. 728-738; and

V.R. Basili and H.D. Rombach, "The TAME Project: Towards Improvement-Oriented Software Environments," *IEEE Transactions on Software Engineering*, June 1988, pp. 758-773.

[7] Basili (1989).

[8] V.R. Basili, G. Caldiera, F. McGarry, R. Pajerski, J. Page, and S. Waligora, "The Software Engineering Laboratory — An Operational Software Experience Factory" (Melbourne, Australia: Proceedings of the Fourteenth International Conference on Software Engineering, May 1992).

[9] ANSI/MIL-STD-1815A 1983: *Reference Manual for the Ada Programming Language.*

[10] Sommerville, *Software Engineering* (Wokingham, England: Addison-Wesley, 1992).

Section 5: Empirical Studies and Technical Development

Rose Pajerski

Fraunhofer Center for Experimental Software Engineering

This section contains 5 journal articles over a 16 year period, which showcases the maturation of development methods and processes as well as the evolution of the underlying science of empirical studies and software engineering experimentation. This section can only provide a few examples since Vic's contribution to this body of knowledge is immense. His work covers diverse experiments on techniques and approaches over the entire lifecycle from development through sustaining engineering. The articles in this section focus on the collection and analysis of data and experience that can be used to characterize relationships between process and product measures. They highlight the lessons learned using experimental methods and are valuable to both researchers and practitioners.

As a researcher, Vic's objective has always been to build models and increase understanding of the relationship between the process under study and the resultant product. To do this, he has carried out over 100 experiments in the classroom and industrial settings in different contexts and application areas. This represents a huge amount of raw data to evaluate; however, Vic's analyses always consider the human factors as well as the statistical results to provide valuable qualitative and quantitative feedback to the practitioner community.

The articles describe individual experiments and aggregated groups of experiments, providing a historical perspective on the evolution of empirical studies driven by Vic's work. As the software engineering discipline has matured, so has the level of sophistication of empirical research. The articles included here show a body of knowledge built carefully over time - from single experiments and from combining and replicating experiments under similar and differing conditions. While the scope of the studies varies from complete methodologies to specific techniques, the study methodology evinces many common characteristics: goal-based objectives considering both process and product elements; quantitative and subjective data collection; and, perhaps most importantly, careful conclusions that do not extend beyond the data and scope of study.

In the first article selected, from 1981, then-current development methods were compared in a controlled experiment report by Basili and Reiter entitled "A Controlled Experiment Quantitatively Comparing Software Development Approaches." The study evaluated the effectiveness of using structured programming practices in small teams against more ad hoc, less disciplined approaches. Evaluation criteria included both process (e.g., effort, number of computer runs, changes made) and product measures (e.g., lines of code, statement types) that were collected automatically and used to confirm/disprove the 7 initial hypotheses. The rigor of this controlled experiment, coupled with the extent of the data collected, provided a valuable template for other studies to follow and garnered the IEEE Computer Society Outstanding Paper Award in 1981.

From 1986, the second selection "Experimentation in Software Engineering" surveys the early years of software engineering studies. In this article, Basili, Selby and Hutchens integrate previous experimental design studies and lessons-learned from a number of researchers to present a comprehensive framework for carrying out and evaluating future experimental studies. This broad ranging empirical survey summarizes the key work, issues, challenges and conclusions that can be drawn from the previous 10 years of empirical studies. Its bibliography alone provides a valuable "Who's who" of researchers and their work for others to reference.

Testing methods are the focus of the third selection. In 1987, Basili and Selby published a study of several testing methods employed at the University of Maryland and in the NASA Software Engineering Laboratory (SEL) to determine their strengths and weaknesses. "Comparing the Effectiveness of Software Testing Strategies" analyzes the effectiveness of these testing methods from several perspectives/objectives and provides a template for future "series of experiments" studies. This ambitious research project spanned several years and was conducted in both university and industrial settings. The three phases incorporated different testing techniques along with different levels of developer expertise, different types of applications, and fault types (e.g., interface versus control, real versus seeded). This study emphasized the value of code reading as an effective testing technique and formed the basis for Vic's continuing experimentation with and evolution of reading techniques.

The fourth selection, "Cleanroom Software Development: An Empirical Evaluation", from 1987 by Selby, Basili, and Baker, provides an analysis of the IBM-developed Cleanroom methodology based on classroom experiments at the University of Maryland (UMD). Over 2 semesters, the Cleanroom method was used by 10 programmer teams and compared with a control group of 5 teams to develop a small system. Individual elements of the methodology were evaluated with respect to their impact on product quality and process effectiveness, incorporating extensive feedback from the teams. The results validated experiences by IBM and highlighted the importance of using developer feedback in implementing process changes.

The final selection, Basili's "Evolving and Packaging Reading Technologies, published in 1997, describes the maturation of reading techniques over a 10 year period as practiced in the SEL and at the UMD. This report describes a number of experiments in testing techniques and perspective-based reading approaches. Vic provides a unifying context for these studies in terms of the Quality Improvement Paradigm (QIP). During successive QIP cycles, the results from previous experiments are used to refine the goals of the next series of experiments, resulting in a set of tailored reading techniques that can be applied to many types of documents such as requirements specifications and design diagrams.

In this section, we see that Vic is a true experimentalist as, in his own words, "Experimentalists observe and measure, i.e., carry out studies to test or disprove a theory or to explore a new domain. But at whatever point the cycle is entered there is a pattern of modeling, experimenting, learning and remodeling.[1]" We also see ample proof that the experimental cycle continues as we enjoy the journey along with Vic.

[1] V. R. Basili, Editorial in *Empirical Software Engineering* (1)2, 1996 Kluwer

A Controlled Experiment Quantitatively Comparing Software Development Approaches

Victor R. Basili and Robert W. Reiter, Jr., Member, IEEE

Abstract. A software engineering research study has been undertaken to empirically analyze and compare various software development approaches; its fundamental features and initial findings are presented in this paper. An experiment was designed and conducted to confirm certain suppositions concerning the beneficial effects of a particular disciplined methodology for software development. The disciplined methodology consisted of programming teams employing certain techniques and organizations commonly defined under the umbrella term structured programming. Other programming teams and individual programmers both served as control groups for comparison. The experimentally tested hypotheses involved a number of quantitative, objective, unobtrusive, and automatable measures of programming aspects dealing with the software development process and the developed software product. The experiment's results revealed several programming aspects for which statistically significant differences existed between the disciplined methodology and the control groups. The results were interpreted as confirmation of the original suppositions and evidence in favor of the disciplined methodology. This paper describes the specific features of the experiment; outlines the investigative approach used to plan, execute, and analyze it; reports its immediate results; and interprets them according to intuitions regarding the disciplined methodology.

Key Words: Controlled experimentation, empirical study, programming measurement, programming methodology, programming teams, software development, software metrics, structured programming practices.

Manuscript received June 30, 1979; revised January 15, 1980. This work was supported in part by the Air Force Office of Scientific Research under Grant AFSOR-77-3181A to the University of Maryland. Computer time was supported in part through the facilities of the Computer Science Center of the University of Maryland. At the time this work was done, both authors were with the University of Maryland.
V. R. Basili is with the Department of Computer Science, University of Maryland, College Park, MD 20742.
R. W. Reiter, Jr. was with the Department of Computer Science, University of Maryland, College Park, MD 20742. He is now with the Software Engineering and Technology Department, IBM Federal Systems Division, Bethesda, MD 20034.

I. Introduction

Much has been written about methodologies for developing computer software (e.g., [9], [11], [15], [17], [20], [28]). Most of these methodologies are founded on sound logical principles. Case studies have occasionally been conducted to demonstrate their effectiveness (e.g., [1], [6]). Their adoption within production ("real-world") environments has generally been successful. Having practiced adaptations of these methodologies, software designers and programmers have often asserted qualitatively that they got the job done faster, made fewer errors, or produced a better product (e.g., [12]). Unfortunately, solid empirical evidence that comparatively and quantitatively assesses any particular methodology is scarce (e.g., [18], [21], [23], [24]). This is due partially to the cost and impracticality of a valid experimental setup within a production environment.

Thus the question remains, are measurable benefits derived from programming methodologies, with respect to either the software development process or the developed software product? Even if the perceived benefits are real, it is not clear that they can be quantified or monitored, in order to confirm the effectiveness of the methodologies. Software development is still too artistic, in the aesthetic or spontaneous sense. In order to understand it more fully, manage it more cost-effectively, and adapt it more readily to challenging applications or situations, software development must become more scientific, in the engineered and deliberate sense. More empirical study, data collection, and experimental analysis are required to achieve this goal.

The purpose of the research reported in this paper is 1) to quantitatively investigate the effect of methodologies and programming environments on software development and 2) to develop an investigative methodology based on scientific experimentation and tailored to this particular application. It involves the measurement and analysis of both the software process and the software product in a manner which is minimally obtrusive (to those developing the software), objective, and automatable. The goal of the research was to verify the effectiveness of a particular programming methodology and to identify various quantifiable aspects that could demonstrate such effectiveness.

To this end, a controlled experiment was conducted involving several replications of a specific software development task under varying programming environments. The experiment compared three distinct groupings of software developers: individual programmers, three-person programming teams, and three-person programming teams using a disciplined methodology. The disciplined methodology consisted of an integrated set of software development techniques and team organizations, including top-down design, process design language, structured programming, code reading, and chief programmer teams.

The study examines differences in the expectancy of software development behavior under the programming environments represented by these groups. The basic premise is that distinctions among the groups exist both in the process and in the product. With respect to the software development process, a disciplined team should have advantages over both an individual and an ordinary team, displaying superior performance on cost factors such as computer usage and number of errors made. This is because of the discipline itself and because of the ability to use team members as resources for validation. With respect to the developed software product, it is believed that a disciplined team should approximate an individual with regard to design and source code characteristics (such as decision structure and global data accessibility) and at the very least lie somewhere between an individual and an ordinary team. This is because the disciplined methodology should enable the team to act as a mentally cohesive unit during the design, coding, and testing phases.

The study's findings reveal several programming characteristics for which statistically significant differences do exist among the groups and tend to support these basic premises.

The investigation has been conducted in a laboratory or proving-ground fashion, in order to achieve some statistical significance and scientific respectability without sacrificing production realism and professional applicability. By scaling down a typical production environment while retaining its important characteristics, the laboratory setting provides for a reasonable compromise between the extremes of

1) "toy" experiments, which can afford elaborate experimental designs and large sample sizes but often suffer from a basic task that is rather unrelated to production situations or involve a context from which it is difficult to extrapolate or scale up (e.g., introductory computer course students taking multiple-choice quizzes based on 30-line programs), and
2) "production" experiments, which offer a high degree of realism by definition but incur prohibitively high costs even for the simplest and weakest experimental designs (i.e., replication of a nontrivial programming project is clearly expensive).

The experiment in this study was conducted within an academic environment where it was possible to achieve an adequate experimental design and still simulate key elements of a production environment.

An initial phase of investigative effort has been completed and its prominent features are presented in the remainder of this paper. Section II gives details pertaining to the experiment itself. Section III describes the investigative methodology used to plan, execute, and analyze the experiment. Sections IV and V present the experiment's findings, segregated into empirical results (resulting from statistical analysis of the measurements) and intuitive judgments (resulting from interpretation of the empirical results), respectively. (Different statistical analyses and additional interpretations of the same experimental data have appeared in [5], [22] as explained below.) Section VI makes some concluding remarks and mentions further work planned for the study. Appendices I and II explain concisely what programming aspects were measured and contain the observed raw data scores.

It should be noted that the terms "methodology" and "methodological" (in reference to software development) are used herein to connote a comprehensive integrated set of development techniques as well as team organizations, rather than a particular technique or organization in isolation.

II. Specifics

Experimental Design

The basic task involved in the experiment was the completion of a specific software development project. There were 19 replications of the basic task, each performed concurrently and independently by a separate software development "team." There were two experimental treatment factors (independent variables): size of the development "team" and degree of methodological discipline. For each factor, there were two experimental treatment factor levels: for the size factor, a single individual and a three-person team; for the degree-of-discipline factor, an ad hoc approach and a disciplined methodology.

The experiment was embedded within two academic courses, and every student enrolled in those courses participated in the experiment. Development "teams" were formed among the subjects: in one course, the .students were allowed to choose between segregating themselves as individual programmers or combining with two other classmates as three-person programming teams; in the other course, the students were assigned (by the researchers) into three-person teams. The experiment was designed in this manner because the two academic courses themselves provided the two levels of the second experimental treatment factor. This scheme yielded three groups of 6, 6, and 7 "teams," designated AI, AT, and DT, respectively. Each group was exposed to a particular combined factor-level treatment according to the following partial factorial arrangement:

(AI) single individuals using an ad hoc approach,

(AT) three-person teams using an ad hoc approach, and

(DT) three-person teams using a particular disciplined methodology.

A set of experimental observations (dependent variables), composed of 35 programming aspects related to the development process and the software product, had been identified prior to conducting the experiment. The performance of each development "team" was quantified according to each programming aspect. The overall experiment thus technically consisted of a series of simultaneous univariate experiments, one for each observed programming aspect, all sharing a common experimental design and a common raw data sample.

Although this experimental design basically followed the reductionist paradigm, in which most variables are controlled so that the relationships among the remaining few can be isolated, the ideal was only approximated. Specifically, there were two variables which the design did not explicitly control: the personal ability/experience of the participants and the amount of actual time/effort they devoted to the project. These variables could only be allowed to vary among the groups in what was assumed to be a random manner. However, information from a pretest questionnaire was used to balance the personal ability/experience of the group DT participants (only) across those seven teams. As a reasonable measure of individual programmer skill levels, the participants' grades from a pertinent prerequisite course provided a post-experimental confirmation that programming ability was fairly evenly distributed among the groups.

Software Development Methodologies

The disciplined methodology imposed on teams in group DT consisted of an integrated set of state-of-the-art techniques, including top-down design, process design language (PDL), functional expansion, design and code reading, walk-throughs, and chief programmer team organization. These were taught as an integral part of the course that the subjects were taking, and the course material was organized around [2], [9], [17] as textbooks. Since the subjects were novices in the methodology, they executed the techniques and organizations to varying degrees of thoroughness and were not always as successful as seasoned users of the methodology would be.

Specifically, the disciplined methodology prescribed the use of a PDL for expressing the design of the problem solution. The design was expressed in a top-down manner, each level representing a solution to the problem at a particular level of abstraction and specifying the functions to be expanded at the next level. The PDL consisted of a specific set of structured control and data structures, plus an open-ended designer-defined set of operators and operands corresponding to the level of the solution and the particular application. Design and code reading involved the critical review of each team member's PDL or code by at least one other member of the team. Walk-throughs represented a more formalized presentation of an individual's work to the other team members in which the PDL or code was explained step by step. Under the chief programmer team organization, one team member was responsible for designing and refining the top-level solution to the problem in PDL, identifying system components to be implemented, defining their interfaces, and implementing the key code; the other team members were each responsible for designing or coding various system components, as assigned by the chief programmer. Responsibility for librarian activities (entering or revising code stored on-line, making test runs, etc.) was allocated among the three team members in the manner most comfortable for them.

Each individual or team in groups AI and AT was allowed to develop the software in a manner entirely of their own choosing, which is herein referred to as an ad hoc approach. No methodology was taught in the course these subjects were taking. Informal observation by the researchers confirmed that approaches used by the individuals and ad hoc teams were indeed lacking in discipline and did not utilize the key elements of the disciplined methodology (e.g., an individual working alone cannot practice code reading, and it was evident that the ad hoc teams did not use a PDL or formally do a top-down design).

Programming Environment

Several particulars of the experimental programming environment contribute significantly to the context in which the experiment's results must be appraised. These include the setting in which the experiment was conducted, the software development project that served as the experimental task, the people who participated as subjects, the computer system access mode they used, and the computer programming language in which the software was written.

The experiment was conducted during the Spring 1976 semester, January through May, within regular academic courses given by the Department of Computer Science on the College Park campus of the University of Maryland. Two comparable advanced elective courses were utilized, each with the same academic prerequisites. The experimental task and treatments were built into the course material and assignments. Everyone in the two classes participated in the experiment; they were aware of being monitored, but had no knowledge of what was being observed or why.

The programming application was a compiler for a small high-level language and a simple stack machine; it involved string processing and language translation (via scanning, parsing, code generation, and symbol table management). The total task was to design, implement, test, and debug the complete computer software system from given specifications. The scope of the project excluded both extensive error handling and user documentation. The project was of modest but non-negligible difficulty, requiring roughly a two man-month effort and resulting in systems that averaged over 1200 lines of high-level-language source code. All facets of the project itself were fixed and uniform across all development "teams." Each "team" worked independently to build its own system, using the same specifications, computer resource allocation, calendar time allotment, implementation language, debugging tools, etc. The delivered systems each passed an independent acceptance test.

The participants were advanced undergraduate and graduate students in the Department of Computer Science, a few with as much as three years' professional programming experience. Generally speaking, they were all familiar with both the implementation language and the host computer system, but inexperienced in team programming and the disciplined methodology. A reasonable degree of homogeneity seemed to exist among the participants with respect to personal factors such as ability/experience, motivation, time/effort devoted to the project, etc. If anything, based on the researchers' subjective judgment, the participants in groups AI and AT seemed to have a slight edge over those in group DT with respect to native programming ability and formal training in the application area.

The host computer system used by all "teams" was a Univac 1100 machine with the usual Exec operating system, supporting both batch and interactive access. It was observed that almost all "teams" consistently preferred the interactive access mode; only one of AI "teams" used the batch access mode extensively.

The implementation language was the high-level, structured-programming language SIMPL-T [7], taught and used extensively in regular course work at the University. SIMPL-T contains the following control constructs: sequence, ifthen, ifthenelse, whiledo, case, exit from loop, and return from routine (but no go to). SIMPL-T allows basically two levels of data declaration scope, local to an individual routine or global across several routines, but routines may not be nested. The language adheres to a philosophy of "strong data typing" and supports integer, character, and string data types and single dimension array data structures. It provides the programmer with both recursion and string-processing capabilities similar to PL/I.

Data Collection and Reduction

During the course of the experiment, while the software projects were being developed, the computer activities of each "team" were automatically and unobtrusively monitored. Special module compilation and program execution processors (invoked by very slight changes to the regular command language) created an historical database, consisting of all source code and test data accumulated throughout the project development period, for each development "team." The raw information in this database was subsequently reduced to obtain the experimental observations. The final products were isolated from the database and measured for various syntactic and organizational aspects of the finished product source code. Effort and cost measurements were also extracted from the database. The inputs to the analysis, in the form of scores for the various programming aspects, reflect the quantitatively measured character of the product and effort of the process. (These raw data scores are presented in Appendix II.) Much of this data reduction was done automatically within a specially instrumented compiler. The same collection and reduction mechanism was uniformly applied to all development teams, ensuring the objectivity of the observations and measurements.

Programming Aspects and Metrics

The dependent variables studied in this experiment are called programming aspects. They represent specific isolatable and observable features of programming phenomena. Furthermore, they are measured in a manner that may be characterized as quantitative (on at least an interval scale [10, pp. 65-67], objective (without inaccuracy due to human subjectivity), unobtrusive (to those developing the software), and automatable (not depending on human agency).

The variables fall into two categories: process aspects and product aspects. Process aspects represent characteristics of the development process itself, in particular, the cost and required effort as reflected in the number of computer job steps (or runs) and the amount of textual revision of source code during development. Product aspects represent characteristics of the final product that was developed, in particular, the syntactic content and organization of the symbolic source code itself. Examples of product aspects are number of lines, frequency of particular statement types, average size of data variables' scope, etc. For each programming aspect there exists an associated metric, a specific algorithm which ultimately defines that aspect and by which it is measured.

Table I lists the particular programming aspects examined in this investigation. They appear grouped by category, with indented qualifying phrases to specify particular variants of certain general aspects. When referring to an individual aspect, a concatenation of the heading line with the qualifying phrases (separated by \ symbols) is used; for example, COMPUTER JOB STEPS\MODULE COMPILATION\UNIQUE denotes the number of COMPUTER JOB STEPS that were MODULE COMPILATIONS in which the source code was UNIQUE from all other compiled versions. Explanatory notes (keyed to the list in Table I) about the programming aspects are given in Appendix I, with definitions for the nontrivial or unfamiliar metrics. Technical meanings for various system- or language-dependent terms (e.g., module, segment) also appear there. Since computer programming terminology is not particularly standardized, the reader is cautioned against drawing inferences not based on this paper's definitions.

The programming aspects had been consciously planned in advance of collecting and extracting data because intuition suggested that they would serve well as quantitative indicators of important qualitative characteristics of software development phenomena. It was predicted a priori that these so-called "confirmatory" aspects would verify the study's basic premises regarding the programming methodologies being investigated.

The overall study also examined many so-called "exploratory" programming aspects: measurements which could be collected and extracted cheaply (even as a natural by-product sometimes) along with the "confirmatory" aspects, but for which there was little serious expectation that they would be useful indicators of differences among the groups. They were included in the overall study with the intent of observing as many aspects as possible on the off chance of discovering any unexpected tendency or difference, thus combining elements of both confirmatory and exploratory data analysis within one common experimental setting [27]. For these "exploratory" programming aspects and their results, interested readers are referred to [5], [22].

III. Approach

The investigative methodology can be characterized as an empirical study based on the "construction" paradigm in which multiple subjects are closely monitored during actual "production" experiences, each subject performing the same task, with controlled variation in specific variables. It uses scientific experimentation and statistical analysis based on a "differentiation among groups by aspects" paradigm in which possible differences among the groups, as indicated by differences in certain quantitatively measured aspects of the observed phenomena, are the target of the analysis. This use of "difference discrimination" as the analytical technique dictates a model of homogeneity hypothesis testing that influences nearly every element (or step) of the methodology.

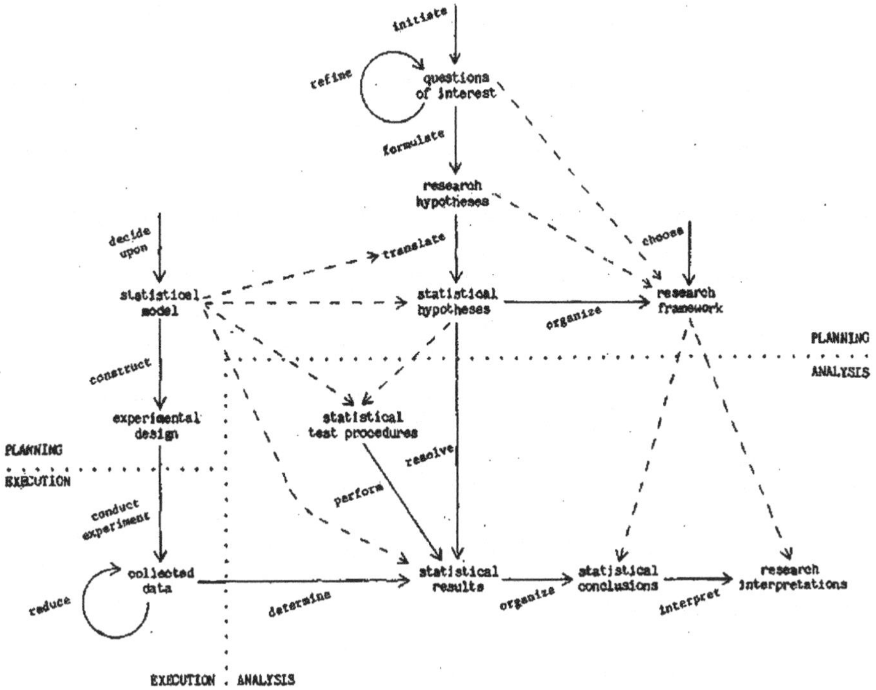

Fig. 1. Approach schematic.

Fig. 1, the approach schematic, charts some of the relationships among the various steps of the investigative methodology. The remainder of this section outlines the approach by briefly defining each step and discussing how it was applied in the research effort at hand.

Step 1-Questions of Interest: Several questions of interest were initiated and refined so that answers could be given in the form of statistical conclusions and research interpretations. The final questions of interest culminated in the form "during software development, what comparisons between the effects of the three factor-level combinations a) single individuals, b) ad hoc teams, and c) disciplined teams appear as differences in the various quantitatively measurable aspects of the software development process and product? Furthermore, what kind of differences are exhibited and what is the direction of these differences?"

Step 2-Research Hypotheses: Based upon the questions of interest, precise research hypotheses were formulated as disjoint pairs designated null and alternative, to be supported or refuted by the evidence.

A precise meaning was given to the notion "what kind of difference." In order to address the expectancy of behavior under the experimental treatments, the investigation focused on differences in central tendency or average value of the quantifiable programming aspects. These "location" comparisons and their results are the topic of this paper. The overall study also addressed the predictability of behavior under the experimental treatments by considering differences in variability around the central tendency of observed values of the programming aspects. For these "dispersion" comparisons and their results, interested readers are referred to [5], [22].

The schema for the research hypotheses may be stated as follows. "In the context of a one-person do-able software development project, there < is not | is > a difference in the location of the measurements on programming aspect <X> between individuals (AI), ad hoc teams (AT), and disciplined teams (DT)." For each programming aspect "X" in the set under consideration, this schema generates a pair of nondirectional research hypotheses, depending upon the selection of "is not" or "is" corresponding to the null and alternative hypothesis.

Step 3-Statistical Model: The choice of a statistical model makes explicit various assumptions regarding the experimental design, the dependent variables, the underlying population distributions, etc. Because the study involves a homogeneity-of-populations problem with shift alternative, the multisample model used here requires the following criteria: independent populations, independent and random sampling within each population, continuous underlying distributions for each population, homoscedasticity (equal variances) of underlying distributions, and interval scale of measurement [10, pp. 65-67] for each programming aspect. Although random sampling was not explicitly achieved in this study by rigorous sampling procedures, it was nonetheless assumed on the basis of the apparent representativeness of the subject pool and the lack of obvious reasons to doubt otherwise. Due to the small sample sizes and the unknown shape of the underlying distributions, a nonparametric statistical model was used.

Whenever statistics is employed to "prove" that some systematic effect — in this case, a difference among the groups — exists, it is important to measure the risk of error. This is usually done by reporting a significance level α [10, p. 79], which represents the probability of deciding that a systematic effect exists when in fact it does not. In the model, the hypothesis testing for each programming aspect was regarded as a separate independent experiment. Consequently, the significance level is controlled and reported experiment wise (i.e., per aspect). While the assumption of independence between such experiments is not entirely supportable, this procedure is valid as long as statistical inferences that couple two or more of the programming aspects are avoided or properly qualified.

Step 4-Statistical Hypotheses: The research hypotheses must be translated into statistically tractable form, called statistical hypotheses. In this study, the research hypotheses are concerned with directional differences among three programming environments. Since the corresponding mathematical statements are not directly tractable, they were broken down into the set of four statistical hypotheses pairs shown below. The hypotheses pair

null: $AI = AT = DT$ alternative: $\sim(AI = AT = DT)$

addresses the existence of an overall difference among the groups. The hypotheses pairs

null: $AI = AT$ alternative: $AI \neq AT$ or

$AI < AT$ or $AT < AI$

null: AT = DT alternative: AT $\neq$ DT or
AT < DT or DT < AT

null: AI =DT alternative: AI $\neq$ DT or
AI < DT or DT < AI

address the existence and direction of pair wise differences between groups. The results of these pair wise comparisons were used to explicate the overall comparison.

Thus, for any particular programming aspect, the research hypotheses pair corresponds to four different pairs (null and alternative) of scientific hypotheses. The results of testing each set of four hypotheses must be abstracted and organized into one statistical conclusion using the first research framework discussed in the next step.

Step 5-Research Frameworks: The research frameworks provide the necessary organizational basis for abstracting and conceptualizing the volume of statistical hypotheses (and statistical results that follow) into a smaller and more intellectually manageable set of conclusions. Two separate research frameworks have been chosen: 1) the framework of possible overall comparison outcomes for a given programming aspect and 2) the framework of general beliefs regarding expected effects of the experimental treatments on the comparison outcomes for the entire set of programming aspects. The first framework is employed in the statistical conclusions step because it can be applied in a statistically tractable manner, while the second framework is reserved for the research interpretations step since it is not statistically tractable and involves subjective judgment.

Since a finite set of three different programming environments (the AI, AT, and DT groups) are being compared, there exists a finite set of nineteen possible overall comparison outcomes for each aspect considered, as displayed in the following chart:

The level number associated (in the chart) with each outcome "equation" is exactly the number of statistically significant (pair wise) differences implied by or stated in that equation.

The level-0 equation indicates no distinction among the three groups. The level-1 equations indicate a difference between the two extreme groups, with the third group (designated in lowercase letters within parentheses) lying in between. The level-2 equations indicate that one group is different from each of the other two, while the level-3 equations indicate that all three groups are differentiated from one another. The equations appearing in boxes provide a direction-free "summary" of the corresponding set of equations. These 19 possible overall comparison outcomes comprise the first research framework and may be viewed as providing a complete "answer space" for the questions of interest. This framework is the basis for organizing and condensing the four statistical results into one statistical conclusion for each programming aspect considered.

The design of the experiments, the choice of treatment factors, etc., were partially motivated by certain general beliefs regarding software development, such as "disciplined methodology reduces software development costs." The implications, relative to these beliefs, of the possible outcomes of each aspect's experiment provide a second research framework. This framework is the basis for interpreting the study's findings in terms of evidence in favor of the general beliefs; details are given in Section V, Interpretation.

The overall study also employed a third research framework, based on abstracting what the study's findings indicate about certain higher level programming issues (such as data variable organization or intersegment communication). For this third framework and the corresponding interpretation, interested readers are referred to [5], [22].

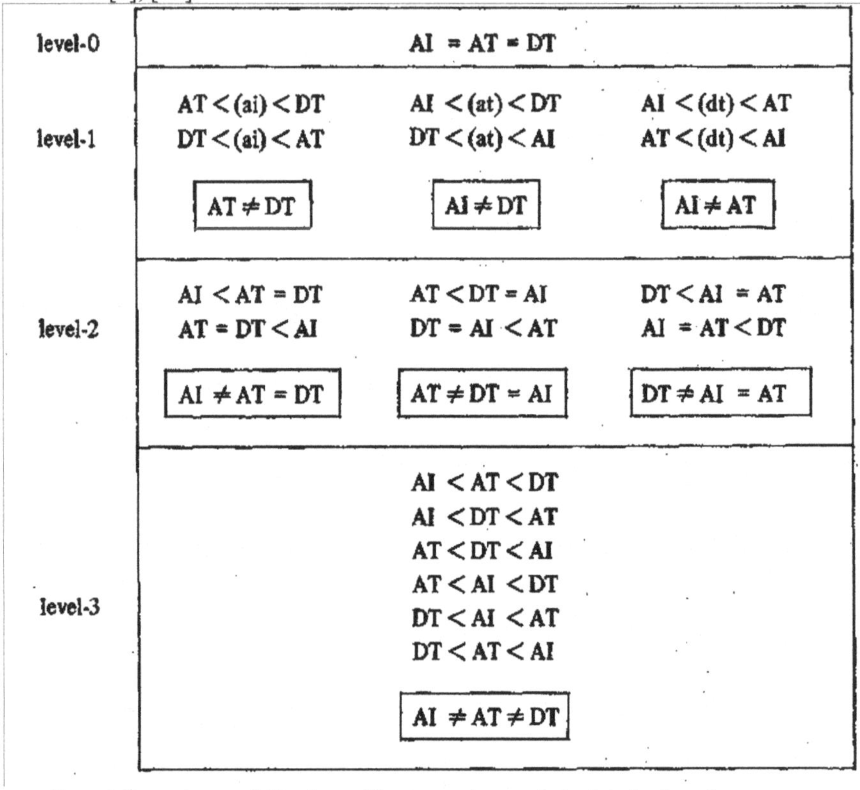

Step 6-Experimental Design: The experimental design is the plan or setup according to which the experiment is actually conducted or executed. It is based upon the statistical model, and deals with practical issues such as experimental units, treatment factors and levels, experimental local control, etc. The experimental design employed for this study has been discussed in Section II, Specifics.

Step 7-Collected Data: The pertinent data to carry out the experimental design are collected and processed to yield the information to which the statistical test procedures were applied. Some details of this execution phase have been given in Section II, Specifics. The data themselves are listed in Appendix II.

Step 8-Statistical Test Procedures: As dictated by the statistical model, the statistical tests used in the study were nonparametric tests of homogeneity of populations against shift alternatives for small samples. In particular, the standard

Kruskal-Wallis H-test [25, pp. 184-193] and Mann-Whitney U-test [25, pp. 116-127] were employed in the statistical results step. Ryan's method of adjusted significance levels [16, pp. 97, 495-497], a standard procedure for controlling the experiment wise significance level when several tests are performed on the same scores as one experiment, was also employed in the statistical conclusions step. As part of Ryan's method, the rank means within the groups were used a posteriori to determine the direction of significant differences.

The critical level α [10, p. 81] is defined as the minimum significance level at which the statistical test procedure would allow the null hypothesis to be rejected (in favor of the alternative) for the given sample data. It is a concise standardized way to state the full result of any statistical test procedure. A decision to reject the null hypothesis and accept the alternative is mandated if the critical level is low enough to be tolerated; otherwise a decision to retain the null hypothesis is made.

A different statistical analysis has been performed [5], [22], which postulated directional alternative hypotheses (and used one-tailed tests). Taking a slightly more conservative tack, this present paper makes no a priori assumptions regarding direction of observed differences (and uses two-tailed tests). It should be noted that, since the study's a priori general beliefs (see Section V, Interpretation) did involve differences in particular directions, some justification exists for using one-tailed tests in the statistical analysis. This would roughly halve the critical levels shown throughout this paper. However, results based on two-tailed tests are presented herein in order to avoid any objections concerning statistical technique.

Step 9—Statistical Results: For each pair of statistical hypotheses, there is one statistical result consisting of four components: 1) the null hypothesis itself; 2) the alternative hypothesis itself; 3) the critical level, stated as a probability value between 0 and 1; and 4) a decision either to retain the null hypothesis or to reject it in favor of (i.e., accept) the alternative hypothesis.

By convention, the null hypothesis purports that no systematic difference appears to exist, and the alternative hypothesis purports that some systematic difference seems to exist. The critical level is associated with erroneously accepting the alternative hypothesis (i.e., claiming a systematic difference when none in fact exists). The decision to retain or reject is reached on the basis of some tolerable level of significance, with which the critical level is compared to see if it is low enough. In cases where a null hypothesis is rejected, the appropriate directional alternative hypothesis (if any) is given to indicate the direction of the systematic difference.

Conventional practice is to fix an arbitrary significance level (e.g., 0.05 or 0.01) in advance, to be used as the tolerable level; critical levels then serve only as stepping-stones toward reaching decisions and are not reported. For this study, it was deemed more appropriate to fix a tolerable level only for the purpose of a screening decision (simply to purge those results with intolerably high critical levels) and to explicitly retain a surviving critical level with each statistical result. The tolerable level of significance used throughout this study to screen critical levels was fixed at under 0.20. A critical level of 0.20 means that the odds of obtaining test scores exhibiting the same degree of difference, due to random chance fluctuations alone, are one in five.

As an example, the four statistical results for the programming aspect STATEMENT TYPE COUNTS\IF are shown below.

Null hypothesis	alternative hypothesis	Critical level	(screening) decision
AI=AT=DT	~(AI=AT=DT)	0.063	reject
AI=AT	AI<AT	0.139	reject
AI=AT	AI≠DT	>0.999	retain
AT=DT	DT<AT	0.066	reject

Observe that the stated decisions reflect the application of the 0.20 tolerable level to the stated critical levels. Results under more stringent levels of significance can easily be determined by simply applying a lower tolerable level to form the decisions, e.g., at the 0.10 significance level, only the AI = AT = DT and AT = DT null hypothesis would be rejected.

Step 10-Statistical Conclusions: The volume of statistical results are organized and condensed into statistical conclusions according to the prearranged research framework(s). Specifically, the first research framework mentioned above was employed to reduce the four statistical results (with four individual critical levels) for each programming aspect to a single conclusion (with one overall critical level) for that aspect. The statement portion of a statistical conclusion is simply one of the nineteen possible overall comparison outcomes. Each overall comparison outcome is associated with a particular set of statistical results whose outcomes support the overall comparison outcome in a natural way. For example, the DT = AI<AT conclusion is associated with the following results:

reject AI = AT = DT in favor of ~ (AI = AT = DT),
reject AI = AT in favor of AI< AT,
retain AI =DT, and
reject AT = DT in favor of DT < AT.

Continuing the example started in Step 9, the statistical results shown there for the STATEMENT TYPE COUNTS\IF aspect are reduced to the statistical conclusion DT = AI < AT with 0.139 critical level overall. The four results match those associated above with the DT = AI < AT outcome. Following Ryan's procedure, the corresponding critical levels for those four results are adjusted to compute the overall critical level associated with this conclusion.

Thus, the statistical conclusions are in one-to-one correspondence with the research hypotheses and provide concise answers on a "per aspect" basis to the questions of interest. Further details and complete listing of the statistical conclusions for this study are presented in Section IV, Results.

Step 11-Research Interpretations: The final step in the approach is to interpret the statistical conclusions in view of any remaining research framework(s). These research interpretations provide the opportunity to augment the objective findings of the study with the researcher's own subjective judgments and interpretations. The second research framework mentioned above, namely, the general beliefs governing the expected outcomes for the entire set of programming aspects, was considered important. However, this particular research framework can only be utilized for research interpretations, since it is not amenable to rigorous manipulation. Nonetheless, within this framework which is based upon intuitive understanding about the software development environments under consideration, the study bears its most interesting results and implications. Further details and discussion of the research interpretations of this study appear in Section V, Interpretation.

IV. Results

The immediate results of the study are the statistical conclusions inferred from the experiment for each programming aspect considered. They state any observed differences, and the directions thereof, among the programming environments represented by the three groups examined in the study: ad hoc individuals (AI), ad hoc teams (AT), and disciplined teams (DT). Each statistical conclusion is expressed in the concise form of a three-way comparison outcome "equation." The equality AI = AT = DT expresses the null conclusion that there is no systematic difference among the groups. An inequality, e.g., AT < (ai) < DT, AI < AT = DT, or DT < AI < AT, expresses a no null (or alternative) conclusion that there are certain systematic difference(s) among the groups in stated direction(s). A critical level (or risk) value is also associated with each no null (or alternative) conclusion, indicating its individual reliability. This value is the probability of having erroneously rejected the null conclusion in favor of the alternative; it also provides a relative index of how pronounced the differences were in the sample data.

Table I gives the complete set of statistical conclusions, arranged by programming aspect. Instances of no null (or alternative) conclusions, indicating some distinction among the groups on the basis of a particular programming aspect, are itemized in English prose form at the end of this section.

Examination of the table immediately indicates that roughly half of the programming aspects (particularly product aspects), which were all expected a priori to show some distinction among the groups, failed in actuality to do so. However, several of the null conclusions may indicate characteristics inherent to the application itself. As one example, the basic symbol-table/scanner/parser/code-generator nature of a compiler strongly influences the way the system is modularized and thus practically determines the number of modules in the final product (give or take some occasional slight variation due to other design decisions).

Impact Evaluation

These statistical conclusions have a certain objective character — since they are statistically inferred from empirical data — and their collective inpact may be objectively evaluated according to the following statistical principle [27, p. 84-85].

Whenever a series of statistical tests (or experiments) are made, all at a fixed level of significance (for example, 0.10), a corresponding percentage (in the example, 10 percent) of the tests are expected a priori to reject the null hypothesis in the complete absence of any true effect (i.e., due to chance alone). This expected rejection percentage provides a comparative index of the true impact of the test results as a whole (in the example, a 25 percent actual rejection percentage would indicate that a truly significant effect, other than chance alone, was operative).

The details of this impact evaluation for the study's objective results, broken down into appropriate categories, are presented in the following table. The evaluation was performed at the $\alpha = 0.20$ significance level used for screening purposes, hence the expected rejection percentage for any category was 20 percent. For each category of aspects, the table gives the number of programming aspects, the expected (rounded to whole numbers) and actual numbers of rejections (of the null conclusion in favor of a directional alternative), and the expected and actual rejection percentages. Strong statistical impact is demonstrated by an actual rejection percentage well above the expected rejection percentage.

Category	number of aspects	expected number of rejections	actual number of rejections	expected rejection percentage	actual rejection percentage
"confirmatory" aspects	35	7	19	20.0	54.3
process aspects only	6	1	6	20.0	100.0
product aspects only	29	6	13	20.0	44.8

The table shows that the results do have strong statistical impact. On the whole, process aspects have more impact than product aspects, but all of the observed quantitative distinctions among the three groups bear statistical impact. They are better explained as consequences of some true effect related to the experimental treatments, rather than as random phenomena.

Individual Highlights

The purpose of this subsection is simply to highlight the individual differences observed in the study, by itemizing the no null conclusions in English.

1. According to the DT < AI = AT outcome on the computer job steps aspect, the disciplined teams used very noticeably fewer computer job steps (i.e., module compilations, program executions, and miscellaneous job steps) than both the ad hoc individuals and the ad hoc teams. As metrics, this aspect and its sub classifications directly represent machine costs, in units of basic computer system operations, and indirectly reflect human costs, since each operation necessitates a certain expenditure of programmer time/effort.
2. This same difference was apparent in the total number of module compilations, the number of unique (i.e., not an identical recompilation of a previ-

ously compiled module) module compilations, the number of program executions, and the number of essential job steps (i.e., unique module compilations plus program executions), according to the DT < AT = AI outcomes on the COMPUTER JOB STEPS\MODULE COMPILATION, COMPUTER JOB STEPS\MODULE COMPILATION\UNIQUE, COMPUTER JOB STEPS\PROGRAM EXECUTION, and COMPUTER JOB STEPS/ESSENTIAL/ aspects, respectively.

3. According to the DT < AI = AT outcome on the PROGRAM CHANGES aspect [13] the disciplined teams required very noticeably fewer textural revisions to build and debug the software than the ad hoc individuals and the ad hoc teams. As a metric, this aspect has been shown to correlate well with total number of error occurrences determined via human inspection.
4. There was a definite trend for the ad hoc individuals and disciplined teams to have produced fewer total symbolic lines (including comments, compiler directives, statements, declarations, etc.) than the ad hoc teams, according to the DT = AI < AT outcome on the LINES aspect. There is evidence, as indicated by the lower critical level, of a stronger pair wise difference between ad hoc individuals and ad hoc teams than between disciplined teams and ad hoc teams. This aspect measures the size of the software product.
5. According to the AI < AT = DT outcome on the segments aspect, the ad hoc individuals organized their software into noticeably fewer routines (i.e., functions or procedures) than either the ad hoc teams or the disciplined teams. In addition to measuring the size of the software product, this aspect reflects its modularity.
6. The ad hoc individuals displayed a trend toward having a greater number of executable statements per routine than did the ad hoc teams, according to the AT < (dt) < AI outcome on the AVERAGE STATEMENTS PER SEGMENT aspect. As a metric, this aspect represents the length of a typical routine in the delivered source code.
7. According to the DT = AI < AT outcomes on the STATEMENT TYPE COUNTS\IF and STATEMENT TYPE PERCENTAGE\IF aspects, both the ad hoc individuals and the disciplined teams coded noticeably fewer IF statements than the ad hoc teams, in terms of both total number and percentage of total statements. In both cases, it should be noted that the more significant pair wise difference lies between disciplined teams and ad hoc teams. These aspects are two of the earliest proposed and more commonly accepted measures of program complexity.
8. According to the DT < (ai) < AT outcome on the decisions aspect, the disciplined teams tended to code fewer decisions (i.e., IF, WHILE, or CASE statements) than the ad hoc teams. As a metric, this aspect represents control flow complexity; it is closely associated with a recently proposed graph theoretic complexity measure [19].
9. The disciplined teams and the ad hoc individuals both coded fewer return statements than the ad hoc teams, according to the DT = AI < AT outcome on the STATEMENT TYPE COUNTS\RETURN aspect, with the stronger pair

wise difference separating disciplined teams and ad hoc teams. This aspect reflects a degree of deviation from rigorously structured code.

10. The disciplined teams coded a higher percentage of case statements than the ad hoc teams, according to the AT < (ai) < DT outcome on the STATEMENT TYPE PERCENTAGES\CASE aspect. This aspect reflects the organization of low-level tests into a more concise control structure.
11. The ad hoc individuals tended to use fewer global variables than the ad hoc teams, according to the AI < (dt) < AT outcome on the DATA VARIABLE SCOPE COUNTS\GLOBAL aspect. As metrics, this aspect and the others dealing with scope reflect the organization and accessibility of data within a program.
12. The ad hoc individuals also tended to use fewer parameter variables than the ad hoc teams, in terms of both total number and percentage of declared data variables, according to the AI (dt) < AT outcomes on the DATA VARIABLE SCOPE COUNTS\PARAMETER and DATA VARIABLE SCOPE PERCENTAGES\PARAMETER aspects.
13. According to the AT = DT < AI outcome on the DATA VARIABLE SCOPE PERCENTAGES\LOCAL aspect, the ad hoc individuals had a larger percentage of local variables compared to the total number of declared data variables than either the ad hoc teams or the disciplined teams. The stronger pair wise differentiation lies between disciplined teams and ad hoc individuals.
14. There was a slight trend for the ad hoc individuals to have fewer potential data bindings [26] (i.e., occurrences of the situation where a global variable could be modified by one segment and accessed by another due to the software's modularization) than the ad hoc teams, according to the AI < (dt) < AT outcome on the (SEG, GLOBAL, SEG) DATA BINDINGS\POSSIBLE aspect. As a metric, this aspect represents the potential number of unique communication paths via globals between pairs of segments.

V. Interpretation

The study's derived results, called research interpretations, consist of an evaluation of the statistical conclusions presented in Section IV, based upon a set of general beliefs regarding software development. These beliefs were formulated by the researchers prior to conducting the experiment. Pertaining to both the process and product of software development, the beliefs are

(Bl) that methodological discipline is a key influence on the general efficiency of the software process;

(B2) that the disciplined methodology reduces the cost and complication of the process;

(B3) that the preferred direction of differences on process aspects is clear and undebatable, due to the tangibleness of the process aspects themselves and the direct applicability of expected values in terms of average cost estimates;

(B4) that "mental cohesiveness" (or conceptual integrity [9, pp. 41-50]) is a key influence on the general quality of the software product;

TABLE 1
PROGRAMMING ASPECTS AND STATISTICAL CONCLUSIONS

N.B.: The parenthesized numbers to the right refer to the explanatory notes in Appendix I. A simple pair of equal signs (= =) appears in place of the null outcome AI = AT = DT to avoid unnecessary clutter.

Programming Aspect	Location Comparison Outcome	Critical Level	
Development Process Aspects			
COMPUTER JOB STEPS	DT < AI = AT DT <(at)< AI DT <(ai)< AT	0.006 0.006 0.003	(1)
MODULE COMPILATION	DT < AI = AT DT <(at)< AI DT <(ai)< AT	0.042 0.042 0.005	(2)
UNIQUE	DT < AI = AT DT <(at)< AI DT <(ai)< AT	0.020 0.020 0.004	(3)
PROGRAM EXECUTION	DT < AI = AT DT <(at)< AI DT <(ai)< AT	0.041 0.011 0.041	(4)
ESSENTIAL	DT < AI = AT DT <(at)< AI DT <(ai)< AT	0.007 0.003 0.007	(5)
PROGRAM CHANGES	DT < AI = AT DT <(at)< AI DT <(ai)< AT	0.006 0.006 0.003	(6)
Final Product Aspects			
MODULES	= =		(7)
SEGMENTS	AI < AT = DT AI <(dt)< AT AI <(at)< DT	0.109 0.077 0.109	(8)
LINES	DT = AI < AT AI <(dt)< AT DT <(ai)< AT	0.109 0.045 0.109	(9)
STATEMENTS	= =		(10)

Programming Aspect	Location Comparison Outcome	Critical Level	
Final Product Aspects			
STATEMENT TYPE COUNTS :			(11)
IF	DT = AI < AT AI <(dt)< AT DT <(ai)< AT	0.139 0.139 0.066	(12)
CASE	= =		(13)
WHILE	= =		(14)
EXIT	= =		(15)
RETURN	DT = AI < AT AI <(dt)< AT DT <(ai)< AT	0.159 0.159 0.047	(16)
STATEMENT TYPE PERCENTAGES :			(11)
IF	DT = AI < AT AI <(dt)< AT DT <(ai)< AT	0.197 0.197 0.054	(12)
CASE	AT <(ai)< DT	0.157	(13)
WHILE	= =		(14)

TABLE I (Continued)

Programming Aspect	Location Comparison Outcome	Critical Level	
Final Product Aspects			
EXIT	= =		(15)
RETURN	= =		(16)
AVERAGE STATEMENTS PER SEGMENT	AT <(dt)< AI	0.139	(17)
AVERAGE STATEMENT NESTING LEVEL	= =		(18)
DECISIONS	DT <(ai)< AT	0.090	(19)
TOKENS	= =		(20)
AVERAGE TOKENS PER STATEMENT	= =		(20)
DATA VARIABLE SCOPE COUNTS :			(21)
GLOBAL	AI <(dt)< AT	0.085	(22)
PARAMETER	AI <(dt)< AT	0.123	(22)
LOCAL	= =		(22)
DATA VARIABLE SCOPE PERCENTAGES :			(21)
GLOBAL	= =		(22)
PARAMETER	AI <(dt)< AT	0.111	(22)
LOCAL	AT =DT< AI AT <(dt)< AI DT <(at)< AI	0.197 0.197 0.066	(22)
(SEGMENT, GLOBAL) USAGE PAIR RELATIVE PERCENTAGE			(23)
(SEGMENT, GLOBAL, SEGMENT) DATA BINDINGS :			(24)
ACTUAL			(25)
POSSIBLE	AI <(dt)< AT	0.197	(25)
RELATIVE PERCENTAGE			(25)

(B5) that a programming team is naturally burdened (relative to an individual programmer) by the organizational overhead and risk of error-prone misunderstanding inherent in coordinating and interfacing the thoughts and efforts of those on the team;
(B6) that the disciplined methodology induces an effective mental cohesiveness, enabling a programming team to behave more like an individual programmer with respect to conceptual control over the program, its design, its structure, etc., because of the discipline's antiregressive, complexity-controlling effects that compensate for the inherent organization overhead of a team; and
(B7) that the preferred direction of differences on product aspects is not always clear (occasionally even subject to diverging viewpoints), due to the intangibleness of many of the product aspects.

In relation to these general beliefs, each possible comparison outcome acquires additional meaning, either substantiating or contravening some subset of the beliefs. For process aspects and beliefs (B1)-(B3)

a) the level-2 outcome $DT < AI = AT$ is directly supportive of these beliefs;
b) the level-3 outcomes $DT < AI < AT$ and $DT < AT < AI$ and the level-1 outcomes $DT < (ai) < AT$ and $DT < (at) < AI$ are indirectly supportive of these beliefs;
c) the level-0 outcome $AI = AT = DT$ may discredit these beliefs, or it may be considered neutral for anyone of several possible reasons [1) the critical level for a no null outcome is just not low enough, so the aspect defaults to the null outcome; 2) the aspect simply reflects something characteristic of the application itself (or another factor common to all the groups in the experiment); or 3) the aspect actually measures something fundamental to software development phenomena in general and would always result in the null outcome]; and
d) all other outcomes discredit these beliefs.

For product aspects and beliefs (B4)-(B7)

a) the level-2 outcome $AT \neq DT = AI$, which is equivalent to $AT < DT = AI$ or $DT = AI < AT$, is directly supportive of these beliefs;
bl) the level-3 outcomes $AI < DT < AT$ and $AT < DT < AI$ may be considered as approximations to the "preferred" level-2 outcome in a) above [DT is distinct from AT but falls short of AI, due to lack of experience or maturity in the disciplined methodology.];
b2) the level-1 outcomes $AT \neq DT$ and $AI \neq AT$ may also be considered as approximations to the "preferred" level-2 outcome in a) above [$AI \neq AT$, which is equivalent to $AI < (dt) < AT$ or $AT < (dt) < AI$, supports the beliefs (B4), (B5) that mental cohesiveness influences the quality of a product and that an ad hoc team is burdened by its organizational overhead. $DT \neq AT$, which is equivalent to $DT < (ai) < AT$ or $AT < (ai) < DT$, supports the belief (B6) that the disciplined methodology affects the behavior of a team.];
c) the level-0 outcome $AI = AT = DT$ may discredit these beliefs, or it may be considered neutral for anyone of several possible reasons [as given in c) above]; and
d) all other outcomes discredit one or more of these beliefs.

The study's interpretation therefore consists of a general assessment of how well the research conclusions have borne out the general beliefs. On the whole, the study's findings do support the general beliefs presented above, although a few conclusions exist which are inconsistent with them.

Overwhelming support comes in the category of comparisons on process aspects, in which the research conclusions are distinguished by their low critical levels and by their unanimous $DT < AI = AT$ outcome. Fairly strong support also comes in the category of comparisons on product aspects, for which the only negative evidence (besides the neutral $AI = AT \neq DT$ outcomes) appeared in the form of two $AI \neq AT = DT$ outcomes. These indicate some areas in which the disciplined methodology was apparently ineffective in modifying a team's behavior toward that of an individual, possibly due to a lack of fully developed training/experience with the methodology.

Thus, according to this interpretation, the study's findings strongly substantiate the claims
(Cl) that methodological discipline is a key influence on the general efficiency of the software development process, and
(C2) that the disciplined methodology significantly reduces the material costs of software development.

The claims
(C3) that mental cohesiveness is a key influence on the general quality of the software development product,
(C4) that, relative to an individual programmer, an ad hoc programming team is mentally burdened by its organizational overhead, and
(C5) that the disciplined methodology offsets the mental burden of organizational overhead and enables a disciplined programming team to behave more like an individual programmer relative to the developed software product are moderately substantiated by the study's findings.

It should be noted that there is a simpler (albeit weaker) interpretive model that covers all of the experimental results. With the beliefs that a disciplined methodology provides for the minimum process cost and results in a product which in some aspects approximates the product of an individual and at worst approximates the product developed by an ad hoc team, the suppositions are $DT < AI$ *and* $DT < AT$ with respect to process and $AI \leq DT \leq AT$ or $AT \leq DT \leq AI$ with respect to product. The study's statistical conclusions fit this model without exception.

The interpretations presented here are neither exhaustive nor unique. They express the researchers' own estimation of the study's implications and general import, according to their professional intuitions about programming and software. It is anticipated that the reader and other researchers might formulate additional or alternative interpretations of the study's empirical results, using their own intuitive judgments. Other interpretations may be found in [5], [22].

VI. Conclusion

A practical methodology was designed and developed for experimentally and quantitatively investigating software development phenomena. It was employed to compare three particular software development environments and to evaluate the relative impact of a particular disciplined methodology (made up of so-called structured programming practices). The experiments were successful in measuring differences among programming environments and the results support the claim that disciplined methodology effectively improves both the process and product of software development. It must be remembered, however, that the results and interpretation of this study are derived from a limited subject population and a set of measures assumed to be associated with software cost and quality. Further studies replicating these experiments in other environments should be performed.

One way to substantiate the claim for improved process is to measure the effectiveness of the particular programming methodology via the number of bugs initially in the system (i.e., in the initial source code) and the amount of effort required to remove them. These measures are assumed to be associated with process aspects considered in the study, namely, PROGRAM CHANGES and COMPUTER JOB STEPS/ESSENTIAL, respectively. The statistical conclusions for both these aspects affirmed DT < AI = AT outcomes at very low (<0.01) significance levels, indicating that on the average the disciplined programming teams "scored" lower than either the ad hoc individual programmers or the ad hoc programming teams, which both "scored" about the same. Thus, the evidence collected in this study confirms the effectiveness of the disciplined methodology in building reliable software efficiently.

The second claim, that the product of a disciplined team should closely resemble that of a single individual since the disciplined methodology assures a semblance of conceptual integrity within a programming team, was partially substantiated. In many of this study's product aspects, the products developed using the disciplined methodology were either similar to or tended toward the products developed by the individuals. In no case did any of the measures show the disciplined teams' products to be worse than those developed by the ad hoc teams. The superficiality of many of the product measures, together with the small sample sizes, may be largely responsible for the lack of stronger support for this second claim. The need for product measures with increased sensitivity to critical characteristics of software is very evident.

It is important that quantitative evidence be gathered to evaluate software methods and tools. The results of these experiments are being used to guide further experiments and will act as a basis for analysis of software development products and processes in the Software Engineering Laboratory at NASA/GSFC [8]. This type of research is being pursued [3], [4], extending the study to include more sophisticated and promising aspects, such as Halstead's software science quantities [14] and other software complexity metrics [19].

Appendix I

Explanatory notes for the programming aspects

The following numbered paragraphs, keyed to the list of aspects in Table I and in Appendix II, describe each of the programming aspects considered in the study. Various system-or language-dependent terms (e.g., module, segment) are also defined here.

1. *A computer job step* is a single indivisible activity performed on a computer at the operating system command level which is nonincidental to the development effort and involves a nontrivial expenditure of computer or human resources. Only module compilations and program executions are counted as COMPUTER JOB STEPS.
2. *A module compilation* is an invocation of the implementation language processor on the source code of an individual module. Only compilations of modules comprising the final software product (or logical predecessors thereof) are counted as COMPUTER JOB STEPS\MODULE COMPILATION.
3. A *unique* module compilation is one in which the source code compiled is textually distinct from that of any previous compilation.
4. A *program execution* is an invocation of a complete programmer-developed program (after the necessary compilation(s) and collection or link-editing) upon some test data.
5. An *essential job step* is a computer job step that involves the final software product (or logical predecessors thereof) and could not have been avoided (by off-line computation or by on-line storage of previous compilations or results).
6. The *program changes* metric [13] is defined in terms of textual revisions made to the source code of a module during the development period, from the time that module is first presented to the computer system, to the completion of the project. The rules for counting program changes are such that one program change should represent approximately one conceptual change to the program.
7. A *module* is a separately compiled portion of the complete software system. In the implementation language SIMPL-T, a typical module is a collection of the declarations of several global variables and the definitions of several segments.
8. A *segment* is a collection of source code statements, together with declarations for the formal parameters and local variables manipulated by those statements, that may be invoked as an operational unit. In the implementation language SIMPL-T, a segment is either a value-returning/function (invoked via reference in an expression) or else a non-value-returning *procedure* (invoked via the call statement); recursive segments are allowed and fully supported. The segment, function, and procedure of SIMPL-T correspond to the (sub)program, function, and subroutine of Fortran, respectively.
9. The LINES aspect counts every textual line in the source code of the complete program, including comments, compiler directives, variable declarations, executable statements, etc.

10. The STATEMENTS aspect counts only the executable constructs in the source code of the complete program. These are high-level, structured-programming statements, including simple statements — such as assignment and procedure call-as well as compound statements — such as ifthenelse and whiledo— which have other statements nested within them. The implementation language SIMPL-T allows exactly seven different statement types (referred to by their distinguishing keyword or symbol) covering assignment (:=), alternation-selection (IF, CASE), iteration (WHILE, EXIT), and procedure invocation (CALL, RETURN). Input-output operations are accomplished via calls to certain intrinsic procedures.
11. The group of aspects named STATEMENT TYPE COUNTS, etc., gives the absolute number of executable statements of certain types. The group of aspects named STATEMENT TYPE PERCENTAGES, etc., gives the relative percentage of certain types of statements, compared with the total number of executable statements.
12. Both ifthen and ifthenelse constructs are counted as IF statements.
13. The CASE statement provides for selection from several alternatives, depending upon the value of an expression. A case construct with n alternatives is logically and semantically equivalent to a certain pattern of n nested ifthenelse constructs.
14. The WHILE statement is the only iteration or looping construct provided by the implementation language SIMPL-T.
15. The EXIT statement allows the abnormal termination of iteration loops by unconditional transfer of control to the statement immediately following the WHILE statement. Thus it is a very restricted form of got.
16. The RETURN statement allows the abnormal termination of the current segment by unconditional resumption of the previously executing segment. Thus, it is another very restricted form of go to.
17. The AVERAGE STATEMENTS PER SEGMENT aspect provides a way of normalizing the number of statements relative to their natural enclosure in a program, the segment.
18. In the implementation language SIMPL-T, both simple (e.g., assignment) and compound (e.g., ifthenelse) statements may be nested inside other compound statements. A particular *nesting level* is associated with each statement, starting at 1 for a statement at the outermost level of each segment and increasing by 1 for successively nested statements.
19. The DECISIONS aspect simply counts the total number of IF, CASE, and WHILE statements within the complete source code.
20. *Tokens* are the basic syntactic entities—such as keywords, operators, parentheses, identifiers, etc. — that occur in a program statement.
21. A *data variable* is an individually named scalar or array of scalars. In the implementation language SIMPL-T, there are three data *types* for scalars: integer, character, and (varying length) string; there is one kind of data *structure* (besides scalar): single dimensional array, with zero-origin subscript range; and there are several levels of *scope* for data variables (as explained in note (22) below). In addition, all data variables in a SIMPL-T program must be explic-

itly declared, with attributes fully specified. The total number of data variables includes each data variable declared in the complete program once, regardless of its type, structure, or scope. Note that each array is counted as a single data variable.

The group of aspects named DATA VARIABLE SCOPE COUNTS, etc., gives the absolute number of declared data variables according to each level of scope. The group of aspects named DATA VARIABLE SCOPE PERCENTAGES, etc., gives the relative percentage of variables at each scope level, compared with the total number of declared variables.

22. In the implementation language SIMPL-T, data variables can have any one of three levels of *scope* — global, parameter, and local — depending on where and how they are declared in the program. Note that the notion of scope deals only with static accessibility by name; the effective accessibility of any variable can always be extended by passing it as a parameter between segments. *Global* variables are accessible by name to each of the segments in the module(s) in which they are declared, and their values are usually manipulated by several segments. Formal *parameters* are accessible by name only within the enclosing (called) segment, but their values are not completely unrelated to the calling segment (since parameters are passed either by value or by reference). *Locals* are accessible by name only within the enclosing segment, and their values are completely isolated from any other segment.
23. A segment-global *usage pair* (p, r) is an instance of a global variable r being used by a segment p (i.e., the global is either modified (set) or accessed (fetched) at least once within the statements of the segment). Each usage pair represents a unique "use connection" between a global and a segment.

    The *actual* usage pair count is the absolute number of true usage pairs (p, r): the global variable r is actually used by segment p. The *possible* usage pair count is the absolute number of potential usage pairs (p, r), given the program's global variables and their declared scope: if the scope of global variable r contains segment p, then p could potentially modify or access r. The count of possible usage pairs is computed as the sum of the number of segments in each global variable's scope. The (SEG, GLOBAL) USAGE RELATIVE PERCENTAGE count is a way of normalizing the number of usage pairs since it is simply the ratio (expressed as a percentage) of actual usage pairs to possible usage pairs.
24. A segment-global-segment *data binding* (p,r,q) [26] is an occurrence of the following arrangement in a program: a segment p modifies (sets) a global variable r which is also accessed (fetched) by a segment q, with segment p different from segment q. The binding (p, r, p) is different from the binding (q, r, p) which may also exist; occurrences such as (p, r, q) are not counted as data bindings.
25. In this study, segment-global-segment data bindings were counted in three different ways. First, the ACTUAL count is the absolute number of true data bindings (p, r, q): the global variable r is actually modified by segment p and actually accessed by segment q. Second, the POSSIBLE count is the absolute number of potential data bindings (p, r, q), given the program's global variables

and their declared scope: the scope of global variable r simply contains both segment p and segment q, so that segment p could potentially modify r and segment q could potentially access r. This count of POSSIBLE data bindings is computed as the sum of terms s*(s - 1) for each global, where s is the number of segments in that global's scope; thus, it is fairly sensitive (numerically speaking) to the total number of SEGMENTS in a program. Third, the RELATIVE PERCENTAGE is a way of normalizing the number of data bindings since it is simply the quotient (expressed as a percentage) of the actual data bindings divided by the possible data bindings.

Appendix II

Raw data for the programming aspects

For each measured programming aspect considered in the study and reported in this paper, the observed raw data scores are listed below in ascending order and identified both as to the type of programming environment — ad hoc individuals (AI), ad hoc teams (AT), or disciplined teams (DT) — and as to the particular numbered subject (an individual or a team) within that environment. For example, "AT(4)" identifies the fourth ad hoc team participating in the experiment.

N.B.: The parenthesized numbers to the right of the programming aspect labels refer to the explanatory notes in Appendix I.

COMPUTER JOB STEPS		COMPUTER JOB STEPS \ MODULE COMPILATION (1), (2)	
DT(2) =	44	DT(2) =	32
DT(6) =	58	AI (6) =	34
DT(1) =	67	DT(1) =	34
DT(3) =	68	DT(6) =	38
DT(4) =	79	DT(5) =	49
AI (6) =	87	DT(3) =	51
DT(5) =	90	DT(4) =	52
DT(7) =	123	DT(7) =	70
AT(5) =	150	AT(4) =	74
AI (3) =	151	AI (1) =	83
AI (1) =	159	AI (3) =	87
AT(6) =	164	AT(5) =	104
AT(4) =	173	AI (5) =	110
AI (5) =	176	AI (4) =	123
AI (4) =	183	AT(6) =	133
AT(1) =	216	AT(1) =	147
AT(3) =	266	AT(3) =	162
AI (2) =	357	AI (2) =	176
AT(2) =	372	AT(2) =	199

COMPUTER JOB STEPS \
ESSENTIAL (1),(5)

DT(2)	=	37
DT(3)	=	46
DT(6)	=	55
DT(1)	=	60
DT(4)	=	65
DT(5)	=	72
AI (6)	=	83
AT(6)	=	102
DT(7)	=	112
AI (4)	=	123
AI (3)	=	128
AT(5)	=	140
AI(1)	=	155
AT(4)	=	158
AI(5)	=	163
AT(1)	=	182
AT(3)	=	230
AI (2)	=	292
AT(2)	=	332

COMPUTER JOB STEPS \
PROGRAM EXECUTION (1), (4)

DT(2)	=	12
DT(3)	=	16
DT(6)	=	20
DT(4)	=	23
AT(6)	=	29
DT(1)	=	33
DT(5)	=	39
AT(5)	=	42
AI (3)	=	49
AI(6)	=	52
AI(4)	=	53
DT(7)	=	53
AI(5)	=	63
AT(1)	=	64
AI(1)	=	76
AT(3)	=	90
AT(4)	=	96
AI(2)	=	163
AT(2)	=	173

MODULES (7)

AT(1)	=	1
AT(2)	=	1
AI(1)	=	2
AI (5)	=	2
AI (6)	=	2
AT(4)	=	2
DT(1)	=	2
AI (2)	=	3
DT(2)	=	3
DT(5)	=	3
DT(7)	=	3
AI (4)	=	4
AT(3)	=	4
DT(6)	=	5
DT(4)	=	6
DT(3)	=	8
AT(5)	=	9
AI (3)	=	10
AT(6)	=	15

PROGRAM CHANGES (6)

DT(4)	=	111
DT(7)	=	114
DT(2)	=	120
DT(3)	=	136
DT(6)	=	159
AI(6)	=	187
DT(1)	=	223
DT(5)	=	251
AI(3)	=	270
AI(2)	=	281
AT(6)	=	287
AT(1)	=	301
AI(4)	=	316
AT(4)	=	394
AT(5)	=	493
AI(5)	=	525
AI(1)	=	539
AT(3)	=	554
AT(2)	=	1107

SEGMENTS (8)		
AI(2)	=	21
AI(1)	=	24
AI (6)	=	25
AI (5)	=	33
DT(2)	=	33
DT(6)	=	33
AI (3)	=	34
AT(2)	=	38
DT(3)	=	38
AT(3)	=	39
AT(6)	=	42
DT(4)	=	42
DT(7)	=	42
AT(1)	=	45
AI (4)	=	47
AT(4)	=	48
DT(1)	=	52
DT(5)	=	52
AT(5)	=	74

LINES (9)		
AI (6)	=	579
AI(1)	=	836
DT(2)	=	894
AI(2)	=	944
DT(3)	=	1083
AI(5)	=	1087
AT(1)	=	1138
AI(4)	=	1155
DT(7)	=	1235
DT(4)	=	1267
DT(5)	=	1269
AT(3)	=	1394
AI(3)	=	1559
DT(1)	=	1579
AT(2)	=	1588
DT(6)	=	1600
AT(6)	=	1675
AT(5)	=	2078
AT(4)	=	2186

STATEMENT TYPE COUNTS\ IF (11), (12)		
AI (6)	=	27
DT(7)	=	38
AI(2)	=	43
DT(3)	=	44
AI (1)	=	49
DT(2)	=	62
DT(4)	=	63
AT(4)	=	78
AI (4)	=	80
DT(1)	=	83
AT(1)	=	88
DT(5)	=	89
DT(6)	=	90
AT(3)	=	97
AI(5)	=	100
AI(3)	=	110
AT(5)	=	114
AT(2)	=	116
AT(6)	=	124

STATEMENT TYPE COUNTS \ WHILE (11), (14)		
DT(4)	=	17
AI(6)	=	18
AI(l)	=	19
AI(5)	=	21
AT(4)	=	21
DT(6)	=	21
DT(3)	=	22
DT(5)	=	22
AT(2)	=	24
AT(6)	=	24
DT(2)	=	24
DT(7)	=	25
AT(5)	=	28
AI(2)	=	29
AI (4)	=	30
AT(1)	=	31
AI (3)	=	34
DT(1)	=	34
AT(3)	=	35

STATEMENTS (10)

AI(6)	=	378
AI(1)	=	432
DT(3)	=	456
DT(7)	=	499
DT(2)	=	502
AI(2)	=	556
AT(4)	=	590
DT(4)	=	617
AI(5)	=	629
AT(1)	=	631
DT(5)	=	640
DT(6)	=	643
AI(4)	=	647
AT(2)	=	654
AT(6)	=	681
AT(3)	=	691
AI(3)	=	738
AT(5)	=	798
DT(1)	=	800

STATEMENT TYPE COUNTS \ CASE (11), (13)

AI(5)	=	1
AT(l)	=	1
AT(2)	=	4
AT(6)	=	4
DT(2)	=	4
DT(3)	=	4
DT(7)	=	4
AI (3)	=	6
AI(6)	=	6
AT(4)	=	6
AT(5)	=	6
AI(1)	=	7
DT(4)	=	7
DT(6)	=	7
AT(3)	=	10
AI(2)	=	11
AI(4)	=	11
DT(5)	=	12
DT(1)	=	14

STATEMENT TYPE COUNTS\ EXIT (11),(15)

AI (6)	=	0
AT(1)	=	0
AT(2)	=	0
AT(3)	=	0
AT(4)	=	0
DT(1)	=	0
DT(2)	=	0
DT(3)	=	0
DT(4)	=	0
DT(5)	=	0
AI(1)	=	1
AI (2)	=	1
DT(7)	=	2
AI (4)	=	3
DT(6)	=	3
AT(6)	=	6
AI(5)	=	8
AT(5)	=	13
AI (3)	=	15

STATEMENT TYPE COUNTS \ RETURN (11), (16)

AI(6)	=	36
AI (2)	=	47
AI (3)	=	47
DT(2)	=	47
DT(3)	=	47
DT(4)	=	48
DT(6)	=	48
AT(4)	=	50
DT(7)	=	50
AI(1)	=	53
AT(2)	=	53
DT(1)	=	54
AI (5)	=	59
AI (4)	=	60
AT(3)	=	64
DT(5)	=	65
AT(1)	=	99
AT(6)	=	109
AT(5)	=	118

STATEMENT TYPE PERCENTAGES \ CASE (11),(13)		
AI(5)	=	0.2
AT(1)	=	0.2
AT(2)	=	0.6
AT(6)	=	0.6
AI (3)	=	0.8
AT(5)	=	0.8
DT(2)	=	0.8
DT(7)	=	0.8
DT(3)	=	0.9
AT(4)	=	1.0
DT(4)	=	1.1
DT(6)	=	1.1
AT(3)	=	1.4
AI(1)	=	1.6
AI(6)	=	1.6
AI(4)	=	1.7
DT(1)	=	1.8
DT(5)	=	1.9
AI (2)	=	2.0

STATEMENT TYPE PERCENTAGES \ EXIT (11), (15)		
AI (6)	=	0.0
AT(1)	=	0.0
AT(2)	=	0.0
AT(3)	=	0.0
AT(4)	=	0.0
DT(1)	=	0.0
DT(2)	=	0.0
DT(3)	=	0.0
DT(4)	=	0.0
DT(5)	=	0.0
AI(1)	=	0.2
AI (2)	=	0.2
DT(7)	=	0.4
AI(4)	=	0.5
DT(6)	=	0.5
AT(6)	=	0.9
AI(5)	=	1.3
AT(5)	=	1.6
AI (3)	=	2.0

STATEMENT TYPE PERCENTAGES \ IF (11), (12)		
AI(6)	=	7.1
DT(7)	=	7.6
AI (2)	=	7.7
DT(3)	=	9.6
DT(4)	=	10.2
DT(1)	=	10.4
AI(1)	=	11.3
AI(4)	=	12.4
DT(2)	=	12.4
AT(4)	=	13.2
AT(1)	=	13.9
DT(5)	=	13.9
AT(3)	=	14.0
DT(6)	=	14.0
AT(5)	=	14.3
AI (3)	=	14.9
AI(5)	=	15.9
AT(2)	=	17.7
AT(6)	=	18.2

STATEMENT TYPE PERCENTAGES \ WHILE (11), (14)		
DT(4)	=	2.8
AI(5)	=	3.3
DT(6)	=	3.3
DT(5)	=	3.4
AT(5)	=	3.5
AT(6)	=	3.5
AT(4)	=	3.6
AT(2)	=	3.7
DT(1)	=	4.3
AI(1)	=	4.4
AI (3)	=	4.6
Al(4)	=	4.6
AI (6)	=	4.8
DT(2)	=	4.8
DT(3)	=	4.8
AT(1)	=	4.9
DT(7)	=	5.0
AT(3)	=	5.1
AT(2)	=	5.2

STATEMENT TYPE PERCENTAGES \ RETURN (11), (16)

AI(3)	=	6.4
DT(1)	=	6.8
DT(6)	=	7.5
DT(4)	=	7.8
AT(2)	=	8.1
AI(2)	=	8.5
AT(4)	=	8.5
AI (4)	=	9.3
AT(3)	=	9.3
AI(5)	=	9.4
DT(2)	=	9.4
AI (6)	=	9.5
DT(7)	=	10.0
DT(5)	=	10.2
DT(3)	=	10.3
AI(1)	=	12.3
AT(5)	=	14.8
AT(1)	=	15.7
AT(6)	=	16.0

AVERAGE STATEMENTS PER SEGMENT (17)

AT(5)	=	10.8
DT(7)	=	11.9
DT(3)	=	12.6
AT(4)	=	12.3
DT(5)	=	12.3
AI(4)	=	13.8
AT(1)	=	14.0
DT(4)	=	14.7
AI(6)	=	15.1
DT(2)	=	15.2
DT(1)	=	15.4
AT(6)	=	16.2
AT(2)	=	17.2
AT(3)	=	17.7
AI(1)	=	18.0
AI(5)	=	19.1
DT(6)	=	19.5
AI(3)	=	21.7
AI (2)	=	26.5

DECISIONS (19)

AI(6)	=	51
DT(7)	=	67
DT(3)	=	70
AI(1)	=	75
AI (2)	=	83
DT(4)	=	87
DT(2)	=	90
AT(4)	=	105
DT(6)	=	118
AT(1)	=	120
AI(4)	=	121
AI(5)	=	122
DT(5)	=	123
DT(1)	=	131
AT(3)	=	142
AT(2)	=	144
AT(5)	=	148
AI(3)	=	150
AT(6)	=	152

AVERAGE TOKENS PER STATEMENT (20)

DT(7)	=	4.2
DT(2)	=	4.7
AI (6)	=	5.0
AT(4)	=	5.0
DT(3)	=	5.0
AI(5)	=	5.2
AT(6)	=	5.2
AI (3)	=	5.3
AT(5)	=	5.3
AI(1)	=	5.4
AT(2)	=	5.6
DT(1)	=	5.6
AT(1)	=	5.7
AI (2)	=	5.9
AI(4)	=	5.9
DT(5)	=	5.9
DT(6)	=	5.9
AT(3)	=	6.2
DT(4)	=	6.5

AVERAGE STATEMENT NESTING LEVEL (18)

AT(1)	=	1.9
AT(5)	=	1.9
AT(4)	=	2.0
DT(2)	=	2.0
DT(3)	=	2.0
DT(7)	=	2.0
AI(6)	=	2.1
DT(4)	=	2.1
AI (4)	=	2.2
DT(5)	=	2.2
AI(5)	=	2.3
AT(2)	=	2.3
AT(3)	=	2.3
DT(1)	=	2.3
AL(1)	=	2.4
AI (2)	=	2.4
DT(6)	=	2.4
AI(3)	=	2.6
AT(6)	=	2.7

TOKENS (20)

AI(6)	=	1878
DT(7)	=	2113
DT(3)	=	2268
AI(1)	=	2313
DT(2)	=	2348
AT(4)	=	2976
AI(5)	=	3270
AI(2)	=	3277
AT(6)	=	3508
AT(1)	=	3622
AT(2)	=	3669
DT(5)	=	3777
AI (4)	=	3792
DT(6)	=	3792
AI(3)	=	3907
DT(4)	=	4016
AT(5)	=	4198
AT(3)	=	4269
DT(1)	=	4471

DATA VARIABLE SCOPE COUNTS \ GLOBAL (21), (22)

AI(6)	=	15
DT(3)	=	21
AI (2)	=	23
AI (5)	=	23
AT(2)	=	24
DT(5)	=	24
DT(1)	=	26
AI(1)	=	28
AI (3)	=	29
AI(4)	=	30
AT(4)	=	32
DT(7)	=	33
AT(6)	=	35
AT(5)	=	37
AT(3)	=	38
DT(6)	=	38
AT(1)	=	46
DT(4)	=	86
DT(2)	=	91

DATA VARIABLE SCOPE COUNTS \ PARAMETER (21), (22)

AI (5)	=	4
AI (6)	=	4
DT(2)	=	6
DT(7)	=	8
AI(1)	=-	10
AI (2)	=	11
AT(6)	=	13
AI(3)	=	15
AT(2)	=	20
DT(6)	=	24
DT(3)	=	26
AT(1)	=	31
AT(4)	=	33
AI(4)	=	34
AT(3)	=	38
AT(5)	=	41
DT(5)	=	51
DT(1)	=	54
DT(4)	=	54

DATA VARIABLE SCOPE PERCENTAGES \ GLOBAL (21), (22)

DT(1)	=	19.5
DT(5)	=	24.0
AI(4)	=	26.5
AT(2)	=	27.9
DT(3)	=	29.2
AT(5)	=	30.1
AI (2)	=	30.3
AT(4)	=	31.7
AT(3)	=	35.8
AT(1)	=	36.2
AI(3)	=	37.2
DT(6)	=	38.4
AI (6)	=	39.5
AT(6)	=	44.3
AI(1)	=	45.9
DT(7)	=	47.8
DT(4)	=	49.4
AI(5)	=	53.5
DT(2)	=	75.8

DATA VARIABLE SCOPE PERCENTAGES \ LOCAL (21), (22)

DT(2)	=	19.2
DT(4)	=	19.5
DT(5)	=	25.0
AT(3)	=	28.3
DT(3)	=	34.7
AT(4)	=	35.6
AT(5)	=	36.6
AI(5)	=	37.2
DT(6)	=	37.4
AI(1)	=	37.7
AT(6)	=	39.2
AT(1)	=	39.4
DT(1)	=	39.8
DT(7)	=	40.6
AI(4)	=	43.4
AI(3)	=	43.6
AT(2)	=	48.8
AI(6)	=	50.0
AI(2)	=	55.3

DATA VARIABLE SCOPE COUNTS \ LOCAL (21), (22)

AI(5)	=	16
AI(6)	=	19
AI(1)	=	23
DT(2)	=	23
DT(3)	=	25
DT(5)	=	25
DT(7)	=	28
AT(3)	=	30
AT(6)	=	31
AI(3)	=	34
DT(4)	=	34
AT(4)	=	36
DT(6)	=	37
AI (2)	=	42
AT(2)	=	42
AT(5)	=	45
AI(4)	=	49
AT(1)	=	50
DT(1)	=	53

DATA VARIABLE SCOPE PERCENTAGES \ PARAMETER (21), (22)

DT(2)	=	5.0
AI(5)	=	9.3
AI (6)	=	10.5
DT(7)	=	11.6
AI(2)	=	14.5
AI(1)	=	16.4
AT(6)	=	16.5
AI(3)	=	19.2
AT(2)	=	23.3
DT(6)	=	24.2
AT(1)	=	24.4
AI(4)	=	30.1
DT(4)	=	31.0
AT(4)	=	32.7
AT(5)	=	33.3
AT(3)	=	35.8
DT(3)	=	36.1
DT(1)	=	40.6
DT(5)	=	51.0

(SEGMENT, GLOBAL) USAGE PAIR RELATIVE PERCENTAGE (23)

AT(1)	=	7.8
AT(5)	=	9.6
AT(4)	=	11.4
DT(7)	=	13.0
AT(2)	=	14.7
DT(1)	=	15.6
AI(1)	=	15.7
DT(2)	=	17.6
DT(4)	=	18.3
AI(4)	=	21.4
DT(5)	=	25.0
AI (5)	=	25.8
AI (6)	=	26.8
AT(3)	=	27.2
DT(6)	=	27.6
AT(6)	=	30.1
AI(3)	=	31.5
AI(2)	=	37.1
DT(3)	=	43.2

(SEGMENT, GLOBAL, SEGMENT) DATA BINDINGS \ RELATIVE PERCENTAGE (24), (25)

AT(5)	=	0.3
AT(2)	=	0.7
DT(7)	=	0.7
AT(4)	=	0.8
AI(4)	=	2.1
DT(2)	=	2.1
DT(4)	=	2.2
DT(6)	=	2.4
AI(1)	=	2.5
AT(1)	=	2.6
AI(3)	=	3.1
AI (6)	=	3.2
AT(6)	=	3.5
AT(3)	=	3.6
AI (5)	=	3.7
DT(3)	=	4.3
DT(5)	=	7.9
AI (2)	=	8.4
DT(1)	=	15.4

(SEGMENT, GLOBAL, SEGMENT) DATA BINDINGS \ ACTUAL (24), (25)

DT(3)	=	121
DT(2)	=	154
DT(4)	=	164
AT(3)	=	184
DT(7)	=	210
AI (6)	=	214
AT(2)	=	221
AI(1)	=	244
DT(6)	=	260
AI (3)	=	280
AI (2)	=	302
AT(6)	=	310
AT(5)	=	360
AT(4)	=	398
AI (4)	=	438
AI (5)	=	590
AT(1)	=	1087
DT(1)	=	1104
DT(5)	=	1337

(SEGMENT, GLOBAL, SEGMENT) DATA BINDINGS \ POSSIBLE (24), (25)

DT(3)	=	2812
AI (2)	=	3588
AT(3)	=	5164
AI(6)	=	6612
DT(1)	=	7166
DT(2)	=	7434
DT(4)	=	7500
AI (3)	=	8922
AT(6)	=	8974
AI (1)	=	9798
DT(6)	=	10834
AI (5)	=	15852
DT(5)	=	17008
AI(4)	=	21309
DT(7)	=	31704
AT(2)	=	33744
AT(1)	=	41500
AT(4)	=	49782
AT(5)	=	115182

Acknowledgement

It is a pleasure to acknowledge colleagues Dr. J. D. Gannon (University of Maryland) and Dr. H. E. Dunsmore (Purdue University) for the constructive criticism and insightful discussion they provided throughout this study. The authors are indebted to Mr. W. D. Brooks (IBM Federal Systems Division) for his technical assistance regarding the statistical data analysis. The authors also thank the referees for their helpful suggestions on improving the presentation of this paper.

References

[1] F. T. Baker, "Structured programming to a production programming environment," *IEEE Trans. Software Eng.*, vol. SE-1, pp. 241-252, June 1975.
[2] V. R. Basili and F. T. Baker, *Tutorial of Structured Programming*, Tutorial from the llth IEEE Comput. Soc. Conf. (COMPCON 75 Fall), IEEE Cat. 75CH1049-6, revised 1977.
[3] V. R. Basili and D. H. Hutchens, "A study of a family of structural complexity metrics," in *Proc. 19th Annu. ACM/NBS Tech. Symp., Pathways to System Integrity.* Washington, DC, June 1980, pp. 13-15.
[4] V. R. Basili and R. W. Reiter, Jr., "Evaluating automatable measures of software development," in *Proc. IEEE/Poly Workshop on Quantitative Software Models for Reliability, Complexity, and Cost*, Kiameshia Lake, NY, Oct. 1979, IEEE Cat. TH0067-9, pp. 107-116.
[5] —, "An investigation of human factors in software development," *Computer*, vol. 12, pp. 21-38, Dec. 1979.
[6] V. R. Basili and A. J. Turner, "Iterative enhancement: A practical technique for software development," *IEEE Trans. Software Eng.*, vol. SE-1, pp. 390-396, Dec. 1975.
[7] V. R. Basili and A. J. Turner, *SIMPL-T, A Structured Programming Language*. Geneva, IL: Paladin House, 1976.
[8] V. R. Basili and M. V. Zelkowitz, "Analyzing medium-scale software development," in *Proc. 3rd Int. Conf. Software Eng.*, Atlanta, GA, May 1978, IEEE Cat. 78CH1317-7C, pp. 116-123.
[9] F. P. Brooks, Jr., *The Mythical Man-Month*. Reading, MA: Addison-Wesley, 1975.
[10] W. J. Conover, *Practical Nonparametric Statistics*. New York: Wiley, 1971.
[11] O.-J. Dahl, E. W. Dijkstra, and C.A.R. Hoare, *Structured Programming*. New York: Academic, 1972.
[12] E. B. Daley, "Management of software development," *IEEE Trans. Software Eng.*, vol. SE-3, pp. 229-242, May 1977.
[13] H. E. Dunsmore and J. D. Gannon, "Experimental investigation of programming complexity," in *Proc. 16th Annu. ACM/NBS Tech. Symp., Systems and Software*, Washington, DC, June 1977, pp. 117-125.
[14] M. Halstead, *Elements of Software Science*. New York: Elsevier, 1977.
[15] M. A. Jackson, *Principles of Program Design*. New York: Academic, 1975.
[16] R. E. Kirk, *Experimental Design: Procedures for the Behavioral Sciences*. Belmont, CA: Wadsworth, 1968.
[17] R. C. Linger, H. D. Mills, and B. I. Witt, *Structured Programming: Theory and Practice*. Reading, MA: Addison-Wesley, 1979.

[18] H. C. Lucas and R. B. Kaplan, "A structured programming experiment," *Comput. J.*, vol. 19, pp. 136-138, May 1976.

[19] T. J. McCabe, "A complexity measure," *IEEE Trans. Software Eng.*, vol. SE-2, pp. 308-320, Dec. 1976.

[20] G. J. Myers, *Reliable Software through Composite Design*. New York: Petrocelli/Charter, 1975.

[21] G. J. Myers, "A controlled experiment in program testing and code walk-throughs/inspections," *Commun. Ass. Comput. Mach.*, vol. 21, pp. 760-768, Sept. 1978.

[22] R. W. Reiter, Jr., "An experimental investigation of computer program development approaches and computer programming metrics," Ph.D. dissertation (308), Dep. Comput. Sci., Univ. Maryland, Dec. 1979 (forthcoming as Tech. Rep. TR-853).

[23] S. B. Sheppard, B. Curtis, P. Milliman, and T. Love, "Modern coding practices and programmer performance," *Computer*, vol. 12, pp. 41-49, Dec. 1979.

[24] B. Shneiderman, R. Mayer, D. McKay, and P. Heller, "Experimental investigations of the utility of detailed flowcharts in programming," *Commun. Ass. Comput. Mach.*, vol. 20, pp. 373-381, June 1977.

[25] S. Siegel, *Nonparametric Statistics: For the Behavioral Sciences*. New York: McGraw-Hill, 1956.

[26] W. P. Stevens, G. J. Myers, and L. L. Constantine, "Structured design," *IBM Syst. J.*, vol. 13, no. 2, pp. 115-139,1974.

[27] J. W. Tukey, "Analyzing data: Sanctification or detective work*?," Amer. Psychol*, vol. 24, pp. 83-91, Feb. 1969.

[28] N. Wirth, "Program development by stepwise refinement," *Commun. Ass. Comput. Mach.,* vol. 14, pp. 221-227, Apr. 1971.

Experimentation in Software Engineering

Victor R. Basili, Richard W. Selby, Member, and David H. Hutchins

Abstract. Experimentation in software engineering supports the advancement of the field through an iterative learning process. In this paper we present a framework for analyzing most of the experimental work performed in software engineering over the past several years. We describe a variety of experiments in the framework and discuss their contribution to the software engineering discipline. Some useful recommendations for the application of the experimental process in software engineering are included.

Key Words: Controlled experiment, data collection and analysis, empirical study, experimental design, software metrics, software technology measurement and evaluation.

I. Introduction

As any area matures, there is the need to understand its components and their relationships. An experimental process provides a basis for the needed advancement in knowledge and understanding. Since software engineering is in its adolescence, it is certainly a candidate for the experimental method of analysis. Experimentation is performed in order to help us better evaluate, predict, understand, control, and improve the software development process and product.

Experimentation in software engineering, as with any other experimental procedure, involves an iteration of a hypothesize and test process. Models of the software process or product are built, hypotheses about these models are tested, and the information learned is used to refine the old hypotheses or develop new ones. In an area like software engineering, this approach takes on special im-

---

Manuscript received July 15. 1985; revised January 15, 1986. This work was supported in part by the Air Force Office of Scientific Research under Contract AFOSR-F49620-80-C-001 and by the National Aeronautics and Space Administration under Grant NSG-5123 to the University of Maryland. Computer support was provided in part by the Computer Science Center at the University of Maryland.

V. R. Basili, Senior Member, IEEE, is with the Department of Computer Science, University of Maryland, College Park, MD 20742.

R. W. Selby, Member, IEEE, was with the Department of Computer Science, University of Maryland, College Park, MD 20742. He is now with the Department of Information and Computer Science, University of California, Irvine, CA 92717.

D. H. Hutchens, Member, IEEE, is with the Department of Computer Science, Clemson University, Clemson, SC 29634.

importance because we greatly need to improve our knowledge of how software is developed, the effect of various technologies, and what areas most need improvement. There is a great deal to be learned and intuition is not always the best teacher.

In this paper we lay out a framework for analyzing most of the experimental work that has been performed in software engineering over the past several years. We then discuss a variety of these experiments, their results, and the impact they have had on our knowledge of the software engineering discipline.

II. Objectives

There are three overall goals for this work. The first objective is to describe a framework for experimentation in software engineering. The framework for experimentation is intended to help structure the experimental process and to provide a classification scheme for understanding and evaluating experimental studies. The second objective is to classify and discuss a variety of experiments from the literature according to the framework. The description of several software engineering studies is intended to provide an overview of the knowledge resulting from experimental work, a summary of current research directions, and a basis for learning from past experience with experimentation. The third objective is to identify problem areas and lessons learned in experimentation in software engineering. The presentation of problem areas and lessons learned is intended to focus attention on general trends in the field and to provide the experimenter with useful recommendations for performing future studies. The following three sections address these goals.

III. Experimentation Framework

The framework of experimentation, summarized in Fig. 1, consists of four categories corresponding to phases of the experimentation process: 1) definition, 2) planning, 3) operation, and 4) interpretation. The following sections discuss each of these four phases.

A. Experiment Definition

The first phase of the experimental process is the study definition phase. The study definition phase contains six parts: 1) motivation, 2) object, 3) purpose, 4) perspective, 5) domain, and 6) scope. Most study definitions contain each of the six parts; an example definition appears in Fig. 2.

I. Definition

Motivation	Object	Purpose	Perspective	Domain	Scope
Understand	Product	Characterize	Developer	Programmer	Single project
Assess	Process	Evaluate	Modifier	Program/project	Multi-project
Manage	Model	Predict	Maintainer		Replicated project
Engineer	Metric	Motivate	Project manager		Blocked subject-project
Learn	Theory		Corporate manager		
Improve			Customer		
Validate			User		
Assure			Researcher		

II. Planning

Design	Criteria	Measurement
Experimental designs	Direct reflections of cost/quality	Metric definition
Incomplete block	Cost	Goal-question-metric
Completely randomized	Errors	Factor-criteria-metric
Randomized block	Changes	Metric validation
Fractional factorial	Reliability	Data collection
Multivariate analysis	Correctness	Automatability
Correlation	Indirect reflections of cost/quality	Form design and test
Factor analysis	Data coupling	Objective vs. subjective
Regression	Information visibility	Level of measurement
Statistical models	Programmer comprehension	Nominal/classificatory
Non-parametric	Execution coverage	Ordinal/ranking
Sampling	Size	Interval
	Complexity	Ratio

III. Operation

Preparation	Execution	Analysis
Pilot study	Data collection	Quantitative vs. qualitative
	Data validation	Preliminary data analysis
		Plots and histograms
		Model assumptions
		Primary data analysis
		Model application

IV. Interpretation

Interpretation context	Extrapolation	Impact
Statistical framework	Sample representativeness	Visibility
Study purpose		Replication
Field of research		Application

Fig. 1. Summary of the framework of experimentation

There can be several motivations, objects, purposes, or perspectives in an experimental study. For example, the motivation of a study may be to understand, assess, or improve the effect of a certain technology. The "object of study" is the primary entity examined in a study. A study may examine the final software product, a development process (e.g., inspection process, change process), a model (e.g., software reliability model), etc. The purpose of a study may he to characterize the change in a system over time, to evaluate the effectiveness of testing processes, to predict system development cost by using a cost model, to motivate[1] the validity of a theory by analyzing empirical evidence, etc. In experimental studies that examine "software quality," the interpretation usually includes correctness if it is from the perspective of a developer or reliability if it is from the perspective of a customer. Studies that examine metrics for a given project type from the perspective of the project manager may interest certain project managers, while corpo-

[1] For clarification, the usage of the word "motivate" as a study purpose is distinct from the study "motivation."

rate managers may only be interested if the metrics apply across several project types.

Definition element	example
Motivation	To improve the unit testing process,
Purpose	characterize and evaluate
Object	the processes of functional and structural testing
Perspective	from the perspective of the developer
Domain: programmer	as they are applied by experienced programmers
Domain: program	to unit-size software
Scope	in a blocked subject-project study.

Fig. 2. Study definition example

#Teams per project	#Projects: one	#Projects: more than one
one	Single project	Multi-project variation
more than one	Replicated project	Blocked subject-project

Fig. 3. Experimental scopes.

Two important domains that are considered in experimental studies of software are 1) the individual programmers or programming teams (the "teams") and 2) the programs or projects (the "projects"). "Teams" are (possibly single-person) groups that work separately, and "projects" are separate programs or problems on which teams work. Teams may be characterized by experience, size, organization, etc., and projects may be characterized by size, complexity, application, etc. A general classification of the scopes of experimental studies can be obtained by examining the sizes of these two domains considered (see Fig. 3). Blocked subject-project studies examine one or more objects across a set of teams and a set of projects. Replicated project studies examine object(s) across a set of teams and a single project, while multiproject variation studies examine object(s) across a single team and a set of projects. Single project studies examine object(s) on a single team and a single project. As the representativeness of the samples examined and the scope of examination increase, the wider-reaching a study's conclusions become.

B. Experiment Planning

The second phase of the experimental process is the study planning phase. The following sections discuss aspects of the experiment planning phase: 1) design, 2) criteria, and 3) measurement.

The design of an experiment couples the study scope with analytical methods and indicates the domain samples to be examined. Fractional factorial or randomized block designs usually apply in blocked subject-project studies, while completely randomized or incomplete block designs usually apply in multiproject and replicated project studies [33], [41]. Multivariate analysis methods, including correlation, factor analysis, and regression [75], [80], [89], generally may be used across all experimental scopes. Statistical models may be formulated and customized as appropriate [89]. Nonparametric methods should be planned when only limited data may be available or distributional assumptions may not be met [100]. Sampling techniques [40] may be used to select representative programmers and programs/projects to examine.

Different motivations, objects, purposes, perspectives, domains, and scopes require the examination of different criteria. Criteria that tend to be direct reflections of cost/ quality include cost [114], [108], [86], [5], [28], errors/changes [49], [24], [112], [2], [81], [13], reliability [42], [64], [56], [69], [70], [76], [77], [95], and correctness [51], [61], [68]. Criteria that tend to be indirect reflections of cost/quality include data coupling [62], [48], [104], [78], information visibility [85], [83], [55], programmer understanding [99], [103], [109], [113], execution coverage [105], [15], [18], and size/complexity [11], [59], [71].

The concrete manifestations of the cost/quality aspects examined in the experiment are captured through measurement. Paradigms assist in the metric definition process: the goal-question-metric paradigm [17], [25[], [19], [93] and the factor-criteria-metric paradigm [39], [72]. Once appropriate metrics have been defined, they may be validated to show that they capture what is intended [7], [21], [45], [50], [108], [116]. The data collection process includes developing automated collection schemes [16] and designing and testing data collection forms [25], [27]. The required data may include both objective and subjective data and different levels of measurement: nominal (or classificatory), ordinal (or ranking), interval, or ratio [100].

C. Experiment Operation

The third phase of the experimental process is the study operation phase. The operation of the experiment consists of 1) preparation, 2) execution, and 3) analysis. Before conducting the actual experiment, preparation may include a pilot study to confirm the experimental scenario, help organize experimental factors (e.g., subject expertise), or inoculate the subjects [45], [44], [63], [18], [113], [73]. Experimenters collect and validate the defined data during the execution of the study [21], [112]. The analysis of the data may include a combination of quantitative and qualitative methods [30]. The preliminary screening of the data, probably using plots and histograms, usually precedes the formal data analysis. The process of analyzing the data requires the investigation of any underlying assumptions (e.g., distributional) before the application of the statistical models and tests.

D. Experiment Interpretation

The fourth phase of the experimental process is the study interpretation phase. The interpretation of the experiment consists of 1) interpretation context, 2) extrapolation, and 3) impact. The results of the data analysis from a study are interpreted in a broadening series of contexts. These contexts of interpretation are the statistical framework in which the result is derived, the purpose of the particular study, and the knowledge in the field of research [16]. The representativeness of the sampling analyzed in a study qualifies the extrapolation of the results to other environments [17]. Several follow-up activities contribute to the impact of a study: presenting/publishing the results for feedback, replicating the experiment [33], [41], and actually applying the results by modifying methods for software development, maintenance, management, and research.

IV. Classification of Analyses

Several investigators have published studies in the four general scopes of examination: blocked subject-project, replicated project, multiproject variation, or single project. The following sections cite studies from each of these categories. Note that surveys on experimentation methodology in empirical studies include [35], [96], [74], [98]. Each of the sections first discusses one experiment in moderate depth, using italicized keywords from the framework for experimentation, and then chronologically presents an overview of several others in the category. In any survey of this type it is almost certain that some deserving work has been accidentally omitted. For this, we apologize in advance.

A. Blocked Subject-Project Studies

With a motivation to improve and better understand unit testing, Basili and Selby [18] conducted a study whose *purpose* was to characterize and evaluate the processes (i.e., *objects*) of code reading, functional testing, and structural testing from the *perspective* of the developer. The testing processes were examined in a blocked subject-project *scope*, where 74 student through professional programmers (from the programmer *domain*) tested four unit-size programs (from the program *domain*) in a replicated fractional factorial *design*. Objective *measurement* of the testing processes was in several *criteria* areas: fault detection effectiveness, fault detection cost, and classes of faults detected. Experiment *preparation* included a pilot study [63], *execution* incorporated both manual and automated monitoring of testing activity, and *analysis* used analysis of variance methods [33], [90]. The major results (in the *interpretation context* of the study purpose) included: 1) with the professionals, code reading detected more software faults and had a higher fault detection rate than did the other methods; 2) with the professionals, functional testing detected more faults than did structural testing, but they were not different in fault detection rate; 3) with the students, the three techniques were not different in performance, except that structural testing detected fewer faults than did the others in one study phase; and 4) overall, code reading detected more interface faults and functional testing detected more control faults than did the other methods. A major result (in the *interpretation context* of the field of research) was that the study suggested that nonexecution based fault detection, as in code reading, is at least as effective as on-line methods. The particular programmers and programs sampled qualify the *extrapolation* of the results. The *impact* of the study was an advancement in the understanding of effective software testing methods.

In order to understand program debugging, Gould and Drongowski [58] evaluated several related factors, including effect of debugging aids, effect of fault type, and effect of particular program debugged from the perspective of the developer and maintainer. Thirty experienced programmers independently debugged one of four one-page programs that contained a single fault from one of three classes. The major results of these studies were: 1) debugging is much faster if the programmer has had previous experience with the program, 2) assignment bugs were harder to find than other kinds, and 3) debugging aids did not seem to help programmers debug faster. Consistent results were obtained when the study was conducted on ten additional experienced programmers [57]. These results and the identification of possible "principles" of debugging contributed to the understanding of debugging methodology.

In order to improve experimentation methodology and its application, Weissman [113] evaluated programmers' ability to understand and modify a program from the perspective of the developer and modifier. Various measures of programmer understanding were calculated, in a series of factorial design experiments, on groups of 16-48 university students performing tasks on two small programs. The study emphasized the need for well-structured and well-documented programs and provided valuable testimony on and worked toward a suitable experimentation methodology.

In order to assess the impact of language features on the programming process, Gannon and Horning [54] characterized the relationship of language features to software reliability from the perspective of the developer. Based on an analysis of the deficiencies in a programming language, nine different features were modified to produce a new version. Fifty-one advanced students were divided into two groups and asked to complete implementations of two small but sophisticated programs (75-200 line) in the original language and its modified version. The redesigned features in the two languages were contrasted in program fault frequency, type, and persistence. The experiment identified several language-design decisions that significantly affected reliability, which contributed to the understanding of language design for reliable software.

In order to understand the unit testing process better, Hetzel [60] evaluated a reading technique and functional and "selective" testing (a composite approach) from the perspective of the developer. Thirty-nine university students applied the techniques to three unit-size programs in a Latin square design. Functional and "selective" testing were equally effective and both superior to the reading technique, which contributed to our understanding of testing methodology.

In order to improve and better understand the maintenance process, Curtis et al. [44] conducted two experiments to evaluate factors that influence two aspects of software maintenance, program understanding, and modification, from the perspective of the developer and maintainer. Thirty-six junior through advanced professional programmers in each experiment examined three classes of small (36-57 source line) programs in a factorial design. The factors examined include control flow complexity, variable name mnemonicity, type of modification, degree of commenting, and the relationship of programmer performance to various complexity metrics. In [45] they continued the investigation of how software characteristics relate to psychological complexity and presented a third experiment to evaluate the ability of 54 professional programmers to detect program bugs in three programs in a factorial design. The series of experiments suggested that software science [59] and cyclomatic complexity [71] measures were related to the difficulty experienced by programmers in locating errors in code.

In order to improve and better understand program debugging, Weiser [110] evaluated the theory that "programmers use 'sliding' (stripping away a program's statements that do not influence a given variable at a given statement) when debugging" from the perspective of the developer, maintainer, and researcher. Twenty-one university graduate students and programming staff debugged a fault in three unit-size (75-150 source line) programs in a nonparametric design. The study results supported the slicing theory, that is, programmers during debugging routinely partitioned programs into a coherent, discontiguous piece (or slice). The results advanced the understanding of software debugging methodology.

In order to improve design techniques, Ramsey, Atwood, and Van Doren [87] evaluated flowcharts and program design languages (PDL) from the perspective of the developer. Twenty-two graduate students designed two small (approximately 1000 source line) projects, one using flowcharts and the other using PDL. Overall, the results suggested that design performance and designer-programmer communication were better for projects using PDL.

In order to validate a theory of programming knowledge, Soloway and Ehrlich [102] conducted two studies, using 139 novices and 41 professional programmers, to evaluate programmer behavior from the perspective of the researcher. The theory was that programming knowledge contained programming plans (generic program fragments representing common sequences of actions) and rules of programming discourse (conventions used in composing plans into programs). The results supported the existence and use of such plans and rules by both novice and advanced programmers.

Other blocked subject-project studies include [82], [115], and [111].

B. Replicated Project Studies

With a *motivation* to assess and better understand team software development methodologies, Basili and Reiter [16] conducted a study whose *purpose* was to characterize and evaluate the development processes (i.e., *objects*) of a 1) disciplined-methodology team approach, 2) ad hoc team approach, and 3) ad hoc individual approach from the *perspective* of the developer and project manager. The development processes were examined in a replicated project *scope*, in which advanced university students comprising seven three-person teams, six three-person teams, and six individuals (from the programmer domain) used the approaches, respectively. They separately developed a small (600-2200 line) compiler (from the program *domain*) in a nonparametric *design*. Objective *measurement* of the development approaches was in several *criteria* areas: number of changes, number of program runs, program data usage, program data coupling/binding, static program size/complexity metrics, language usage, and modularity. Experiment *preparation* included presentation of relevant material [68], [8], [34], *execution* included automated monitoring of on-line development activity and *analysis* used nonparametric comparison methods. The major results (in the *interpretation context* of the study purpose) included: 1) the methodological discipline was a key influence on the general efficiency of the software development process; 2) the disciplined team methodology significantly reduced the costs of software development as reflected in program runs and changes; and 3) the examination of the effect of the development approaches was accomplished by the use of quantitative, objective, unobtrusive, and automatable process and product metrics. A major result (in the *interpretation context* of the field of research) was that the study supported the belief that incorporating discipline in software development reflects positively on both the development process and final product. The particular programmers and program sampled qualify the *extrapolation* of the results. The *impact* of the study was an advancement in the understanding of software development methodologies and their evaluation.

In order to improve the design and implementation processes, Parnas [84] evaluated system modularity from the perspective of the developer. Twenty university undergraduates each developed one of four different types of implementations for one of five different small modules. Then each of the modules were combined with others to form several versions of the whole system. The results were that minor effort was required in assembling the systems and that major system changes were confined to small, well-defined subsystems. The results supported the ideas on formal specifications and modularity discussed in [83] and [85], and advanced the understanding of design methodology.

In order to assess the impact of static typing of programming languages in the development process, Gannon [53] evaluated the use of a statically typed language (having integers and strings) and a "typeless" language (e.g., arbitrary subscripting of memory) from the perspective of the developer. Thirty-eight students programmed a small (48-297 source line) problem in both languages, with half doing it in each order. The two languages were compared in the resulting program faults, the number of runs containing faults, and the relation of subject experience to fault proneness. The major result was that the use of a statically typed language can increase programming reliability, which improved our understanding of the design and use of programming languages.

In order to improve program composition, comprehension, debugging, and modification, Shneiderman [99] evaluated the use of detailed flowcharts in these tasks from the perspective of the developer, maintainer, modifier, and researcher. Groups of 53-70 novice through intermediate subjects, in a series of five experiments, performed various tasks using small programs. No significant differences were found between groups that used and those that did not use flowcharts, questioning the merit of using detailed flowcharts.

In order to improve and better understand the unit testing process, Myers [79] evaluated the techniques of three-person walk-throughs, functional testing, and a control group from the perspective of the developer. Fifty-nine junior through advanced professional programmers applied the techniques to test a small (100 source line) but nontrivial program. The techniques were not different in the number of faults they detected, all pairings of techniques were superior to single techniques, and code reviews were less cost-effective than the others. These results improved our understanding of the selection of appropriate software testing techniques.

In order to validate a particular metric family, Basili and Hutchens [11] evaluated the ability of a proposed metric family to explain differences in system development methodologies and system changes from the perspective of the developer, project manager, and researcher. The metrics were applied to 19 versions of a small (600-2200) compiler, which were developed by teams of advanced university students using three different development approaches (see the first study [16] described in this section). The major results included: 1) the metrics were able to differentiate among projects developed with different development methodologies; and 2) the differences among individuals had a large effect on the relationships between the metrics and aspects of system development. These results provided insights into the formulation and appropriate use of software metrics.

In order to improve the understanding of why software errors occur, Soloway et al. [65], [101] characterized programmer misconceptions, cognitive strategies, and their manifestations as bugs in programs from the perspective of the developer and researcher. Two hundred and four novice programmers separately attempted implementations of an elementary program. The results supported the programmers' intended use of "programming plans" [103] and revealed that most people preferred a read-process strategy over a process-read strategy. The results advanced the understanding of how individuals write programs, why they sometimes make errors, and what programming language constructs should be available.

In order to understand the effect of coding conventions on program comprehensibility, Miara et al. [73] conducted a study to evaluate the relationship between indentation levels and program comprehension from the perspective of the developer. Eighty-six novice through professional subjects answered questions about one of seven program variations with different level and type of indentation. The major result was that an indentation level of two or four spaces was preferred over zero or six spaces.

In order to improve software development approaches, Boehm, Gray, and Seewaldt [29] characterized and evaluated the prototyping and specifying development approaches from the perspective of the developer, project manager, and user. Seven two- and three-person teams, consisting of university graduate students, developed versions of the same application software system (2000-4000 line); four teams used a requirement/design specifying approach and three teams used a prototyping approach. The systems developed by prototyping were smaller, required less development effort, and were easier to use. The systems developed by specifying had more coherent designs, more complete functionality, and software that was easier to integrate. These results contributed to the understanding of the merits and appropriateness of software development approaches.

In order to validate the theoretical model for *N*-version programming [3], [66], Knight and Leveson [67] conducted a study to evaluate the effectiveness of *N*-version programming for reliability from the perspective of the customer and user. *N*-version programming uses a high-level driver to connect several separately designed versions of the same system, the systems "vote" on the correct solution, and the solution provided by the majority of the systems is output. Twenty-seven graduate students were asked to independently design an 800 source line system. The factors examined included individual system reliability, total *N*-version system reliability, and classes of faults that occurred in systems simultaneously. The major result was that the assumption of independence of the faults in the programs was not justified, and therefore, the reliability of the combined "voting" system was not as high as given by the model.

In order to improve and better understand software development approaches, Selby, Basili, and Baker [94] characterized and evaluated the Cleanroom development approach [46], [47], in which software is developed without execution (i.e., completely off-line), from the perspective of the developer, project manager, and customer. Fifteen three-person teams of advanced university students separately developed a small system (800-2300 source line); ten teams used Cleanroom and five teams used a traditional development approach in a nonparametric design. The major results included: 1) most developers using the Cleanroom approach were able to build systems without program execution; and 2) the Cleanroom teams' products met system requirements more completely and succeeded on more operational test cases than did those developed with a traditional approach. The results suggested the feasibility of complete off-line development, as in Cleanroom, and advanced the understanding of software development methodology.

Other replicated project studies include [37], [4], and [63].

C. Multiproject Variation Studies

With a *motivation* to improve the understanding of resource usage during software development, Bailey and Basili [5] conducted a study whose *purpose* was to predict development cost by using a particular model (i.e., *object*) and to evaluate it from the *perspective* of the project manager, corporate manager, and researcher. The particular model generation method was examined in a multi-project *scope*, with baseline data from 18 large (2500-100 000 source line) software projects in the NASA S.E.L. [27], [26], [38], [91] production environment (from the program *domain*), in which teams contained from two to ten programmers (from the programmer *domain*). The study *design* incorporated multivariate methods to parameterize the model. Objective and subjective *measurement* of the projects was based on 21 criteria[2] in three areas: methodology, complexity, and personnel experience. Study *preparation* included preliminary work [52], *execution* included an established set of data collection forms [27], and *analysis* used forward multivariate regression methods. The major results (in the *interpretation context* of the study purpose) included 1) the estimation of software development resource usage improved by considering a set of both baseline and customization factors; 2) the application in the NASA environment of the proposed model generation method, which considers both types of factors, produced a resource usage estimate for a future project within one standard deviation of the actual; and 3) the confirmation of the NASA S.E.L. formula that the cost per line of reusing code is 20 percent of that of developing new code. A major result (in the *interpretation context* of the field of research) was that the study highlighted the difference of each software development environment, which improved the selection and use of resource estimation models. The particular programming environment and projects sampled qualify the *extrapolation* of the results. The *impact* of the study was an advancement in the understanding of estimating software development resource expenditure.

In order to assess, manage, and improve multiproject environments, several researchers [28], [20], [108], [10], [36], [21], [62], [112], [97], [107] have characterized, evaluated, and/or predicted the effect of several factors from the perspective of the developer, modifier, project manager, and corporate manager. All the studies examined moderate to large projects from production environments. The relationships investigated were among various factors, including structured programming, personnel background, development process and product constraints, project complexity, human and computer resource consumption, error-prone software identification, error/change distributions, data coupling/binding, project duration, staff size, degree of management control, and productivity. These studies have provided increased project visibility, greater understanding of classes of factors sensitive to project performance, awareness of the need for project measure-

---

2 Twenty-one factors were selected after examining a total of 82 factors that possibly contributed to project resource expenditure, including 36 from [108] and 16 from [28].

ment, and efforts for standardization of definitions. Analysis has begun on incorporating project variation information into a management tool [9], [14].

In order to improve and better understand the software maintenance process, Vessey and Weber [106] conducted an experiment to evaluate the relationship between the rate of maintenance repair and various product and process metrics from the perspective of the developer, user, and the project manager. A total of 447 small (up to 600 statements) commercial and clerical Cobol programs from one Australian organization and two U.S. organizations were analyzed. The product and process metrics included program complexity, programming style, programmer quality, and number of system releases. The major results were: 1) in the Australian organization, program complexity and programming style significantly affected the maintenance repair rate; and 2) in the U.S. organizations, the number of times a system was released significantly affected the maintenance repair rate.

In order to improve the software maintenance process, Adams [1] evaluated operational faults from the perspective of the user, customer, project manager, and corporate manager. The fault history for nine large production products (e.g., operating system releases or their major components) were empirically modeled. He developed an approach for estimating whether and under what circumstances preventively fixing faults in operational software in the field was appropriate. Preventively fixing faults consisted of installing fixes to faults that had yet to be discovered by particular users, but had been discovered by the vendor or other users. The major result was that for the typical user, corrective service was a reasonable way of dealing with most faults after the code had been in use for a fairly long period of time, while preventively fixing high-rate faults was advantageous during the time immediately following initial release.

In order to assess the effectiveness of the testing process, Bowen [31] evaluated estimations of the number of residual faults in a system from the perspective of the customer, developer, and project manager. The study was based on fault data collected from three large (2000-6000 module) systems developed in the Hughes-Fullerton environment. The study partitioned the faults based on severity and analyzed the differences in estimates of remaining faults according to stage of testing. Insights were gained into relationships between fault detection rates and residual faults.

D. Single Project Studies

With a *motivation* to improve software development methodology, Basili and Turner [22] conducted a study whose *purpose* was to characterize the process (i.e., *object*) of iterative enhancement in conjunction with a top-down, stepwise refinement development approach from the *perspective* of the developer. The development process was examined in a single project *scope*, where the authors, two experienced individuals (from the programmer *domain*), built a 17 000 line compiler (from the program *domain*). The study *design* incorporated descriptive methods to capture system evolution. Objective *measurement* of the system was in several *criteria* areas: size, modularity, local/global data usage, and data binding/coupling

[62], [104]. Study *preparation* included language design [23], *execution* incorporated static analysis of system snapshots, and *analysis* used descriptive statistics. The results (in the *interpretation context* of the statistical framework) included: 1) the percentage of global variables decreased over time while the percentage of actual versus possible data couplings across modules increased, suggesting the usage of global data became more appropriate over time; and 2) the number of procedures and functions rose over time while the number of statements per procedure or function decreased, suggesting increased modularity. The major result of the study (in the *interpretation context* of the study purpose) was that the iterative enhancement technique encouraged the development of a software product that had several generally desirable aspects of system structure. A major result (in the *interpretation context* of the field of research) was that the study demonstrated the feasibility of iterative enhancement. The particular programming team and project examined qualify the *extrapolation* of the results. The *impact* of the study was an advancement in the understanding of software development approaches.

In order to improve, better understand, and manage the software development process, Baker [6] evaluated the effect of applying chief programming teams and structured programming in system development from the perspective of the user, developer, project manager, and corporate manager. The large (83 000 line) system, known as "The New York Times Project," was developed by a team of professionals organized as a chief programmer team, using structured code, top-down design, walk-throughs, and program libraries. Several benefits were identified, including reduced development time and cost, reduced time in system integration, and reduced fault detection in acceptance testing and field use. The results of the study demonstrated the feasibility of the chief programmer team concept and the accompanying methodologies in a production environment.

In order to improve their development environments, several researchers [49], [24], [2], [81], [13] have each conducted single project studies to characterize the errors and changes made during a development project. They examined the development of a moderate to large software project, done by a multiperson team, in a production environment. They analyzed the frequency and distribution of errors during development and their relationship with several factors, including module size, software complexity, developer experience, method of detection and isolation, effort for isolation and correction, phase of entrance into the system and observance, reuse of existing design and code, and role of the requirements document. Such analyses have produced fault categorization schemes and have been useful in understanding and improving a development environment.

In order to better understand and improve the use of the Ada®[3] language, Basili et al. [55], [12] examined a ground-support system written in Ada to characterize the use of Ada packages from the perspective of the developer. Four professional programmers developed a project of 10 000 source lines of code. Factors such as how package use affected the ease of system modification and how to measure

[3] Ada is a registered trademark of the U.S. Department of Defense (Ada Joint Program Office).

module change resistance were identified, as well as how these observations related to aspects of development and training. The major results were 1) several measures of Ada programs were developed, and 2) there was an indication that a lot of training will be necessary if we are to expect the facilities of Ada to be properly used.

In order to assess and improve software testing methodology, Basili and Ramsey [15], [88] characterized and evaluated the relationship between system acceptance tests and operational usage from the perspective of the developer, project manager, customer, and researcher. The execution coverage of functionally generated acceptance test cases and a sample of operational usage cases was monitored for a medium-size (10 000 line) software system developed in a production environment. The results calculated that 64 percent of the program statements were executed during system operation and that the acceptance test cases corresponded reasonably well to the operational usage. The results gave insights into the relationships among structural coverage, fault detection, system testing, and system usage.

V. Problem Areas in Experimentation

The following sections identify several problem areas of experimentation in software engineering. These areas may serve as guidelines in the performance of future studies. After mentioning some overall observations, considerations in each of the areas of experiment definition, planning, operation, and interpretation are discussed.

A. Experimentation Overall

There appears to be no "universal model" or "silver bullet" in software engineering. There are an enormous number of factors that differ across environments, in terms of desired cost/quality goals, methodology, experience, problem domain, constraints, etc. [108], [20], [5], [10], [28], This results in every software development/maintenance environment being different. Another area of wide variation is the many-to-one (e.g., 10:1) differential in human performance [11], [43], [18]. The particular individuals examined in an empirical study can make an enormous difference. Among other considerations, these variations suggest that metrics need to be validated for a particular environment and a particular person to show that they capture what is intended [11], [21]. Thus, experimental studies should consider the potentially vast differences among environments and among people.

B. Experiment Definition

In the definition of the purpose for the experiment, the formulation of intuitive problems into precisely stated goals is a nontrivial task [17], [25]. Defining the purpose of a study often requires the articulation of what is meant by "software quality." The many interpretations and perceptions of quality [32], [39], [72] highlight the need for considering whose perspective of quality is being examined. Thus, a precise specification of the problem to be investigated is a major step toward its solution.

C. Experiment Planning

Experimental planning should have a horizon beyond a first experiment. Controlled studies may be used to focus on the effect of certain factors, while their results may be confirmed in replications [92], [99], [102], [113], [58], [57], [45], [44], [18] and/or larger case studies [5], [16]. When designing studies, consider that a combination of factors may be effective as a "critical mass," even though the particular factors may be ineffective when treated in isolation [16], [107]. Note that formal designs and the resulting statistical robustness are desirable, but we should not be driven exclusively by the achievement of statistical significance. Common sense must be maintained, which allows us, for example, to experiment just to help develop and refine hypotheses [13], [112]. Thus, the experimental planning process should include a series of experiments for exploration, verification, and application.

D. Experiment Operation

The collection of the required data constitutes the primary result of the study operation phase. The data must be carefully defined, validated, and communicated to ensure their consistent interpretation by all persons associated with the experiment: subjects under observation, experimenters, and literature audience [21]. There have been papers in the literature that do not define their data well enough to enable a comparison of results across many projects and environments. We have often contacted experimenters and discovered that different entities were being measured in different studies. Thus, the experimenter should be cautious about the definition, validation, and communication of data, since they play a fundamental role in the experimental process.

E. Experiment Interpretation

The appropriate presentation of results from experiments contributes to their correct interpretation. Experimental results need to be qualified by the particular samples (e.g., programmers, programs) analyzed [17]. The extrapolation of results from a particular sample must consider the representativeness of the sample to other environments [40], [114], [108], [86], [5], [28]. The visibility of the experimental results in professional forums and the open literature provides valuable feedback and constructive criticism. Thus, the presentation of experimental results should include appropriate qualification and adequate exposure to support their proper interpretation.

VI. Conclusion

Experimentation in software engineering supports the advancement of the field through an iterative learning process. The experimental process has begun to be applied in a multiplicity of environments to study a variety of software technology areas. From the studies presented, it is clear that experimentation has proven effective in providing insights and furthering our domain of knowledge about the software process and product. In fact, there is a learning process in the experimentation approach itself, as has been shown in this paper.

We have described a framework for experimentation to provide a structure for presenting previous studies. We also recommend the framework as a mechanism to facilitate the definition, planning, operation, and interpretation of past and future studies. The problem areas discussed are meant to provide some useful recommendations for the application of the experimental process in software engineering. The experimental framework cannot be used in a vacuum; the framework and the lessons learned complement one another and should be used in a synergistic fashion.

References

[1] E. N. Adams, "Optimizing preventive service of software products," *IBMJ. Res. Develop.,* vol. 28, no. 1, pp. 2-14, Jan. 1984.

[2] J.-L. Albin and R. Ferreol, "Collecte et analyse de mesures de logiciel (Collection and analysis of software data)," *Technique et Science Informatiques,* vol. 1, no. 4, pp. 297-313, 1982 (Rairo ISSN 0752-4072).

[3] A. Avizienis, P. Gunningberg, J. P. J. Kelly, L. Strigini, P. J. Traverse, K. S. Tso, and U. Voges, "The UCLA Dedix system: A distributed testbed for multiple-version software," in *Dig. 15th Int. Symp. Fault-Tolerant Comput.,* Ann Arbor, MI, June 19-21, 1985.

[4] J. W. Bailey, "Teaching Ada: A comparison of two approaches," in *Proc. Washington Ada Symp.,* Washington, DC, 1984.

[5] J. W. Bailey and V. R. Basili, "A meta-model for software development resource expenditures," in *Proc. 5th Int. Conf. Software Eng.,* San Diego, CA, 1981, pp. 107-116.

[6] F. T. Baker, "System quality through structured programming," *in AfIPS Proc. 1972 Fall Joint Comput. Conf.,* vol. 41, 1972, pp. 339-343.

[7] V. R. Basili, *Tutorial on Models and Metrics for Software Management and Engineering.* New York: IEEE Computer Society, 1980.

[8] V. R. Basili and F. T. Baker, "Tutorial of structured programming," in *Proc. 11th IEEE COMPCON,* IEEE Cat. No. 75CH1049-6, 1975.

[9] V. R. Basili and C. Doerflinger, "Monitoring software development through dynamic variables," in *Proc. COMPSAC,* Chicago, IL, 1983.

[10] V. R. Basili and K. Freburger, "Programming measurement and estimation in the software engineering laboratory," *J. Syst. Software, vol.* 2, pp. 47-57, 1981.

[11] V. R. Basili and D. H. Hutchens, "An empirical study of a syntactic metric family," *IEEE Trans. Software Eng.,* vol. SE-9, pp. 664-672, Nov. 1983.

[12] V. R. Basili, E. E. Katz, N. M. Panilio-Yap, C. L. Ramsey, and S. Chang, "A quantitative characterization and evaluation of a software development in Ada," *Computer,* Sept. 1985.

[13] V. R. Basili and B. T. Perricone, "Software errors and complexity: An empirical investigation," *Commun. ACM,* vol. 27, no. 1, pp. 42-52,Jan. 1984.

[14] V. R. Basili and C. L. Ramsey, "Arrowsmith-P—A prototype expert system for software engineering management," in *Proc. Symp. Expert Systems in Government,* Mclean, VA, Oct. 1985.

[15] V. R. Basili and J. R. Ramsey, "Analyzing the test process using structural coverage," in *Proc. 8th Int. Conf. Software Eng.,* London, Aug. 28-30, 1985, pp. 306-312.

[16] V. R. Basili and R. W. Reiter, "A controlled experiment quantitatively comparing software development approaches," *IEEE Trans. Software Eng.,* vol. SE-7, May 1981.

[17] V. R. Basili and R. W. Selby, "Data collection and analysis in software research and management," *Proc. Amer. Statistical Association and Biometric Society Joint Statistical Meetings,* Philadelphia, PA, August 13-16, 1984.

[18] ——,"Comparing the effectiveness of software testing strategies," Dep. Comput. Sci. Univ. Maryland, College Park/Tech. Rep. TR-1501, May 1985.

[19] ——,"Four applications of a software data collection and analysis methodology," in *Proc. NATO Advanced Study Institute: The Challenge of Advanced Computing Technology to System Design Methods,* Durham, U.K., July 29-Aug. 10, 1985.

[20] ——,"Calculation and use of an environment's characteristic software metric set," in *Proc. 8th Int. Conf. Software Eng.,* London, Aug. 28-30, 1985, pp. 386-393.

[21] V. R. Basili, R. W. Selby, and T. Y. Phillips, "Metric analysis and data validation across FORTRAN projects," *IEEE Trans. Software Eng.,* vol. SE-9, pp. 652-663, Nov. 1983.

[22] V. R. Basili and A. J. Turner, "Iterative enhancement: A practical technique for software development," *IEEE Trans. Software Eng.,* vol. SE-1, Dec. 1975.

[23] ——,*SIMPL-T: A Structured Programming Language.* Geneva, IL: Paladin House, 1976.

[24] V. R. Basili and D. M. Weiss, "Evaluation of a software requirements document by analysis of change data," in *Proc. 5th Int. Conf. Software Eng.,* San Diego, CA, Mar. 9-12, 1981, pp. 314-323.

[25] ——,"A methodology for collecting valid software engineering data*," *IEEE Trans. Software Eng.,* vol. SE-10, pp. 728-738, Nov.1984.(

[26] V. R. Basili and M. V. Zelkowitz, "Analyzing medium-scale software developments," in *Proc. 3rd Int. Conf. Software Eng.,* Atlanta, GA, May 1078, pp. 116-123.

[27] V. R. Basili, M. y. Zelkowitz, F. E. McGarry, R. W. Reiter, Jr., W. F. Truszkowski, and D. L. Weiss,."The software engineering laboratory," Software Eng. Lab., NASA/Goddard Space Flight Center, Greenbelt, MD, Rep. SEL-77-001, May 1977.

[28] B. W. Boehm, *Software Engineering Economics.* Englewood Cliffs, NJ: Prentice-Hall, 1981.

[29] B. W. Boehm, T. E. Gray, and T. Seewaldt, "Prototyping versus specifying: A multiproject experiment," *IEEE Trans. Software Eng.,* vol. SE-10, pp. 290-303, May 1984.

[30] R. C. Bogdan and S. K. Biklen, *Qualitative Research for Education: An Introduction to Theory and Methods.* Boston, MA: Allyn and Bacon, 1982.

[31] J. Bowen, "Estimation of residual faults and testing effectiveness," in *Proc. 7th Minnowbrook Workshop Software Performance Evaluation,* Blue Mountain Lake, NY, July 24-27, 1984.

[32] T. P. Bowen, G. B. Wigle, and J. T. Tsai, "Specification of software quality attributes," Rome Air Development Center, Griffiss Air Force Base, NY, Tech. Rep. RADC-TR-85-37 (3 vols.), Feb. 1985.

[33] G. E. P. Box, W. G. Hunter, and J. S. Hunter, *Statistics for Experimenters.* New York: Wiley, 1978.

[34] F. P. Brooks, Jr., *The Mythical Man-Month.* Reading, MA: Addison-Wesley, 1975.

[35] R. E. Brooks, "Studying programmer behavior: The problem of proper methodology, *Common. ACM,* vol. 23, no. 4, pp. 207-213, 1980.

[36] W. D. Brooks, "Software technology payoff: Some statistical evidence," *J. Syst. Software,* vol. 2, pp. 3-9, 1981.

[37] F. O. Buck, "Indicators of quality inspections," IBM Systems Products Division, Kingston, NY, Tech. Rep. 21.802, Sept. 1981.

[38] D. N. Card, F. E. McGarry, J. Page, S. Eslinger, and V. R. Basili, "The software engineering laboratory," Software Eng. Lab., NASA/Goddard Space Flight Center, Greenbelt, MD, Rep. SEL-81-104, Feb. 1982.

[39] J. P. Cavano and J. A. McCall, "A Framework for the measurement of software quality," in *Proc. Software Quality and Assurance Workshop,* San Diego, CA, Nov. 1978, pp. 133-139.

[40] W. G. Cochran, *Sampling Techniques.* New York: Wiley, 1953.

[41] W. G. Cochran and G. M. Cox, *Experimental Designs.* New York: Wiley, 1950.

[42] P. A. Currit, M. Dyer, and H. D. Mills, "Certifying the reliability of software," *IEEE Trans. Software Eng.,* vol. SE-12, pp. 3-11, Jan. 1986.

[43] B. Curtis, "Cognitive science of programming," *6th Minnowbrook Workshop Software Performance Evaluation,* Blue Mountain Lake, NY, July 19-22, 1983.

[44] B. Curtis, S. B. Sheppard, P. Milliman, M. A. Borst, and T. Love, "Measuring the psychological complexity of software maintenance tasks with the Halstead and McCabe metrics," *IEEE Trans. Software Eng.,* pp. 96-104, Mar. 1979.

[45] B. Curtis, S. B. Sheppard, and P. M. Milliman, "Third time charm: Stronger replication of the ability of software complexity metrics to predict programmer performance," *in Proc. 4th Int. Conf. Software Eng.,* Sept. 1979, pp. 356-360.

[46] M. Dyer, "Cleanroom software development method," IBM Federal Systems Division, Bethesda, MD, Oct. 14, 1982.

[47] M. Dyer and H. D. Mills, "Developing electronic systems with certifiable reliability," in *Proc. NATO Conf.,* Summer 1982.

[48] T. Emerson, "A discriminant metric for module cohesion," in *Proc. 7th Int. Conf. Software Eng.,* Orlando, FL, 1984, pp. 294-303.

[49] A. Endres, "An analysis of errors and their causes in systems programs," *IEEE Trans. Software Eng.,* pp. 140-149, vol. SE-1, June 1975.

[50] A. R. Feuer and E. B. Fowlkes, "Some results from an empirical study of computer software," in *Proc. 4th Int. Conf. Software Eng.,* 1979, pp. 351-355.

[51] R. W. Floyd, "Assigning meaning to programs," *Amer. Math. Soc.,* vol. 19, J. T. Schwartz, Ed., Providence, Rl, 1967.

[52] K. Freburger and V. R. Basili, "The software engineering laboratory: Relationship equations," Dep. Comput. Sci., Univ. Maryland, College Park, Tech. Rep. TR-764, May 1979.

[53] J. D. Gannon, "An experimental evaluation of data type conventions," *Commun. ACM,* vol. 20, no. 8, pp. 584-595, 1977.
[54] J. D. Gannon and J. J. Homing, "The impact of language design on the production of reliable software," *IEEE Trans. Software Eng.,* vol. SE-1, pp. 179-191, 1975.
[55] J. D. Gannon, E. E. Katz, and V. R. Basili, "Characterizing Ada programs: Packages," in *The Measurement of Computer Software Performance,* Los Alamos Nat. Lab., Aug. 1983.
[56] A. L. Goel, "Software reliability and estimation techniques," Rome Air Development Center, Griffiss Air Force Base, NY, Rep. RADC-TR-82-263, Oct. 1982.
[57] J. D. Gould, "Some psychological evidence on how people debug computer programs," *Int. J. Man-Machine Studies,* vol. 7, pp. 151-182, 1975.
[58] J. D. Gould and P. Drongowski, "An exploratory study of computer program debugging," *Human Factors,* vol. 16, no. 3, pp. 258-277, 1974.
[59] M. H. Halstead, *Elements of Software Science.* New York: North-Holland, 1977.
[60] W. C. Hetzel, "An experimental analysis of program verification methods," Ph.D. dissertation, Univ. North Carolina, Chapel Hill, 1976.
[61] C. A. R. Hoare, "An axiomatic basis for computer programming," *Commun. ACM,* vol. 12, no. 10, pp. 576-583, Oct. 1969.
[62] D. H. Hutchens and V. R. Basili, "System structure analysis: Clustering with data bindings," *IEEE Trans. Software Eng.,* vol. SE-11, Aug. 1985.
[63] S.-S. V. Hwang, "An empirical study in functional testing, structural testing, and code reading/inspection*," Dep. Comput. Sci., Univ. Maryland, College Park, Scholarly Paper 362, Dec. 1981.
[64] Z. Jelinski and P. B. Moranda, "Applications of a probability-based model to a code reading experiment," in *Proc. IEEE Symp. Comput. Software Rel.,* New York, 1973, pp. 78-81.
[65] W. L. Johnson, S. Draper, and E. Soloway, "An effective bug classification scheme must take the programmer into account," in *Proc. Workshop High-level Debugging,* Palo Alto, CA, 1983.
[66] J. P. J. Kelly, "Specification of fault-tolerant multi-version software: Experimental studies of a design diversity approach," Ph.D. dissertation, Univ. California, Los Angeles, 1982.
[67] J. C. Knight and N. G. Leveson, "An experimental evaluation of the assumption of independence in multiversion programming," *IEEE Trans. Software Eng.,* vol. SE-12, pp. 96-109, Jan. 1986.
[68] R. C. Linger, H. D. Mills, and B. I. Witt, *Structured Programming: Theory and Practice.* Reading, MA: Addison-Wesley, 1979.
[69] B. Littlewood, "Stochastic reliability growth: A model for fault renovation computer programs and hardware designs," *IEEE Trans. Rel.,* vol. R-30, Oct. 1981.
[70] B. Littlewood and J. L. Verrall, "A Bayesian reliability growth model for computer software," *Appl. Statist.,* vol. 22, no. 3, 1973.
[71] T. J. McCabe, "A complexity measure," *IEEE Trans. Software Eng.,* vol. SE-2, pp. 308-320, Dec. 1976.
[72] J. A. McCall, P. Richards, and G. Walters, "Factors in software quality," Rome Air Development Center, Griffiss Air Force Base, NY, Tech. Rep. RADC-TR-77-369, Nov. 1977.
[73] R. J. Miara, J. A. Musselman, J. A. Navarro, and B. Shneiderman, "Program indentation and comprehensibility," *Commun. ACM,* vol. 26, no. 11, pp. 861-867, Nov. 1983.
[74] T. Moher and G. M. Schneider, "Methodology and experimental research in software engineering," *Int. J. Man-Machine Studies,* vol. 16, no. 1, pp. 65-87, 1982.
[75] S. A. Mulaik, *The Foundations of Factor Analysis.* New York: McGraw-Hill, 1972.

[76] J. D. Musa, "A theory of software reliability and its application," *IEEE Trans. Software Eng.,* vol. SE-1, pp. 312-327, 1975.
[77] ——, "Software reliability measurement," *J. Syst. Software,* vol. l. no. 3, pp. 223-241, 1980.
[78] G. L. Myers, *Composite/Structured Design.* New York: Van Nostrand Reinhold, 1978.
[79] ——, "A controlled experiment in program testing and code walkthroughs/inspections," *Commun. ACM,* pp. 760-768, Sept. 1978.
[80] J. Neter and W. Wasserman, *Applied Linear Statistical Models.* Homewood, IL: Richard D. Irwin, 1974.
[81] T. J. Ostrand and E. J. Weyuker, "Collecting and categorizing software error data in an industrial environment*," *J. Syst. Software,* vol. 4, pp. 289-300, 1983.
[82] D. J. Panzl, "Experience with automatic program testing," in *Proc. NBS Trends and Applications,* Nat. Bureau Standards, Gaithersburg, MD, May 28, 1981, pp. 25-28.
[83] D. L. Pamas, "On the criteria to be used in decomposing systems into modules," *Commun. ACM,* vol. 15, no. 12, pp. 1053-1058, 1972.
[84] ——,"Some conclusions from an experiment in software engineering techniques," in *AFIPS Proc. 1972 Fall Joint Comput. Conf.,* vol. 41, 1972, pp. 325-329.
[85] ——,"A technique for module specification with examples," *Commun. ACM,* vol. 15, May 1972.
[86] L. Putnam, "A general empirical solution to the macro software sizing and estimating problem," *IEEE Trans. Software Eng.,* vol. SE-4, July 1978.
[87] H. R. Ramsey, M. E. Atwood, and J. R. Van Doren, "Flowcharts versus program design languages: An experimental comparison," *Commun. ACM,* vol. 26, no.6, pp. 445-449, June 1983.
[88] J. Ramsey, "Structural coverage of functional testing," in *Proc. 7th Minnowbrook Workshop Software Perform. Eval.,* Blue Mountain Lake, NY, July 24-27, 1984.
[89] *Statistical Analysis System (SAS) User's Guide,* SAS Inst. Inc., Box 8000, Gary, NC 27511, 1982.
[90] H. Scheffe, *The Analysis of Variance.* New York: Wiley, 1959.
[91] "Annotated bibliography of software engineering laboratory (SEL) literature," Software Eng. Lab., NASA/Goddard Space Flight Center, Greenbelt, MD, Rep. SEL-82-006, Nov. 1982.
[92] R. W. Selby, "An empirical study comparing software testing techniques," in *Proc. 6th Minnowbrook Workshop Software Perform. Eval.,* Blue Mountain Lake, NY, July 19-22, 1983.
[93] ——,"Evaluations of software technologies: Testing, CLEANROOM, and metrics," Ph.D. dissertation, Dep. Comput. Sci., Univ. Maryland, College Park, Tech. Rep. TR-1500, 1985.
[94] R. W. Selby, V. R. Basili, and F. T. Baker, "CLEANROOM software development: An empirical evaluation," Dep. Comput. Sci., Univ. Maryland, College Park, Tech. Rep. TR-1415, Feb. 1985.
[95] J. G. Shanthikumar, "A statisical time dependent error occurrence rate software reliability model with imperfect debugging," in *Proc. 1981 Nat. Comput. Conf.,* June 1981.
[96] B. A. Sheil, "The psychological study of programming," *Comput. Surveys,* vol. 13, pp. 101-120, Mar. 1981.
[97] V. Y. Shen, T. J. Yu, S. M. Thebaut, and L. R. Paulsen, "Identifying error-prone software—An empirical study," *IEEE Trans. Software Eng.,* vol. SE-11, pp. 317-324, Apr. 1985.
[98] B. Shneiderman, *Software Psychology: Human Factors in Computer and Information Systems.* Winthrop, 1980.

[99] B. Shneiderman, R. E. Mayer, D. McKay, and P. Heller, "Experimental investigations of the utility of detailed flowcharts in programming," *Commun. ACM,* vol. 20, no. 6, pp. 373-381, 1977.

[100] S. Siegel, *Nonparametric Statistics for the Behavioral Sciences.* New York: McGraw-Hill, 1955.

[101] E. Soloway, J. Bonar, and K. Ehrlich, "Cognitive strategies and looping constructs: An empirical study," *Commun. ACM,* vol. 26, no.11, pp. 853-860, Nov. 1983.

[102] E. Soloway and K. Ehrlich, "Empirical studies of programming knowledge," *IEEE Trans. Software Eng.,* vol. SE-10, pp. 595-609, Sept. 1984.

[103] E. Soloway, K. Ehrlich, J. Bonar, and J. Greenspan, "What do novices know about programming?" in *Directions in Human-Computer Interactions,* A. Badre and B. Shneiderman, Eds. Norwood, NJ: Ablex, 1982.

[104] W. P. Stevens, G. L. Myers, and L. L. Constantine, "Structural design, " *IBM Syst. J.,* vol. 13, no. 2, pp. 115-139. 1974.

[105] L. G. Stucki, "New directions in automated tools for improving software quality," in *Current Trends in Programming Methodology,* R. T. Yeh, Ed. Englewood Cliffs, NJ: Prentice-Hall, 1977.

[106] I. Vessey and R. Weber, "Some factors affecting program repair maintenance: An empirical study," *Commun. ACM,* vol. 26, no. 2, pp. 128-134, Feb. 1983.

[107] J. Vosburgh, B. Curtis, R. Wolverton, B. Albert, H. Malec, S. Hoben, and Y. Liu, "Productivity factors and programming environments," in *Proc. 7th Int. Conf. Software Eng.,* Orlando, FL, 1984, pp. 143-152.

[108] C. E. Walston and C. P. Felix, "A method of programming measurement and estimation," *IBM Syst. J.,* vol. 16, no. 1, pp. 54-73, 1977.

[109] G. Weinberg, *The Psychology of Computer Programming.* New York: Van Nostrand Rheinhold, 1971.

[110] M. Weiser, "Programmers use slices when debugging," *Commun. ACM,* vol. 25, pp. 446-452, July 1982.

[111] M. Weiser and J. Shertz, "Programming problem representation in novice and expert programmers," *Int. J. Man-Machine Studies,* vol. 19. pp. 391-398, 1983.

[112] D. M. Weiss and V. R. Basili, "Evaluating software development by analysis of changes: Some data from the software engineering laboratory," *IEEE Trans. Software Eng.,* vol. SE-11, pp. 157-168, Feb. 1985.

[113] L. Weissman, "Psychological complexity of computer programs: An experimental methodology," *SIGPLAN Notices,* vol. 9, no. 6, pp. 25-36, June 1974.

[114] R. Wolverton. "The cost of developing large scale software," *IEEE Trans. Comput.,* vol. C-23, June 1974.

[115] S. N. Woodfield, H. E. Dunsmore, and V. Y. Shen, "The effect of modularization and comments on program comprehension," Dep. Comput. Sci., Arizona State Univ., Tempe, AZ, Working Paper, 1981.

[116] J. C. Zolnowski and D. B. Simmons, "Taking the measure of program complexity," in *Proc. Nat. Comput. Conf.,* 1981, pp. 329-336.

Comparing the Effectiveness of Software Testing Strategies

Victor R. Basil and Richard W. Selby

Abstract. This study applies an experimentation methodology to compare three state-of-the-practice software testing techniques: a) code reading by stepwise abstraction, b) functional testing using equivalence partitioning and boundary value analysis, and c) structural testing using 100 percent statement coverage criteria. The study compares the strategies in three aspects of software testing: fault detection effectiveness, fault detection cost, and classes of faults detected. Thirty-two professional programmers and 42 advanced students applied the three techniques to four unit-sized programs in a fractional factorial experimental design. The major results of this study are the following. 1) With the professional programmers, code reading detected more software faults and had a higher fault detection rate than did functional or structural testing, while functional testing detected more faults than did structural testing, but functional and structural testing were not different in fault detection rate. 2) In one advanced student subject group, code reading and functional testing were not different in faults found, but were both superior to structural testing, while in the other advanced student subject group there was no difference among the techniques. 3) With the advanced student subjects, the three techniques were not different in fault detection rate. 4) Number of faults observed, fault detection rate, and total effort in detection depended on the type of software tested. 5) Code reading detected more interface faults than did the other methods. 6) Functional testing detected more control faults than did the other methods. 7) When asked to estimate the percentage of faults detected, code readers gave the most accurate estimates while functional testers gave the least accurate estimates.

Key Words: Code reading, empirical study, functional testing, methodology evaluation, off-line software review, software measurement, software testing, structural testing.

Manuscript received May 31, 1985; revised June 30, 1986. This work was supported in part by the Air Force Office of Scientific Research under Contract AFOSR-F49620-80-C-001, the National Aeronautics and Space Administration under Grant NSG-5123, and the University of California Faculty Research Fellowship Program. Computer support was provided in part by the NASA/Goddard Space Flight Center, the Computer Science Center at the University of Maryland, and the University of California.

V. R. Basili, senior member, IEEE, is with the Department of Computer Science, University of Maryland, College Park, MD 20742.

R. W. Selby, member, IEEE, is with the Department of Information and Computer Science, University of California, Irvine, CA 92717.

I. Introduction

The processes of software testing and fault detection continue to challenge the software community. Even though the software testing and fault detection activities are inexact and inadequately understood, they are crucial to the success of a software project. This paper presents a controlled study where an experimentation methodology was applied to address the uncertainty of how to test software effectively. In this investigation, common testing techniques were applied to different types of software by subjects that had a wide range of professional experiments. This controlled study is intended to evaluate different testing methods that are actually used by software developers, "state-of-the-practice" methods, as opposed to state-of-the-art techniques.

This work is intended to characterize how testing effectiveness relates to several factors: testing technique, software type, fault type, tester experience, and any interactions among these factors. The study presented extends previous work by incorporating different testing techniques and a greater number of persons and programs, while broadening the scope of issues examined and adding statistical significance to the conclusions.

There are multiple perspectives from which to view empirical studies of software development techniques, including the study presented in this paper.

Experimenter—An experimenter may view the study as a demonstration of how a software development technique (or methodology, tool, etc.) can be empirically evaluated. Experimenters may examine the work as an example application of a particular experimentation methodology that may be reused in future studies.

Researcher—A researcher may view the study as an empirical basis to refine theories of software testing. Researchers formulate software testing theories that have a horizon across multiple studies. As a consequence, they examine data from a variety of sources and focus on data that either support or refute proposed theories.

Practitioner—A practitioner may view the study as a source of information about which approaches to testing should be applied in practice. Practitioners may focus on the particular quantifications and comparisons provided by the results. They then consider the relationship of the programs and programmers examined to the particular environment or projects in which the results might be applied.

The following sections describe the testing techniques examined, the investigation goals, the experimental design, operation, analysis, and conclusions.

II. Testing Techniques

To demonstrate that a particular program actually meets its specifications, professional software developers currently utilize many different testing methods. The controlled study presented analyzes three common software testing techniques, which will be referred to as functional testing, structural testing, and code reading. Before presenting the goals for the empirical study comparing the techniques, a description will be given of the testing strategies and their different capabilities (see Fig. 1.). In functional testing, which is a "black box" approach, a programmer constructs test data from the program's specification through methods such as equivalence partitioning and boundary value analysis [42]. The programmer then executes the program and contrasts its actual behavior with that indicated in the specification. In structural testing, which is a "white box" approach [25], [29], a programmer inspects the source code and then devises and executes test cases based on the percentage of the program's statements or expressions executed (the "test set coverage") [52]. The structural coverage criteria used was 100 percent statement coverage. In code reading by step-wise abstraction, a person identifies prime subprograms in the software, determines their functions, and composes these functions to determine a function for the entire program [35], [39]. The code reader then compares this derived function and the specifications (the intended function).

	code reading	functional testing	structural testing
view program specification	X	X	X
view source code	X		X
execute program		X	X

Fig. 1. Capabilities of the testing method

The controlled study presented analyzes, therefore, 1) the functional testing technique of using equivalence class partitioning and boundary value analysis, 2) the structural testing technique of using 100 percent statement coverage criteria, and 3) the code reading technique of reading by stepwise abstraction. Certainly more advanced methods of testing software have been proposed (for example, see [10]). The intention of the controlled study, however, is to apply an experimentation methodology to analyze testing methods that are actually being used by developers to test software [56]. Note that alternate forms exist for each of the three methods described, for example, functional testing that takes into consideration the program design [27], structural testing that uses branch or data flow criteria [16], and code reading in multiperson inspections [14]. With the above descriptions in mind, we will refer to the three testing methods as functional testing, structural testing, and code reading.

A. Investigation Coals

The goals of this study comprise three different aspects of software testing: fault detection effectiveness, fault detection cost, and classes of faults detected. An application of the goal/question/metric paradigm [2], [6] leads to the framework of goals and questions for this study appearing in Fig. 2.

The first goal area is performance oriented and includes a natural first question (I-A): which of the techniques detects the most faults in the programs? The comparison between the techniques is being made across programs, each with a different number of faults. An alternate interpretation would then be to compare the percentage of faults found in the programs (question I-A-1). The number of faults that a technique exposes should also be compared; that is, faults that are made observable but not necessarily observed and reported by a tester (I-A-2). Because of the differences in types of software and in testers' abilities, it is relevant to determine whether the number of the faults detected is either program or programmer dependent (I-B, I-C). Since one technique may find a few more faults than another, it becomes useful to know how much effort that technique requires (II-A). Awareness of what types of software require more effort to test (II-B) and what types of programmer backgrounds require less effort in fault uncovering (II-C) is also quite useful. If one is interested in detecting certain classes of faults, such as in error-based testing [15], [53] it is appropriate to apply a technique sensitive to that particular type (III-A). Classifying the types of faults that are observable yet go unreported could help focus and increase testing effectiveness (III-B).

I. Fault detection effectiveness

- A. For programmers doing unit testing, which of the testing techniques (code reading, functional testing, or structural testing) detects the most faults in programs?
  - 1. Which of the techniques detects the greatest percentage of faults in the programs (the programs each contain a different number of faults)?
  - 2. Which of the techniques exposes the greatest number (or percentage) of program faults (faults that are observable but not necessarily reported)?
- B. Is the number of faults observed dependent on software type?
- C. Is the number of faults observed dependent on the expertise level of the person testing?

II. Fault detection cost

- A. For programmers doing unit testing, which of the testing techniques (code reading, functional testing, or structural testing) detects the faults at the highest rate (#faults/effort)?
- B. Is the fault detection rate dependent on software type?
- C. Is the fault detection rate dependent on the expertise level of the person testing?

III. Classes of faults observed

- A. For programmers doing unit testing, do the methods tend to capture different classes of faults?
- B. What classes of faults are observable but go unreported?

Fig. 2. Outline of goals / subgoals /questions for testing experiment.

III. Empirical Study

Admittedly, the goals stated here are quite ambitious. In no way is it implied that this study can definitively answer all of these questions for all environments. It is intended, however, that the statistically significant analysis presented lends insights into their answers and into the merit and appropriateness of each of the techniques. Note that this study compares the individual application of the three testing techniques in order to identify their distinct advantages and disadvantages. This approach is a first step toward proposing a composite testing strategy, which possibly incorporates several testing methods. The following sections describe the empirical study undertaken to pursue these goals and questions, including the selection of subjects, programs, and experimental design, and the overall operation of the study. For an overview of the experimentation methodology applied in this study, as well as a discussion of numerous software engineering experiments, see [4].

A. Iterative Experimentation

The empirical study consisted of three phases. The first and second phases of the study took place at the University of Maryland in the Fall of 1982 and 1983, respectively. The third phase took place at Computer Sciences Corporation (Silver Spring, MD) and NASA Goddard Space Flight Center (Greenbelt, MD) in the Fall of 1984. The sequential experimentation supported the iterative nature of the learning process, and enabled the initial set of goals and questions to be expanded and resolved by further analysis. The goals were further refined by discussions of the preliminary results [47], [51]. These three phases enabled the pursuit pf result reproducibility across environments having subjects with a wide range of experience.

B. Subject and Program/Fault Selection

A primary consideration in this study was to use a realistic testing environment to assess the effectiveness of these different testing strategies, as opposed to creating a best possible testing situation [23]. Thus, 1) the subjects for the study were chosen to be representative of different levels of expertise, 2) the programs tested correspond to different types of software and reflect common programming style, and 3) the faults in the programs were representative of those frequently occurring in software. Sampling the subjects, programs, and faults in this manner is intended to evaluate the testing methods reasonably, and to facilitate the generalization of the results to other environments.

1) *Subjects*: The three phases of the study incorporated a total of 74 subjects; the individual phases had 29, 13, and 32 subjects, respectively. The subjects were selected, based on several criteria, to be representative of three different levels of

computer science expertise: advanced, intermediate, and junior. The number of subjects in each level of expertise for the different phases appears in Fig. 3.

The 42 subjects in the first two phases of the study were the members of the upper level "Software Design and Development" course at the University of Maryland in the falls of 1982 and 1983. The individuals were either upper-level computer science majors or graduate students; some were working part-time and all were in good academic standing. The topics of the course included structured programming practices, functional correctness, top-down design, modular specification and design, step-wise refinement, and PDL, in addition to the presentation of the techniques of code reading, functional testing, and structural testing. The references for the testing methods were [40], [14], [42], [27], and the lectures were presented by V. R. Basili and F. T. Baker. The subjects from the University of Maryland spanned the intermediate and junior levels of computer science expertise. The assignment of individuals to levels of expertise was based on professional experience and prior academic performance in relevant computer science courses. The individuals in the first and second phases had overall averages of 1.7 (SD = 1.7) and 1.5 (SD = 1.5) years of professional experience. The nine intermediate subjects in the first phase had from 2.8 to 7 years of professional experience (average of 3.9 years, SD = 1.3), and the four in the second phase had from 2.3 to 5.5 years of professional experience (average of 3.2, SD = 1.5). The 20 junior subjects in the first phases and the nine in the second phase both had from 0 to 2 years professional experience (averages of 0.7, SD = 0.6, and 0.8, SD = 0.8, respectively).

	Phase			
Level of Expertise	1 (Univ. MD)	2 (Univ. MD)	3 (NASA/CSC)	total
Advanced	0	0	8	8
Intermediate	9	4	11	24
Junior	20	9	13	42
Total	29	13	32	74

Fig. 3. Expertise levels of subjects.

The 32 subjects in the third phase of the study were programming professionals from NASA and Computer Sciences Corporation. These individuals were mathematicians, physicists, and engineers that develop ground support software for satellites. They were familiar with all three testing techniques, but had used functional testing primarily. A four hour tutorial on the testing techniques was conducted for the subjects by R. W. Selby. This group of subjects, examined in the third phase of the experiment, spanned all three expertise levels and had an overall average of 10.0 (SD = 5.7) years professional experience. Several criteria were considered in the assignment of subjects to expertise levels, including years of professional experience, degree background, and their manager's suggested assignment. The eight advanced subjects ranged from 9.5 to 20.5 years professional experience (average of 15.0, SD = 4.1). The eleven intermediate subjects ranged from 3.5 to 17.5 years experience (average of 10.9, SD = 4.9). The 13 junior subjects ranged from 1.5 to 13.5 years experience (average of 6.1, SD = 4.4).

2) *Programs*: The experimental design enables the distinction of the testing techniques while allowing for the effects of the different programs being tested. The four programs used in the investigation were chosen to be representative of several different types of software. The programs were selected specially for the study and were provided to the subjects for testing; the subjects did not test programs that they had written. All programs were written in a high-level language with which the subjects were familiar. The three programs tested in the CSC/NASA phase were written in Fortran, and the programs tested in the University of Maryland phase were written in the Simpl-T structured programming language [5][1]. The four programs tested were P_1) a text processor, P_2) a mathematical plotting routine, P_3) a numeric abstract data type, and P_4) a database maintainer. The programs are summarized in Fig. 4. There exists some differentiation in size, and the programs are a realistic size for unit testing. Each of the subjects tested three programs, but a total of four programs was used across the three phases of the study. The programs tested in each of the three phases of the study appear in Fig. 5. The specifications for the programs appear in the Appendix, and their source code appears in [3], [48].

program	source lines	executable statements	cyclomatic complexity	# routines	# faults
P_1=text formatter	169	33	18	3	9
P_2=mathematical plotting	145	93	32	9	5
P_3=numeric data abstraction	147	48	13	9	7
P_4=database maintainer	293	144	37	7	12

Fig. 4. The programs tested.

Program	Phase 1 (Univ. MD)	Phase 2 (Univ. MD)	Phase 3 (NASA/CSC)
P_1=text formatter	X	X	X
P_2=mathematical plotting	X	X	
P_3=numeric data abstraction	X		X
P_4=database maintainer		X	X

Fig. 5. Programs tested in each phase of the analysis.

The first program is a text formatting program, which also appeared in [41]. A version of this program, originally written by [43] using techniques of program correctness proofs, was analyzed in [19]. The second program is a mathematical plotting routine. This program was written by R. W. Selby. based roughly on a

[1] Simpl-T is a structured language that supports several string and tile handling primitives, in addition to the usual control flow constructs available, for example, in Pascal.

sample program in [33]. The third program is a numeric data abstraction consisting of a set of list processing utilities. This program was submitted for a class project by a member of an intermediate level programming course at the University of Maryland [36]. The fourth program is a maintainer for a database of bibliographic references. This program was analyzed in [23], and was written by a systems programmer at the University of North Carolina computation center.

Note that the source code for the programs contains no comments. This creates a worst-case situation for the code readers. In an environment where code contained helpful comments, performance of code readers would likely improve, especially if the source code contained as comments the intermediate functions of the program segments. In an environment where the comments were at all suspect, they could then be ignored.

3) *Faults*: The faults contained in the programs tested represent a reasonable distribution of faults that commonly occur in software [1], [54]. All the faults in the database maintainer and the numeric abstract data type were made during the actual development of the programs. The other two programs contain a mix of faults made by the original programmer and faults seeded in the code. The programs contained a total of 34 faults: the text formatter had nine, the plotting routine had six, the abstract data type had seven, and the database maintainer had twelve.

a) *Fault Origin*: The faults in the text formatter were preserved from the article in which it appeared [41], except for some of the more controversial ones [9]. In the mathematical plotter, faults made during program translation were supplemented by additional representative faults. The faults in the abstract data type were the original ones made by the program's author during the development of the program. The faults in the database maintainer were recorded during the development of the program, and then reinserted into the program. The next section describes a classification of the different types of faults in the programs. Note that this investigation of the fault detecting ability of these techniques involves only those types occurring in the source code, not other types such as those in the requirements or the specifications.

b) *Fault Classification*: The faults in the programs are classified according to two different abstract classification schemes [1]. One fault categorization method separates faults of omission from faults of commission. Faults of commission are those faults present as a result of an incorrect segment of existing code. For example, the wrong arithmetic operator is used for a computation in the right-hand-side of an assignment statement. Faults of omission are those faults present as a result of a programmer's forgetting to include some entity in a module. For example, a statement is missing from the code that would assign the proper value to a variable.

A second fault categorization scheme partitions software faults into the six classes of 1) initialization, 2) computation, 3) control, 4) interface, 5) data, and 6) cosmetic. Improperly initializing a data structure constitutes an initialization fault. For example, assigning a variable the wrong value on entry to a module. Computation faults are those that cause a calculation to evaluate the value for a variable incorrectly. The above example of a wrong arithmetic operator in the right-hand-side of an assignment statement would be a computation fault. A control fault causes the wrong control flow path in a program to be taken for some input. An incorrect predicate in an IF-THEN-ELSE statement would be a control fault. Interface faults result when a module uses and makes assumptions about entities outside the module's local environment. Interface faults would be, for example, passing an incorrect argument to a procedure, or assuming in a module that an array passed as an argument was filled with blanks by the passing routine. A data fault are those that result from the incorrect use of a data structure. For example, incorrectly determining the index for the last element in an array. Finally, cosmetic faults are clerical mistakes when entering the program. A spelling mistake in an error message would be a cosmetic fault.

Interpreting and classifying faults in software is a difficult and inexact task. The categorization process often requires trying to recreate the original programmer's misunderstanding of the problem [34]. The above two fault classification schemes attempt to distinguish among different reasons that programmers make faults in software development. They were applied to the faults in the programs in a consistent interpretation; it is certainly possible that another analyst could have interpreted them differently. The separate application of each of the two classification schemes to the faults categorized them in a mutually exclusive and exhaustive manner. Fig. 6 displays the distribution of faults in the programs according to these schemes.

	Omission	Commission	Total
Initialization	0	2	2
Computation	4	4	8
Control	2	5	7
Interface	2	11	13
Data	2	1	3
Cosmetic	0	1	1
Total	10	24	34

Fig. 6. Distribution of faults in the programs.

c) *Fault Description*: The faults in the programs are described in Fig. 7. There have been various efforts to determine a precise counting scheme for "defects" in software [18], [31], [13]. According to the IEEE explanations given, a software "fault" is a specific manifestation in the source code of a programmer "error." For example, due to a misconception or document discrepancy, a programmer makes an "error" (in his/her head) that may result in more than one "fault" in a program. Using this interpretation, software "faults" reflect the correctness, or lack thereof, of a program. A program input may reveal a software "fault" by causing a software "failure." A software "failure" is therefore a manifestation of a software "fault." The entities examined in this analysis are software faults.

Fault	Program	Omission/ Commission	Class	Description
a	P1	omission	control	a blank is printed before the first word on the first line unless the first word is 30 characters long; in the latter case, a blank line is printed before the first word
b	P1	commission	initialization	the character & (not $) is the new-line character
c	P1	commission	initialization	the line size is 31 characters (not 30); this fault causes the references to the number 30 in the other faults to be actually the number 31
d	P1	commission	interface	since the program pads an empty input buffer with the character "z," it ignores a valid input line that has a "z" as a first character
e	P1	omission	control	successive break characters are not condensed in the output
f	P1	commission	cosmetic	spelling mistake in the error message "*** word to long ***"
g	P1	commission	computation	after detecting a word in the input longer than 30 characters, the message "*** word to long ***" is printed once for every character over 30, and the processing of the text does not terminate
h	P1	omission	interface	after detecting a word in the input longer than 30 characters, the program prints whatever is residing in its output buffer
i	P1	commission	control	after detecting an input line without an end-of-text character, the program erroneously increments its buffer pointer and replaces the first character of the next input line with a "z"
j	P3	commission	interface	routine FIRST returns zero (0) when the list has one element
k	P3	commission	interface	routine ISEMPTY returns true (1) when the list has one element
l	P3	commission	interface	routine DELETEFIRST can not delete the first list element when the list has only one element
m	P3	commission	interface	routine LISTLENGTH returns one less than the actual length of the list
n	P3	commission	interface	routine ADDFIRST can add more than the specified five elements to the list
o	P3	commission	interface	routine ADDLAST can add more than the specified five elements to the list
p	P3	omission	computation	routine REVERSE does not reverse the list properly when the list has more than one element

Fault	Program	Omission/ Commission	Class	Description
q	P4	commission	computation	words greater than or equal to three characters (not strictly greater than) are treated as cross reference keywords
r	P4	commission	interface	since the program uses the key "ZZZ" as an end-of-input sentinel, it does not process a valid record with key "ZZZ" and ignores any following records
s	P4	commission	control	update action add with the error condition "key already in the master file" replaces the existing record; the update record is not ignored
t	P4	commission	control	update action replace with the error condition "key not found in the master file" adds the record; the update record is not ignored
u	P4	omission	data	the number of references and number of words in the dictionary are not checked for overflow
v	P4	omission	computation	two or more update transactions for the same master record give incorrect results
w	P4	commission	interface	keywords longer than 12 characters are truncated and not distinguished
x	P4	commission	control	an update record with column 80 neither an add action "A" nor replace action "R" acts like an add transaction
y	P4	commission	interface	keyword indices appear in reverse alphabetical order
z	P4	omission	interface	no check is made for unique keys in the master file
A	P4	commission	interface	punctuation is made a part of the keyword
B	P4	omission	data	words appearing twice in a title get two cross reference entries
C	P2	commission	computation	the x and y axes are mislabeled
D	P2	omission	computation	points with negative y-values are not processed and do not appear on the graph
E	P2	commission	control	the origin (0,0) appears on the graph regardless of whether it is an input point
F	P2	commission	data	no points can appear on the vertical axis
G	P2	commission	computation	the vertical and horizontal scaling for the pixels are calculated incorrectly, causing some points not to appear in the proper pixel
H	P2	omission	computation	when more than one point would appear in a given pixel, only an asterisk (*) appears, not an appropriate integer

Fig. 7. Fault classification and description.

C. Experimental Design

The experimental design applied for each of the three phases of the study was a fractional factorial design [7], [12]. This experimental design distinguishes among the testing techniques, while allowing for variation in the ability of the particular individual testing or in the program being tested. Fig. 8 displays the fractional factorial design appropriate for the third phase of the study. Subject S_1, is in the advanced expertise level, and he structurally tested program P_1, functionally tested program P_3, and code read program P_4. Notice that all of the subjects tested each of the three programs and used each of the three techniques. Of course, no one tests a given program more than once. The design appropriate for the third phase is discussed in the following paragraphs, with the minor differences between this design and the ones applied in the first two phases being discussed at the end of the section.

1) *Independent and Dependent Variables*: The experimental design has the three independent variables of testing technique, software type, and level of expertise. For the design appearing in Fig. 8, appropriate for the third phase of the study, the three main effects have the following levels:
   1) testing technique: code reading, functional testing, and structural testing.
   2) software types: (*P1*) text processing, (*P3*) numeric abstract data type, and (*P4*) database maintainer.
   3) level of expertise: advanced, intermediate, and junior.

   Every combination of these levels occurs in the design. That is, programmers in all three levels of expertise applied all three testing techniques on all programs. In addition to these three main effects, a factorial analysis of variance (ANOVA) model supports the analysis of interactions among each of these main effects. Thus, the interaction effects of testing technique * software type, testing technique* expertise level, software type * expertise level, and the three-way interaction of testing technique * software type * expertise level are included in the model. There are several dependent variables examined in the study, including number of faults detected, percentage of faults detected, total fault detection time, and fault detection rate. Observations from the on-line methods of functional and structural testing also had as dependent variables number of computer runs, amount of cpu-time consumed, maximum statement coverage achieved, connect time used, number of faults that were observable from the test data, percentage of faults that were observable from the test data, and percentage of faults observable from the test data, and percentage of faults observable from the test data that were actually observed by the tester.
2) *Analysis of Variance Model:* The three main effects and all the two-way and three-way interactions effects are called fixed effects in this factorial analysis of variance model. The levels of these effects given above represent all levels of interest in the investigation. For example, the effect of testing technique has as particular levels code reading, functional testing, and structural testing; these particular testing techniques are the only ones under comparison in this study. The effect of the particular subjects that participated in this study re-

quires a little different interpretation. The subjects examined in the study were random samples of programmers from the large population of programmers at each of the levels of expertise. Thus, the effect of the subjects on the various dependent variables is a random variable, and this effect therefore is called a random effect. If the samples examined are truly representative of the population of subjects at each expertise level, the inferences from the analysis can then be generalized across the whole population of subjects at each expertise level, not just across the particular subjects in the sample chosen. Since this analysis of variance model contains both fixed and random effects, it is called a mixed model. The additive ANOVA model for the design appearing in Fig. 8 is given below [7], [12].

		Code Reading			Functional Testing			Structural Testing		
		P_1	P_3	P_4	P_1	P_3	P_4	P_1	P_3	P_4
Advanced Subjects	S_1			X		X		X		
	S_2		X		X					X
	.					. . .				
	.					. . .				
	S_8	X					X		X	
Intermediate Subjects	S_9		X		X					X
	S_{10}			X		X		X		
	.					. . .				
	.					. . .				
	S_{19}	X					X		X	
Junior Subjects	S_{20}		X		X					X
	S_{21}	X					X		X	
	.					. . .				
	.					. . .				
	S_{32}			X		X		X		

Fig. 8. Fractional factorial design.

$$\gamma_{ijk} = \mu + \alpha_i + \beta_j + \gamma_k + \delta_{kl} + \alpha\beta_{ij} + \alpha\gamma_{ik} + \beta\gamma_{jk} + \alpha\beta\gamma_{ijk} + \varepsilon_{ijkl}$$

where

γ_{ijk} is the observed response from subject *l* of expertise level *k* using technique *i* on program *j*.

μ is the overall mean response.

α_i is the main effect of testing technique *i* ($i = 1, 2, 3$)

β_j is the main effect of program *j* ($j = 1, 3, 4$).

γ_k is the main effect of expertise level *k* ($k = 1, 2, 3$).

δ_{kl} is the random effect of subject *l* within expertise level *k*, a random variable ($l = 1, 2, \cdots, 32$: $k = 1, 2, 3$).

$\alpha\beta_{\eta}$ is the interaction effect of testing technique i with program j (i = 1, 2, 3;
j = 1, 3, 4).

$\alpha\gamma_{ik}$ is the interaction effect of testing technique i with expertise level k (i = 1, 2, 3; k = 1,2, 3).

$\beta\gamma_{jk}$ is the interaction effect of program j with expertise level k (j = 1, 3, 4; k = 1, 2, 3).

$\alpha\beta\gamma_{ijk}$ is the interaction effect of testing technique i program j with expertise level k (i = 1, 2, 3; j = 1, 3, 4; k = 1, 2, 3).

ε_{ijkl} is the experimental error for each observation, a random variable.

The tests of hypotheses on all the fixed effects mentioned above are referred to as F-tests [46]. The F-tests use the error (residual) mean square in the denominator, except for the test of the expertise level effect. The expected mean square for the expertise level effect contains a component for the actual variance of subjects within expertise level. In order to select the appropriate term for the denominator of the expertise level F-test, the mean square for the effect of subjects nested within expertise level is chosen. The parameters for the random effect of subjects within expertise level are assumed to be drawn from a normally distributed random process with mean zero and common variance. The experimental error terms are assumed to have mean zero and common variance.

The fractional factorial design applied in the first two phases of the analysis differed slightly from the one presented above for the third phase[2]. In the third phase of the study, programs P_1, P_3, and P_4 were tested by subjects in three levels of expertise. In both phases one and two, there were only subjects from the levels of intermediate and junior expertise. In phase one, programs P_1, P_3, and P_2 were tested. In phase two, the programs tested were P_1, P_2, and P_4. The only modifications necessary to the above explanation for phases one and two are 1) eliminating the advanced expertise level, 2) changing the program P subscripts appropriately, and 3) leaving out the three way interaction term in phase two, because of the reduced number of subjects. In all three of the phases, all subjects used each of the three techniques and tested each of the three programs for that phase. Also, within all three phrases, all possible combinations of expertise level, testing techniques, and programs occurred.

The order of presentation of the testing techniques was randomized among the subjects in each level of expertise in each phase of the study. However, the integrity of the results would have suffered if each of the programs in a given phase was tested at different times by different subjects. Note that each of the testing sessions took place on a different day because of the amount of effort required. If different programs would have been tested on different days, any discussion about the programs among subjects between testing sessions would have affected the fu-

[2] Although the data from all the phases can be analyzed together, the number of empty cells resulting from not having all three experience levels and all four programs in all phases limits the number of parameters that can be estimated and causes nonunique Type IV partial sums of squares.

ture performance of others. Therefore, all subjects in a phase tested the same program on the same day. The actual order of program presentation was the order in which the programs are listed in the previous paragraph.

D. Experimental Operation

Each of the three phases were broken into five distinct pieces: training, three testing sessions, and a follow-up session. All groups of subjects were exposed to a similar amount of training on the testing techniques before the study began. As mentioned earlier, the University of Maryland subjects were enrolled in the "Software Design and Development" course, and the NASA/CSC subjects were given a four-hour tutorial. Background information on the subjects was captured through a questionnaire. Elementary exercises followed by a pretest covering all techniques were administered to all subjects after the training and before the testing sessions. Reasonable effort on the part of the University of Maryland subjects was enforced by their being graded on the work and by their needing to use the techniques in a major class project. Reasonable effort on the part of the NASA/CSC subjects was certain because of their desire for the study's outcome to improve their software testing environment. All subjects' groups were judged highly motivated during the study. The subjects were all familiar with the editors, terminals, machines, and the programs' implementation language.

The individuals were requested to use the three testing techniques to the best of their ability. Every subject participated in all three testing sessions of his/her phase, using all techniques but each on a separate program. The individuals using code reading were each given the specification for the program and its source code. They were then asked to apply the methods of code reading by step-wise abstraction to detect discrepancies between the program's abstracted function and the specification. The functional testers were each given a specification and the ability to execute the program. They were asked to perform equivalence partitioning and boundary value analysis to select a set of test data for the program. Then they executed the program on this collection of test data, and inconsistencies between what the program actually performed and what they thought the specification said it should perform were noted. The structural testers were given the source code for the program, the ability to execute it, and a description of the input format for the program. The structural testers were asked to examine the source and generate a set of test cases that cumulatively execute 100 percent of the program's statements. When the subjects were applying an on-line technique, they generated and executed their own test data; no test data sets were provided. The programs were invoked through a test driver that supported the use of the multiple input data sets. This test driver, unbeknown to the subjects, drained off the input cases submitted to the program for the experimenter's later analysis; the programs could only be accessed through a test driver.

A structural coverage tool calculated the actual statement coverage of the test set and which statements were left unexecuted for the structural testers[3]. After the structural testers generated a collection of test data that met (or almost met) the 100 percent coverage criteria, no further execution of the program or reference to the source code was allowed.

They retained the program's output from the test cases they had generated. These testers were then provided with the program's specification. Now that they knew what the program was intended to do, they were asked to contrast the program's specification with the behavior of the program on the test data they derived. This scenario for the structural testers was necessary so that "observed" faults could be compared.

At the end of each of the testing sessions, the subjects were asked to give a reasonable estimate of the amount of time spent detecting faults with a given testing technique. The University of Maryland subjects were assured that this had nothing to with the grading of the work. There seemed to be little incentive for the subjects in any of the groups not to be truthful. At the completion of each testing session, the NASA/CSC subjects were also asked what percentage of the faults in the program that they thought were uncovered. After all three testing sessions in a given phase were completed, the subjects were requested to critique and evaluate the three testing techniques regarding their understandability, naturalness, and effectiveness. The University of Maryland subjects submitted a written critique, while a two hour debriefing forum was conducted for the NASA/CSC individuals. In addition to obtaining the impressions of the individuals, these follow-up procedures gave an understanding of how well the subjects were comprehending and applying the methods. These final sessions also afforded the participants an opportunity to comment on any particular problems they had with the techniques or in applying them to the given programs.

IV. Data Analysis

The analysis of the data collected from the various phases of the experiment is presented according to the goal and question framework discussed earlier.

A. Fault Detection Effectiveness

The first goal area addresses the fault detection effectiveness of each of the techniques. Fig. 9 presents a summary of the measures that were examined to pursue

---

[3] Program statements within the body of a WHILE statement were considered unexecuted if the Boolean condition of the WHILE statement was false. Having the Boolean condition of the WHILE statement become true at some point was a prerequisite for executing the statements with the body of the WHILE.

this goal area. A brief description of each measure is as follows; an asterisk (*) means only relevant for on-line testing.

a) Number of faults detected = the number of faults detected by a subject applying a given testing technique on a given program.
b) Percentage of faults detected = the percentage of a program's faults that a subject detected by applying a testing technique to the program.
c) Number of faults observable (*) = the number of faults that were observable from the program's behavior given the input data submitted.
d) Percentage of faults observable (*) = the percentage of a program's faults that were observable from the program's behavior given the input data submitted.
e) Percentage detected/observable (*) = the percentage of faults observable from the program's behavior on the given input set that were actually observed by a subject.
f) Percentage faults felt found = a subject's estimate of the percentage of a program's faults that he/she thought were detected by his/her testing.
g) Maximum statement coverage (*) = the maximum percentage of a program's statements that were executed in a set of test cases.

1) *Data Distributions:* The actual distribution of the number of faults observed by the subjects appears in Fig. 10, broken down by phase. From Figs. 9 and 10, the large variation in performance among the subjects is clearly seen. The

Phase	#Subj.	Measure	Mean	SD	Min.	Max.
1	29	# Faults detected	3.94	1.82	0.00	7.00
1	29	% Faults detected	54.78	28.11	0.00	100.00
1	29(*)	# Faults observable	5.38	1.51	3.00	8.00
1	29(*)	% Faults observable	74.59	20.54	33.33	100.00
1	29(*)	% Detected/observable	70.99	24.01	0.00	100.00
2	13	# Faults detected	3.28	1.98	0.00	7.00
2	13	% Faults detected	39.53	27.25	0.00	100.00
3	32	# Faults detected	4.27	1.86	0.00	8.00
3	32	% Faults detected	49.82	27.44	0.00	100.00
3	32	% Faults felt found	75.10	24.07	0.00	100.00
3	32(*)	# Faults observable	5.61	1.52	3.00	9.00
3	32(*)	% Faults observable	62.11	18.30	25.00	100.00
3	32(*)	% Detected/observable	69.67	27.14	0.00	100.00
3	32(*)	Max. % stmt. covered	97.02	7.83	48.00	100.00
Ave	74	# Faults detected	3.97	1.88	0.00	8.00
Ave	74	% Faults detected	49.98	27.29	0.00	100.00
Ave	61(*)	# Faults observable	5.5	1.5	3.00	9.00
Ave	61(*)	% Faults observable	68.0	20.3	25.0	100.0
Ave	61(*)	% Detected/observable	70.3	25.6	0.0	100.0

Fig. 9. Overall summary of detection effectiveness data. Note: some data pertain only to on-line techniques (*), and some data were collected only in certain phases.

mean number of faults detected by the subjects is displayed in Fig. 11, broken down by technique, program, expertise level, and phase.

2) *Number of Faults Detected:* The first question under this goal area asks which of the testing techniques detected the most faults in the programs. The overall F-test of the techniques detecting an equal number of faults in the programs is rejected in the first and third phases of the study ($\alpha < 0.024$ and $\alpha < 0.0001$, respectively; not rejected in phase two, $\alpha > 0.05$). Recall that the phase three data was collected from 32 NASA/CSC subjects, and the phase one data was from 29 University of Maryland subjects. With the phase three data, the contrast of "reading - 0.5 * (functional + structural)" estimates that the technique of code reading by stepwise abstraction detected 1.24 more faults per program than did either of the other techniques ($\alpha < 0.0001$, c.i. 0.73-1.75)[4].

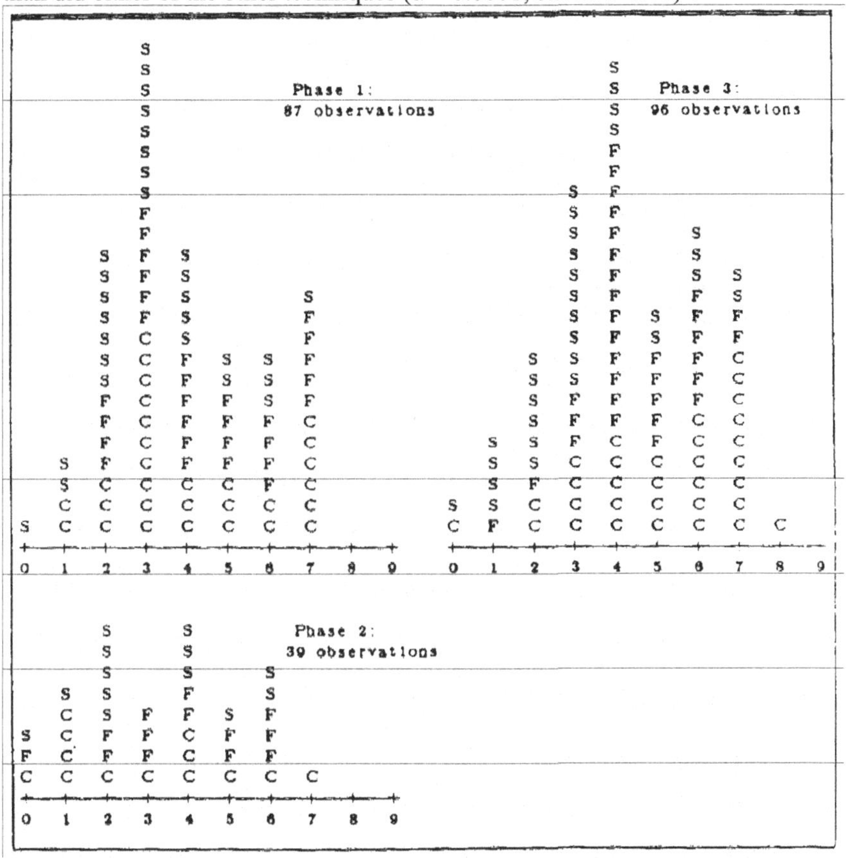

Fig. 10. Distribution of the number of faults detected broken down by phase. Key: code readers (C), functional testers (F), and structural testers (S).

[4] The probability of Type 1 error is reported, the probability of erroneously rejecting the null hypothesis. The abbreviation "c.i." stands for 95 percent confidence interval.

Note that code reading performed well even though the professional subjects' primary experience was with functional testing. Also with the phase three data, the contrast of "functional — structural" estimates that the technique of functional testing detected 1.11 more faults per program than did structural testing ($\alpha < 0.0007$, c.i. 0.52-1.70).

In the phase one data, the contrast of "0.5 * (reading + functional) — structural^' estimates that the technique of structural testing detected 1.00 fault less per program than did either reading or functional testing (a < 0.0065, c.i. 0.31-1.69). In the phase one data, the contrast of "reading — functional" was not statistically different from zero ($\alpha > 0.05$). The poor performance of structural testing across the phases suggests the inadequacy of using statement coverage criteria. The above pairs of contrasts were chosen because they are linearly independent.

		Phase		
		1	2	3
Effect	Level	Mean(SD)	Mean(SD)	Mean(SD)
Technique	Reading	4.10 (1.93)	3.00 (2.20)	5.09 (1.92)
	Functional	4.45 (1.70)	3.77 (1.83)	4.47 (1.34)
	Structural	3.28 (1.67)	3.08 (1.89)	3.25 (1.80)
Program	Formatter	4.07 (1.62)	3.23 (2.20)	4.19 (1.73)
	Plotter	3.48 (1.45)	3.31 (1.97)	. (.)
	Data type	4.28 (2.25)	. (.)	5.22 (1.75)
	Database	. (.)	3.31 (1.84)	3.41 (1.66)
Expertise	Junior	3.88 (1.89)	3.04 (2.07)	3.90 (1.83)
	Intermed.	4.07 (1.69)	3.83 (1.64)	4.18 (1.99)
	Advanced	. (.)	. (.)	5.00 (1.53)

Fig. 11. Overall summary for number of faults detected (SD = std. dev.).

3) *Percentage of Faults Detected:* Since the programs tested each had a different number of faults, a question in the earlier goal/question framework asks which technique detected the greatest percentage of faults in the programs. The order of performance of the techniques is the same as above when the percentage of the program's faults detected are compared. The overall F-tests for phases one and three were rejected as before ($\alpha < 0.037$ and $\alpha < 0.0001$. respectively; not rejected in phase two, $\alpha > 0.05$). Applying the same contrasts as above: a) in phase three, reading detected 16.0 percent more faults per program than did the other techniques ($\alpha < 0.0001$, c.i. 9.9-22.1), and functional detected 11.2 percent more faults than did structural ($\alpha < 0.003$, c.i. 4.1-18.3); b) in phase one, structural detected 13.2 percent fewer of a program's faults than did the other methods ($\alpha < 0.011$, c.i. 3.5-22.9), and reading and functional were not statistically different as before.

4) *Dependence on Software Type:* Another question in this goal area queries whether the number or percentage of faults detected depends on the program being tested. The overall F-test that the number of faults detected is not program dependent is rejected only in the phase three data ($\alpha < 0.0001$). Applying Tukey's multiple comparison on the phase three data reveals that the most faults were detected in the abstract data type, the second most in the text formatter, and the least number of faults were found in the database maintainer (simultaneous $\alpha < 0.05$). When the percentage of faults found in a program is considered, however, the overall F-tests for the three phases are all rejected ($\alpha < 0.027$, $\alpha < 0.01$, and $\alpha < 0.0001$ in respective order). Tukey's multiple comparison yields the following orderings on the programs (all simultaneous $\alpha < 0.05$). In the phase one data, the ordering was (data type = plotter) > text formatter; that is, a higher percentage of faults were detected in either the abstract data type or the plotter than were found in the text formatter; there was no difference between the abstract data type and the plotter in the percentage found. In the phase two data, the ordering of percentage of faults detected was plotter > (text formatter = database maintainer). In the phase three data, the ordering of percentage of faults found in the programs was the same as the number of faults found, abstract data type > text formatter > database maintainer. Summarizing the effect of the type of software on the percentage of faults observed: 1) the programs with the highest percentage of their faults detected were the abstract data type and the mathematical plotter, the percentage detected between these two was not statistically different; 2) the programs with the lowest percentage of their faults detected were the text formatter and the database maintainer; the percentage detected between these two was not statistically different in the phase two data, but a higher percentage of faults in the text formatter was detected in the phase three data.
5) *Observable Versus Observed Faults*: One evaluation criteria of the success of a software testing session is the number of faults detected. An evaluation criteria of the particular test data generated, however, is the ability of the test data to reveal faults in the program. A test data set's ability to reveal faults in a program can be measured by the number or percentage of a program's faults that are made observable from execution on that input[5]. Distinguishing the faults observable in a program from the faults actually observed by a tester highlights the differences in the activities of test data generation and program behavior examination. As shown in Fig. 8, the average number of the programs' faults observable was 68.0 percent when individuals were either functional testing or structural testing. Of course, with a nonexecution-based technique such as code reading, 100 percent of the faults are observable. Test data generated by subjects using the technique of functional listing resulted in 1.4

[5] Test data "reveal a fault" or "make a fault observable" by making a fault be manifested as a program failure (see the explanation in the earlier section entitled Fault Description). Since the analysis is focusing on the number of distinct software faults revealed—and for purposes of readability—this paragraph uses the single word "fault."

more observable faults ($\alpha < 0.0002$, c.i. 0.79-2.01) than did the use of structural testing in phase one of the study; the percentage difference of functional over structural was estimated at 20.0 percent ($\alpha <$ 0.,0002, c.i. 11.2-28.8). The techniques did not differ in these two measures in the third phase of the study. However, just considering the faults that were observable from the submitted test data, functional testers detected 18.5 percent more of these observable faults than did structural testers in the phase three data ($\alpha < 0.0016$, cj.i. 8.9-28.1); they did not differ in the phase one data.

Note that all faults in the programs could be observed in the programs' output given the proper input data. When using the on-line techniques of functional and structural testing, subjects detected 70.3 percent of the faults observable in the program's output. In order to conduct a successful testing session, faults in a program must be both revealed and subsequently observed.

6) *Dependence on Program Coverage*: Another measure of the ability of a test set to reveal a program's faults is the percentage of a program's statements that are executed by the test set. The average maximum statement coverage achieved by the functional and structural testers was 97.0 percent. The maximum statement coverage from the submitted test data was not statistically different between the functional and structural testers ($\alpha > 0.05$). Also, there was no correlation between maximum statement coverage achieved and either number or percentage of faults found ($\alpha > 0.05$).
7) *Dependence on Programmer Expertise:* A final question in this goal area concerns the contribution of programmer expertise to fault detection effectiveness. In the phase three data from the NASA/CSC professional environment, subjects of advanced expertise detected more faults than did either the subjects of intermediate or junior expertise ($\alpha < 0.05$). When the percentage faults detected is compared, however, the advanced subjects performed better than the junior subjects ($\alpha < 0.05$), but were not statistically different from the intermediate subjects ($\alpha > 0.05$). The intermediate and junior subjects were not statistically different in any of the three phases of the study in terms of number or percentage faults observed. When several subject background attributes were correlated with the number of faults found, total years of professional experience had a minor relationship (Pearson R - 0.22, $\alpha < 0.05$). Correspondence of performance with background aspects was examined across all observations, and within each of the phases, including previous academic performance for the University of Maryland subjects. Other than the above, no relationships were found.
8) *Accuracy of Self-Estimates*: Recall that the NASA/CSC subjects in the phase three data estimated, at the completion of a testing session, the percentage of a program's faults they thought they had uncovered. This estimation of the number of faults uncovered correlated reasonably well with the actual percentage of faults detected ($R = 0.57$, $\alpha < 0.0001$). Investigating further, individuals using the different techniques were able to give better estimates: code readers gave the best estimates ($R = 0.79$, $\alpha < 0.0001$), structural testers gave the second best estimates ($R = 0.57$, $\alpha < 0.0007$), and functional testers gave the worst estimates (no correlation, $\alpha > 0.05$). This last observation suggests

that the code readers were more certain of the effectiveness they had in revealing faults in the programs.

9) *Dependence on Interactions:* There were few significant interactions between the main effects of testing technique, program, and expertise level. In the phase two data, there was an interaction between testing technique and program in both the number and percentage of faults found ($\alpha < 0.0013$, $\alpha < 0.0014$, respectively). The effectiveness of code reading increased on the text formatter. In the phase three data, there was a slight three-way interaction between testing technique, program, and expertise level for both the number and percentage of faults found ($\alpha < 0.05$, $\alpha < 0.04$ respectively).
10) *Summary of Fault Detection Effectiveness*: Summarizing the major results of the comparison of fault detection effectiveness: 1) in the phase three data, code reading detected a greater number and percentage of faults than the other methods, with functional detecting more than structural; 2) in the phase one data, code reading and functional were equally effective, while structural was inferior to both—there were no differences among the three techniques in phase two: 3) the number of faults observed depends on the type of software; the most faults were detected in the abstract data type and the mathematical plotter, the second most in the text formatter, and (in the case of the phase three data) the least were found in the database maintainer; 4) functionally generated test data revealed more observable faults than did structurally generated test data in phase one, but not in phase three; 5) subjects of intermediate and junior expertise were equally effective in detecting faults, while advanced subjects found a greater number of faults than did either group; 6) self-estimates of faults detected were most accurate from subjects applying code reading, followed by those doing structural testing, with estimates from persons functionally testing having no relationship.

B. Fault Detection Cost

The second goal area examines the fault detection cost of each of the techniques. Fig. 12 presents a summary of the measures that were examined to investigate this goal area. A brief description of each measure is as follows; an asterisk (*) means only relevant for on-line testing. All of the on-line statistics were monitored by the operating systems of the machines.

a) Number of faults/hour = the number of faults detected by a subject applying a given technique normalized by the effort in hours required, called the fault detection rate.
b) Detection time = the total number of hours that a subject spent in testing a program using a technique.
c) Cpu-time (*) = the cpu-time in seconds used during the testing session.

Phase	#Subj.	Measure	Mean	SD	Min.	Max.
1	29	# Faults / hour	1.63	1.28	0.00	7.00
1	29	Detection time (hrs)	3.33	2.09	0.75	10.00
2	13	# Faults / hour	0.99	0.81	0.00	3.00
2	13	Detection time (hrs)	4.70	3.02	1.00	14.00
3	32	# Faults / hour	2.33	2.28	0.00	14.00
3	32	Detection time (hrs)	2.75	1.57	0.50	7.25
3	32(*)	Cpu-time (sec)	45.2	56.1	3.0	283.0
3	32(*)	Cpu-time (sec; norm.)	38.5	51.7	2.9	314.4
3	32(*)	Connect time (min)	65.83	50.21	3.50	214.00
3	32(*)	# program runs	5.45	5.00	1.00	24.00
Ave	74	# Faults / hour	1.82	1.90	0.00	14.00
Ave	74	Detection time (hrs)	3.32	2.19	0.50	14.00

Fig. 12. Overall summary of fault detection cost data. Note: some data pertain only to on-line techniques (*), and some data were collected only in certain phases.

d) Normalized cpu-time (*) = the cpu-time in seconds used during the testing session, normalized by a factor for machine speed[6].
e) Connect time (*) = the number of minutes that a individual spent on-line while testing a program.
f) Number of program runs (*) = the number of executions of the program test driver; note that the driver supported multiple sets of input data.

1) *Data Distributions:* The actual distribution of the fault detection rates for the subjects appears in Fig. 13, broken down by phase. Once again, note the many-to-one differential in subject performance. Fig. 14 displays the mean fault detection fate for the subjects, broken down by technique, program. expertise level, and phase.
2) *Fault Detection Rate and Total Time:* The first question in this goal area asks which testing technique had the highest fault detection rate. The overall F-test of the techniques having the same detection rate was rejected in the phase three data ($\alpha < 0.0014$). but not in the other two phases ($\alpha > 0.05$). As before, the two contrasts of "reading - 0.5 * (functional + structural)" and "functional - structural" were examined to detect differences among the techniques. The technique of code reading was estimated at detecting 1.49 more faults per hour than did the other techniques in the phase three data ($\alpha < 0.0003$, c.i. 0.75-2.23). The techniques of functional and structural testing were not statistically different ($\alpha > 0.05$). Comparing the total time spent in fault detection, the techniques were not statistically different in the phase two and three data;

[6] In the phase three data, testing was done on both a VAX 11/780 and an IBM 4341. As suggested by benchmark comparisons [11], the VAX cpu-times were divided by 1.6 and the IBM cpu-times were divided by 0.9.

the overall F-test for the phase one data was rejected ($\alpha < 0.013$). In the phase one data, structural testers spent an estimated 1.08 hours less testing than did the other techniques ($\alpha < 0.004$, c.i. 0.39-1.78), while code readers were not statistically different from functional testers. Recall that in phase one, the structural testers observed both a lower number and percentage of the programs' faults than did the other techniques.

3) *Dependence on Software Type*: Another question in this area focuses on how fault detection rate depends on software type. The overall F-test that the detection rate is the same for the programs is rejected in the phase one and phase three data ($\alpha < 0.01$ and $\alpha < 0.0001$, respectively); the detection rate among the programs was not statistically different in phase two ($\alpha > 0.05$). Applying Tukey's multiple comparison on the phase one data finds that the fault detection rate was greater on the abstract data type than on the plotter, while there was no difference either between the abstract data type and the text formatter or between the text formatter and the plotter (simultaneous $\alpha < 0.05$). In the phase three data, the fault detection rate was higher in the abstract data type

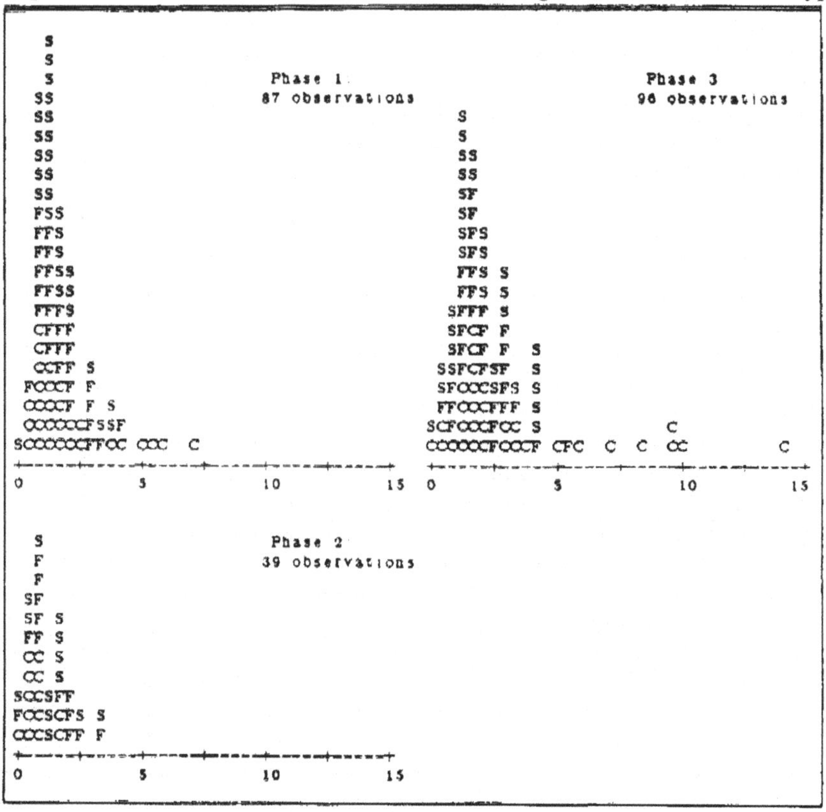

Fig. 13. Distribution of the fault detection rate (number of faults detected per hour) broken down by phase. Key: code readers (C), functional testers (F), and structural testers (S).

than it was for the text formatter and the database maintainer, with the text formatter and the database maintainer not being statistically different (simultaneous $\alpha < 0.05$). The overall effort spent in fault detection was different among the programs in phases one and three ($\alpha < 0.012$ and $\alpha < 0.0001$, respectively), while there was no difference in phase two. In phase one, more effort was spent testing the plotter than the abstract data type, while there was no statistical difference either between the plotter and the text formatter or between the text formatter and the abstract data type (simultaneous $\alpha < 0.05$). In phase three, more time was spent testing the database maintainer than was spent on either the text formatter or on the abstract data type, with the text formatter not differing from the abstract data type (simultaneous $\alpha < 0.05$). Summarizing the dependence of fault detection cost on software type, 1) the abstract data type had a higher detection rate and less total detection effort than did either the plotter or the database maintainer, the latter two were not different in either detection rate or total detection time; 2) the text formatter and the plotter did not differ in fault detection rate or total detection effort; 3) the text formatter and the database maintainer did not differ in fault detection rate overall and did not differ in total detection effort in phase two, but the database maintainer had a higher total detection effort in phase three; 4) the text formatter and the abstract data type did not differ in total detection effort overall and did not differ in fault detection rate in phase one, but the abstract data type had a higher detection rate in phase three.

		Phase		
		1	2	3
Effect	Level	Mean(SD)	Mean(SD)	Mean(SD)
Technique	Reading	1.90 (1.83)	0.56 (0.46)	3.33 (3.42)
	Functional	1.38 (0.90)	1.22 (0.91)	1.84 (1.06)
	Structural	1.40 (0.87)	1.18 (0.84)	1.82 (1.24)
Program	Formatter	1.60 (1.39)	0.98 (0.67)	2.15 (1.10)
	Plotter	1.19 (0.83)	0.92 (0.71)	. (.)
	Data type	2.09 (1.42)	. (.)	3.70 (3.26)
	Database	. (.)	1.05 (1.04)	1.14 (0.79)
Expertise	Junior	1.36 (0.97)	1.00 (0.85)	2.14 (2.48)
	Intermed.	3.22 (1.66)	0.96 (0.74)	2.53 (2.48)
	Advanced	. (.)	. (.)	2.36 (1.61)

Fig. 14. Overall summary for fault detection rate (number of faults detected per hour) (SD = std. dev).

3) *Computer Costs:* In addition to the effort spent by individuals in software testing, online methods incur machine costs. The machine cost measures of cpu-time, connect time, and the number of runs were compared across the on-line techniques of functional and structural testing in phase three of the study. A nonexecution-based technique such as code reading, of course, incurs no machine time costs. When the machine speeds are normalized (see measure definitions above), the technique of functional testing used 26.0 more seconds of cpu-time than did the technique of structural testing ($\alpha < 0.016$, c.i. 7.0-45.0). The estimate of the difference is 29.6 seconds when the cpu-times are not normalized ($\alpha < 0.012$, c.i. 9.0-50.2). Individuals using functional testing used 28.4 more minutes of connect time than did those using structural testing ($\alpha < 0.004$, c.i. 11.7-45.1). The number of computer runs of a program's test driver was not different between the two techniques ($\alpha > 0.05$). These results suggest that individuals using functional testing spent more time on-line and used more cpu-time per computer run than did those structurally testing.
4) *Dependence on Programmer Expertise*: The relation of programmer expertise to cost of fault detection is another question in this goal section. The expertise level of the subjects had no relation to the fault detection rate in phases two and three ($\alpha > 0.05$ for both F-tests). Recall that phase three of the study used 32 professional subjects with all three levels of computer science expertise. In phase one, however, the intermediate subjects detected faults at a faster rate than did the junior subjects ($\alpha < 0.005$). The total effort spent in fault detection was not different among the expertise levels in any of the phases ($\alpha > 0.05$ for all three F-tests). When all 74 subjects are considered, years of professional experience correlates positively with fault detection rate ($R = 0.41$, $\alpha < 0.0002$) and correlates negatively with total detection time ($R = -0.25$, $\alpha < 0.03$). These last two observations suggest that persons with more years of professional experience detected the faults faster and spent less total time doing so. Several other subject background measures showed no relationship with fault detection rate or total detection time ($\alpha > 0.05$). Background measures were examined across all subjects and within the groups of NASA/CSC subjects and University of Maryland subjects.
5) *Dependence on Interactions:* There were few significant interactions between the main effects of testing technique, program, and expertise level. There was an interaction between testing technique and software type in terms of fault detection rate and total detection cost for the phase three data ($\alpha < 0.003$ and $\alpha < 0.007$, respectively). Subjects using code reading on the abstract data type had an increased fault detection rate and a decreased total detection time.
6) *Relationships between Fault Detection Effectiveness and Cost:* There were several correlations between fault detection cost measures and performance measures. Fault detection rate correlated overall with number of faults detected ($R = 0.48$, $\alpha < 0{,}0001$), percentage of faults detected ($R = 0.48$, $\alpha < 0.0001$), and total detection time ($R = -0.53$, $\alpha < 0.0001$), but not with normalized cpu-time, raw cpu-time, connect time, or number of computer runs ($\alpha > 0.05$). Total detection time correlated with normalized cpu-time ($R = 0.36$, $\alpha < 0.04$) and raw cpu-time ($R = 0.37$, $\alpha < 0.04$), but not with connect time, num-

ber of runs, number of faults detected, or percentage of faults detected ($\alpha > 0.05$). The number of faults detected in the programs correlated with the amount of machine resources used: normalized cpu-time ($R = 0.47$, $\alpha < 0.007$), raw cpu-time ($R = 0.52$, $\alpha < 0.002$), and connect time ($R = 0.49$, $\alpha < 0.003$), but not with the number of computer runs ($\alpha > 0.05$). The correlations for percentage of faults detected with machine resources used were similar. Although most of these correlations are weak, they suggest that 1) the higher the fault detection rate, the more faults found and the less time spent in fault detection; 2) fault detection rate had no relationship with use of machine resources; 3) spending more time in detecting faults had no relationship with the amount of faults detected; and 4) the more cpu-time and connect time used, the more faults found.

7) *Summary of Fault Detection Cost*: Summarizing the major results of the comparison of fault detection cost: 1) in the phase three data, code reading had a higher fault detection rate than the other methods, with no difference between functional testing and structural testing; 2) in the phase one and two data, the three techniques were not different in fault detection rate; 3) in the phase two and three data, total detection effort was not different among the techniques, but in phase one less effort was spent for structural testing than for the other techniques, while reading and functional were not different; 4) fault detection rate and total effort in detection depended on the type of software: the abstract data type had the highest detection rate and lowest total detection effort, the plotter and the database maintainer had the lowest detection rate and the highest total detection effort, and the text formatter was somewhere in between depending on the phase; 5) in phase three, functional testing used more cpu-time and connect time than did structural testing, but they were not different in the number of runs; 6) in phases two and three, subjects across expertise levels were not different in fault detection rate or total detection time, in phase one intermediate subjects had a higher detection rate; and 7) there was a moderate correlation between fault detection rate and years of professional experience across all subjects.

C. Characterization of Faults Detected

The third goal area focuses on determining what classes of faults are detected by the different techniques. In the earlier section on the faults in the software, the faults were characterized by two different classification schemes: omission or commission; and initialization, control, data, computation, interface, or cosmetic. The faults detected across all three study phases are broken down by the two fault classification schemes in Fig. 15. The entries in the figure are the average percentage (with standard deviation) of faults in a given class observed when a particular technique was being used. Note that when a subject tested a program that had no faults in a given class, he/she was excluded from the calculation of this average.

1) *Omission Versus Commission Classification:* When the faults are partitioned according to the omission/commission scheme, there is a distinction among

the techniques. Both code readers and functional testers observed more omission faults than did structural testers ($\alpha < 0.001$). with code readers and functional testers not being different ($\alpha > 0.05$). Since a fault of omission occurs as a result of some segment of code being left out, you would not expect structurally generated test data to find such faults. In fact, 44 percent of the subjects applying structural testing found zero faults of omission when testing a program. A distribution of the faults observed according to this classification scheme appears in Fig. 16.

2) *Six-Part Fault Classification*: When the faults are divided according to the second fault classification scheme, several differences are apparent. Both code reading and functional testing found more initialization faults than did structural testing ($\alpha < 0.05$), with code reading and functional testing not being different ($\alpha > 0.05$). Code reading detected more interface faults than did either of the other methods ($\alpha < 0.01$), with no difference between functional and structural testing ($\alpha > 0.05$). This suggests that the code reading process of abstracting and composing program functions across modules must be an effective technique for finding interface faults. Functional testing detected more control faults than did either of the other methods ($\alpha < 0.01$), with code reading and structural testing not being different ($\alpha > 0.05$). Recall that the structural test data generation criteria examined is based on determining the execution paths in a program and deriving test data that execute 100 percent of the program's statements. One would expect that more control path faults would be found by such a technique. However, structural testing did not do as well as functional testing in this fault class. The technique of code reading found more computation faults than did structural testing ($\alpha < 0.05$), with functional testing not being different from either of the other two methods ($\alpha > 0.05$). The three techniques were not statistically different in the percentage of faults they detected in either the data or cosmetic fault classes ($\alpha > 0.05$ for both). A distribution of the faults observed according to this classification scheme appears in Fig. 17.

3) *Observable Fault Classification:* Fig. 18 displays the average percentage (with standard deviation) of faults from each class that were observable from the test data submitted, yet were not reported by the tester[7]. The two on-line techniques of functional and structural testing were not different in any of the faults classes ($\alpha > 0.05$). Note that there was only one fault in the cosmetic class.

4) *Summary of Characterization of Faults Detected:* Summarizing the major results of the comparison of classes of faults detected: 1) code reading and functional testing both detected more omission faults and initialization faults than did structural testing; 2) code reading detected more interface faults than did the other methods; 3) functional testing detected more control faults than did the other methods; 4) code reading detected more computation faults than did

[7] The standard deviations presented in the figure are high because of the several instances in which all observable faults were reported.

structural testing; and 5) the on-line techniques of functional and structural testing were not different in any classes of faults observable but not reported.

	Code Reading	Functional Testing	Structural Testing	Overall
Omission	55.6 (40.1)	61.0 (39.5)	39.2 (41.6)	52.0 (41.3)
Commission	54.3 (32.1)	53.5 (25.4)	44.3 (26.8)	50.7 (28.4)
Total	54.1 (29.2)	54.6 (24.5)	41.2 (26.1)	50.0 (27.3)
Initial.	64.6 (40.3)	75.0 (36.1)	46.2 (39.8)	61.5 (40.2)
Control	42.8 (36.6)	66.7 (34.9)	48.8 (36.5)	52.8 (37.2)
Data	20.7 (36.6)	28.3 (44.9)	26.8 (41.9)	25.3 (41.0)
Computat.	70.9 (37.0)	64.2 (40.8)	58.8 (43.5)	64.6 (40.6)
Interface	46.7 (38.5)	30.7 (33.5)	24.6 (29.4)	34.1 (35.1)
Cosmetic	16.7 (38.1)	8.3 (28.2)	7.7 (27.2)	10.8 (31.3)
Total	54.1 (29.2)	54.6 (24.5)	41.2 (26.1)	50.0 (27.3)

Fig. 15. Characterization of the faults detected. Mean (and std. dev.) of the percentage of faults in each class that were detected.

	Reading	Functional	Structural
100%			
	O	OxO	
	xxxx	Oxxx	Ox
	Oxxx		x
	O	x	x
75%	x	xOxxx	x
	xO	x	O
	xxx	xx	xxx
	xx		xx
		x	x
50%		Oxx	
		xxxO	xOxxx
	Ox		x
	x		Ox.
		xx	x
25%	Oxx		xxx
	xxxx		xO
	O		O
		xOOxO	OxOO
0%	xOOxO	xOx	Oxx

Fig. 16. Characterization of faults detected by the three techniques: 10 omissions (0) versus 24 commission (x). The vertical axis is the percentage of persons using the particular technique that detected the fault.

	Reading	Functional	Structural
100%			
	P	PIP	
	PIII	PIIC	PC
	CIII		I
	P	A	P
75%	C	ACPPC	C
	AP	C	P
	AIP	CC	PCP
	CC		PC
		D	A
50%		CPI	
		IIII	DPIII
	CP		A
	D	.	CI
		PI	I
25%	DCI		IIC
	SPII		II
	I		D
		SIPID	CSDI
0%	CPIID	IDI	PII

Fig. 17. Characterization of faults detected by the three techniques. Initialization (2-A). computation (8-P), control (7-C), data (3-D), interface (13-I). and cosmetic (1-S). The vertical axis is the percentage of the persons using the particular technique that detected the fault.

	Functional Testing	Structural Testing	Overall
Omission	15.7 (25.4)	21.3 (31.8)	18.5 (28.8)
Commission	19.1 (20.0)	20.1 (16.6)	19.6 (18.3)
Total	18.1 (17.8)	19.9 (16.8)	19.0 (17.3)
Initial.	5.0 (15.4)	14.3 (32.2)	9.8 (25.5)
Control	20.3 (30.6)	21.1 (31.4)	20.7 (30.8)
Data	28.6 (43.5)	7.5 (24.5)	18.3 (36.7)
Computat.	16.0 (31.3)	20.1 (37.6)	18.0 (34.5)
Interface	16.1 (20.0)	20.3 (21.5)	18.2 (20.8)
Cosmetic	60.0 (50.3)	85.7 (35.9)	73.2 (44.9)
Total	18.1 (17.8)	19.9 (16.8)	19.0 (17.3)

Fig. 18. Characterization of the faults observable but not reported. The mean (and std. dev.) of the percentage of such faults in each class are given. (With the appropriate inputs, all faults could be made observable in the program output. The faults included here are those that were observable given the program inputs selected by the testers yet were unreported.)

V. Conclusions

This study compares the strategies of code reading by stepwise abstraction, functional testing using equivalence class partitioning and boundary value analysis, and structural testing using 100 percent statement coverage. The study evaluates the techniques across three data sets in three different aspects of software testing: fault detection effectiveness, fault detection cost, and classes of faults detected. The three data sets involved a total of 74 programmers applying each of the three testing techniques on unit-sized software; therefore, the analysis and results presented were based on observations from a total of 222 testing sessions. The investigation is intended to compare the different testing strategies in representative testing situations, using programmers with a wide range of experience, different software types, and common software faults.

In this controlled study, an experimentation methodology was applied to compare the effectiveness of three testing techniques; for an overview of the experimentation methodology, see [4]. Based on our experience and observation [56], the three testing techniques represent the high end of the range of testing methods that are actually being used by developers to test software. The techniques examined correspond, therefore, to the state-of-the-practice of software testing rather than the state-of-the-art. As mentioned earlier, there exist alternate forms for each of the three testing methods.

There are several perspectives from which to view empirical studies of software development techniques. Three example perspectives given were that of the experimenter, researcher, and practitioner. One key aspect of the study presented, especially from an experimenter's perspective, was the use of an experimentation methodology and a formal statistical design. The actual empirical results from the study, which are summarized below, may be used to refine a researcher's theories about software testing or to guide a practitioner's application of the techniques.

Each of the three testing techniques showed some merit in this evaluation. The major empirical results of this study are the following. 1) With the professional programmers, code reading detected more software faults and had a higher fault detection rate than did functional or structural testing, while functional testing detected more faults than did structural testing, but functional and structural testing were not different in fault detection rate. 2) In one University of Maryland (UoM) subject group, code reading and functional testing were not different in faults found, but were both superior to structural testing, while in the other UoM subject group there was no difference among the techniques. 3) With the UoM subjects, the three techniques were not different in fault detection rate. 4) Number of faults observed, fault detection rate, and total effort in detection depended on the type of software tested. 5) Code reading detected more interface faults than did the other methods. 6) Functional testing detected more control faults than did the other methods. 7) When asked to estimate the percentage of faults detected, code readers gave the most accurate estimates while functional testers gave the least accurate estimates.

The results suggest that code reading by stepwise abstraction (a nonexecution-based method) is at least as effective as on-line functional and structural testing in terms of number and cost of faults observed. They also suggest the inadequacy of using 100 percent statement coverage criteria for structural testing. Note that the professional programmers examined preferred the use of functional testing because they felt is was the most effective technique; their intuition, however, turned out to be incorrect. Recall that the code reading was performed on uncommented programs, which could be considered a worst-case scenario for code reading.

In comparing the results to related studies, there are mixed conclusions. A prototype analysis done at the University of Maryland in the Fall of 1981 [30] supported the belief that code reading by stepwise abstraction does as well as the computer-based methods, with each strategy having its own advantages. In the Myers experiment [41], the three techniques compared (functional testing, 3-person code reviews, control group) were equally effective. He also calculated that code reviews were less cost effective than the computer-based testing approaches. The first observation is supported in one study phase here, but the other observation is not. A study conducted by Hetzel [23] compared functional testing, code reading, and "selective" testing (a composite of functional, structural, and reading techniques). He observed that functional and "selective" testing were equally effective, with code reading being inferior. As noted earlier, this is not supported by this analysis. The study described in this analysis examined the technique of code reading by stepwise abstraction, while both the Myers and Hetzel studies examined alternate approaches to off-line (nonexecution-based) review/reading. Other studies that have compared the effectiveness of software testing strategies include [22], [32], [21], [20], [24], [8], [26], [28], [55], [38], [45], [17].

A few remarks are appropriate about the comparison of the cost-effectiveness and phase-availability of these testing techniques. When examining the effort associated with a technique, both fault detection and fault isolation costs should be compared. The code readers have both detected and isolated a fault; they located it in the source code. Thus, the reading process condenses fault detection and isolation into one activity. Functional and structural testers have only detected a fault; they need to delve into the source code and expend additional effort in order to isolate the fault. Moreover, the code reading process corresponds more closely to the activity of program proving than do the other methods. Also, a non execution-based reading process can be applied to any document produced during the development process (e.g., high-level design document, low-level design document, source code document). While functional and structural execution-based techniques may only be applied to documents that are executable (e.g., source code), which are usually available later in the development process.

Investigations related to this work include studies of fault classification [54], [34], [44], [1] and Cleanroom software development [50]. In the Cleanroom software development approach, techniques such as code reading are used in the development of software completely offline (i.e., without program execution). In [50], systems developed using Cleanroom met system requirements more completely and had a higher percentage of successful operational test cases than did systems developed with a more traditional approach.

The work presented in this paper differs from previous studies in several ways. 1) The non execution-based software review technique used was code reading by stepwise abstraction. 2) The study was based on programmers — including professionals — having varying expertise, different software types, and programs having a representative profile of common software faults. 3) A very sensitive statistical design was employed to account for differences in individual performance and interactions among testing technique, software type, and subject expertise level. 4) The study was conducted in multiple phases in order to refine experimentation methods. 5) The scope of issues examined was broadened (e.g., observed versus observable faults, structural coverage of functional testing, multiple fault classification schemes).

The empirical study presented is intended to advance the understanding of how various software testing strategies contribute to the software development process and to one another. The results given were calculated from a set of individuals applying the three techniques to unit-sized programs—the direct extrapolation of the findings to other testing environments is not implied. Further work applying these and other results to devise effective testing environments is underway [49].

Appendix

The Specifications for the Programs

Program 1[8]

Given an input text of up to 80 characters consisting of words separated by blanks or new-line characters, the program formats it into a line-by-line form such that 1) each output line has a maximum of 30 characters, 2) a word in the input text is placed on a single output line, and 3) each output line is filled with as many words as possible.

The input text is a stream of characters, where the characters are categorized as either break or nonbreak characters. A break character is a blank, a new-line character (&), or an end-of-text character (/). New-line characters have no special significance; they are treated as blanks by the program. The characters & and / should not appear in the output.

A word is defined is a nonempty sequence of nonbreak characters. A break is a sequence of one or more break characters and is reduced to a single blank character or start of a new line in the output.

When the program is invoked, the user types the input line, followed by a / (end-of-text) and a carriage return. The program then echoes the text input and formats it on the terminal.

[8] Note that this specification was rewritten in [37].

If the input text contains a word that is too long to fit on a single output line, an error message is typed and the program terminates. If the end-of-text character is missing, an error message is issued and the program awaits the input of properly terminated line of text.

Program 2

Given ordered pairs (x, y) of either positive or negative integers as input, the program plots them on a grid with a horizontal *x*-axis and a vertical *y*-axis which are appropriately labeled. A plotted point on the grid should appear as an asterisk (*).

The vertical and horizontal scaling is handled as follows. If the maximum absolute value of any *y*-value is less than or equal to 20, the scale for vertical spacing will be one line per integral unit [e.g., the point (3, 6) should be plotted on the sixth line, two lines above the point (3, 4)]. Note that the origin [point (0, 0)] would correspond to an asterisk at the intersection of the axes (the *x*-axis is referred to as the 0th line). If the maximum absolute value of any *x*-value is less than or equal to 30, the scale for horizontal spacing will be one space per integral unit [e.g., the point (4, 5) should be plotted four spaces to the right of the *y*-axis, two spaces to the right of (2, 5)]. However, if the maximum absolute value of any *y*-value is greater than 20, the scale for vertical spacing will be one line per every (max absolute value of *y*-values)/20 rounded-up. [e.g., If the maximum absolute value of any *y*-value to be plotted is 66, the vertical line spacing will be a line for every 4 integral units. In such a data set, points with *y*-values greater than or equal to eight and less than twelve will show up as asterisks in the second line, points with *y*-values greater than or equal to twelve and less than sixteen will show up as asterisks in the third line, etc. Continuing the example, the point (3, 15) should be plotted on the third line, two lines above the point (3, 5).] Horizontal scaling is handled analogously.

If two or more of the points to be plotted would show up as the same asterisk in the grid (like the points (9, 13) and (9, 15) in the above example), a number "2" (or whatever number is appropriate) should be printed instead of the asterisk. Points whose asterisks will lie on an axis or grid marker should show up in place of the marker.

Program 3

A list is defined to be an ordered collection of integer elements which may have elements annexed and deleted at either end, but not in the middle. The operations that need to be available are ADDFIRST, ADDLAST, DELETEFIRST, DELETELAST, FIRST, ISEMPTY, LISTLENGTH, REVERSE, and NEWLIST. Each operation is described in detail below. The lists are to contain up to a maximum of 5 elements. If an element is added to the front of a "full" list (one containing five elements already), the element at the back of the list is to be discarded. Elements to be added to the back of a full list are discarded. Requests to delete elements from empty lists result in an empty list, and requests for the first element of an empty list results in the integer 0 being returned. The detailed operation descriptions are as below:

ADDFIRST(LIST L, INTEGER I)
    Returns the list L with I as its first element followed by all the elements of L. If L is "full" to begin with, L's last element is lost.

ADDLAST(LIST L, INTEGER I)
    Returns the list with all of the elements of L followed by I. If L is full to begin with, L is returned (i.e., I is ignored).

DELETEFIRST(LIST L)
    Returns the list containing all but the first element of L. If L is empty, then an empty list is returned.

DELETELAST(LIST L)
    Returns the list containing all but the last element of L. If L is empty, then an empty list is returned.

FIRST(LIST L)
    Returns the first element in L. If L is empty, then it returns zero.

ISEMPTY(LIST L)
    Returns one if L is empty, zero otherwise.

LISTLENGTH(LIST L)
    Returns the number of elements in L. An empty list has zero elements.

NEWLIST(LIST L)
    Returns an empty list.

REVERSE(LIST L)
    Returns a list containing the elements of L in reverse order.

Program 4

(Note that a "file" is the same thing as an IBM "dataset.")

The program maintains a database of bibliographic references. It first reads a master file of current references, then reads a file of reference updates, merges the two, and produces an updated master file and a cross reference table of keywords. The first input file, the master, contains records of 74 characters with the following format:

Column	comment
1-3	Each reference has a unique reference key
4-14	Author of publication
15-72	Title of publication
73-74	Year issued

The key should be a three character unique identifier consisting of letters between A-Z. The next input file, the update file, contains records of 75 characters in length. The only difference from a master file record is that an update record has either an "A" (capital A meaning add) or an "R" (capital R meaning replace) in column 75. Both the master and update files are expected to be already sorted alphabetically by reference key when read into the program. Update records with action replace are substituted for the matching key record in the master file. Records with action add are added to the master file at the appropriate location so that the file remains sorted on the key field. For example, a valid update record to be read would be

BITbaker an introduction to program testing 83A

The program should produce two pieces of output. It should first print the sorted list of records in the updated master file in the same format as the original master file. It should then print a keyword cross reference list. All words greater than three characters in a publication's title are keywords. These keywords are listed alphabetically followed by the key fields from the applicable updated master file entries. For example, if the updated master file contained two records,

ABCkermit introduction to software testing 82
DDXjones the realities of software management 81

then the keywords are introduction, testing, realities, software, and management. The cross reference list should look like

introduction
ABC
management
DDX
realities
DDX
software
ABC
DDX
testing
ABC

Some possible error conditions that could arise and the subsequent actions include the following. The master and update files should be checked for sequence, and if a record out of sequence is found, a message similar to "key ABC out of sequence" should appear and the record should be discarded. If an update record indicates replace and the matching key can not be found, a message similar to "update key ABC not found" should appear and the update record should be ignored. If an update record indicates add and a matching key is found, something like "key ABC already in file" should appear and the record should be ignored. (End of specification.)

Acknowledgment

The authors are grateful to F. T. Baker, F. E. McGarry, and G. Page for their assistance in the organization of the study. The authors appreciate the comments from J. D. Gannon, H. D. Mills, and R. N. Taylor on an earlier version of this paper. The authors are grateful to the subjects from Computer Sciences Corporation,

NASA Goddard, and the University of Maryland for their enthusiastic participation in the study.

References

[1] V. R. Basili and B. T. Perricone, "Software errors and complexity: An empirical investigation," *Commun. ACM,* vol. 27, no. 1, pp. 42-52, Jan. 1984.
[2] V. R. Basili and R. W. Selby, "Data collection and analysis in software research and management," in *Proc. Amer. Statist. Ass. and Biometric Soc. Joint Statistical Meetings,* Philadelphia, PA, Aug. 13-16, 1984.
[3] — "Comparing the effectiveness of software testing strategies," Dep. Comput. Sci., Univ. Maryland, College Park, Tech. Rep. TR-1501, May 1985.
[4] V. R. Basili, R. W. Selby, and D. H. Hutchens, "Experimentation in software engineering," *IEEE Trans. Software Eng.,* vol. SE-12, no. 7, pp. 733-743, July 1986.
[5] V. R. Basili and A. J. Turner, *SIMPL-T: A Structured Programming Language.* Paladin House, 1976.
[6] V. R. Basili and D. M. Weiss, "A methodology for collecting valid software engineering data," *IEEE Trans. Software Eng.,* vol. SE-10, no. 6, pp. 728-738, Nov. 1984.
[7] G. E. P. Box. W. G. Hunter, and J. S. Hunter, *Statistics for Experimenters.* New York: Wiley, 1978.
[8] T. A. Budd, R. J. Lipton, F. G. Sayward, and R. DeMillo, "The design of a prototype mutation system for program testing," *Proc. AFIPS Conf.,* vol. 47, pp. 623-627, 1978.
[9] R. Cailliau and F. Rubin, "ACM forum: On a controlled experiment in program testing," *Commun. ACM,* vol. 22, pp. 687-688, Dec. 1979.
[10] L. A. Clarke, Program Chair, *Proc. Workshop Software Testing,* Banff, Alta., Canada, July 15-17, 1986.
[11] V. Church, "Benchmark statistics for the VAX 11/780 and the IBM 4341," Computer Sciences Corporation, Silver Spring, MD, Internal Memo, 1984.
[12] W. G. Cochran and G. M. Cox. *Experimental Designs.* New York: Wiley, 1950.
[13] J. C. Deprie, "Report from the IFIP Working Group on Terminology," in *Proc. 15th Annu. Int. Symp. Fault Tolerant Computing,* University of Michigan, Ann Arbor, MI, June 19-21, 1985.
[14] M. E. Fagan, "Design and code inspections to reduce errors in program development," *IBM Sys. J.,* vol. 15, no. 3, pp. 182-211, 1976.
[15] K. A. Foster, "Error sensitive test cases," *IEEE Trans. Software Eng.,* vol. SE-6, no. 3, pp. 258-264, 1980.
[16] P. G. Frankl and E. J. Weyuker, "Data flow testing in the presence of unexecutable paths," in *Proc. Workshop Software Testing,* Banff, Alta., Canada, July 15-17, 1986, pp. 4-13.
[17] M. R. Girgis and M. R. Woodward. "An experimental comparison of the error exposing ability of program testing criteria," in *Proc. Workshop Software Testing,* Banff, Alta., Canada, July 15-17, 1986, pp. 64-73.
[18] S. A. Gloss-Soler, 'The DACS glossary: A bibliography of software engineering terms. Data & Analysis Center for Software," Griffiss Air Force Base. NY, Rep. GLOS-1, Oct. 1979.
[19] J. B. Goodenough and S. L. Gerhart, "Toward a theory of test data selection," *IEEE Trans. Software Eng.,* vol. SE-1, pp. 156-173, June 1975.

{20] J. D. Gould, "Some psychological evidence on how people debug computer programs," *Int. J. Man-Machine Studies,* vol. 7, pp. 151-182, 1975.
[21] J. D. Gould and P. Drongowski, "An exploratory study of computer program debugging," *Human Factors,* vol. 16, no. 3, pp. 258-277, 1974.
[23] W. C. Hetzel, "An experimental analysis of program verification problem solving capabilities as they relate to programmer efficiency," *Comput. Personnel,* vol. 3, no. 3, pp. 10-15. 1972.
[23] W. C. Hetzel, "An experimental analysis of program verification methods," Ph.D. dissertation, Univ. North Carolina, Chapel Hill, 1976.
[24] W. E. Howden, "Symbolic testing and the DISSECT symbolic evaluation system," *IEEE Trans. Software Eng.,* vol. SE-3, no. 4, pp. 266-278,1977.
[25] — "Algebraic program testing," *Acta Inform.,* vol. 10, 1978.
[26] — "An evaluation of the effectiveness of symbolic testing," *Software—Practice and Experience,* vol. 8, pp. 381-397, 1978.
[27] — "Functional program testing," *IEEE Trans. Software Eng., vol.* SE-6, pp. 162-169, Mar. 1980.
[28] — "Applicability of software validation techniques to scientific programs," *ACM Trans. Program. Lang. Syst.,* vol. 2, no. 3, pp. 307-320, July 1980
[29] — "A survey of dynamic analysis methods," in *Tutorial: Software Testing & Validation Techniques,* 2nd ed., E. Miller and W. E. Howden, Eds. Washington. DC: IEEE Computer Society Press, 1981, pp. 209-231.
[30] S-S. V. Hwang, "An empirical study in functional testing, structural testing, and code reading inspection*," Dep. Comput. Sci., Univ. Maryland, College Park. Scholarly Paper 362, Dec. 1981.
[31] *IEEE Standard Glossary of Software Engineering Terminology,* IEEE, New York, Rep. IEEE-STD-729-I983, 1983.
[32] Z. Jelinski and P. B. Moranda, "Applications of a probability-based model to a code reading experiment," in *Proc. IEEE Symp. Computer Software Reliability,* New York, 1973, pp. 78-81.
[33] K. Jensen and N. Wirth. *Pascal User Manual and Report,* 2nd ed. New York: Springer Verlag. 1974.
[34] W. L. Johnson. S. Draper, and E. Soloway, "An effective bug classification scheme must take the programmer into account," in *Proc. Workshop High-Level Debugging,* Palo Alto, CA, 1983.
[35] R. C. Linger, H. D. Mills, and B. I. Witt, *Structured Programming: Theory and Practice.* Reading, MA: Addison-Wesley, 1979.
[36] P. R. McMullin and J. D. Gannon, "Evaluating a data abstraction testing system based on formal specifications," Dep. Comput. Sci., Univ. Maryland, College Park, Tech. Rep. TR-993, Dec. 1980.
[37] B. Meyer, "On formalism in specifications," *IEEE Software,* vol. 2, pp. 6-26, Jan. 1985.
[38] E. Miller and W. E. Howden, *Tutorial: Software Testing & Validation Techniques,* 2nd ed., IEEE Catalog No. EHO 180-0. Washington. D.C: IEEE Computer Society Press, 1981.
[39] H. D. Mills. "Mathematical foundations for structural programming." IBM Rep. FSL 72-6021, 1972.
[40] — "How to write correct programs and know it," in *Proc. Int. Conf. Reliable Software,* Los Angeles, CA, 1975, pp. 363-370.
|41] G. J. Myers, "A controlled experiment in program testing and code walkthroughs inspections," *Commun. ACM,* pp. 760-768, Sept. 1978.
[42] —, *The Art of Software Testing*, New York: Wiley, 1979.

[43] P. Naur, "Programming by action clusters," *BIT*, vol. 9, no. 3, pp. 250-258, 1969.
[44] T. J. Ostrand and E. J. Weyuker, "Collecting and categorizing software error data in an industrial environment*," *J. Syst. Software*, vol. 4, pp. 289-300, 1984.
[45] D. J. Panzl, "Experience with automatic program testing," in *Proc. NBS Trends and Applications*, Nat. Bureau Standards, Gaithersburg, MD, May 28, 1981, pp. 25-28.
[46] H. Scheffe, *The Analysis of Variance*. New York: Wiley, 1959.
[47] R. W. Selby, "An empirical study comparing software testing techniques," in *Proc. Sixth Minnowbrook Workshop Software Performance Evaluation*, Blue Mountain Lake, NY, July 19-22, 1983.
[48] — "Evaluations of software technologies: Testing, CLEANROOM, and metrics," Ph.D. dissertation, Dep. Comput. Sci. Univ. Maryland, College Park, Tech. Rep. TR-1500, 1985.
[49] — "Combining software testing strategies: An empirical evaluation," in *Proc. Workshop Software Testing*, Banff, Alba., Canada, July 15-17, 1986, pp. 82-91.
[50] R. W. Selby, V. R. Basili, and F. T. Baker, "Cleanroom software development: An empirical evaluation," *IEEE Trans. Software Eng.*, vol. SE-13, pp. 1027-1037, Sept. 1987.
[51] R. W. Selby, V. R. Basili, J. Page, and F. E. Mc Garry, "Evaluating software testing strategies," in *Proc. Ninth Annu. Software Eng. Workshop*, NASA/GSFC, Greenbelt, MD, Nov. 1984.
[52] L. G. Stucki, "New directions in automated tools for improving software quality," in *Current Trends in Programming Methodology*, R. T. Yeh, Ed. Englewood Cliffs, NJ: Prentice Hall, 1977.
[53] P. M. Valdes and A. L. Goel, "An error-specific approach to testing," in *Proc. 8th Annu. Software Eng. Workshop*, NASA/GSFC, Greenbelt, MD, Nov. 1983.
[54] D. M. Weiss and V. R. Basili, "Evaluating software development by analysis of changes: Some data from the software engineering laboratory," *IEEE Trans. Software Eng.*, vol. SE-11, no. 2, pp. 157-168, Feb. 1985.
[55] M. R. Woodward, D. Hedley, and M. A. Henncll. "Experience with path analysis and testing of programs," *IEEE Trans. Software Eng.*, vol. SE-6, no. 3, pp. 278-286, May 1980.
[56] M. V. Zelkowitz, R. T. Yeh, R. G. Hamlet, J. D. Gannon, and V. R. Basili, "Software engineering practices in the US and Japan," *Computer*, vol. 17, no. 6, pp. 57-66, June 1984.

Cleanroom Software Development: An Empirical Evaluation

Richard W. Selby, Victor R. Basili and F. Terry Baker

Abstract. The Cleanroom software development approach is intended to produce highly reliable software by integrating formal methods for specification and design, nonexecution-based program development, and statistically based independent testing. In an empirical study, 15 three-person teams developed versions of the same software system (800-2300 source lines); ten teams applied Cleanroom, while five applied a more traditional approach. This analysis characterizes the effect of Cleanroom on the delivered product, the software development process, and the developers.

The major results of this study are the following. 1) Most of the developers were able to apply the techniques of Cleanroom effectively (six of the ten Cleanroom teams delivered at least 91 percent of the required system functions). 2) The Cleanroom teams' products met system requirements more completely and had a higher percentage of successful operationally generated test cases. 3) The source code developed using Cleanroom had more comments and less dense control-flow complexity. 4) The more successful Cleanroom developers modified their use of the implementation language; they used more procedure calls and IF statements, used fewer CASE and WHILE statements, and had a lower frequency of variable reuse (average number of occurrences per variable). 5) All ten Cleanroom teams made all of their scheduled intermediate product deliveries, while only two of the five non-Cleanroom teams did. 6) Although 86 percent of the Cleanroom developers indicated that they missed the satisfaction of program execution to some extent, this had no relation to the product quality measures of implementation completeness and successful operational tests. 7) Eighty-one percent of the Cleanroom developers said that they would use the approach again.

Key Words: Empirical study, methodology evaluation, off-line software review, software development methodology, software management, software measurement, software testing.

Manuscript received February 28, 1985; revised May 30, 1986. This work was supported in part by the Air Force Office of Scientific Research under Contract AFOSR-F49620-80-C-001 to the University of Maryland and the University of California Faculty Research Fellowship Program. Computer support was provided in part by the Computer Science Center at the University of Maryland.
R. W. Selby, Member, IEEE, is with the Department of Information and Computer Science. University of California, Irvine, CA 92717.
V. R. Basili, Senior Member, IEEE, and F. T. Baker are with the Department of Computer Science, University of Maryland, College Park, MD 20742.

I. Introduction

The need for discipline in the software development process and for high quality software motivates the Cleanroom software development approach. In addition to improving the control during development, this approach is intended to deliver a product that meets several quality aspects: a system that conforms with the requirements, a system with high operational reliability, and source code that is easily readable.

Section II describes the Cleanroom approach and Section III presents a framework of goals for characterizing its effect. Section IV describes an empirical study using the approach. Section V gives the results of the analysis comparing projects developed using Cleanroom with those of a control group. The overall conclusions appear in Section VI.

II. Cleanroom Development

The following sections describe the Cleanroom software development approach, discuss its introduction to an environment, describe the relationship of Cleanroom to software prototyping, and explain the role of software tools in Cleanroom development.

A. Cleanroom Software Development

The IBM Federal Systems Division (FSD) [23], [19], [24], [21], [16] presents the Cleanroom software development method as a technical and organizational approach to developing software with certifiable reliability. The idea is to deny the entry of defects during the development of software, hence the term "Cleanroom." The focus of the method, which is an extension of the FSD software engineering program [22], is imposing discipline on the development process by integrating formal methods for specification and design, nonexecution-based program development, and statistically based independent testing. These components are intended to contribute to a software product that has a high probability of zero defects and consequently a high measure of operational reliability.

1. *Software Life Cycle of Executable Increments*: In the Cleanroom approach, software development is organized around the incremental development of the software product [16]. Instead of considering software design, implementation, and testing as sequential stages in a software life cycle, software development is considered as a sequence of executable product increments. The increments accumulate over the development life cycle and result in a final product with full functionality.
2. *Formal Methods for Specification and Design:* In order to support the life cycle of executable increments, Cleanroom developers utilize "structured specifications" to divide the product functionality into deeply nested subsets that

can be developed incrementally. The mathematically based design methodology in Cleanroom [22] incorporates the use of both structured specifications and state machine models [26]. A systems engineer introduces the structured specifications to restate the system requirements precisely and organize the complex problems into manageable parts [41]. The specifications determine the "system architecture" of the interconnections and groupings of capabilities to which state machine design practices can be applied. System implementation and test data formulation can then proceed from the structured specifications independently.

3. *Development without Program Execution*: The right-the-first-time programming methods used in Cleanroom are the ideas of functionally based programming in [38], [32]. The testing process is completely separated from the development process by not allowing the developers to test and debug their programs. The developers focus on the techniques of code reading by stepwise abstraction [32], code inspections [25], group walkthroughs [40], and formal verification [29], [32], [44], [20] to assert the correctness of their implementation. These non-execution-based methods are referred to as "off-line software review techniques" in this paper. These constructive techniques apply throughout all phases of development, and condense the activities of defect detection and isolation into one operation. Empirical evaluations have suggested that the software review method of code reading by stepwise abstraction is at least as effective in detecting faults as execution-based methods [7], [43]. The intention in Cleanroom is to impose discipline on software development so that system correctness results from a coherent, readable design rather than from a reliance on execution-based testing. The notion that "Well, the software should always be tested to find the faults" is eliminated.
4. *Statistically Based, Independent Testing:* In the statistically based testing strategy of Cleanroom, independent testers simulate the operational environment of the system with random testing. This testing process includes defining the frequency distribution of inputs to the system, the frequency distribution of different system states, and the expanding range of developed system capabilities. Test cases then are chosen randomly and presented to the series of product increments, while concentrating on functions most recently delivered and maintaining the overall composite distribution of inputs. The independent testers then record observed failures and determine an objective measure of product reliability. Since software errors tend to vary widely in how frequently they are manifested as failures [1], operational testing is especially useful to assess the impact of software errors on product reliability. In addition to the statistical testing approach, the independent testers submit a limited number of test cases to ensure correct system operation for situations in which a software failure would be catastrophic. It is believed that the prior knowledge that a system will be evaluated by random testing will affect system reliability by enforcing a new discipline into the system developers.

The independent testing group operationally tests the software product increments from a perspective of reliability assessment, rather than a perspective of error detection. The responsibility of the test group is, therefore, to certify the reliability of the increments and final product rather than assist the development group in getting the product to an acceptable level of quality. One approach for measuring the reliability of the increments is through the use of a projected mean-time-between-failure (MTBF). MTBF estimations, based on user representative testing, provide both development managers and users with a useful, readily interpretable product reliability measure. Statistical models for calculating MTBF's projections include [34], [39], [33], [45], [15], [27], [16].

B. Introducing Cleanroom into a Development Environment

Before introducing the Cleanroom methodology into a software production environment, the developers need to be educated in the supporting technology areas. The technology areas consist of the development techniques and methods outlined in the above sections describing the components of Cleanroom. Potential Cleanroom users should also understand the goals of the development approach and be motivated to deliver high quality software products. One fundamental aspect of motivating the developers is to convince them that they can incorporate error prevention into the software process and actually produce error-free software. This "error-free perspective" is a departure from a current view that software errors are always present and error detection is the critical consideration.

C. Cleanroom versus Prototyping

The Cleanroom methodology and software prototyping are not mutually exclusive methods for developing software—the two approaches may be used together. The starting point for Cleanroom development is a document that states the user requirements. The production of that requirement document is an important portion of the software development process. Software prototyping is one approach that may be used to determine or refine the user requirements, and hence, produce the system requirements document [31], [47]. After the production of the requirements document, the prototype would be discarded and the Cleanroom methodology could be applied.

D. Tool Use in Cleanroom

Since Cleanroom developers do not execute their source code, does that mean that Cleanroom prohibits the use of tools during development? No—software tools can play an important role in the Cleanroom development approach. Various software tools can be used to help construct and manipulate the system design and source code. These tools can also be used to detect several types of errors that commonly occur in the system design and source code. The use of such tools facilitates the process of reviewing the system design and source code prior to submission for testing by the independent group. Some of the tools that may assist Cleanroom developers include various static analyzers, data flow analyzers, syntax checkers, type checkers, formal verification checkers, concurrency analyzers, and modeling tools.

III. Investigation Goals

Some intriguing aspects of the Cleanroom approach include 1) development without testing and debugging of programs, 2) independent program testing for quality assurance (rather than to find faults or to prove "correctness" [30]), and 3) certification of system reliability before product delivery. In order to understand the effects of using Cleanroom, we proposed the following three goals: 1) characterize the effect of Cleanroom on the delivered product, 2) characterize the effect of Cleanroom on the software development process, and 3) characterize the effect of Cleanroom on the developers. An application of the goal/question/metric paradigm [6], [10] lead to the framework of goals and questions for this study which appears in Fig. 1. The empirical study executed to pursue these goals is described in the following section.

IV. Empirical Study Using Cleanroom

This section describes an empirical study comparing team projects developed using Cleanroom with those using a more conventional approach.

A. Subjects

Subjects for the empirical study came from the "Software Design and Development" course taught by F. T. Baker and V. R. Basili at the University of Maryland in the Falls of 1982 and 1983. The initial segment of the course was devoted to the presentation of several software development methodologies, including top-down design, modular specification and design, PDL, chief programmer teams, program correctness, code reading, walkthroughs, and functional and structural testing strategies. For the latter part of the course, the individuals were divided into three-person chief programmer teams for a group project [2], [37], [3]. We attempted to divide the teams equally according to professional experience, academic performance, and implementation language experience. The subjects had an average of 1.6 years professional experience and were university computer science students with graduate, senior, or junior standing. The subjects' professional experience predominantly came from government organizations and private software contractors in the Washington, DC area. Fig. 2 displays the distribution of the subjects' professional experience.

B. Project Developed

A requirements document for an electronic message system (read, send, mailing lists, authorized capabilities, etc.) was distributed to each of the teams. The project was to be completed in six weeks and was expected to be about 1500 lines of

Simpl-T[1] source code [9]. The development machine was a Univac 1100/82 running EXEC VIII, with 1200 baud interactive and remote access available.

I. Characterize the effect of Cleanroom on the delivered product.
  A. For intermediate and novice programmers building a small system, what were the operational properties of the product?
    1. Did the product meet the system requirements?
    2. How did the operational testing results compare with those of a control group?
  B. What were the static properties of the product?
    1. Were the size properties of the product any different from what would be observed in a traditional development?
    2. Were the readability properties of the product any different?
    3. Was the control complexity any different?
    4. Was the data usage any different?
    5. Was the implementation language used differently?
  C. What contribution did programmer background have on the final product quality?

II. Characterize the effect of Cleanroom on the software development process.
  A. For intermediate and novice programmers building a small system, what techniques were used to prepare the developing system for testing submissions?
  B. What role did the computer play in development?
  C. Did the developers meet their delivery schedule?

III. Characterize the effect of Cleanroom on the developers.
  A. When intermediate and novice programmers built a small system, did the developers miss the satisfaction of executing their own programs?
    1. Did the missing of program execution have any relationship to programmer background or to aspects of the delivered product?
  B. How was the design and coding style of the developers affected by not being able to test and debug?
  C. Would the developers use Cleanroom again?

Fig. 1. Framework of goals and questions for Cleanroom development approach analysis.

C. Cleanroom Development Approach versus Traditional Approach

The ten teams in the Fall 1982 course applied the Cleanroom software development approach, while the five teams in the Fall 1983 course served as a control group (non-Cleanroom). All other aspects of the developments were the same. The

[1]Simpl-T is a structured language that supports several string and file handling primitives, in addition to the usual control flow constructs available, for example, in Pascal. If Pascal or Fortran had been chosen, it would have been very likely that some individuals would have had extensive experience with the language, and this would have biased the comparison. Also, restricting access to a compiler that produced executable code would have been very difficult.

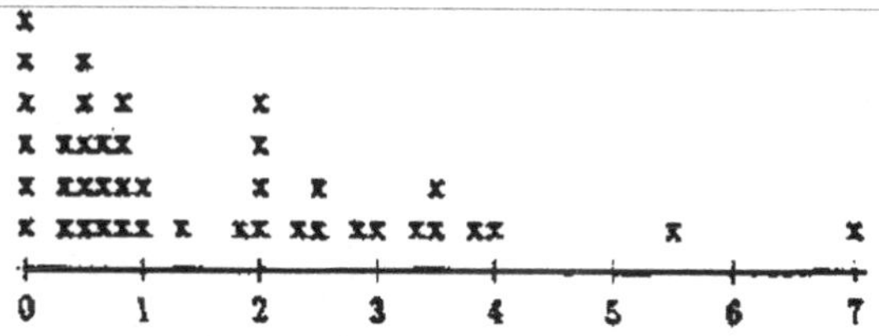

Fig. 2. Subjects' professional experience in years.

two groups of teams were not statistically different in terms of professional experience, academic performance, or implementation language experience. If there were any bias between the two times the course was taught, it would be in favor of the 1983 (non-Cleanroom) group because the modular design portion of the course was presented earlier. It was also the second time F. T. Baker had taught the course.

The Cleanroom teams entered their source code on-line, used a syntax-checker (but did not do automated type checking across modules), and were not able to execute their programs. The Cleanroom teams relied on the techniques of code reading, structured walkthroughs, and inspections to prepare their evolving systems before submission for independent testing. The non-Cleanroom teams were able to execute and debug their programs and applied several modern programming practices: modular design, top-down development, data abstraction, PDL, functional testing, design reviews, etc. The non-Cleanroom method was intended to reflect a software development approach that is currently in use in several software development organizations. Note that the non-Cleanroom method was roughly similar to the "disciplined team" development methodology examined in an earlier study [5].

One issue to consider when comparing a "newer" approach with an existing one is whether one group will try harder just because they are using the newer approach. This effect is referred to as the Hawthorne effect. In order to combat this potential effect, we decided to have all the members of one course apply the same development approach[2]. In order to diffuse any of the Cleanroom developers from thinking that they were being compared relative to a previously applied approach, we decided that Cleanroom would be used in the earlier (1982) course. Therefore, there was no obvious competing arrangement in terms of approaches that were newer versus controlled.

D. Project Milestones

The objective for all teams from both groups was to develop the full system described in the requirements document. The first document every team in either group turned in contained a system specification, composite design diagram, and

[2] This decision also happened to result in the two groups not being as close in terms of size as they could have been.

implementation plan. The implementation plan was a series of milestones chosen by the individual teams which described when the various functions within the system would be available. At these various dates—minimum one week apart, maximum two—teams from the groups would then submit their systems for independent testing. Note that both the Cleanroom and non-Cleanroom teams had the benefit of the independent testing throughout development. An independent party would apply statistically based testing to each of the deliveries and report to the team members both the successful and unsuccessful test cases. The unsuccessful test cases would be included in a team's next test session for verification. The following section briefly describes the operationally based testing process applied to all projects by the independent tester.

E. Operational Testing of Projects

The testing approach used in Cleanroom is to simulate the developing system's environment by randomly selecting test data from an "operational profile", a frequency distribution of inputs to the system [46], [18]. The projects from both groups were tested interactively by an independent party (i.e., R. W. Selby) at the milestones chosen by each team. A distribution of inputs to the system was obtained by identifying the logical functions in the system and assigning each a frequency. This frequency assignment was accomplished by polling eleven well-seasoned users of a University of Maryland Vax 11 /780 mailing system. Then test data were generated randomly from this profile and presented to the system. Recording of failure severity and times between failure took place during the testing process. The operational statistics referred to later were calculated from 50 user-session test cases run on the final system release of each team. For a complete explanation of the operationally based testing process applied to the projects, including test data selection, testing procedure, and failure observation, see [42].

F. Project Evaluation

All team projects were evaluated on their use of the particular software development techniques, the independent testing results, and a final oral interview. Both groups of subjects were judged to be highly motivated during the development of their systems. One reason for their motivation was their being graded based on the evaluation of their team projects. Information on the team projects was also collected from a background questionnaire, a post-development attitude survey, static source code analysis, and operating system statistics.

V. Data Analysis and Interpretation

The analysis and interpretation of the data collected from the study appear in the following sections, organized by the goal areas outlined earlier. In order to address the various questions posed under each of the goals, some raw data usually will be presented and then interpreted. Fig. 3 presents the number of source lines, executable statements, and procedures and functions to give a rough view of the systems developed.

A. Characterization of the Effect on the Product Developed

This section characterizes the differences between the products delivered by the two development groups. Researchers have delineated numerous perspectives of software product quality [36], [14], [13], and the following sections examine aspects of several of these perspectives. Initially we examine some operational properties of the products, followed by a comparison of some of their static properties.

1) *Operational System Properties:* In order to contrast the operational properties of the systems delivered by the two groups, both completeness of implementation and operational testing results were examined. A measure of implementation completeness was calculated by partitioning the required system into 16 logical functions (e.g., send mail to an individual, read a piece of mail, respond, add yourself to a mailing list, . . .). Each function in an implementation was then assigned a value of two if it completely met its requirements, a value of one if it partially met them, or zero if it was inoperable. The total for each system was calculated; a maximum score of 32 was possible. Fig. 4 displays this subjective measure of requirement conformance for the systems. Note that in all figures presented, the ten teams using Cleanroom are in upper case and the five teams using a more conventional approach are in lower case. A first observation is that six of the ten Cleanroom teams built very close to the entire system. While not all of the Cleanroom teams performed equally well, a majority of them applied the approach effectively enough to develop nearly the whole product. More importantly, the Cleanroom teams met the requirements of the system more completely than did the non-Cleanroom teams.

To compare testing results among the systems developed in the two groups, 50 random user-session test cases were executed on the final release of each system to simulate its operational environment. If the final release of a system performed to expectations on a test case, the outcome was called a "success;" if not, the outcome was a "failure." If the outcome was a "failure" but the same failure was observed on an earlier test case run on the final release, the outcome was termed a "duplicate failure." Fig. 5 shows the percentage of successful test cases when duplicate failures are not included. The figure displays that Cleanroom projects had a higher percentage of successful test cases at system delivery[3]. When duplicate failures are included, however, the better performance of the Cleanroom systems is not nearly as significant (MW = 0.134).[4] This is caused by the Cleanroom projects having a

[3]Although not considered here, various software reliability models have been proposed to forecast system reliability based on failure data (see Section JI-A-4)

[4] To be more succinct, MW will sometimes be used to abbreviate the significance level of the Mann-Whitney statistic. The significance levels for the Mann-Whitney statistics reported are the probability of Type 1 error in a one-tailed test.

Team	Cleanroom	Source Lines	Executable Statements	Procedures & Functions
A	yes	1681	813	55
B	yes	1626	717	42
C	yes	1118	573	12
D	yes	1046	477	30
E	yes	1087	624	32
F	yes	1214	440	35
G	yes	1196	581	31
H	yes	1870	550	51
I	yes	1305	608	23
J	yes	1052	658	21
a	no	904	410	26
b	no	1429	633	18
c	no	2264	999	46
d	no	1629	626	67
e	no	1310	459	43

Fig. 3. System statistics

relatively higher proportion of duplicate failures, even though they did better overall. This demonstrates that while reviewing the code, the Cleanroom developers focused less than the other group on certain parts of the system. The more uniform review of the whole system makes the performance of the system less sensitive to its operational profile. Note that operational environments of systems are usually difficult to define a priori and are subject to change.

In both of the product quality measures of implementation completeness and operational testing results, there was quite a variation in performance.[5] A wide variation may have been expected with an unfamiliar development technique, but the developers using a more traditional approach had a wider range of performance than did those using Cleanroom in both of the measures even with there being twice as many Cleanroom teams. All of the above differences are magnified by recalling that the non-Cleanroom teams did not develop their systems in one monolithic step, they (also) had the benefit of periodic operational testing by independent testers. Since both groups of teams had independent testing of all their deliveries, the early testing of deliveries must have revealed most faults overlooked by the Cleanroom developers.

[5] An alternate perspective includes only the more successful projects from each group in the comparison of operational product quality. When the best 60 percent from each approach are examined (i.e., removing teams "d," "e," "A," "E," "F," and "1"), the Mann-Whitney significance level for comparing implementation completeness becomes 0.045 and the significance level for comparing successful test cases (without duplicate failures) becomes 0.034. Thus, comparing the best teams from each approach increases the evidence in favor of Cleanroom in both of these product quality measures.

These comparisons suggest that the non-Cleanroom developers focused on a "perspective of the tester," sometimes leaving out classes of functions and causing a less completely implemented product and more (especially unique) failures. Off-line software review techniques, however, are more general and their use contributed to more complete requirement conformance and fewer failures in the Cleanroom products. In addition to examining the operational properties of the product, various static properties were compared.

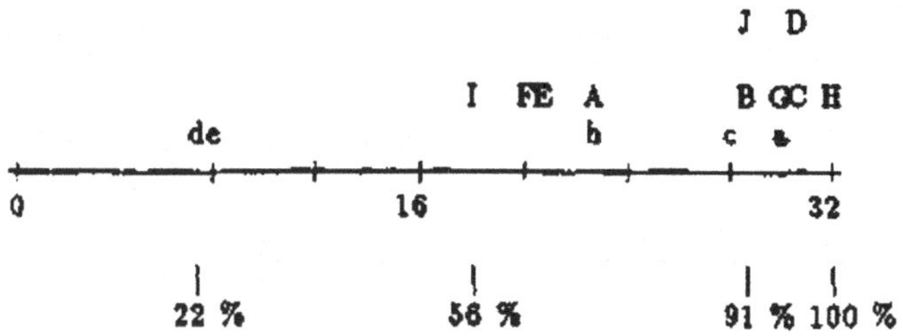

Mann-Whitney [5] signif. = .088

Fig. 4. Requirement conformance of the systems.

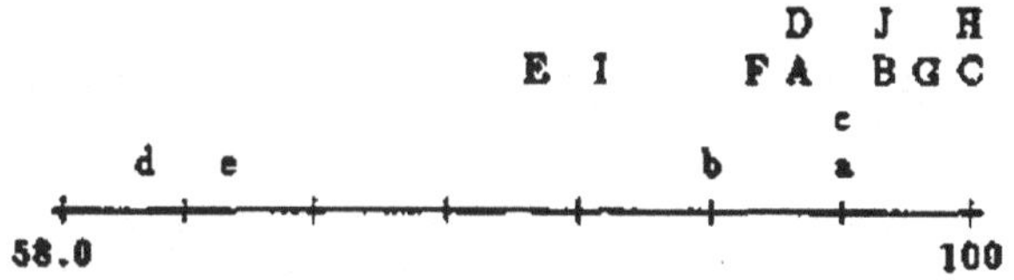

Mann-Whitney signif. = .055

Fig. 5. Percentage of successful test cases during operational testing (without duplicate failures).

2) *Static System Properties:* The first question in this goal area concerns the size of the final systems. Fig. 3 showed the number of source lines, executable statements, and procedures and functions for the various systems. The projects from the two groups were not statistically different (MW > 0.10) in any of these three size attributes. Another question in this goal area concerns the readability of the delivered source code. Although readability is not equivalent to maintainability, modifiability, or reusability, it is a central component of each of these software quality aspects. Two aspects of reading and altering source code are the number of comments present and the density of the "complexity." In an attempt to capture the complexity density, syntactic complexity [4] was calculated and normalized by the number of executable statements. In addition to control-flow complexity, the syntactic complexity metric considers nesting depth and prime program decomposition [32]. The developers using Cleanroom wrote code that was more highly commented (MW = 0.089) and had a lower complexity density (MW = 0.079) than did those using the traditional approach. A calculation of either software science effort [28], cyc-

lomatic complexity [35], or syntactic complexity without any size normalization, however, produced no significant differences (MW > 0.10). This seems as expected because all the systems were built to meet the same requirements. Comparing the data usage in the systems, Cleanroom developers used a greater number of nonlocal data items (MW = 0.071). Also, Cleanroom projects possessed a higher percentage of assignment statements (MW = 0.056). These last two observations could be a manifestation of teaching the Cleanroom subjects modular design later in the course (see Section IV-C), or possibly an indication of using the approach. One interpretation of the Cleanroom developers' use of more nonlocal data could be that the resulting software would be less reusable and less portable. In fact, however, the increased use of nonlocal data by some Cleanroom developers was because of their use of data abstraction. In order to incorporate data abstraction into a system implemented in the Simpl-T programming language, developers may create independently compilable program units that have retained nonlocal data and associated accessing routines.

Some interesting observations surface when the operational quality measures of just the Cleanroom products are correlated with the usage of the implementation language. Both percentage of successful test cases (without duplicate failures) and implementation completeness correlated with percentage of procedure calls (Spearman R = 0.65, signif. = 0.044. and R = 0.57, signif. = 0.08, respectively) and with percentage of IF statements (R = 0.62, signif. = 0.058, and R = 0.55, signif. = 0.10, respectively). However, both of these two product quality measures correlated negatively with percentage of CASE statements (R = -0.86, signif. = 0.001, and R = -0.69, signif. = 0.027, respectively) and with percentage of WHILE statements (R = -0.65, signif. = 0.044. and R = -0.49, signif. = 0.15, respectively). There were also some negative correlations between the product quality measures and the average software science effort per subroutine (R = -0.52, signif. = 0.12, and R = -0.74. signif. = 0.013, respectively) and the average number of occurrences of a variable (R = -0.54, signif. = 0.11, and R = -0.56, signif. = 0.09, respectively). Considering the products from all teams, both percentage of successful test cases (without duplicate failures) and implementation completeness had some correlation with percentage of IF statements (R = 0.48, signif. = 0.07, and R = 0.45, signif. = 0.09, respectively) and some negative correlation with percentage of CASE statements (R = -0.48, signif. = 0.07, and R = -0.42, signif. = 0.12, respectively). Neither of the operational product quality measures correlated with percentage of assignment statements when either all products or just Cleanroom products were considered. These observations suggest that the more successful Cleanroom developers simplified their use of the implementation language; i.e., they used more procedure calls and IF statements, used fewer CASE and WHILE statements, had a lower frequency of variable reuse, and wrote subroutines requiring less software science effort to comprehend.

3) *Contribution of Programmer Background:* When examining the contribution of the Cleanroom programmers background to the quality of their final products, general programming language experience correlated with percentage of

successful operational tests (without duplicate failures: Spearman $R = 0.66$, signif. = 0.04; with duplicates: $R = 0.70$, signif. = 0.03) and with implementation completeness ($R = 0.55$; signif. = 0.10). No relationship appears between either operational testing results or implementation completeness and either professional[7] or testing experience. These background/quality relations seem consistent with other studies [17].

4) *Summary of the Effect on the Product Developed*: In summary, Cleanroom developers delivered a product that 1) met system requirements more completely, 2) had a higher percentage of successful test cases, 3) had more comments and less dense control-flow complexity, and 4) used more nonlocal data items and a higher percentage of assignment statements. The more successful Cleanroom developers 1) used more procedure calls and IF statements, 2) used fewer CASE and WHILE statements, 3) reused variables less frequently, 4) developed subroutines requiring less software science effort to comprehend, and 5) had more general programming language experience.

B. Characterization of the Effect on the Development Process

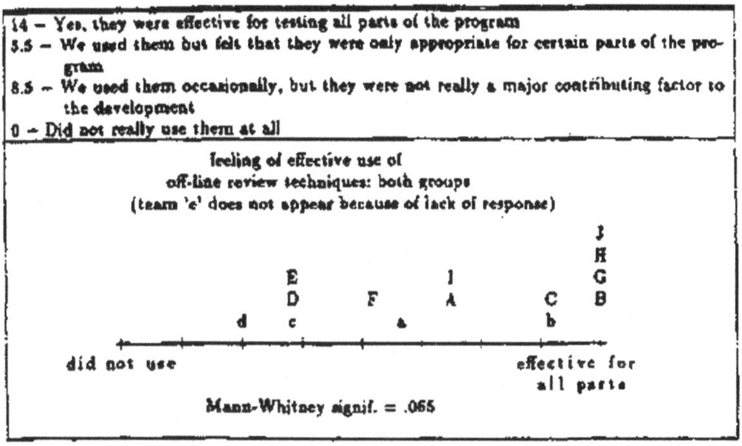

Fig. 6. Breakdown of responses to the attitude survey question, "Did you feel that you and your team members effectively used off-line review techniques in testing your project?" (Responses are from Cleanroom teams.)[8]

In a post development attitude survey, the developers were asked how effectively they felt they applied off-line software review techniques in testing their projects (see Fig. 6). This was an attempt to capture some of the information necessary to answer the first question under this goal (question II-A). In order to make comparisons at the team level, the responses from the members of a team are composed into an average for the team. The responses to the question appear on a team basis in a histogram in the second part of the figure. Of the Cleanroom developers, teams "A," "D," "E," "F," and "I" were the least confident in their use of the off-line review techniques and these teams also performed the worst in terms of operational testing results; four of these five teams performed the worst in terms of implementation completeness. Offline review effectiveness correlated with percentage of successful operational tests (without duplicate failures) for the Cleanroom teams (Spearman $R = 0.74$; signif. = 0.014) and for all the teams ($R = 0.76$; signif. = 0.001); it correlated with implementation completeness for all the teams ($R = 0.58$; signif. = 0.023). Neither professional nor testing experience correlated with off-line review effectiveness when either all teams or just Cleanroom teams were considered.

The histogram in Fig. 6 shows that the Cleanroom developers felt they applied the off-line review techniques more effectively than did the non-Cleanroom teams. The non-Cleanroom developers were asked to give a relative breakdown of the amount of time spent applying testing and off-line review techniques. Their aggregate response was 39 percent off-line review, 52 percent functional testing, and 9 percent structural testing. From this breakdown, we observe that the non-Cleanroom teams primarily relied on functional testing to prepare their systems for independent testing. Since the Cleanroom teams were unable to rely on testing methods, they may have (felt they had) applied the off-line review techniques more effectively.

Since the role of the computer is more controlled when using Cleanroom, one would expect a difference in online activity between the two groups. Fig. 7 displays the amount of connect time that each of the teams cumulatively used. A comparison of the cpu-time used by the teams was less statistically significant (MW = 0.110). Neither of these measures of on-line activity related to how effectively a team felt they had used the off-line review techniques when either all teams or just Cleanroom teams were considered. Although non-Cleanroom team "d" did a lot of on-line testing and non-Cleanroom team "e" did little, both teams performed poorly in the measures of operational product quality discussed earlier. The operating system of the development machine captured these system usage statistics. Note that the time the independent party spent testing is included.[6] These observations exhibit that Cleanroom developers spent less time on-line and used fewer computer resources. These results empirically support the reduced role of the computer in Cleanroom development.

Schedule slippage continues to be a problem in software development. It would be interesting to see whether the Cleanroom teams demonstrated any more discipline by maintaining their original schedules. All of the teams from both groups planned four releases of their evolving system, except for team "G" which planned five. Recall that at each delivery an independent party would operationally test the functions currently available in the system, according to the team's implementation plan. In Fig. 8, we observe that all the teams using Cleanroom kept to their original schedules by making all planned deliveries; only two non-Cleanroom teams made all their scheduled deliveries.

[6] When the time the independent tester spent is not included, the significance levels for the nonparametric statistics do not change.

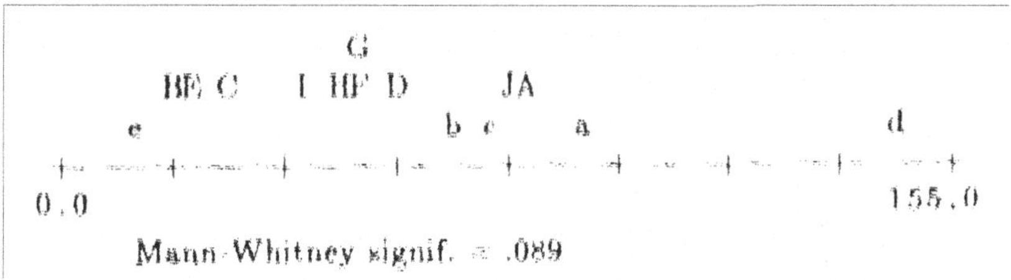

Fig. 7. Connect time in hours during project development.[7]

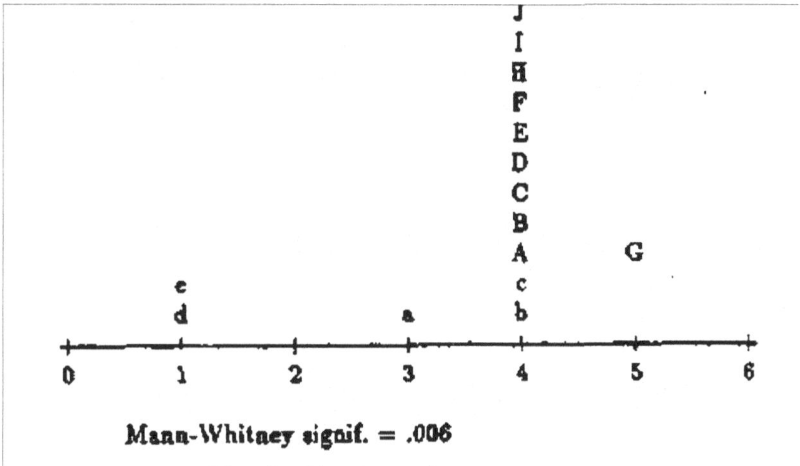

Fig. 8. Number of system releases.

1) *Summary of the Effect on the Development Process:* Summarizing the effect on the development process, Cleanroom developers 1) felt they applied off-line review techniques more effectively, while non-Cleanroom teams focused on functional testing; 2) spent less time online and used fewer computer resources; and 3) made all their scheduled deliveries.

C. Characterization of the Effect on the Developers

The first question posed in this goal area is whether the individuals using Cleanroom missed the satisfaction of executing their own programs. Fig. 9 presents the responses to a question included in the post development attitude survey on this issue. As might be expected, almost all the individuals missed some aspect of program execution. As might not be expected, however, this missing of program exe-

24 Non-Cleanroom team "e" entered a substantial portion of its system on a remote machine, only using the Univac computer mainly for compilation and execution. Team "e" was the only team that used any machine other than the Univac. (See Section V-D.)

cution had no relation to either the product quality measures mentioned earlier or the teams' professional or testing experience. Also, missing program execution did not increase with respect to program size (see Fig. 10).

13 – Yes, I missed the satisfaction of program execution.
11 – I somewhat missed the satisfaction of program execution.
4 – No, I did not miss the satisfaction of program execution.

Fig. 9. Breakdown of responses to the attitude survey question, "Did you miss the satisfaction of executing your own programs?"

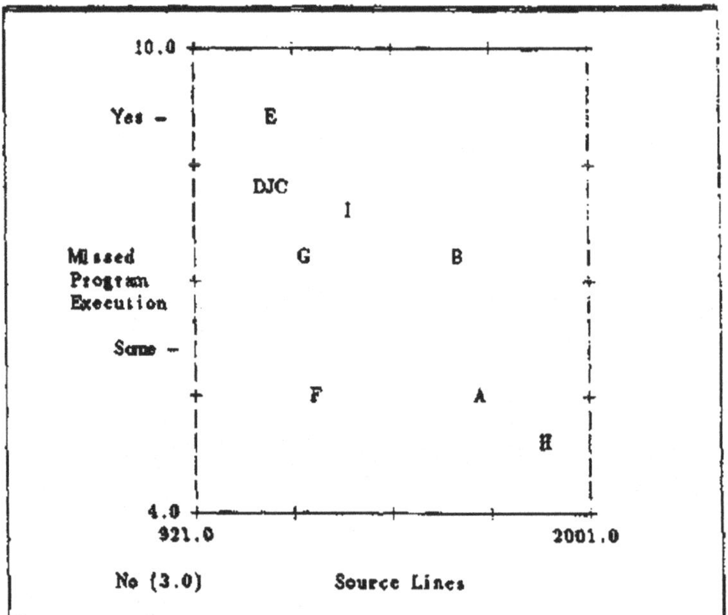

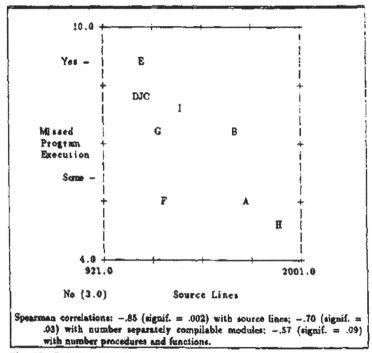

Spearman correlations: –.85 (signif. = .002) with source lines; –.70 (signif. = .03) with number separately compilable modules; –.57 (signif. = .09) with number procedures and functions.

Fig. 10. Relationship of program size versus missing program execution.

Fig. 11 displays the replies of the developers when they were asked how their design and coding style was affected by not being able to test and debug. At first it would seem surprising that more people did not modify their development style when applying the techniques of Cleanroom. Several persons mentioned, however, that they already utilized some of the ideas in Cleanroom. Keeping a simple design supports readability of the product and facilitates the processes of modification and verification. Although some of the objective product measures presented earlier showed differences in development style, these subjective ones are interesting and lend insight into actual programmer behavior.

One indicator of the impression that something new leaves on people is whether they would do it again. Fig. 12 presents the responses of the individuals when they were asked whether they would choose to use Cleanroom again as either a software development manager or as a programmer. Even though these responses were gathered (immediately) after course completion, subjects desiring to "please the instructor" may have responded favorably to this type of question regardless of their true feelings. Practically everyone indicated a willingness to apply the approach again. It is interesting to note that a greater number of persons in a managerial role would choose to always use it. Of the persons that ranked the reuse of Cleanroom fairly low in each category, four of the five were the same people. Of the six people that ranked reuse low, four were from less successful projects (one from team "A," one from team "E" and two from team "I"), but the other two came from reasonably successful developments (one from team "C" and one from team "J"). The particular individuals on teams "E," "I," and "J" were the four that rated reuse fairly low in both categories.

1) *Summary of the Effect on the Developers:* In summary of the effect on the developers, most Cleanroom developers 1) partially modified their development style, 2) missed program execution, and 3) indicated that they would use the approach again.

7 – Yes, my style was substantially revised.
15 – I modified some of my tendencies.
11 – It did not affect my style at all.

Frequently mentioned responses include
- kept design simple, attempted nothing fancy
- kept readability of code in mind
- already was a user of off-line review techniques
- very careful scrutiny of code for potential mistakes
- prepared for a larger range of inputs

Fig. 11. Breakdown of responses to the attitude survey question. "How was your design and coding style affected by not being able to test and debug?"

As a software development manager?
8 – Yes, at all times
14 – Yes, but only for certain projects
5 – Not at all

As a programmer?
4 – Yes, for all projects
18 – Yes, but not all the time
5 – Only if I had to
0 – I would leave if I had to

Fig. 12. Breakdown of responses to the attitude survey question. "Would you use Cleanroom again?" (One person did not respond to this question.)

D. Distinction Among Teams

In spite of efforts to balance the teams according to various factors (see Section IV-A), a few differences among the teams were apparent. Two separate Cleanroom teams, "H" and "I," each lost a member late in the project. Thus at project completion, there were eight three-person and two two-person Cleanroom teams. Recall that team "H" performed quite well according to requirement conformance and testing results, while team "I" did poorly. Also, the second group of subjects did not divide evenly into three-person teams. Since one of those individuals had extensive professional experience, non-Cleanroom team "e" consisted of that one highly experienced person. Thus at project completion, there were four three-person and one one-person non-Cleanroom teams. Although team "e" wrote over 1300 source lines, this highly experienced person did not do as well as the other teams in some respects. This is consistent with another study in which teams applying a "disciplined methodology" in development outperformed individuals [5]. Appendix A contains the significance levels for the results of the analysis presented when team "e", when teams "H" and "I", and when teams "e", "H," and "I" are removed from the analysis. Removing teams "H" and "I" has little effect on the significance levels, while the removal of team "e" causes a decrease in all of the significance levels except for executable statements, software science effort, cyclomatic complexity, syntactic complexity, connect-time, and cpu-time.

VI. Conclusions

This paper describes "Cleanroom" software development—an approach intended to produce highly reliable software by integrating formal methods for specification and design, nonexecution-based program development, and statistically based independent testing. The goal structure, experimental approach, data analysis, and conclusions are presented for a replicated-project study examining the Cleanroom approach. This is the first investigation known to the authors that applied Cleanroom and characterized its effect relative to a more traditional development approach.

The data analysis presented and the testimony provided by the developers suggest that the major results of this study are the following. 1) Most of the developers were able to apply the techniques of Cleanroom effectively (six of the ten Cleanroom teams delivered at least 91 percent of the required system functions). 2) The Cleanroom teams' products met system requirements more completely and had a higher percentage of successful operationally generated test cases. 3) The source code developed using Cleanroom had more comments and less dense control-flow complexity. 4) The more successful Cleanroom developers modified their use of the implementation language; they used more procedure calls and IF statements, used fewer CASE and WHILE statements, and had a lower frequency of variable reuse (average number of occurrences per variable). 5) All ten Cleanroom teams made all of their scheduled intermediate product deliveries, while only two of the five non-Cleanroom teams did. 6) Although 86 percent of the Cleanroom developers indicated that they missed the satisfaction of program execution to some extent, this had no relation to the product quality measures of implementation completeness and successful operational tests. 7) Eighty-one percent of the Cleanroom developers said that they would use the approach again.

Based on the experience of applying Cleanroom in this study, some potential areas for improving the methodology are as follows. 1) As mentioned above, several Cleanroom developers tended to miss the satisfaction of program execution. In order to circumvent a potential long-term psychological effect, a method for providing such satisfaction to the developers would be useful. One suggestion would be for developers to witness, but not influence, program execution by the independent testers. 2) Several of the persons applying the Cleanroom approach mentioned that they had some difficulty visualizing the user interface, and hence, felt that the systems suffered in terms of "user-friendliness." One suggestion would be to prototype the user interfaces as part of the requirement determination phase, and then describe the interfaces in the requirements document, possibly using an interactive display specification language [11]. 3) A few of the Cleanroom developers said that they did not feel subjected to a "full test." Recall that the reliability certification component of the Cleanroom approach stands on the premise that operationally-based testing is sufficient to assess system reliability. One suggestion may be to augment the testing process with methods that enforce increased coverage of the system requirements, design, and implementation and/or methods that utilize frequent error profiles.

Overall, it seems that the ideas in Cleanroom help attain the goals of producing high quality software and increasing the discipline in the software development process. The complete separation of development from testing appears to cause a modification in the developers' behavior, resulting in increased process control and in more effective use of methods for software specification, design, off-line review, and verification. It seems that system modification and maintenance would be more easily done on a product developed in the Cleanroom method, because of the product's thoroughly conceived design and higher readability. Facilitating the software modification and maintenance tasks results in a corresponding reduction in associated costs to users. The amount of development effort required by the Cleanroom approach was not gathered in this study because its purpose was to examine the feasibility of Cleanroom and to characterize its effect. However, even if using Cleanroom required additional development effort, it seems that the potential reduction in maintenance and enhancement costs may result in an overall decrease in software life cycle cost. Thus, achieving high requirement conformance and high operational reliability coupled with low maintenance costs would help reduce overall costs, satisfy the user community, and support a long product lifetime.

Other studies which have compared software development methodologies include [5] and [12].[8] In [5] three software development approaches were compared: a disciplined-methodology team approach, an ad hoc team approach, and an ad hoc individual approach.

The development approaches were applied by advanced university students comprising seven three-person teams, six three-person teams, and six individuals,

---

[8] For a survey of controlled, empirical studies that have been conducted in software engineering, see [8].

respectively. They separately built a small (600-2200 line) compiler. The disciplined-methodology team approach significantly reduced the development costs as reflected in program changes and runs. The resulting designs from the disciplined-methodology teams and the ad hoc individuals were more coherent than the disjointed designs developed by the ad hoc teams. In [12] two software development approaches were compared: prototyping and specifying. Seven two- and three-person teams, consisting of university graduate students, developed separate versions of the same (2000-4000 line) application program. The systems developed by prototyping were smaller, required less development effort, and were easier to use. The systems developed by specifying had more coherent designs, more complete functionality, and software that was easier to integrate.

Measure	Average		Mann-Whitney significance levels			
	Clean-room Teams	Non-Clean-room Teams	All Teams	With-out Team e	With-out Teams H,I	With-out Teams e,H,I
Source lines	1320.0	1491.2	.196	.240	.153	.198
Executable stmts	604.1	625.4	.500	.286	.442	.367
Procedures & functions	36.5	40.0	.357	.500	.330	.500
%Implementation completeness	82.5	60.0	.088	.197	.093	.196
%Successful tests (w/o duplicate failures)	92.5	80.8	.055	.128	.053	.116
%Successful tests (w/ duplicate failures)	78.7	59.2	.134	.285	.151	.304
Comments	194.9	122.2	.089	.102	.190	.198
Syntactic complexity/ executable stmts	1.5	1.6	.079	.179	.082	.175
Software Science E	6728.6e3	7355.4e3	.451	.240	.442	.248
Cyclomatic complexity	196.8	212.2	.250	.198	.255	.248
Syntactic complexity	917.5	1017.0	.500	.286	.500	.305
Non-local data items	37.6	24.2	.071	.129	.053	.117
%Assignment stmts	34.2	26.6	.056	.129	.040	.087
Off-line effectiveness	3.2	2.5	.065	.065	.098	.098
Connect-time (hr.)	41.0	71.3	.089	.012	.121	.021
Cpu-time (min.)	71.7	136.1	.110	.017	.072	.009
Deliveries	4.1	2.6	.006	.015	.010	.022

Fig. 13. Summary of measure averages and significance levels.

Future possible research directions include 1) assessment of the applicability of Cleanroom to larger software developments (note that aspects of the Cleanroom approach are being used in a 30 000 source line project [21], [16]); 2) empirical evaluation of the effect of Cleanroom from additional software quality perspectives, including reusability and modifiability; and 3) further characterization of the number and types of errors that occur when Cleanroom is or is not used.

This empirical study is intended to advance the understanding of the relationship between introducing discipline into the development process, as in Cleanroom, and several aspects of product quality: conformance with requirements, high operational reliability, and easily readable source code. The results given were calculated from a set of teams applying Cleanroom development on a relatively small project—the direct extrapolation of the findings to other projects and development environments is not implied.

Appendix A

Fig. 13 presents the measure averages and the significance levels for the above comparisons when team "e," when teams "H" and "I," and when teams "e," "H," and "I" are removed. The significance levels for the Mann-Whitney statistics reported are the probability of Type I error in a one-tailed test.

Acknowledgment

The authors are grateful to D. H. Hutchens and R. W. Reiter for the use of their static analysis program in this study.

References

[1] E. N. Adams. “Optimizing preventive service of software products,” *IBM J. Res. Develop.*, vol. 28, no. 1, pp. 2-14, Jan. 1984.

[2] F. T. Baker. "Chief programmer team management of production programming," *IBM Syst. J.*, vol. 11, no. 1, pp. 131-149, 1972.

[3] ——, "Chief programmer teams," in *Tutorial on Structured Programming: Integrated Practices*. V. R. Basili and F. T. Baker, Eds. New York: IEEE, 1981.

[4] V. R. Basili and D. H. Hutchens. "An empirical study of a syntactic metric family," *IEEE Trans. Software Eng.*, vol. SE-9, pp. 664-672, Nov. 1983.

[5] V. R. Basili and R. W. Reiter. "A controlled experiment quantitatively comparing software development approaches," *IEEE Trans. Software Eng.*, vol. SE-7, May 1981.

[6] V. R. Basili and R. W. Selby. "Data collection and analysis in software research and management." in *Proc. Amer. Statist. Ass. and Biometric Sov. Joint Statist. Meetings*, Philadelphia, PA, August 13-16, 1984.

[7] ——, "Comparing the effectiveness of software testing strategies, "Dep. Comput. Sci.. Univ. Maryland, College Park, Tech. Rep. TR-1501, May 1985; to appear in *IEEE Trans. Software Eng.*

[8] V. R. Basili, R. W. Selby, and D. H. Hutchens, "Experimentation in software engineering," *IEEE Trans. Software Eng.*, vol. SE-I2, pp. 733-743, July 1986.

[9] V. R. Basili and A. J. Turner. SIMPL-*T: A Structured Programming Language*. Geneva, IL: Paladin House. 1976.

[10] V. R. Basili and D. M. Weiss, "A methodology for collecting valid software engineering data, "*IEEE Trans. Software-Eng.*, vol. SE-10, pp. 728-738, Nov. 1984.

[11] L. J. Bass, "An approach to user specification of interactive display interfaces," *IEEE Trans. Software Eng.*, vol. SE-11, pp. 686-698, Aug. 1985,

[12] B. .W, Boehm, T. E. Gray, and T. Seewaldt, "Prototyping versus specifying: A multiproject experiment," *IEEE Trans. Software Eng.*, vol. SE-10, pp. 290-303, May 1984.

[13] T. P. Bowen, G. B. Wigle, and J. T. Tsai, "Specification of software quality attributes," Rome Air Development Center, Griffiss Air Force Base, NY, Tech. Rep. RADC-TR-85-37 (3 volumes), Feb. 1985.

[14] J. P. Cavano and J. A. McCall. "A framework for the measurement of software quality," in *Proc. Software Quality and Assurance Workshop*, San Diego, CA, Nov. 1978, pp. 133-139.

[15] P. A. Currit, "Cleanroom certification model." in *Proc. 8th Annu. Software Eng. Workshop*, NASA/GSFC, Greenbelt, MD, Nov. 1983.

[16] P. A. Currit, M. Dyer, and H. D. Mills, "Certifying the reliability of software," *IEEE Trans. Software Eng.*, vol. SE-12, pp. 3-11, Jan. 1986.

[17] B. Curtis, "Cognitive science of programming," in *Sixth Minnowbrook Workshop Software Performance Evaluation*, Blue Mountain Lake, NY, July 19-22, 1983.

[18] J. W. Duran and S. Ntafos. "A report on random testing*," in *Proc. Fifth Int. Conf. Software Eng.*, San Diego, CA, Mar. 9-12, 1981, pp. 179-183.

[19] M. Dyer, "Cleanroom software development method," IBM Federal Systems Division, Bethesda. MD, Oct. 14, 1982.

[20] ——, "Software validation in the Cleanroom development method," IBM-FSD Tech. Rep. 86.0003, Aug. 19, 1983.

[21] ——, "Software development under statistical quality control," *In Proc. NATO Advanced Study Institute: The Challenge of Advanced Computing Technology to System Design Methods*. Durham, UK, July 29-Aug. 10, 1985.

[22] M. Dyer, R. C. Linger, H. D. Mills. D. O'Neill, and R. E. Quinnan. "The management of software engineering," *IBM Syst. J.*, vol. 19, no. 4, 1980.

[23] M. Dyer and H. D. Mills. "The Cleanroom approach to reliable software development," in *Proc. Validation Methods Research for Fault-Tolerant Avionics and Control Systems Sub-Working-Group Meeting: Production of Reliable Flight-Crucial Software*, Research Triangle Institute, NC, Nov. 2-4, 1981.

[24] ——, "Developing electronic systems with certifiable reliability," in *Proc. NATO Conf.*, Summer 1982.

[25] M. E. Pagan, "Design and code inspections to reduce errors in program development," *IBM Syst. J.*, vol. 15, no. 3, pp. 182-211, 1976.

[26] A. B. Ferrentino and H. D. Mills, "State machines and their semantics in software engineering," in *Proc. IEEE COMPSAC*, 1977.

[27] A. L. Goel. "A guidebook for software reliability assessment," Dep. Industrial Eng. and Oper. Res., Syracuse Univ., New York, Tech. Rep. 83-11, Apr. 1983.

[28] M. H. Halstead. *Elements of Software Science*. New York: North-Holland, 1977.

[29] C. A. R. Hoare. "An axiomatic basis for computer programming," *Commun. ACM*, vol. 12, no. 10. pp. 576-583, Oct. 1969.

[30] W. E. Howden, "Reliability of the path analysis testing strategy," *IEEE Trans. Software Eng.*, vol. SE-2. no. 3, Sept. 1976.

[31] P. Kerola and P. Freeman. "A comparison of lifecycle models," in *Proc. 5th Int. Conf. Software Eng.*, Mar. 1981, pp. 90-99.

[32] R. C. Linger, H. D. Mills, and B. I. Witt, *Structured Programming: Theory and Practice*. Reading, MA: Addison-Wesley, 1979.

[33] B. Littlewood, "Stochastic reliability growth: A model for fault renovation computer programs and hardware designs." *IEEE Trans. Rel.*, vol. R-30, Oct. 1981.

[34] B. Littlewood and J. L. Verrall. "A Bayesian reliability growth model for computer software." *Appl. Statist.*, vol. 22, no. 3, 1973.

[35] T. J. McCabe, "A complexity measure." *IEEE Trans. Software Eng.*, vol. SE-2, pp. 308-320, Dec. 1976.

[36] J. A. McCall. P. Richards, and G. Walters. "Factors in software quality," Rome Air Development Center, Griffiss Air Force Base, NY, Tech. Rep. RADC-TR-77-369, Nov. 1977.

[37] H. D. Mills, "Chief programmer teams: Principles and procedures." IBM Corp., Gaithersburg, MD, Rep. FSC 71-6012, 1972.

[38] ——. "Mathematical foundations for structural programming," IBM Rep. FSL 72-6021, 1972.

[39] J. D. Musa. "A theory of software reliability and its application." *IEEE Trans. Software Eng.*, vol. SE-1, no. 3, pp. 312-327, 1975.

[40] G. J. Myers, *Software Reliability: Principles & Practices*. New York: Wiley, 1976.

[41] D. L. Parnas. "On the criteria to be used in decomposing systems into modules," *Commun. ACM*, vol. 15, no. 12, pp. 1053-1058, 1972.

[42] R. W. Selby, "Evaluations of software technologies: Testing, CLEANROOM, and metrics," Ph.D. dissertation, Dep. Comput. Sci., Univ. Maryland, College Park, Tech. Rep. TR-1500, 1985.

[43] —— "Combining software testing strategies: An empirical evaluation," in *Proc. Workshop Software Testing*, Banff, Alta., Canada, July 15-17, 1986, pp. 82-91.

[44] K. S. Shankar, "A functional approach to module verification," *IEEE Trans. Software Eng.*, vol. SE-8, Mar. 1982.

[45] J. G. Shanthikumar, "A statistical time dependent error occurrence rate software reliability model with imperfect debugging," *in Proc. 1981 Nat. Comput. Conf.*, June 1981.

[46] R. A. Thayer, M. Lipow, and E. C. Nelson, *Software Reliability*. Amsterdam, The Netherlands: North-Holland, 1978.

[47] M. V. Zelkowitz and M. Branstad, in *Proc. ACM SIGSOFT Rapid Prototyping Symp.*, Apr. 1982.

Evolving and Packaging Reading Technologies

Victor R. Basili

Department of Computer Science and Institute for Advanced Computer Studies
University of Maryland, College Park, MD

Abstract Reading is a fundamental technology for achieving quality software. This paper provides a motivation for reading as a quality improvement technology, based upon experiences in the Software Engineering Laboratory at NASA Goddard Space Flight Center, and shows the evolution of our study of reading via a series of experiments. The experiments range from early reading vs. testing experiments to various Cleanroom experiments that employed reading to the development of new reading technologies currently under study.

1. Introduction

Reading is a fundamental technology for achieving quality software. It is the only analysis technology we can use throughout the entire life cycle of the software development and maintenance processes. And yet, very little attention has been paid to the technologies that underlie the reading of software documents. For example, where is software reading taught? What technologies have been developed for software reading? In fact, what is software reading?

During most of our lives, we learned to read before we learned to write. Reading formed a model for writing. This was true from our first learning of a language (reading precedes writing and provides simple models for writing) to our study of the great literature (reading provides us with models of how to write well). Yet, in the software domain, we never learned to read, e.g., we learn to write programs in a programming language, but never how to read them.

We have not developed reading-based models for writing. For example, we are not conscious of our audience when we write a requirements document. How will they read it? What is the difference between reading a requirements document and reading a code document? We all know that one reads a novel differently than one reads a text book. We know that we review a technical paper differently than we review a newspaper article. But how do we read a requirements document, a code document, or a test plan? There are many factors that affect the way we read.

Address correspondence to Victor R. Basili, Department of Computer Science / Institute for Advanced Computer Studies, University of Maryland, AV Williams Building 115, College Park, MD 20742

Let us define some terms so that we understand what we mean by reading. We differentiate a technique from a method, from a life cycle model. A technique is the most primitive. It is an algorithm, a series of steps producing the desired effect, and requires skill. A method is a management procedure for applying techniques, organized by a set of rules stating how and when to apply and when to stop applying the technique (entry and exit criteria), when the technique is appropriate, and how to evaluate it. We will define a technology as a collection of techniques and methods. A life cycle model is a set of methods that covers the entire life cycle of a software product.

For example, reading by step-wise abstraction (Linger, et al. 1979) is a technique for assessing code. Reading by step-wise abstraction requires the development of personal skills; one gets better with practice. A code inspection is a method that is defined around a reading technique, which has a well defined set of entry and exit criteria and a set of management supports specifying how and when to use the technique. Reading by stepwise abstraction and code inspections together form a technology. Inspections are embedded in a life cycle model, such as the Cleanroom development approach, which is highly dependent on reading techniques and methods. That is, reading technology is fundamental to Cleanroom development.

In what follows, we will discuss the evolution and packaging of reading as a technology in the Software Engineering Laboratory (SEL) (Basili, et al. 1992; Basili, et al. 1994) via a series of experiments from some early reading vs. testing technique experiments, to various Cleanroom experiments, to the development of new reading techniques currently under study.

In the SEL, we have been working with a set of experimental learning approaches: the Quality Improvement Paradigm, the Goal Question Metric Paradigm, the Experience Factory Organization, and various experimental frameworks to evolve our knowledge and the effectiveness of various life cycle models, methods, techniques, and tools (Basili, 1985; Basili and Weiss 1984; Basili and Rombach 1988; Basili 1989). All of these approaches have been applied to the series of experiments we've conducted at the University of Maryland and at NASA to learn about, evaluate, and evolve reading as a technology.

2. Reading Studies

Figure 1 provides a characterization of various types of experiments we have run in the SEL. They define different scopes of evaluation representing different levels of confidence in the results. They are characterized by the number of teams replicating each project and the number of different projects analyzed yielding four different experimental treatments: blocked subject-project, replicated project, multi-project variation, and single project case study. The approaches vary in cost, level of confidence in the results, insights gained, and the balance between quantitative and qualitative research methods. Clearly, an analysis of several replicated projects costs more money but provides a better basis for quantitative analysis and can generate stronger statistical confidence in the conclusions. Unfortunately, since a blocked subject-project experiment is so expensive, the projects studied tend to be small. To increase the size of the projects, keep the costs reasonable, and allow us to better simulate the effects of the treatment variables in a realistic environment, we can study very large single project case studies and even multi-project studies if the right environment can be found. These larger projects tend to involve more qualitative analysis along with some more primitive quantitative analysis.

Because of the desire for statistical confidence in the results, the problems with scale up, and the need to test in a realistic environment, one approach to experimentation is to choose one of the multiple team treatments (a controlled experiment) to demonstrate feasibility (statistical significance) in the small project, and then to try a case study or multi-project variation to analyze whether the results scale up in a realistic environment—a major problem in studying the effects of techniques, methods and life cycle models.

Scopes of Evaluation

		# Projects	
		One	More than one
# of Teams per Project	One	Single Project	Multi-Project Variation
	More than one	Replicated Project	Blocked Subject-Project

Figure 1. Classes of studies.

2.1 Reading by Step-wise Abstraction

In order to improve the quality of our software products at NASA, we have studied various approaches. One area of interest was to understand the relationship between reading and testing in our environment. Early experiments showed very little difference between reading and testing (Hetzel 1972; Myers 1978). But reading in these studies was simply reading, without a technological base. Thus we attempted to study the differences between various specific technology based approaches. Our goal was to analyze code reading, functional testing and structural testing to evaluate and compare them with respect to their effect on fault detection effectiveness, fault detection cost and classes of faults detected from the viewpoint of the researchers (Basili and Selby 1987). The study was conducted in the SEL, using three different programs: a text formatter, a plotter, and a small database.

The programs were seeded with software faults, (9, 6, and 12 faults respectively), and ranged in size from 145 to 365 LOG. The experimental design was a blocked subject-project, using a fractional factorial design. There were 32 subjects.

Specific techniques were used for each of the three approaches studied. Code reading was done by step-wise abstraction, i.e., reading a sequence of statements and abstracting the function they compute and repeating the process until the function of the entire program has been abstracted and can be compared with the specification. Functional testing was performed using boundary value, equivalence partition testing, i.e., dividing the requirements into valid and invalid equivalence classes and making up tests that check the boundaries of the classes. Structural testing was performed to achieve 100% statement coverage, i.e., making up a set of tests to guarantee that 100% of the statements in the program have been executed.

As a blocked subject-project study, each subject used each technique and tested each program. The results were that code reading found more faults than functional testing, and functional testing found more faults than structural testing. Also, code reading found more faults per unit of time spent than either of the other two techniques. Different techniques seemed to be more effective for different classes of faults. For example, code reading was more effective for interface faults and functional testing more effective for control flow faults.

A second set of conclusions, based upon the perception of the readers and testers, was that code readers were better able to assess the actual quality of the code that they analyzed than the testers. And in fact, the structural testers were better able to assess the actual quality of the code they analyzed than the functional testers. That is, the code readers felt they only found about half the faults (and they were right), where the functional testers felt that had found about all the faults (and they were wrong). Also, after the completion of the study, over 90% of the participants thought functional testing worked best. This was a case where perception or intuition was clearly wrong.

Based upon this study, reading was implemented as part of the SEL development process. However, much to our surprise, reading appeared to have very little effect on reducing defects. It should be noted that the SEL keeps baselines of defect rates for project sets. This leads us to two possible hypotheses:

> *Hypothesis 1:* People did not read as well as they should have because they believed that testing would make up for their mistakes.

To test this first hypothesis, we ran an experiment that showed that if a developer reads and cannot test they do a more effective job of reading than if they read and know they can test later. This supported hypothesis 1.

> *Hypothesis 2:* There is a confusion between reading as a technique and the method in which it is embedded, e.g., inspections.

This addresses the concern that we often use a reading method (e.g., inspections or walk-through) but do not often have a reading technique (e.g., reading by step-wise abstraction) sufficiently defined within the method. To some extent, this might explain the success of reading in this experiment (Basili and Selby 1987) over the studies by Hetzel (Hetzel 1972) and Myers (Myers 1978).

Thus we derived the following conclusions from the studies described thus far:

- Reading using a particular technique is more effective and more cost effective than specific testing techniques, i.e., the reading technique is important. However, different approaches may be effective for different types of defects.
- Readers need to be motivated to read better, i.e., the ability to read a document effectively seems to be related to the readers' belief that their reading of the document is important.
- We may need to better support the reading process, i.e., the reading technique may be different from the reading method.

2.2 The Cleanroom Approach

The Cleanroom approach, as proposed by Harlan Mills (Currit, et al., 1986) addressed the above issues by providing a particular reading technique (step-wise abstraction) and a motivation for reading (the developer cannot test). To study the effects of the approach and reduce the risk of applying it in the SEL, we ran a controlled experiment at the University of Maryland.

The goal of this study was to analyze the Cleanroom process in order to evaluate and compare it to a non-Cleanroom process with respect to the effects on the process, product and developers from the point of view of the researchers (Selby, et al., 1987). This study was conducted using upper division and graduate students at the University of Maryland. The problem studied was an electronic message system of about 1500 LOC. The experimental design was a replicated project using 15 three-person teams (10 used Cleanroom). They were allowed 3 to 5 test submissions to an independent tester. We collected data on the participants' background, attitudes, online activities, and testing results.

The major results were:

- With regard to process, the Cleanroom developers (1) felt they more effectively applied off-line review techniques, while others focused on functional testing, (2) spent less time on-line and used fewer computer resources, and (3) tended to make all their scheduled deliveries.
- With regard to the delivered product, the Cleanroom products tended to have the following static properties: less dense complexity, higher percentage of assignment statements, more global data, more comments; and the following operational properties: the products more completely met the requirements and a higher percentage of test cases succeeded.
- With regard to the effect on the developers, most Cleanroom developers missed program execution, modified their development style, but said they would use the Cleanroom approach again.

2.3 Cleanroom in the SEL

Based upon this success, we decided to try the Cleanroom approach in the SEL (Basili and Green, 1994). The study goal was to analyze the *Cleanroom process* in order to *evaluate and compare it to the standard SEL development process* with respect to the *effects on the effort distribution, cost, and reliability* from the point of view of the *SEL organization*. This was the basis for a single-project case study in which Cleanroom was applied to a 40 KLOC ground support system. To evaluate and integrate Cleanroom into the SEL we used the Quality Improvement Paradigm to set up our learning process. We define the six steps of the QIP as they apply to the introduction of Cleanroom into the SEL:

Characterize: Describe the product and its environment. For example, what are the relevant models, baselines and measures, what are the existing processes, what is the standard cost, relative effort for activities, reliability, what are the high risk areas? (See the sample measures and baselines in Figure 2).

Set goals: Define the goals to be achieved. For example, what are the expectations, relative to the baselines, what do we hope to learn or gain, how will Cleanroom perform with respect to changing requirements? (See the sample expectations in Figure 2).

Choose process: Select the best mix of methods and techniques to achieve the goals relative to the environment. That is, how should the Cleanroom process be modified and tailored relative to the environment? For example, formal methods are hard to apply and require skill; we may have insufficient data to measure reliability; therefore, we might allow back-out options for unit testing certain modules.

Execute: Collect and analyze data based upon the goals, making changes to the process in real time.

Analyze: Try to characterize and understand what happened relative to the goals; write lessons learned.

Package: Modify the process for future use.

	Sample Measures	Sample Baseline	Sample Expectation
PROCESS	Effort distribution Change profile	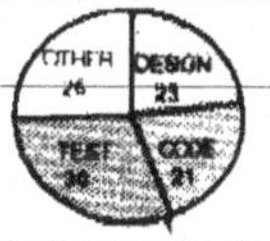	Increased design % due to emphasis on peer review process
COST	Productivity Level of rework Impact of spec changes	Historically, 26 DLOC per day	No degradation from current level
RELIABILITY	Error rate Error distribution Error source	Historically, 7 errors per KDLOC	Decreased error rate

Figure 2. Sample measures, baselines, and expectations.

There were many lessons learned during this first application of the Cleanroom approach in the SEL. However, the most relevant to reading were that the failure rate during test was reduced by 25% and productivity increased by about 30%, mostly due to fact that there was a reduction in the rework effort, i.e., 95% as opposed to 58% of the faults took less than 1 hour to fix. About 50% of code time was spent reading, as opposed to the normal 10%. All code was read by 2 developers. However, even though the developers were taught reading by step-wise abstraction for coding reading, only 26% of the faults were found by both readers. This implied to us that the reading technique was not applied as effectively as it should have been, as we expected a more consistent reading result.

During this case study, problems, as specified by the users, were recorded and the process was modified in real time. As well, notes were made as to how to improve the process for its next application. For example, better training and skill development was needed for the methods and techniques, better mechanisms were needed to upload the code to the testers and testers needed to be able to add requirements to help them analyze output.

Based upon the success of the first Cleanroom case study, we began to define new studies with the goal of applying the reading technique more effectively. A second and third Cleanroom project were initiated. Changes to the process involved better training, a solution to the uploading problem, and allowing testers to add requirements. The project leaders for the first project became process modelers for the next two and we began to generate the evolved version of the SEL Cleanroom Process Model. Thus, experimentally, we moved from a case study to a multi-project analysis study.

Figure 3 gives an overview of the projects studied to date. Figure 4 gives the effects of Cleanroom on error rate and productivity. Like the first Cleanroom project, the second was done in-house at NASA, and was successful with regard to reducing error rate but was not as productive as the first. The third project was done totally by the contractor. It appeared to be less successful on both counts, partly because it was our first experience with a project of that size (160 KLOC) and partly because it was done off site with less access to support. Based upon these projects, other modifications were made to the method, e.g., allowing a clean compile before reading.

A fourth Cleanroom project was recently completed. Again, like the third, it was large and totally developed by the contractor. As can be seen in Figure 4, the results here were very positive.

Cleanroom has been successful in the SEL. Although there is still room for improvement in reading and abstracting code formally, a more major concern is the lack of techniques for reading documents other than code, e.g., requirements, design, test plans.

This has generated a motivation for the continual evolution of reading techniques in the SEL, both inside and outside the Cleanroom life cycle model. Specific emphasis is on improving reading technology for requirements and design documents.

2.4 Scenario-Based Reading

The experiments described above convinced us that reading is a key, if not the key technical activity for verifying and validating software work products. However, there has been little research focus on the development of reading techniques, with the possible exception of reading by step-wise abstraction, as developed by Harlan Mills.

	1st Cleanroom	2nd Cleanroom	3rd Cleanroom	4th Cleanroom
Project	ACME	SAMPEX	WIND/POLAR	SOHO AGSS
Size (developed lines)	40 KSLOC	23 KSLOC	160 KSLOC	141 KSLOC
Size (total lines)	60 KLOC	39 KLOC	201 KLOC	485 KLOC
Dates	1988-90	1990-91	1990-92	1993-1995
Function	Attitude determination (Math)	Telemetry processing (data processing)	Full attitude (two missions)	Full attitude

Figure 3. Multi-project analysis study of cleanroom in the SEL.

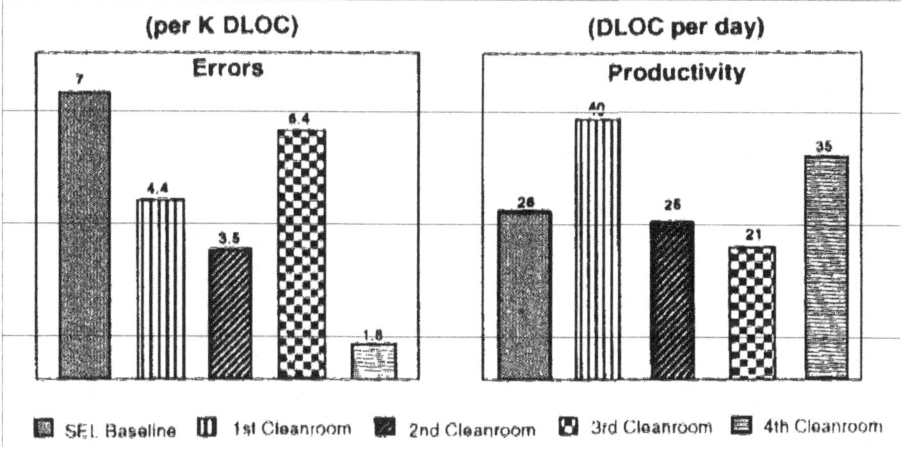

Figure 4. Effects of Cleanroom on error rate and productivity.

The ultimate goal here is to understand the best way to read for a particular set of conditions. That is, we are not only interested in how to develop techniques for reading such documents as requirements documents, but under what conditions are each of the techniques most effective and how might they be combined in a method, such as inspections, to provide a more effective reading technology for the particular problem and environment.

The idea is to provide a flexible framework for defining the reading technology so that the definer of the technology for a particular project has the appropriate information for selecting the right techniques and method characteristics. Thus, the process definition may change depending on the project characteristics. For example, if a higher number of omission faults are expected, we might emphasize a traceability reading approach embedded in design inspections; when embedding traceability reading in design inspections, we might make sure a traceability matrix exists.

As stated in the introduction, we believe there are many factors that affect the way a person reads, e.g., the reviewer's role, the reading goals, the work product. Based upon these studies, we also believe that techniques can be developed that will allow us to better define how we should read, and that using these techniques, effectively embedded in the appropriate methods, can improve the effects of reading. For example, reading techniques for end-users reading a software requirements document should be different than the reading techniques for software testers reading a requirements document; reading techniques for developers reading for interface faults should be different than reading techniques for developers reading for missing initialization. Also, if we know that reading by step-wise refinement is more effective for interface faults, and, based upon past history, we anticipate a large number of interface faults for a particular project, then we can assign more than one reader to use step-wise abstraction reading in our inspection team.

Thus we need to improve the reading of all kinds of documents from various points of view. To do this, we need to more deeply understand the relationship between techniques and methods and the dimensions of both. That is, what are the things we can vary when dealing with a technique? For example, consider the following dimensions of a reading technique:

Input object: any document, e.g., requirements, design, code, test plan, etc.

Output object: a set of defects or anomalies

Technique: some specific procedure, e.g., sequential reading, path analysis, step-wise abstraction, etc.

Formality: the degree of rigor, e.g., proof, correctness demonstration, etc.

Goals: the purpose for reading, e.g., fault detection, traceability, performance, understanding reuse, etc.

Method: the method the technique is embedded in, e.g., walk-through, inspections, reviews, etc.

Perspective: the role of the reader, e.g., user, designer, tester, maintainer, etc.

Context: anticipated problems, application domain, organization, etc.

Product qualities: correctness, reliability, efficiency, portability, etc.

Process qualities: process conformance, integration with other processes, etc.

When defining a technique, what are the values of the various dimensions? We have been developing and studying reading techniques that take into account the various dimensions, as well as the historical data of the environment where the technique will be applied. The goal is to define a set of reading techniques that can be tailored to the document being read and the goals of the organization for that document, and that are usable in existing methods, such as inspections or reviews.

To this end, we have been working on an approach to generating families of reading techniques, based upon the values of different dimensional attributes. At the top level, each family of techniques is based upon combining two primary dimensions, e.g., the goal and the perspective, to generate a procedure, or operational scenario (Figure 5). The operational scenario requires the reader to (1) create an abstraction (based on a model building or abstraction dimension) of the product, and (2) answer questions (based on an analysis dimension) while building that abstraction. Each reading technique in the family can be based upon a different abstraction and question set.

Each family (and thus each technique) is tailored based upon other dimensions as well, e.g., the input dimension, the context dimension. So, based upon the input dimension, a family of techniques can be instantiated for a particular document (e.g., requirements, design) and notation (e.g., English text, a formal notation) in which the document is written. Based upon the context dimension, a family of techniques can be tailored to react appropriately to the project and environment characteristics. The choice of primary, and secondary dimensions, as well as abstractions and the types of questions asked depend on the organization's needs and concerns.

Thus each technique within the family is (1) tailorable, based upon the values of various dimensions, (2) detailed, in that it provides the reader a well-defined set of steps to follow, (3) specific, in that the reader has a particular purpose or goal for reading the document and the procedures support that goal, (4) focused, in that it provides a particular coverage of the document, and a combination of techniques in the family provides coverage of the entire document, (5) studied empirically to determine if and when it is most effective.

So far, two different families of reading techniques have been defined for requirements documents: defect-based reading and perspective-based reading.

Perspective-based reading focuses on different product customer perspectives, e.g., reading from the perspective of the software designer, the tester, the end-user, the maintainer, the hardware engineer, representing the perspective dimension. The analysis questions were generated by focusing predominantly on various requirements type errors, e.g., incorrect fact, omission, ambiguity, and inconsistency (Basili and Weiss 1981), representing the goal dimension.

Defect-based reading focuses on a model of the data and functions of the requirements in a form of state machine notation. The different model views were based upon focusing on a variation of the defect classes given above: data type inconsistency, incorrect functions, an ambiguity or missing information, representing the goal dimension. The analysis questions were generated by combining/abstracting a set of questions that were used in checklists for evaluating the correctness and reliability of requirements documents, representing an existing technique dimension.

To provide a little more detail into the approach for generating reading techniques, consider the following example of the generation of test-based reading, one member of the family of perspective-based reading. The object is the requirements document, the model-base is a testing technique, (e.g., equivalence partitioning, boundary-value testing), and the analysis dimensions are the correctness, completeness, consistency, and unambiguity of the requirements.

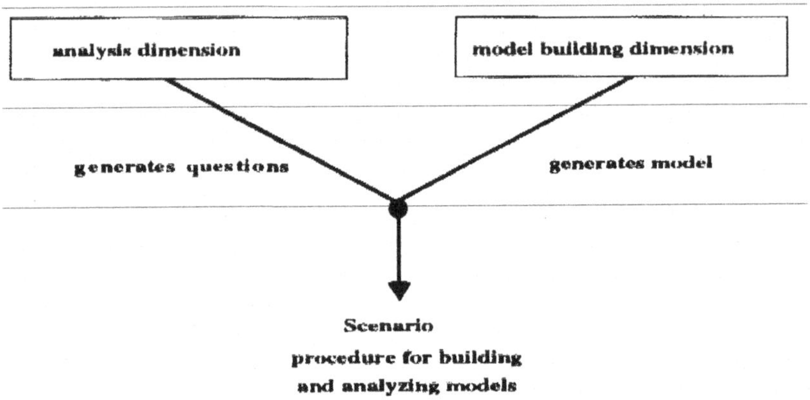

Figure 5. Building focused tailored reading techniques.

The operational scenario of reading procedure is defined as follows: for each requirement, make up a test or set of tests that will allow you to ensure that the implementation satisfies the requirement. Use equivalence partitioning, boundary-value testing criteria to make up the test suite.

The second dimension is based upon defect classes, specifically incorrect fact, omission, ambiguity, and inconsistency. These generated the following questions, which the reader should ask while building the test plan model:

a) Do I have all the information necessary to divide the requirement into a valid equivalence class and invalid equivalence classes? Can I make up reasonable test cases for each based upon the criteria?
b) Can I be sure that the test I generated will yield the correct value in the correct units?
c) Does the requirement make sense from what I know about the application and from what is specified in the overview?
d) Are there other interpretations of this requirement that the implementor might make based upon the way the requirement is defined?
e) Is there another requirement for which the equivalence class is defined differently, i.e., in which the test case you generate should give a contradictory response for the other equivalence class?

The model for developer-based reading might be to perform a high level design using structured analysis or object oriented design. The model for the use-based reading might be to develop a user's manual. Although in each case the questions are derived from trying to identify omission, incorrect facts, etc., the opportunities for such discoveries, and thus the questions, will vary, depending on the model used.

Specific members of each of the families have been studied experimentally. In the defect-based reading study, the goal was to analyze *defect-based reading, ad hoc reading* and *checklist-based reading* in order to *evaluate and compare* them with respect to their *effect on fault detection effectiveness in the context of an inspection team* from the viewpoint of the *researcher*. The three defect-based reading techniques stated above were applied. The study was applied using graduate students at the University of Maryland. The requirements documents were written in the SCR notation (Henninger 1980). They were a Water Level Monitoring System and a Cruise Control System. The experimental design is a blocked subject-project: Partial factorial design, replicated twice with a total of 48 subjects (Porter, et al., 1995).

Major results were that (1) the defect-based readers performed better than ad hoc and checklist readers with an improvement in defect detection rate of about 35%, (2) the defect-based reading procedures helped reviewers focus on specific fault classes but were no less effective at detecting other faults, and (3) checklist reading was no more effective than ad hoc reading.

In the perspective-based reading study, the goal was to analyze *perspective-based reading* and *NASA's current reading technique* in order to *evaluate and compare* them with respect to their *effect on fault detection effectiveness in the context of an inspection team* from the viewpoint of the *researcher and the SEL*. Three perspective-based reading techniques (test-based, developer-based, and use-based reading) were defined and studied. Studies have been performed in the SEL environment using generic requirements documents written in English (ATM machine, Parking Garage) and NASA type functional specifications (two ground support AGSS sub-systems). The experimental design is again a blocked subject-project using a partial factorial design. It has been applied twice, with a total of 25 subjects (Basili, et al., 1996).

Major results are that perspective-based reading (1) is effective for generic documents both at the individual and team level, i.e., taking each technique in the family individually as compared with the standard approach, and combining the three perspectives for full coverage against a team of standard readers, (2) catches different types of defects depending on the perspective, (3) is effective for the NASA documents at the team level. It was felt that the techniques could be better tailored for the NASA style document to improve individual scores.

We will continue to evolve and study various families and various techniques within the families. The first series of experiments described above is aimed at discovering if scenario-based reading is more effective than current practices. Early results are promising. A second series will be used to discover under which circumstances each of the various scenario-based reading techniques, or families of techniques, is most effective.

We hope to replicate these experiments in different environments, replacing the NASA documents with documents from other organizations. We also hope to run a case study at NASA to better understand how to tailor the techniques to the documents.

We will continue to develop operational scenarios for other document types, e.g., design document, and test their effectiveness in experiments. We will eventually consider tool support for the techniques developed.

Scopes of Evaluation

		# Projects	
		One	More than one
# of Teams per Project	One	3. Cleanroom (SEL Project 1)	4. Cleanroom (SEL Projects, 2,3,4,...)
	More than one	2. Cleanroom at Maryland	1. Reading vs. Testing 5. Scenario reading vs. ...

Figure 6. Series of studies.

3. Conclusion

In our attempt to better understand the effects of software reading techniques, we have run the experimental gamut from blocked subject-project experiments (reading vs. testing) to replicated projects (University of Maryland Cleanroom study) to a case study (the first SEL Cleanroom study) to multi-project variation (the set of SEL Cleanroom projects) and now back to blocked subject-project experiments (for scenario-based reading). (See Figure 6).

As we learn, as we move through each cycle of the Quality Improvement Paradigm, the level of sophistication of our reading goals is maturing. Our ability to understand things about reading is evolving. A pattern of knowledge is being built from a series of experiments.

Various groups at different sites are already replicating some of the experiments. Most of these are members of ISERN, the International Software Engineering Research Network, whose goal is specifically to perform and share the results of empirical studies.

Acknowledgements

I would like to thank Forrest Shull and Carolyn Seaman for reviewing the drafts of this paper. This work was supported in part by NASA grant NSG-5123, UMIACS, NSF grant 01-5-24845.

References

Basili, V. R., Green, S., Laitenberger, O. U., Lanubile, F., Shull, F. Sorumgaard, S. and Zelkowitz, The Empirical Investigation of Perspective-Based Reading. *Journal of Empirical Software Engineering*, Volume 1, Issue 2 (1996).

Basili, V. R. and Green, S., Software Process Evolution at the SEL. *IEEE Software*, pp. 58-66 (1994).

Basili, V. R., Zelkowitz, M. V., McGarry, F., Pajerski, R., Page, J., Waligora, S., SEL'S Software Process-Improvement Program. *IEEE Software*, pp. 83-87 (1994).

Basili, V. R., Caldiera, G., McGarry, F., Pajerski, R., Page, G., Waligora, S., The Software Engineering Laboratory —An Operational Software Experience Factory, 14th International Conference on Software Engineering (1992).

Basili, V. R., Software Development: A Paradigm for the Future, COMPSAC '89, Orlando, Florida, pp. 471-485 (1989).

Basili, V. R., and Rombach, H. D., The TAME Project: Towards Improvement-Oriented Software Environment. *IEEE Transactions on Software Engineering*, vol. 14, no. 6 (1988).

Basili, V. R., and Selby, R., Comparing the Effectiveness of Software Testing Strategies. *IEEE Transactions on Software Engineering*, pp. 1278-1296 (1987).

Basili, V. R., Quantitative Evaluation of Software Methodology, Keynote Address, First Pan Pacific Computer Conference, Melbourne, Australia (1985).

Basili, V. R. and Weiss, D. M., A Methodology for Collecting Valid Software Engineering Data. *IEEE Transactions on Software Engineering*, pp. 728-738 (1984).

Basili, V. R., Weiss, D. M., Evaluation of a Software Requirements Document by Analysis of Change Data, Proceedings of the Fifth International Conference on Software Engineering, pp. 314-323 (1981).

Currit, P. A., Dyer, M. and Mills, H. D., Certifying the Reliability of Software. *IEEE Transactions on Software Engineering*, vol. SE-12, pp. 3-11 (1986).

Henninger, K. L., Specifying Software Requirements for Complex Systems: New Techniques and Their Application. *IEEE TSE*, vol. SE-6, no. 1, pp. 2-13 (1980).

Linger, R. C., Mills, H. D. and Witt, B. I., Structured Programming: Theory and Practice. *IEEE TSE*, Reading, MA: Addison-Wesley (1979).

Myers, G. J., A Controlled Experiment in Program Testing and Code Walkthrough Inspections. *Communications ACM*, pp. 760-768 (1978).

Hetzel, W. C., An Experimental Analysis of Program Verification Problem Solving Capabilities as They Relate to Programmer Efficiency. *Computer Personnel*, vol. 3, pp. 10-15 (1972).

Porter, A. A., Votta, L. G. and Basili, V. R., Comparing Detection Methods for Software Requirements Inspections: A Replicated Experiment. *IEEE Transactions on Software Engineering*, vol. 21, no. 6, pp. 563-575 (1995).

Selby, R., Basili, V. R. and Baker, T., Cleanroom Software Development: An Empirical Evaluation. *IEEE Transactions on Software Engineering*, pp. 1027-1037 (1987).

Section 6. Experience Base

Barry Boehm

University of Southern California

The Experience Base in Context

It's impossible to discuss a piece of Vic's work without relating it to the other pieces. Everything fits together within an overall strategy of applying the empirical scientific method to the challenge of continuously improving an organization's software processes and products.

The Goal-Question-Metric approach recognizes that "improvement" requires metrics, but that every organization has its own set of goals and environmental influences. This means that "improvement" metrics may be anything from meaningless to dysfunctional if they aren't related to the organization's goals and to questions about the organization's current state and evolving environment. The Quality Improvement Paradigm recognizes that continuous process and product improvement needs to fit within a framework involving the scientific method of hypothesis formulation, test, and closed-loop feedback control. The Experience Factory recognizes that continuous improvement, as with any other investment to achieve results, should have a business plan, management commitment to the plan, and an infrastructure of policies, processes, procedures, facilities, tools, management information systems, staffing, training, and incentives to get best results. The Software Engineering Laboratory (SEL) has been a marvelous example of successfully applying, evaluating, learning about, and evolving all of these concepts and capabilities in the area of software development and evolution. It justly deserved being the first recipient of the IEEE Software Process Achievement Award.

In this context, a narrow definition of an Experience Base is that it serves as the management information system for the continuous process and product improvement enterprise. This includes the data definitions, data base organization and content, database management capabilities, and analysis tools for formulating, testing, and evolving hypotheses about improving the organization's processes and products. But I think a broader definition is more appropriate; the entire infrastructure of product, process, data, and personnel assets that evolve to enable the organization to most rapidly and cost-effectively improve its capabilities to adapt to its changing goals and environment.

Paper 1: Software Engineering Practices in the U.S. and Japan

The first paper in this chapter, "Software Engineering practices in the U.S. and Japan," reflects this holistic view of an organization's experience base. The paper's author list (Zelkowitz, Yeh, Hamlet, Gannon, and Basili) also reflects Vic's gracious pro-active efforts to avoid alphabetical bias in team-authored papers.

The paper is based on a University of Maryland study sponsored by IBM of software practices across 25 organizations in the U.S. and Japan. It was performed in the somewhat heady days of the "Software Factory" concept as the silver bullet for solving the software engineering problem. It was also a time of some concern that the Japanese investments in Fifth Generation Computing Technology and Japanese Software Factories would cause U.S. leadership in computers and software to go the way of its leadership in automobile and consumer electronics production [Feigenbaum-McCorduck, 1983; Cusumano, 1991]. IBM was making significant investments in software processes and support environments at the time, along with other leading software producers such as Hughes, System Development Corporation, and TRW, and was interested in an external perspective on which practices were most widely used and most effective.

Under Vic's and Frank McGarry's leadership, the NASA/University of Maryland/Computer Sciences Corporation Software Engineering Lab was already producing measured results on such issues as the relative effectiveness of peer reviews and testing for identifying defects. It came as an eye-opener to Vic and the Maryland study group not only that such data were relatively scarce among even the more advanced software organizations that participated in the study, but also that many well-known practices were not much used. The organizations had high usage rates for high-level languages, on-line development, and some kind of reviews, but only 45% of the organizations had formally-defined software methods, only 27% used test tools, and only 18% used automated code auditors to check for standards compliance. It is not clear that the situation has become markedly better since 1988.

In discussing these results with Vic, we concluded that a 2005 industry survey probably would not yield much higher adoption percentages. However, we believe that it would be valuable to have such a comparison study performed and extended to newer techniques such as requirements management tools, architecture definition languages, configuration management, lightweight formal methods, and agile methods.

With respect to comparisons between the U.S. and Japan, the study concluded that Japanese organizations were doing more investments in tools and metrics. Since then, though, the rapid pace of information technology change has made it more difficult to succeed with a factory-type approach to software production, and Japanese as well as U.S. organizations are exploring how to best integrate more agile practices into their software portfolios.

In terms of the effect of the study on my work, it was particularly significant since I was one of the TRW contributors to the study. It was very helpful in benchmarking TRW's practices with those of other organizations, and in providing insights for prioritizing investments in our TRW Software Productivity System (SPS) corporate software support environment [Boehm et al., 1984]. It also helped greatly in explaining our SPS project to TRW management, and in guiding our collaborative explorations of the Computer Aided Software Environment (CASE) and workstation marketplace as part of our TRW-Fujitsu Corp. venture with Fujitsu (which ended up not going forward as a product venture for several good reasons). The study was similarly valuable to the U.S. Department of Defense in providing insights and rationale for its mid-1980's Software Technology for Adaptable, Reliable Systems (STARS) initiative [Druffel et al, 1983].

In terms of the effect of the study on Vic's future work, one can see that it provided a rare perspective and database of software experience across a wide variety of organizations. This led to Vic's conclusion that one-size-fits-all metrics were unworkable, and that each organization needed to examine its own goals and formulate its own improvement questions before adopting improvement metrics. It also gave him the breadth of analyzed experience to be an effective consultant to organizations seeking to measure and improve their processes, further adding to his experience base.

Paper 2: An Evaluation of Expert Systems for Software Engineering Management

Paper 2 builds on some earlier SEL work reported in the 1985 paper, "Monitoring Software Development Through Dynamic Variables" [Doerflinger-Basili, 1985]. The 1985 paper shows the value of having an experience base that includes not only data but also evolving hypotheses about what the data means and what to do about it. By the early 1980's, the SEL was collecting consistent data across a project's development cycle, such as the number of source instructions developed and changed, number of computer runs, number of programmer hours, number of software changes, and amount of computer time expended. This enabled managers of new SEL projects to determine whether their combinations of these variables at a given time (lines of code per software change, programmer hours per line of code, computer runs per software change) were considerably higher or lower than the baseline set of projects. Knowing these facts, they then wanted some interpretation of the likely root causes and likely appropriate corrective actions, if necessary.

The SEL researchers formulated such hypotheses for nine of these combinations. For example, having a relatively large number of lines of code per change might imply one or more of such root causes as having good code, easily developed code, or a poor testing approach. Having a relatively large number of computer runs per software change might imply one or more of such root causes as having good code, lots of testing, or a poor testing approach.

Having a project that exhibited both of these characteristics would then involve taking the intersection of their root causes as potential explanations of the results. In this case, it might imply having good code, a poor testing approach, or both.

When all nine combinations were analyzed for all nine of the projects with comparable data during the code and test phases, the results were not uniform but exhibited fairly consistent data patterns. When the root cause rules were applied at several stages of a tenth project, the results were reasonably consistent with observed project behavior. Thus, the rules appeared to provide good early working indicators about potential problem projects. This led to more extensive effort to develop and evaluate a knowledge base, and an expert system for diagnosing software development project problems, as discussed in Paper 2.

Paper 2 shows all of the hallmarks of a Basili empirical study: explicit hypothesis formulation, comparative technology evaluation, hypothesis-driven data collection and analysis, objective outcome evaluation, and constructive but conservative conclusions. Such studies were relatively rare in the enthusiastic early days of expert systems (with some exceptions such as medical diagnosis).

In this case, two expert-system rule base development approaches were used. One was an extension of the bottom-up symptom-to-root-cause rules in the previous Doerflinger-Basili paper. The other was a separate top-down root-cause-to-symptom rule generation and merger involving two domain experts. The resulting rules were tailored for comparative use in two types of inference mechanisms—rule-based deduction and frame-based abduction—and the comparative results of all four combinations of rule bases and inference mechanisms analyzed.

The results indicated that rule-based deduction performed somewhat better than frame-based abduction, and that the bottom-up rules yielded somewhat better results than the top-down rules. Unfortunately, though, the study also found that none of the combinations did much better at problem identification than did random choice. There are good discussions of why this turned out to be the case. Fundamentally, the deductions can be only as good as the rules. And even within a set of projects as uniform as those in the SEL, the variability across such software projects is considerably higher than the variability within domains where expert systems have performed much better, such as computing platform configuration or medical diagnosis.

The limitations of these software engineering expert systems are nicely summarized on papers 754-755: (1) so much of the knowledge and relationships are unclear in this field, (2) the experts themselves do not agree on much of the knowledge, (3) the expert systems used were only a small number of variables and metrics, (4) the metrics used are not ideal, (5) many of the interpretations in the database are subjective and may not always be correct, and (6) there may be discrepancies in the interpretations at different points in the project.

These results were quite helpful in realigning expectations and identifying pitfalls to avoid in applying expert systems technology to software engineering problems. I found them very useful in running a project course on Knowledge Based Software Engineering in 1993.

Paper 3: Software Defect Reduction Top-10 List

In 2000, Vic and I were awarded an NSF grant to create and operate a Center for Empirically-Based Software Engineering (CeBASE). Its objectives were to develop empirically-based practices for software development, to establish an experience base (eBase) of empirical data on the relative effectiveness of the practices in various domains, and to conduct empirical studies to fill key gaps in the practices and eBase. To avoid getting spread too thin, we initially focused on two high-concern areas: software defect reduction and commercial-off-the-shelf (COTS)-based system development.

Some of our initial steps were to identify key issues in defect reduction and COTS-based development; to integrate our existing experience bases, and to integrate our existing empirical software development guidelines. To summarize and stimulate extensions of our integrated defect reduction and COTS experience bases, we published top-10 lists of the most useful empirical data we could find in each area. Paper 3 covers the defect reduction area; the COTS area is covered in [Basili-Boehm, 2001]. We then followed these up with further studies and electronic workshops (a Basili-team innovation) to extend the experience bases. Examples of the results for defect reduction are in [Shull et al., 2002]; the current eBase content is at http://www.cebase.org.

Item one in Paper 3, "Finding and fixing a software problem after delivery is often more than 100 times more expensive than finding and fixing it during the requirements and design phase," became part of a productive discussion with the agile methods community. In Extreme Programming Explained [Beck, 1999], Kent Beck presented "the technical premise of XP" on page 23: a graph indicating that practicing XP could completely flatten the slope of cost-to-fix-vs.-time curve. Since empirical data to substantiate this graph was lacking, this stimulated some further electronic workshops to capture empirical data on agile methods. This led to some fruitful collaborative work with Laurie Williams, the leading empirical researcher in the agile methods area, and some summaries of empirical findings in agile methods in [Lindvall et. al., 2002] and Appendix E of [Boehm-Turner, 2004].

In terms of the slope of the cost-to-fix-vs.-time curve, we found that the 100:1 slope still held for most large projects, but that the slope could be reduced significantly by early and thorough architecting and risk reduction. For small and agile projects, we found no data confirming a 1:1 slope, but some projects with around a 5:1 slope.

Our efforts to integrate Maryland's and USC's empirical software engineering processes led to a synthesis of Maryland's organization-level Experience Factory/GQM/QIP guidelines with USC's project-level MBASE guidelines into an approach called the CeBASE Method [Boehm et. al., 2002]. This has been applied to several projects as a result of the U.S. Department of Defense's selecting CeBASE to support the efforts of its Software Intensive Systems Office to improve DoD's software engineering practices, especially for projects representing future trends in DoD software intensive systems.

Parts of this effort have involved elaborating our integrated CeBASE Method and mapping it onto the Integrated Capability Maturity model (CMMI) [Ahern et al., 2001; Chrissis et al., 2003], which DoD has been using to stimulate its suppliers' software and system engineering process maturity. Other parts have involved applying and evolving the method on major futures-representative DoD projects, particularly on the U.S. Army/DARPA Future Combat Systems program, a huge, transformational, network-centric system of systems. A summary of this work is [Boehm et al., 2004] (CrossTalk articles are available at www.stsc.hill.af.mil/crosstalk).

We were able to integrate the Maryland and USC models rapidly because we had already been applying Experience Factory techniques to our annual series of real-client USC campus electronic services projects (I have been a big fan of Vic and the SEL group's methods, and had begun applying Experience Factory techniques at TRW in the late 1970's). The annual feedback on these projects enabled us to improve our MBASE Guidelines and improve project performance both at early milestones and in terms of end-product client satisfaction, as shown in Table 2 of [Boehm et. al., 2002].

Unfortunately, NSF support of CeBASE lasted only 2 years, but by then CeBASE was relatively self-sufficient with support from both DoD and the NASA High Dependability Computing Program. CeBASE results have helped Future Combat Systems identify critical risks and avoid significant overruns. They have also provided NASA with useful models of dependability [Basili et al., 2004; Boehm et al., 2004].

Being able to collaborate with Vic has been a highlight of my career. It is rare to find someone with such strong technical capabilities, empathy for people, creativity in finding constructive solutions to complex problems, high standards, joy of living, and ease of collaboration.

Bravissimo, Vic! May you continue to make great contributions and enjoy the best.

References

[1] [Ahern et al., 2001]. D. Ahern, A. Clouse, and R. Turner, CMMI Distilled, Addison Wesley, 2001 (2nd ed., 2004).

[2] [Basili-Boehm, 2001]. V. Basili and B. Boehm, "COTS-Based Systems Top 10 List," Computer, May 2001, pp. 91-93.

[3] [Basili et al., 2004]. V. Basili, P. Donzelli, and S. Asgari, "A Unified Model of Dependability; Capturing Dependability in Context," Software, November/December 2004, pp. 19-25.

[4] [Beck, 1999]. K. Beck, Extreme Programming Explained (1st ed.), Addison-Wesley, 1999.

[5] [Boehm et al, 1984]. B. Boehm, M. Penedo, E.D. Stuckle, R. Williams, and A. Pyster, "A Software Development Environment for Improving Productivity," Computer, June 1984, pp. 30-44.

[6] [Boehm et. al., 2002]. B. Boehm, V. Basili, D. Port, and A. Jain, "Achieving CMMI Level 5 Improvements with MBASE and the CeBASE Method," CrossTalk, May 2002, pp. 9-16.

[7] [Boehm et al., 2004]. B. Boehm, A. W. Brown, V. Basili, and R. Turner, "Spiral Acquisition of Software-Intensive Systems of Systems," CrossTalk, May 2004, pp. 4-9.

[8] [Boehm et al., 2004] B. Boehm, L. Huang, A. Jain, and R. Madachy, "The ROI of Software Dependability: The iDAVE Model," Software, May/June 2004, pp. 54-61.

[9] [Boehm-Turner, 2004]. B. Boehm and R. Turner, Balancing Agility and Discipline, Addison-Wesley, 2004.

[10] [Chrissis et al., 2003]. M. Chrissis, M. Konrad, and S. Shrum, CMMI, Addison Wesley, 2003.

[11] [Cusumano, 1991]. M. Cusumano, Japan's Software Factories, Oxford University Press, 1991.

[12] [Doerflinger-Basili, 1985]. C. Doerflinger and V. Basili, "Monitoring Software Development Through Dynamic Variables," IEEE Transactions on Software Engineering, September 1985, pp. 978-985.

[13] [Druffel et al., 1983]. L. Druffel, S. Redwine, and W. Riddle (eds.), "The DoD-STARS Program," Special Issue, Computer, November 1983.
[14] [Feigenbaum-McCorduck, 1983]. E. Feigenbaum and P. McCorduck, The Fifth Generation, Addison Wesley, 1983.
[15] [Lindvall et. al., 2002]. M. Lindvall, V. Basili, B. Boehm, P. Costa, K. Dangle, F. Shull, R. Tesoriero, L. Williams, and M. Zelkowitz, "Empirical Findings in Agile Methods," in D. Wells and L. Williams (eds.), Extreme Programming and Agile Methods – XP/Agile Universe 2002, Springer Verlag, 2002, pp. 197-207.
[16] [Shull et al, 2002]. F. Shull, V. Basili, M. Zelkowitz, B. Boehm, A. W. Brown, P. Costa, M. Lindvall, D. Port, I. Rus, and R. Tesoreiro, "What We Have Learned About Fighting Defects," Proceedings of International Conference on Software Metrics, June 2002.

The Software Industry: A State of the Art Survey

Marvin V. Zelkowitz, Raymond Yeh, Richard G. Hamlet,
John D. Gannon, Victor R. Basili

Department of Computer Science,
University of Maryland, College Park, MD 20742

1. Introduction

1.1. Goals

The term "software engineering" first appeared in the late 1960s [Naur and Randell 69], [Buxton and Randell 70] to describe ways to develop, manage and maintain software so that the resulting products are reliable, correct, efficient, and flexible. After 15 years of study by the computer science community, it is important to assess the impact that numerous software engineering advances have had on actual software production. The IBM Corporation asked the University of Maryland to conduct a survey of different program development environments in industry in order to determine the state of the art in software development and to ascertain which software engineering techniques are most effective in the non-academic sector. This report contains the results of that survey.

1.2. The Survey Process

This project began during the spring of 1981. The goal was to sample 19 to 20 organizations, including the primary sponsor of this project - IBM, and study their development practices. This was accomplished via a two-step process. A detailed survey form was sent to each of the participating companies. In response to the return of this form, a follow-up visit was made. This visit clarified the answers given on the form. We believe that this process, although limiting the number of places surveyed, resulted in more accurate information being presented than if we had just relied on forms.

Each survey form contains two parts. Section one asks for general comments concerning software development for the organization as a whole. The information described by this part typically represents the "standards and practices" document for the organization. In addition, we also studied several recently completed projects within each company. Each such project completed the second section of the survey form, which described the tools and techniques that were used on that particular project.

A variety of organizations in both the United States and Japan participated in the study. The acknowledgement at the end of this report lists some of the participants. Due to the proprietary nature of part of the information we obtained, some of the participants wish to remain anonymous. Over the life of this project, we surveyed 25 different organizations. Thirteen of them are U.S. companies and 12 were from Japan. Due to the cost and time restrictions, about half of the Japanese companies were not interviewed, and the other half were interviewed in varying degrees of detail.

In addition to our survey form, interviews were held with several company officials, and some published references were used for additional data. Figure 1 lists the basic data processed. In order to characterize the projects we studied, projects and teams are somewhat arbitrarily classified into four groups according to sizes: Small, Medium, Large, and Very Large. Projects are classified according to the number of staff months needed to complete them, and teams according to the numbers of members. This division leads to a breakdown in which there is only one case of a team that is larger than a project (Company U).

After reviewing the basic data, we recognized three different software development environments:

(1) Contract software – Typically Department of Defense and NASA aerospace systems

(2) Data processing applications - Typically software produced by an organization for its own internal business use

(3) Systems software - Typically operating system support software produced by a hardware vendor as part of a total hardware-software package of products for a given operating system.

A single company might be represented in more than one of the above categories. For example, we looked at several Defense-related projects and one internal data processing application at an aerospace company.

This survey is not meant to be all-encompassing; however, we believe that we have surveyed a large enough number of locations to understand software development in industry today. Several companies were concerned about which projects we should study — we left that decision up to them. There was concern that the projects we were looking at were "not typical" of the company. (Interestingly, very few companies claimed to be doing "typical" software. We felt that we were getting to see the "better" developed projects. In general, every company had either a written guideline or unwritten folklore as to how software was developed. Deviations from this policy were rare.

2. General Observations

The literature contains many references to software engineering methodology; including tools support throughout the lifecycle language support in other than source code, testing support, measurement and management practices, and other techniques that will be mentioned throughout this report. But in our survey, we found surprisingly little use of software engineering practices across all companies. No organization fully tries to use the available technology. While some companies had stronger management practices than others, none used tools to support these practices in any significant way.

Table 1. Companies surveyed. The size of the project is in staff-months where (S)mall = < 10, (M)edium = 10-100, (L)arge = 100-1000, and (V)ery (L)arge = > 1000. Team size is in staff members where S = < 10, M = 10-25, L = 25-50, and VL = > 50.

CODE	NO. OF DIVISIONS	NO. OF PROJECTS	INTERVIEWED	PROJECT SIZE	TEAM SIZE
A	2	3	Yes	L	L
B	2	7	Yes	VL	VL
C	1	1	No	S	M
D	1	3	Yes	L	L
E	3	4	Yes	VL	VL
F	1	3	Yes	VL	VL
G	1	2	Yes	L	L
H	1	7	Yes	L	M
I	1	9	Yes	VL	VL
J	1	4	Yes	L	VL
K	1	8	Yes	VL	M
L	1	1	Yes	L	VL
M	1	3	Yes	M	VL
N	1	2	No	S	S
O	1	1	Yes	VL	VL
P	1	1	No	M	-
Q	2	0	No	M	L
R	1	0	No	-	-
S	1	1	Yes	M	S
T	1	4	Yes	VL	VL
U	1	0	Yes	L	VL
V	1	1	Yes	M	S
W	1	1	Yes	L	S
X	1	1	No	L	S
Y	1	1	No	L	-
Z	1	2	Yes	M	S
AA	2	5	Yes	VL	VL
BB	1	1	Yes	M	S
CC	1	1	Yes	L	S
DD	1	7	Yes	VL	VL

Project Size (staff months)	Team Size (staff)
S<10	S<10
M 10-100	M 10-25
L 100-1000	L 25-50
VL>1000	VL>50

Figure 1. Legend

2.1. Organizational Structure

Most companies that we surveyed had an organizational structure similar to the one in Figure 2.

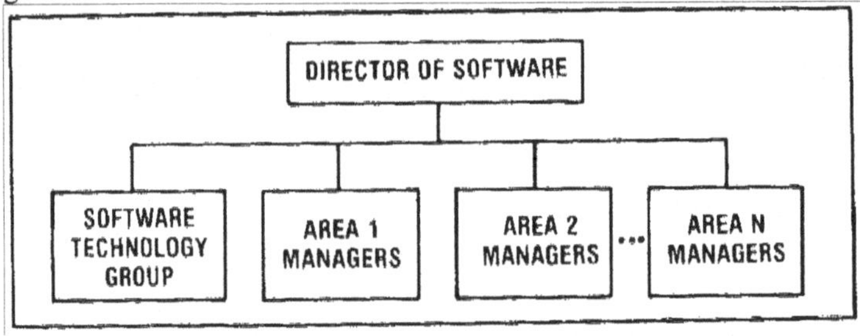

Figure 2. Typical Organization Structure

The software technology group typically has one to five individuals collecting data, modeling resource usage, and generating standards and practices documents. However, this group has no direct authority to enforce adherence to software engineering practices even within a single division. As a result, standards often vary within a single organization.

This structure also explains a current anomaly in the use of software engineering techniques. Although they are frequently mentioned in the literature and at conferences, software engineering techniques are rarely used correctly by the industry at large. Developers of real products often think that the software technology (research) group of Figure 2 (who are the conference attendees and write most of the research papers) is too optimistic about the effects of these techniques and are unrealistic since they have not applied them to real life situations. Managers know their personnel often lack the education and experience needed for successful applications of these techniques. Even the techniques that have been adopted are frequently misused. For example, although many companies used the term "chief programmer" to describe their programming team organization, most bore little resemblance to the technique described in the literature. Generally each project had two to three levels of management who handled staff and resource acquisition, but who did not actively participate in system design.

A further problem in many organizations is that there is generally no one person at the head of the chart of Figure 2 who makes software decisions. Such a person often exists in hardware organizations. For this reason, software standards are generally low and vary across the company.

2.2. Tool Use

Tool use is relatively low across the industry. Not too surprisingly, the use of tools varies inversely from their "distance" from the code and unit test phase of development. That is, tools are most frequently used during the code and unit test phase of software development (e.g., compilers. code auditors, test coverage monitors, etc.). Adjacent phases of the software lifecyle, design and integration, usually have less tool support (e.g., PDL processors and source code control systems). Few requirements or maintenance tools are used. In looking at tool use, Figure 3 gives some indication of which techniques and tools are used:

METHOD OR TOOL	PERCENTAGE OF COMPANIES
High-level languages	100
On-line access	93
Reviews	73
Program design languages	63
Some formal methodology	41
Some test tools	27
Code auditors	18
Chief programmer team	7
Any formal verification	0
Formal requirements or specifications	0

Figure 3. Industrial Method or Tool Use

Time sharing computer systems and compiler writing became practical in the late 1960s and early 1970s; thus online access and high level languages can probably be labeled the successes of the 1960s. Similarly, the widespread use of reviews and pseudo code or program design language (PDL) permits us to call them the successes of the 1970s. It is disappointing that few other tools have been adopted by industry. Testing tools are used by only 27% of the companies, and most of these are simply test data generators. Only one company (in Japan) indicated that it used any form of unit test tool to measure test case coverage. Although many companies claim to use chief programmer teams, few actually do.

While PDLs are heavily used, it is disappointing that the process is not automated. Some PDL processors are simply manual formatters, while some do "pretty print" and indent the code. Often the PDL is only a "coding standard" and not enforced by any tool. Only one location had a PDL processor that checked interfaces and variable use/define patterns.

Tool use generally has the flavor of vintage 1970 time sharing. Jobs have a "batch flavor" in that runs are assembled and then compiled. There is little interactive computing. There is minimal tool support - mostly compilers and simple editors.

The problems in using tools can be attributed to several factors. Corporate management has little (if any) software background and is not sympathetic with the need for tools. No separate corporate entity exists whose charter includes tools so there is no focal point for tool selection, deployment and evaluation, Tools must be paid out of project funds, so there is a fair amount of risk and expenditure for a project manager to adopt a new tool and train his people to use it. Since project management is evaluated on meeting current costs and schedules, and tool use must be amortized across several projects to be effective, a single project manager will almost always stand out as "unproductive. " Companies often work on different hardware, so tools are not transportable, limiting their scope and their perceived advantage. The most striking example of this, was one system where $1M was spent building a data base, yet there was no thought of ever using that data base on another system. The need to maintain large existing source code libraries (generally in assembly code) makes it hard to introduce a new tool that processes a new higher level language. Finally, many of the tools are incomplete and poorly documented. Because such tools fail to live up to promises, project managers are justifiably reluctant to adopt them or consider subsequently developed tools.

2.3. Japan – U.S. Comparisons

There is currently much interest in comparing U. S. and Japanese technology. In general, development practices are similar. Programmers in both countries complain about the amount of money going towards hardware development and the lack of resources for software. However, in comparing U.S. and Japanese software development, we found that Japanese companies typically optimize development across the company rather than within a single project. One effect of this is that tools become a capitalized investment paid far or developed out of company overhead rather than project funds. The cost of using tools is spread among more projects, knowledge about tools is known to more in the company, and project management is more willing to use tools since the risk is lower. Thus, tool development and use is more widespread in Japan.

2.4. Review

At the end of each phase (and sometimes within a phase) the evolving software product (i.e., requirements, design, code, test cases, see for example [Belady and Lehman 76]) is subjected to a review process, trying to uncover problems as soon as possible. ("Inspection" and "walkthrough" [Fagan 76] are other terms used for reviews without regard to the distinctions made in the software-engineering literature.) Nearly everyone agrees that reviews work, and nearly everyone uses them, but there is a wide variety in the ways that reviews are conducted. There seems to be an agreement that they allow the routine completion of software projects within time and budget constraints that only a few years ago could be managed only by luck and sweat. Reviews were first instituted for code, then extended to design. Extensions to requirements and test-case design are not universal, and some feel that the technique may have been pushed beyond its usefulness. Managers would like to extend the review process, while the technical people are more inclined to limit it to the best-understood phases of development.

Two aspects of reviews must be separated: one is management control and the other is technical utility. Managers must be concerned with both aspects, but technical success cannot be assured by insisting that certain forms be completed. If the tasks assigned to the reviewers are ill-defined, or the form of the product reviewed inappropriate, the review will waste valuable people's time. Lower-level managers prefer to use reviews where they think reviews are appropriate, and avoid them in other situations.

The technical success of the review process rests squarely on the expertise and interest of the people conducting the review, not on the mechanism itself. The review process is refined by continually changing it to reflect past successes and failures, and much of this information is subjective, implicitly known to experienced participants. Some historical information is encoded in review checklists, which newcomers can be trained to use. However, subjective items like the "completeness" of requirements are of little help to a novice.

2.5. Data Collection

Every company collects some data, but little data becomes part of the corporate memory to be used beyond the project on which it was collected. Data generally belongs to individual managers, and it is their option as to what to do with it. Data is rarely evaluated and used in a postmortem analysis of a project. After a project is completed, it is rarely subjected to an analysis to see if the process could have been improved. This is not the case in Japanese companies, in which postmortem analysis was more frequently performed.

Several companies are experimenting with various resource models (e.g., SLIM [Putnam 79], PRICE S [Freiman and Park 79], etc.). No company seems to trust any model enough to use it on a full proposal; instead the models are used to check manual estimates. Figure 4 shows that little data is being collected across all companies.

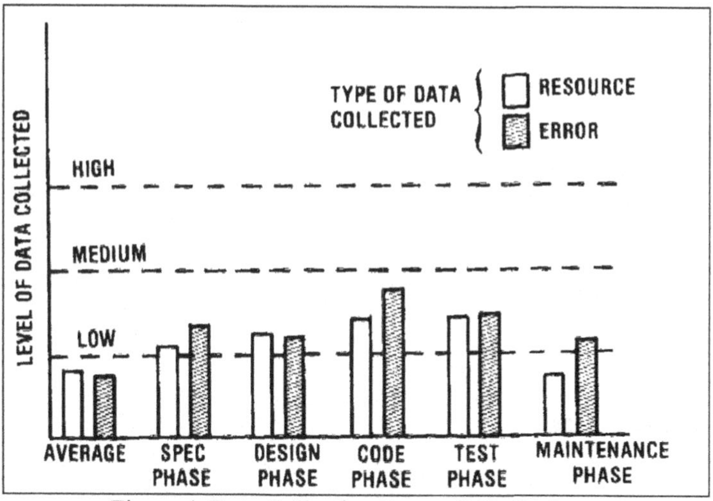

Figure 4. Data Collection Across Life Cycle

In general, we found it extremely difficult to acquire data. First of all, quantitative data is quite rare within most companies. In addition each company has different definitions for most of the measured quantities, such as:

(1) **Lines of code** is defined as source lines, comment lines with or without data declarations, executable lines or generated lines.

(2) **Milestone dates** depend on the local software life cycle used by the company. Whether requirements, specification, or maintenance data is included will have a significant effect upon the results.

(3) **Personnel** might include programmers, analysts, typists, librarians, managers, etc.

Much of this data is proprietary. The differing definitions of quantities for which data was collected prevent any meaningful comparison. It is quite evident that the computer industry needs more work on the standardization of terms in order to be able to address these quantitative issues in the future.

3. Software Development Environments

In the following section general characteristics about most software environments are described. The last sections outline particular characteristics of the three classes of environments that we studied in detail.

3.1. General Life Cycle

3.1.1. Requirements and Specification

In all places we contacted, requirements were in natural language text (English in the US and Kanji in Japan). Some projects had machine-processable requirements, documents, but tool support was limited to interactive text editors. No analysis tools (e.g., SREM [Alford 77], PSL/PSA [Teichroew and Hersey 77]) were used except on "toy" projects. Projects were either too small to make the use of such a processor valuable, or else too large to make use of the processor economical.

Reviews determine if the system architecture is complete, if the specifications are "complete", the internal and external interfaces are defined, and the system can be implemented. These reviews are the most difficult to perform and their results are highly dependent on the quality of people doing the review because the specifications are not formal. There is little traceability between specifications and designs.

3.1.2. Design Phase

Most designs were expressed in some form of Program Design Language (PDL) or pseudo code, which made design reviews effective. Tools that manipulated PDL varied from editors to simple text formatters. Only one company extended its PDL processor to analyze interfaces and the dataflow in the resulting design.

While using PDL seems to be accepted practice, its effective use is not a foregone conclusion. For example, we consider the expansion of PDL to code a reasonable measure of the level of a design. A 1:1 PDL to source code expansion ratio indicates that the design was essentially code instead of design. Figure 5 indicates the ranges of expansions of PDL to code found at several locations that provided such data.

Location	PDL to Code Ratio
1	to 5-10
2	to 3-10
3	to 1.5(!!)-3

Figure 5. Expansion of PDL to Code

Customer involvement with design varied greatly even within installations. Producing lots of detailed PDL is much the same as producing lots of detailed flowcharts. (Nobody cares, but it's in the contract.)

3.1.3. Code and Unit Test

Most code that we saw was in higher level languages - Fortran for scientific applications or some local variation of PL/I for systems work.

In the aerospace industry FORTRAN was the predominant language. People who normally worked in assembly language thought that FORTRAN and PL/I significantly enhanced their productivity. Historical studies have shown that programmers produce an average of one line of debugged source code per hour regardless of the language. ([Brooks 75] contains a concise review of this work.)

Despite claims that they used, chief programmer teams in development, very few first or second-line managers ever wrote any PDL or code themselves. We heard complaints that chief programmer teams worked well only with small groups of 6-9 people, and on projects in which a person's responsibility was not divided between different groups.

Much of the code and unit test phase lacks proper machine support. Code auditors could greatly enhance the code review process. We studied one code review form and found that 13 of 32 checks could be automated. Manual checks are currently performed for proper indentation of the source code, initialization of variables, interface consistency between the calling and called modules, etc.

Most unit testing could be called adversary testing. The programmer claims to have tested a module and the manager either believes the programmer or not. No unit test tools are used to measure how effectively the tests devised by a programmer exercise his source code. While a test coverage measure like statement or branch coverage is nominally required during the review of unit test, mechanisms are rarely available to assure that such criteria have been met.

3.1.4. Integration Test

Integration testing is mostly stress testing — running the product on as much real or simulated data as is possible. The data processing environment had the highest level of stress testing during integration tasting. Systems software projects were relatively slack in integration testing compared to the banking industry.

3.2. Resources

Office space for programmers varied from 1 to 2 programmers sharing a "Santa-Teresa" style office [McCue 1978] with a terminal to large bullpens divided by low, moveable partitions. Terminals were the dominant mode for computer access. Some sites had terminals in offices, while others had large terminal rooms. The current average seems to be about two to seven programmers per terminal. Within the last two years most companies have realized the cost-effectiveness of giving programmers adequate computer access via terminals, but have still not provided adequate response time. Ten to twenty second response time was considered "good" at some places, where sub-second response could be used [Thadani 82].

It seems worth noting that most companies were willing to invest in hardware (e. g, » terminals) to assist their programmers, but were reluctant to invest in software that might be as beneficial.

3.3. Education

Most companies had agreements with a local university to send employees for advanced training (e.g., MS degrees). Most brought in special speakers. However, there was little training for project management. Only one company had a fairly extensive training policy for all software personnel.

Many companies had the following problems with their educational program:

(1) Programmers were sent to courses with little or no follow-up experience. Thus what they learned was rarely put into practice, and was often forgotten.

(2) Some locations complained about their distance from any quality university, and the difficulties that such isolation brought.

3.4. Data Collection Efforts

The data typically collected on projects includes the number of lines of PDL for each level of design, the number of lines of source code produced per staff-month, the number and kinds of errors found in reviews, and a variety of measures on program trouble reports. The deficiency of lines of code as a measure can be indicated by the range in values of "good" developments, as given by Figure 6:

LINES OF CODE	APPLICATION AND LANGUAGE
75	OS in Assembly
91	I/O controller in HLL
142-167	OS in HLL
182-280	Assembly applications

Figure 6. Source Code per Staff-Month

Due to the differing application areas, it is not really possible to compare these numbers. However, it does seem obvious that the difficulty of the application area (e.g., operating systems and other real-time programs being the most difficult) has more impact on productivity than does the implementation language used.

One location reports the following figures for errors found during reviews.

Phase	**Defects/1000 Lines**
Design	2 major, 5 minor
Code	5 major, 8 minor

Figure .7 Defects Discovered During Reviews

The classification of errors into categories like "major" and "minor" is actuarial. While the classification is useful for putting priorities on changes, it sheds little light onto the causes and possible treatments of these errors.

4. Three Development Environments

4.1. Applications Software

We studied 13 projects in 4 companies that produce applications software. In this area, software is contracted from the organization by a Federal agency, typically the Department of Defense or NASA. Software is developed and "thrown over the wall" to the agency for operation and maintenance. Typically, none of the organizations we surveyed were interested in maintenance activities. All believed that the payoff in maintenance was too low, and smaller software houses could fill that void.

Since contracts are awarded after a competitive bidding cycle (after a Request For Proposal) and requirements analysis is typically charged against company overhead, analysis was kept to a minimum before the contract was awarded. In addition, since the goal was to win a contract, there was a clear distinction between cost and price. **Cost** was the amount needed to build a product - a technical process at which most companies believed they were reasonably proficient. On the other hand, **price** was a marketing strategy needed to win a bid. The price had to be low enough to win, but not too low to either lose money on the project or else be deemed "not responsive" to the requirements of the RFP. Thus many of the ideas of software engineering developed during the 1970s on resource estimation and workload characterization are not meaningful in this environment due to the competitive process of winning bids.

In addition, two distinct types of companies emerged within this group - **system developers** and **software developers**. The system developers would package both hardware and software for a government agency, e.g., a communications network. In this case, most of the costs were for hardware with software not considered significant. On the other hand, the software developers simply built systems on existing hardware systems; DEC's PDP/11 series seemed to be the most popular with system builders that were not hardware vendors.

All of the companies surveyed had a methodology manual, however, they were either out of date, were just in the process of being updated. In this environment, Department of Defense MIL specifications were a dominant driving force and most standards were oriented around government policies. The methodology manuals were often policy documents outlining the type of information to be produced by a project, but not how to obtain that information.

As stated previously, most organizations bid on RFPs from government agencies. Because of that, requirement analysis is kept to a minimum. Requirements are written in English and no formal tool is used to process the requirements.

Except for one company, FORTRAN seemed to be the dominant programming language. Two tools did seem to be used. Due to DoD specifications, most had some sort of management reporting forms on resource utilization. However, these generally did not report on programmer activities. PDL was the one tool many companies did depend on - probably because the cost was low.

Staff turnover was uniformly low - generally 5% to 10% a year. Space for programmers seemed adequate, with 1 to 2 per office being typical. All locations, except one, used terminals for all computer access, and that one site had a pilot project to build "Santa Teresa"-style offices connected to a local minicomputer.

4.2. Systems Software

We studied eight projects produced by three vendors. All of the projects were for large machines, and operating systems for those machines were the most important projects studied. The other projects, mostly compilers and utilities, did not follow the same development rules as did operating systems projects, because they were considered to be small and their designs well-understood.

The software is generally written on hardware similar to the target machine. Terminals are universally used and the ratio of programmers to terminals varies from almost 1:1 to 3:1. Getting a terminal is frequently less of a problem than getting CPU cycles to do development.

Software support is generally limited to line-oriented text editors and interactive compilers. High-level development languages exist, and in most cases there is a policy that they be used; however, a substantial portion of operating systems remains in assembler language (20% to 90% depending upon company). The reasons are partly good ones (such as the prior existence of assembler code) and partly the usual one: alternatives have never been considered at the technical level. Text formatting programs are in wide use, but analysis of machine-readable text other than source code is virtually nonexistent.

Most testing is considered part of the development effort. There may be a separate test group, but it reports to the development managers. Only a final "field" test may be under the control of an independent quality-control group.

Maintenance is usually handled by the development staff. A field support group obtains trouble reports from the field, and then forwards them on to the development organization for correction. In many cases, the developers, even if working on a new project, handle errors.

Programmers are usually organized into (usually) small teams by project, and usually stick with a project until it is completed. The term "chief programmer team" is used incorrectly to describe conventional organizations: a chain of managers (the number depends on project size) who do not program, and small groups of programmers with little responsibility for organization.

Staff turnover is relatively high (up to 20% per year) compared to the applications software area. Most programmers typically have private cubicles paralleled out of large open areas. The lack of privacy is often stated as a negative factor.

Software engineering practices vary widely among the projects we investigated. There was a strong negative correlation between the age of the system and the amount of software engineering used.

4.3. Data Processing

We studied 6 data processing projects at 4 locations, although every location had some data processing activities for its own internal use. Most data processing software that we studied was developed in COBOL, although some systems are written in FORTRAN, and used to provide internal data processing services for the company. These systems did not produce revenue for the company, and were all "company overhead." There was a need to maintain the code throughout the life cycle.

Requirements were mostly in English and unstructured, although one financial company structured specifications by user function. Designs, especially for terminal-oriented products, were relatively similar - a set of simulated screen displays and menus to which the user could respond. The most striking difference in the data processing environment was the heavy involvement of users in the two development steps. The success of the project depended upon the degree of user involvement before integration testing. One site clearly had a "success" and a "failure" on two different projects that used the same methodology. The company directly attributed the success and failure to the interest (or lack of interest, respectively) to the user assigned to the development team during development.

All usage that we observed was via terminals. Office space was more varied than in the other two environments we observed. Some places used one and two-person offices, while others partitioned large open areas into cubicles. "Stress" was often high in that overtime was more common, and turnover was the highest in this environment - often up to 30% per year, although one location had a low turnover rate which they attributed to relatively higher salaries than comparable companies.

Data processing environments often used a phased approach to development, and quality control was especially important. One location, which had numerous failures in the past, attributed their recent successes to never attempting any development that would require more than 18 months. Since these systems often managed the company's finances, the need for reliability was most critical and stress testing was higher than in other areas.

5. Conclusions

We feel there are both short and long-term remedies to raise the level of methodology and tool use throughout industry. The short-term suggestions are relatively conservative; however, we feel they can improve productivity. While we can point to no empirical evidence that will permit us to forecast gains, there is a general consensus in the software community (like that for the use of high level languages) to support these ideas. Our long-term suggestions could form the basis for a research effort.

5.1. Short Term

(1) **More and better computer resources should be made available for development.** The computer systems being used for development are comparable with the best of those available in the late 1960's or early 1970's timesharing on large machines. The use of screen editors at some locations has been a major improvement, but other tools seem limited to batch compilers and primitive debugging systems. Response time seems to be a major complaint at many development installations.

(2) **Methods and tools should be evaluated.** A separate organization with this charter should be established. As of now, it does not appear that any one group in most companies has the responsibility to study the research literature and try promising techniques. Since the most successful tools have been high level language compilers, the first tools to be developed should be integrated into compilers. Thus these tools should concentrate on the design and unit test phases of development during which formal languages exist and compiler extensions are relatively straightforward. This organization could both acquire and evaluate the tools via case studies and/or experiments.

(3) **Tool support should be built for a common high level language.** The tools we would pick first include a PDL processor, a code auditor, and a unit test coverage monitor. The PDL processor should at least check interfaces. Unfortunately, commercially available processors do little more than format a listing; however, interface checking is nothing more than 20-year-old compiler technology. The processor should also construct graphs of the flow of data through the design and extract PDL from source code so that while both are maintained together they can be viewed separately. Code auditors can be used to check that source code meets accepted standards and practices. Many of these checks are boring to perform manually (e.g., checking whether BEGIN-END blocks are aligned) and thus become error prone. Unit testing tools can evaluate how thoroughly a program has been exercised. These tools are easy to build and should meet with quick acceptance since many managers require statement or branch coverage during unit test.

PDL processors should support an automated set of metrics that cover the design and coding process. The metrics in turn can monitor progress, characterize the intermediate products (e.g., the design, source code, etc.), and attempt to predict the characteristics of the next phase of development. Possible metrics include design change counts, control and data complexity metrics for source code, structural coverage metrics for test data, etc. [Basili 80].

(4) **Improve the review process.** Reviews or inspections are a strong part of current methodology. The review process can be strengthened by the use of the tools mentioned above. This would permit reviewers to spend more time on the major purpose of the review — the detection of logical errors, and avoid the distractions of formatting or syntactic anomalies.

(5) **Use incremental development** (e.g., iterative enhancement [Basili and Turner 75]). One data processing location, after repeatedly failing to deliver software, made a decision never to build anything that had a chunk larger than those requiring 18 staff months. Since then they have been successful.

(6) **Collect and analyze data.** Most of the data being collected now is used primarily to schedule work assignments. Measurement data can be used to classify projects, evaluate methods and tools, and provide feedback to project managers. Data should be collected across projects to evaluate and help predict the productivity and quality of software. The kind of data collected and analysis performed should be driven by a set of questions that need answers rather than what is convenient to collect and analyze. For example, classifying errors into "major" and "minor" categories does not answer any useful questions. A more detailed examination of error data can determine the causes of common errors, many of which may have remedies. Project post mortems should be conducted.

5.2. Long Term

(1) **Compiler technology should be maintained.** Many companies seem to "contract" out compiler development to smaller software houses due to "pedestrian" nature of building most compilers. While compiler technology is relatively straightforward and perhaps cheaper to contract to a software house, the implications are far reaching. Software research is heading towards an integrated environment covering the entire life cycle of software development. Research papers are now being written about requirements and specification languages, design languages, program complexity measurement, knowledge based Japanese "fifth generation" [Karatsu 82] languages, etc. All of these depend upon mundane compiler technology as their base.

(2) **Prototyping should by tried.** It was **never** mentioned during our visits.

(3) **Develop a test and evaluation methodology.** Test data has to be designed and evaluated. While the current software development process provides for the design of test data in conjunction with the design of the software, there is little tool support for this effort. As a result, almost every project builds its own test data generator and a few even build test evaluators. Concepts like attribute grammars may provide the basis for a tool to support test data generation.

(4) **Examine the maintenance process.** The maintenance process should be formalized as part of the continuing development process. Maintenance was rarely mentioned in our interview process, although there is a project in Japan to build

maintenance workstations. Their view is that development is a subset of maintenance. This implies that the successful methods and tools used in development should be adapted for use in this stage of the process.

(5) **Encourage innovation.** Experimental software development facilities are needed. Management should be encouraged to use new techniques on small funded-risk projects.

6. Acknowledgements

This project was sponsored by a contract from the IBM Corporation to the University of Maryland. We also wish to acknowledge the cooperation of the following organizations in addition to IBM for allowing us to survey their development activities: Bankers Trust Company, Honeywell Large Information Systems Division, Kozo Keikaku Kenkyujo, Japan Information Processing Service, Nomura Computer Systems Ltd., Software Research Associates (Japan), Sperry Univac, System Development Corporation, Tokyo Electric Power Company, Toshiba Corporation, TRW, Xerox, and several other organizations who wish to remain anonymous. This project would not have been possible without their help.

7. References

[Alford 77] M. W. Alford. A Requirements Engineering Methodology for Real-time Processing Requirements. IEEE Transactions on Software Engineering SE-3, (January, 1977), 60-69.

[Basili 80] V. R, Basili. Models and Metrics for Software Management and Engineering. IEEE Computer Society Press, 1980.

[Basili and Turner 75] V. R. Basili and A. J. Turner. Iterative Enhancement: A Practical Technique for Software Development. IEEE Transactions on Software Engineering SE-1, 4, (December 1975), 390-396.

[Belady and Lehman 76] L. A. Belady and M. M. Lehman. A model of Large Program Development. IBM Systems Journal 15, 3, (September, 1976), 225-252.

[Boehm 81] B. W. Boehm. Software Engineering Economics. Prentice-Hall, Inc., Englewood Cliffs, N. J., (1981).

[Brooks 75] F.P. Brooks, Jr. The Mythical Man-Month. Addison-Wesley Publishing Company, Reading, MA, (1975).

[Buxton and Randell 70] J. N. Buxton and B. Randell (ed.). Software Engineering Techniques. NATO Scientific Affairs Division, Brussels, (1970).

[Fagan 76] M. E. Fagan. Design and Code Inspections to Reduce Errors in Program Development. IBM Systems Journal 15, 3, (1976), 182-211.

[Freiman and Park 79] F. Freiman and Park. PRICE Software Model Overview. RCA, (February 1979).

[Halstead 77] M. H. Halstead. Elements of Software Science. Elsevier, New York, (1977).

[Karatsu 82] H. Karatsu, What is required of the 5th generation computer - social needs and its impact, Fifth Generation Computer Systems, North Holland, 1982.

[McCue 1978] G. M. McCue, IBM's Santa Teresa Laboratory -Architectural design for program development, IBM systems Journal 17, 1 (1978) 4-25.

[Naur and Randell 69] P. Naur and B. Randell (ed.). Software Engineering. NATO Scientific Affairs Division, Brussels, (1969).

[Putnam 79] L. Putnam. SLIM Software Life Cycle Management Estimating Model: User's Guide. Quantitative Software Management, (July 1979).

[Teichroew and Hersey 77] D. Teichroew and E. A. Hersey III. PSL/PSA: A Computer-Aided Technique for Structured Documentation and Analysis of Information Processing Systems. IEEE Transactions on Software Engineering, SE-3, 1, (January 1977), 41-48.

[Thadani 81] A. J. Thadani. Interactive User Productivity. IBM Systems Journal, 20, 4, (1981), 407-423.

An Evaluation of Expert Systems for Software Engineering Management

Connie Loggia Ramsey and Victor R. Basili

Abstract. Although the field of software engineering is relatively new, it can benefit from the use of expert systems because of the ability to learn from them. We believe that a major limitation to building expert systems for software engineering is the fact that much of the knowledge in this field is not well understood yet. Therefore, the development of expert systems in this field must be considered exploratory. This project focused on the development of four separate, prototype expert systems to aid in software engineering management. Given the values for certain metrics, these systems provide interpretations which explain any abnormal patterns of these values during the development of a software project. The four expert systems, which solve the same problem, were built using two different approaches to knowledge acquisition, a bottom-up approach and a top-down approach, and two different expert system methods, rule-based deduction and frame-based abduction. In a comparison to see which methods might better suit the needs of this field, it was found that the bottom-up approach led to better results than did the top-down approach, and the rule-based deduction systems using simple rules provided more complete and correct solutions than did the frame-based abduction systems.

Key Words: Expert systems, software development, software engineering management.

I. Introduction

The importance of expert systems is growing in industrial, medical, scientific, and other fields. Several major reasons for this are: 1) the necessity of handling an overwhelming amount of knowledge in these areas, 2) the potential of expert systems to train new experts, 3) the potential to learn more about a field while organizing knowledge for the development of expert systems, 4) cost reductions

Manuscript received November 10, 1986; revised January 31, 1989. This work was supported in part by the National Aeronautics and Space Administration under Grant NSG-5123 to the University of Maryland. Computer support was provided in part by the Computer Science Center of the University of Maryland.
C. L. Ramsey, Member, IEEE, is with the Navy Center for Applied Research in Artificial Intelligence, Naval Research Laboratory, Washington, DC 20375.
V. R. Basili, Senior Member, IEEE, is with the Institute for Advanced Computer Studies and the Department of Computer Science, University of Maryland, College Park, MD 20742.

sometimes provided by expert systems, and 5) the desire to capture corporate knowledge so it is not lost as personnel changes.

Although the field of software engineering is still relatively new, it can certainly benefit from the use of expert systems because of the ability to learn from them. The development of any expert system requires organized knowledge; therefore, the knowledge engineer can learn more about the field of software engineering as he is forced to develop, understand, and organize relationships between various pieces of knowledge.

On another level, the expert systems in this field can be used to train and help people, including software managers. They can contain general software engineering principles as well, as a history of information from a particular software development environment which can be particularly helpful to inexperienced managers and developers.

Since software engineering is still such a new field with much of its knowledge unclear, expert systems developed in this field must be considered exploratory prototypes. This project focused on software engineering management. A first attempt was made at creating and systematically analyzing and comparing expert systems which intelligently relate software engineering project measurements and explanations of project behavior. This was an exploratory learning experience which has provided an initial baseline for future work [4], [29].

The high level goal of this project was to examine different approaches to expert system development for software engineering management and determine strengths and limits of the various approaches as they relate to the field. Some of the questions this study tried to answer were: 1) Are expert systems for software engineering management feasible at this time? 2) What methodology should be used for knowledge acquisition? 3) What type of expert system methodology best suits software engineering management? 4) Do the experts themselves agree on the information to be used? 5) Are certain software environments more suited for expert systems than others? 6) Are we ready to develop systems with environment-independent, general truths? 7) What information should be included in the system?

This paper will discuss the comparison of several prototype expert systems, collectively named ARROW-SMITH-P.[1] Earlier versions of these expert systems are described in [3]. ARROWSMITH-P is intended to aid the manager of a software development project in an automated manner. The goal of these systems is to help detect and assess the problems which might occur during the coding and testing of a project as early as possible. The systems work as follows. First, it is determined whether or not a software project is following normal development patterns by comparing measures such as programmer hours per line of source code against historical, environment-specific baselines of such measures. Then, the "manifestations" detected by this comparison, such as an abnormally high rate of

[1] Martin Arrowsmith, created by Sinclair Lewis in the novel *Arrowsmith*, was in constant search of truth in scientific fields. The "P" stands for Prototype.

programmer hours per line of source code, serve as input to each expert system, and each system attempts to determine the reasons, such as *high complexity* or *low productivity,* for any abnormal software development patterns. Early detection of potential problems can provide invaluable assistance to the manager of a software development project. These expert systems should be updated as the environment changes and as more is learned in the field of software engineering.

The rest of this paper is organized as follows. Section II provides a brief overview of the underlying methodologies used to build the expert systems discussed in this paper. The knowledge representation and inference techniques of the methodologies are presented here. Section III describes aspects of the software engineering development environment used for this study. Section IV details the implementations of ARROWSMITH-P, i.e., how the different approaches were utilized to build the expert systems. In Section V, some of the technical issues and problems associated with this process are discussed. Section VI furnishes the details for the evaluation of the expert systems. Section VII then discusses results and conclusions from the development and testing of the expert systems. Finally, Section VIII discusses current and future research needs.

II. Background on Expert Systems

In general, an expert system consists of two basic components, a domain-specific knowledge base and a domain-independent inference mechanism. The knowledge base consists of data structures which represent general problem-solving information for some application area. The inference mechanism uses the information in the knowledge base along with problem-specific input data to generate useful information about a specific case.

The set of expert systems in ARROWSMITH-P was constructed using KMS [25], an experimental domain-independent expert system generator which can be used to build rule-based, frame-based and Bayesian systems. The ARROWSMITH-P systems were built using two different methods: rule-based deduction and frame-based abduction. These two methods are briefly described below.

A. Rule-Based Deduction

A common method for expert systems is rule-based deduction. In this approach, domain-specific problem-solving knowledge is represented in rules which are basically of the form:

"IF <antecedents> THEN <Consequents>",

although the exact syntax used may be quite different (e.g., PROLOG). If the antecedents of such a rule are determined to be true, then it logically follows that the consequents are also true. Note that these rules are not branching points in a program, but are nonprocedural statements of fact.

The inference mechanism consists of a rule interpreter which, when given a specific set of problem features, determines applicable rules and applies them in some specified order to reach conclusions about the case at hand. Rule-based deduction can be performed in a variety of ways, and rules can be chained together to make multiple-step deductions. (For a fuller description, see [13].) In addition, in many systems one can attach "certainty factors" to rules to capture probabilistic information, and a variety of mechanisms can be used to propagate certainty measures during problem solving. MYCIN [26] and PROSPECTOR [8] are two well-known examples of expert systems which incorporate rule-based deduction.

B. Frame-Based Abduction

Another important method for implementing expert systems is frame-based abduction. Here, the domain-specific problem-solving knowledge is represented in descriptive "frames" of information [15], and inference is typically based on hypothesize-and-test cycles which model human reasoning as follows. Given one or more initial problem features, the expert system generates a set of potential hypotheses or "causes" which can explain the problem features. These hypotheses are then tested by 1) the use of various procedures which measure their ability to account for the known features, and 2) the generation of new questions which will help to discriminate among the most likely hypotheses. This cycle is then repeated with the additional information acquired. This type of reasoning is used in diagnostic problem solving (see [22] for a review). INTERNIST [14], KMS.HT [25], [23], PIP [17], and IDT [27] are typical systems using frame-based abduction.

In order to simulate hypothesize-and-test reasoning, KMS employs a generalized set covering model in which there is a universe of all possible manifestations (symptoms) and a universe which contains all possible causes (disorders). For each possible cause, there is a set of manifestations which that cause can explain. Likewise, for each possible manifestation, there is a set of causes which could explain the manifestation. Given a diagnostic problem with a specific set of manifestations which are present, the inference mechanism finds all sets of causes with minimum cardinality[2] which could explain (cover) all of the manifestations. For a more detailed explanation of the theory underlying this approach and the problem-solving algorithms, see [23], [24], [16], and [18].

III. Background on Software Environment

The software which provided the data for this study was developed at the NASA Goddard Space Flight Center. This software development environment is homogeneous, i.e., many similar projects are developed for the same application area.

---

[2] Ockham's razor, which states that the simplest explanation is usually the correct one, together with the assumption of independence among causes motivate the requirement of minimum cardinality.

There has been a standard process model developed over the years; the methodology for development is similar across projects, and there is a great deal of reuse of code from prior projects. The NASA Software Engineering Laboratory has been collecting reliable software project data such as programmer hours and lines of code for approximately fifteen years. The data used for the knowledge bases of the expert systems was chosen from this database of information because it was standard data for the environment and covered a great deal of the software life cycle phases being studied.

The experts who aided in knowledge acquisition were two managers who had successfully supervised software development in this environment for many years. They were also involved in the collection and analysis of data for prior projects and therefore understood the implications of the information in the database.

IV. Implementations

In this section, we will first present the methodology developed for building expert systems for software engineering management. Then we will discuss the actual implementations of ARROWSMITH-P.

A. Methodology

The following two methodologies of knowledge acquisition for constructing expert systems for software engineering management were developed. They can best be described as a bottom-up methodology and a top-down methodology. (An earlier version of the bottom-up reasoning was developed by Doerflinger and Basili [12].)

1) Bottom-Up Methodology: Given a homogeneous environment, it is possible to produce historical, environment-specific baselines of normalized metrics from the data of past software projects. Normalized metrics are derived by comparing variables such as programmer hours and lines of code against each other. This is done so influences such as the size of the individual project are factored out. The baseline for each metric is defined as the average value of that metric for the past projects at various discrete time intervals (such as early coding or acceptance testing). Only those metrics which exhibit baselines with reasonable standard deviations should be used; too little variety in the values of the measures proves uninteresting, while too much variety is not very meaningful. In addition, one ideally wants a relatively small number of meaningful metrics whose values are easily obtainable.

Next, experts can determine interpretations, such as *unstable specifications* or *good testing,* which would explain any significant deviation (more than one standard deviation less than or greater than the average) of a particular metric from the historical baseline. The deviation of some metric can be thought of as a manifestation or symptom which can be "diagnosed" as certain interpretations or causes. Furthermore, these relationships between interpretations and manifestations should be made time-line specific because, for example, an interpretation during early coding might not be valid during acceptance testing. In addition, measures to indicate how certain one is that the deviation of a particular metric has resulted from a particular interpretation can be included.

The approach, described above, can be classified as a bottom-up approach because it seems to go in the opposite direction of cause-and-effect. First the symptoms (deviant metric values) that something is abnormal are explored, and then the underlying interpretations or diagnoses of the abnormalities are developed. This approach to knowledge acquisition is reasonable in a homogeneous environment because the metrics are homogeneous, and deviations are indicative that something is wrong. However, this approach contrasts with the development of expert systems in other fields, such as medicine, which typically use a top-down approach.

2) Top-Down Methodology: A top-down approach to knowledge acquisition can be similar to the bottom-up approach in that the same manifestations and causes can be used. However, it would first define the various interpretations or diagnoses and then indicate the metrics which would be likely to have abnormal values for each interpretation.

Using the top-down approach, the experts view the knowledge from a different perspective when defining the relationships that exist between the interpretations and manifestations. This approach can be seen as a more general approach than the bottom-up approach is to knowledge acquisition in the field of software engineering management. In the bottom-up methodology, the metrics are analyzed first and these are, by their nature, environment-specific. The focus is automatically limited to the specific environment. Conversely, in the top-down methodology, the experts think first of the causes or interpretations and then indicate the effects or likely metrics which would show deviant values if a certain interpretation existed. This generalizes the problem across environments somewhat because the emphasis seems to be switched to the interpretations which can be universal.

3) Using the Expert Systems: Once the expert systems have been developed, the input to each expert system would then consist of those metrics from a current project which deviate from a historical baseline of the same metrics at the same time of development for similar projects. The knowledge bases consist of information about various potential causes; such as *poor testing* or *unstable, specifications,* for any abnormally high or low measures, and the expert system provides explanations for any abnormal software development patterns.

B. Actual Implementations

ARROWSMITH-P consists of four independent expert systems, one using a bottom-up approach to knowledge acquisition and rule-based deduction, a second using the bottom-up approach and frame-based abduction, a third using a top-down approach to knowledge acquisition and rule-based deduction, and a fourth using the top-down approach and frame-based abduction.

The bottom-up methodology described above was based on previous research conducted on the NASA Goddard Space Flight Center Software Engineering Laboratory (SEL) environment [12]. Since the SEL environment is homogeneous, it was possible to produce historical, environment-specific baselines of normalized metrics from the highly reliable data of nine software projects. (See [7], [5], [6], [9], and [1] for fuller descriptions of the SEL environment.)

The bottom-up development was performed first, and nine metrics, derived from five variables, were chosen because they were standard data measurements for the environment and covered a great deal of the software life cycle phases being studied. They also proved satisfactory because they exhibited baselines with reasonable standard deviations. The metrics are displayed in Table I. These same metrics were later used during the top-down development to ensure consistency and to allow a comparative study to be performed. The time-line for the baselines was divided (after a slight modification) into the following five discrete intervals: early code, middle code, late code, systems test, and acceptance test.

The initial sets of interpretations and the relationships between the interpretations and the abnormal values of metrics were mainly derived from two experts who have had a great deal of experience in this field and particularly in the SEL environment. The experts were asked what they thought high and low values of metrics might mean, and the interpretations they suggested were used in the experiment [12]. During the bottom-up development of ARROWSMITH-P, mainly one of these experts modified the existing sets and made them time-line specific. In addition, measures to indicate how certain one is that the interpretation and the abnormal metric value are connected were included. During the top-down development, the same two experts were again asked to provide the relationships for all five time phases, and the intersection of their responses was used for the expert systems. Some of their other indicated relationships were used as well; when the experts did not agree on a relationship, we discussed the situation to understand the reasoning behind the relationship and to see how certain an expert felt about the relationship. The list of interpretations used and tested in the bottom-up and top-down expert systems is displayed in Table II. (Other interpretations were used as well, but these could not be tested. See [3] for the complete list.)

As stated previously, two different expert system methods were used to build the expert systems for this application in order to determine which method better suits the needs of this field. The two methods used were rule-based deduction and frame-based abduction which were described in Section II. In the rule-based systems, the rules are of the form "IF manifestations THEN interpretations," while in the frame-based systems, there is one frame (containing a list of manifestations) for each interpretation. Please note that these formats are independent of whether the relationships between manifestations and interpretations were defined using a bottom-up or a top-down approach to knowledge acquisition. The rule-based and frame-based systems which used the bottom-up approach were intentionally built to be as consistent with one another as possible. The causes and manifestations used were identical in both cases, as were the relationships between them. The same was true for the two expert systems which employed the top-down approach. However, the certainty factors attached to the rules and the measures of likelihood in the frames could not be directly translated to each other so some of these measures were omitted. For example, within the bottom-up approach we were relatively certain that an abnormally high value of computer time per software change is caused by good, reliable code so this was given a certainty factor of 0.75. However, if that particular metric appears abnormally high very infrequently and that particular interpretation is common, then we would not be able to state that good, reliable code generally results in an abnormally high value of computer time per software change. (For a discussion of similar problems see [21].) Fig. 1 shows a sample section of a rule-based and a frame-based knowledge base. Example sessions with the expert systems are provided in the Appendix.

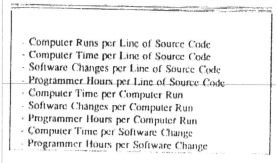

- Computer Runs per Line of Source Code
- Computer Time per Line of Source Code
- Software Changes per Line of Source Code
- Programmer Hours per Line of Source Code
- Computer Time per Computer Run
- Software Changes per Computer Run
- Programmer Hours per Computer Run
- Computer Time per Software Change
- Programmer Hours per Software Change

TABLE I. Metrics used in expert system

Unstable Specifications
Low Productivity
High Productivity
High Complexity or Tough Problem
High Complexity or Compute Bound Algorithms Run or Tested
Low Complexity
Simple System
Error Prone Code
Good Solid and Reliable Code
Large Portion of Reused Code
Lots of Testing
Little Testing
Good Testing or Good Test Plan
Lack of Thorough Testing
Poor Testing Program
Changes Hard to Make
Loose Configuration Management or Unstructured Development
Tight Configuration Management or Control
Computer Problems or Inaccessibility or Environmental Constraints
Lots of Terminal Jockeys

TABLE II. Interpretations used in expert system

V. Research Issues and Problems

The field of expert systems is relatively new, and therefore, the development process of expert systems still faces many problems. The selection of which method to use for building them is not generally clear, although an attempt has been made to provide guidelines for the selection of an appropriate method in [21]. Furthermore, most expert systems are shallow in nature and cannot handle temporal or spatial information well.

In addition to general problems, negative effects are compounded when the knowledge to be included in such systems is incomplete. The science of software engineering is not well-defined yet, and therefore many details about the relationships between various components are often unclear. The experts themselves may not even agree on the information used in the expert systems. As a result, the knowledge base of any expert system developed in this field is particularly exploratory and prototypical in nature. This is in contrast to expert systems developed in established fields such as medicine where the information contained in the knowledge base is based on many years of experience.

Due to the uncertainty of the data in the knowledge base for a field such as software engineering, one must deal with the issues of completeness versus correctness and completeness versus minimality. When dealing with a diagnostic problem, the more certain one is of relationships between causes and manifestations, the more exact the answer can be, ultimately leading to the one correct answer. However, when dealing with very uncertain relationships, it is preferable to list many outcomes so as to avoid missing the correct explanation, and to let the experienced person using the expert system decide what the correct explanation really is. Therefore, rules with simple antecedents were used in the rule-based deduction systems [see Fig. I (a)] because the more involved patterns needed for complex antecedents are not yet known. If one tried to "guess" what these patterns are without actually being certain, this would lead to incomplete solutions which miss some of the correct interpretations. For example, a high value for computer runs per line of code, a high value for computer time per line of code, and a high value for programmer hours per line of code are all indications of *low productivity*. So, we might construct the following rule for this pattern:

IF computer runs per line of code is above normal,
and computer time per line of code is above normal,
and programmer hours per line of code is above normal,
THEN the interpretation is *Low Productivity*.

However, what if it turns out that computer time per line of code is almost never above normal? Then this rule will almost never succeed, and we will miss the interpretation of *low productivity* even if it happens to be true.

This issue also leads to concern in the frame-based abduction systems which provide all answers of minimum cardinality. This inference mechanism works well for most diagnostic problem solving, but one must be cautiously aware of the fact that not all possible explanations are provided by this expert system. For example, if an abnormally high value of computer runs per line of code and an

```
ATTRIBUTES:

/* INPUT ATTRIBUTES */
COMPUTER RUNS PER LINE OF SOURCE CODE (SGL)
    ABOVE NORMAL,
    NORMAL,
    BELOW NORMAL.
                    .
                    .
                    .
/* INFERRED ATTRIBUTE */
INTERPRETATION (MLT):
    UNSTABLE SPECIFICATIONS
    LOW PRODUCTIVITY
    HIGH PRODUCTIVITY
    GOOD TESTING OR GOOD TEST PLAN
                    .
                    .
                    .
RULES:
CRLC1 IF COMPUTER RUNS PER LINE OF CODE = ABOVE NORMAL,
        & TIME = EARLY CODING
        THEN INTERPRETATION = LOW PRODUCTIVITY <0.25>,
        & INTERPRETATION = ERROR PRONE CODE <0.75>.
                    .
                    .
                    .
SCLC3 IF SOFTWARE CHANGES PER LINE OF CODE = ABOVE NORMAL,
        & TIME = LATE CODING
        THEN INTERPRETATION = GOOD TESTING OR GOOD TEST PLAN <0.25>,
        & INTERPRETATION = ERROR PRONE CODE <0.75>.
                    .
                    .
                    .
                              (a)
ATTRIBUTES:

/* INPUT ATTRIBUTES */
COMPUTER RUNS PER LINE OF SOURCE CODE (SGL):
    ABOVE NORMAL,
    * NORMAL,
    BELOW NORMAL.
                    .
                    .
                    .
/* INFERRED ATTRIBUTE - FRAMES */
INTERPRETATION (MLT):
    LOW PRODUCTIVITY
     [DESCRIPTION:
          COMPUTER RUNS PER LINE OF CODE = ABOVE NORMAL;
          COMPUTER TIME PER LINE OF CODE = ABOVE NORMAL;
          PROGRAMMER HOURS PER LINE OF CODE = ABOVE NORMAL ].
    GOOD TESTING OR GOOD TEST PLAN
     [DESCRIPTION:
          SOFTWARE CHANGES PER LINE OF CODE = ABOVE NORMAL,
          SOFTWARE CHANGES PER COMPUTER RUN = ABOVE NORMAL;
          COMPUTER TIME PER SOFTWARE CHANGE = BELOW NORMAL;
          PROGRAMMER HOURS PER SOFTWARE CHANGE = BELOW NORMAL ].
                    .
                    .
                    .
                              (b)
```

Fig. 1. (a) Small section of (a) rule-based deduction expert system, (b) frame-based abduction expert system.

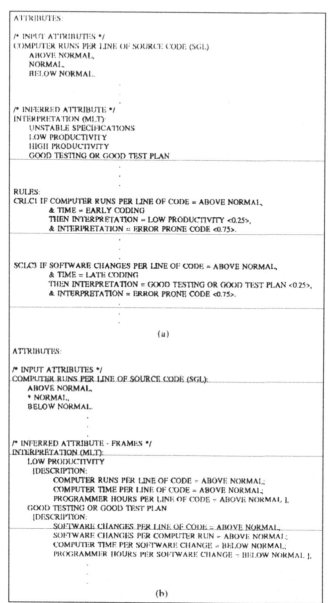

abnormally low value of programmer hours per software change can be explained by the combination of two interpretations, *low productivity,* and *good testing,* and also by a single interpretation, *error prone code* alone, then only the single interpretation will be provided by this system. This is because the single interpretation has a lower cardinality than the two interpretations together. As was the case in this study, some researchers now feel that the idea of providing only answers of minimum cardinality (minimal set covers) is inadequate sometimes. Research is currently being performed on a newer and better method called *irredundant covers* which provides all irredundant sets of causes which cover all of the manifestations [19], [11]. (A set of interpretations which covers all of the manifestations is *irredundant* if none of its proper subsets also cover all of the manifestations.)

One final, but very important, fact should be noted here. ARROWSMITH-P was built using the data from one particular homogeneous environment. Therefore, the information in the knowledge base reflects this one environment and would not be transportable to other environments. However, the ideas and methods used to build ARROWSMITH-P are transportable, and that is what is important.

VI. Evaluation of Expert Systems

A. Methods of Evaluation

ARROWSMITH-P has been evaluated in several ways. The correctness of each system was measured by comparing the interpretations provided by the expert system against what actually happened during the development of the projects, thereby obtaining a measure of agreement. This analysis was performed for ten projects (the original nine plus a newer project which was completed after the development of the expert systems) in all five time phases for each of the four expert systems. Each of the original nine projects was compared against historical baselines of the remaining eight projects to determine abnormal metric values, and the tenth project, which was tested later, was compared against the original nine. A total set of 50 cases was tested on each of the four expert systems.

The actual results of what took place during development were gathered from information in another section of the database, mostly from subjective evaluation forms and project statistics forms. The subjective evaluation form contains mostly subjective information (such as a rating of the programming team's performance) and some objective numbers (such as total number of errors) concerning the project's overall development. Since the vast majority of the ratings in the subjective evaluation form is not divided by phase of the project, there probably exist some discrepancies between the results indicated in the forms and the actual interpretations for a particular phase. However, these are the closest data that are available, so we must assume that most of the interpretations for each phase are similar to the interpretations for the entire project.

The results from the expert systems were also analyzed statistically by using a Kappa statistic test [28], [10] on each interpretation. The Kappa statistic determines whether the results are better or worse than chance agreement. It takes into account the number of correct answers and the number of incorrect answers with respect to each interpretation, and it determines the amount of agreement which can be attributable to chance alone. The formula for the Kappa statistic is:

$$K = \frac{P_0 - P_c}{1 - P_c}$$

where P_0 is the observed proportion of agreement, and Pc is the proportion (of agreement expected by chance.

TABLE III
(a) COMPARISON OF RESPONSES PROVIDED BY EXPERTS IN EACH OF THE FIVE TIME PHASES FOR THE TOP-DOWN EXPERT SYSTEMS. (b) COMPARISON OF FINAL BOTTOM-UP AND FINAL TOP-DOWN EXPERT SYSTEMS

	Number of Relationships Indicated by Experts		
Time Phase	Expert 1	Expert 2	Intersection
Early Coding	66	60	23
Middle Coding	78	65	28
Late Coding	81	68	38
Systems Test	79	48	30
Acceptance Test	68	42	23

(a)

	Number of Relationships Used in Each Approach		
Time Phase	Bottom-Up	Top Down	Intersection
Early Coding	61	35	15
Middle Coding	65	43	19
Late Coding	63	50	23
Systems Test	65	40	17
Acceptance Test	62	37	17

(b)

A value of 1 for *K* indicates perfect agreement, a value of 0 indicates that the results can be due to chance alone, and a value less than 0 indicates worse than chance agreement. The Kappa statistic was used for each interpretation in each of the four expert systems. This was done to determine whether certain interpretations are better understood than others.

In addition to testing the performance of the expert systems, an analysis was performed to compare the information provided by the two experts for the systems. This was performed by comparing the relationships indicated by each of the experts against each other and also by comparing the relationships indicated in the bottom-up systems against those indicated using the top-down approach.

B. Results

The first results we would like to discuss are those comparing information provided by the experts. This is essential because the expert systems can only perform as well as the knowledge contained in the systems permits. The experts were asked to fill in grids (one for each time phase for the bottom-up approach and one for each time phase for the top-down approach) indicating the relationships between the interpretations and the manifestations as described in Section IV. The comparison between the sets of grids for the top-down approach is provided in Table III(a). (The data for one of the experts using the bottom-up approach is incomplete, so a comparison between the two experts was not made there.) The experts only agreed in about 1/3-1/2 of their indicated relationships. Furthermore, the final set of relationships for the top-down approach is very different from the final set for the bottom-up approach. [See Table III(b).] When deciding on the relationships during the top-down development, the experts even decided to combine some of the interpretations used in the bottom-up approach, feeling there was too little difference in meaning between them to be significant, and they also dismissed several interpretations during certain time phases (and *tight management* during all time phases) because they felt that the meaning of those interpretations could not be captured by the available metrics in those particular time periods. We believe that the differences between the two approaches are mainly due to two facts: 1) the experts were seeing the data from a very different point of view, and 2) the metrics are not ideal in that some of the interpretations could not be adequately described in terms of the available metrics, so the experts were not completely certain of all of the relationships that they stated and they changed their opinions over time.

TABLE IV
AGREEMENT BETWEEN EXPERT SYSTEM AND INFORMATION IN DATABASE
BOTTOM-UP SYSTEMS, (a) EARLY CODING PHASE, (b) MIDDLE CODING PHASE, (c) LATE CODING PHASE, (d) SYSTEMS TEST PHASE, (e) ACCEPTANCE TEST PHASE

	Rule Based Deduction System			Frame Based Abduction System		
Project	Agreement	Disagreement	Extra	Agreement	Disagreement	Extra
1	1	0	2	1	0	2
2	3	4	7	0	7	1
3	1	0	9	1	0	5
4	0	4	0	0	4	0
5	2	2	5	1	1	3
6	1	3	1	1	3	3
7	1	5	3	1	5	1
8	0	4	0	0	4	0
9	4	2	8	0	6	1
10	7	2	4	1	8	0
Total	20	26	39	6	40	16
Percent Agreement	43% (20/46)			13% (6/46)		

(a)

	Rule Based Deduction System			Frame Based Abduction System		
Project	Agreement	Disagreement	Extra	Agreement	Disagreement	Extra
1	3	0	7	0	3	1
2	0	7	0	0	7	0
3	1	1	11	0	2	1
4	2	2	1	2	2	1
5	0	5	0	0	5	0
6	4	0	7	0	4	1
7	2	4	4	0	6	2
8	5	3	2	1	7	0
9	2	4	2	2	4	2
10	5	4	5	1	8	3
Total	24	30	39	6	48	11
Percent Agreement	44% (24/54)			11% (6/54)		

(b)

	Rule Based Deduction System			Frame Based Abduction System		
Project	Agreement	Disagreement	Extra	Agreement	Disagreement	Extra
1	2	1	6	0	1	2
2	4	3	8	2	5	4
3	0	2	0	0	7	0
4	1	3	3	1	1	0
5	0	6	5	0	6	5
6	3	1	5	1	3	1
7	1	5	0	1	5	0
8	3	5	3	1	7	2
9	1	5	2	1	4	1
10	1	8	3	1	8	3
Total	16	39	35	8	47	18
Percent Agreement	29% (16/55)			15% (8/55)		

(c)

	Rule Based Deduction System			Frame Based Abduction System		
Project	Agreement	Disagreement	Extra	Agreement	Disagreement	Extra
1	1	2	8	1	2	6
2	3	4	7	0	7	1
3	0	1	0	0	1	0
4	2	2	4	1	3	0
5	1	5	0	1	5	0
6	3	1	5	0	4	1
7	2	4	3	2	4	3
8	3	5	1	3	5	1
9	2	4	6	2	4	6
10	1	8	1	1	8	3
Total	18	36	37	11	43	21
Percent Agreement	33% (18/54)			20% (11/54)		

(d)

	Rule Based Deduction System			Frame Based Abduction System		
Project	Agreement	Disagreement	Extra	Agreement	Disagreement	Extra
1	1	6	2	1	6	2
2	3	4	9	2	5	1
3	0	2	4	0	2	4
4	0	4	0	0	4	0
5	3	3	5	3	3	5
6	2	2	2	2	2	2
7	5	1	3	1	5	1
8	1	7	1	1	7	1
9	1	5	2	1	5	1
10	1	8	3	1	8	3
Total	17	42	31	12	47	22
Percent Agreement	29% (17/59)			20% (12/59)		

(e)

However, there were certain relationships which proved more consistent than others. For example, the two experts had strong agreement over the relationships involving programmer hours per line of code, software changes per line of code, and computer time per computer run. These metrics seem to be better understood than the others probably because they are often used for evaluation and comparisons in this field. They also had fairly good agreement with the interpretations of *error prone code, lots of reused code*, and *loose management*. The top-down and bottom-up expert systems had good agreement over programmer hours per line of code and software changes per line of code and over the interpretations of *error prone code* and *good solid code*.

TABLE V
AGREEMENT BETWEEN EXPERT SYSTEM AND INFORMATION IN DATABASE TOP DOWN SYSTEMS. (a) EARLY CODING PHASE, (b) MIDDLE CODING PHASE, (c) LATE CODING PHASE, (d) SYSTEMS TEST PHASE, (e) ACCEPTANCE TEST PHASE

	Rule Based Deduction System			Frame Based Abduction System		
Project	Agreement	Disagreement	Extra	Agreement	Disagreement	Extra
1	0	3	2	0	1	2
2	1	1	5	1	1	2
3	0	1	5	0	1	1
4	0	4	0	0	4	0
5	1	1	1	0	2	7
6	1	2	2	1	2	2
7	1	2	2	1	2	2
8	0	3	0	0	3	0
9	2	2	6	0	4	7
10	3	2	4	2	1	1
Total	9	23	29	5	27	14
Percent Agreement	28% (9/32)			16% (5/32)		

(a)

	Rule Based Deduction System			Frame Based Abduction System		
Project	Agreement	Disagreement	Extra	Agreement	Disagreement	Extra
1	2	2	6	0	4	4
2	0	5	0	0	5	0
3	1	1	7	1	1	3
4	0	2	1	0	2	1
5	0	4	0	0	4	0
6	4	1	6	0	4	1
7	0	4	4	0	4	2
8	3	4	0	2	5	0
9	1	4	3	1	4	3
10	5	1	3	1	5	2
Total	15	30	40	7	38	16
Percent Agreement	33% (15/45)			16% (7/45)		

(b)

	Rule Based Deduction System			Frame Based Abduction System		
Project	Agreement	Disagreement	Extra	Agreement	Disagreement	Extra
1	2	3	6	0	5	4
2	4	2	8	2	4	1
3	0	2	0	0	2	0
4	1	1	1	1	3	1
5	0	5	3	0	5	1
6	3	1	5	1	3	2
7	0	6	2	0	6	2
8	3	5	1	1	7	0
9	1	2	3	0	3	1
10	1	8	3	0	9	1
Total	15	37	37	5	47	15
Percent Agreement	29% (15/52)			10% (5/52)		

(c)

	Rule Based Deduction System			Frame Based Abduction System		
Project	Agreement	Disagreement	Extra	Agreement	Disagreement	Extra
1	2	3	5	1	4	4
2	4	1	8	0	5	2
3	0	0	0	0	0	0
4	1	3	3	0	4	1
5	0	5	3	0	5	3
6	1	2	5	0	3	3
7	3	5	4	0	6	3
8	1	7	0	1	7	0
9	1	3	5	1	3	3
10	1	7	3	0	8	2
Total	12	36	36	3	45	21
Percent Agreement	25% (12/48)			6% (3/48)		

(d)

	Rule Based Deduction System			Frame Based Abduction System		
Project	Agreement	Disagreement	Extra	Agreement	Disagreement	Extra
1	0	5	5	0	5	5
2	3	1	8	1	3	0
3	0	0	1	0	0	1
4	0	3	0	0	3	0
5	1	4	6	1	4	1
6	0	2	1	0	2	1
7	2	4	4	2	4	4
8	2	4	0	2	4	0
9	0	1	2	0	1	1
10	0	7	3	0	7	1
Total	8	33	30	6	35	16
Percent Agreement	20% (8/41)			15% (6/41)		

(e)

The results of evaluating the four expert systems are displayed in Tables IV and V. (An expanded version of this data is presented in the technical report version of this paper [20].) The entries in the agreement column are the number of interpretations which were indicated by both the expert system and the information in the database.

The entries in the disagreement column are those interpretations indicated by the database, but not listed by the expert system. Finally, the column labeled "Extra" specifies the number of extra interpretations listed by the expert system. This number is not that meaningful in determining the performance of the rule-based systems at this time because, as discussed previously, the rule-based systems were built to provide as complete a list of interpretations as possible. The manager would then have to decide which interpretations are meaningful and disregard the others. However, in general, it is better to have as few extra interpretations as possible. It should be noted that the total number of interpretations varies from table to table. This is because certain metrics were not available for some projects in some of the time phases. It would be unfair to say the expert systems did not detect certain interpretations if they were not given the manifestations necessary to do so, so these interpretations were not included in the results of the evaluation for those particular cases.

The expert systems performed moderately well given the following limitations: 1) so much of the knowledge and relationships are unclear in this field, 2) the experts themselves do not agree on much of the knowledge, 3) the expert systems used only five variables and only nine metrics derived from these variables to achieve the list of interpretations, 4) the metrics used are not ideal, 5) many of the interpretations in the database are subjective in nature and therefore may not always be correct, and 6) there may be discrepancies between the interpretations of the particular time phase and the overall interpretations for the project.

The systems which were developed with the bottom-up approach performed better than those developed with the top-down approach, and the rule-based deduction systems performed better than the frame-based abduction systems. Both the bottom-up and top-down rule-based systems performed better than either of the frame-based systems. The bottom-up rule-based system performed best, agreeing with an average of 36 percent (ranging from 29 to 44 percent depending on time phase) of the actual interpretations indicated in the subjective evaluation forms and project statistics forms in the database, and the top-down rule-based system agreed with an average of 27 percent (ranging from 20 to 33 percent) of the database conclusions. The bottom-up frame-based system agreed with an average of 16 percent (ranging from 11 to 20 percent) of the database interpretations, and the top-down frame-based system agreed with an average of 13 percent (ranging from 6 to 16 percent) of the database conclusions. It should be pointed out that each expert system produced relatively consistent results throughout its five time phases.

The bottom-up systems contained more relationships between manifestations and interpretations than did the top-down systems. One might assume that the only reason the bottom-up systems agreed with a higher percentage of the database conclusions was that the bottom-up systems would list more interpretations for the same input manifestations (test case). If it listed more interpretations, it would get more right by chance. However, there was not that big a difference between the number of manifestations per interpretation for the bottom-up systems which was 3.16 and the number for the top-down systems which was 2.77. As mentioned before, during the top-down development, the experts combined certain interpretations and dismissed others altogether during certain time phases so there were fewer interpretations for each phase. Although the intent was to throw out inappropriate interpretations and make the top-down systems that much better, the bottom-up systems still captured a higher percentage of correct relationships than did the top-down systems. The total number of interpretations listed by the bottom-up rule-based system was 276 in the 50 test cases. Of these, 95 were in agreement with the database conclusions. The total number of interpretations listed by the top-down rule-based system was 216, and of these, 59 agreed with the database conclusions. Therefore, the bottom-up rule-based system had an average of 34 percent (95/276) correct interpretations out of all those listed, while the top-down rule-based system averaged only 27 percent (59/216) correct interpretations.

It is interesting to observe that within both the bottom-up and top-down sets of systems the frame-based system always provided a subset of the interpretations listed by the rule-based system (although in 48 percent of the combined bottom-up

TABLE VI

KAPPA STATISTIC VALUES OF EACH INTERPRETATION IN EACH OF THE FOUR EXPERT SYSTEMS

Interpretation	Bottom-Up Systems RBD	Bottom-Up Systems FBA	Top-Down Systems RBD	Top-Down Systems FBA
Unstable Specifications	0.120	0.000	-0.065	-0.158
Low Productivity	0.270	-0.065	0.369	0.023
High Productivity	0.000	0.000	0.000	0.000
High Complexity (Tough Problem)	-0.261	-0.236	-0.346	-0.160
Compute Bound Algorithm	-0.139	-0.154	-0.253	-0.168
Low Complexity	0.122	-0.066	0.016	0.155
Simple System	0.121	0.124	***	***
Error Prone Code	0.178	0.118	0.046	0.130
Good Solid Code	-0.134	-0.174	-0.372	-0.082
Lots of Reused Code	-0.121	-0.109	-0.075	-0.163
Lots of Testing	-0.040	0.000	-0.273	-0.205
Little Testing	0.051	-0.144	-0.308	-0.238
Good Testing	0.231	0.296	-0.326	-0.198
Poor Testing	0.186	0.188	-0.241	-0.267
Lack of Thorough Testing	-0.190	-0.061	***	***
Changes Hard to Make	0.000	-0.092	0.211	0.149
Loose Management	0.124	0.123	0.427	0.194
Tight Management	-0.062	-0.114	***	***
Computer Problems	0.235	0.091	0.104	-0.092
Lots of Terminal Jockeys	0.049	-0.087	0.052	0.107

Note - $K > 0$ indicates better than chance agreement: $K = 0$ indicates chance agreement; $K < 0$ indicates worse than chance agreement.
RBD - Rule-Based Deduction; FBA - Frame-Based Abduction
*** - these interpretations were not used in the top-down systems

and top-down cases, the rule-based and frame-based systems listed the exact same interpretations). As stated previously, the relationships between the manifestations and interpretations were identical in the frame-based and rule-based systems within each knowledge acquisition approach used. Then, by the nature of the expert system methodologies, the rule-based system always listed every interpretation associated with every input manifestation, while the frame-based system only provided answers of minimum cardinality which explained all of the manifestations. Since the relationships in the two systems were identical, the frame-based systems could only list the exact same interpretations or a proper subset of those listed by the rule-based systems. As a result, the frame-based systems could not perform better than the rule-based systems with respect to agreement with the database conclusions. The frame-based systems listed an average of 50 percent fewer extra interpretations (ranging from 29 percent to 72 percent depending on time phase) for the bottom-up approach and an average of 48 percent fewer extra interpretations (ranging from 42 to 53 percent) for the top-down approach. However, it is better to have extra interpretations than to miss correct interpretations.

The results of using the Kappa statistic to evaluate the expert systems is shown in Table VI. According to these results, the bottom-up rule-based system performed best again, indicating better than chance agreement for more of the interpretations than the other systems did. A few of the interpretations performed relatively well in all or most of the expert systems. These were *low productivity, loose management, error prone code*, and *computer problems*. The experts had fairly good agreement with each other and also over time (between the bottom-up and the top-down approaches) on the manifestations for *loose management* and *error prone code*. They agreed less on *low productivity* and mostly disagreed on *computer problems*. The interpretations of *low complexity*, *simple system*, and *changes hard to make* also did a little better than chance agreement. The experts had fair agreement with each other and over time concerning *changes hard to make*, but mostly disagreed over *low complexity* and *simple system*. It is interesting to note that the interpretations involving testing performed better in both bottom-up systems than in the top-down systems in general. Perhaps testing is better understood using a very environment-specific approach. Several of the interpretations did not perform well in any of the expert systems, doing worse than chance agreement in all or most cases. These were *high complexity (tough problem), compute bound algorithm, good solid code, lots of reused code, lots of testing, little testing, lack of thorough testing*, and *tight management*.

VII. Discussion

The goal of this study was to determine whether it is possible to build useful expert systems for software engineering management. Some of the questions which we tried to resolve involved determining how to do the knowledge acquisition and what type of expert system methodology might be best suited for this field. We used two approaches to knowledge acquisition and two expert system methodologies. The reader should be careful in drawing too strong a set of conclusions, however, because this was an exploratory experiment using a limited number of techniques for expert systems. It is very possible that other representations of the knowledge using the same or other inference mechanisms would lead to different results. Additionally, it is clear that a better and more extensive set of metrics would provide a more successful management system. This work is being continued on the TAME project [4] where various methods for structuring knowledge are being analyzed. Based upon this study, good results have also been obtained at NASA using a similar system [29].

We believe that a major limitation to developing expert systems for software engineering in general is the fact that much of the knowledge in this field is not well understood yet. Knowledge was gathered from two experts who have had a great deal of experience in this field, and it was found that they did not agree with each other about many of the relationships we were trying to determine. Furthermore, they did not always agree with themselves when looking at the data from a different point of view at a later date.

The expert systems performed moderately well, especially when one considers that many of the relationships between the metrics and the interpretations are unclear. The experts did not agree on many of the relationships, and the expert systems cannot perform better than the information included in them. Indeed, the bottom-up rule-based system performed about as well as the experts agreed with each other. In addition, a relatively small number of metrics were used to suggest many interpretations, and the metrics used were not ideal. The experts felt that some of the interpretations could not be adequately described in terms of the available metrics. For example, it was felt that the complexity interpretations could not be adequately captured without error metric data. The experts even threw out one of the interpretations altogether when they were determining relationships using the top-down approach. However, the five variables used in the metrics were easily obtainable, and this is an important consideration when creating expert systems.

Another fact we would like to stress is that the expert systems for the earlier time phases also performed well. This is especially important because a manager should learn of potential problems as early in the development process as possible. Expert systems can be very helpful because they may detect problems which a manager may not recognize early on.

Two approaches to knowledge acquisition were used and compared. The bottom-up approach produced better results than did the top-down approach. This may well be because the bottom-up approach is more environment-specific. Since the field of software engineering is still new, it is probably better to develop expert systems for one homogeneous environment rather than trying to determine general truths across different environments. In general, it may be advantageous to work with small domains when building expert systems for fields with uncertain knowledge.

The two expert system methodologies, rule-based deduction and frame-based abduction, were also compared with respect to ease of implementation and accuracy of results. The initial knowledge was derived from empirical software engineering research and organized in a table format, so the very first sets of simple rules and frames which were not time-line specific were straightforward to develop. The situation became more complex when the interpretations were made time-line specific. A time phase was added to the antecedent of each rule, so there were five times as many rules as before, specializing for each of the five time phases. Each frame-based system was divided into five systems based on time period because the second dimension of time could not be incorporated into the frames in a reasonable manner. Furthermore, an attempt was made to rewrite the rules to contain more meaningful and complex relationships among the manifestation in the antecedents. However, it was decided to retain the format of simple rules in order to be as complete as possible. It should be noted that for this type of diagnostic problem in a well-defined domain, it is generally much easier and more natural to write frames than to encode the same information in complex rules [21].

In 48 percent of the cases, the rule-based and frame-based systems provided the same interpretations. However, when analyzing the results from all projects, the rule-based systems provided more interpretations and exhibited a higher rate of agreement with the database than did the frame-based systems. This is directly attributable to the fact that simple rules containing one manifestation in the antecedents were used in the rule-based systems, leading to solutions which contained the complete list of all possible interpretations associated with the manifestations, while the frame-based systems provided only those explanations of minimum cardinality and often missed correct interpretations because the relationships between interpretations and manifestations were not always correct. It is better to have extra interpretations than to miss correct interpretations, so we conclude that a rule-based system with simple rules is probably more applicable to newer fields with unclear knowledge, such as software engineering. However, as a field becomes more established, a frame-based system may provide better solutions. Also, newer methods of implementing frame-based abduction with irredundant covers should provide better results than those currently provided by frame-based abduction using minimal set covers.

This study has provided many additional new insights into the development of expert systems for software engineering management. It is feasible to develop prototype expert systems at this point in time, but one must realize that in any new field with uncertain knowledge, the expert systems cannot perform better than the state of knowledge in the field permits. One of the best reasons to develop these systems may be to learn from their development. The knowledge engineer can learn a great deal about a field as he organizes the information. Then, analyzing the performance of the working systems can give further insight about what is and what is not understood. In order to develop better expert systems for software engineering management, one needs to define fully the relationships that exist between the components. In particular one must define what development characteristics would result in what types of abnormal measures, how this changes through various project development phases, and how certain one is that an abnormal measure results from a certain characteristic. As more is learned about software engineering management, more can be incorporated into useful expert systems.

VIII. Future Research Directions

The development of ARROWSMITH-P was a preliminary attempt at constructing expert systems for software engineering management. Replications of this experiment using varying approaches to building the expert systems will lead to stronger confidence in the results and a better understanding of the effects.

There is certainly a need for further research in the field of software engineering. As more is learned, the information contained in the knowledge bases can be refined, and new knowledge, such as information about error metrics [30], [2] or information about other phases of development such as requirements or design, can be incorporated into the expert systems to make them stronger. As incorrect relationships are brought to the surface, the systems can be changed to incorporate the knowledge gained from testing. Eventually, the rules should become more complex as relationships between manifestations and causes become better defined. In addition, the testing of current, ongoing projects can be performed on the expert systems. The data from the new projects can then be incorporated into the environment-specific baselines of metrics so the systems continue to be updated as the environment changes.

In a more general sense, a theoretical framework for developing export systems for software engineering is needed. For example, a categorization scheme, which would address such issues as when a top-down system is better than a bottom-up system and vice versa, should be built. Also, perhaps a new and different type of inference mechanism or method for building expert systems would better suit the needs of some aspects in this field. All of these issues require a great deal of further research and analysis.

Appendix A

A sample interactive session with the rule-based deduction expert system

THIS EXPERT SYSTEM WILL HELP A MANAGER OF A SOFTWARE PROJECT DETERMINE IF THE PROJECT IS ON SCHEDULE OR IN TROUBLE.

PLEASE ANSWER THE FOLLOWING QUESTIONS.
COMPUTER RUNS PER LJNE OF SOURCE CODE:
(1) ABOVE NORMAL
(2) NORMAL
(3) BELOW NORMAL
=?
2.
COMPUTER TIME PER LINE OF SOURCE CODE:
(1) ABOVE NORMAL
(2) NORMAL
(3) BELOW NORMAL
=?
2.

SOFTWARE CHANGES PER LINE OF SOURCE CODE:
(1) ABOVE NORMAL
(2) NORMAL
(3) BELOW NORMAL
=?
2.

PROGRAMMER HOURS PER LINE OF SOURCE CODE:
(1) ABOVE NORMAL
(2) NORMAL
(3) BELOW NORMAL
=?
2.

COMPUTER TIME PER COMPUTER RUN:
(1) ABOVE NORMAL
(2) NORMAL
(3) BELOW NORMAL
=?
2.

SOFTWARE CHANGES PER COMPUTER RUN:
(1) ABOVE NORMAL
(2) NORMAL
(3) BELOW NORMAL
=?
2.

PROGRAMMER HOURS PER COMPUTER RUN:
(1) ABOVE NORMAL
(2) NORMAL
(3) BELOW NORMAL
=?
3.

PROJECT TIMEPHASE:
(1) EARLY CODE PHASE
(2) MIDDLE CODE PHASE
(3) LATE CODE PHASE
(4) SYSTEMS TEST PHASE
(5) ACCEPTANCE TEST PHASE
=?
2.

COMPUTER TIME PER SOFTWARE CHANGE:
(1) ABOVE NORMAL
(2) NORMAL
(3) BELOW NORMAL
=?
2.

PROGRAMMER HOURS PER SOFTWARE CHANGE:
(1) ABOVE NORMAL
(2) NORMAL
(3) BELOW NORMAL
=?
3.

POSSIBLE INTERPRETATIONS ARE:
ERROR PRONE CODE <0.94>
EASY ERRORS OR CHANGES BEING FOUND OR FIXED <0.81>
LOTS OF TESTING <0.75>
LOTS OF TERMINAL JOCKEYS <0.75>
UNSTABLE SPECIFICATIONS <0.50>
NEAR BUILD OR MILESTONE DATA <0.50>
GOOD TESTING OR GOOD TEST PLAN <0.25>
MODIFICATIONS BEING MADE TO RECENTLY TRANSPORTED CODE <0.25>
Note – User answers are in boldface.

Appendix B

A sample interactive session with the frame-based abduction expert system

THIS EXPERT SYSTEM WILL HELP A MANAGER OF A SOFTWARE PROJECT DETERMINE IF THE PROJECT IS ON SCHEDULE OR IN TROUBLE.
THIS PARTICULAR SYSTEM SHOULD BE USED FOR THE MIDDLE CODING PHASE.
PLEASE ANSWER THE FOLLOWING QUESTIONS.
FOCUS OF SUBPROBLEM:
THIS SUBPROBLEM IS CURRENTLY ACTIVE
GENERATOR:
COMPETING POSSIBILITIES:
UNSTABLE SPECIFICATIONS
LATE DESIGN
NEW OR LATE DEVELOPMENT
LOW PRODUCTIVITY
HIGH PRODUCTIVITY
HIGH COMPLEXITY OR TOUGH PROBLEM
HIGH COMP OR COMPUTE BOUND ALGORITHMS RUN OR TESTED
LOW COMPLEXITY
SIMPLE SYSTEM
REMOVAL OF CODE BY TESTING OR TRANSPORTING
INFLUX OF TRANSPORTED CODE
LITTLE EXECUTABLE CODE BEING DEVELOPED
ERROR PRONE CODE
GOOD SOLID AND RELIABLE CODE
NEAR BUILD OR MILESTONE DATE
LARGE PORTION OF REUSED CODE OR EARLY AND LARGER TESTS

LOTS OF TESTING
LITTLE OR NOT ENOUGH ONLINE TESTING BEING DONE
GOOD TESTING OR GOOD TEST PLAN
UNIT TESTING BEING DONE
LACK OF THOROUGH TESTING
POOR TESTING PROGRAM
SYSTEM AND INTEGRATION TESTING STARTED EARLY
CHANGE BACKLOG OR HOLDING CHANGES
CHANGE BACKLOG OR HOLDING CODE
CHANGES HARD TO ISOLATE
CHANGES HARD TO MAKE
EASY ERRORS OR CHANGES BEING FOUND OR FIXED
MODIFICATIONS BEING MADE TO RECENTLY TRANSPORTED CODE
LOOSE CONFIGURATION MANAGEMENT OR UNSTRUCTURED DEV
TIGHT MANAGEMENT PLAN OR GOOD CONFIGURATION CONTROL
COMPUTER PROBLEMS OR INACCESSIBILITY OR ENV CONSTRAINTS
LOTS OF TERMINAL JOCKEYS

COMPUTER RUNS PER LINE OF SOURCE CODE:
(0)ABOVE NORMAL
(1)NORMAL
(2)BELOW NORMAL
= ?
2.
COMPUTER TIME PER LINE OF SOURCE CODE:
(0)ABOVE NORMAL
(1)NORMAL
(2)BELOW NORMAL
= ?
2.
SOFTWARE CHANGES PER LINE OF SOURCE CODE:
(0)ABOVE NORMAL
(1)NORMAL
(2)BELOW NORMAL
= ?
2.
PROGRAMMER HOURS PER LINE OF SOURCE CODE:
(1) ABOVE NORMAL
(2) NORMAL
(3) BELOW NORMAL
= ?
2.
SOFTWARE CHANGES PER COMPUTER RUN:
(1) ABOVE NORMAL
(2) NORMAL
(3) BELOW NORMAL
= ?

2.
COMPUTER TIME PER COMPUTER RUN:
(1) ABOVE NORMAL
(2) NORMAL
(3) BELOW NORMAL
= ?
2.
PROGRAMMER HOURS PER COMPUTER RUN:
(1) ABOVE NORMAL
(2) NORMAL
(3) BELOW NORMAL
= ?
3.
FOCUS OF SUBPROBLEM:
GENERATOR:
COMPETING POSSIBILITIES:
LOTS OF TERMINAL JOCKEYS
EASY ERRORS OR CHANGES BEING FOUND OR FIXED
LOTS OF TESTING
ERROR PRONE CODE
UNSTABLE SPECIFICATIONS
PROGRAMMER HOURS PER SOFTWARE CHANGE:
(0)ABOVE NORMAL
(1)NORMAL
(2)BELOW NORMAL
= ?
3.
FOCUS OF SUBPROBLEM:
GENERATOR:
COMPETING POSSIBILITIES:
EASY ERRORS OR CHANGES BEING FOUND OR FIXED
ERROR PRONE CODE
COMPUTER TIME PER SOFTWARE CHANGE:
(0)ABOVE NORMAL
(1)NORMAL
(2)BELOW NORMAL
= ?
2.
POSSIBLE INTERPRETATIONS ARE:
EASY ERRORS OR CHANGES BEING FOUND OR FIXED <H>
ERROR PRONE CODE. <L>

Note – User answers are in boldface.

- Both interpretations listed as solutions can explain all of the manifestations, but the first is given a high measure of likelihood (shown by the ⟨H⟩) of being correct, while Error Prone Code is rated low.

Acknowledgment

The authors are grateful to F. McGarry, Dr. J. Page, Dr. J. Reggia, J. Ramsey, B. Decker, and D. Card for their invaluable assistance in this project. The authors would also like to thank the members of their research group for enlightening comments and ideas.

References

[1] "Annotated bibliography of Software Engineering Laboratory (SEL) literature, SEL-82-006," Software Eng. Lab.. NASA Goddard Space Flight Center, Greenbelt, MD, Nov. 1982.

[2] V. R. Basili and B. T. Perricone, "Software errors and complexity: An empirical investigation," *Commun. ACM.,* vol. 27, no. 1, pp. 42-52, Jan. 1984.

[3] V. R. Basili and C. L. Ramsey, "ARROWSMITH-P-A prototype expert system for software engineering management," in *Proc. Expert Systems in Government Symposium,* IEEE, McLean, VA, Oct. 1985, pp. 252-264.

[4] V. R. Basili and H. D. Rombach, "The TAME project: Towards improvement-oriented software environments," *IEEE Trans. Software Eng..* vol. SE-14. no. 6, pp. 758-773, June 1988.

[5] V. R. Basili and D. M. Weiss, "A methodology for collecting valid software engineering data," *IEEE Trans. Software Eng.,* vol. SE-10, no. 6, pp. 728-738, Nov. 1984.

[6] V. R. Basili and M. V. Zelkowitz, "Analyzing medium scale software developments," in *Proc. Third Int. Conf. Software Engineering,* Atlanta. GA, May 1978, pp. 116-123.

[7] V. R. Basili. M. V. Zelkowitz, F. E. McGarry, R. W, Reiter, Jr., W. F. Truszkowksi, and D. M. Weiss, "The Software Engineering Laboratory, SEL-77-001," Software Eng. Lab., NASA Goddard Space Flight Center, Greenbelt, MD, May 1977.

[8] A. N. Campbell. V. F. Hollister, R. O. Duda, and P. E. Hart, "Recognition of a hidden mineral deposit by an artificial program," *Science,* vol. 217, pp. 927-928, Sept. 1982.

[9] D. N. Card, F. E. McGarry, J. Page, S. Eslinger, and V. R. Basili, "The Software Engineering Laboratory, SEL-81-104," Software Eng. Lab., NASA Goddard Space Flight Center, Greenbelt, MD, Feb. 1982.

[10] J. Cohen, "Weighted Kappa: Nominal scale agreement with provision for scaled disagreement or partial credit," *Psychol. Bull.,* vol. 70, pp. 213-220, 1968.

[11] J. deKleer and B. Williams, "Reasoning about multiple faults," in *Proc. Fifth Nat. Conf. Artificial Intelligence,* Philadelphia, PA, Aug. 11-15, 1986, pp. 132-139.

[12] C. Doerflinger and V. R. Basili, "Monitoring software development through dynamic variables," *IEEE Trans. Software Eng.,* vol. 11, no. 9, pp. 978-985, Sept. 1985.

[13] F. Hayes-Roth, D. Waterman, and D. Lenat, "Principles of Pattern-directed inference systems," in *Pattern-Directed Inference Systems,* Waterman and Hayes-Roth, Eds. New York: Academic, 1978, pp. 577-601.

[14] R. Miller, H. Pople, and J. Myers, "Internist-1: An experimental computer-based diagnostic consultant for general internal medicine," *New England J. Med.,* vol. 307, pp. 468-476, 1982.

[15] M. Minsky, "A framework for representing knowledge," in *The Psychology of Computer Vision,* P. Winston, Ed. New York: McGraw-Hill, 1975. pp. 211-277.
[16] D. S. Nau and J. A. Reggia, "Relationships between deductive and abductive inference in knowledge-based diagnostic expert systems," in *Proc. First Int. Workshop Expert Database Systems,* 1984, pp. 500-509.
[17] S. G. Pauker, G. A. Gorry, J. P. Kassirer, and W. B. Schwartz, "Towards the simulation of clinical cognition," *Amer. J. Med.,* vol. 60, no. 7, pp. 981-996, June 1976.
[18] Y. Peng and J. A. Reggia, "A probabilistic causal model for diagnostic problem-solving," *IEEE Trans. Syst., Man, Cybern.,* vol. 17, pp. 146-162, 395-406. 1987.
[19] Y. Peng and J. A. Reggia, "Plausibility of diagnostic hypotheses: The nature of simplicity," in *Proc. Fifth Nat. Conf. Artificial Intelligence,* Philadelphia. PA. Aug. 11-15, 1986. pp. 140-145.
[20] C. L. Ramsey and V. R. Basili. "An evaluation of expert systems for software engineering management," Dep. Comput. Sci., Univ. Maryland, College Park, Tech. Rep. TR-1708, Sept. 1986.
[21] C. L. Ramsey, J. A. Reggia, D. S. Nau, and A. Ferrentino, "A comparative analysis of methods for expert systems," *Int. J. Man-Machine Studies,* vol. 24, no. 5, pp. 475-499, May 1986.
[22] J. Reggia, "Computer-assisted medical decision making," in *Application of Computers in Medicine,* M. Schwartz, Ed. New York: IEEE Press, 1982, pp. 198-213.
[23] J. A. Reggia, D. S. Nau, and P. Wang, "Diagnostic expert systems based on a set covering model," *Int. J. Man-Machine Studies,* vol. 19, no. 5, pp. 437-460, Nov. 1983.
[24] J. A. Reggia, D; S. Nau, P. Wang, and Y. Peng, "A formal model of diagnostic inference," *Inform. Sci.,* vol. 37, pp. 227-285, 1985.
[25] J. A. Reggia and B. Perricone, "KMS reference manual," Dep. Comput. Sci., Univ. Maryland, College Park, Tech. Rep. TR-1136, 1982.
[26] E. Shortliffe, *Computer-Based Medical Consultations; MYCIN.* New York: Elsevier, 1976.
[27] H. Shubin and J. Ulrich, "IDT: An intelligent diagnostic tool," in *Proc. Nat. Conf. Artificial Intelligence,* AAAI, 1982, pp. 290-295.
[28] R. Spitzer, J. Cohen, J. Fleiss, and J. Endicott. "Quantification of agreement in psychiatric diagnosis." *Archives General Psychiatry,* vol. 17, pp. 83-87, 1967.
[29] J. D. Valett, W. Decker, and J. Buell, "Software management environment," in *Proc. SEL Workshop 1988,* NASA Goddard Space Flight Center, Greenbelt, MD, Dec. 1988.
[30] D. M. Weiss and V. R. Basili, "Evaluating software development by analysis of changes: Some data from the software engineering laboratory," *IEEE Trans. Software Eng.,* vol. SE-11, no. 2, pp. 157-168, Feb. 1985.

Software Defect Reduction Top-10 List

Barry Boehm and Victor Basili

Recently a grant from NSF enabled us to establish a national center for Empirically-Based Software Engineering (CeBASE). The CeBASE objective is to transform software engineering as much as possible from a fad-based practice to an engineering-based practice through derivation, organization, and dissemination of empirical data on software development and evolution phenomenology.

"As much as possible" reflects the fact that software development will always remain a people-intensive and continuously changing field. However, we have found that people in the field have been able to establish objective and quantitative data, relationships, and predictive models which have helped many software developers to avoid predictable pitfalls and improve their ability to predict and control efficient software projects.

As a way of illustrating this, we are devoting this column to an update of one of our previous columns ("Industrial Metrics Top-10 List," by Barry Boehm, IEEE Software, September 1987, pp. 84-85) which provided a concise selection of empirical data which many software practitioners found very helpful. As a major CeBASE focus is on software defect reduction, here is a software defect reduction top 10-list, in rough priority order. More details and references can be found in an expanded Web version of this column, at http://www.cebase.org/defectreduction/top10.

1. Finding and fixing a software problem after delivery is often 100 times more expensive than finding and fixing it during the requirements and design phase.

This was also the top-priority item in the 1987 list. As in 1987, "This insight has been a major driver in focusing industrial software practice on thorough requirements analysis and design, on early verification and validation, and on up-front prototyping and simulation to avoid costly downstream fixes."

The only thing we have changed since 1987 is to add the word "often," to reflect additional insights on the relationship. For one, the cost-escalation factor for small, noncritical software systems is more like 5:1 than 100:1, enabling such systems to be developed most efficiently in a less formal, "continuous prototype" mode -- but still with emphasis on getting things right early rather than late. Another is that the cost-escalation factor can be reduced significantly even for large critical systems via good architectural practices. These reduce the cost of most fixes by confining them to small, well-encapsulated modules. An excellent example was the million-line TRW CCPDS-R project described in Appendix D of

---

Dr. Boehm is with the University of Southern California and Dr. Basili is with the University of Maryland.

Walker Royce's Software Project Management: A Unified Approach, Addison-Wesley, 1988, where the cost-escalation factor was only about 2:1.

2. About 40-50% of the effort on current software projects is spent on avoidable rework.

"Avoidable rework" is effort spent fixing difficulties with the software that could have been avoided or discovered earlier and less expensively. This implies that there is such a thing as "unavoidable rework." This fact has been increasingly appreciated with the growing realization that better user-interactive systems result from "emergent" processes (where the requirements emerge from prototyping and other multi-stakeholder shared learning activities) than from "reductionist" processes (where the requirements are stipulated in advance and then reduced to practice via design and coding). We believe that this distinction is essential to a modern theory and practice of software defect reduction. Changes to the definition of a system that make it more cost-effective should not be discouraged by classifying them as defects to be avoided.

Reducing avoidable rework is thus a major source of software productivity improvement. In our behavioral analysis of the effects of software cost drivers on effort for the COCOMO II model (B. Boehm et al., *Software Cost Estimation with COCOMO II*, Prentice Hall, 2000) most of the effort savings from improving software process maturity, software architectures, and software risk management came from reductions in avoidable rework.

3. About 80% of the avoidable rework comes from 20% of the defects.

For smaller systems, the 80% number may be lower; for very large systems, it may be higher. Two major sources of avoidable rework are hastily-specified requirements and nominal-case design and development (where late accommodation of off-nominal requirements causes major architecture, design, and code breakage). If you have a software problem report tracking system which records the effort to fix each defect, it is fairly easy for you to analyze the data to determine and address additional major sources of rework in your organization.

4. About 80% of the defects come from 20% of the modules and about half the modules are defect free.

Studies from different environments over many years have been amazingly consistent, with figures between 60% and 90% of the defects coming from 20% of the modules, and a median of about 80%. What also appears to be consistent is that all of the defects are contained in about half of the modules. This data is representative of each of the studies cited in the web version of this paper.

Thus, it is worth the effort to identify the characteristics of error prone modules in a particular environment. There are a variety of factors that contribute to error-proneness that appear to be context dependent. However, some factors that usually contribute to error-proneness are the level of data coupling and cohesion, size, complexity, and amount of change to reused code.

5. About 90% of the downtime comes from at most 10% of the defects.

It is obvious that all faults are not equal in terms of their rate of occurrence. That is, some defects have a disproportionate effect on downtime and reliability of a system than others. An analysis of the software failure history of nine large IBM software products, found that about .3% of the defects accounted for about 90% of the downtime. Thus risk-based testing, including understanding the operational profiles of a system and emphasizing testing of high-risk scenarios, is clearly cost effective.

6. Peer reviews catch 60% of the defects.

Given that the cost of finding and fixing most defects rises the later we find them in the lifecycle, we are interested in techniques that find defects earlier in the lifecycle. Numerous studies have confirmed that peer reviews are very effective in this regard. The data range from catching 31% to 93% of the defects, with a median of around 60%. Thus the 60% number, which comes from the 1987 column, is still a reasonable estimate.

Factors effecting the percentage of defects caught include the number and type of peer reviews performed, the size and complexity of the system, and the frequency of defects better caught by execution (e.g., concurrency and algorithm defects). Our studies have provided evidence that peer reviews, analysis tools, and testing catch different classes of defects at different points in the development cycle. Further empirical research is needed to help choose the best mixed strategy for defect reduction investments.

7. Perspective-based reviews catch 35% more defects than non-directed reviews.

A scenario based reading technique (Basili, V. R., Evolving and Packaging Reading Technologies, Journal of Systems and Software, vol. 38, no. 1, pp. 3-12, July 1997) offers a reviewer a set of formal procedures for defect detection based upon varying perspectives. The union of several perspectives into a single inspection offers broad, yet focused coverage of the document being reviewed. The goal is to generate focused techniques aimed at specific defect detection goals, taking advantage of the existing defect history in an organization.

Scenario-based reading techniques have been applied in requirements and object oriented design inspections, as well as user interface inspections. Improvement results vary from 15% to 50% in fault detection rate. Further benefits of focused reading techniques are that they facilitate training of inexperienced personnel, better communication about the process, and continual improvement over time.

8. Practice Disciplined personas can reduce defect introduction rates by up to 75%.

Several disciplined personal processes have been introduced into practice. These include Harlan Mills' Cleanroom software development process and Watts Humphrey's Personal Software Process (PSP). Data from both of them support the concept that personal discipline can greatly reduce the introduction of defects into software products. Data from the use of Cleanroom at NASA have shown failure rates during test reduced by 25% to 75%. Use of Cleanroom also showed a reduction in rework effort, i.e., only 5% of the fixes took more than an hour to fix as opposed to the standard of over 60% of the fixes taking over an hour to fix.

PSP's strong focus on root-cause analysis of an individual's software defects and overruns, and on developing personal checklists and practices to avoid future reoccurrence, has a significant effect on personal defect rates. Reductions of 10:1 are common between exercises 1 and 10 of the PSP training course.

Effects at the project level are more scattered. They depend on such factors as the organizations' existing software maturity level and the people's and organizations' willingness to operate within a highly structured software culture. When PSP is coupled with the strongly compatible Team Software Process (TSP), defect reduction rates can be factors of 10 or higher for organizations operating at modest maturity levels, but less if organizations already have highly mature processes. The June 2000 special issue of CrossTalk, "Keeping Time with PSP and TSP," has a good set of relevant discussions, including experience showing that adding PSP and TSP to a CMM Level 5 organization reduced acceptance test defects by about 50% overall, and about 75% for high-priority defects.

9. All other things being equal, it costs 50% more per source instruction to develop high-dependability software products than to develop low-dependability software products. However, the investment is more than worth it if significant operations and maintenance costs are involved.

The analysis of 161 project data points for the COCOMO II model referenced above resulted in an added cost of 53% for its "Required Reliability" factor, while normalizing for the effects of 22 other factors. Does this mean that Philip Crosby's landmark book, Quality Is Free (Mentor, 1980), had it all wrong? Maybe for some low-criticality, short-lifetime software, but not for the most important cases.

First, in the COCOMO II maintenance model, low-dependability software is about 50% per instruction more expensive to maintain than to develop, while high-dependability software is about 15% less expensive to maintain than to develop. For a typical life cycle cost distribution of 30% development and 70% maintenance, low-dependability software becomes about the same in cost per instruction as high-dependability software (again, assuming all other factors are equal).

Second, in the COCOMO II-related quality model, high-dependability software removes about 4 times as many defects as average-dependability software, which in turn removes about 4 times as many defects as low-dependability software. Thus, if the operational cost of software defects (due to lost worker time, lost sales, recalls, added customer service costs, litigation costs, loss of repeat business, etc.) is roughly equal to life-cycle software development and maintenance costs for average-dependability software, the increased defect rate of low-dependability software will make its ownership costs roughly three times higher than the ownership costs of high-dependability software.

10. About 40-50% of user programs have nontrivial defects.

A landmark 1987 study in this area found that 44% of 27 spreadsheet programs produced by experienced spreadsheet developers had nontrivial defects: mostly errors in spreadsheet formulas. The developers were quite confident that their spreadsheets were accurate. Subsequent laboratory experiments have reported defective spreadsheet rates between 35% and 90%. Analysis of operational spreadsheets have reported defectiveness rates between 21% and 26%; the lower rates are probably due to corrections already made during operation.

Nowadays and increasingly in the future, user programs will escalate from spreadsheets to Web/Internet scripting languages capable of sending agents into cyberspace to make deals for you. And there will be many more "sorcerer's apprentice" user-programmers with tremendous power to create high-risk defects and little training or expertise in how to avoid or detect them. One of our studies for the COCOMO II book (page 6) estimated that there would be 55 million user-programmers in the U.S. by the year 2005. Including active Web-page developers as user-programmers, this prediction is basically on-track.

Thus, another challenge for the creators of web-programming facilities is to provide them with the equivalent of seat belts and air bags, plus safe-driving aids and rules of the road. This is one of several software engineering research challenges identified by a National Science Foundation study, "Gaining Intellectual Control of Software Development," which we recently summarized in Computer (May 2000, pp. 27-33).

There is a great need to refine and expand this top-10 list and related empirical research on defect reduction.

Clearly, much of the data reported above does not take into account the interaction of many of the variables. Some further things you would like to know, for example, are, "If I invest in peer reviewing, Cleanroom, and PSP, am I paying for the same defects to be removed three times? Will this enable me to avoid doing (some) testing?" Further empirical research in defect reduction is needed to be able to answer questions like these.

We hope to involve the software community in a process of expanding the top-10 defect reduction list and other currently-available data into a continually evolving, open-source, Web-accessible handbook of empirical results on software defect reduction strategies. We also plan to initiate counterpart handbooks for COTS-based systems and other future software areas. We would welcome your participation in this effort; please see the CeBASE web site (http://www.cebase.org) for further information and ways of participating.

Summary: Software Defect Reduction Top-10 List

1. Finding and fixing a software problem after delivery is often 100 times more expensive than finding and fixing it during the requirements and design phase.

2. About 40-50% of the effort on current software projects is spent on avoidable rework.

3. About 80% of the avoidable rework comes from 20% of the defects.

4. About 80% of the defects come from 20% of the modules and about half the modules are defect free.

5. About 90% of the downtime comes from at most 10% of the defects.

6. Peer reviews catch 60% of the defects.

7. Perspective-based reviews catch 35% more defects than non-directed reviews.

8. Disciplined personal practices can reduce defect introduction rates by up to 75%.

9. All other things being equal, it costs 50% more per source instruction to develop high-dependability software products than to develop low-dependability software products. However, the investment is more than worth it if significant operations and maintenance costs are involved.

10. About 40-50% of user programs have nontrivial defects.